Paths to a New Europe

Also by the same author

Catherine the Great and the Russian Nobility (Cambridge, 1967)
The Emergence of the Superpowers (London, 1970)
Russia under Catherine the Great, 2 vols. (Newtonville, MA, 1978)
October and the World: Perspectives on the Russian Revolution (London, 1979)
The Last Great Game: USA versus USSR (London, 1989)
The Making of Russian Absolutism, 1613–1801, 2nd edn (London, 1990)
World Order in History: Russia and the West (London, 1996)
A History of Russia, 3rd edn (London, 1998)
The Superpowers: A Short History (London, 2000)

Paul Dukes

Paths to a New Europe

From Premodern to Postmodern Times

First published 2004 by
PALGRAVE MACMILLAN
Houndmills, Basingstoke, Hampshire RG21 6XS and
175 Fifth Avenue, New York, N. Y. 10010
Companies and representatives throughout the world

PALGRAVE MACMILLAN is the global academic imprint of the Palgrave
Macmillan division of St. Martin's Press, LLC and of Palgrave Macmillan Ltd.
Macmillan® is a registered trademark in the United States, United Kingdom
and other countries. Palgrave is a registered trademark in the European
Union and other countries.

ISBN 1–4039–0248–8 hardback
ISBN 1–4039–0249–6 paperback

This book is printed on paper suitable for recycling and made from fully
managed and sustained forest sources.

A catalogue record for this book is available from the British Library.

A catalog record for this book is available from the Library of Congress.

10   9   8   7   6   5   4   3   2   1
13   12   11   10   09   08   07   06   05   04

Printed in China

CONTENTS

LIST OF MAPS

Abbreviations

EB   *Encyclopaedia Britannica*, 11th edn, 29 vols (Cambridge, 1910–11)

EB 12   Volumes 30–32 added to form 12th edn (London and New York, 1922)

EB 13   Volumes I–III added to form 13th edn (London and New York, 1926)

NE   R. C. Bridges, J. D. Hargreaves, Paul Dukes and William Scott, *Nations and Empires: Documents on the History of Europe and on its Relations with the World since 1648* (London, 1969)

PREFACE

The aim of this book is to consider the development of Europe from its origins through premodern to postmodern times. The pace of this process accelerated from about the middle of the seventeenth century with the formation of the nation state accompanied by the growth of empires. By the beginning of the twentieth century, European empires had arisen to dominate most of planet earth's land and water surfaces. However, the two world wars brought the continent down from its peak of power. From 1945 to 1989, Europe lost its empires and fell under the influence of the two peripheral superpowers, the USA and the USSR. Then, with the decline and fall of the USSR by 1991, it moved towards a new unity as the USA exerted global hegemony. However, a new question arose: was the nation state under threat from the external process of globalisation, and the internal pressures of regionalisation? Even if it could not supply a full answer, history would retain its high value, since the new Europe would retain significant features of the old. A Chinese proverb puts the point well: to look back makes you blind in one eye, not to look back makes you blind in both.

The basic story is one of power relationships, and therefore primarily political. But economic forces and cultural considerations also form important parts of the plot.

In the telling of the tale, balance and perspective are pursued through consideration of the relationship between the continent as a whole and its constituent parts: south-western, north-western, northern, central, south-eastern and east.

In the completion of *Paths to a New Europe: From Premodern to Postmodern Times*, I have made considerable use of *A History of Europe 1648–1948: The Arrival, The Rise, The Fall*, published in 1985. However, changes and additions are significant enough to justify the new title. I have indicated the sources for the book in the notes and Suggestions for Further Reading. The use of these sources reflects my belief that a work is not necessarily good because it is new, nor bad because it is old. Inevitably, in a subject of this scale, many works of high quality, both new and old, have been omitted. While accepting full responsibility for the finished product, I acknowledge with deep gratitude the generous advice given by Jeremy Black, Roy Bridges, Michael Broers, Christoph Dartmann, Nicholas Fisher, Ron Grant, John Hargreaves, Graeme Herd, John Hiden, John Kent, Evan Mawdsley, Ian Mitchell, Roy Porter, Hamish Scott, William Scott and others. Associates of the University of Aberdeen's Directorate of Information Services, especially its librarians and IT support staff, have been most helpful too, as have the administrative and secretarial support of the History Department, Janet Hendry, Gillian Brown and Barbara McGillivray. Most of the writing has been completed in the mostly peaceful setting of the Scottish hills, thanks to my partner, Cathryn Brennan, and her late mother, Mary Berry. My debt to them is incalculable.

King's College, Old Aberdeen

1

ORIGINS: EUROPE BEFORE 1648: MID-CENTURY CRISIS

ORIGINS

The idea of Europe first took shape where so many of the origins of civilisation are to be found, in the eastern Mediterranean. However, the origins of the name itself are uncertain. One possible derivation is from the Semitic *ereb*, meaning 'evening' or 'west'. Certainly from the Greeks, via the Romans, we have received the name as Europe.

Classical civilisation was based mainly on the sea, and more certain settlement of the question of land boundaries was put off until a fuller consciousness emerged of the continent as a whole. Now, when awareness of the rest of Europe beyond Greece and Rome has broadened, and awareness of the rest of the world beyond Europe and its transoceanic offshoots has also developed, we can more completely appreciate that the origins of Europe were by no means exclusively Mediterranean. The Celtic, Germanic, Norse and Slavonic components in the culture of the continent as well as influences from outside can now be given their fuller due. For example, everyday English language is more German than Latin; women played a greater part in the other components than in Greece and Rome.

Old structures have combined with others more recent to make a complex patchwork of ancient and medieval, modern and contemporary buildings in Europe today. And what goes for the buildings applies to other aspects of the environment that have been fashioned by human beings, including much of the land – to give just one instance, bare Scottish moors of primeval aspect were once richly endowed with forest. If we extend our concept of time beyond history into geology, yet another patchwork can be found: of mountains, plains and other physical features moulded by ice, wind and weather over the course of a chronological period far too long for the mind trained to deal in centuries to grasp. More than 600 million years ago, the pre-Cambrian mountain chain was formed in the outer Hebrides, northern Norway, the Kola Peninsula and elsewhere, but is now in places so worn down as hardly to qualify as hills. The coastline has been shifting continually: the port that gave its name in the days of classical Greece to the Adriatic Sea is now 20 kilometres inland; the Low Countries have lost more land than they have gained during the past 2000 years.

Encroaching or receding, the coastline is probably Europe's most distinctive geographical feature – over 75,000 kilometres of it according to one calculation, which is almost twice the length of the earth's circumference. The continent, often formed into peninsulas, abuts vast expanses of water, varying from the warm Mediterranean Sea to the freezing Arctic Ocean, and the waterborne activities of many of its peoples have played as important a part in their development as those on land, especially if we include navigation of the rivers, from the Volga to the Tagus. Moving ashore, we should note that more often than not the surrounding terrain is low-lying rather than elevated. That is to say, the lowlands of Europe cover a vaster area than its mountains, particularly to the north: the great European plain occupies well over 3 million square kilometres, while the highlands take up little more than 800,000 and apart from Scotland and Scandinavia are to be found mainly to the centre or the south. Moreover, the alignment of the Pyrenees, Alps and Carpathians, to take the principal ranges, facilitates the penetration of the prevailing south-westerly winds, which bring both warmth and rain. However, the Gulf Stream has been a more important influence on the maintenance throughout much of the continent of a moderate climate, the regions most remote from it tending to suffer the greatest extremes of temperature and unreliability of precipitation.

The consequent distribution of Europe's agriculture, as well as the exploitation of the mineral resources with which it has been endowed, especially coal and iron ore, has contributed much to its development. Altogether, the importance of geography for history can hardly be exaggerated. However, one problem of definition arises: while Capes Nordkinn, Roca and Tarifa stand out clearly as northern, western and southern terminal points for the continent, demarcation to the east is debatable. Here, the convention will be followed for Europe to stop at the Urals, the Caspian, the Caucasus and the Bosporus, even though this leaves many jagged edges as far as race, language and other human distribution characteristics are concerned. And while the last three of these boundary features, like the aforementioned capes, are distinctive enough, the first of them, although considered a mountain chain, is in many places no more than a gentle incline: travellers on the trans-Siberian railway have to be informed by signpost that they are leaving Europe.

The problem of the eastern boundary of Europe arises in history as much as geography. After the collapse of classical civilisation, the inheritance was claimed not only by Rome itself, which became a centre of Christianity, but also by Byzantium (or Constantinople, later Istanbul) by the Bosporus which claimed from AD 330 onwards to be New Rome, in both secular and religious senses. The Byzantine emperors, who were to assert both secular and religious supremacy, established in the eastern Mediterranean a sphere of influence on the fringe of which was the cradle of Russian civilisation, the city of Kiev.

To the west, in the year AD 800, with the blessing of the Pope, Charlemagne became the first Holy Roman Emperor, exercising power over an area which, broken up soon after his death, ultimately became France and Germany. The process took much longer in the case of Germany, for until the middle of the nineteenth century the centre of Europe remained an area consisting mostly of weak political units given only an artificial cohesion by the continued existence of the Holy Roman Empire. Even France would take several hundred years to become recognisable as a nation state. The collapse of Charlemagne's legacy involved movement among his own people, the Germanic Franks, and others such as the Norsemen (who became known also as the Vikings and the Normans). For some time before Charlemagne until well after him, there was a Moslem Arab presence in Europe, especially in the south-west and south-east, in spite of the Christian Crusades.

During the Middle Ages, the population of Europe was thinly spread. The largest social class, made up of peasants, was bound in a number of ways to the smallest but most influential class, consisting of the landlords – mostly the nobility and the princes. There were exceptions to this general rule, notably the persistence of ancient communal rights and the existence of independent towns, and the apartness of the Church, but most people were bound together in a service relationship, the upper levels of which were involved in a pyramid of loyalties. A serviceman would pledge himself to a master in return for protection – the minor members of the nobility to the major, and so on up to the prince. These ties came together to make up what was later called the feudal system. However, under the surface of ideals of chivalry and complicated rules and regulations there were many disagreements, rivalries and struggles for power, so many that the ignorant might be forgiven for thinking that the system consisted of nothing but feuds. Like most other -isms, feudalism has been given a wide range of interpretations. Some have stressed the economic aspect, the relationship between peasants and landlords. Others have concentrated on the social aspect, the relationship between serviceman and master, tending to argue that this was to be found much more in the West of Europe than in the East.

A great blow was struck in the East in 1453, against Byzantium, the self-styled New Rome, the headquarters of Orthodoxy – as the eastern branch of Christianity called itself after the final split with the Pope in old Rome. After a long period of decline and retreat before Moslem invaders in the shape of the Ottoman Turks, the city finally fell. By this time, the Italian city states were achieving that remarkable cultural upsurge known as the Renaissance, although nobody now would support the old argument that this rebirth occurred in Florence, Venice and elsewhere as a direct result of the death of Byzantium. By this time, too, in East as well as West, the nation state was taking on a firmer shape, to some extent because of a clearer social structure. This was reflected in the emergence of assemblies giving a voice to representatives of the three estates: the first being the clergy, the second the nobility, and the third everybody else, but especially members of professions and trades. Here again, such assemblies as well as such estates would be found more in the West than in the East. Even if stress is placed on economic development, on the formation of a national market as a foundation of the nation state, this characteristic would also have a similarly unbalanced distribution between the two principal parts of Europe.

The great divide appears clearly when Europe is placed in the setting of the wider world, with the celebrated voyages of exploration and discovery of the fifteenth and sixteenth centuries. These were of the greatest importance for the West, first for Portugal and Spain, then for Holland, England and France. For some analysts, the extremity of eastern Europe was 'discovered' along with Asia, Africa and the Americas. Nevertheless, we must recall that the Russians played a part in the process of expansion, opening up Siberia and maintaining the old overland routes to Asia. Generally speaking, the two major sections of Europe had more in common than apart. East was East and West was West, but often the twain did meet.

In 1596, after the death of the first great mapmaker, Mercator, the first part of his *Cosmographia,* entitled *Atlas,* was published by his son. The title page includes the mythical Atlas with the celestial globe on his knee and the terrestrial globe at his feet, while the Foreword suggests that the person who is really wise tries to harmonise his knowledge of heaven and earth. After discussion of creation, the book of Genesis and the four Gospels, Europe and the other known continents are set out in a further four parts as in previous publications. In 1625, Samuel Purchas published a large number of travel stories, commenting: 'The Qualitie of Europe exceeds her Quantitie, in this the least, in that the Best of the world'.[1] The manner in which the opening up of the world influenced the imagination is illustrated further in the work of John Donne (1571?–1613), who wrote the following lines of verse:

> On a round ball
> A Workeman that hath copies by, can lay
> An Europe, Afrique and an Asia,
> And quickly make that, which was nothing, *All.*

and of prose: 'No man is an *Iland,* intire of it selfe; every man is a peece of the *Continent,* a part of the *maine;* if a *Clod* bee washed away by the *Sea, Europe* is the lesse ...'

Still, however, the significance of the wider world was as yet dimly appreciated: beyond Christendom there were Moslem infidels, and beyond them in Asia lesser civilisations, in Africa benighted savages. The earth was no longer the fixed centre of the universe for the educated, who nevertheless hesitated in their acceptance of this loss of status. The leading authorities for enquiry remained the Scriptures and the classics, and time was generally believed to stretch no further back than the year of the Creation – for the Catholic West, 4004 BC, for the Orthodox East, 5509 BC. In most parts of Europe, new ideas could be discussed only in private. Yet a great breakthrough was about to arrive, encouraged by such individuals as Francis Bacon (1561–1626), Lord Chancellor under James I of Great Britain. Bacon argued that the book of nature should be studied along with the revered texts. The enquirer should be like a bee, collecting as many pieces of observation as possible for storing in an encyclopaedic hive. Careful analysis, based on experiment and reason, could then ensue to the benefit of mankind and the glory of God.

The glory of God meant different things to different branches of Christendom, since by the early seventeenth century the great schism between East and West had not been mended, and other schisms had developed. In particular, the Protestant Reformation began, with Martin Luther from 1517, and with Jean Calvin about two decades later. From around the middle of the sixteenth century the Roman Catholic Church made a vigorous response in the Counter-Reformation. On all sides of the divisions of Christendom, however, there were at least some hoping for a general reconciliation, possibly through the revival of the anti-Moslem Crusades.

EUROPE BEFORE 1618

An actual journey through Europe as it was in the period leading up to the Thirty Years War would have presented a challenge of discomforts, delays and dangers insupportable for all but the most intrepid. Here, not courage but suspension of disbelief is called for as we embark upon the attempt to summarise a complex situation in just a few words. To simplify the task, let us divide the continent, West and East, into smaller areas: south-western – Portugal, Spain and Italy; north-western – France, the British Isles and the Low Countries; central – Germany, Austria and Poland; northern – Denmark and Sweden; eastern – Russia; and south-eastern – the Ottoman Empire.

To turn first to the West, we can hardly fail to note that its political arrangement in the early seventeenth century was not very different from what it is in the early twenty-first century (unlike the centre and the East, where great changes have taken place). Ireland and Belgium had still to be created as independent states, while Italy was fragmented enough to be little more than a geographical expression, and many significant boundary changes were to come. However, all this amounted to very little in comparison with those huge alterations to be made in the configuration of Germany, Poland and Russia, and other transformations brought about by the rise and fall of the Ottoman and Austrian empires.

With its long Atlantic coastline, Portugal was exceptionally well placed to gain from the great voyages of discovery and exploration. Like many other states, it drew some sustenance from a romantic view of ancient history, claiming descent from the revolt of Lusitania against Rome in the second century BC, but in fact it appears to have been closely associated with the rest of Iberia until the eleventh century. From then until the beginning of the fourteenth century, the Portuguese monarchy was able to achieve some consolidation of a varied society in spite of internal opposition from the first two estates, Church and nobility, and the external rivalry of Castile. In the first half of the fifteenth century, Portugal constituted the cutting edge of European maritime expansion down the coast of Africa under the energetic leadership of Prince Henry the Navigator, and by the end of the century his successors had rounded Cape Horn to reach India after Portugal and Spain had agreed to divide the wider world between themselves in 1494. In 1500 King Emanuel took the title 'Lord of the conquest, navigation and commerce of India, Ethiopia, Arabia and Persia', and the Portuguese adventurers set about their worldly business with an energy spiritually refreshed by the ardour of missionaries. However, the strength of Portugal was overextended in Latin America as well as in areas of Asia and Africa; it was a military empire not well enough endowed with natural resources. A tendency towards depopulation was reinforced by the insistence on religious purity, which meant the banishment or forcible conversion of the Jews who had played an active part in trade and finance. This reduction in population was less than compensated by the import of large numbers of slaves. The death of Sebastian, the last male member of the royal line, appropriately enough on an imperial adventure in Morocco in 1578, led by 1581 to the inauguration of the 'Sixty Years Captivity' as the Portuguese crown was assumed by Philip II of Spain.

Spain now seemed to be experiencing its greatest age; in fact, as in the case of Portugal, its undoubted grandeur led to delusions. Phoenician, Roman, Visigothic and especially Moslem conquests had all left their mark, and the business of the unification could hardly be said to have reached completion at the time of the celebrated marriage of Queen Isabella of Castile to King Ferdinand of Aragon in 1469. And although their even more celebrated patronage of Columbus led to the acquisition of colonies and of a goodly Spanish share of the division of the world with Portugal in 1494, involvement in almost continuous war on the Italian peninsula was a drain on resources while weakening internal stability. Then, with the premature death of the only son of Ferdinand and Isabella, the crown passed to Charles of Habsburg, the Holy Roman Emperor Charles V, and Spanish involvement in European wars widened, especially those concerning the Netherlands, which Charles left to his son Philip II. Meanwhile, the Inquisition played a modest part in the attack on Spanish Moslems and Jews (as economically active as their counterparts in Portugal) and became an important weapon of the Counter-Reformation, even if less through the notorious torture and execution of heretics than through guardianship of religious orthodoxy and public morals. As for the second estate, the nobles were conducting themselves in a manner which was to inspire Cervantes to create Don Quixote, who like all good caricatures emphasises reality rather than ignoring it. Also, some of them spent more time around court looking for places which would bring monetary rewards than at large seeking out opportunities for the performance of knightly deeds with remunerations for their honour only; their consumption was more conspicuous than their valour. Of course, there were a few good officers and administrators, but Spanish Habsburg aspirations and commitments could not be sustained by the governmental system that Philip was trying to control at the same time as fighting the Netherlands, France, England and other European enemies while posing as the champion of Christendom against the Moslem Turks.

Italy, much more than Portugal and Spain, was trying to live on past glories at the beginning of the seventeenth century. Soon after the sack of Rome in 1527, the peninsula became little more than a number of client states with virtually no power to stop foreign patrons battling on their soil. The lion's share went to the Habsburgs but the French Bourbons were soon to challenge that apportionment. Whatever the abiding splendours of the Renaissance, and however large its population, politically Italy was now to have little history exclusively of its own for some hundreds of years. However, the papacy remained a powerful influence throughout much of Europe, especially during the Counter-Reformation, and some of the other Italian states did what they could to play off one invader against another in order to retain a measure of independence – Piedmont and Venice enjoying the greatest degree of success in this regard. Already, the division was apparent between a richer North and a poorer South.

Across the Pyrenees or the Alps, and away from the Mediterranean, feudalism was to be found in its purest form, risen from the western ruins of the empire of Charlemagne. All Gaul had been divided in Roman times into three parts, said Caesar; from about the end of the ninth century onwards, it had been divided into many more. However, after the Duchy of France had established its authority over other provinces such as Flanders, Normandy and Burgundy, Aquitaine and Toulouse, something like national unity was established on a still localised base, even though internal conflict, often closely linked with foreign wars, threatened dismemberment on many occasions. Joan of Arc was a powerful symbol of the struggle for unification. At the beginning of the sixteenth century, Francis I was a powerful rival to Emperor Charles V, flexing his muscles in Italy at the same time as trying to behave like a Caesar at home in relation to both Church and nobility. But the repetition and savagery of the religious wars later on in that century, with social tensions added to the struggle between Catholics and Protestants, starkly revealed that centrifugal forces were still strong, and the stabilising achievement of Henry IV at the century's end was far from conclusive.

Although Henry IV and later members of the Bourbon dynasty promoted expeditions to the New World, they exerted their strength mostly in Europe itself, looking on maritime activity as something of secondary importance. Not so the later Tudors over the small but significant stretch of water that separated the British Isles from the continent, for theirs was an inheritance intimately linked with the sea from time immemorial. Successive waves of invasion – British, Roman,

Anglo-Saxon and Scandinavian – had culminated in the final Norman Conquest of the eleventh century. Then, a feudal order was successfully superimposed on the already existing structure of common law. In order to strengthen their position the English monarchs moved their forces in the direction of the Celtic fringes, northwards towards Scotland, westwards to Wales and across the sea to Ireland. Moving back over the Channel, they attempted to claim for themselves an inheritance that they were reluctant to realise was no longer theirs: Calais, the last foothold, was only given up as late as 1558. By this time, various companies of entrepreneurs were developing from such activities as the European woollen cloth trade into ventures directed further outwards. At the turn of the century, results still pointed towards potential rather than achievement (although Shakespeare had taken the English language to new heights). Yet it was the financial power and reformed religion of many of the merchants as well as the hybrid nature of English feudalism that encouraged Queen Elizabeth I to make at least limited compromises with Catholicism on behalf of the Protestant Church first introduced by her father, Henry VIII, as well as with her parliaments evolved over several centuries. At her death in 1603, James VI of Scotland, son of the ill-fated Mary Stewart, was invited to come to London to become James I of England. He soon pronounced himself King of Great Britain.

The power of the merchants was an even greater obstacle to absolutism in the low-lying northern Netherlands, which broke from their southern neighbours towards the end of the sixteenth century to form the United Provinces. Their easy access to the sea and the great use that they had previously made of it in fishing and commerce combined with the more recent enthusiastic reception of Calvinism to give the United Provinces (commonly known as Holland after the chief of them) the will and wherewithal to survive in the difficult years following their formal creation in 1579–81. Even though William of Orange (William the Silent) was a member of the high nobility who had performed important courtly and diplomatic services for Charles V and then became Stadholder or Governor of the north-western Dutch provinces of Philip II, his leadership of the revolt of the Netherlands could never have been successful without the support of the middle class as well as of society at large. Meanwhile, the Spanish Habsburgs managed to maintain their hold on the southern Netherlands (which would later form the basis of Belgium).

France, Great Britain and the United Provinces had more in common with each other than with any of the other sections into which we have divided Europe. In the seventeenth century, many of the most progressive practices in both civil administration and military organisation were to be found in this north-western part of the continent.

To turn to the centre, the great European plain with no natural boundaries to speak of and limited access to the Atlantic and other oceans was a difficult setting for the development of an effective government. Certainly there had been a German consciousness of law and society before the *Reich* of Charlemagne claimed the classical inheritance for itself in the year 800. In the thirteenth century, the Teutonic Knights superimposed their order upon Slavs and other peoples to the East. More peacefully, the Hanseatic towns around the Baltic Sea and beyond were among those to share in medieval commercial prosperity, especially in the fourteenth century. In the 1520s, according to some accounts, during the first years of the reign of Emperor Charles V and, more significantly, the first years of the spread of the doctrines of Martin Luther, the possibility of a new national movement appeared to arise among the German people. However, after the Peasant War of 1524–5 and Luther's declaration in favour of the princes, continued conflict led to the compromise peace of Augsburg in 1555 which allowed each prince to choose either the Catholic or Lutheran faith for his region. Protestant and Catholic political units continued an uneasy coexistence within the loose framework of the Holy Roman Empire, from which neither Brandenburg–Prussia nor Austria had yet emerged with anything like the clarity that they would later assume.

A word should perhaps be spoken in passing about Switzerland, strategically placed at one of the crossroads of Europe but to some extent protected by mountainous inaccessibility. From the beginning of the sixteenth century, virtually separated from the empire, the confederation of Swiss cantons had attempted to adhere to a policy of balanced neutrality amid the wars raging around them, with some success. Religious and other internal problems would continue to exist, especially after Jean Calvin began to promulgate his doctrines of the Reformation from the late 1530s onwards. But on the whole the confederation was able to survive without any of these problems approaching crisis point.

In and around the Baltic, after the decline of the Norse Vikings, feudalism had developed comparatively late, and the power of the Hanseatic League had been at times almost dominant. It was through the assistance of one of the league's outstanding members, the city of Lübeck, that Sweden after more than a century of dependence was able to break from Denmark in the 1520s. Then a powerful new dynasty, the Vasas, with the support of a mostly compliant nobility and the comparative absence of domestic opposition, rural or urban, was able to make use of the ideology of the Reformation as well as of the compact peninsular position and natural resources of the country to make Sweden into a centralised state that could throw off the demanding patronage of Lübeck and constitute a rival for dominance in the Baltic to a still formidable Denmark and to other neighbours.

Of these, although no better blessed with natural boundaries than Germany, Poland had a continuous history stretching back to the tenth century and was able to enjoy something of a Golden Age throughout most of the sixteenth century. The decline of the Teutonic Order of Knights had been signalled by their defeat at the Battle of Grünwald (Tannenberg) in 1410, and the joint victors, Poland and Lithuania, were mostly in collaboration from some time before the solemnising Union of Lublin in 1569. Yet the *Rzesczpospolita Polska* (literally Republic of Poland) developed as anything but an absolutist regime. The nobility was divided among itself while giving far less than consistent support to the central monarchy, even under Sigismund II, who was perhaps the most successful king. There were religious problems among people mostly Roman Catholic but also Protestant and Orthodox, Jewish and even Moslem. The population, while largely Slavonic, was also Germanic and Baltic. To survive economically, Poland had to participate in international trade, especially in grain: this necessity in turn led to the inordinate exploitation of the peasants by the noble landlords and gave such importance to the city of Gdańsk (Danzig) that it became almost an independent principality. Rivalry with Sweden to the north, the Ottoman Empire to the south and Russia to the east, not to mention sometimes difficult relations with states to the west, meant that the Golden Age could never be enjoyed with any great degree of relaxation.

Comfort was even more lacking in the fellow Slav state of Muscovite Russia. Here, geography had shown its meanest face, so much so indeed that its intemperate climate, interminable distances and landlocked remoteness have often persuaded analysts to exclude it from Europe entirely for these reasons alone, or in addition to the powerful prejudice that has entered discussion of this extremity of the continent with unusual frequency. True, too, the Russians themselves (in this respect at least similar to the inhabitants of Great Britain) have often made the distinction between their own country and Europe, and this distinction must have been forced upon them wittingly or unwittingly during the centuries of the Mongol or Tatar yoke which broke most of the contacts made during the preceding Kievan period, when Viking, Byzantine Orthodox and other influences had combined with a sturdy native tradition to produce a remarkable medieval civilisation. By the end of the fifteenth century Ivan III and his adherents brought near to completion the process of the ingathering of the Russian lands, which involved not only the reduction of the Asiatic hordes but also the suppression of independent principalities and cities. Muscovy claimed a classical inheritance as a Third Rome now that the second – Byzantium – had fallen. Then, in the second half of the sixteenth century, Ivan IV (Ivan the Terrible) led a bold attempt to continue the work of his predecessors in establishing control over Muscovite Russia at the same time as pushing out its boundaries to the east, where he took Kazan and Astrakhan on the Volga from the Tatars, and to the west, where he enjoyed less lasting success in the attempt to establish a foothold on the Baltic. Soon after his death, however, the virtually enserfed peasants as well as dissident nobles and the Cossacks all in their various ways demonstrated their discontent in the Time of Troubles, of which more later.

For the moment, we must complete our brief journey around Europe by moving to its south-eastern area under the control of the Ottoman Empire, which by the mid-sixteenth century under Suleiman I (Suleiman the Magnificent) was probably the most powerful political organisation on earth. Its influence spread throughout the Mediterranean to affect developments in many parts of Europe, of course, but nowhere so intimately as in the Balkans and Hungary. For a time, under Suleiman's despotism, with a mighty army and navy, the empire was able to make best use of both its rural-nomadic and urban-settled characteristics. Soon after his death a decline set in, but not without some intermittent revival. As the Moslem Empire began to recede, Christian neighbours grew anxious to move in for the kill. We shall consider each part of that disintegrating empire as it emerged from Ottoman control, pausing here only to note that as states were either reborn or born for the first time, considerable use was made by them of historic precedents, sometimes distorted and on occasion even manufactured. In this respect, they were not unlike the states already in existence.

THE THIRTY YEARS WAR

On 23 May 1618, a group of Protestant nobles threw three Roman Catholic officials from a window of the royal palace in Prague. The miraculous survival of the officials appeared to confirm that God was on their side, but their opponents believed in divine support, too. A revolt enveloping much of Bohemia (Czechia) led to a counterattack from Ferdinand II, elected Holy Roman Emperor on 28 August 1619, just two days after he had been deposed as king of Bohemia. From such beginnings there developed a war involving in some way or another virtually the whole of Europe.

The scene had already been set. Just before the turn of the century, the frail edifice of Muscovy gave way under the strain of dynastic confusion and domestic strife. Ambitious invaders, notably Poles and Swedes, broke in to seize the spoils, and were not successfully driven out and deprived of their gains until after the election of a new dynasty, the Romanovs, in 1613. Poland and Sweden now turned on each other again to resume their struggle for dominance in the Baltic and its hinterland, while the Holy Roman Emperor was stung into action not only by the action of the Bohemian Protestants but also by his realisation that reverses for his fellow Roman Catholics in Poland meant setbacks for the Habsburg strategy in central and eastern Europe as a whole. Meanwhile, although there were not so many immediate preliminary hostilities to the west of the continent, the Spanish Habsburgs believed that the time was ripe for a further strike against their rebellious Dutch provinces and were prepared to give full assistance to their Holy Roman relations, while the French monarch and his advisers believed that the moment was approaching for them to make another attempt to break out from Habsburg encirclement.

Already the features that were to characterise the Thirty Years War were apparent: political, national, religious and social. Most obviously, the war consisted of a struggle between various European states for dominance in certain strategically vital areas of the continent. However, some of the parties involved were less than states, notably most of the German principalities, and at least one of the major participants was more than a state, the Holy Roman Empire. While Ferdinand II and his successor attempted to keep together what was left of the empire, Czechs, Hungarians and other subject nationalities did what they could to achieve the greatest possible measure of independence. In both East and West, the Habsburgs fought for the faith of their fathers as well as their property. Religious affiliation was strong, yet it could yield to other considerations. Most notoriously, Cardinal Richelieu on behalf of France gave much support to what was widely seen as the Protestant cause, while in the estimation of some historians, the most fundamental allegiance of those involved in the conflict was not to their government, their people or their confession but to their class. At least one analyst has asserted that to a significant extent the war constituted 'a punitive expedition against the German peasants', culminating in their enserfment.[2]

The hostilities begun in Bohemia in 1618 culminated in defeat for the Czech rebels and their all too few Hungarian and other allies at the Battle of the White Mountain in November 1620. From 1621 to 1623, the Habsburgs took their victory further in the upper Rhine and in the neighbourhood of Bavaria, the Dutch promoting the principal opposition. The period 1624–9, customarily known as the Danish War, shifted the centre of attention to the north-west of Germany, where the Dutch continued to provide much of the finance while the Danes and others did most of the fighting, with mixed success. By 1629 the imperial forces had established themselves firmly on the Baltic Sea, and their leader, Wallenstein, had acquired for himself the title 'General of the Whole Imperial Fleet and Lord of the Ocean'. Neither Wallenstein nor any of his side in the war did in fact lord it over the Atlantic Ocean, where the Dutch were infiltrating Spanish American colonies. Meanwhile, by no means everything was going the way of the Habsburgs on European land, yet Emperor Ferdinand was confident enough at the end of the 1620s once again to assert Roman Catholic ascendancy in the empire.

Although Denmark was now knocked out, a new Protestant champion entered the fray in the shape of the Lion of the North, Gustavus Adolphus of Sweden, who put his firm stamp on the next major series of hostilities, the Swedish War from 1630 to 1635. However, the Swedish lion could not have performed his great deeds without the financial assistance of the French fox, Richelieu, their joint aims being listed in the treaty of alliance as 'the safeguarding of the Baltic and the Oceanic Seas, the liberty of commerce, and the relief of the oppressed states of the Holy Roman Empire'.[3] Gustavus Adolphus now made his greatest contribution to the relief of the 'oppressed states', penetrating deep into the heart of Germany with the help not only of French money but also of Muscovy, in two ways: certainly with the engagement of Poland in a war for the frontier fortress of Smolensk; and probably with the supply of grain at low prices that could be sold at great profit in the international markets of Amsterdam and Antwerp. With the untimely death of Gustavus Adolphus in November 1632, the Swedes and their allies suffered several reverses, especially after the vain and erratic Wallenstein had been assassinated and the command of their enemies' forces taken over by the emperor's son, the future Ferdinand III. The present emperor, Ferdinand II, made at least some concessions to his Protestant princes, and in May 1635 Prague gave its name to a treaty bringing hostilities to a temporary uneasy end, 17 years almost to the day after they had begun in the same city.

The final 13 of the 30 years are usually known as the Franco-Habsburg War, 1635–48. During them, in alliance with Sweden and Holland in particular, Bourbon France attempted to weaken the Habsburg encirclement and to strengthen its own frontiers. While the Swedes continued to make sorties into the empire, more than once penetrating as far as Vienna, the Dutch struggled on sea and land to loosen the Spanish grip on the Netherlands, and the French pushed towards the Pyrenees on the one hand and the Rhine on the other. There was fighting also in Italy to the south-west and in Bohemia and Hungary to the south-east, as well as across the Atlantic Ocean.

Then, after years of talk that threatened to be as prolonged as the action, a series of agreements, the most important of which comprised the Peace of Westphalia, brought the war in general to an end in October 1648, although Spain and France in particular were to keep it going until November 1659. By the principal terms of the peace, France gained Alsace, the Dutch Republic consolidated its rise and Sweden retained a foothold in northern Germany. Switzerland achieved formal separation from the empire while Brandenburg expanded within it. The Austrian and Spanish Habsburgs lost some of their pretensions, although Ferdinand III, Holy Roman Emperor since 1637, gained some consolation from his confirmation as king of Bohemia, where upstart Protestantism had been suppressed, as well as in Hungary and Austria. Outside these hereditary dominions, however, both Lutheran and Calvinist heresies continued to thrive as the local rulers saw fit. According to Heinhard Steiger, the Roman Catholic Counter-Reformation could not now achieve complete success; indeed, the Pope was involved in the peace 'not as the religious leader of Europe or the world, but as the secular ruler of a territory'. And so, the 'Christian Peace' of Westphalia was 'general', not 'denominational': Catholics, Lutherans and Calvinists were 'partners in the treaties', while the Orthodox were also included and 'thereby joined the community of international law'. Even the Ottoman sultan 'formed a part, if only in a modified manner, of the community of law'. In the view of John Elliott:

> This Europe, as shaped by the Peace of Westphalia, was to be a continent in which the secular interests of states were to be of more importance in the conduct of international affairs than their religious differences. In this more secularised continent, the papacy, which had been relegated to the sidelines in the Westphalia negotiations, ceased to be even the nominal arbitrator of Christendom. Indeed, it was a symptom of the changing times that the very term 'Christendom' was more and more to yield pride of place to 'Europe'.[4]

The misery inflicted by the Thirty Years War on all ranks and orders of men, women and children is incalculable. Hostilities by no means enveloped the whole of Germany; nevertheless, just the simple task of keeping the various armies and their horses fed visited great hardships on those provinces through which they were passing. To quote from the well-known literary account, Grimmelshausen's *Simplicius Simplicissimus*, first published in 1669:

> Foraging is defined as riding out to the villages and, with danger
> to life and limb, threshing, grinding, and baking, grabbing and
> stealing whatever is handy, maltreating and abusing peasants and
> even ruining their women, daughters and hired girls ... And when
> the poor peasants object to this treatment or get bold enough to
> rap some forager's knuckles while he is at work ... then you strike
> them down – provided you can – or at least make their houses go
> up in smoke.[5]

Even though armies were not as large as they later became, Gustavus
Adolphus was leading a force of about 100,000 men in 1632 (with
perhaps half as many horses) and each man alone would require a daily
ration of 1 kilogram of bread and 300 grams of meat.[6] Such a basic
requirement dictated the war's strategy as well as contributing to many
of its hardships, both for the peasants and for the soldiers and horses,
with the not infrequent consequence of starvation and epidemic.

The Thirty Years War was an important stage in military development, Gustavus Adolphus showing the way with a well-drilled and
disciplined army which possessed a national core even though it contained many mercenaries. More generally, that long series of hostilities
marked a significant step forward towards the formation of the absolutist state, of which the national army would be an essential part.
To pay for it and other vital needs, improvements in the economy had
to be encouraged and more efficient means of taxation had to be
devised. These in turn made necessary a more smoothly working
administration and improved system of law. The monarch, previously
exercising a personal rule through divine right, now had to look for
additional support in secular ideas as his commands merged with the
edicts of the state. Agreement had to be reached with the clergy, the
nobility and leading burghers, since absolutism needed a firm social
basis. But national assemblies were often restricted in the interests of
centralisation. More coercive methods often had to be found for keeping the peasantry in subjection, especially in the centre and the East,
where serfdom became entrenched.

All these characteristics of absolutism varied throughout Europe in
the timing, pace and intensity of their development. Moreover, as
always in history, as the new appeared, the old did not completely
disappear. The privileges belonging to the clergy, the nobility and the

townsfolk would be jealously guarded; whole provinces would attempt to maintain their separate existence; 90 per cent or so of the people of the continent were still peasants. Many believers set in their ways would resist cultural change; along with the arrival of modern science came waves of witch-hunting. The normal area of circulation and consciousness for as much as 80 per cent of Europeans would still be no more than 5 kilometres from the centre of the parish. Yet for a considerable proportion of the other 20 per cent, horizons could envelop large parts of the continent, even the whole of it or in some cases much of the world. Even when most of the fifth of the world's total population that lived in Europe (approximately 100 million out of 500 million) were unaware of it, their destinies could be affected through interaction with Asia, Africa and the Americas.[7]

Within the area between the Atlantic and the Urals, there was more evident interaction. For example, of the officers of the Scottish army moving into England to support the parliamentary cause in 1644, according to one detailed calculation, all the generals, every lieutenant-colonel but two, and every major but one had served in the continental wars. Their military expertise, which included knowledge of fighting in the most up-to-date fashion, was joined to an often fervent religious faith to produce a fighting force that was formidable indeed. As John Morrill rightly observes, the civil wars that took place in Scotland and Ireland as well as England were 'a peripheral but actual part of the Thirty Years War, the greatest of all continental European wars before the era of Bonaparte'.[8] Economic connections were well established too, as witnessed by Sir Thomas Roe, itinerant ambassador extraordinary, writing at the end of the 1620s:

> The loss of the free trade of the Balticque sea is more dangerous to the kingdome of England and the United Provinces than any other prosperity of the house of Austria, being the Indyes of the materialls of shipping, and consequently, both of their strength, riches, and subsistence.[9]

English and Dutch interest in the grain market of the Baltic was also considerable. In general, the peninsular nature of its geography and the closer nature of its relations persuaded Philip Cluver, born in Danzig and living in the United Provinces, to liken the European body politic in

1629 to the body of a woman whose 'head is Spain ... bosom is France, arms are Italy and Britain, stomach is Germany, navel is Bohemia', with other parts including Denmark, Sweden, Prussia, Poland, Hungary and Muscovy.[10]

Cluver was among a number of scholars who managed to turn their often painful experiences during the Thirty Years War to constructive advantage, helping to beat the swords into ploughshares. For example, the French philosopher René Descartes was attracted into Bavarian service and then encouraged by his solitude in winter quarters along the Danube in the year 1619 to move towards the famous conclusion: *cogito ergo sum* – I think, therefore I exist. According to his own account, he was filled with enthusiasm, and discovered the foundations of a marvellous science. He went on to spend much of his working life in Holland, publishing in Leyden in 1637 a collection of *Philosophical Essays* that included 'Discourse on the Method of Using One's Reason Well and Searching for the Truth in the Sciences'. Because of a desire for self-protection rather than through modesty, Descartes brought out his work anonymously, but he has since been widely celebrated for having begun with it the Age of Reason. The Dutch thinker Hugo de Groot (known as Grotius) managed to escape from prison to complete *On the Law of War and Peace*, first published in Latin in Paris in 1625. 'Throughout Christendom', he wrote, 'I saw a readiness to make war of which even barbarians might be ashamed ... The sight of such atrocities has induced a good many truly reputable writers to forbid Christian men all recourse to arms since it is their special duty to love all men.' To stop war was impossible, Grotius conceded, but it should be possible to establish that men should not be killed on neutral territory and that women should not be violated or killed anywhere.[11] This was by no means the first word on this important subject, but it was further clear evidence that, amid all the tumult and the agony, the still, small voice of reason was attempting to argue its way towards the establishment of a lasting peace.

MID-CENTURY CRISIS

The political impact of the Thirty Years War was felt throughout the continent; the states that comprised it and the frontiers that separated them both took on more definitive shape: France especially benefited from the ultimate victory over the Habsburgs. While the Swedish triumph was to be shorter-lived owing to the rise of Brandenburg–Prussia, the United Provinces of the Netherlands continued to prosper. Even the defeated Habsburgs learned from their painful experience, giving up their ambition to achieve imperial hegemony over Germany and Europe to establish themselves on a more secure and separated footing in Austria, and for a briefer period in Spain. In eastern Europe the scale of the changes arising from the war was greatest, much of the Ukraine breaking away from Poland only to be incorporated in Muscovite Russia. Yet the significance of the events taking place in the much smaller area of the British Isles was arguably equally considerable, if not more so. If the connection between the Thirty Years War and the civil war breaking out in the offshore kingdoms was not obvious and direct, it was certainly there, as were connections between the social disturbances leading up to the execution of Charles I in London and other upsets occurring in Paris and many other cities throughout Europe.

This is not to suggest a conspiracy, but rather a series of comparable reactions to attempts by governments under severe strain to extract more obedience and more money from their subjects. These were not just rural and urban lower-class revolts, which occurred with remarkable frequency in the seventeenth and eighteenth centuries, but movements involving the upper ranks of society, too. The intensity of the crisis may have arisen partly from the weather, especially the onset of the 'Little Ice Age' which affected harvests, and partly from longer-term economic problems involving money supply and prices. Possibly, great upsets in Asia, even dynastic change as far away as China, and developments across the Atlantic Ocean had some kind of knock-on effect. However, war in Europe itself was of primary importance.

France's predecessor as leading power had been Spain, but its ambitions had recently been greater than its achievements, and under the pressure of trying to maintain its leadership into the seventeenth century, Spain was falling apart. The government had never been consolidated, and now Catalonia and Portugal were breaking away from the control of Castile. Already a decline had set in through the loss of some of the riches of the wider world, and Spain did not possess the resources to control and protect overseas dominions at the same time as fighting the Dutch and the French nearer home. Moreover, domestic problems had been made worse by the expulsion in 1609 of the Moriscos, the Moors who retained cultural apartness even if they had officially accepted Christianity. They had been a sizeable and economically active segment of the population, and their departure meant a human and financial shortage. Then, in the late 1630s, dissatisfaction at tax and other demands from Madrid led to unrest in many areas, especially Catalonia and Portugal. The proximity of Catalonia to France gave it strategic priority, and the government attempted to solve its problems there by involving the people of the province more deeply in the war. But the Catalans turned their arms against their own king. Meanwhile, with no smaller fervour, the Portuguese were taking the opportunity to bring to an end the 'Sixty Years Captivity'. The Duke of Braganza became John IV in 1640 and set about maintaining Portuguese independence with widespread domestic support and the encouragement of Spain's enemies.

With the lack of homage from Catalonia continuing into the 1640s, King Philip IV was to suffer from disloyalty on the part of his further flung subjects in the Kingdom of Naples, although Don Juan of Austria, the King of Spain's son, was able to restore order by the beginning of 1648. Towards the end of that year, Pope Innocent X issued a bull denouncing the Peace of Westphalia as 'null and void, accursed and without any influence or result for the past, the present or the future',[12] the thoroughness of his condemnation being a measure of his inability to do anything about what he perceived as the growing power of Protestantism. At this time, no state in Italy, even Venice, could claim to be pursuing policies independent of the great European powers that still continued their struggle for dominance in the peninsula. Piedmont, it is true, retained something of a distinctive character in its role as a buffer state with France, which, however, was encroaching in all directions after surmounting the crisis, or series of crises, known as the Fronde (1648–53).

These were set off perhaps by problems stemming from the minority of Louis XIV, who had been a young boy at the time of his accession in 1643, but there were deeper-seated causes for discontent. In France as elsewhere this arose from the complex international conflict that was the Thirty Years War, and more exclusively from the war with Spain that continued beyond 1648. Popular uprisings of the period formed an important accompaniment to the struggle that took place at the higher levels of society and perhaps gave it an urgency and a seriousness that it would not otherwise have possessed. The background to the Fronde was also provided by the tension between province and centre, between old nobility and new nobility, between Catholics and Protestants.

Taxation and other economic circumstances were as significant in France as elsewhere, as both a general and a specific cause of trouble. In the summer of 1648, leadership was given to rising discontent, perhaps unwittingly, by the *parlement* of Paris. This high court and executive council had never, like its parliamentary counterpart over the Channel, developed an elective representative element, since its members often purchased their places and then made them hereditary. Nevertheless, it had assumed from its function of the registration of royal edicts a measure of legislative action and even of political power, and because of the nature of the process of centralisation in France, it exercised an authority far greater than the other *parlements* distributed among the provinces. Thus, as Cardinal Mazarin, the young king's chief minister, attempted to establish absolutist control through the use of appointed officials bypassing the authority of the *parlements* and through the imposition of higher taxes, especially an increase of the *paulette* levied on hereditary office holding, the *parlement* of Paris led a constitutional movement of protest, which enjoyed early success and came near to reducing monarchical sovereignty. However, as already indicated, the circumstances of the time would not allow the struggle to be simply king versus *parlement*, and it soon broadened to include rural and urban insurgents from some of the meanest peasants to the highest princes of the blood. Having won at least a technical victory, the *parlement* now became alarmed at the increasing level of illegal activity, and made a deal with the government early in 1649. Although the princes of the blood shared a haughty disdain of the upstart nobility of the robe in the *parlement*, they could never agree how best to defend their time-honoured privileges and fell out among themselves for reasons varying from family honour to religious affiliation. Cardinal Mazarin was forced to go into temporary exile, but Louis enjoyed enough support to secure his own reputation in a triumphant entry into Paris late in 1652 after the leader of the opposition had been forced to seek refuge with the Spanish in the Netherlands. The cardinal came back to Paris to join his more confident master at the beginning of 1653. After order had been restored throughout the provinces, Louis XIV and his chief minister set about the construction of a more permanent absolutism, although vivid memories of the Fronde made it necessary for them to proceed warily at the same time as gaining for them a large measure of support.

The nature of the regime that emerged from the mid-century crisis on the other side of the Channel was determined by a compromise less favourable to absolutism (at least of the monarchical type – it is possible to argue that in its place there developed a parliamentary variety of this form of government). However, although the resolution may have been distinctive, and although the crisis may have been – in the execution of Charles I – unique, the British Isles were by no means immune from the widely shared problems stemming from the Thirty Years War. The British king's troubles deepened in the mid-1630s when he attempted to finance his personal rule through, among other extraordinary taxation measures, the levy of ship money. He had already incurred widespread displeasure because of the royal favourite Buckingham's overadventurous foreign policy a decade or so before. Even if the support that he had given to the Protestant cause in the great continental conflict had pleased at least some of his people, his arbitrary decision now to use the navy on the Spanish and Catholic side led to the outrage of far many more, and to an almost general refusal to pay ship money.

The royal predicament was made even worse by the king's evident misunderstanding of the importance of both the outlying areas and the centre of his kingdom. When Charles attempted to interfere with the direction taken north of the border in church matters, he offended the national pride as well as the religious faith of a large number of his fellow countrymen (he had been born in Dunfermline, the medieval seat of Scottish kings). The Scots raised an army to resist the imposition of bishops, and the king was obliged to give way. His English subjects were now emboldened to show their resistance when a penniless Charles was faced with no alternative but to call parliament again in 1640. In 1641, following the Scottish example, the Irish rose in a rebellion that was to last until 1652. A comment of the royalist Clarendon on later developments is applicable here: 'though Scotland blew the first trumpet, it was Ireland that drew the first blood'.[13] At the beginning of 1642, after the Long Parliament had abolished ship money and many of the other foundations of the king's attempt at personal absolutism, Charles made another great error in the shape of his decision to quit London. True enough, his supporters there were in a minority, and he was opposed by the City as well as by parliament. But London was the commercial as well as the administrative capital, and because of the nature of previous economic and political history, it was more dominant over the rest of the country than its continental counterparts. While to have remained there would have called for a measure of boldness even greater than Louis XIV was to show in his entry into Paris in 1652, Charles lost much of what initiative was left to him by leaving London. He was to return there only in late 1648 for imprisonment, trial and execution. Possibly, in the years between, a more fluid strategy and less opportunistic tactics could have saved him. But, already perhaps courting martyrdom, Charles refused to yield his ultimate control over army and Church, while all too often revealing in a far less idealistic desire for victory at any price the willingness to co-operate with many groups who did not share his fundamental views about sovereignty. In the confused aftermath that followed the execution of Charles I at the beginning of 1649, power went to a Lord Protector ruling in a manner which, at least for a time, was more successfully absolutist than that of his royal predecessor.

Oliver Cromwell's early problems, again following precedent, were foreign as well as domestic. At the same time as controlling parliament and the army, he had to deal with conflict stemming from commercial and political rivalry stronger than religious sympathy and social affinity with the Dutch. War broke out in 1652, and the fact that the Dutch also had emerged with new strength from their own internal crisis meant that they made formidable opponents. For the United Provinces had been able to exploit the interaction of forces during the Thirty Years War to achieve confirmation and even extension of their independence from Spain. However, after everything that they had sought seemed to have been gained, the Dutch fell into deep disagreement among themselves about how to proceed after peace was made with Spain in the Treaty of Münster at the beginning of 1648. William II, who had succeeded his father as Prince of Orange about a year earlier, was anxious to keep to an earlier agreement with France. He told Mazarin that he would carry the war to Spain until France had achieved satisfaction; he would then in conjunction with Louis XIV pursue a policy of intervention in the British civil war on the side of Charles I, whose eldest daughter was his own wife. At the same time, he was hoping that the city of Amsterdam and its hinterland province of Holland, which were in favour of peace and reluctant to finance any military adventures, could be brought to heel. Undismayed by the difficulties of Louis XIV and the execution of Charles I, he moved into Holland in the summer of 1650 and arrested six of the leading members of its States. An uneasy compromise led in August to the release of the prisoners, but William's relations with both the States of Holland and the States General were still unsettled at the time of his sudden death from smallpox in November.

Turmoil to the north-west was in many ways a reflector of progress, while stability in the centre was an indicator of stagnation. The stability was no more than relative and was more clearly apparent on the region's own terms than on those of Europe in general. Moreover, the stability was deceptive in the sense that its largest political unit, the Holy Roman Empire, had been since the Treaty of Westphalia even less actually in control of its several constituent parts than it had been previously, while none of these was yet by itself in a position to make any challenge to its supremacy. Bavaria and Saxony would perhaps exert most influence beyond their boundaries at mid-century. But before the century was completed, a greater degree of physical might was probably concentrated in Brandenburg–Prussia, beginning to take on formidable shape with the acquisition of the undistinguished looking but strategically well-placed coastal province of eastern Pomerania.

Sweden acquired the more immediately useful western Pomerania and other footholds on the southern shores of the Baltic Sea, but wisely modified its earlier ambitions for extended empire in Germany, even if it was necessarily involved in the complicated politics of the Holy Roman Empire. The Swedish government's top priority remained domination of the Baltic Sea, an ambition that continued to antagonise the traditional enemy, Denmark, and began to arouse the suspicion of a former ally, the Dutch Republic. In common with many other European states, Denmark and Sweden felt the strains of continued warfare to the full. The death of the long-reigning Christian IV of Denmark in 1648 was followed by strong pressure on his heir from the nobility, which was in turn under threat of dissent from below. The crisis in Sweden was made more serious by the strong will of Queen Christina, a young girl at the death of her father Gustavus Adolphus in 1632 but by now very much her own woman, almost, according to some evaluations, her own man. By supporting the cause of the religious and commoner Estates in the Diet of 1650, she alarmed the nobility, but once all the Estates and the Council had recognised her cousin Charles Gustavus as hereditary heir, she resumed her patronage of blue blood, and returned the clergy, burghers and peasants to their former status before giving up the throne in 1654 and becoming a Catholic.

On the other side of the Baltic Sea, Poland, which had been able to make Muscovy a puppet state during the Time of Troubles, was experiencing its own grievous problems. The seventeenth century was by no means a continuation of the 'Golden Age' and Poland had been deeply involved in the Thirty Years War, even if the years 1638–48 nevertheless became known as a decade of 'golden peace' at least as far as relations were concerned between the government and its most troublesome subjects, the Cossacks. In 1648 the newly elected king, John Casimir, found himself confronted by a revolt of the Cossacks and unrest among many other of his subjects, at the same time beset by a series of international problems left over from the Thirty Years War. Under a vigorous leader, Bogdan Khmelnitsky, whose fame spread throughout Europe, the Cossacks of the Ukraine, joined by the local peasants, rose to restore old freedoms and gain new privileges, quickly forcing John Casimir to make several concessions.

The struggle was by no means over, and was complicated by the intervention of other interested parties: the Crimean Tatars found Khmelnitsky too ambitious an ally and switched their allegiance from him to John Casimir; the Muscovite Russians took the opportunity to tie Khmelnitsky's ambitions to their own, helping him to sever much of the Ukraine from Poland only for them virtually to annex it in the agreement reached at Pereiaslavl in 1654. The government of Tsar Alexis, who had succeeded to the throne in 1645, was at first somewhat reluctant to become too closely involved in the Ukrainian problem since it already had more than enough troubles of its own. Attempts to reduce financial arrears, incurred as elsewhere to a significant extent by an expensive foreign policy, led to social unrest which culminated in the summer of 1648 in a revolt in the city of Moscow itself. The young and inexperienced tsar was forced to hand over some officials to be executed by an incensed crowd, and to send his chief adviser into exile to avoid a similar fate. After the revolt died down a *zemsky sobor* (national assembly) was convened in September 1648 to complete the restoration of order: most of the wishes of the nobility, many of those of the merchants and other members of the middle orders, and some of those of the clergy were satisfied, while the peasants found themselves subjected to serfdom, in the Code of Laws drawn up in the *zemsky sobor* by January 1649.

The acquisition of the Ukraine both added to and detracted from the security of the Muscovite state. On the one hand, it meant the addition of a significant buffer area manned by the usually co-operative Cossacks against enemies to the south; on the other hand, it led to the provocation of the Crimean Tatars and, more ominously, to that of their patrons, the Ottoman Turks. However, in the short run there was to be no major confrontation, partly because the major thrust of the Turks at that time was in another direction, and partly because, as in the case of most of their European neighbours, the strenuous efforts involved in international activities had led to severe social strains at home. Wars against Persia and Venice, accompanied by rumours of new crusades, as well as problems stemming from the administration of an empire in which the Turks themselves were a minority and the subject peoples numbered more than 20 millions, contributed to a crisis in which the Sultan Ibrahim was deposed and then murdered in the summer of 1648 and his seven-year-old son installed as Mehmed IV.

Crisis in history, as well as in medicine, is followed by resolution, and after the disturbances accompanying the conclusion of the Thirty Years War, Europe entered a period of by no means complete but at least comparative calm: ensuing conflicts enveloped parts of the continent rather than the whole, even though there were some connections between them. Roughly speaking, there was a certain similarity in the shape of the two major divisions, with France at the centre to the west and Poland at the centre to the east. However, we must remember that frontiers to the east were much more fluid than those to the west. Moreover, Poland was in decline while France was on the rise.

Looking back at Europe in the middle of the seventeenth century from the vantage point of the beginning of the twenty-first, we must recall, too, that none of the states of today existed in their present form, while some of them were still in embryo. We look further back for origins used in the making of later nationalisms. The Roman imprint was strong not only in the south-west, but also in Romania and Moldova. Celtic ancestry may be found not only to the north-west but also in the centre and south-east around the Carpathians in Hungary, the Czech republic. Germanic and Nordic influences intermix to the north as well as in the centre, in Scandinavia as well as in Germany itself, while Slavonic roots may be found throughout the centre and east, in Belarus and Ukraine as well as Russia, in Slovakia and the former Yugoslavia as well as Poland, the Czech Republic and Bulgaria. Hungary, Finland and Estonia share a linguistic legacy, as do Latvia and Lithuania. As we shall see in our final chapter, origins both real and imagined are important in the making not only of the nations that comprise Europe but also in the construction of the continent as a whole.

2

THE FRENCH CHALLENGE: RESPONSES EAST AND WEST, 1648–1721

THE FRENCH CHALLENGE

Louis XIV was 16 years old when he was crowned in Rheims Cathedral in July 1654. Still learning the craft of kingship, however, he was to defer to his advisers – Mazarin especially – until the cardinal died in 1661. As far as foreign policy was concerned, the major problem of these still early years was to bring to a conclusion the war against Spain. During the troublesome years of the Fronde, the French had suffered some reverses, which persuaded Mazarin that final victory could not be won without allies. Having recognised Cromwell's Commonwealth in 1652, he made a treaty of friendship with it in 1655, expanding commerce and expelling the Stuarts. In 1657 he agreed to co-operate in the conquest of Dunkirk and other cities in Flanders, then part of the Spanish Netherlands. A joint force was successful at the Battle of the Dunes and the allied aims were achieved in the summer of 1658. At this time, Mazarin also obliged Leopold I at his election as Holy Roman Emperor to forswear further assistance to Spain against France. An alliance with Brandenburg–Prussia which had been arranged at the beginning of 1656 was now supplemented by a League of the Rhine in which France combined with Sweden and a number of German associates in order to force Leopold I to keep his word. A beleaguered Spain had no alternative but to make peace, and in the Treaty of the Pyrenees of November 1659 agreed to make that mountain range the south-west frontier of France while also making concessions in the north-east and allowing Lorraine to move further into the French sphere of influence. France agreed to abandon support for the Catalans beyond the Pyrenees and the Portuguese by the Atlantic, and to give up most claims in Italy and some of them in the neighbourhood of Switzerland. In 1660, peace with Spain was consolidated by the marriage of Louis XIV to Maria Theresa, daughter of Philip IV, and France on its side of the Pyrenees was strengthened by the final pacification of Provence. Mazarin was able to avoid any clash with the restored Stuart King Charles II and to contribute to peace in the Baltic before his death in March 1661.

At home after the Fronde, Mazarin was able for the most part to maintain some kind of order in the royal administration, filling the royal coffers while lining his own pockets, as in the provinces collectors and farmers of the royal taxes did their best to squeeze hard cash out of a much put upon people and to retain as much of it as possible for their own establishments. In 1661, when Mazarin died, Louis XIV resolved not to appoint another first minister but to take personal charge of the councils dealing with the disorder which he found everywhere. Yet one of those among whom the king divided the administration of his chaotic kingdom was soon to attain pre-eminence and then to retain it until his death in 1683. This man, Jean-Baptiste Colbert, who had been on Mazarin's staff, devised great schemes for the introduction of smooth efficiency into the governance of the king's dominions at home and abroad. The chief aim was to untie the great knot of the purse-strings, especially by reducing the number of fingers on them. For example, an amalgamation of the many private tax-collecting agencies into one General Farm was gradually approached, then finally achieved in 1680. Colbert made vigorous attempts to reduce tax fraud and evasion, and to improve the keeping of accounts. He did not shrink from recourse to time-honoured methods of raising revenue such as an increase in the size of the royal domain and of the income from it, especially the forests, and manipulation of the currency. But in a country which was still not a uniform nation state with many different provinces separated by poor communications, customs barriers and diversity of weights and measures and legal systems, even by linguistic variations which made mutual understanding difficult, the strongest will and the highest principles were not enough to bring balance to the books, let alone comprehensive rearrangement of them.

Similarly, Colbert had little chance of achieving any great measure of success for his schemes in commerce and industry. He was basically a mercantilist in outlook, believing that the international cake was of fixed dimensions, and that the largest slices with the richest ingredients went to those who attempted to deny others more than the merest crumbs. He looked in envy at the Dutch United Provinces: if they could attract to themselves an impressive level of prosperity, including a thriving trade and a large amount of gold and silver, then how much more should France be able to surpass them. Thus he entertained the hope of building up a strong merchant fleet, which would carry abroad large quantities of manufactured goods and then sail home with their holds brimming with useful raw materials and precious metals. Skilled craftsmen would be encouraged to come into and forbidden to leave the country, subsidies would be given and monopolies granted, appropriate construction projects would be carried out in France while suitable colonies would be developed overseas, to east and west. The whole system would be protected by tariffs and a navy. Here again, bright ideas ran up against dull reality. For example, none of the overseas trading companies that were set up achieved much prosperity, partly because of lack of investment, partly because of overabundance of government regulation; only one of them, the East India Company, survived Colbert's death. As before, local and sectional interest conflicted with the concept of concerted national policy. Certainly some progress was made towards economic unification, for example in the construction of a canal linking the Mediterranean with the Atlantic. But how could the merchants of Marseille on the Mediterranean see eye to eye with their counterparts at Rouen near the Channel, let alone members of other classes or a minister in Paris?

As for the peasants, the circumstance that they were mostly downtrodden was regrettable not only from a humanitarian point of view, since they provided the bulk of many sources of state income, including most of the *taille*, the principal direct tax, and much of indirect taxes, the *gabelle* on salt and others. Such attempts as there were to make taxation more equitable need to be examined in conjunction with any existing social policy. There certainly were attempts at judicial reform, especially in the late 1660s, culminating in the Civil Ordinance of 1667 and the Criminal Ordinance of 1670. Unfortunately, war intervened to hinder the implementation of these law codes.

Colbert also attempted to make more general use throughout the kingdom of those officials known as *intendants*, who have often been seen as the linchpins that kept the wheels of absolutism turning smoothly on their bureaucratic axles. They were no novelty in the reign of Louis XIV, but more use than before was made of their direct responsibility to the crown and their independence from the localities. The *intendants* were not gods from the machine of ideal government, not even for the most part new men with new ideas, but, used by Colbert along with the other officials at his disposal, they certainly gave the administration a largely unprecedented degree of control over the provinces. At the centre, however, the continued sale and hereditary tenure of offices by the nobility of the robe made it difficult for Colbert to make much progress with schemes for reform. Also there were further theoretical weaknesses in his outlook, including too strong a belief in the power of rules and orders. This belief was a failing of his age, for it was shared by many of his contemporaries, including the military architect Vauban, who built several castles in the air with the aim of increasing the national prosperity through more peaceful pursuits. Whether to increase the number of pigs in metropolitan France or the number of colonists in New France over in Canada, Vauban made recommendations stretching as far as the merest detail. He also made a worthwhile attempt to propose more equitable taxation – *la dîme royale* (royal tithe).

Colbert's achievement was considerable, even if he attempted too much too quickly, taking on responsibility for the development of the arts and the construction of palaces in addition to all his other concerns. Appropriately enough, Louis XIV was to take up residence at about the time of Colbert's death in 1683 at the palace most associated with the Sun King's glory, Versailles. Here, Louis was able to take to a new level the ceremony and etiquette that enhanced his position at the head of French society. Moreover, the pursuit of glory much further from Paris had in fact led even before 1683 to a decline in the influence of Colbert and a rise in that of Louvois, the secretary of state for war. Louis was increasingly concerned that his armed forces should spread his fame and majesty by carrying the fight to anybody rash enough to stand in the way. Although he was not averse to war where necessary, Colbert hoped to overtake rivals primarily by means of commerce and industry; Louvois planned to crush them more exclusively in battle.

To carry out his task, Louvois needed to deal as effectively with the nobility of the sword as Colbert had attempted to manage that of the robe. He did indeed make considerable progress between the Treaty of the Pyrenees in 1659 and the outbreak of the next war against Spain in 1667, tackling in particular the problem of the contractors, who were in relation to military organisation comparable with that of the tax-farmers to financial administration. As far as he could, Louvois introduced the appointment of regimental officers directly responsible to the crown. A new hierarchy of ranks went further to reduce the influence of birth and money, and a tendency towards standardisation of drill, uniform and weaponry was sufficient to give the officer in charge immortality, the inspector-general of infantry from 1667 onwards being Colonel Jean Martinet. As in the civil sphere so in the military, the completeness of the reform must not be exaggerated. The old system was sufficiently alive for the nobility of the sword to give enthusiastic support to their king's wars, and to bask in his glory.

The official reason for carrying the fight to Spain again in 1667 was the claim that Louis could make to the rights of his Spanish wife, Maria Theresa, especially in the Spanish Netherlands. A list of demands was sent off to Madrid, and a French attack launched before a reply could arrive. Louis was not deterred by the circumstance that a British–Dutch war had just been brought to an end, nor by the British–Dutch alliance with Sweden in 1668 which was opposed to French expansionism, since he himself had made an advantageous accommodation with the Holy Roman Emperor Leopold I. But then, somewhat surprisingly, Louis listened to those advisers in favour of concluding peace rather than to those in favour of prosecution of the war. The Treaty of Aix-la-Chapelle was drawn up by May 1668, allowing France to keep Lille and some other conquests in the Netherlands. The pause gave Louis time for further preparation, while also allowing resentment of his unsatisfied ambition to build up among his rivals and enemies.

Four years after the conclusion of the War of Devolution, as the conflict of 1667–8 is known, hostilities were resumed again, this time specifically against the United Provinces, or Holland, which had replaced Spain as prime enemy for reasons both economic and political. For some years before the shooting started, commercial rivalry had already led to a trade war. Moreover, the Dutch parliamentary regime was hateful to the French king, one of whose secretaries wrote disparagingly: 'These bodies formed of so many heads have no heart that could be warmed by the fire of beautiful passions.'[1] At the beginning of the Franco-Dutch War of 1672–9, Holland was almost completely isolated as France invaded and Britain resumed its former attack from the sea, although some support for the Dutch cause was received from Brandenburg–Prussia. As before, however, other powers soon took alarm at the French advance. In particular, the Emperor, Leopold I, encouraged many of the German states to join him in a coalition after making a pact with the Elector of Brandenburg in the summer of 1672. Spain entered the war officially in the summer of 1673, after which the struggle increasingly took on the complexion of the old rivalry between Bourbon and Habsburg. The 'many heads' in Great Britain had 'no heart' for the war, from which Charles II was obliged to withdraw in 1674, by which time the French forces were making fresh advances towards the Rhine and across it. The conflict widened to the Baltic Sea as France's ally Sweden struggled with Denmark for dominance over Scania, the southern tip of the Scandinavian peninsula, and with Brandenburg–Prussia for Pomerania on the Baltic's southern shore. In the Mediterranean, France helped rebellious forces in Sicily, attacked Naples and invaded Catalonia in Spain itself. The Dutch fleet met with defeat in the Mediterranean, but enjoyed more success in attacks on overseas French colonies. After delays brought about by fluctuating fortunes on the battlefields and many arguments over protocol and procedure around conference tables, a series of treaties drawn up principally at Nymegen (Nijmegen) brought the war to an end in 1678–9. France kept some gains and gave up or exchanged others in such a manner that its frontiers could now be made more secure by Vauban and his fellow military architects. Holland gained no actual ground, but its commercial position with regard to France was restored to an extent sufficient to worry Colbert towards the time of his death. Spain kept Catalonia and Sicily but lost provinces next to Switzerland and along the Rhine to France. The other Habsburg power ruled by Leopold I managed to retain what was still left to it of the Holy Roman Empire and, although menaced by Turkish advances, Hungarian insurgency and other problems around its Austrian capital,

Vienna, managed to pose a threat sufficient to keep French hands off even more traditional imperial possessions. Sweden regained losses inflicted by Denmark and by Brandenburg–Prussia, which nevertheless deemed the moment appropriate to stop taking subsidies from Holland and to begin taking them from France.

The end of the 1670s marked the peak of Louis XIV's glory, as special tribunals were set up to interpret the treaties in France's favour, and force was used whenever necessary to implement their decisions. Of course, the taxes imposed to pay for the war were far from popular, and there were violent protests against them, especially in the provinces. Yet, a few years earlier, the chief of police in Paris had declared, not without much fawning exaggeration but also with some basis in reality, that

> there is nobody who is not extremely pleased to think of what all Europe is going to say of a prince capable of himself forming, conducting and executing such enterprises, and who, in reuniting to France the important places that he has just taken by force, does more for the grandeur of his State in the commencement of a single campaign, than was done during all the wars of the preceding reigns.[2]

Similar in vein to the chief of police although vastly superior in literary talent, the playwright Racine could declare of his labours on the dictionary being prepared under the auspices of the recently formed French Academy: 'Every word in the language, every syllable, is precious to us, because we consider them as the instruments which must serve the glory of our august protector.'[3] Again, there might have been a grain of true feeling here, as well as a servile flattery and an inclination towards acceptance of rigid rules. As for the king himself, his love of glory appears to have been great, even insatiable; certainly, according to his reputed deathbed declaration, it was excessive. To what extent his own ambition overlapped with the real interests of France is a more difficult question to tackle. Such ambiguity does not disappear when we turn to consider an important further constituent of Louis XIV's outlook, his religion. While the faith of the Glorious King in the King of Glory was probably genuine enough, his confidence in his vicars the popes of Rome at times wavered. Devout Catholic though he may have been, Louis sometimes regretted that an authority higher than his own had to be recognised beyond the Alps, and he was not happy with dissident co-religionists at home, still less with heretic Protestant Huguenots. He grew increasingly discontented with the toleration introduced at the end of the sixteenth century in the Edict of Nantes by his sometime Protestant predecessor Henry IV. And, although he often managed to keep the affairs of his heart away from affairs of state, it is possible that his secret marriage in or around 1683 to a pious mistress, Madame de Maintenon, inclined him closer to the edict's revocation, duly carried out in October 1685. But he received other advice based on considerations of foreign policy, too. Meanwhile, in 1682, prompted by the Dauphin's tutor, the former Bishop Bossuet, the Assembly of the Clergy had issued a Declaration of the king's supremacy in matters temporal, at the same time challenging the Pope's authority in some matters spiritual, especially in France. Bossuet had his own version of the Trinity 'The king, Jesus Christ and the Church, God in these three names' – and also declared in more down-to-earth fashion: 'The whole state is in the person of the prince.' If Louis XIV did not for certain utter the most famous phrase attributed to him, 'l'état c'est moi', Bossuet said it, and much else besides, for him.[4]

The French king's appetite for glory, with or without religious over-tones, left his neighbours in Europe in some doubt about his ultimate intentions. Did he really wish to become ruler of the continent, even of the wider world, as was sometimes suggested? Or was his ambition more narrowly confined to territories nearer home? The second alternative seems nearer the truth, but the answer cannot and could not be specifically given. The vagueness of 'glory' as a strategic concept makes it difficult for historians today and made it difficult for states-men at the time to assess the extent to which glory meant expansion. For this reason, Louis XIV cut a figure somewhat larger than life in seventeenth-century Europe, in many parts of which, not just those adjacent to France but also more remote, his name evoked apprehen-sion. Solid, down-to-earth reasons for this uneasy feeling were that, for all its faults, the French administration was comparatively well organ-ised and, even more, that it was attempting to mobilise the energies of up to 20 million people as opposed to less than a third of that number in each of its immediate neighbours across mountain, river and sea: Spain, Holland and Great Britain respectively. Even vast Russia had at that time a population totalling little more than 15 million, and other loose conglomerations such as Germany and Italy probably each had a considerably smaller combined number. And so, at a time when most peaceful and much wartime labour was still manual, the balance of power in population as well as politics was in France's favour: it could be resisted only by alliances. For this reason, relations between the states, especially in western Europe, are most appropriately examined with a French pivot.

RESPONSES TO THE FRENCH CHALLENGE

Beyond the Pyrenees came Spain, ruled in name by the last of the Habsburg kings, Charles II, but in fact by a series of royal favourites and aristocratic factions. In many assessments, this reign from 1665 to 1700 marked a low point in Spanish history: certainly, most of the Spanish glory had faded before the reign began. As we have just seen, during the Franco-Dutch War of 1672–9 the old enemy Bourbon France had attacked some of the outlying possessions and had even invaded Catalonia. Much hereditary territory on the other side of France had been lost, and some of it in Italy had been retained only with great difficulty. Moreover, accompanying military and diplomatic reverses abroad was a decline of no small proportion in Spain itself. Both the extent and the nature of this decline remain matters of debate; there was certainly something of a revival in the eighteenth century. But there can be little doubt that Spain was not the power it had been nor the power that others, especially France, had become. On the other hand, in spite of losses in Europe and threats to its overseas empire centred in South America, it could by no means be left out of the reckoning. Similarly, although experiencing some internal and overseas problems after its newly regained independence, Portugal was a force to be taken into account from Brazil through Africa and India to China and Japan.

Little need be said of Italy, which was in more thorough decline. It had become less the arena in which the great states of Europe fought out their rivalries, while none of its several parts had yet asserted complete independence from them. Venice attempted to hold on to Crete and other Mediterranean possessions without much Christian support against Ottoman Muslim encroachment; Piedmont tried without much initial success to emulate in miniature the achievement of

France; the papacy could not retain its former moral and political influence. In the later part of the seventeenth century, 'Italy lived through a time of political immobility during which, at least to all outward appearances, virtually nothing happened'.[5]

The Italian cities had given way in prestige to those of the north-west: Paris, Amsterdam and especially London, which doubled its population during the seventeenth century to reach a total of over half a million and become Europe's largest city. This expansion was not only a reflection of increased commercial activity in the city itself but also a measure of political cohesion in neighbouring Westminster. British government, however, did not involve bureaucratic centralisation: the English provinces retained a considerable measure of self-government and Scotland preserved some of its ancient independence, even if Ireland was administered like a colony. Cromwell's Commonwealth and Protectorate had turned out to be far less revolutionary than opponents feared and supporters hoped, both at home and abroad. Louis XIV's government had been prepared to co-operate with Cromwell to the point of expelling the Stuarts from France in 1655, and made no great effort to support the Stuart restoration in Britain in 1660. If Charles II became the ally of Louis XIV in 1670, this was for reasons of state and cash that Cromwell would have understood, as much as out of mutual monarchical sympathy, which would have been alien to him. Cromwell's colonial policy foreshadowed that of the restored monarchy, concentrating on maintaining a system closed to the Dutch and other rivals, especially in the Atlantic triangular trade involving raw materials such as sugar, manufactured goods such as cloth, and human beings – African slaves. To protect this system, in the reign of Charles II a modern army was raised on the lines of Cromwell's New Model Army, while the navy developed by Cromwell was expanded in the often inhuman but ultimately successful manner recorded by Samuel Pepys, the great diarist.

The relationship between Britain and France was one of envy but sometimes convenience, that between Britain and Holland more one of love and hate. From the Baltic and Mediterranean to the Far East, they were commercial rivals, and the series of wars between them in 1652–4, 1665–7 and 1672–4 was concerned with trade as well as with political rivalry. Yet Sir William Temple, English ambassador to The Hague on a number of occasions during this period, subjected the

Dutch government and people to a sympathetic analysis which, first published in 1674 as *Observations upon the United Provinces of the Netherlands* and soon running through several editions, revealed an affinity with Temple's own government and people. This affinity made easier the British–Dutch reconciliation consequent upon the marriage in 1677 of William III, Prince of Orange, and Mary, eldest daughter of the Stuart Duke of York, later James II. One observation that would be well received in certain quarters over the water ran as follows: 'Their common Riches lye in every Man's having more than he spends; or, to say it more properly, In evry man's spending less than he has coming in, be that what it will ... This enables every Man to bear their extream Taxes, and makes them less sensible than they would be in other places ...'[6] Here are sentiments that would be after the heart of many Londoners and other Britons, and to some extent it was the failure of the later Stuart monarchs to take them closely into consideration that led to their unpopularity.

Soon after the death of William II of Orange in 1650 and up to the accession of William III in 1672, the virtual ruler of the United Provinces was one of the six members of the States of Holland imprisoned by William II just a few months before he died, Johan de Witt. For 20 years or so he made good use of considerable managerial capabilities during a period that was full of international problems but also marked the greatest economic and cultural achievements of the United Provinces. His rule involved constant manipulation of the decentralised form of government, with a fair measure of bribery and corruption, and it stirred up a strong resentment against him which led to an inglorious end, torn to pieces by a crowd made additionally excitable by the reverses suffered at the beginning of the war against France.

If the decline of the United Provinces towards the end of the seventeenth century was a case 'of a small and far from well-endowed people which had, by an earlier opportunism of genius, created a position for itself higher than was warranted in terms of crude power, and was now overtaken by the nemesis of normality',[7] another such case was that of Sweden. Meanwhile, because of endowments not yet completely apparent, Brandenburg–Prussia was, like Britain, on the rise at this time. If we then compare Spain at one end of Europe to Russia at the other, we note a difference in relative international strength: that of the state at the western end was failing while that of the state at the eastern end was just about to exert itself. From the point of view of size and central position, Poland was the pivot for relations between the states in the east as France was in the west – though it must be emphasised that while French influence was at its peak, Polish influence was long past it.

The Polish predicament was intensified by the fact that no sooner was its southern problem at least temporarily settled with the loss of the Ukraine than trouble came from the north. In 1655, the Swedes launched an invasion, the official reason being the disputed claim of John Casimir to the Swedish throne, the unofficial aim the capture of the Baltic provinces. Other powers joined in, and great efforts were needed to bring the war to an end. With France as mediator, the Peace of Oliwa was agreed in 1660, restoring the status quo, or as much of it as was left after economic ruin and political weakening. Meanwhile, hostilities with Russia had been resumed in 1659 and were not brought to an end until the Peace of Andrusovo in 1667, by the terms of which Poland ceded the left-bank Ukraine and Kiev, as well as Smolensk and some of Belorussia. A year later, confronted by internal rebellion, John Casimir left for exile in France. Soon after this, another French client, John Sobieski, was elected king in 1674, having just made himself popular at home through a splendid victory over yet another invader, this time Ottoman Turkey. A few years later, still greater glory was to come for John Sobieski as he led a successful coalition against the Ottoman Turks besieging Vienna in 1683. But this famous victory was of less benefit to Poland than to Austria and Hungary.

Muscovite Russia was comparatively remote from the world view of Europe's greatest power, France. Nevertheless, during the reign of Tsar Alexis (1645–76), father of the future Peter the Great, the double-headed eagle of the Romanovs began to flap its wings in a manner distinctly felt by Russia's more immediate neighbours: Poland, Sweden, the Crimean Tatars and Turkey. Moreover, the reforms associated with Peter the Great were clearly foreshadowed during the reign of Alexis and his immediate successors. The army began to take on regular shape, and in the construction of some ships to patrol the rivers Volga and Don might be seen the beginnings of the navy. There was at least some rationalisation of the central administrative system, while the *voevoda* (sheriff) was a rough equivalent of the French *intendant* in the provinces. The *zemsky sobor* (national assembly) was in decline, and the old method of appointment to places in government was abolished in 1682 as an absolutist establishment composed of the leading members of the nobility showed signs of consolidation. The assimilation of the Ukraine was of tremendous importance in many ways, not least economically and culturally. A national market connected mostly by river now dealt in many items from grain to furs. The Orthodox Church was reformed, with those adhering to the old ways bringing about a schism, and through the Ukraine and Poland were channelled not only several new ideas in religion but at least a few in secular thought as well. There was a handful of well-educated and widely aware individuals as well as a great mass of enserfed peasants adhering to their old folk ways, normally peaceful except at such times as the Razin Revolt of 1670–1.

The completion of many of the processes just listed would depend on Russia's acquisition of a permanent foothold on the Baltic. During the late seventeenth century Sweden and Brandenburg–Prussia succeeded in excluding Russia at the same time as reducing the Polish presence. France frequently intervened in the Baltic struggle for power, as did other states, notably the Dutch United Provinces, which at times maintained a virtual monopoly of commerce there, in spite of vigorous British attempts at infiltration. However, Sweden was moving down the international league table while Brandenburg–Prussia was embarking on its ascent to the top under the resolute leadership of Frederick William, the Great Elector. A disciplined social system with the Junkers (nobles) performing the combined role of army officers and landlords was matched by an integrated bureaucratic machine in which the chief cog from 1679 onwards was the General War Commissariat. As in Russia and most of eastern Europe, the bulk of the population had been held in serfdom during the course of the seventeenth century. Nevertheless, the Pietist Protestant ideas of some of the leading lights in Königsberg and other cities were to be found in cameralism, the concept of a police service combining law and order with a primitive kind of regulatory social welfare.

Frederick William, like some other German princes, was aware of a world beyond the Baltic, and made some efforts to promote overseas companies and to secure colonies, with little success. But much of the energy of rulers and people alike was taken up by more local enterprise, which included mercenary warfare and the cultivation of often refractory sandy marshes. To the south, where the terrain could be mountainous, there was the additional problem for the Austrian

Habsburg emperors of coping with incursions from the Ottoman Turks even after the siege of Vienna was lifted in 1683.

For several hundred years, the greatest threat to Europe from outside had been the Ottoman Turks. However, although they had taken Crete in the Mediterranean from Venice and also made gains by the Black Sea, they had appeared to be in decline as far as the continent as a whole was concerned during the latter part of the seventeenth century. But in 1683, old nightmares concerning the extension of their European empire were revived by the grand vizier to Sultan Mehmed IV, Kara Mustafa. Fame through conquest having been denied him in the Ukraine after the Treaty of Bakhchisarai with Russia in 1681, Kara Mustafa persuaded the sultan to move his restless forces westwards. Taking advantage of Hungarian disaffection with Habsburg domination, especially among the Protestants, the grand vizier led the army into Hungary in the summer of 1682. In the words of an eminent Turkish historian, 'The most important campaign in Turkish history had begun'. As he began the advance on Vienna, Kara Mustafa declared that with its fall, 'all the Christians would obey the Ottomans'.[8]

The Habsburg Emperor Leopold I was almost as concerned with French encroachments to the west as he was with the Ottoman approach from the east, and so the lead in the organisation of a Christian coalition to repel the infidel was taken by a new pope, Innocent XI, the most energetic crusading pontiff in centuries. At the end of March 1683, King John Sobieski of Poland joined members of the Holy Roman Empire in an anti-Turkish alliance, just a few months before the siege of Vienna began in mid-July. Had Kara Mustafa invested the city earlier, or had his men been convinced that there was enough booty within it to justify the necessary sacrifices in breaking through its defences, possibly he would have realised a long-held Ottoman aim whose attainment had evaded even Suleiman the Magnificent. As it was, the garrison bravely held out until 12 September, when a relief force under John Sobieski swept the Turks away, a victory which brought about as much rejoicing as had Lepanto in 1571, and with more significant consequences than that great naval battle:

> Like Lepanto it was a joint victory of pope and Emperor. Moreover it marked the advent of Austria to the position of a great power. It was Leopold, and not Louis XIV, who now stood at the pinnacle of glory,

and in the years that followed, while Louis' great armies were struggling obscurely and unsuccessfully in the labyrinth of the War of the League of Augsburg, Leopold's army under the aegis of the refurbished Crown of St. Stephen was hammering the Infidel back beyond the Danube and the Carpathians. The war of Hungarian liberation was veritably a crusade, the final achievement of the victorious Counter Reformation.[9]

WARS EAST AND WEST, 1683–1721

In the East, a Treaty of Eternal Peace confirming earlier rapprochement was signed by Russia and Poland in the spring of 1686. Among the commitments made by Russia in return for concessions by Poland was the launching of a war against the Crimean Tatars. But continued discussions with other European powers came to little or nothing. In 1689, much further afield, the Treaty of Nerchinsk with China limited Russian expansion in the Far East.

In the West, by 1685, a configuration of European power that would facilitate a seizure of power in Britain was already emerging in the shape of a new resistance to French expansionism, which itself had been revitalised by the accession of Louis XIV's ally and co-religionist, James VII and II. This did not mean a new unity for Roman Catholicism as a whole, even though the Revocation of the Edict of Nantes (of the limited toleration of the Huguenots) in October 1685 might appear at first glance to be an additional move in that direction. In fact, the Pope was not reconciled to Louis, while the refusal of the French king to support the relief of the siege of Vienna by the Turks in 1683, indeed his taking advantage of that embarrassment to consolidate earlier gains along the Rhine and elsewhere, had alienated many potential friends as well as annoying most of his foes. Thus, in July 1686, Protestant and Catholic powers came together in the defensive League of Augsburg, determined to maintain the status quo against any further French aggression. The Turks suffered further reverses in 1687. While the Russians invaded the Crimea, the hero of Vienna, John Sobieski, led a successful Polish expedition to the south, and Venetian forces invaded the Peloponnese and then took Athens. The Austrian Habsburgs, having occupied Buda in 1686, now invaded Transylvania and crushed the Turks in southern Hungary in August.

All this helped produce alarm and disorder involving Constantinople itself. Back in western Europe, the Marquis of Halifax, one of his promoters, noted in a letter to William of Orange dated 1687:

> We are full of the news from Hungary, which is not equally welcome to the several princes of Christendom. We think it may have a considerable influence upon this part of the world, and if the season was not too far advanced, we are apt to believe France might this very year give some trouble to its neighbours.[10]

War was already expected in 1688. Among William's allies in the League of Augsburg, the most important, Brandenburg–Prussia, was to hold firm after the death in late April of the Great Elector, Frederick William, who allegedly gave as the last password and countersign to his guards the indicative words: 'London: Amsterdam'. Meanwhile, money appears to have come to William from the papal treasury on condition that he would be prepared to lead a coalition against the French on the Rhine. Throughout 1688, the anti-Turkish coalition continued to make progress. For example, it seized the important fortress of Belgrade in the late summer, although it did not drive the advantage home as much as might have been expected, partly because of misunderstandings among its members, partly because Turkish resolve was strengthened when, after the fall of Belgrade, Louis XIV sent his troops into the Rhineland in September. The Austrians and the Brandenburgers now found it necessary to divert a considerable amount of their forces to resist the French, the Brandenburgers in particular providing cover for William's invasion of Great Britain, which was finally successful in November. James VII and II, who according to one account had been most dismissive of the advice 'Better a vassal of France than a slave of the Demon',[11] realising that to be too close to Louis would be to alienate the bulk of his subjects at least as much as his adherence to Roman Catholicism, now found it necessary to cross the Channel to become the French king's abject creature.

The War of the League of Augsburg (Nine Years War) was brought to an end in 1697, with Louis XIV giving up some of his acquisitions from former wars in the Treaty of Ryswick. In 1699, by the Peace of Carlowitz, Austria retained Transylvania and most of Hungary. Hostilities had ranged from the Mediterranean and Italy through the Balkans,

Germany and the Low Countries over the sea to Ireland and over the ocean to the Americas, Africa and India. A brief respite now ensued, during which attempts were made to stabilise Europe through partial partition. Soon, however, another conflict commenced, concerned officially with the age-old rivalry between the Bourbon and Habsburg families, this time over the question of the succession to the throne of Spain. Before his death in 1700, King Charles II of Spain named as his sole heir Louis XIV's grandson Philip of Anjou, a disposition which met with the strong disapproval of Emperor Leopold and the increasing alarm of King William of Great Britain and the United Provinces, who were the leading members of a strong anti-French Grand Alliance which survived the deaths of its principal promoters.

The War of the Spanish Succession, which broke out in 1702, once again enveloped much of Europe and penetrated the overseas colonies as well. The most significant land battle took place in 1704, when a Franco-Bavarian thrust down the Danube towards Vienna, which was also under threat from Hungarian separatists on the other side, met with a severe check from a coalition force under the Duke of Marlborough at Blenheim. At sea in 1704, after Piedmont and Portugal had been lured away from attachment to France, the British navy took Gibraltar, from which it could dominate the western Mediterranean, even if no comparable success was achieved on the wider waterways of the world. Then, after some years of virtual stalemate, the war came to an end in a manner very similar to that in which it had begun, through the death of a monarch. The Emperor Joseph I, who had succeeded his father Leopold I in 1705, died suddenly in 1711, to be succeeded by his brother Charles, who had already been recognised by some of the belligerents as king of Spain. The consequent threat of a revived Habsburg Empire stretching from Vienna to Madrid contributed to a degree of alarm sufficient for the wide recognition as king of Spain of Philip of Anjou, who made the counterbalancing renunciation of his right to the French throne. So now, in 1713 and 1714, negotiations for a restoration of peace could be brought to a head, in the Treaty of Utrecht and other agreements. King Philip V retained Spain and Spanish America, while the Emperor Charles VI acquired Milan, Naples, Sardinia and the Spanish Netherlands. Louis XIV gave up his previous gains across the Rhine but did not have to move back from the others to the east and north-east. The Elector of Brandenburg was confirmed as king of

Prussia, while the Elector of Hanover was recognised as King George I of Britain, to the detriment of the house of Stuart. In addition, George I received confirmation of the addition to the growing British Empire of Gibraltar and Minorca, as well as Nova Scotia, Newfoundland and Hudson Bay, and important trading rights within the Spanish Empire.

In some ways, Utrecht could be interpreted as a general recognition of the diplomatic importance over the preceding decades of Louis XIV's France, not least in the wider acceptance of many of its negotiating practices and of French as the language of diplomacy *par excellence*. One of the French delegation at Utrecht, the Abbé de Saint-Pierre, put forward ideas on international co-operation in his project for a perpetual peace. But in fact the last years of the Sun King were setting rather than rising, especially for his own glory, but not a little for the comfort and liberty of his subjects. In the early 1690s there was a series of poor harvests and consequent famine, especially in 1694. There were widespread food riots, and protests from at least some of the king's own former supporters. Archbishop Fénelon wrote:

> your people, whom you should love as your children, and who have up till now been so devoted to you, are dying of hunger. The cultivation of the countryside is almost abandoned; towns and countryside are becoming depopulated; all trades are stagnant and no longer sustain the workers. All commerce is annihilated. Thus you have destroyed half of the real internal strength of your State, to make and defend useless external conquests. Instead of extracting money from this poor people, you should give them alms and nourish them. The whole of France is nothing but a huge hospital, desolate and without succour.

Not only had recent unnecessary war led towards ruin, but for about 30 years in Fénelon's estimation the king's chief ministers had 'shaken and overturned all the former principles of government in order to build up your authority to a zenith, because your authority had become their own, being in their hands'. Moreover, revenues and expenditures had increased beyond all bounds, and all France had been impoverished 'in order to introduce at Court a monstrous and incurable luxury'.[12]

In spite of such disorder and protest, Louis XIV was to remain in power for a further 20 years. But soon after his death in 1715, his declining reputation was further eclipsed by rival emperors. Charles VI pushed Austrian influence deep into the Balkans in a war against Turkey which ended in 1718 with the Peace of Passarowitz. Austria now gained the remainder of Hungary, Belgrade, northern Serbia and western Wallachia. Meanwhile, Peter the Great moved towards the triumphant conclusion of the Great Northern War against Sweden in 1721. We must turn to examine that war and its preliminaries.

John Sobieski died in 1696 unable to secure the Polish succession for his son, and Poland revealed that it had become a passive object of international rivalries with the election to the throne in 1697 of the Elector of Saxony, supported by a coalition in which the participation of Peter the Great probably tipped the scales against a rival candidate promoted by Louis XIV. Meanwhile, Charles XI of Sweden (1660–97) was able to avoid entanglement in European wars to an extent suffic- ient for him to embark upon a series of reforms that enabled him to make his country once again a force to be reckoned with. In combina- tion with the lower nobility and commoner estates, he managed to reduce the pretensions of the high nobility and at the same time develop an army and a bureaucracy with a Table of Ranks. The prema- ture death of Charles XI in 1697 brought to the throne the 15-year-old Charles XII (1697–1718), who was to spend three-quarters of his reign absent from Sweden owing to his deep involvement in the Great Northern War, which preoccupied Peter the Great of Russia as well.

Peter's Great Embassy to western Europe of 1697–8 was aimed to a considerable extent at the revival of the Christian coalition against the Turks and their allies after two expeditions to the Crimea in 1695 and 1696. However, potential members of such a coalition were interested primarily in ending their war with Turkey or with Turkey's ally, France. While no doubt disappointed by the failure of his major aim, and of his connected purpose of acquiring Kerch at the mouth of the Sea of Azov, Peter did nevertheless manage to take advantage of Turkish war- weariness to arrive at the Treaty of Constantinople in the summer of 1700. This was not the end of the conflict with the Crimean Tatars, still less with their patrons the Turks, but a fairly important point had been reached in the long story of the stabilisation of the southern steppe. Russia was to retain the fortress of Azov, although it could not move from it out into the open Black Sea. There were to be no more tributes to the Crimean Tatars, but they were to withdraw from the lower Dnepr. Russia was to be represented at Constantinople on a regular basis.

On his way back home from the Great Embassy, Peter's thoughts turned to war against Sweden. After long and often intense hostilities involving not just the two major belligerents but many other European states both nearby and more remote, Russia was to achieve on a lasting basis its access to the Baltic Sea, its famous 'window on the west' symbolised by the construction of a new capital city, St Petersburg. To begin with, Charles XII was able to use his greater mobility and more informed military intelligence in a crushing victory at Narva in 1700, but then, after arduous years of preparation, the verdict was resoundingly reversed at Poltava in 1709. The war might have come to a quicker conclusion had it not been for the defection of Mazepa, Hetman of the Ukrainian Cossacks, and the involvement of Turkey. The Turks inflicted a humiliation on Peter the Great at the River Prut beyond the Ukraine in 1711, forcing Russia to give up Azov and other acquisitions on the Black Sea. Then, with the end of war in the west in 1714 and a worsening crisis in the Baltic after the sudden death of Charles XII in 1718, both France and Britain used their influence to restrict Peter the Great's victory. Finally, by the Treaty of Nystad of 1721, Russia gained the Baltic shores from Riga in Latvia to Vyborg in Finland, making commercial and financial concessions to Sweden in return. Voltaire considered the outcome of the Great Northern War to be perhaps the most important turning point for Europe after the discovery of the New World.

Having established Russia on the Baltic, Peter now pushed towards the Caspian. In the spring of 1722, taking advantage of instability in Persia, he launched a campaign to the western and southern shores of that sea with the support of Armenia and Georgia. Soon after his death, however, Russia was obliged to pull back.

PETER THE GREAT AND RUSSIA

Towards the end of his reign, 'Peter's court was not so different in spirit from that of Louis XIV, which provided the model for much of the rest of Europe'.[13] Possibly, his encouragement of assemblies and ceremonies indicated just one of the ways in which Peter wanted to catch up and then surpass the achievement of the Sun King, although he also criticised Louis for not leading his troops into battle enough and for not mastering any useful trades. Certainly, he himself worked hard throughout his reign at building up the armed services and the economy while developing an educational system and secular culture.

Early on, during the Great Embassy to the West of 1697–8, the tsar-carpenter enthusiastically applied himself to learning shipbuilding and other such 'useful trades'. However, he was already showing an interest in other branches of the Christian church as well as wanting to take the process of reform further in his own. One approach already undertaken was the creation of the 'Most Drunken Synod of Fools and Jesters', a weird private club which made fun of old church rituals as well as bringing in extravagant secular ceremonies. However, during his visit to England, he impressed Gilbert Burnet, Bishop of Salisbury, with 'a degree of knowledge I did not think him capable of ... He hearkened to no part of what I told him more attentively than when I explained the authority that the Christian Emperors assumed in matters of religion and the supremacy of our Kings.'[14] However, whatever the curiosity they showed in matters secular as well as spiritual, the abiding memory left by the young tsar and his entourage was of a violent drunken mob despoiling the house that they rented and laying waste to its garden.

Back in Russia, Peter first completed the suppression of a revolt in favour of the old ways. Then, without forsaking his own bluff faith, he was also to work for the completion of the state structure on a secular basis. However, a perceptive Scottish mercenary, Alexander Gordon, was to observe:

> It is morally impossible that such a country as Russia was, could be more speedily reduced to a regular and consistent plan of government; but the extremity of arbitrary power, which had long subsisted, and the unpolished manners which had for so many ages prevailed, seemed to have established a rule of Asiatick policy, which Peter was not able, or not willing to destroy.

Thus the tsar connived

> in seeing the grandees pillage the lower classes of the people, according as their offices might afford them an occasion; but when they had thus accumulated wealth, and rendered themselves obnoxious to the laws, their sovereign came in for the plunder, either by

degrading the offender, or suffering him to ransom one part by delivering up the other.[15]

How far this was 'Asiatick policy' could be a matter for debate, since something like it could be found in many European countries beyond Russia, especially in the centre, where the institution of serfdom had been introduced or reintroduced a half-century or more previously. In these regions, the 'grandees' (members of the nobility) usually combined the role of landlord with that of officer in the armed forces or leading official in the bureaucracy. The nobility as a whole was therefore in an advantageous position for the exploitation of the serfs, even if through abuse of the system or fall from favour individuals from the ruling class could suffer the penalty of reduction to the rank of commoner. Such was the social basis of absolutism not only in Russia but also in Brandenburg–Prussia and Austria.

Peter was less than a superman, but much more than a nobody. Even if his efforts were far from unaided and more than a few hints of modern practice had penetrated Muscovy before he came to maturity, there is little doubt that he himself contributed to the moulding of society and government that took place during his reign. To take first the ruling class, Peter gave the nobility both a name and a structure. A new label – dvoriantsvo, from dvor, the household or court – did not mean instant coherence for the class, which stemmed from varied national origins (Polish–Lithuanian, German and Scandinavian among them) and various elements of the service people (top officials from the chancelleries and military and naval officers, all of which categories could overlap). Deference was still paid to family origin, but more emphasis was given to contributions to the state, a tendency reinforced by the regularisation of military service and the introduction of naval service during the Petrine wars. Foreigners, who had provided most of the famous members of Peter the Great's early entourage such as Patrick Gordon and Franz Lefort, diminished in numbers and importance as the reign wore on. These tendencies were taken to a climax with the lengthy preparation of the Table of Ranks, in which close attention was paid to Russian precedents as well as to foreign models, especially the Prussian, Swedish and Danish. In its final version, the Table of Ranks was set out in three principal columns: the armed forces, the civil service and the court, with the first of them given most emphasis. The Table's basic assertion was put forcefully enough: 'We do not allow anybody rank, until he has rendered service to Us and to the Fatherland.'

The Table of Ranks was a lasting enactment, partly because it had been thoroughly prepared, partly because it was the culmination of an evolutionary development stretching far back into the seventeenth century. For example, ranks such as *kapitan, major* and even *kvartermeister* had been introduced into the Russian army as far back as the 1630s. A less durable decree from Petrine times was that of 1714 which introduced a version of the virtually pan-European system of passing family property from one individual member to another with the aim of avoiding ruinous subdivision. However, equal division of property among all children had long been considered in Russia a principle of divine justice. For this reason, the decree was resisted and manipulated by the *dvorianstvo* with such stubbornness that it was rescinded just over 15 years later, in 1730. Moreover, not only ancient Russian family tradition but also the pre-eminence of service made it impossible for single succession to be adapted to Russian conditions, and therefore Russian *dvoriane* were set somewhat apart from many of their European counterparts.

Due deference having been paid to the nobility, we move on to an all too brief note about the peasants. Constituting over 90 per cent of the approximately 16 million inhabitants of the Russian Empire towards the end of Peter the Great's reign, they were either enserfed to noble landlords or bound in a similar manner to the state. A considerable number of them showed what they thought of their predicament in such outbreaks of violence as the widespread Bulavin Revolt of 1707–9, but most usually accepted their unfair lot in silent obedience. Legislation on the peasants concentrated on them not as subjects but as objects, as property to be put into one category or another, as payers of taxes, as slave labour or cannon fodder. Even in these respects, legislation was far from complete, since it was based on the assumption that most of the activities of their human property would be regulated by landlords or by state officials. To take direct taxation as an example, this had been levied in the last part of the seventeenth century on the basis of households, but it was then realised that taxation by head would produce a better income for the state. So in 1718–19 a new tax was levied on all male 'souls'. State bureaucrats at the centre, along with landlords and army officers in the localities, were all involved in squeezing taxes from the peasants, who also owed dues of labour, kind and money to their superiors. The latter were, naturally enough, excused payment of the poll tax, although it was levied on various categories of Russia's urban population. This was officially about 3 per cent of the total according to the census, but was in fact somewhat larger. Peter the Great's government was aware of the necessity of promoting a middle class, but its restrictions and controls were not very helpful in this respect.

Some of Peter's first attempts at reform of governmental institutions were directed at the towns, officials known by the Dutch title of *burgmester* being introduced in 1699. Their title might as well have been double Dutch as far as many urban dwellers were concerned, although in some towns there might have been at least a marginal improvement in tax collection and the administration of justice. A more comprehensive reform was introduced towards the end of Peter's reign, from 1718 onwards, the models this time being Riga and other German–Swedish cities on the Baltic. Urban administration was based now on the *magistrat* or town council, while the urban population was divided into three guilds separated by qualifications of property and status. The first and second guilds would elect members of the first guild to the *magistrat*, while well over half the town dwellers had no vote. Even the limited independence envisaged for the *magistrat* proved too much for the bureaucratic Russian tradition, and the reform was withdrawn soon after Peter's death. The same fate was met by the more ambitious attempts at reform of local government in general. Just as the guild or *tsech* (from the German *Zeche)* was spoilt in the import, so too the Swedish parish *(socken* or *kirchspiel)* was marred by its crossing of the frontier. Having from 1708 to 1710 divided the empire up into eight large provinces, each of which was to be controlled by one of his trusted associates and all of which except Moscow were to comprise at least part of the empire's periphery, Peter then attempted from 1718 onwards to increase the number of provinces to 12 and also to introduce intermediate and lower levels of administration right down to the parish. However, not only was the parish in the Swedish sense totally without precedent in Russian practice, the introduction of whole new ranges of officials looking after law and order and tax collection together with education and social welfare besides would have made impossible demands on Russia's financial resources and also on the firmly set attitudes of the functionaries.

For similar reasons, not too much success or innovation can be attributed to Peter the Great's famous reforms of central government. The final departure of the Boyar Council and the arrival of the Senate, the disappearance of the chancelleries known as *prikazy* and the arrival of the Colleges, too easily suggest a clean break, an ordered structure. If one looks at the personnel rather than the institutions, a strong measure of continuity is apparent between the former system of administration and that now introduced. There were some 'new men', but members of old families were also to be found both in the tsar's immediate informal entourage and in the formal bodies such as the Senate and the Colleges. The Senate was originally introduced as a stop-gap measure when Peter went off on an ill-fated campaign against the Turks in 1711, and was also from the beginning subject to interference from various kinds of agents and inspectors directly responsible to the tsar. The Colleges were originally constructed after foreign models, chiefly Swedish, but the basic concept of a board taking decisions by majority vote fell somewhat short of implementation. Moreover, some of the nine Colleges set up from 1718 onwards were more successful than others, those responsible for the conduct of foreign affairs, the army and the navy proving active and even enterprising while some of those dealing with economic affairs finding their assignments too much for them. Peter's demands for the development of commerce and industry through a rigid policy of mercantilism were far from easy to translate into action. In 1721, a collegial body, the Holy Synod, was created to complete the subjection of the Church to the state. Also in 1721, the Colleges were subordinated to the Senate, but in 1722 the Senate itself was placed under the supervision of a newly created Procurator-General, who headed a network of inspectors of various kinds. As in ancient Rome, so in imperial Russia, a fundamental question was *quis custodiet ipsos custodes?* – who will guard the guards themselves? Senators and Collegians as well as their lesser colleagues were constantly looking over their shoulders to see whose eyes were on them. Nevertheless, the Russian administration contrived to suffer from more than its fair share of bribery and corruption which, as Alexander Gordon pointed out, Peter himself was either unwilling or unable to destroy.

Like Louis XIV, Peter the Great was seen by his contemporaries as the heart of the body politic. His top PR man was Feofan Prokopovich, Bishop of Novgorod, who in the composition of *The Justice of the Monarch's Right*, published in 1722, made use not only of the scriptures but also of the writings of the Sun King himself and of Bossuet, together with a wide range of other sources – 'from a Renaissance background of classical and civic humanism and neo-stoicism, from a view of world history, ancient and modern, as a well-spring of philosophy and a school of virtue; from the study of Roman law and the development of natural law concepts'. The work concludes:

> As for all other true sons of the Russian fatherland, as staunch supporters of the Russian good, we need not expatiate on where their duty lies: for they themselves, clearly seeing the great advantage to the whole of Russia from the Monarch's statute, know that they must thank the Heavenly King with all their heart, who has so wonderfully glorified our Sovereign, and has inspired him to introduce this most useful enactment; and as for the Father of our Fatherland himself, His Imperial Majesty, Peter the Great, they must wish him a long and victorious reign, crowned with success in this regard, and worthy successors, that is, successors like himself.[16]

We will see how the latter part of this wish was granted in later chapters. For the moment, we should note that Peter did not help the situation by taking unto himself the right to name his successor, but then failing to do so.

THE OTHER POWERS, 1689–1721

When we turn to consider Brandenburg–Prussia and the Hohenzollern dynasty and its supporters, we find as great an emphasis on discipline and service as in Russia, and probably more success in achieving them. Frederick William I (1713–40), the 'Sergeant King', as he became known, did not except himself from the rigours of service to the state, proclaiming: 'I am the finance minister and field marshal of the King of Prussia.' But he also insisted: 'I must be served with life and limb, with house and wealth, with honour and conscience, everything must be committed except eternal salvation – that belongs to God, but all else is mine.' Therefore his 'servants' were necessarily more conscious than their predecessors of the 'burdensome properties' of 'Prussian Puritanism', especially since all the king's private secretaries and personal assistants were commoners, dependent on him for their eminent position. The army was a different kettle of fish, with the Junkers acquiring an almost exclusive hold on all commissioned ranks from captain upwards. And the army was always given top priority, even the 'father of Prussian bureaucracy', as Frederick William I has been called, spending 80 per cent of the state income on it, and giving it pride of place in his Table of Ranks introduced in 1713. Moreover, the Junkers were dominant in the provinces, both in the boards and councils controlled by the government and even more in their private domains where they exerted unchallenged authority. Even after the institution in 1723 of the General Directory of Finance, War and Domains had given more opportunities for advancement to commoners, the Junkers were still very much in evidence in Berlin and unrivalled in their authority in most places outside, where the importance of state commissars was diminishing. If the reign of Frederick William witnessed the 'complete intermarriage of army and state' that constitutes the 'real meaning of militarism', there is no doubt that the Junkers were the most honoured celebrants of the wedding. The 'second-class people' of the towns were given a distinctly lower position, while the bulk of the population, the enserfed peasant masses, had to snatch what crumbs they could from the rich folk's tables, for whose adornment they with their taxes had provided the largest share. They also helped to pay for the chief acquisition of the reign, Stettin and part of west Pomerania, from Sweden in 1720.[17]

The Prussian example was not followed under Emperor Leopold I, whose long reign lasted from 1658 to 1705. As a younger son, Leopold had at first been intended for the Church rather than headed for the throne. After his coronation as Holy Roman Emperor, his devotion to the cause of the Counter-Reformation was relieved by a love of literature and music rather than of war, even of government. But he made a conscientious attempt to carry out his difficult assignment, combining the narrower concern for the monarchy of Austria with his wider imperial responsibilities. His administration was inevitably far less centralised than that of Prussia or Russia. King of Austria, Leopold also wore the crowns of Bohemia and Hungary. Perhaps the Habsburg imperial eagle should have been adorned by three heads rather than two. Certainly, the imperial government was far less integrated and the nobility far more mixed in origins and status than in the case of the more successful examples of east and central European absolutism. But the embellishment of Vienna in the late seventeenth century created an impressive imperial capital. And there were to be more vigorous attempts at reform in the eighteenth century.

Not every power in the early eighteenth century was monarchist–absolutist. Although parliamentary government in Great Britain could trace its infancy both real and imaginary to medieval times, and although the important years of adolescence may be said to have been spent during the reigns of the Tudors and the early Stuarts, there can be little doubt that maturity was reached after the arrival of William and Mary in the 'Bloodless and Glorious Revolution' of 1688. The Acts passed almost immediately and in succeeding years made it certain that monarchical absolutism could not be imposed. The Bill of Rights of 1689, among other measures, laid down an order of succession from William and Mary to Anne which was supplemented in 1701 by the Act of Settlement, which asserted the Hanoverian succession to the exclusion of Catholic claimants to the throne. The Toleration Act of 1689 did much to end persecution of dissenters, both Catholic and Protestant nonconformist, although the only believers not disadvantaged in some way were loyal members of the Church of England. While the common law and other protective traditions were respected, both judges and judged were given protection from arbitrary royal interference, the control of the monarch over the army and navy was restricted, and the freedom of the press was guaranteed. Above all, regular parliaments were to be held, representing the needs and wishes of at least some strata of society and maintaining control over the monarch especially through management of the country's finances. These were put on a firmer footing by the introduction of the National Debt in 1693, the incorporation of the Bank of England in 1694 and the reform of the coinage in 1696. To cope with the administration of the army and navy and of finances in general, the executive arm of government was strengthened, but attached to the main body politic through the acceptance of ministerial responsibility. An increased electorate used its frequent opportunities to maintain some influence over parliament, and set a good example to the vast majority of the

people still without a vote in the payment of direct land taxes and indirect impositions such as customs and excise. London and provincial
towns alike grew with the increased opportunities afforded for trade in
Europe and overseas, while better internal communications by water,
if not yet over land, allowed the still more important home markets to
thrive and prosper. Undoubtedly, compact insularity was of enormous
benefit to both the economic and political situations. United for the
moment in peace and war, England was joined in 1707 with a sufficient amount of harmony by Scotland.

Unfortunately, 1688 and after was not really as smooth a process
as the above summary suggests. The Acts of those years were aiming
at stability rather than stemming from it. At the turn of the century,
monarchical absolutism may not have been a threat, but there remained the distinct possibility of renewed dislocation, even anarchy,
and the exiled Stuarts had great hopes for a second restoration. To
become and remain an MP took a lot of money, so both the Members
of Parliament and their patrons were anxious to get their hands on as
much of the spoils of the expanded governmental machine as possible. For this purpose at least as much as through political belief, they
moved towards the formation of parties – Tories and Whigs. Thus
while there was widespread agreement that life, liberty and property
should be respected, there was also furious argument about the size of
the share-out of these rights, about who should get the better deal
from the social contract, whether in an open manner or through the
more secret route of bribery and corruption. Then there were those,
possibly the majority of the population, who felt alienated from the
contract, who felt unfree to assign even the minimum amount of
property that they possessed, that is their own labour, and who, at a
time when mortality rates in general were high, maintained the weak-
est of holds on life itself. Sometimes in London and the lesser towns,
sometimes in the rural areas, they would vent their frustration and
annoyance in individual violence or collective riot. Meanwhile, Scotland was by no means unanimously reconciled to the Union, as the
Jacobite risings of 1715 and 1745 clearly showed, and Ireland was
extremely unhappy for the most part with its predicament. The
government's aim remained the preservation of Protestantism at home
and resistance of Catholic encroachments from abroad, especially from
France.

From 1648 to 1721, France, Austria and Russia all achieved great victories with disciplined armed forces. Already, however, 'Europe's dominant maritime and colonial power' was Britain, 'poised to create the greatest Empire in terms of territories, trade and shipping that the world had ever seen'.[18]

3

THE GROWTH OF EMPIRE, 1721–1763

THE BRITISH EMPIRE

Empire had been expanding the horizons of Europe for several centuries. As we have already seen, voyages of exploration laid the foundations of colonial acquisitions which were sufficient by the beginning of the sixteenth century for the Spanish and the Portuguese to have made several attempts at dividing the world between them. However, before the sixteenth century was over, there had been many assaults on this Iberian dominance, especially by the Italian city states and, from the north-west of Europe, by the French, the British and the Dutch. Moreover, the movement of Europe outwards was by no means confined to the sea. At a time when Drake, Hawkins and their like were voyaging on behalf of Queen Elizabeth, an equally doughty Cossack named Yermak was penetrating deep into Siberia in the name of Ivan the Terrible, while the footsteps of Marco Polo overland to China were also being followed.

Right from the start, the courage and skill of explorers were accompanied by the less attractive characteristics of intolerance and callousness. Moreover, as consciousness grew in Europe of the profit and advantage to be gained from infiltration into the wider world, the conflict between its several parts was extended beyond the confines of the continent. Already apparent before the Thirty Years War of

1618–48, the struggle for empire became especially pronounced with the Seven Years War of 1756–63. The purpose of this chapter will be to investigate the context of the significant struggle for empire in the 40 years or so leading up to the Treaty of Paris of 1763, and although some attention will be given to landward expansion by Russia, Austria and Prussia and to seaborne empires such as the Spanish, Portuguese, French and Dutch, first emphasis will be given to that small set of offshore islands that were to acquire dominance in the imperial world. We will see how not only Great Britain but also the other great powers in Europe were becoming connected in an inextricable manner among themselves and with almost every part of the globe.

When exactly Britain first arose from out the azure main is difficult to say, and whether or not it was at heaven's command is impossible even to conjecture. Beyond all reasonable doubt, however, these famous lines and the rest of the song 'Rule Britannia' (the chorus of which has been adopted by English football fans) were written in or about the year 1740 for a masque celebrating King Alfred. By that time, the ninth-century monarch had confirmed his reputation not only for carelessly burning cakes while making plans for the defeat of the invading Danes but also for inflicting that defeat and following it with a consolidation of the boundaries of England. Other national heroes had joined him in a patriotic ideology that was to blossom and flourish into the nineteenth century, as Britannia did indeed rule the waves. 1740 or soon after was also the time at which 'God Save the King' was first sung, originating perhaps from an air composed over 120 years before by a man bearing the name of the essence of the English character, John Bull.

The mastery of the waterways that was established near the beginning of the eighteenth century was a necessary accompaniment to the successful extension of the British Empire. So was an appropriate social and political arrangement that was completed at the same time to facilitate the growth of constitutional monarchy and parliamentary democracy. For these reasons, the British Empire was a comparatively late developer. In the days when the Elizabethan sea-dogs were singeing the King of Spain's beard, they were also plundering his treasure galleons rather than stealing his colonies. Early British settlement in North America and the West Indies was largely under the auspices of private enterprise and without much mercantilist regulation until

Cromwell's Navigation Act of 1651. The restored Stuarts took this further in their own Acts of Trade and Navigation to embody from 1660 onwards what came to be known as the Old Colonial System, which made it difficult for foreigners to participate in a largely closed arrangement of trade and manufacture. Moreover, such an arrangement could be extended to the east and south as well as to the west and north. This was clearly shown by the successful foundation of the Hudson's Bay Company in 1670 to exploit the Canadian fur trade and of the Royal African Company in 1672 to take care of the commerce in slaves. Meanwhile, the East India Company, which had been set up in 1600, gained new prosperity on the mainland of India with the acquisition of Bombay in 1668 and the development of Calcutta from 1690. The Board of Trade and Plantations was set up in 1696. In 1714 the Treaty of Utrecht brought gains especially in the eastern Mediterranean and Canada, together with some right of entry into the still rich economic network of the Spanish Empire.

However, the rise of Great Britain was by no means all plain sailing. Not only were there social and political difficulties at home, there were also huge problems connected with expansion abroad. Even the successes could not always be easily accommodated, while the failures led to dislocation of considerable proportions. For example, in 1695 the royal assent was given to an 'Act for a Company Trading to Africa and the Indies with the Sceptre of Scotland'. Both English and Dutch rivals did much to undermine the company before its assets were recklessly thrown into the Darien Scheme for taking over the isthmus between North and South America, 'this door of the seas, and the key of the Universe' as it was called by the scheme's principal promoter, William Paterson.[1] Possibly he and his unfortunate colleagues received some posthumous vindication two centuries or so later with the construction of the Panama Canal, but neither the position of world commerce nor the pattern of international relations was ripe for such a venture at the end of the seventeenth century. Therefore a sufficient number of influential Scotsmen decided that they could no longer go it alone, and accepted with resignation (in some cases welcoming with enthusiasm) the Union with England that was concluded in 1707. From then on, and even more after 1745, the empire was British indeed.[2]

In 1720, the United Kingdom and British Empire were shaken to their new foundations by another great storm of financial speculation that blew up quickly into the South Sea Bubble and then burst with devastating suddenness. In the aftermath of the Treaty of Utrecht, there seemed to be rich returns on offer for those investing in overseas commerce, while the National Debt had risen during the preceding war to an astronomical total approaching £10 million. In a neat attempt to balance the books the South Sea Company, which had been set up in 1711, took over much of the debt in return for a monopoly of the trade to Spanish America. Unfortunately, with the renewed outbreak of war in 1718, the Spanish government seized the company's effects, and little commerce ensued. Meanwhile, however, financial speculation rose to dizzy heights, and the South Sea Company could be detected through its size alone in the midst of a veritable ocean of bubbles. Change Alley in London in early 1720 was similar to Wall Street in New York in the first months of 1929. Then came the great crash, the bubbles exploded and thousands of investors rich and not so rich were soaked. The so-called Bubble Act was quickly passed, prohibiting the formation of joint-stock companies without royal charter, but confidence was not sufficiently restored for those who still had money to lend it to British commerce or industry.

That the panic did not intensify or continue was largely the consequence of the support given by the men of power and influence in the City of London to a skilful politician, Sir Robert Walpole. Having rejoined the government as Paymaster-General in June 1720 and quickly earned the nickname of 'Skreen-Master General' for his adroitness in the mounting of a comprehensive cover-up operation that saved fellow MPs and even the highest-placed personages at court from the embarrassment of a parliamentary enquiry, Walpole soon rose to become in fact if not in name Britain's first prime minister.

After a restless period of ministerial leapfrog, two decades of comparative tranquillity were to be achieved by Walpole, a 20-stone incarnation of John Bull full of good English roast beef (even if washed down by vintage French claret). He engineered his rise to power largely through doing down the Tories, taking advantage of the fact that some of them were Jacobites to tar most of the rest of them with the same brush. Walpole made full use of the sentiments expressed in the preamble of the Septennial Act of 1716 which had increased the length that parliaments could run to seven years, commenting on the previous stipulation of three:

> the said clause hath proved very grievous and burthensome, by occasioning much greater and more continued expenses in order to elections of members to serve in parliament, and more violent and lasting heats and animosities among the subjects of this realm, than were ever known before the said clause was enacted; and the said provision, if it should continue, may probably at this juncture, when a restless and popish faction are designing and endeavouring to renew the rebellion within this kingdom and an invasion from abroad, be destructive to the peace and security of the government.[3]

The shouting may have been louder than ever, but the planning of rebellion and invasion were almost certainly an invention as far as 1716 were concerned, though real enough before and after. The recurring possibility of a Jacobite rising or French attack was used by Walpole to the full in order to gain power and then to hold on to it; for what he represented as the national good, he would happily extend parliaments beyond seven years to infinity. True, Walpole had real enough problems closer to home: if the Tories were out, the Whigs were far from united and in any case it would be misleading to look upon both of them as in any way comparable to political parties as they developed a century or so later.

The First Lord of the Treasury in name and Prime Minister in fact needed to balance one faction against another to maintain majority support in parliament, which was his most difficult political task, and to retain the favour of the first two Hanoverian Georges (I, 1714–27; II, 1727–60), which was achieved more simply through catching the ear of the monarch or of his friends or mistresses, often by the simple strategem of filling the appropriate purses. Simultaneously, Walpole had to work for a sufficient level of support outside parliament by keeping the influential City of London on his side, and by protecting commercial and other interests in the provinces, too. Under the latter heading, for example, the Black Act of 1723 introduced stringent protection of landed estates for the following 100 years; E. P. Thompson suggested that the act was 'an expression of a Whig oligarchy, which created new laws and bent old legal forms in order to legitimize its own property and status'.[4]

During the 20 years or so in which Walpole exercised power, entrepreneurs were normally able to profit, and while many of them made their money in domestic markets and invested it in land, the opportunities for dealing with customers abroad also increased. To revert to the major theme of this chapter, the years from 1721 to 1763 marked a period during which there was a significant growth in the size and strength of the British Empire, from North America to the Far East. To consider first North America, where the most significant developments of the eighteenth century were to take place, the population rose from less than half a million in 1721 to nearly a million and a half by 1756. A new colony, Georgia, was founded in 1732, simultaneously aimed at providing a new start for the poor, the needy and the criminal, while affording stronger protection for the Carolinas which formed the southern flank of the British colonies against their Spanish and more especially their French rivals. This threat was perceived even more keenly in the offshore colonies in the West Indies, which at the time were believed to be of prime importance for British security and prosperity, as indeed had been the case from the time of Cromwell. In the West Indies as in the mainland colonies, the population was rising quickly, although the bulk of the increase in the islands came from the import of human beings from Africa. Of the approximately 50,000 slaves brought over the Atlantic in each average year during the period under consideration, the vast majority were taken to the Caribbean, a minority finding their new home in the southern mainland colonies. Just a few years later, the Abbé Raynal observed:

> The labours of the people settled in those islands are the sole basis of the African trade, they extend the fisheries and the culture of North America, afford a good market for the manufactures of Asia, and double, perhaps treble, the activity of all Europe. They may be considered as the principal cause of the rapid motion which now agitates our globe.[5]

In his enthusiasm, Raynal exaggerated the proportions of the commerce, but there can be little doubt that the West Indies constituted a key segment of what came to be known as the triangular trade, which played an increasingly important part in the economies of several European states, especially Britain. One triangle consisted of slaves from West Africa to the West Indies, sugar from the plantations of the Caribbean to the New England colonies of North America, and rum from them to purchase more slaves in Africa. Another triangle, not involving slaves, would take manufactured goods from north-western Europe to be exchanged for colonial fish, meat, timber and grain, which were then carried back across the ocean to south-western Europe to be exchanged in turn for wines and fruits. There were in fact many triangles, and a fair proportion of the activity was not triangular at all, but bilateral or even unilateral. For example, ships might carry goods from British ports to the West Indies and then go straight back again with sugar or even in ballast. And if throughout much of the eighteenth century the West Indies were believed to be the finest jewel in the British crown, the American continental colonies were far more important as a market for British manufactures by the middle of that century, while the East India Company in Bombay, Calcutta and other *entrepôts* was already extracting significant profits from trade with the Orient. Moreover, it must not be forgotten that eastern Europe, especially Russia, continued to be an important source of naval stores in particular.

Altogether, sugar, tobacco, indigo (a blue dye plant grown mostly in the Carolinas), coffee, tea and other colonial products were involved with manufactured goods from the metropolis in a network which soon after 1750 approached one-third of the total of British overseas commercial activity. While London was as ever the busiest town, Bristol, Liverpool and Glasgow were all deriving prosperity from their transoceanic connections. Especially controversial among the calculations that have attempted to establish the most accurate accounts have been those concerned with the amount of profit extracted from the slave economy. If the already great city of Bristol rose to be second in size to London from the sale of slaves and the fruits of their labour, Liverpool was little more than a village before it became involved in the buying and selling of human beings, deriving benefits at the same time from its proximity to the manufacturing centre of Manchester. Glasgow began its rise from village to Scotland's largest conurbation after the Union of 1707 on the basis of the sugar and tobacco trade, even if it was not so directly involved in the slave trade. Some Britons never would be wage slaves because their masters had comprehensively enslaved many Africans, and the social mobility of British society as a whole received some impetus from the immobility of the society of the plantations. But the seeds of British liberties had been sown and successfully nurtured before any significant involvement in colonial trade. Moreover, as already observed above, even in the middle of the eighteenth century more than two-thirds of British overseas commercial intercourse was with Europe, from the Baltic to the Mediterranean, while the most important of all markets were still to be found at home. Therefore the argument that the British industrial revolution was launched on the wealth extracted from slavery remains powerful but cannot be accepted as overwhelming.

British imperial interests as a whole, strategic as well as economic, grew at a great rate from the 1730s onwards, and thenceforth occupied a larger place than hitherto in the decision of international conflicts. The shift of emphasis is reflected in the pantheon of British heroes: Marlborough in Europe at the beginning of the eighteenth century, Wolfe in Canada and Clive in India soon after the middle of it. Yet the prime enemy remained the same, whether fought in the valley of the Danube near Vienna, on the heights of Montcalm outside Quebec, or at the walls of Trichinopoly in India. For France too, the 1730s were significant as the colonial and commercial rivalry with Britain moved from the periphery of concern much nearer to the centre.

However, when war broke out in 1739 after two decades of comparative peace and some friendship, including alliance with France from 1716 to 1731, the immediate enemy was not France but Spain. Nor was the direct cause commerce or colonies but the ear of the British Captain Jenkins, removed by Spanish freebooters some eight years earlier. Pickled in a bottle, the severed organ was brandished by its owner in the House of Commons as part of a campaign to rouse the sleeping old bulldog Walpole and to renew the traditional anti-Spanish frenzy among the public at large. For its part, the Spanish government was keen to avoid hostilities, and offered considerable monetary compensation for losses incurred by the British in the Caribbean, including presumably the ear of Captain Jenkins. But the South Sea Company refused to pay the Spanish government its rightful share of the proceeds accruing from its 'annual ship' to the Caribbean, and so that privilege of *asiento* was withdrawn. Inevitably, once war was joined between Britain and Spain the involvement of France could be only a matter of time, especially since the opportunity had now been presented for British naval superiority to be pressed home, especially across the Atlantic.

Delay, disease and indecision meant that in fact little was achieved and, partly in consequence, if more through electoral reverses, Walpole was forced to resign early in 1742. However, across the Channel apprehension grew rather than abated, and in 1744 what had become fierce colonial rivalry between France and Britain erupted into open warfare. In 1745, a great fear arose concerning the possibility of French support for the Jacobite rising in Scotland. The primary centre of overseas attention was the West Indies, in which the French had sugar and other interests greater than the British. Although there was still more bark than bite, by 1747 the British navy was able to extend its dominance in the seas around Europe over to the Caribbean. Further to the north, there was some consideration of advance inland on French Canada, following up the capture of the fortress of Louisburg on Cape Breton Island in 1745. But when final peace negotiations began in 1748, Louisburg was returned to France and a stalemate or compromise agreement was arranged with France and Spain for other overseas theatres of war. Britain made these concessions because of growing concern about developments on the continent of Europe.

The Treaty of Aix-la-Chapelle (or Aachen) of October 1748 brought to an end not only the war that had commenced with outrage at the loss of an ear but also another that had arisen from arguments concerning the acquisition of a throne. We will turn in due course to consider the War of the Austrian Succession, as it was known. For the moment, all we need to know is that France overran the Austrian Netherlands and threatened the Dutch Republic with a similar fate, to forestall which Britain was prepared to sacrifice its newly won prize of Louisburg. Now, although peace was agreed, the signatories to the treaty of 1748 all realised that this was more of a lull in hostilities than a complete cessation of them. By 1756, the conflict had been fully rejoined in the Americas and India as well as in Europe.

OTHER EMPIRES

The attempts by Colbert in the seventeenth century to develop an empire for France in a formal manner had been overshadowed by the informal extensions of French interest in the New World by Canadian fur-traders and fishermen. John Law's grandiose scheme for the development of Louisiana collapsed soon after the British South Sea Bubble in 1720, but New Orleans struggled on as the centre for a modest amount of commercial activity up the Mississippi. However, as with the British, the focus of French overseas attention in the period after 1720 was the West Indies, especially the slave sugar economy, and the ports of Nantes, La Rochelle and Bordeaux shared the prosperity of Bristol, Liverpool and Glasgow. Even if the French population of some 23 million was about three times greater than the British and therefore capable of developing a more significant internal economy, there can be little doubt that the expansion around and after mid-century was sufficiently connected with overseas activity for the French government to be prepared to put a considerable amount of effort and resources into its protection, both across the Atlantic and over the Indian Ocean. Such concern also reflected a continuing formal concept of empire.

Meanwhile, the Dutch could still be found in many parts of the world, but they were no longer as dominant as round about the middle of the seventeenth century, either in the Baltic, the Atlantic or the East Indies. The domestic market was not big enough to launch large-scale industrial development, and the British and French had caught up and even overtaken the Dutch in what had previously been almost a monopoly of their merchant navy as freight carrier. By 1750, Hamburg as a port was busier than Amsterdam, although the Dutch city had become one of Europe's principal financial centres, handling credit for its partners and rivals, and also extending foreign loans.

Just as Holland had lost its former pre-eminence but was still of central importance in the European commercial network from some points of view, so the once dominant Spain and Portugal must not be forgotten even if their decline was relatively greater. Access to the old Spanish Empire had been of benefit to its newer British counterpart, a popular caricature around 1700 depicting a fat, contented Hispanic cow being milked by British, French and Dutch calves. Beyond the official concessions, there was much smuggling, estimated later at no less than two-thirds of the total commerce of Spanish America. In theory the empire, like its European counterparts, was a closed system – in this case the largest of them, stretching from Florida and Mexico through Cuba and South America over the Pacific Ocean to the Philippines. Powerful viceroys, supported by the various branches of the Church, were expected to exert a close control. In fact, there were not only external infringements of the Spanish variety of bureaucratic control, but also many kinds of internal tension: between rich and poor; between white settlers, black slaves and brown natives, as well as a wide range of mixtures; even in the ranks of the ruling class, between those born locally and those from over the water. Moreover, Spain itself lacked the basic wherewithal for successful empire – the raw materials and processing industries as well as the thrusting enterprise.

Portugal's plight was if anything worse – both a weaker metropolis and a more overextended empire. Brazil was still a most worthwhile possession, especially perhaps after the discovery of gold there at the end of the seventeenth century, and profit could be extracted from footholds in Africa, India and further to the east. But the Dutch and the British had taken over several former Portuguese colonies in the Orient, and the central government encountered even more difficulties than its Spanish counterpart in the maintenance of supervision and control.

Before we turn to examine the continental empires, let us put those overseas in a clearer perspective by glancing at them from outside, from the point of view of those parts of the world into which they had already penetrated. This will omit large areas as yet untouched, even unknown. Apart from associates of the Hudson's Bay Company and a further handful of intrepid explorers, non-European segments of the Arctic Circle were barely infiltrated by the middle of the eighteenth century, while the continent of Antarctica was imagined rather than discovered and Australasia still peripheral to the European consciousness. China, Japan, India and Africa had not yet been significantly probed beyond the coasts. Ships from most European seafaring nations were to be found in Canton while the Portuguese for the most part concentrated on Macao. However, from soon after 1720 onwards, Christianity was banned from the Chinese Empire, and foreign merchants were obliged to hear the edicts of the emperor on their knees. During the eighteenth century, successive representatives of the Manchu dynasty were concentrating much effort on the subjugation of the unruly Mongol tribes to the north, where overland contact was maintained with Russia, but the frontier made secure. Thus, for the time being, the universal empire could continue on its own way with the material basis of agriculture and the moral basis of Confucianism. Meanwhile, Japan was in almost complete seclusion, a few Dutch merchants maintaining bare contact via a minute artificial island in Nagasaki harbour. India, on the other hand, was poised for surrender to the victor in the struggle between the British and the French. The once all-powerful Moghul Empire was breaking up through internal conflict and landward invasion from the north, leaving it open to European conquest. As for Africa, the only major European settlement was by Dutch farmers at the Cape of Good Hope. Along the east and west coasts, the Portuguese kept a tenuous hold on a few bases, and the French were strategically poised in the large eastern offshore island of Madagascar. A much higher level of activity was to be found on that strip of the west coast where the British and other slavers plied their human trade. Local society, although by no means pure and peaceful in earlier times, was now more corrupt and turbulent, and possibly the malign influence of slavery spread a considerable distance inland. But Europeans did not move far beyond the sea before the end of the eighteenth century.

Therefore in the period when overseas European empire, especially the British and French, assumed greater importance in the affairs of the continent than formerly, the world at large had yet to feel the impact of European incursions in a direct manner. Most attention was paid to the Indies, the East far less than the West, and to the seaboard regions of North and South America. The principal cockpit of rivalry between the British and the French was the Caribbean, previously dominated by the Spanish, stretching out into the Atlantic. Meanwhile, in a barely perceptible manner the 13 colonies of British settlement from Massachusetts to Georgia were undergoing the formative experience of most long-term significance, and were soon to feel the first intimations of independence.

Further important developments not fully appreciated at the time or since by those accustomed to think in terms of exploration and exploitation by sea were occurring in the second quarter of the eighteenth century in central and eastern Europe. Here, the expansion of Russia, Austria and Prussia was mostly by land. The greatest spread, which was looked at in the previous chapter and noticed in passing two paragraphs above, was that of Russia. In the Far East, the Treaty of Nerchinsk of 1689 defined the boundary between Russia and China for nearly two centuries, during which contact between the two powers was no more than intermittent. A Danish explorer in Russian service,

Vitus Bering, made the acquaintance of the strait that bears his name soon after the death of Peter the Great in 1725, and in 1741, just before his own death, led an expedition that sighted the coast of Alaska. Entrepreneurs, looking especially for furs, soon followed in his wake. While Siberia experienced the increasing presence of Russian immigrants, there was also significant activity to the west of the Urals with the foundation in 1735 of the fortress of Orenburg at the confluence of the Rivers Or and Yaik (later Ural) and the extension on either side of a line of defence against marauders from central Asia. From the point of view of the Bashkirs and other peoples of the neighbourhood, the marauders were of course the Russians. Attitudes would have been similar at the Caucasus Mountains and on the shores of the Caspian and Black Seas on either side of them. Of some importance was the peace established with Persia by 1735 and the war with the Turks and their clients the Crimean Tatars in 1736–9. Even though the Treaty of Belgrade, which brought the war to a conclusion, restored the previous situation by excluding Russia from the Black Sea, a further stage was reached in the softening up of the Muslim enemies of the Orthodox Church. Much the same stalemate resulted from the next in the series of wars with Poland, 1733–6, and with Sweden, 1741–3, two more traditional enemies revealing their failing strength. The Turks and the Swedes were in touch about possible co-operation against their mutual foe, a liaison encouraged by the French, who were alarmed at the prospect of further expansion by the Russians as well as by the Austrians, who were allies of the Russians in the war against Turkey.

In fact, Austria was about to shrink. During the reign of Charles VI (1711–40), there were at first some grandiose dreams of spreading the empire overseas, building on the confidence of the new Vienna and the gains from the Treaty of Utrecht. An Oriental Company and an East India Company were founded, and Trieste and Fiume on the Adriatic were made free ports with the acquiescence of Venice. But such projects aroused the suspicions of maritime powers whose support would be necessary for a vital ambition of this last male in the Habsburg line, the succession of his daughter Maria Theresa. The nascent Austrian fleet was sold to Venice. After a promising beginning Charles made very little progress for Austria in the wider world or nearer home. His involvement in a series of wars in Europe was not successful. By the end of his reign, the Habsburgs had lost Lorraine, southern Italy and much of southern Hungary. Charles made many concessions to other powers, either because of his fundamental aim of recognition for the Pragmatic Sanction, the device for keeping the provinces of the Austrian monarchy indivisible and inseparable, or because of his realisation that their stronger might left him with no alternative.

The achievements of Maria Theresa, empress from 1740 to 1780, were considerable. A formidable wife and mother (16 children in 20 years), she also took a most active interest in the affairs of her widespread dominions in both war and peace. She gave her full support to capable ministers. For example, Haugwitz strove to arrange tax assessment and collection directly by the state. Estates throughout the empire were unhappy at these and other encroachments on their self-government, and compromises were necessarily made. In 1749, older chancelleries were replaced by a *Directorium* under Haugwitz for administration and finance, and an *Oberste Justizstelle* for justice. Austrian, Bohemian and German provinces were subject to the same jurisdiction centred on Vienna. There were attempts to boost the economy and to regulate society, even to remove some of the worst excesses of serfdom. However, Hungary, Italy and the Netherlands retained most of their separate administration. Moreover, there had to be give and take throughout the empire, bound together by an elaborate system of patronage over which Maria Theresa kept as tight control as possible.

GERMANY: FROM OLD EMPIRE TOWARDS NEW

Upstart Prussia was another power that had contemplated joining its European fellows in the search for overseas empire, but was ultimately to take little action. As far back as 1682, the Great Elector of Brandenburg (1640–88) was the first shareholder in the African Company, which established a couple of bases on the Guinea coast and broadened its modest interests to include a foothold in the West Indies. But the great elector's grandson, Frederick William I of Prussia (1713–40), soon sold the company at a modest price to the rival Dutch, observing that for his kingdom colonial enterprise was a 'chimera'. In turn his son, Frederick II (Frederick the Great, 1740–86), took the first stride towards the acquisition of his outstanding reputation, not over the oceans but in the immediate vicinity, by extending his inheritance at the expense of that of Maria Theresa of Austria.

Before the descent on Silesia, the Prussian lands had been gathered together during the course of the previous century. Why was it that Prussia rather than Bavaria or Saxony was emerging as the dynamic state in Germany, now capable of pushing back Austria from one of its most valued provinces? And why was it that nearly 1000 years after the foundation of the first *Reich* by Charlemagne, the German people were soon to be on their way to a further union, a second *Reich* under the leadership of Brandenburg–Prussia? To take the second question first, sooner or later (sooner in the West, later in the East), out of the varied patchwork of the crumbling medieval giant that was the Holy Roman Empire, some modern political arrangement was bound to arise. The implication of inevitability in that bald statement may be counter-balanced by a visit to the site of the unpromising beginnings of Brandenburg–Prussia's rise to world power, the sandy, marshy flat-lands between the Rivers Elbe and Oder. Here, emerging from the Thirty Years War with the acquisition of the eastern part of Pomerania by the Baltic Sea, was the Duchy of Brandenburg, ruled by the Great Elector Frederick William. At this time, Bavaria and Saxony were more prominent in the affairs of Germany, but they started to fade from view as Brandenburg became more conspicuous.

Neither of Brandenburg's rivals was helped by its pretensions. During the Thirty Years War, Duke Maximilian I of Bavaria had been the leader of the Catholic members of the Holy Roman Empire against the Bohemian Protestants and their allies, a distinction that had cost him dearly in money and men. Saxony, once among the most prosperous and advanced of German states, with Leipzig a flourishing commercial centre, was not helped by the involvement of its elector, once he had gained a royal title as King Augustus II towards the end of the seventeenth century, in the affairs of Poland. Meanwhile, Frederick William was husbanding his resources and augmenting them. However, the difference between the candidates for pre-eminence in Germany went beyond the policies and personalities of their rulers, important though they may have been. There were important social variations, too: for example, in Bavaria, a basic structure of 'small noble estates, small towns and small peasants'[6] militated in favour of ducal absolutism but against its progressive evolution, while in Saxony the nobility did not establish its dominance over the peasants and burghers. Strategically, its rivals were not as well placed as Brandenburg, being both surrounded on all sides by potentially hostile neighbours and remote from any outlet to the sea. Strategic considerations also weighed heavily against the German principalities on the Rhine, which was a centre of contention over many centuries, while the prosperity of the towns along this economically important river was a further barrier to the superimposition of absolutism.

Brandenburg took a step towards prominence with its acquisition of eastern Pomerania at the end of the Thirty Years War. The other results of that great conflict produced a configuration in Europe that was also favourable to the ambitions of the great elector, especially the reduction of Habsburg ambitions and the decline of the power of Poland, soon to be followed by that of Sweden. It was through the playing off of these two rival neighbours that Frederick William was able in 1656 to acquire full control over East Prussia, the Polish province whose name was to replace Brandenburg as that given to the inheritance of his successors. Originally peopled by Slavs, after the thirteenth century East Prussia took on a distinctive Germanic character as the area of settlement of the Teutonic Knights and other colonists, whose descendants were reunited with their long-lost brothers and sisters in 1618 as a result of a family marriage. The full control over East Prussia acquired in war with Sweden against Poland in 1656 was confirmed in war with Poland against Sweden in 1660, and the Elector of Brandenburg could now add the title of a European prince to that which he possessed as member of the Holy Roman Empire. His son, Frederick III, became king in East Prussia in 1701, and Brandenburg began to take lesser precedence in the Hohenzollern family's titles, even if the capital city remained Berlin. It was not until the First Partition of Poland in 1772 that Frederick the Great gained West Prussia. His father, Frederick William I, paid Sweden compensation in 1720 for its cession of Stettin (Szczecin) and part of western Pomerania.

Thus the long march towards the German Empire under Prussian domination had taken several strides forward before the launching of the war on Austria in 1740, even if there had been no such clear aim at the time. Just as in the case of the relative failure of Bavaria and Saxony, however, the success of Prussia cannot be ascribed to the personalities and the policies of the rulers alone. They themselves were more interested in advancing the claims of their families than of their peoples. Moreover, capable though most members of the Hohenzollern dynasty in the seventeenth and eighteenth centuries were, they were fortunate in being able to make advantageous use of a favourable social system, in which the dominant part was played by the Junkers. These celebrated noblemen possessed no superhuman talents; indeed, their success may be said to have lain in their very ordinariness. They were not great landowners, but middling; they were prepared to work hard on their estates as well as leading the army and participating in civil administration. Most of the 2 million or so inhabitants of Prussia on the eve of the War of the Austrian Succession were enserfed peasants, whom the Junkers had little difficulty in keeping in subjection; there was somewhat more tension between the nobles and the townsfolk. On the whole, Prussian society possessed an unusual degree of cohesion, a very necessary attribute in some of the difficulties that were to be encountered in the later years of Frederick the Great's reign following its most successful beginning.

There was no valid excuse for the invasion of Silesia in December 1740 beyond the desire of Frederick and his advisers for power and glory. Might was right as the first victories went to Prussia and, in a treaty of June 1741, France recognised Prussia's acquisition of Lower Silesia in exchange for Frederick's vote in the forthcoming imperial election for Charles Albert of Bavaria. Saxony also voted for Charles Albert, and George II of Britain in his capacity as Elector of Hanover was obliged to do likewise to guarantee the neutrality of his fatherland, even though his sympathies were with France's enemy, Austria. Charles Albert was duly elected Charles VII in January 1742 after the allied forces had taken Prague and Bohemia a couple of months previously. Meanwhile, Maria Theresa had withdrawn to Hungary and awarded herself the crown of St Stephen in the summer of 1741. An attempt to reach accommodation with Frederick II, not yet the Great, in the autumn of 1741 had failed, but after some further bruising hostilities Maria Theresa was forced in the summer of 1742 to recognise the king's acquisition of virtually all Silesia.

Bohemia was retaken by the Austrians who in turn were soon to be driven out of Bavaria. But the British were not satisfied that the balance between the Austrians and the French was being maintained and were also, as described above, about to become involved in a war with the French overseas. With Hanoverian and Hessian troops in support, the British drove the French from the Rhine in the summer of 1743. Previously worried about what she could hold on to, Maria Theresa now became interested in what she could take. Possibly she could recapture the old Habsburg dominions of Alsace and Lorraine, annex Bavaria and even expand in Italy. Nearer home, she managed to secure the alliance of Saxony, which would help her defence against any further attacks from Prussia. Since the Elector of Saxony was also King of Poland with the support of Russia, the alliance was wider ranging. However, Maria Theresa's dreams of Habsburg restoration and growth were abruptly halted by a new attack by the Prussians and their occupation of Bohemia in the late summer of 1744. Fortunately for Maria Theresa, the French were preoccupied with involvement in the Netherlands and overseas problems, and did not give Frederick their promised support. With the help of the Saxons, the Austrian army was able to drive the Prussians out of Bohemia again.

The death of the Emperor Charles VII at the beginning of 1745 brought an end to the conflict between his native Bavaria and Austria, which encouraged Maria Theresa to take the fight to Frederick II in Silesia. But the Prussian forces stood firm, and launched a counter-attack into Saxony. Maria Theresa had to be satisfied with the election of her husband as Emperor Francis I, some limited gains in Italy and the renewal of her grasp on the Netherlands. These were the terms of the Treaty of Aachen or Aix-la-Chapelle in 1748 as far as Austria was concerned, while Prussia retained Silesia and received a large payment for withdrawal from Saxony. We have already seen how Britain gave up some overseas gains in order once again to achieve this satisfactory balance of power in Europe. To some extent for the same reason, although probably more from military exhaustion, Prussia stopped short of imposing more punitive terms on Austria. Certainly, even if none of the signatory parties could be completely happy at the manner in which the war was brought to a conclusion, the question of the Austrian succession was now settled, and something like a new balance of power achieved both in the continent and in the wider world. However, little more than a decade later, a new and greater conflict was to break out.

THE SEVEN YEARS WAR, 1756–63

To say that the Seven Years War began an era in the development of Europe is also to repeat that epochs in history evolve more often than they are created. The conflict that broke out in 1756 was the culmination of a process inaugurated by the Thirty Years War (1618–48). Yet, more definitely than its predecessors, the Seven Years War involved the major powers of the continent while at the same time extending their struggle into the wider world. Two of those powers could derive special satisfaction from the peace, even if neither was happy about the specific terms of the treaties. Most clearly, the British Empire established its predominance in North America and India. Less obviously, since it gained no further territory and achieved no decisive military victory, Prussia was able through its very survival to consolidate its position in central Europe.

The Seven Years War began with a revolution in diplomacy: just before the war broke out officially, the age-old enemies Bourbon France and Habsburg Austria agreed to a defensive alliance on 1 May 1756. The credit for this about-turn has often been given to the Austrian Chancellor Kaunitz, who was certainly a man with distinctive attitudes and ideas: according to the 'political algebra' that he had devised, every possible move and countermove of the powers of Europe could be clearly calculated, and his complex continental equation indicated beyond all doubt that Prussia must be destroyed. Still smarting from the humiliation of the loss of Silesia in the War of the Austrian Succession, many of the chancellor's fellow Austrians had arrived at the same conclusion by a simpler route, and were fully prepared to see old enemies placated so that the dangerous new foe could be put back in its place. For France, Prussian expansionism was a greater threat than the latter-day enfeebled version of the pretension of the Austrians, who were not by themselves powerful enough to resist further attacks on their fragile empire. Turkey and Poland could not now be used as counterweights to a power threatening to dominate central Europe, while Russia was if anything no more attractive a proposition than Prussia. Therefore there was a certain logic in France's participation in the diplomatic revolution; even if several of his ministers were not immediately convinced by the arguments of the Austrian negotiators, Louis XV had a personal preference for Maria Theresa over Frederick II which helped push France in the direction ordained by the 'political algebra' of Kaunitz. But the Bourbons and Habsburgs did not complete their reconciliation until they received the news of a rival agreement made with Prussia by Britain, with whom France was already informally at war.

From the British point of view, France was undoubtedly enemy number one, and so the preferred ally was France's traditional chief enemy, Austria. Realising, however, that Austria was not the force that it had formerly been, Britain gave renewed attention to another ally, Russia, to which it agreed at the end of September 1755 to pay subsidies in return for the presence on the Prussian border of an army ready to attack if Prussia invaded Hanover, the ancestral home of the British dynasty. Alarmed at the prospect of a new powerful combination poised to beat him, Frederick II joined it, at least to the extent of signing the Treaty of Westminster at the beginning of 1756 whereby Prussia contracted with Britain to forego mutual hostilities in Germany. This northern accord was viewed in Paris with surprise and shock, causing France to move towards closer relationship with its former rival Austria, signing a defensive Treaty of Versailles in May 1756. Meanwhile, Empress Elizabeth of Russia and her advisers in St Petersburg decided that they could not sit idly by while Prussia was gaining strength and confidence from its closer ties with Britain. Russian mobilisation began in earnest, and according to some analysts, this was the move that pushed Europe from diplomatic manoeuvres into war. Austria was less than fully encouraging to Russia until full accord was reached with France, which was already concerned with its colonial war against Britain and therefore anxious not to commit itself too readily to a provocative anti-Prussian coalition. But Frederick the Great took appearances for reality, and decided to make what later became known in strategic jargon as a pre-emptive first strike. At the end of August he invaded Saxony and, after some hesitation, France signed a second Treaty of Versailles with Austria, this time an offensive one, on 1 May 1757. Kaunitz had squared his circle: the diplomatic revolution was now complete, and war was more generally joined.

It was not so much one war as two, one in Europe, the other overseas. Britain, the ultimate victor in the struggle for empire, gave money to Prussia and others to keep France busy in Europe while itself harrying the French fleet and making sorties directed at the French coast.

William Pitt the Elder was now in charge of operations, constantly sick in body and intermittently in mind, but of persistently bold spirit in his implementation of the policy forced upon him by circumstances – 'to win Canada on the banks of the Elbe'. Before the first shots were fired in Europe, the army detachments in North America were already engaged with some of the local colonists against a dual enemy in what became known on the far side of the Atlantic as the French and Indian War. With their native allies, the French in Canada were trying to establish contact by way of the Ohio and Mississippi river valleys with their fellow-countrymen in Louisiana. From the summer of 1757, Pitt inaugurated a policy not only of breaking the French lines of communication but also of removing the French presence completely from Canada. In India, after the widely publicised humiliation of the nearly 150 British citizens imprisoned overnight in the Black Hole of Calcutta, Robert Clive recaptured that British station and drove the French from theirs at the same time as defeating the jailer Nawab of Bengal. In West Africa, the British enjoyed early successes in Senegal and Dakar, but were not able to make much headway at first in the more important theatre of war in the West Indies.

Meanwhile, back in Europe, in November 1757 Prussia inflicted a shattering defeat on France at Rossbach that 'destroyed her military reputation for a generation and thereby undermined her position as the leading continental state'.[7] However, Prussia soon had to withdraw from its first advances and was soon under counter-attack from its wide range of enemies. Its cause was not helped by the Duke of Cumberland, who found the French in Hanover a more formidable enemy than the Jacobites at Culloden and made dangerous concessions to them. Not only Russia but also Sweden was harrying Prussia from the north while Austria penetrated from the south as far as Berlin. But Pitt gave the allied forces a new commander and fresh heart, and the French were pushed back from Hanover, while the Prussians were further encouraged by the second Treaty of Westminster of April 1758, which gave them an annual subsidy. With continued great difficulties and heavy losses, Frederick earned some of his reputed greatness by calling for constant efforts by his armies to keep their various enemies at bay.

The second phase of the Seven Years War brought little immediate relief to the Prussian king and his subjects, although Pitt's new French counterpart Choiseul decided to give most emphasis to the defeat of

Britain and therefore lowered the level of financial and other assistance given to Austria. The British-supported force from Hanover and elsewhere pushed the French back in the summer of 1759 to weaken their interest in the continental war even further and to justify Pitt's policy of supporting an allied force as well as the Prussians. Nevertheless, Frederick the Great suffered a crushing defeat at the same time, and was saved only by the failure of the Austrians and the Russians to agree on how to follow up their victory. As it was, Frederick and his adherents had to leave Berlin briefly in the autumn of 1760, although they then managed an at least partially successful counter-attack. Away from Europe in 1759, Clive and his comrades swept the French before them in India while in Canada another British hero, General Wolfe, with his men achieved victory at the cost of his own life at Quebec. There were victories too in the West Indies, while in European waters a considerable part of the French fleet was taken out before it could cross the Atlantic to afford relief or cross the Channel to effect a diversionary invasion of England.

From late 1760 onwards, the war moved into its final phase amid a number of monarchical and ministerial changes. In October, two weeks after the Austro-Russian occupation of Berlin, George III (1760–1820) ascended the throne at the death of his grandfather George II. The new king and his advisers were not as interested in the war as the old king and the elder Pitt, and about a year after George III's accession, unable to secure continued support for his active policies, Pitt resigned. He had wanted to declare war on Spain which, itself under a new monarch, Charles III, moved close to France: it had promised to enter the war if negotiations begun between the British and French in March 1761 had not led to peace by 1 April 1762. The new British government actually declared war against Spain at the beginning of 1762, but reduced its subsidies to Prussia. Frederick the Great was still hard pressed on all fronts, but was then saved by another monarchical changeover at the beginning of 1762, the death of his bitter enemy the Empress Elizabeth of Russia and the accession of his devoted admirer Peter III. The new Russian emperor soon withdrew his forces from the war and made peace with his hero early in May. Sweden soon did the same, having made little impact on the war since its entry into it in 1757. The British forces continued their successes over the Atlantic and elsewhere, but now that the war on the continent was coming to an end, there was not enough enthusiasm to keep it going across the seas.

Two treaties of February 1763 brought the Seven Years War to an end. In Paris it was agreed that Canada and the area as far west as the Mississippi should be ceded by France to Britain. According to a later concession, Britain received Florida from Spain, which gained Louisiana from France. In the West Indies, and to a lesser extent in West Africa, Britain made gains at the expense of France, while in India British conquests were restored – 'The Seven Years War was the most dramatically successful war the British ever fought.'[8] While the power of France was undermined by a prohibition of its refortification in India, back in Europe it had to fall back from Germany across the Rhine. In the second treaty, signed at Hubertusburg, Prussia and Austria agreed to restore the pre-war situation. By implication, the Prussian gain of Silesia during the previous War of the Austrian Succession was confirmed. Explicitly, the official reason for that previous war was nullified as a possible reason for a future war by Prussia's promise of support for Maria Theresa's son as a future Holy Roman Emperor, Joseph II.

The entrances and exits of monarchs and ministers that accompanied the final stages of the Seven Years War and the concluding peace treaties must not conceal some of the wider issues involved, which may conveniently be put under the heading of the balance of power system. Consider first the difficulties faced towards the end of hostilities by Prussia. Why was Frederick the Great not completely humiliated, as on several occasions seemed possible? What had gone wrong with the 'political algebra' of Kaunitz? Resourceful as ever, the Austrian chancellor had come to Hubertusburg with five different equations of peace, but was more than a little disappointed to be forced to accept the least welcome of them, the restoration of the status quo. To a certain extent, Kaunitz himself was responsible for the failure to destroy Prussia: he had got his earlier sums wrong. Minus for Prussia meant plus for Russia, and the thought of Russia in charge of Poland and the Baltic was if anything an even more undesirable solution to the problems of central and eastern Europe than an expanding Prussia. As for Russian policy towards the end of the war, its withdrawal was not just the consequence of Peter III's Prussophilia, for when he was removed after a reign of only a few months by his ambitious wife and none too reluctant widow, this new Empress Catherine II (not yet except perhaps in her own estimation the Great) made no move towards re-entry into the final hostilities. With the understanding that she and her ministers already possessed, Catherine realised that an overextension of Russian influence would make her by no means completely secure position at home even more difficult as well as alarming the rest of Europe at a time when she needed its acquiescence. Moreover, if Prussia were removed from central Europe, the major share of the spoils would probably go to Austria, which in that case would pose at least as great a threat as that already constituted by Prussia. To turn to the international order emerging from the Treaty of Paris, the elder Pitt was not alone in wanting to assert British imperial might on a greater scale at the expense of the French, but the alternative view prevailed that France had already been forced to her knees and that to make the proud lady grovel would certainly exhaust British treasure and perhaps provoke French vengeance. As for France itself, the terms of the treaty had to be accepted in the unfavourable circumstances, but there were indeed already thoughts of revenge, as well as the strong feeling on the part of Choiseul and other ministers, even on the part of Louis XV himself, that the old order would have to be reformed to meet the challenges of the post-war age.

THE BALANCE OF POWER

We must be careful not to make the principle of 'the balance of power' as inflexible and comprehensive as it sometimes appears, although we should also recognise it as 'one of the essential conditions of the sovereign independence of the nations of Europe'. As W. L. Dorn elaborated this observation in 1940:

> The historian of the eighteenth century would do wrong either to deride it as a scarecrow or to worship it as a totem. As a restraining influence it was even more useful than international law, which, in this epoch at least, was nothing more than a war code. Like private persons engaged in a duel, the states of Europe created this war code to govern their international relations, a code which they invoked prior to an appeal to arms, and reaffirmed or modified after a fight.

This code laid down the principles and rules, but never quite obtained the force of law, because legal procedure and penalties were utterly lacking. The principle of balance of power, too, was not an end in itself, but only a means to an end and as such necessarily imperfect. At its best it created a certain common consciousness, a certain feeling of solidarity among the peoples of Europe. In spite of their babel of tongues, their bloody and endless quarrels, Europe still remained a vital and organic unity. The wrongs and injuries which these peoples had done to one another in the past, their conquests and reconquests, groupings and regroupings, their occasional fierce hatreds arising from balked ambitions, had welded them into a kind of union from which even Englishmen [Britons], in spite of their insularity, have been unable to escape to this day.[9]

Another, more recent, authority, Michael Sheehan, has traced the emergence of the term from classical times through to the eighteenth century, near the beginning of which he notes that the Treaty of Utrecht (1713) aimed explicitly at 'a just Balance of Power (which is the best and most solid foundation of mutual friendship and a lasting general concord)'.[10]

The great powers of the eighteenth century, especially Britain and France, strove to maintain a balance in which, nevertheless, the scales would be weighted on their side. Britain moved from its maritime base towards great power status during a long series of wars against France, which had been dominant in the continent in the earlier part of the reign of Louis XIV but now, during the reign of his less competent successor, Louis XV (1715–74), attempted to seek compensation in overseas commercial and colonial activities. And so the 'second Hundred Years War', as it has often been called, fought on and off from 1689 to 1815, was concerned with balance not only in Europe but also in North America, India and elsewhere. Meanwhile, the major more landlocked powers, Russia, Austria and Prussia, devoted their attentions to the more local issue of how to share out the pieces of central and eastern Europe. These two sets of concerns were closely interlocked. They were also influenced by the relative decline of a number of former great powers which had had their moments in the seventeenth century or before: Spain and the Dutch United Provinces, Sweden and Poland. The once all-conquering Ottoman Empire was now on its way to becoming the sick man of Europe, and no longer posed a threat sufficient for there to be any further talk of a pan-European crusade against the infidel.

Accompanying or perhaps underlying the principle of the balance of power was that economic system known as mercantilism, the concept of what might be called 'the balance of trade' still in operation many years after its first formulation. As with the balance of power, however, we must be careful not to elevate what was a rough guiding line into a rigid regulation. To resume the analogy we used in an earlier chapter, an international cake of large but fixed dimensions was widely believed to be up for grabs by those with the strongest and longest reach. Realisation was beginning to spread that the cake would become bigger and richer if all trading nations worked on their appetites together, collecting more ingredients and processing them in a common enterprise. But individual greed and envy were still powerful, and blinded the states of Europe to the mutual benefits of opening up their respective closed economic units. However, before the century was over the advantages of free trade would be realised by at least some members of the European community.

Mercantilism served its purpose in its time: it was the stronger rather than the weaker who tended to lower their trade barriers first, and their strength at least partly arose from the commerce carried on in colonial networks fenced off from competitors. The states without such opportunities for development had to look inward to their own resources, and this necessity made for disagreeable social consequences. For example, while the lot of the home subjects of the British and French maritime empires was eased by the spread of the overseas institution of slavery, the peoples of the more landlocked states – Russia, Austria and Prussia – found themselves restricted by the continued imposition of the comparable institution of serfdom.

True, there were other pressures making for the retention of serfdom: the sparsely populated nature of the vast plains of central and eastern Europe put human beings at a premium too high for liberty. In other words, if they had not been obliged to toil in the fields and, to a much less extent, in the factories, the peasants might have moved on too readily from one master to another, or even joined the Cossacks and other groups of bandits and freebooters that were to be found in these areas. The Cossacks and their like illustrate another distinctive feature of their part of the continent, namely its continually moving frontiers, which in their turn present another reason for serfdom, on this occasion military. In order to acquire a sufficient supply of cannon fodder for their new regular armies, Russia, Austria and Prussia had to make use of a recruitment method that recalled the old feudal levies, with the exception that now a larger part was played by the state and a smaller one by the landlords, who tended to become officers in the monarch's army rather than the leaders of their own private detachments. The armies thus manned and staffed were kept continually busy quelling domestic disturbance and struggling with their counterparts for more favourable frontiers.

Land war in the eighteenth century was by no means the gentlemanly affair that has too often been suggested, with greater exchange of compliments than of gunfire. There has been a tendency to look upon the eighteenth century as a less military age than most, a period when armies became isolated from societies and more akin to the toys of kings. Perhaps the most enduring image has been of French and British officers doffing their tricorn hats and politely inviting each other to fire first. But, just as the fact that soldiers from both sets of trenches shared their Christmas fare in 1914 did not make the First World War into a picnic, so the occasional act of good manners did not transform the armed conflicts of the eighteenth century into schools of etiquette. War at that time as at any other, we can be certain, was hell, and any limitation on it was not so much by quality of mercy as by quantity of cash. The horrors of the Thirty Years War were repeated over and over again in the next century and a half, if usually on a smaller scale, and the troops of monarchs who considered themselves enlightened amply demonstrated that they could put the boot and bayonet in with the best or the worst of them. In this, the ultimate test, some great powers of earlier times, Spain, Sweden, Poland and the Ottoman Empire, made less impact, while survivors such as France and Austria were joined by upstarts such as Russia, Prussia and Britain.

War at sea, whose increased significance was indicated by the arrival and growth of regular navies, was also extremely unpleasant for those obliged to take part in it. In Britain, press gangs searched for ablebodied and not so able-bodied seamen in ports and fishing villages, and Jack Tar's life expectancy was no greater than that of Johnny Soldier. To protect the lifelines of colonial commerce, the British navy, followed by its major French enemy, took to most of the world's high seas, and while at this point in their development ships could easily be converted from peacetime to wartime use and back again, permanent squadrons of fighting vessels began to be kept at stations abroad as the war between Britain and France grew more intense, especially in the West Indies from the 1740s onwards. For this reason, Britain had to maintain contact with Russia, its principal supplier of naval stores, however difficult the relationship became. By the eighteenth century, consciousness of the importance of navies had widened throughout Europe. At its beginning, for example, Peter the Great created a formidable Russian force virtually from scratch to win its first victories in the Baltic; it later saw action in the Mediterranean.

Armies and navies needed not only raw materials and people, but administration and control: service had to be civil, too. Therefore a further consequence of the incessant struggle for the balance of land and sea power was a considerable growth in the activity and influence of the state, absolutist and otherwise. For example, in Russia, the governmental system created by Peter the Great would probably have fallen apart if such pressures had not been operating upon it, since after his death, the throne passed to a series of rulers far less capable than he. In 1730, with the death of his young grandson Peter II, power appeared to be moving to the members of a recently created Supreme Privy Council. However, after a brief interlude in which the councillors imposed restrictive 'Conditions' upon the heir designate, Anna, Duchess of Courland, the supporters of absolutism were able to restore it and the 'Conditions' were torn up. Both Anna and her principal successor, Peter the Great's daughter Elizabeth, managed to maintain their hold on power in alliance with the nobility as it had been organised through the Table of Ranks.

To turn briefly to the major imperial powers, during the years of Walpole's ascendancy the settlement arrived at with William III in 1688 and succeeding years had been confirmed and strengthened. Just after Walpole's fall, the final failure of the exiled Stuarts to effect a return to power in Bonnie Prince Charlie's uprising of 1745 demonstrated clearly enough the thoroughness of Walpole's overall success. Meanwhile, in the country where the Stuarts found their refuge, Louis XV was at the same time attempting to hold back the deluge promised him by his great-grandfather Louis XIV and to preside over an evolution of the bureaucracy devised by Colbert and others during his forbear's reign. After a couple of ineffective regents had come and gone, a prime minister in name if not in title, Cardinal Fleury, conducted policies in the Colbert tradition from 1726 to 1743: peace if possible and a balanced budget in the framework of mercantilism. If Fleury met with a degree of success no smaller than that of Colbert, the degree of comparative failure was at least as great in the later years of Louis XV as it had been in those of Louis XIV, as the one followed the other in attempting to exert a more personal rule. Financial, administrative and religious problems continued to dog the French monarchy along with those of international relations. Towards the end of his reign, it is true, Louis XV made a last strenuous effort at reform.

The continuing struggle among the leading nations for the realisation of their own versions of the balance of power led thinkers in the second half of the eighteenth century to continue to address the age-old question of a more lasting and more profound equilibrium. For example, in 1758 the Swiss jurist Emeric de Vattel produced *The Law of Nations or the Principles of Natural Law Applied to the Conduct and Affairs of Nations and Sovereigns*, demonstrating that as European empires were fighting each other to achieve maximum growth, at least some individuals were carrying on the work of such predecessors as Grotius and the Abbé de Saint-Pierre in the cause of peace, even if through a somewhat different approach. Meanwhile, no less interested in peace than Vattel, the greatest European minds at the middle of the century were applying themselves to a wide range of fundamental problems. For example, in 1756, Voltaire brought out a version of his 'universal history' (*Essai sur les moeurs*) in which he attempted to describe the contribution of the world's major civilisations to its development. In this way, Voltaire showed that the increasing dominance of European empires did not stem from moral or cultural superiority, but from social and political systems capable of generating the appropriate measure of force. As he also pointed out in a sardonic comment on the infinite capacity of great powers for self-justification, when attacked by the sheep, the wolf defends itself with great courage.

4

ENLIGHTENED GOVERNMENTS, THEIR CONFLICTS AND THEIR CRITICS, 1763–1789

AFTER THE SEVEN YEARS WAR

The consequences of the Seven Years War and of later conflicts were of considerable importance, since both those who did well out of them and those who did not were obliged to examine the degree to which their systems of government matched up to the demands of the times. To an extent greater than ever before, politicians from Lisbon to St Petersburg were persuaded to have recourse to ideas being put forward by a wide variety of thinkers in the vast and many-sided intellectual movement known as the Enlightenment, which we will examine more broadly in the next chapter. The outstanding examples of such adoption were made by those monarchs who became known as enlightened despots or absolutists – Catherine II (the Great) of Russia, Frederick II (the Great) of Prussia and Joseph II of Austria (remarkable enough if never dubbed the Great). The Enlightenment also exerted its influence on a number of statesmen in Europe as well as crossing the Atlantic to the British mainland colonies in particular. There, ideas both new and old were used to assert the independence of the United States of America in 1776. Later, they were employed at the beginning of an even greater upset, the French Revolution of 1789. To trace the manner in which the Enlightenment was used to support monarchy as well as to overthrow it will be a major purpose of this chapter.

First, however, we must stress that international relations played a significant part in this process. Therefore, we will begin with a quick sketch of them during the period from the end of the Seven Years War in 1763 to the outbreak of the French Revolution in 1789. Although Europe was now integrated in its mutual contacts as never before, the international relations of the period in question can be divided into two sections, those arising from the Treaty of Hubertusburg and those arising from the Treaty of Paris. To describe first the centre and the East, three great powers by the standards of the age, Austria, Prussia and Russia, were making the attempt to readjust their positions in the light of the accommodation they had reached in 1763 and in the circumstance of the decline of three great powers by the standards of a former age, Sweden, Poland and the Ottoman Empire.

Even before the Seven Years War had begun, Frederick the Great had written in his *Political Testament* of 1752 that Polish Prussia should be eaten 'like an artichoke, leaf by leaf ... now a town, now a district, until the whole has been eaten up'.[1] Then, at the end of the Seven Years War, Catherine made the Duchy of Courland immediately to the west of her Baltic provinces into a virtual Russian protectorate. Later in the year 1763, another of the crowned heads of Europe breathed his last, this time Augustus III, King of Poland, Elector of Saxony and feudal superior of the Duchy of Courland. As the election of a successor approached, Austria and France gave their support to the son of Augustus III, while Prussia and Russia grew close enough together to sign a treaty of mutual defence and protection concerning Poland and Sweden early in 1764 and then to work together for the candidacy of one of Catherine's former lovers. Stanisław Poniatowski duly became King Stanisław later in 1764, but soon revealed himself to be no puppet of his former mistress and her ally; indeed, he worked for improved relations with Austria and France and shared at least some of the patriotic fervour of his fellow Poles as they struggled to maintain their independence. By 1768 Russian forces were deeply involved in Polish civil disturbances, which alarmed Austria sufficiently to move in and claim for itself a Polish province adjacent to its own frontier while provoking the Ottoman Turks into a declaration of war on Russia, encouraged by France. Meanwhile, Prussia also was moving in to extend its interests, and by the spring of 1771 had agreed with Russia on the first partition of Poland. By holding out longer, Austria was able to claim the largest cut in land and people when the three-way share-out with the other two interested powers was finally agreed in 1772. But Prussia was satisfied with its leaves from the artichoke, since the acquisition of West Prussia meant that an awkward gap in its territories was now closed. And Russia was happy to extend its frontiers in a manner that improved its strategic position and also effected a reunion with a largely Orthodox group of Slavs whom it looked on as its own.

The Russian war with Turkey that had broken out in 1768 was still in progress, becoming rather more like stalemate, however, after some early spectacular Russian victories on land and sea. Out of practice in such large-scale fighting as well as generally in decline, the Ottoman Turks had reeled back along the Black Sea coast and up the Danube and been smitten by two naval defeats off their own Mediterranean coast. Some of the bolder Russian leaders now revived old dreams of retaking Constantinople for Orthodoxy. But with France still support-ing Turkey and Sweden threatening war in the north, with military reverses counterbalancing victories and severe domestic problems overtaking stability at home, the Empress Catherine moved towards conclusion of hostilities. The Turks were in no position to insist on a return to the pre-war situation, and made concessions in the Black Sea and along its shores, with Azov firmly reincorporated in the empire and the Crimea made independent. They retained formal jurisdiction along the Danube, but gave the Russians right of protection over the Orthodox in their principalities.

After the Treaty of Kuchuk Kainardzhi in 1774, the Eastern Question remained uneasily dormant for 13 years, during which Russia annexed the Crimea in 1783 and contemplated the seizure of more parts of the ailing Ottoman Empire, increasingly in partnership with Austria, which moved closer to Russia as Prussia drifted away. By the time of the death of Frederick the Great in 1786, Russia's intercession in quarrels between Austria and Prussia concerning Austria's designs on Bavaria and in the Netherlands, together with Catherine's involvement in the affairs of the Holy Roman Empire and her alliance with Maria Theresa's successor, Joseph II, had brought a cooling of relations with Prussia, which was also suspicious of a partition of Turkey after the pattern of that of Poland. So when the Turks were provoked to launch an offensive in 1787, Prussia joined Britain in encouraging them and the Swedes to carry the fight to Russia in particular. Austria, weakened by the death of Joseph II in 1790 and by a series of internal difficulties, made peace with Turkey by 1791. Russia came to status quo terms around the Baltic Sea with Sweden in 1790, but kept the war going with Turkey until 1792, when the Treaty of Jassy confirmed and extended Russia's Black Sea presence, although doing nothing to advance the cause of the Ottoman Empire's more complete dismemberment.

While all the major states of Europe were interested in the manner in which the Eastern Question was posed and solved, France and Britain had more pressing problems to consider in the period following the Seven Years War. As before, these concerned their imperial rivalry in the wider world as well as such preoccupations as they had nearer home. Before the beginning of the French Revolution in 1789, the most important conflict between the two old rivals surrounded the outbreak of a similar upset across the Atlantic, the American Revolution of 1776. The new French king, Louis XVI, who had succeeded his grandfather Louis XV in 1774, was encouraged by the early successes of George Washington's army to look upon an American alliance as an outstanding opportunity not so much for the extension of the French Empire as for sapping the strength and reducing the size of the British Empire. The alliance was concluded early in 1778, and war broke out soon afterwards. The army and navy reformed after the Seven Years War by Choiseul now passed their practical examinations with flying colours, especially in 1781, when the American victory at Yorktown was made all the more conclusive by an army that was half French and a blockading navy that was almost completely French. By this time the Franco-American cause had been actively joined by both Spain and the United Provinces, and passively supported by the Armed Neutrality of 1780 in which an important part was played by Russia. Britain suffered reverses not only on the American mainland but also in the West Indies and West Africa. By the Treaty of Paris in 1783, the United States of America consummated independence and won the West from Canada. Her allies made modest gains, Spain reacquiring Florida and France getting Tobago in the West Indies as well as reacquiring Senegal in West Africa, for example. Britain's humiliation was profound.

At last, the British government moved to overcome the dangers of diplomatic isolation from the continent, which had followed from its desertion of Prussia in the later stages of the Seven Years War. When the new Prussian king, Frederick William II, intervened in the United Provinces on behalf of the House of Orange in 1787, he readily received the British support for which he had been hoping. France, which had been exhausted financially by its war expenditure earlier in the decade, was now too feeble to follow up protest with action as the Patriot side that it had supported in the Dutch conflict was declared illegal.

ENLIGHTENED GOVERNMENTS

The fact that most of the outstanding figures in that intellectual movement known as the Enlightenment were against war and in favour of peace has tended to discourage the observation that the hostilities occurring at its peak inspired many of their ideas and also brought at least some of them nearer to implementation. For governments throughout Europe during the Seven Years War and after discovered that in an increasingly competitive world reforms were necessary if they were to survive and prosper, while many of the Enlightenment's brightest stars were always ready to cast their light wherever it was welcomed. Moreover, in order to understand the opposition and revolutionary movements of the period that we shall be looking at next, it is necessary to realise that the governments opposed and overturned were themselves often attempting within traditional social and political frameworks to adapt themselves to the demands of their time. The American and French revolutions, to take the most famous examples, broke out against governments that had made great efforts to solve the problems that led in the end to their extreme solutions.

Before looking at the British and French monarchies and their policies at the end of the Seven Years War, let us turn to the east and centre of Europe, where we will find the three best-known representatives of that royal approach to ruling known as enlightened absolutism or despotism. The first point to make here is that the location of this trio is by no means accidental, for as we have already seen, on the foundation of an enserfed peasantry and a service nobility there had been erected in Russia, Prussia and Austria a type of state in which the government attempted to be more centralised and more dominant than its counterparts to the West. However, we must not mistake the attempt for actual achievement: both the enlightenment and the absolutism were aspirations rather than realities. Moreover, the centre and especially the East were comparatively isolated from the mainstream of European and worldwide interaction. They were therefore obliged to force the pace of development in order to keep up. Such pressure intensified during the Seven Years War. All these circumstances combined to produce an emphasis on sets of ideas that were less significant to the West – Pietism, Cameralism and Jansenism.

Pietism was a movement for religious reform arising within the Lutheran church and developing social and political aims, too. It gave emphasis to the principle of service to others in general and to the state in particular. In Catholic lands, a comparable part was played by Jansenist ideas of a return to the simplicities of the early church including useful labour. Cameralism gave secular emphasis to service while offering a justification for bureaucracy as well as monarchy. A strong 'police state' (not the same as the police state of the twentieth century) could be achieved by detailed regulation which would also promote the general welfare: the whole edifice would run like clockwork with the ruler providing the mainspring. Pietist and Cameralist ideas permeated university teaching in Prussia and Austria, helping to produce well-trained civil servants. But their influence was also to be found in Russia.

When Catherine II (the Great, 1762–96) and her adherents seized power from Peter III in the summer of 1762, they began to think almost as much through necessity as inclination of taking steps not only to maintain their hold on power but also to buttress that power through reform. A measure taken by Peter III's government, perhaps with the same end in view, called for special and immediate attention. This was the so-called Emancipation of the Nobility (*dvorianstvo*) announced in February 1762, which ostensibly allowed Russian nobles 'freedom and liberty' but in practice restricted the usage of such rights with so many qualifications as to make the appearance deceptive in the extreme. Whatever interpretations could be placed on Peter III's decree, Catherine II would be obliged sooner or later to make her own arrangements for the part to be played by her leading class. With the armed forces out of the final stages of the Seven Years War and no other large-scale conflict in the immediate offing, there was a certain amount of demobilisation. The empress turned first to the civil administration, on which in any case she was receiving a considerable amount of well-intentioned advice from some of her supporters. At the end of 1763 there was a reform of the Senate with some rationalisation of its various duties. Moves were made towards the creation of a State Council (completed in 1768), and a certain amount of readjustment of provincial government was carried out. On the nobility in particular, a special commission was set up in 1763 to look again at the emancipation question, although it spent much less time on the manner of withdrawal from service than on the advantages to be secured in it. In 1764, the all-important Table of Ranks was subjected to its most comprehensive reform since the 1720s, with emphasis on the nobility in the civil service.

To continue the discussion of the leading part to be played by the nobility as well as the supporting parts to be played by the middle class and the peasantry, in 1767 Catherine convened a Legislative Commission for the Composition of a New Law Code. By such a step, she took up a problem that had been addressed by her predecessors, including the Empress Elizabeth, and at the same time injected fresh considerations into it. For example, her own hold on the throne was secure enough but still awaited the full stamp of legitimacy. The outlying provinces of her expanding empire needed to be persuaded to accept more complete incorporation. Could not aims like these be realised at the same time as achieving a new definition for the classes composing Russian society? Would it not be possible to proceed towards these desirable goals while projecting to the rest of Europe the image of an enlightened and conscientious absolute ruler? To reinforce these aims, particularly the last perhaps, the empress composed an Instruction for the commission adapted from Montesquieu and other leading thinkers of the day, including the Italian writer on crime and punishment, Beccaria, and the central European Cameralists. She found it difficult to combine the Western ideas with those coming from Austria and Prussia: the former encouraged freedom and justice, the latter a broad concept of 'police' extending regulation into many aspects of public and even private life. However, she insisted at the outset that Russia was a European state: this was indicated by the ease with which Peter the Great had introduced his reforms. As described in the Instruction, Catherine's enlightened absolutism would consist of an all-powerful monarch ruling in the interests of all her people with the help of intermediate governmental bodies and appropriate legislation.

The actual experience of the Legislative Commission, which met in plenary session from the summer of 1767 to the end of 1768, was very educational for Catherine, who secretly listened to some of the debates and made the acquaintance of some of the written complaints and wishes of her subjects that had been submitted to the commission at her invitation. Sadly, even the moderate hopes that she herself had held out for the limited acquisition of property rights by peasants were dashed by the passionate opposition of most of the noble deputies, who were also deeply suspicious of mild suggestions put forward by the empress for the consolidation of the middle class. In the event, the influence of the dominant noble class was if anything strengthened by the experience of the Legislative Commission.

By the time of the commission's adjournment at the end of 1768, this tendency had been reinforced by the outbreak of war with Turkey. Dependence on nobles as officers in the armed forces continued as that war came to an end but domestic peace needed to be restored and maintained in the face of the threat posed by the Cossack and peasant Revolt of 1773–5 led by Emelian Pugachev. Employment of the noble landlords in the provincial bureaucracy was an essential feature of the reform of local government, which was announced in 1775. Here, one of Catherine's sources was Sir William Blackstone's *Commentaries on the Laws of England*. Although Russian squires could not be made into Justices of the Peace on the English model, there was an attempt to use them, as well as townspeople and state peasants, in a series of courts as well as in general administration, including law and order as well as social welfare. Needless to say, the implementation of this ambitious reform was often beyond the resources of provincial society. The Police Ordinance of 1782, with detailed regulations on such matters as public hygiene and street lighting, was another example of the difficulty, even the impossibility, of introducing bureaucratic controls imperfectly realised in central and western Europe.

Then, in 1785, the most prominent members of Russian society were given a definitive statement of their position in the Charter of the Nobility, which guaranteed to the class property rights and other advantages in return for its service to the state. And the state, it should be emphasised, can hardly be seen as exercising its authority in a manner completely independent of the nobility. The class and the state's absolute ruler were fundamentally interdependent, indeed, as was generally the case in the monarchical system of government as analysed by Montesquieu and other *philosophes* of the Enlightenment. A Charter of the Towns, also promulgated in 1785, and a Charter for the State Peasants, which was never promulgated, completed Catherine's scheme for a society that would possess a restricted measure of self-reliance.

Catherine the Great did not use the ideas of Montesquieu and his fellows either to the extent or in the manner that they would have approved. As she herself said, it was much easier to discuss the problems of government than actually to govern. Nevertheless, we would be unjustified in going to the opposite extreme in dismissing Catherine as nothing but a vain hypocrite. At least some of the ideas of the Enlightenment on society and government, not to mention on education and culture in the wider sense, helped to give her more than 30 years of tenure of the Russian throne and to lend her policies a cohesion and direction that they might otherwise have lacked. Catherine also made some attempt to use her sovereign power to help the economy move forward. Even though she was hampered by her failure to reform the institution of serfdom, which had a malign influence stretching into most aspects of the national life, she attempted to encourage those who possessed property and wealth to use them in an active manner.

Born a German Protestant, converting to Russian Orthodoxy and assimilating European culture, Catherine contained within her intellectual contradictions brought about by her own experience as well as by her wide reading. Like Peter the Great before her, she invoked the deity as a fundamental sanction of her rule, and closely followed the observances of the Orthodox Church. She also made frequent acknowledgements to the authority of her distinguished predecessor. However, as O. A. Omelchenko makes clear, there was a clear difference between Peter's military–bureaucratic police absolutism and Catherine's 'enlightened' legal absolutism.[2]

Another generation gap may be found in Prussia. Although differing radically from his father in his youth, Frederick II (the Great, 1740–86) came to share Frederick William I's fundamental outlook, declaring in his *Essay on the Forms of Government and the Duties of Sovereigns* in 1777 that a prince

> should often recall to mind that he is a man like the least of his subjects; if he is not the first judge, the first general, the first minister of society, it is not that he can indulge himself, but so that he can fulfil the duties involved. He is only the first servant of the state, obliged to act with honesty, wisdom and with a complete lack of self-interest, as if at every moment he might be called upon to render an account of his stewardship to his fellow-citizens.

However, there remained key differences between father and son, as T. C. W. Blanning points out. Frederick William I believed that his 'theoretical omnipotence was limited by three powerful constraints: respect for the Holy Roman Empire, concern for the Hohenzollern family and, above all, fear of his terrible Calvinist God'. But 'Imperial law, dynasticism and Christianity mean nothing to his son, who despised all three. Where Frederick William's thinking was prescriptive, particularist and pious, Frederick's was rational, universal and secular.' Moreover, while the father's German spelling and grammar were deficient, the son, like Catherine the Great, was the correspondent of Voltaire and other leading figures of the Enlightenment and wrote works on a considerable range of subjects in French.

Frederick's new thinking was demonstrated in his religious toleration, for which he was praised by the leading German intellectual, Immanuel Kant. For his part, Kant argued in favour of obedience to the state by those in public service, who would include many university-trained members of the intelligentsia. Many of these would have liked to have embraced more completely the concept of free trade, to give an important example, but were obliged to exercise restraint: *raison d'état* prevented *laissez-faire*. In other words, Prussian enlightened absolutism was limited by its insecure position in Europe, which encouraged the persistence of old thinking.

As before, the Junkers were expected to combine the functions of landlord, officer and bureaucrat in a manner not dissimilar from that of the *dvoriane*. In return, Frederick declared in his 'Political Testament' of 1752: 'a sovereign should regard it as his duty to protect the nobility, who form the finest jewel in his crown and the lustre of his army'. The army was his first consideration: Frederick himself always wore military uniform, and made Prussia a byword for militarism.[3]

Frederick looked upon peasants primarily as recruits, and was anxious therefore that they should not starve. But he did not interfere with the Prussian variant of the institution of serfdom: unlike Joseph II in Austria, he did not contemplate emancipation; he probably gave the matter less thought than Catherine in Russia. On the other hand, he encouraged the contribution of the middle class to the development of the economy, and made as much use as possible of immigrant merchants and manufacturers. Unprepossessing though some of the Prussian terrain was, it must have appeared far less remote than the banks of the Volga, to which the Russian empress was attempting to entice colonists. Communications were easier in Prussia, too, and access to the sea closer.

However, Frederick's government remained mercantilistic in its outlook and policies. Some of his advisers wanted to move beyond the Cameralism that had been the basis of the philosophy of government in the earlier part of the eighteenth century to incorporate in the courts and chancelleries at least some of the ideas of the later Enlightenment. To give an important example, after several years of preparation during Frederick the Great's lifetime, the Prussian Code was finally promulgated in 1794 some eight years after his death. The announcement was made that 'The general rights of man are founded on the natural freedom to seek and advance his own welfare without interfering with the rights of others'. However, once again Montesquieu's recommendation of divided intermediary powers was unrealised, and, while the 'citizens' were divided into three 'estates', the particular rights of the peasants remained much more circumscribed than those of the middle class and the Junkers.[4] General rights of man came nearest to recognition in religious toleration and in education, even if their implementation did not penetrate very deeply into the mass of the peasantry. Like their ancestors, they tended to follow the faith of their landlords as they followed their ploughs, while very few learned to read or write or to assimilate the simple moral instruction prepared for them. In spite of these and other deficiencies, the Prussian Code marked an advance in efficiency and justice for a state which, without any strong tradition of representative government, depended on its own self-restraint and good order.

Our third example of an enlightened despot or absolutist, Joseph II of Austria (1780–90), was also the most determined to introduce reform that went further than administrative readjustment and social redefinition. Here was a monarch who had served a long apprenticeship during the reign of his mother, Maria Theresa (1740–80). Although Holy Roman Emperor since 1765, he did not assume exclusive authority in Austria until 1780. Lonely and sick, he could hardly believe as he approached the age of 40 that his life was about to begin anew. Nevertheless, he harboured the grand design of removing from what was left of the Habsburg dominions the outdated ideas and practices that had accumulated over previous centuries and during the reign of his mother, who had resisted the joint efforts of Kaunitz and himself to bring the Enlightenment fully into Vienna and other governmental centres. As we have seen, there had been some changes in the earlier part of Maria Theresa's reign, and there were more towards the end of the Seven Years War as Kaunitz adapted the Directory previously formed along Prussian lines into the United Bohemian and Austrian Chancellery, a year or so after creating an eight-man Council of State as the chief advisory body in 1760. There were corresponding rearrangements in other parts of the empire.

The arrival of peace in 1763 gave the opportunity (and to an extent underlined the necessity) of taking reform further. For example, Maria Theresa attempted to convert the forced labour of the peasants into money payments and to divert as high a proportion as possible of these to the state; she also tried to extend taxation to the property of the nobility and the Church. Her success was extremely limited in Austria, even more so in Hungary.

A woman of strict religious observance, Maria Theresa had nevertheless been prepared to override papal protests to apply the doctrine that all Church business except that specifically entrusted by Christ to his apostles should be rendered unto Caesar, or in this case, the kaiser's widow – herself, first in the Duchy of Milan, 1765, then in the regions closer to home. When the Pope dissolved the Jesuits in 1773, their property was taken over to swell an Education Fund, and the General Education Regulation of 1774 set up a hierarchy of primary and secondary schools and training colleges that was most impressive on paper if not by the blackboard. From 1778 onwards, Protestants were allowed to take degrees at the University of Vienna, which provided at least some of the graduates in law who busied themselves with constant discussions of legal reform.

At his accession to exclusive power with the death of Maria Theresa in 1780, Joseph II immediately resolved to press home the drive towards equality under the law, and under himself too, for like his fellow enlightened despots or absolutists Catherine the Great and Frederick the Great, he believed that he alone could be the impartial guarantor of justice and harmony. Beginning with the Penal Code of 1781, he proceeded to the Civil Code of 1786 and the Code of Criminal Procedure of 1788. The death penalty was prohibited for civilians, for whom generally the quality of mercy was now considered to be less strained. However, Joseph did not stop here: he attempted to continue and extend his mother's work in all significant directions. At the centre of government, the United Chancellery took on more functions but was also reorganised into a number of departments, while the Council of State was reduced in size. The number of provinces was meanwhile halved as a further move towards bureaucratic uniformity, which was also encouraged in the municipalities: representative assemblies were everywhere giving way to groups of civil servants, who themselves were in turn under surveillance from the police.

Partly because he accepted the argument of some of the *philosophes* that peasants would work hardest when their own self-interest was involved, Joseph strove mightily to improve their position not only in law but also in fact. The Patent to Abolish Serfdom of 1781 allowed those previously subject to the institution to join themselves in marriage or in labour to whomsoever they wished. Other patents of the same year encouraged serfs to buy land with government protection, and enabled them to appeal before the courts of the state against judgements of the courts of the lords. In 1781, these courts were restricted in the punishments that they could order. Not satisfied with stopping there, Joseph tried to accelerate the process already begun in Maria Theresa's reign of reducing the amount of compulsory labour undertaken by the serfs; indeed, he tried to do away with it altogether. Then in 1789, after a census of the population and a register of landed property had been completed, he issued the Tax and Agrarian Regulation, which attempted to reduce the dues of at least the more prosperous peasants to both the state and their noble or Church landlords. Not surprisingly, the landlords opposed Joseph at every step:

much less expected was the violent reaction of the very people that the Regulation was intended to help. Before his death in February 1790, Joseph II had begun to learn the hard way that monarchs, however all-powerful they believed themselves to be, could tamper with the bases of the old regime evolved over the course of centuries only at great risk to themselves. Joseph did not need to look at France for the lesson, it was being taught him at home.

Already, in the 1780s, he had received early warning in the response to his religious policy. Joseph probably had a more genuine belief in God than either Catherine or Frederick, but his respect for the Church was severely limited. Extending a policy of toleration adopted in a limited manner by Maria Theresa, he gave civil equality to Protestant and Orthodox Christians in 1781, reduced the power of Roman Catholic bishops and the size of their dioceses, and began to dissolve the monasteries, assigning the income thus received to social welfare and education. He was not diverted from his chosen course by the visit to Vienna in 1782 of Pope Pius VI, but penetrated even deeper into the sphere of influence of the Church, attempting to reduce the number of its special saints' days, even trying to restrict the use of candles and images. Here he was driven by his desire for economy as well as by his religious views. But he was opposed not only by the Church but by many of his secular subjects, whose simple faith contained a strong admixture of superstition and paganism. To tamper with their observances appeared to them to be the work of the devil, or of hobgoblins. Aware of such ignorant opposition, and because he believed in any case in the spreading of the light, Joseph encouraged education, albeit with a strong practical emphasis. He also made use of the censoring power he retained over the press to push such advanced views as helped his cause against that of Church, noble and popular opposition.

Joseph's problems in Austria were accompanied by even greater difficulties in Hungary and the Netherlands. His attempt to make his empire prosperous and its administration efficient was certainly vigorous enough, but it was also insufficiently flexible. Perhaps he should have made his own absolutism give way a little as he attempted to bend his subjects to his will. A further charge that has been levelled against Joseph II is that he wanted to increase the size of the Austrian army up to 300,000, three times what it had been during the Seven Years War, and to assert himself with such backing in diplomatic negotiations as well as on the battlefield. But if he was guilty in this respect, so were Catherine and Frederick. Moreover, we should not forget that the enlightened absolutists themselves found no difficulty in reconciling self-aggrandisement and territorial expansion even when accompanied by the use of force with the support and the use that they gave to a selection of the ideas of the normally peace-loving *philosophes*. For enlightened absolutism may best be defined as the attempt by governments of the old regime to modernise themselves without giving up ambitious aims in foreign policy or changing the social and political bases for their domestic policy. They neither renounced war nor took their efforts on behalf of the vast peasant majority of their people to such a point that the support they received from the powerful noble minority would be placed in jeopardy. This observation applies equally to Frederick who attempted very little, Catherine who attempted rather more and to Joseph who attempted quite a lot. Their plans for economic progress and cultural development alike were necessarily restricted.

Nevertheless, we must not dismiss enlightened absolutism as merely a superficial flirtation of monarchs with some of the outstanding intellectuals of their day. If these monarchs and their advisers did not adopt suggestions as thoroughly and consistently as the *philosophes* would have liked at the time and historians would have preferred since, at least some suggestions were taken very seriously indeed, helping Russia, Prussia and Austria to increase their cohesion and to survive the wrath to come that was embodied in the French Revolution.

Generally speaking, we must understand that it is fundamental to an understanding of the old regime in the years before the French Revolution to realise that it was not immobile, that it did make its own peculiar attempts to adapt to the needs of the new age arriving with the Seven Years War. Such an observation applies not only in the east and centre of Europe but also to the west, where the major challenges of the revolutionary age were to be met. We must not forget it as we turn to consider the governments of Britain and France, and their opponents.

THE CRITICS: THE AMERICAN REVOLUTION

As a result of the Seven Years War (especially by its other name, of the French and Indian War), the British Empire asserted its supremacy over its chief rival in 1763. But success had bred almost as many problems as would have arisen from failure: what to do with the mainland colonies across the Atlantic now that the way west across the North American continent lay open for 2 million or more British subjects? Governor Bernard of Massachusetts sent the message back to the government in London that now was 'the proper and critical time to reform the American governments upon a general, constitutional, firm and durable plan; and if it is not done now, it will probably grow every day more difficult, till at last it becomes impracticable'.[5] However, such messages took several weeks to cross the ocean, and the time lag accompanied, perhaps intensified, mutual difficulties of comprehension. Not surprisingly, none of the leading British statesmen of the time ever made the long and dangerous crossing to the American colonies. Most of them found it difficult to understand why such remote societies were not continually consumed with gratitude for their membership of the British Empire. As for the Americans themselves, although a considerable number of them had visited the home country, their sense of it was often distorted. That is, they could not easily distinguish the Britain that they actually saw from the one in which they believed: distance tended to lend enchantment to their view of the British constitution, the wide gap in miles helping to shorten the passage of years. Consequently, for the colonists, the Bloodless and Glorious Revolution of 1688 retained a vitality that it had largely lost among its more immediate beneficiaries. For example, Bishop Burnet's *History of My Own Time*, which presented a personalised analysis of the great events of 1688 and after, was out of fashion in Britain by the time of Walpole: in the American colonies, it still made a vital impact on its readers, Benjamin Franklin calling it 'seminal' and John Adams deeming it just 'great'.[6] More significantly, the arguments of John Locke concerning the social contract exercised a powerful influence on the minds of the colonists while they were comparatively forgotten by the metropolitans.

However, it would still be some time before Franklin and Adams would assist the young Virginian Thomas Jefferson to adapt the ideas of Locke to assert the basic human rights 'of life, liberty and the pursuit of happiness' in the Declaration of Independence of 4 July 1776. At the beginning of the 1770s, the colonists were for the most part still far from thinking of breaking away from the mother country.

Benjamin Franklin in Philadelphia could assert that he was proud of her, and John Adams could bring himself to act for the defence of the British soldiers arrested in connection with the 'Boston Massacre' of five citizens of Massachusetts. Even as late as Christmas 1775, after the first American shots had been fired and 'heard round the world', after more colonists and some British redcoats had been killed, George Washington and his fellow officers were still drinking to the health of King George III. The British government had been given a respite of a dozen years or so to act on the advice of Governor Bernard and others to reform the government of the colonies.

Immediately after the Treaty of Paris in 1763, the king's ministers were much less interested in constitutional change than in the preservation of peace throughout the empire and the extraction of more money from it. They persuaded His Majesty to issue a royal proclamation forbidding colonial settlement to the west of the Appalachian Mountains, where the French threat had been removed but the Indians or Native Americans were reluctant to yield more of their homelands to the invading white men without a fight. The royal proclamation would therefore reduce the need for military expenditure. Then in the spring of 1764, realising that the American excise taxes cost more than they collected, the First Lord of the Treasury, George Grenville, brought in a Revenue Act (Sugar Act) tightening up the collection of dues not only on sugar but also on molasses and a number of other items. He was no doubt conscious of the competition presented by American, especially New England, merchants to their counterparts in Britain. To the injury of such indirect taxation, Grenville added in 1765 the insult of direct taxation in the Stamp Act, which required the colonists to affix a stamp as evidence of their payment of an imposition to legal documents, newspapers, playing cards and dice. Suspicion and animosity were aroused further in 1765 by the introduction of a Quartering Act obliging the colonists to give board and lodging to the soldiers sent over the ocean to protect them.

To protect or to police? Suspicion changed to alarm. Like the freedom-loving Englishmen, Scotsmen and Irishmen they still believed themselves to be, American colonists made the assertion of 'no taxation without representation' in the Stamp Act Congress of October 1765 in New York and on many other occasions. An organisation known as the Sons of Liberty and determined to fight unto death spread throughout the colonies. There were in fact no immediate fatalities, but there were civil disturbances as well as announcements and boycotts in support of this grand new cause. As a result the Stamp Act was repealed, although not before the British parliament had passed a Declaratory Act asserting its total control early in 1766.

Grenville had risen to be prime minister but then fallen in the summer of 1765. After a year of instability, the king turned to a statesman whose love of the British Empire was accompanied by a strongly expressed sympathy for the American colonists – William Pitt the Elder. Unfortunately, however, Pitt did not enjoy the good health necessary to give firm direction and control to a somewhat motley collection of ministers, among whom the Chancellor of the Exchequer, Charles Townshend, emerged as the leading figure. In a series of Acts of 1767 known by his name, duties were imposed on a number of imports into the colonies, lead, paper, glass and tea. The customs service was reorganised, and the Quartering Act was reinforced, especially in New York. The colonial opposition, which had never disappeared, now gathered new strength, a climax being reached outside a customs house on 5 March 1770 which led to the 'Boston Massacre'.

Soon after the Townshend Acts were passed, their creator died, and not much later, the Pitt government fell. Townshend's successor as chancellor of the exchequer, Lord North, repealed all the duties except that on tea on the very day that the five Bostonians were 'massacred' and a month or so after he himself had become prime minister. The tea duty was expressly retained to indicate the supremacy of parliament in colonial government.

The decade that was to produce the American Revolution opened harmoniously enough, although anybody reading the tea leaves could see that trouble would soon be brewing again. The Sons of Liberty did not disband, and new sources of discord soon arose, although some of these were between or within the colonies, over frontier and religious questions, for example. However, another series of actions by parliament provoked the American colonists into a storm of protest more unified and more radical than ever. Although the Proclamation Line of 1763 was moved westwards from the Appalachian Mountains towards the Ohio River, this was not far enough for those who wanted to develop a new colony there. Annoyance at restriction of movement grew with the passing of the Quebec Act in 1774, which assigned the whole region to the west of the Appalachians and north of the Ohio to Canada. Moreover, the inclusion in that Act of special protection for the Catholic Church and the omission from it of any kind of representative assembly upset the religious and political sensitivities of the colonists at a time when another development in the tea question had already provoked widespread anger. Anxious to do something for the East India Company, which had fallen on hard times, Lord North gave it the right of direct sale to American consumers, cutting out the middlemen. Not only the merchants losing their trade were incensed by this but also the consumers who were prepared to put their principles before their pockets. The Boston Tea Party, with a large quantity of the offending commodity being dumped into the harbour, led to the harbour's closure and then to other impositions collectively known as the Coercive or Intolerable Acts of 1774. These in turn led by September to the First Continental Congress in Philadelphia, where the representatives of the colonists decided to oppose the encroachments by parliament on their British liberties. It was only after the first hostilities at Concord in December 1775 had brought about the more general outbreak of war that the delegates to the Second Continental Congress, already in session in Philadelphia from May 1775 onwards, decided to accept the Declaration of Independence of 4 July 1776 and to carry on the fight for their freedom as Americans.

A history of Europe is no place to tell in detail the story of the War for Independence and of the American Revolution, nor indeed is it appropriate here to go very far into what happened afterwards. Nevertheless, it is important at least to note that by no means all the former colonists supported the war and revolution: John Adams estimated that a third of the population were for, another third against and the rest indifferent. Moreover, after the Treaty of Paris of 1783 had confirmed the achievement of the aims of Washington and his supporters, the Americans discovered that they were even less united in peace, and many old rivalries and animosities forgotten or suppressed during the hostilities came to the surface again. At least some of the Sons of Liberty became anxious that their own particular sacrifices had not brought what they had fought for, especially when the movement in favour of stronger central government gained sufficient momentum for another convention to gather in Philadelphia in the summer of 1787. Disillusionment set in even more for some when the Federal Constitution was produced after a series of debates, and then ratified by the several states after further discussion.

The intellectual influences on the constitution were markedly different from those on the Declaration of Independence, with Jefferson absent in Paris and James Madison and Alexander Hamilton the chief spokesmen for new views. Locke and his view of the social contract and basic human rights was now relegated to the background, comparatively speaking, while Montesquieu with his ideas of balanced government and intermediary powers came more to the fore. There was even some talk of creating an American monarchy, which might have gone further had it not been for the associations created by Washington's first name. More seriously, enough Americans were persuaded that the interests of small states and large states, of the individual and society, were sufficiently protected and proportionately represented, especially when a Bill of Rights was added to the Federal Constitution as its first ten amendments. There was further dissension with the onset of the French Revolution, but the United States of America was able to withstand it quite comfortably at the same time as beginning an expansion which went far beyond the lines of royal proclamations.

THE CRITICS: TOWARDS EUROPEAN REVOLUTION

To recross the Atlantic to the mother country just deprived of its oldest colonial children, we soon notice that in Britain also there was much debate on the question of government, whether it concerned Americans or the British people themselves. To take again the example of William Pitt the Elder (after 1766 the Earl of Chatham), he was not in favour of coercion but was against independence, speaking in such a manner before he collapsed on the floor of the House of Lords in April 1778 and died a month later. Arguably, such conciliators as he had been were defeated not only by the vagaries of a political system heavily dependent on patronage but also by the lack of any coherent imperial policy. It took the defection of the United States of America to persuade British statesmen to move away from the old mercantilist concept of colonies towards ideas more appropriate for the demands of the time.

There were some consistent supporters of the American cause in Britain, but these tended to be individuals and groups who had no great love for the parliamentary system as currently practised. In 1763, John Wilkes, a radical MP of colourful character, was imprisoned in the Tower of London for publishing an article attacking the King's Speech. There were mass demonstrations with the slogan 'Wilkes and Liberty', and a number of people were killed by troops in the 'Massacre of St George's Fields'. Wilkes was expelled from the House of Commons and then fled abroad for four years after being wounded in a duel and pronounced an outlaw by the courts. After some legal rehabilitation, Wilkes was back in 1768 to serve a jail sentence but also to be re-elected to the House of Commons as MP for Middlesex, not once but seven times, in face of opposition from the House of Commons itself. In 1769 he became an alderman of the City of London. Encouraged by the Society of Supporters of the Bill of Rights, he remained a thorn in the side of successive governments for more than a decade, arguing for 'a fair and equal representation of the people in Parliament'. Benjamin Franklin made the observation that if Wilkes had been of good character and George III of bad, the king would have been turned off the throne. As it was, the attempt by George III to restore something like absolutism came to an end in 1780 as the House of Commons passed a resolution 'that the influence of the Crown has increased, is increasing, and ought to be diminished'. However, the Wilkite movement was destroyed in the same year, when anti-Catholic feeling, inspired to some extent by the allegedly pro-popish Quebec Act of 1774 although more by the Catholic Relief Act of 1778 removing certain penalties and disabilities, flared up into scares of a 'Popish plot' involving the government: the ensuing riots under the leadership of Lord George Gordon were named after him. Many Wilkites were involved in disturbances in the House of Commons and elsewhere, but Wilkes himself as alderman of the City of London moved to the side of law and order and led a force that shot down some of the rioters.[7]

The movement associated with Wilkes died away, but some of the ideas persisted. Even some supporters of the government gave way a little, cutting down the number of sinecures and pensions that the king could distribute to bolster his power in the so-called 'economic reformation' Acts of 1782. But these subjects of His Majesty now sang

'God Save the King' more often and with more enthusiasm. Protestant British patriotism centred on the monarchy was in the ascendancy. As for the government's opponents, there was some celebration of the centenary of the Bloodless and Glorious Revolution of 1688, but the outstanding advocate of the rights of man at this time was Tom Paine, who had made a major contribution to the American Revolution with his two publications, *Common Sense* and *The Crisis*, and was now back home, his eloquence unstilled. His devotion to his cause persisted up to the outbreak of the French Revolution in 1789, and beyond.

One of Paine's principal opponents, Edmund Burke, was to assert in 1791 that 'the little catechism of the rights of men is soon learned'. He made this remark in connection with the possibility of the revival in Russia of 'headlong rebellions of the people, such as in the turbinating movement of Pugatchef', expressing the opinion that 'The Muscovites are no great speculators – but I should not much rely on their uninquisitive disposition, if any of their ordinary motives to sedition should arise'.[8] In fact, there were some disturbances in Russia at least partly influenced by the French Revolution, but nothing on the scale of the Pugachev Revolt of 1773–5, which was large-scale and intensive enough to deserve to be called 'peasant war'. Cossacks, tribesmen, Ural factory workers and the serfs were in turn involved in a vast movement that went in a great circle from near the Caspian Sea up through the Urals and round to the Volga, threatening in the summer of 1774 especially to envelop Moscow province and even regions nearer to St Petersburg. The leader, a Cossack claiming to be Peter III in order to appease the primitive constitutional ideas of most of his followers, showed himself in the decrees that he issued to be in no mood for compromise with the government, holding out the hope that with the eradication of opponents and 'villainous nobles', 'each may feel peace and a quiet life, which will continue forever'. Pugachev was betrayed, captured and executed, but his name lived on with its various associations of expectation and fear, as Burke was rightly to point out.

While there was surprisingly little opposition to absolutist policies in Prussia, there was a considerable amount in the Austrian Empire. Indeed, throughout Europe in the period 1763–89, the existence of both governments and various kinds of popular opposition affected to some degree by the ideas of the Enlightenment – as well as by pressing material problems – was the rule rather than the exception, even in the south-west and the north. Among the more vigorous proponents of the ideas of the Enlightenment on the anti-monarchical side was J. D. Van der Capellen tot den Pol, who in his 'Discourse to the People of the Low Countries' in 1781 asserted:

> Ah, my compatriots! Arm yourselves again, and defend the interest of the republic, yours, in a word. The republic is your weal, not at all solely that of the Prince and his court, who consider us all, the Dutch nation in its entirety ... as their hereditary vassals, their sheep and cattle, which they have the right to clip or slaughter as their avarice and resentment inspire in them. ... Now, all men are born free; nobody, by nature, is subservient to the authority of another. ... In these great societies, commonly called civil societies, the members join together to construct their mutual happiness, to defend their goods and the other rights that they have legitimately acquired. ... Arm yourselves; choose leaders; follow the example of the American people where not a drop of blood was spilt, as long as the English had not struck the first blow. ...[9]

As we have already seen, the Dutch movement was crushed in 1787 by the Prussians with British support, a few of the Patriots managing to take refuge in France.

There they would arrive to witness or even to participate in the most significant events of the eighteenth century, the background to which we can only hint at here. After decades of economic growth accompanied by an increase in the population in the earlier part of the century, the later 1770s and 1780s brought about problems for industry and trade in France, made worse by poor credit arrangements and shortage of precious metal for the manufacture of coins. The weather compounded these difficulties by being too dry in 1785 and too wet in 1788 and 1789. Starvation was less widespread than it had been in earlier bad times, but the peasants and other classes had come to expect more whenever it was available. Frustration brought tension between all these classes, especially between the Second Estate, the nobility, and the Third, which was composed of the peasantry and the other lower orders, and of the middle class or bourgeoisie, some of whose members were attempting to break the nobility's stranglehold on the best jobs in the government service. Feeling itself under threat, the nobility itself was to make the first moves, and the king and his advisers intensified the crisis through their own clumsiness and inconsistency.

At the end of the Seven Years War, the attempts at reform by Choiseul and others were carried out against the background of a struggle between Louis XV's administration and the privileged corporations led by the *parlement* of Paris. The virtual abolition of the *parlements* in 1771 was not a good legacy for his successor. Louis XVI (1774–93), who was to lose his head early in 1793, could probably have made better use of it in the years immediately following his accession to the throne in 1774. Even before his accession, in 1770, he was not helped by the death of 132 people in a stampede during the celebrations of his marriage to the Austrian princess Marie-Antoinette. Personally, he appears to have been an amiable enough man, but without much drive or purpose, and so his good intentions led down the road to the guillotine. From the very beginning, Louis attempted to appease those who were unhappy at the state of public affairs, dismissing Louis XV's unpopular ministers and recalling the *parlements*. He also gave his support to an enlightened reforming minister, Turgot, who attempted to abolish old restrictions on trade and manufacture, and to convert the forced labour of the peasants into a money tax. The *parlement* of Paris again led the opposition to this project 'produced by an inadmissible system of equality', and, yielding to such pressure, the king dismissed Turgot in 1776. There ensued the French support of the American War of Independence, which made a desperate financial situation even worse. Furthermore, the lesson that a patriotic liberation movement could succeed across the Atlantic was not lost on French dissidents. After 1783, the French government attempted in its desperation once more to bypass the *parlements* which, still led by Paris, fought back in another and greater 'revolt of the nobles'. As de Tocqueville described the sequel:

> The King still used the language of a master but in actual fact he always deferred to public opinion and was guided by it in his handling of day-to-day affairs. Indeed, he made a point of consulting it, feared it, and bowed to it invariably. Absolute according to the letter of the law, the monarchy was limited in practice. In 1784 Necker frankly recognised this as an accepted fact in an official declaration. 'Few foreigners have any notion of the authority with

which public opinion is invested in present-day France, and they have much difficulty in understanding the nature of this invisible power behind the throne. Yet it most certainly exists.'[10]

But neither Necker nor other director-generals of France – Turgot, Calonne and Brienne – could push through enough reforms to solve the budget deficit and other problems in Paris and the provinces, which were bigger than all of them. The basic problem remained what it had been for some time – a medieval financial system attempting to adapt to a changing society.

On 22 February 1787, Calonne presented a far-reaching programme for a unified land tax and stimulation of the economy through the abolition of internal customs and other measures to an 'Assembly of Notables'. Composed of what Calonne hoped would be people worthy of the public's confidence, the hand-picked notables did not give him theirs. Most of the nobles, priests and magistrates were more worried about their own privileges than the state of the realm. Calonne fell, and Brienne in his turn failed to channel the impulse for reform. Opposition continued, especially from the *parlements*. On 22 May, members of the most important of them, the *parlement* of Paris, were exiled and two of them arrested. The decision to dissolve the Assembly of Notables and to revive the Estates-General was taken during the ensuing confusion as Brienne fell and Necker was recalled.

When it last met, way back in 1614, this old advisory body had consisted of the medieval orders, the clergy, the nobility and the Third Estate – everybody else. The *parlements*, looking upon the Estates-General as a support of their own old privileges, wanted to maintain its former composition. However, many changes had taken place in French society over a century and three-quarters, especially as far as the Third Estate was concerned. Not only was it much more numerous than the First and Second, it also contained a very wide variety of lay commoners ranging from poor peasants through prosperous enough lawyers and functionaries to extremely rich merchants and manufacturers. Under the pressure of events, the Third Estate was obliged to assume a much greater measure of solidarity than it would otherwise have possessed or even chosen. Meanwhile, the king's advisers were aiming for self-imposed reform of the old order rather than reform introduced from outside, and the king himself realised that his own position might be exposed if he threatened the security of its own main props, the clergy and the nobility.

Unfortunately for Louis, he alienated both the First and Second Estates in the spring of 1788 by his adoption of a policy of reducing the power of the *parlements*. Both clergy and nobles in many provinces sprang to the defence of the *parlements* and of their own position in society in the so-called 'noble revolt'. Without support and virtually bankrupt, on 8 August the king followed the advice of Necker to declare the convocation of the Estates-General for 5 May 1789. As Brienne observed, 'Since the Nobility and the Clergy are abandoning the King, who is their natural protector, he must throw himself into the arms of the Commons in order to crush both.'[11] When the *parlements* and the Assembly of the Notables were recalled in September 1788, both bodies insisted that the Estates-General follow the form of 1614. In December 1788, the government gave way before the agitation of the Third Estate to the extent that it conceded double representation to the commons. But since voting was by estate rather than by head, this would not mean much unless the clergy and the nobilty agreed to further reform.

We will take the account into 1789 in the next chapter.

THE ARRIVAL OF EUROPE

The first four chapters of this book have attempted to spell out the argument that European absolutism was the first comparatively successful system of modern central government. In summary form, its characteristics may be presented as follows: an all-powerful figurehead, usually a monarch; an ideology, basically 'divine right' with a growing secular component, for example the 'general good'; an accommodation with the Church, sometimes the assumption of superiority over it; a tendency towards unified law and permanent bureaucracy; a standing army, and sometimes its waterborne counterpart, a fleet in being or in potential readiness; the nobility as a ruling class, although sometimes counterbalanced by a growing middle class or even an unruly peasantry; the beginnings of a national taxation network and a national market; some awareness of the necessity for education and some encouragement of cultural development in general. These characteristics could be found to a greater or lesser extent in both major regions of the continent, east and west. The most dynamic influence on the emergence and evolution of these characteristics was war.

The Thirty Years War ended in 1648 with the failure of the Habsburg dynasty to re-establish the Holy Roman Empire throughout Europe. Under Louis XIV, France rose to dominate the continent for much of the later part of the seventeenth century. Absolutist government which attempted to follow a French pattern became the norm, although Britain and the United Provinces were significant exceptions.

After the failure of the Ottoman Turkish siege of Vienna in 1683, Austria and Russia were able to stabilise Europe's landward frontier and also to respond, both directly and indirectly, to the French challenge. The Dutch and especially the British were able to make their response in the struggle for overseas empire, which culminated in the Seven Years War of 1756–63. Britain emerged triumphant, although it soon lost its American colonies. France was exhausted by its support for the United States of America, and then collapsed. Meanwhile, Prussia was consolidating its rise to great power status by partitioning Poland with Austria and Russia. Further reverses for Ottoman Turkey meant that Europe was establishing itself along the Danube and on the Black Sea.

The cumulative effect of all these and earlier experiences persuaded Edmund Burke to declare in 1796:

> There have been periods of time in which communities apparently in peace with each other, have been more perfectly separated than, in latter times, many nations in Europe have been in the course of long and bloody wars. The cause must be sought in the similitude throughout Europe of religion, laws, and manners. At bottom, these are all the same. ... The whole of the polity and economy of every country in Europe has been derived from the same sources.[12]

This observation calls for some latter-day comment. To take religion first, there is no doubt that Christianity provided the principal identifier of Europe throughout the medieval period up to the later seventeenth century, when it was overtaken by a secular definition exemplified by the replacement of Latin by French as the leading language of international communication. However, there was a counter-culture, too. The vast majority of Europeans at the time when Burke wrote were peasants, often more preoccupied by pagan supernaturalism than by

Church doctrine, as unaware of French as of Latin, still less conscious that there was a family of Indo-European languages to which both Latin and French belonged. Nevertheless, 'outsiders', be they Muslim or Jew, even Catholic or Protestant, were often treated with harsh intolerance by the uneducated and educated alike. Turning to laws, again, as well as the codified and customary common varieties there was another, more basic, kind, exemplified by the almost universal belief of the peasants that the land was theirs. Perhaps Burke had this consideration in mind when he wrote that 'the little catechism of the rights of men is soon learned'. As far as manners were concerned, in the narrower sense etiquette was as yet beyond the reach of the majority. In the wider sense in which Burke meant it – what the French call *moeurs* – there was possibly more generally shared throughout the whole continent. Before the agricultural improvements of the eighteenth century, the main occupation tended to follow comparable patterns and engendered comparable outlooks. But here we move from the territory of the historian towards that of the anthropologist. The same consideration might apply to the analysis of popular archetypal heroes, the German Herman, the Bulgarian Marko, and so on. At the highest level, a kind of European culture was in process of formation by the time of the French Revolution, and at least there was interaction between national cultures exemplified by the influence of individuals such as Shakespeare and Cervantes. Sadly, here too, as in other spheres, we have to recognise the influence of war, or at least to acknowledge that Goethe had a point when he observed that 'The first true and really vital material of the higher order came into German literature through Frederick the Great and the deeds of the Seven Years War'.[13]

Burke asserted that 'No citizen of Europe could be altogether an exile in any part of it'. Nevertheless, such a citizen could still feel himself completely abroad when he travelled for whatever purpose beyond Europe. On the other hand, by the time of the French Revolution, Europeans were becoming more aware of their commanding relationship with most of the rest of the world: in short, Europe had arrived. Already, however, it was possible to perceive that the global dominance of the continent would not last forever. During the great debate on the American Constitution in 1787, Alexander Hamilton accused Europe of extending her domination over Africa, Asia and America by arms and negotiations, force and fraud, alleging: 'The superiority she has long maintained has tempted her to plume herself as the Mistress of the World, and to consider the rest of mankind as created for her benefit.' However, Hamilton went on to declare that the 13 states bound together in 'a strict and indissoluble Union' should collaborate in the construction of 'one great American system, superior to the control of all transatlantic force or influence, and able to dictate the terms of the connection between the old and the new world'.[14] Then, at the end of 1790, one of Catherine the Great's correspondents, Baron Melchior von Grimm, wrote to her of a future when:

> Two empires will then share all the advantages of civilisation, of the power of genius, of letters, of arms and industry: Russia on the eastern side and America, become free in our own day, on the western side, and we other peoples of the nucleus will be too degraded, too debased to know otherwise than by a vague and stupid tradition what we have been.

Ironically, Grimm believed that Europe's downfall would stem from the French Revolution. In fact, many of the circumstances that promoted the French Revolution were to enable Europe to complete its rise.[15]

5

EUROPE BEFORE 1789, AND THE ORIGINS OF THE FRENCH REVOLUTION

THE GRAND TOUR

Although travel was established as a normal practice for a young gentleman in the seventeenth century and even in the sixteenth century and before, it did not develop into the Grand Tour until the eighteenth century. The English poet Cowper described the experience of a typical youth going from school to Cambridge or Oxford University, and then on the Tour:

> Returning, he proclaims by many a grace,
> By shrugs and strange contortions of his face,
> How much a dunce that has been set to roam,
> Excels a dunce that has been kept at home.[1]

Hundreds, perhaps thousands, of young men from England, and to a lesser extent from elsewhere, in addition to very few women from anywhere, followed the well-trod roads mostly leading to Rome and the other Italian cities of classical antiquity, usually taking in Paris and other parts of France, something of Switzerland and perhaps of Germany and the Low Countries, but rarely roaming further afield.[2]

It was the post-horses who did most of the treading, with the travellers observing whatever took their fancy from the relative comfort of their chaises. The journey was by no means as smooth as the railway was to make it in the nineteenth century: highwaymen could be encountered on the open road, and problems could be met at overnight stops. As a contemporary guidebook described one possible hazard: 'If the Guest be assaulted and beat within the Inn, he shall have no Action against his Host; for the Charge of the Host extends to the Moveables only, and not the Persons of His Guests.'[3]

Bearing such problems in mind, let us take our own rapid Grand Tour around Europe in the years before the French Revolution, beginning in the south-west. In 1776, Voltaire gave the following advice about going to Spain: 'It is a country of which we know no more than of the most savage parts of Africa, and it is not worth the trouble of being known.' Other advice was less dismissive, but insisted on the necessity of a sound constitution, reliable servants and trusty firearms. Portugal had close commercial relations with Britain, but it was rare for an Englishman or any other foreigner to venture inland from Lisbon and the other coastal towns. On the other hand, as we have already seen, Italy was the principal destination of the Grand Tour, even though it was still far away from political unity and by no means everywhere hospitable, especially south of Naples. In spite of all the discomforts that they might experience, many of his fellow-countrymen and others would have agreed with the observation of Captain John Northall after his travels in 1752:

> Italy, thus enriched by nature and adorned by art, is therefore justly esteemed the most agreeable and most useful part of Europe to a lover of antiquity, and the polite arts and sciences; nor is it strange that it should be much frequented by foreigners of taste in this learned and refined age.

Switzerland was, for the majority, a dangerous country that had to be crossed to reach Venice, Florence, Rome and other Italian cities. Rugged mountains were as yet a minority taste. Similarly, the trip down the Rhine had not achieved much of its later popularity, although old cities like Heidelberg and Cologne had their early advocates. Another route to Vienna and on through Bohemia to Dresden, Leipzig and Berlin was often followed. 'Vienna', claimed Martin Sherlock in 1780, 'is perhaps the best city in Europe to teach a young traveller the manners of the great world', while Thomas Nugent in his guidebook published in 1756 asserted that, although no great pleasure could be extracted from the dreary plains of Bohemia where 'the peasants were all in a state of vassalage to the nobility, and ... a brutish heavy kind of people, pretty much addicted to pilfering and thieving', the city of Prague was beautiful and wealthy, with a greater choice of company than any in the Austrian Empire.[4]

Generally speaking, the centre of Europe was by no means as sought after as Italy in the south-west and France in the north-west, where the Low Countries also held their attractions. Most sea routes led to Amsterdam, but the busy seaport was not as attractive to travellers as the neater and more peaceful Leyden, where in the Physic Garden galleries adjoining the university the visitor would find rarities including two mummies, the skin of a Scotchman, dried, the heart, guts and bowels of a man, also dried, the rib of a 'rinocero', 'a sportful instrument made of straw', the feather of a phoenix, the teeth of a fish called pot, the head of a 'hippopotomie', and a cat with wings.[5] Still in the north-west, quite a few continental Europeans would cross the Channel to return the visit of the English. Among the more famous of such people were Montesquieu and Voltaire. Both of these great men spent years in England, and made its government and society a subject for their serious study. A traveller from the furthest end of Europe, the Russian writer Nikolai Karamzin, escaped over the water from the beginning of the French Revolution in 1789 to observe that 'The English are enlightened ... it is not the constitution but the enlightenment of the English that is their real Palladium', or security. However, Karamzin was also moved to remark: 'An Englishman is a humanitarian in his own country, but in America, Africa and Asia he is all but a wild beast.'[6]

Fortunately for Karamzin and his fellow Russians, English visitors to their country usually treated it as part of the civilised world even if they were by no means always completely convinced that it was part of polite Europe rather than savage Asia. George Macartney, a young diplomat, served in St Petersburg from 1765 to 1767 and wrote:

> The Russian gentlemen are certainly the least informed of all others in Europe; the chief point of their instruction is a knowledge of

modern languages, particularly, the French and German; both which they usually speak with very great facility, tho' incapable of writing either with precision or propriety. Those who can afford the expence, and indeed many who cannot afford it, complete their education by a tour to France ... they rarely acquire more than personal affectation and mental distortion, and after all their travels return home far inferior, in the virtues of a good citizen, to those who have never traveled at all.[7]

Thus, from Cowper's Cambridge or Oxford graduate to Macartney's Russian nobleman, we have come full circle with the Grand Tour. We can be fairly certain that, whether from West or East, most of the participants in the standard European travels of the eighteenth century did not learn very much from their experiences. Even those who went to the more exotic parts of the continent, to the far north through Denmark to Sweden, or to the south-east, through Austria or Poland or the Mediterranean to the Ottoman Empire, did not always change their outlook in any perceptible manner. Moreover, in spite of some interest in such voyages as those of Louis de Bougainville and James Cook into the South Seas, and the vogue for objects from and information about China, Persia and Turkey, concern for the rest of the world was not widespread. Disdain and ignorance were mutual: 'An eighteenth-century Ottoman knew as much of the states and nations of Europe as a nineteenth-century European about the tribes and peoples of Africa, and regarded them with the same slightly amused disdain.'[8] In this case, however, defeat at the hands of Russia in the last quarter of the century and especially the onset of the French Revolution brought about the beginning of a change of attitude.

ARTHUR YOUNG IN FRANCE, 1787–8

It was a rare individual who knew how to keep his eyes open and to describe and analyse what he saw. Let us take as an example an English-man already practised in observation of the British Isles and skilled in the most basic of eighteenth-century occupations, agriculture. We will see how he discerned in the making the great series of events that was to cause an abrupt interruption in the Grand Tour and helped to bring it to an end.

The essential message of Arthur Young's *Travels in France* was conveyed in two of his observations: 'The magic of property turns sand to gold', and 'Whenever you stumble upon a grand seigneur, even one that is worth millions, you are sure to find his property desert'. In other words, he was in favour of a stimulus to peasant-tenant agriculture and against the absentee landowning nobility, welcoming the French Revolution as a movement in the desired direction. Let us begin with his own Preface, the first paragraph of which runs as follows:

> It is a question whether modern history has anything more curious to offer the attention of the politician, than the progress and rivalship of the French and English empires, from the ministry of Colbert to the revolution in France. In the course of these 130 years, both have figured with a degree of splendour that has attracted the admiration of mankind.

'The admiration of mankind' was something of an exaggeration, no doubt, but Young was certainly correct in his assertion that the manner in which the political economy of each nation had affected its prosperity was a subject worthy of practical investigation. Such a question was indeed 'resolved insufficiently by those whose political reveries are spun by their firesides, or caught flying as they are whirled through Europe in post-chaises'. Somebody like himself with a thorough knowledge and experience of agriculture, but also with an interest in government and society, was necessary to carry out the investigation.

Soon after his arrival in France in May 1787, Arthur Young encountered south of Orléans those cultivators called *métayers* – that is, in his own words, 'men who hire the land without ability to stock it; the proprietor is forced to provide cattle and seed, and he and his tenant divide the produce; a miserable system, that perpetuates poverty and excludes instruction'. About a week later, near Limoges he came across a hilly, forested region where there was 'Not a vestige of any human residence; no village: no house or hut, no smoke to raise the idea of a peopled country; an American scene; wild enough for the tomohawk of the savage'. A week later, after crossing the River Dordogne in the province of Lot, he encountered the first evidence of mass misery:

All the country, girls and women, are without shoes or stockings; and the ploughmen at their work have neither sabots nor feet to their stockings. This is a poverty, that strikes at the root of national prosperity; a large consumption among the poor being of more consequence than among the rich: the wealth of a nation lies in its circulation and consumption; and the case of poor people abstaining from the use of manufactures of leather and wool ought to be considered as an evil of the first magnitude.

Near the Pyrenees, Young passed through areas even wilder than those near Limoges, places where shepherds had to face the threat of wolves and carnivorous bears. Communications here were even more difficult than elsewhere, and Young was full of praise for efforts made to improve them, such as the construction of the Canal du Midi during the reign of Louis XIV, linking the Mediterranean with the Atlantic. But the general lack of development was one of the reasons for the staggering ignorance that Young encountered concerning England. One Frenchman asked him, were there any trees in England? He replied that there were a few. And were there any rivers? The exasperated traveller answered, none at all, adding with somewhat exaggerated patriotic pride: 'This incredible ignorance, when compared with the knowledge so universally disseminated in England, is to be attributed, like everything else, to government.' At Mirepoix near Carcassonne, one of the most considerable manufacturing towns in France with 15,000 people, Young could not find a carriage of any kind to carry him, again contrasting the situation with that to be found in England, where he believed that even in a town of 1500 people he could have found a conveyance at a moment's notice: 'What a contrast! This confirms the fact deducible from the little traffic on the roads even around Paris itself. Circulation is stagnant in France.' The wretchedness of the inns underlined this fact, one of them producing the comment: 'Spain brought nothing to my eyes that equalled this sink, from which an English hog would turn with disgust.' In the south, there were 'an incredible number of splendid bridges, and many superb causeways'. But this only demonstrated 'the absurdity and oppression of government', because one-quarter of the expense would have answered 'the purpose of real utility'. Soon came another lament on the road to

Lourdes, not yet a place of pilgrimage, but rather containing a castle for keeping state prisoners, sent there by the notorious warrants known as *lettres de cachet*. Here Young was moved to exclaim:

> Oh, liberty! liberty! – and yet this is the mildest government of any considerable government in Europe, our own excepted. The dispensations of providence seem to have permitted the human race to exist only as the prey of tyrants, as it has made pigeons the prey of hawks.

The travels of 1787 were not all discouraging, however, Young being most impressed by Bordeaux. Much as he had read and heard of the commerce, wealth and magnificence of this city, they greatly passed his expectations. Paris could not be compared with London, but Liverpool could not compete with Bordeaux. Back out in the countryside, however, there was more cause for complaint. Young regretted that 'banishment alone will force the French nobility to execute what the English do for pleasure – reside upon and adorn their estates'. He declared: 'Oh! if I was the legislator of France for a day, I would make the great lords skip again.' For 'Great lords love too much an environ of forest, boars, and huntsmen, instead of marking their residence by the accompanyment of neat and well cultivated farms, clean cottages, and happy peasants'. Having travelled up the Loire valley he reached Paris on 15 September, 'with the same observation I made before, that there is not one-tenth of the motion on the roads around it that there is around London'.

The streets in Paris itself were incredibly dirty and inconvenient and dangerous for walking without a 'foot-pavement'. Young learned that the affairs of the kingdom were in such dire straits that the financial chaos could not be cleared up without the summons of the States-General, and that 'it is impossible for such an assembly to meet without a revolution in the government ensuing'. Further conversations informed him that there were 'a prince on the throne, with excellent dispositions, but without the resources of a mind that could govern in such a moment without ministers'. No capable minister was to be found, while 'a court buried in pleasure and dissipation' added to the distress. Meanwhile, there was 'a great ferment amongst all ranks of men' and 'a strong leaven of liberty, increasing every hour since the American revolution'.

Young was not impressed by Versailles, believing that its palaces were a less worthy achievement of Louis XIV than the Canal du Midi. He did approve, however, of the respect in which persons of science and literature were held, although if the government changed and politics could be discussed more openly, 'academicians will not be held in such estimation, when rivalled in the public esteem by the orators who hold forth liberty and property in a free parliament'. Finally, on his way home at the beginning of November, Young was amazed in Lille to hear the great cry for war against Britain, as a result of the free trade treaty made with that country in 1786: 'The advantages reaped by four-and-twenty millions of consumers are lighter than a feather compared with the inconveniences sustained by half a million of manufacturers.' A week or so later, Young was relieved to reach his home estate at Bradfield in Suffolk, 'having more pleasure in giving my little girl a French doll, than in viewing Versailles'.

In spite of his wide travels in 1787, and while he was drawing 'conclusions relative to the political state of that great country, in every circumstance connected with its husbandry', Arthur Young con-sidered it necessary to make a further visit in 1788 to renew his survey. As before, Young was shocked by what he found in rural areas, both near Calais and in Brittany, but he was more impressed by his urban experiences, exclaiming: 'What a miracle, that all this splendour and wealth of the cities in France should be so unconnected with the country! There are no gentle transitions from ease to comfort, from comfort to wealth: you pass at once from beggary to profusion.' He found some of the buildings in the port of Lorient magnificent, although at times as elsewhere in France there was lacking 'the vigour and vivacity of an active commerce'. Nantes had 'that sign of pros-perity of new buildings, which never deceives'. Nevertheless, it was as excited by talk of liberty as any town in France could be, Young concluding that:

> the conversations I witnessed here, prove how great a change is effected in the minds of the French, nor do I believe it will be possible for the present government to last half a century longer, unless the clearest and most decided talents are at the helm. The American revolution has laid the foundation of another in France, if government does not take care of itself.[9]

Arthur Young returned to France yet again in 1789 to observe that the government could not last even one year longer, and was present in Paris as an eye-witness of many of the events of that momentous year. Among his many discoveries was an enormous number of publications on all kinds of political questions. This marked the popularisation of ideas concerning government and society that had been formed over the course of the preceding century and a half. We shall look at this intellectual evolution before assessing its importance relative to other aspects of the arrival of the French Revolution; we shall then also be in a position to assess the accuracy of Arthur Young's observations in the years 1787 and 1788.

THE AGE OF REASON, 1648–1721

By 1648, the way for a scientific revolution had been prepared by such individuals as Francis Bacon and René Descartes. They in their turn had been influenced by previous developments. Bacon himself referred to the importance of the inventions of the compass, gunpowder and printing. Ultimately, these had all been imported from China. Moreover, advanced ideas in mathematics and other fields had been contributed by Arabic scholars. Undoubtedly, Europe made use of the wider world in working towards its dominance. Thus, the voyages of discovery and exploration symbolised by the compass had stimulated both technical advance and speculation about the nature of the earth and the universe (although the telescope was also of key significance in this regard). Refinement in the use of gunpowder contributed to a military revolution which bore fruit in the armies of the Thirty Years War, for example in that of Gustavus Adolphus of Sweden. Descartes was inspired by his experiences in the Thirty Years War, although he also recommended an intellectual 'grand tour':

> For to converse with those of other centuries is almost the same as to travel. It is a good thing to know something of the customs and manners of various peoples in order to judge of our own more objectively and so not think everything which is contrary to our ways is ridiculous and irrational, as those who have seen nothing are in the habit of doing. But when one spends too much time travelling,

one becomes eventually a stranger in one's own country; and when one is too interested in what went on in past centuries, one usually remains extremely ignorant of what is happening in this century.[10]

Wise words for the seventeenth century, and for the twenty-first century, too!

We have already noted the manner in which the Thirty Years War encouraged thought about the natural world and its human inhabitants. Developments in printing produced a great flood of pamphlets concerning both that war and the civil war in Britain, and considering the fundamental questions provoked by those conflicts. Most of the publication was done in or near the triangle described by London, Paris and Amsterdam, and most of a growing reading public was to be found there, too.

Thomas Hobbes was inspired by his own experiences in such a setting at mid-century to compose his *Leviathan, or the Matter, Form and Power of a Commonwealth, Ecclesiastical and Civil*, first published in London in 1651. The book has a distinctive frontispiece which depicts a landscape of hills overlooking a town and countryside. Above this towers the torso of a bearded giant wearing a crown and what appears to be chain mail but on closer inspection is revealed as a huge cluster of tiny human beings. In the right hand he carries a sword and in the left a crozier or bishop's crook. This is the great Leviathan, the centrepiece of the attempt by Hobbes to set out a regular basis for the state or commonwealth.

As Hobbes himself puts it: 'The skill of making and maintaining Commonwealths consisteth in certain Rules, as doth Arithmetique and Geometry; not ... on Practise onely; which Rules, neither poor men have the leisure, nor men that have had the leisure, have hitherto had the curiosity or the method to find out.' Embarking on his ambitious task, he devotes the first part of his book to a consideration 'Of Man', sense and imagination, reason and science, passions and so on. Towards the end of this part, Hobbes makes his most celebrated observation concerning what is 'consequent to a time of Warre, where every man is Enemy to every man' and also 'consequent to the time, wherein men live without other security, than what their own strength, and their own invention shall furnish them withall'. In such circumstances

> there is no place for Industry; because the fruit thereof is uncertain: and consequently no Culture of the Earth, no Navigation, nor use of the commodities that may be imported by Sea; no commodious Building; no Instruments of moving, and removing such things as require much force; no Knowledge of the face of the Earth; no account of Time; no Arts; no Letters; no Society; and which is worst of all, continuall feare, and danger of violet death; and the life of man, solitary, poore, nasty, brutish, and short.

If there be any doubt that such circumstances ever existed, Hobbes offers the observation that 'the savage people in many places of *America*, except the government of small Families, the concord whereof dependeth on naturall lust, have no government at all; and live at this day in that brutish manner . . .'. Moreover, even if there had never been any time 'wherein particular men were in a condition of warre one against another',

> yet in all times, Kings, and Persons of Soveraigne authority, because of their Independency, are in continuall jealousies, and in the state and posture of Gladiators; having their weapons pointing, and their eyes fixed on one another; that is, their Forts, Garrisons, and Guns, upon the Frontiers of their Kingdomes; and continuall Spyes upon their neighbours; which is a posture of War. But because they uphold thereby, the Industry of their Subjects; there does not follow from it, that misery, which accompanies the Liberty of particular men.

Having remarked upon the war between individuals in distant America, Hobbes describes from personal experience the war between societies in Europe. From such evidence, he deduces as 'a precept, or generall rule of Reason' that every man ought to strive for peace as much as possible, and for the maximum advantage from war when he cannot obtain peace: 'The first branch of which Rule, containeth the first, and Fundamentall Law of Nature; which is, *to seek Peace*, and follow it. The Second, the summe of the Right of Nature; which is, By all means we can, *to defend our selves*.' From the fundamental law of nature derives another, that men are willing for peace and defence to give up much of their own liberty, entering by contract, pact or covenant into an organised state or commonwealth.

In Part Two of his great work, Hobbes considers this common-wealth, and explains the apparition in its frontispiece. The multitude united in one sovereign by contract is called a commonwealth:

> This is the Generation of that great *LEVIATHAN*, or rather (to speake more reverently) of that *Mortall God*, to which wee owe under the *Immortall God*, our peace and defence. For by this Authoritie, given him by every particular man in the Common-Wealth, he hath the use of so much Power and Strength conferred on him, that by terror thereof, he is inabled to forme the wills of them all, to Peace at home, and mutuall ayd against their enemies abroad.

There can be three kinds of commonwealth: monarchy, where sover-eignty is invested in one man; democracy, where it is located in a general assembly; and aristocracy, where it is found in the assembly of a few. However, in all three kinds sovereignty is absolute, without limit or division, and Church must be subordinate to state.

In Part Three, the longest of all, Hobbes proceeds to give a detailed description of 'A Christian Common-Wealth', but makes clear that his purpose is 'onely to shew what are the Consequences that seem to me deducible from the Principles of Christian Politiques, (which are the holy Scriptures,) in confirmation of the Power of Civill Soveraigns, and the Duty of their Subjects'. Part Four, 'Of the Kingdome of Darknesse', is a diatribe against the papacy and the Roman Catholic Church, which had in his view confused the issue of sovereignty. Moreover, there is a hint that their ambitions could lead to the introduction of even more malign influences:

> But who knows that this Spirit of Rome, now gone out, and walking by Missions through the dry places of China, Japan and the Indies, that yeeld him little fruit, may not return, or rather an Assembly of Spirits worse than he, enter, and inhabite this clean swept house, and make the End thereof worse than the Beginning? For it is not the Romane Clergy onely, that pretends the Kingdome of God to be of this World, and thereby to have a Power therein, distinct from that of the Civill State.

Evidently, as well as advancing the first full secular argument for absolute government, Hobbes was also fully immersed in the religious controversies of his time that had raged throughout the civil wars in England, Scotland and Ireland and the Thirty Years War on the European continent. Equally, he was conscious in a general sense of the wider setting of those controversies, both across the Atlantic and across Asia. On the one side, there were 'The Savages of America', who 'are not without some good Morall Sentences; also they have a little Arithmetick, to adde, and divide in Numbers not too great: but they are not therefore Philosophers'. On the other, there had been the wisdom of the ancient East, of India and Persia, but more sinister influences might penetrate from that quarter and beyond in more recent years.

Hobbes ranged freely through time as well as through the world of the mid-seventeenth century. He wrote: 'In a good History, the Judgement must be eminent; because the goodnesse consisteth, in the Method, in the Truth, and in the Choyse of the actions that are most profitable to be known. Fancy has no place, but onely in adorning the stile.' Attempting to carry out his own instructions, he gave full respect to the classical era, but attempted also to give other makers of European civilisation their due. For example, he described the manner in which gentry or nobility, with its sense of honour and coats of arms, was derived from the ancient Germans: 'Amongst the people of *Asia*, *Afrique*, and *America*, there is not, nor was ever, any such thing. The Germans onely had that custome; from whom it has been derived into *England*, *France*, *Spain*, and *Italy*, when in great numbers they either ayded the Romans, or made their own Conquests in these Westerne parts of the world.' Germany, like all other countries in their beginnings, was 'divided amongst an infinite number of little Lords, or Masters of Families, that continually had wars one with another', but then many such families joined together to make 'a greater Monarchy'. And the great monarchies in general, as we have seen, were as much at war with each other as individual men and families in pre-monarchical centuries, or in the state of nature to be found in America and perhaps in pre-history.[11]

Leviathan gives ample proof that at the beginning of the Age of Reason many of the ideas on government and society associated not only with that period but also with the later stages of the Enlightenment were already formed or at least in the process of formation. Among the characteristics still to arrive were religious toleration, secularism and a definition of rights and liberties as well as an objective awareness of the place of Europe in time and space, even a full definition of Europe. Moreover, the message of the Enlightenment had still to be distributed beyond a small intellectual elite. On the other hand, of course, Thomas Hobbes was far from alone, and has been paid special attention here largely in the belief that to begin with one significant figure is more helpful than to give a list of names. Inevitably, however, we shall not be able to accord anything like the same treatment to any other individual, however important.

John Locke took the concept of a social contract further than Hobbes, reserving to the individuals who had made it certain basic inalienable rights, to life, liberty and property, in his second *Treatise of Government*, first published in 1690 as a rationale for the Revolution of 1688. In his *Essay Concerning Human Understanding*, also published in 1690, Locke developed many of the suggestions made by Hobbes and added some of his own, thereby reversing the dictum of Descartes not to assert 'I think, therefore I am', but to imply 'I am, therefore I think'. In his emphasis on the importance of the environment in the development of the individual consciousness, Locke prepared the ground for the emergence of modern ideas concerning education and psychology. His *Letter Concerning Toleration* of 1688 pointed the way forward to the deism (belief based on reason rather than revelation) and even to the materialism of the eighteenth century.

Ideas are not easily attached to single individuals, nor to single countries. In 1700, for example, the Prussian Academy of Sciences was founded in Berlin with Gottfried Wilhelm Leibniz as director. Leibniz made important contributions to a wide range of subjects including mathematics, linguistics and political theory. He corresponded widely throughout Europe, for example making suggestions to Peter the Great for comprehensive reform in Russia. There were other academies, and other correspondents. However, while the works of Hobbes and Locke were not necessarily more remarkable than those of their contemporaries elsewhere during the Age of Reason, at least a brief mention must be made of the contribution of one other Englishman. Sir Isaac Newton (1642–1704) produced precise calculations based on the principles of gravity and motion that made an impact far beyond the minds of those who could understand them. For Newton, God was still very much alive in the infinities of space that formed his temple, and it was God who put life into the mechanical workings of the universe. For educated fellow countrymen and fellow Europeans, Newton himself became a kind of god, since he had combined the Baconian tradition of empirical observation with the Cartesian approach of mathematical, rational science. In other words, while behaving like a bee in the collection of as much information as possible, he also arranged it in a honeycomb more complex than the bee could achieve by itself. In such a manner, moving on from the recommendations of Bacon and Descartes earlier in the seventeenth century, he succeeded in combining induction with deduction, and thus brought a more complete order and harmony to the understanding of creation.

THE ENLIGHTENMENT, 1721–89

Newton's influence made an enormous contribution to the broadening of human enquiry that took place soon after his death. Another stimulus was provided by developments in politics and international relations. The death of Queen Anne in Britain in 1714 and of Louis XIV in France in 1715 led to renewed speculation about government. This was especially the case during the regency set up during the minority of Louis XV (1715–74), who was only five years old at his accession. But the arrival of the Hanoverian Succession in the shape of George I (1714–27), when considered alongside the Union with Scotland in 1707 and the Jacobite Revolt of 1715, was a powerful enough encouragement to profound argument on both sides of the British border. North-west Europe continued to provide the centre for intellectual activity, but the War of the Spanish Succession and the Great Northern War coming to an end in 1714 and 1721 respectively helped to spread the spirit more widely. The growth from Russia to Portugal of secular education from the primary level to that of the academy was another important development, accompanied as it was by a further upsurge in all manner of publications.

The wider world made an even greater impact than before on mental horizons. In his two *Treatises of Government*, John Locke had made no reference to Persia or India, and only one revealing remark about other parts of Asia:

> How many do most of the civilest Nations amount to? and who are they? I fear the *Chineses*, a very great and civil people, as well as

several other People of the *East, West, North* and *South,* trouble not themselves much about this matter. All that believe the Bible, ... must necessarily derive themselves from Noah, but for the rest of the World, they think little of his Sons or Nephews.[12]

In the eighteenth century a keener interest was to develop in other lands and their implications for Europe, while respect for the literal truth of Holy Writ was to diminish. This fresh departure was clearly marked in the work of Charles Louis de Secondat, Baron de la Brède et de Montesquieu. Montesquieu's first important composition was *The Persian Letters,* first published in 1721. These letters purport to be the correspondence of two Persian gentlemen travelling in Europe but thinly disguise a biting satire on aspects of social, political, ecclesiastical and literary life in Regency France. They brought Montesquieu fame but also trouble, for which reason he may well have thought it advisable to turn for his next publication to his own version of the rise and fall of the Roman Empire – *Considerations on the Causes of the Grandeur and the Decadence of the Romans,* which appeared in 1734. Here, Montesquieu showed himself to be moving in the direction of several of his contemporaries, notably the Neapolitan priest Giovanni Battista Vico, whose *New Science* came out in its first edition in 1725, and in its much-altered second edition in 1730. Applying himself like most of his predecessors to the study of Rome and Greece, Vico discerned more clearly than them the evolutionary nature of history and its progression through the centuries, as well as asserting more vigorously than before its cyclical pattern, its rises and falls. Vico was a man before his time, or possibly out of place, since he would probably have received more immediate recognition if he had been a Frenchman, a Dutchman or an Englishman rather than a Neapolitan.

Montesquieu's masterpiece, *The Spirit of the Laws,* which came out in 1748, is less explicitly historical than his work on Rome, but nevertheless shows a full realisation that among the most important conditioning influences on a society are climate, religion, laws, the principles of government, the example of the past and social practices and manners. From these a consequent general spirit is formed. The example of the past takes a leading place in the exposition of his declaration that the more we enter into particulars, the more we can discern the certainty of the principles on which they are founded. *The Spirit of the*

Laws is divided into six parts, considering in turn: laws in general and forms of government, republics, monarchies and despotisms; administration, especially of the army and of taxation; manners and customs, and their dependence on climatic conditions; population and the economy; religion; and the composition of the law, Roman, French and feudal. Montesquieu based his work on voluminous reading of the classics and of travel books, and on personal travel confined to Europe but including a stay of 18 months in England. There, he formed a great respect for the British constitution, discovering in it principles which became basic to his view of good government. These included the separation and balance of powers between the legislative, executive and judicial branches of government. Another means of the preservation of his preferred system of government, monarchy, was the existence of intermediate powers, especially the nobility but also the Church and municipalities. These would provide barriers against despotism and republic, as well as channels of communication between ruler and ruled. Montesquieu's thorough and many-sided exposition of the constituent parts of government gave him some claim to be considered as one of the founders of the modern study of politics and of sociology, as well as a contributor to the emergence of the modern study of history.

The best-known of all the great men of the Enlightenment was François Marie Arouet, or Voltaire. Like Montesquieu, Voltaire was much influenced by a stay in England, where he became closely acquainted with the ideas of Newton and Locke. He wrote voluminously on all kinds of subjects, as well as corresponding with the enlightened despots or absolutists and receiving many visitors from all over Europe at his estate of Ferney near the Swiss frontier. His historical studies included *The Age of Louis XIV* and biographies of Peter the Great of Russia and Charles XII of Sweden. He ranged more widely in his universal history, beginning with chapters on China, India and Persia respectively. A passionate fighter against intolerance and bigotry, Voltaire also showed some scepticism about the power of positive thinking and rational analysis in his novel *Candide*.

The dominance of the Enlightenment by the French in general was reflected in the widespread acceptance of the French term *philosophe* as a description for all the thinkers involved in the movement. Certainly, as before, much of the progress made in human thought was to be found in France, along with its immediate neighbours in the Low Countries and in England. But the area of concentration had now widened to include some of the outlying countries, notably Scotland. Encouraged by the Union with England in 1707 and by the persistence of the Jacobite movement to consider the nature of society and the means of achieving happiness within it, a considerable number of learned men in the major cities and old universities, especially Edinburgh, Glasgow, Aberdeen and St Andrews, made distinctive responses in works of both an historical and a more abstract nature. Both approaches were made by the outstanding Scottish *philosophe* David Hume. Hume was interested in the manner in which men made sense of the world around them, even more in the best mode of approach to the good life. Such virtue was to be achieved by constant critical review of one's beliefs in the light of experience. This approach would lead not only to individual happiness, but also to the better preservation of happiness in society. In his *History of England*, Hume showed that dedication to abstract ideals of liberty rather than its specific manifestations had led to the political upsets of the seventeenth century. In his *Inquiry Concerning Human Understanding*, he argued that 'Mankind are so much the same, in all times and places, that history informs us of nothing new or strange in this particular. Its chief use is only to discover the constant and universal principles of human nature.'[13] Hume also made a sceptical attack on all revealed religion. A most powerful response came from Thomas Reid in Aberdeen, founder of the 'Common sense' school arguing for observation beyond reason. Among Reid's most fervent disciples was Thomas Jefferson, soon to write of 'self-evident truths' in the American Declaration of Independence.

The Enlightenment in Scotland, France and elsewhere consisted of the spread of new ideas as well as of their development. The best-known move in this direction was advertised in 1750 in the Prospectus for *L'Encyclopédie, The Encyclopaedia, or Explanatory Dictionary of the Sciences, Arts and Crafts*. This work originated from another, the *Cyclopaedia, or a Universal Dictionary of Art and Sciences*, brought out first in London in 1728 by the Englishman Ephraim Chambers, and intended for a French edition for which Denis Diderot was made responsible a year or so before he issued the Prospectus. Diderot announced that all previous such projects were realised when

> The true Philosophy was in its infancy; the Geometry of the Infinite did not yet exist; there was no Dialectic; the laws of sound Criticism were entirely unknown. ... Learned men were not moved by the spirit of research and emulation; that other spirit of method and exactness (less fruitful in results perhaps, but still more rare) did not yet govern the various branches of literature; the Academies, whose work has so much advanced the Sciences and the Arts, had not been founded.

Francis Bacon had launched a plan for a universal dictionary of sciences and arts at a time when neither sciences nor arts as such existed, and following both him and Chambers, Diderot offered in his Prospectus a systematic table of human knowledge classified as memory, reason and imagination. His own work would not be a translation of Chambers, however, but a new compilation of matter under three principal headings, the Sciences, the Liberal Arts and the Mechanical Arts, in which 'Facts are cited, experiences compared, methods formulated only to inspire the human spirit to open unknown paths and advance to new discoveries, taking their first step in the last footprints of great predecessors'. History and biography were excluded, again following precedent, while the emphasis on the 'Mechanical Arts' was claimed to be an innovation:

> Recourse was had to the most skilful workers of Paris and the Kingdom. We took the trouble to go into their workshops, question them, write to their dictation, draw out their ideas, extract the terminology appropriate to their profession – draw up tables, settle definitions, to talk with those who had provided us with memoranda, and – an almost indispensable precaution – to correct by long and frequent interviews with one set of informants, the incomplete, obscure and sometimes inaccurate information provided by others.

Whatever care and patience were taken in the compilation, imperfections would exist, and suggestions and criticisms were gratefully received. In fact, such was the pace of innovation that some of the drawings were out of date by the time they were printed. Moreover, some of the representations of animals were inaccurate: for example, the giraffe was not given a long enough neck. Meanwhile, art (in the sense that it was to acquire later) and architecture both followed the strict principles of neoclassicism, thus reflecting and encouraging the aspiration for rational enquiry and structure.

The Prospectus declared: 'the final perfection of an Encyclopaedia must be the work of ages. It has taken centuries to begin the work, it will take centuries to complete it. To Posterity, and the Being who never dies.' Nevertheless, in conclusion, Diderot and his colleagues expressed the hope that

> this Work might serve as a Library in all subjects for a man of the world, and in all subjects save his own for a professional Scholar; that it will replace elementary works; will develop the true principles of things, and demonstrate their relationships; that it will contribute to the certainty and progress of human knowledge, and that by multiplying the number of true Scholars, distinguished Artists and enlightened Amateurs, it will spread new benefits throughout society.

In spite of such good intentions, to compose the *Encyclopaedia* turned out to be a more difficult task than Diderot and his colleagues had expected, while the publication and distribution also ran into formidable obstacles. The first two volumes were suppressed in 1752 as injurious to the king's authority and to religion, and this was only the beginning of a long tale of suppression, censorship and mutilation of the great work. At one point, Diderot seriously considered taking up an invitation from Catherine the Great of Russia and moving the whole operation to St Petersburg, but through perseverance he managed with about 160 collaborators to bring out 35 volumes in Paris and Amsterdam by 1780. By the wish of some of the 4000 subscribers, history was introduced into the subject matter, but 'only the general features which mark epochs in the annals of the world'.

In Britain, translations from the French *l'Encyclopédie* were not a success, but the idea was further embodied in the *Encyclopaedia Britannica*, first completed by 'a society of gentlemen in Scotland' and printed in Edinburgh in three volumes by 1771, with the claim that the editors had 'digested the principles of every science in the form of systems or distinct treatises, and explained the terms as they occur in the order of the alphabet'.[14] We shall see how this project progressed in Chapter 10 of this book by examining the eleventh edition, which was produced in 1910–11. Meanwhile in the second half of the eighteenth century, the knowledge and understanding promoted by the encyclopaedias and other agencies certainly contributed to the spread of the Enlightenment. Beginning for the most part as a movement involving no more than a few individuals in the triangle formed by Amsterdam, London and Paris in the Age of Reason, the spirit of intellectual enquiry moved out to Philadelphia and St Petersburg as well as to most cities in between and, in strong or diluted form, to all educated people, especially among the middle class and nobility, but not excluding a few from the humbler classes of society. Perhaps the most powerful assertion came from outside the triangle, from Königsberg in Prussia. In *What is Enlightenment?* (1784), Immanuel Kant declared: *Sapere aude!* – in other words, enlightenment means the courage to use one's own reason. However, in the same work Kant observed that, as far as government was concerned, one must obey. Moreover, in 1781 he had indicated in his *Critique of Pure Reason* that the senses provide the perceptions that lead to thought, provoked by Hume like Reid before him.

Along with the completion of success for the Enlightenment came the beginning of failure. The international nature of the movement was breaking down in the face of the assertion of national differences. The Seven Years War had a part to play here, as had the onset of the Industrial Revolution, the one asserting not only the maturity of nationhood but also the growth of empire, the other beginning the great transformation that was later to lead to the predominance of town over country, of middle class or bourgeoisie over nobility, of working class or proletariat over peasantry. And so the introduction of secular thought concerning government and society that had gained considerable impetus from the late seventeenth century onwards would take new turns, removing reason from its pedestal.

A distinctive contribution in this direction was made by Jean-Jacques Rousseau. In *The Social Contract*, first published in 1762, Rousseau argued that the views of Hobbes must be rejected, but he went on to produce an adaptation of his predecessor's ideas rather than a complete alternative to them. In place of Leviathan, he introduced the concept of 'general will', to which everybody would surrender individual rights for the common good. The 'general will' would be exercised not through a simple majority, but by some kind of consensus. Rousseau's vagueness on this point was perhaps inevitable. Certainly, it led to *The Social Contract* being looked upon as a pointer towards later political ideologies of widely varying kinds. In other works, Rousseau argued that reason alone was not enough, that there was something to be said for the simple, natural life, that the heart should work along with the head, that the 'inner light' should be consulted as well as the illumination deriving from argument. Here, as in other directions, he would lead the way towards later intellectual developments.

In his educational tract *Émile*, published like *The Social Contract* in 1762, Rousseau wrote: 'The male is male only at certain moments; the female is female her whole life ... The rigid strictness of the duties owed by the sexes is not and cannot be the same.' As Dorinda Outram aptly observes, for the Enlightenment 'biological difference and culturally induced sex roles were seen as one and the same thing'. Today we see things differently, separating nature and nurture and often giving emphasis to the latter. In the eighteenth century, clearly, war and politics were largely matters for men, but the pursuit of peace was shared by both sexes. To quote Outram again, 'The practice of the Enlightenment set the stage for the creation of an entirely masculine political culture during the French Revolution; but its theory of universalism also gave ammunition to those who were to struggle to free women from restrictive definitions of gender'.[15] A powerful shot was fired by Mary Wollstonecraft in 1792 with her *Vindication of the Rights of Women, with Strictures on Political and Moral Subjects*.

However, for the most part, the Enlightenment did not recommend revolutionary action or even thought concerning government and society. *L'Encyclopédie*, in its article on 'Political Economy', was loud in its praise of monarchy: 'It alone has discovered the real means of enabling us to enjoy all the possible happiness and liberty and all the advantages which man in society can enjoy on the earth.' *L'Encyclopédie* also pointed out that 'The progress of enlightenment is limited, it hardly reaches the suburbs; the people there are too stupid. The amount of riff-raff is about always the same ... The multitude is ignorant and doltish.'[16] Yet by 1789 the ideas of Diderot and his fellow editors had reached further than they had intended. Following the lead of the capitals, many provincial cities in France and elsewhere by this time possessed their own academies, libraries and reading societies.

In Paris for many of the events of that momentous year, Arthur Young wrote: 'The spirit of reading political tracts, they say, spreads into the provinces, so that all the presses of France are equally employed. Nineteen-twentieths of these productions are in favour of liberty, and commonly violent against the clergy and nobility.'[17] But the clergy and the nobility were the twin props of the old order whose apex was the monarchy. Thus the attack on the privileges of the first two Estates led easily on to the assault against those of the king himself.

In a somewhat similar manner, the old economic order was undermined along with the social and the political. *L'Encyclopédie* helped to popularise the views of Dr Francois Quesnay and other Physiocrats, who proceeded from the strongly held basic principle that agriculture was the source of all wealth, and that commerce and industry depended on the produce of the land. However, the Physiocrats moved from the argument that landed proprietors were the backbone of the body economic to the conclusion that nothing should be put in the way of such individuals developing their own interests. They therefore wished to sweep away all the traditional seigneurial dues and customs duties, both internal and external. *Laissez-faire*, or free enterprise, was their watchword, and they led on towards the more general, classic statement of that doctrine, with more emphasis on commerce and industry, in the Scotsman Adam Smith's *Inquiry into the Nature and Causes of the Wealth of Nations*, first published in 1776, the year of the American Declaration of Independence. Unfortunately, Smith has been much misunderstood by many who have not read *The Wealth of Nations*, still less other works such as *The Theory of Moral Sentiments*, which extols sympathy, conscience and community. Nevertheless, in addition, he certainly set out a rationale for the economic growth that was soon to ensue in the first industrial revolution.

Thus, the old order was undermined by a 'triple revolution', political, economic and cultural – action, growth and thought, all interdependent.

THE FIRST INDUSTRIAL REVOLUTION AND ITS CONSEQUENCES

The Physiocrats and Adam Smith were observers as well as analysts and prescribers. That is, they could take note of the developments that they were recommending already in progress around them. Especially in Britain if not so much in France, the closed world of mercantilism was on its way out, and a more open commercial system was in process of creation. Moreover, these two national economies at least were poised for the greatest change yet in their history, the first industrial revolution. To a considerable extent, pressure for this was exerted by population growth between 1700 and 1800: in France from more than 20 million to about 28, in Britain from about 5 million to nearly 9, with the total for Europe as a whole approaching 190 million. Consequently, there were more bodies to clothe as well as mouths to feed, the prospect alarming Thomas Malthus (in his *Essay on the Principles of Population as it affects the Future Improvement of Society*, 1798) but affording astute businessmen unprecedented opportunity. The extent of the transformation by the end of the eighteenth century must not be exaggerated, but mechanisation in the textile industry in particular had shown the way towards mass production. Adam Smith's most famous example actually came from another industry, the manufacture of pins, but the principle that he described was capable of application to a whole host of activities, as enterprising businessmen were increasingly to discover as consumers made more demands. However, it was still possible to journey the length and breadth of Britain without being made aware of the scope and nature of the new methods of making money faster, and only a genius such as Adam Smith could achieve such a full understanding of them. He was considerably assisted by the Physiocrats, whom he visited in the 1760s, and possibly he even began the writing of *The Wealth of Nations* in Toulouse, but it appears unlikely that France offered so many examples of the advantages to capitalist expansion of the appropriate kind of setting. Similarly, Arthur Young could not easily estimate the extent to which the stranglehold of the nobility on landed property was undermined under the old regime. The bourgeoisie (middle class) was often more prosperous than lack of official recognition would make it appear.

To revert to the point that Arthur Young made in the Preface to his book, 'It is a question whether modern history has anything more curious to offer the attention of the politician than the progress and rivalship of the French and English empires'. Partly in recognition of this, perhaps, a commercial treaty between the two powers abolished some tariffs and lowered others in 1786. Certainly, there is much to be said for the historian taking this comparison as a basis for attempting to understand the arrival of the fateful course of events that unfolded in France from the end of the 1780s onwards. Arthur Young possibly underestimated the economic progress that France had been able to make during the course of the eighteenth century, for in some respects the volume of its manufactures exceeded that of Britain. Nevertheless, he could appreciate the manner in which that progress was being held back by privilege and restriction. Similarly, he may have exaggerated the degree of freedom of enterprise already existing in Britain, and not given sufficient attention to the advantages that Britain had gained from its compact size, its earlier conquest of the fundamental barrier of subsistence and its control of the seas. French colonial activity was too exclusively concentrated on San Domingo, even if its European commercial connections were more widespread than the British. Britain had also benefited more than France from earlier wars. Moreover, there was no doubt that enterprise and mobility were less restricted in Britain, where political and social revolution had to a certain extent been achieved in the late seventeenth century. Hence, Britain was able to avoid the catastrophe that struck France a century later and seemed also to threaten absolute monarchy in other states.

FRANCE IN 1789 AND THE ORIGINS OF THE FRENCH REVOLUTION

1789 began in France with elections by the three Estates to the Estates-General, followed by the composition in each electoral district of lists of grievances or *cahiers de doléance*, again by each of the three local Estates. As an example of a *cahier*, let us take that from the Third Estate at Rouen, which was described by Arthur Young in 1788 as 'this great, ugly, stinking, close, and ill built town, which is full of nothing but dirt and industry'.[18] We must recall the nature of the Third Estate in the late eighteenth century. Though this was a blanket term for all commoners, it was dominated by members of the legal profession and bureaucrats, to a lesser extent by bankers, businessmen and landowners, with little influence from the rest. Therefore, composed by a commission consisting of merchants and lawyers, our sample *cahier* was a reflection of the complaints and wishes of only a small section of the population of the town and surrounding district. The poor and needy received but little attention.

As far as the First Estate was concerned, the *cahier* asked for the clergy to be subjected to the same taxes and methods of collection as the other two Orders, that bishops, abbots and priors should hold one office only and reside in the appropriate area, that payments to the Church should be regularised in such a way that parish priests would be able to carry out their duties in the appropriate manner, and that interference from Rome should be kept under control. Regarding the Second Estate, the *cahier* wanted the status of nobility to be acquired in future only for long and useful services to the state, no longer by the purchase of offices. Offices should for the most part be open to the Third Estate, while the nobility should be free to enter any employment or profession without losing status.

The interests of the lawyers in the composition commission were reflected in the sections of the *cahier* that dealt with the National Constitution, the Constitution of the Estates-General, the Provincial Estates and Legislation. There was no great revolutionary impulse here, but rather the assertion that 'the principal source of the errors and abuses of the administration resides in the lack of a fundamental law which fixes in a precise and authentic manner the principles of a national constitution and the respective limits of the various powers'. France was an hereditary monarchy which passed from male to male, and the king alone possessed the power to govern according to the laws, with the legislative power belonging to the nation assembled in the Estates-General together with the king. Personal liberty and property should be protected by law, and taxation should be shared out equally, 'without distinctions of rank or order, but according to wealth and ability to pay'. The Estates-General should have control over taxation as well as legislation, and should vote by head, not by Order – that is, as individuals rather than as the Three Estates. Provincial Estates should have control over the internal administration of each region, while the former Estates of Normandy in particular should be re-established in the provincial capital of Rouen, according to its 'primitive constitution, charters and royal promises'. This last measure would be 'to bind the interests of the province to those of the Kingdom as a whole and to facilitate the general regeneration by unifying principles and government'. As far as Legislation was concerned, the *parlements* hence-forth would have no right to modify laws, only to make representations to the Estates-General. Delay and expense in securing justice should be reduced, and justice should be meted out equally to the guilty, without arbitrary arrest, confiscation of property or torture.

The two sections of the *cahier* dealing with Finances and then with Commerce, Industry and Agriculture were probably of greater interest to the merchants in the composition commission. Emphasis was given again to taxation, which should be equitable in its nature and distribution, as well as being levied in such a manner that it would not harm the economy. Accounts of public income and expenditure should be published each year. There was particular concern about the commercial treaty drawn up with Britain in 1786, and protection should be introduced for French manufactures and its merchant fleet, while there should perhaps be a ban on the use of British machines in the kingdom. Internal customs should be abolished, and weights, distances and measures standardised. At least some of these suggestions would be for the general good, as were a further series concerning the prosperity of the peasants who inhabited the rural areas around Rouen. Financial burdens, 'which delay agricultural progress and which alienate certain classes of citizens from exploiting the land', would have to be abolished, as would 'the vexatious and abusive system of the militia, which reduces the population of the countryside and thus weakens the backbone of agriculture'. Provincial Estates should allow or prohibit the export of grain, depending on harvest yields and adequacy of grain stores. A none too indirect blow at the Second Estate's passionate involvement in hunting was taken in the recommendation 'That strict regulations should deal with the damage caused by the multiplicity of pigeons, especially at the time of sowing and of harvesting, with the intolerable abuse of open rabbit warrens and with the devastation caused by wild animals'. A more direct reminder to the First Estate of its charitable duties was contained in the complaint that 'disorders caused by vagabond beggars' were 'one of the great scourges of the countryside', and that therefore 'part of the possessions of the Church shall be recalled to their original purpose'. A final declaration underlined the moderate, constitutional nature of the *cahier*, humbly begging the king, 'because of his virtue and manifest desire to help his people', to accept the title 'Father of the People'.[19]

Not all *cahiers* went quite as far as this in its salute to the monarchy, but on the other hand there was as yet no open challenge to the king's authority. Indeed, the vast majority of the *cahiers*, from all three Estates, were moderate in tone, even though there was much loud debate and even some disturbance at the assemblies approving them and choosing deputies to go to Versailles for the convention of the Estates-General on 5 May 1789. The limited nature of the objectives of the *cahiers* is all the more surprising given that the economic problems were growing worse at the time that they were being composed. The harvest of 1788 had been well below average, and the following winter had been the worst for 80 years. There had been riots in Paris and the provinces. Yet the *cahiers* of the Third Estate were rarely more radical than that from Rouen, partly because, like it, they left out the complaints of the lower elements in society, while those of the clergy and the nobility concentrated on the protection of their own rights and privileges from the encroachments of the monarchy. On the other hand, the sum total of the requests contained in the *cahiers* was greater than their parts. Together, they implied an end to absolutism.

Therefore at the moment of its convention on 5 May 1789 the Estates-General already contained the seeds of its own destruction and that of the absolute monarchy as well. The Third Estate argued from the beginning that it deserved more influence since it represented the majority of the people, even though its deputies included not one single peasant or urban worker and very few merchants and commoner landowners, but were mostly lawyers, eloquent beyond the strict confines of their exclusive social position and with a tendency to abstract speculation and theory. At least a few deputies from the Third Estate opposed the arguments of their colleagues, while some representatives from the Second Estate supported them, even more from the First Estate. For about 200 parish priests were elected as deputies, who were opposed to the power of the bishops and therefore agreed to some extent with their lay, commoner colleagues.

It was indeed a breakaway group composed largely of parish priests that broke the stalemate into which the Estates-General degenerated soon after its ceremonial opening. The now reinforced Third Estate assumed the title of National Assembly, arguing that it represented those who shared the responsibility for paying the national taxes and going on to propose a new collection of taxes. The king attempted to keep the Estates separate at the same time as giving them the encouragement of a promise of reform, but he could not shake the resolve of the National Assembly, which had sworn on a tennis court on 20 June not to dissolve itself until it had worked out a constitution. As even some members of the nobility along with more clergy joined the National Assembly, the king conceded the necessity of the three Estates meeting as one, and indeed ordered them to do so on 27 June. Meanwhile, a large number of troops was mobilised by some of the king's entourage to carry out a counter-revolution, and the dismissal of Necker further intensified the widespread alarm that had risen to a new level along with the price of bread. A climax was reached with the decision of members of the garrison of Paris, the French Guards regiment, to go over to the side of a crowd that had already committed acts of violence against property for the seizure of the most notorious royal possession, the Bastille, on 14 July.

Before we look at the sequel to this opening event of the French Revolution, let us briefly return to the observations of Arthur Young, who returned to France for his third visit in the summer of 1789. When he moved out from Paris to the provinces, he discovered that political reading was not as widespread as he had previously believed, and that there was in particular an absence of newspapers. In Château-Thierry (Aisne), Nancy (Meurthe), Besançon (Doubs), Moulins (Allier), Clermont-Ferrand (Puy de Dôme) and Le Puy (Haute Loire), he found a comparative or complete absence of political information and discussion, although the opposite was more nearly the case in Strasbourg and Marseille. In Nancy, Young reported the answer to his question about developments there, and then made a telling comment:

> We are a provincial town, we must wait to see what is done at Paris; but every thing is to be feared from the people, because bread is so dear, they are half starved, and are consequently ready for commotion.' – This is the general feeling: they are as nearly concerned as Paris; but they dare not stir; they dare not even have an opinion of their own till they know what Paris thinks; so that if a starving populace were not in question, no one would dream of moving. This confirms what I have often remarked, that the deficit would not have produced the revolution but in concurrence with the price of bread. Does this not shew the infinite consequence of great cities to the

liberty of mankind? Without Paris, I question whether the present revolution, which is fast working in France, could possibly have had an origin.[20]

Thus, as well as making an intelligent diagnosis of the ills affecting France throughout its length and breadth, Arthur Young also made the point that the strongest initiative towards a cure would come from the centre. Therefore, while taking into account the more important developments in the provinces during the revolutionary years, we will concentrate on the events unfolding in Paris.

Let us attempt to sum up the reasons why the events of the French Revolution were about to occur. To begin at the top of society, although not at the root of the trouble, let us take the king himself. Louis XVI was neither severe nor flexible enough, and chose the wrong moments to attempt to be either. More fundamentally, the glitter had rubbed off the idea of kingship in general. Old ideas of royal paternalism were also wearing thin, while the spirit of the age had reduced the strength of the concept of divine right. The new secular arguments for monarchy based on variations of the social contract did much to reduce His Majesty's power and glory. Moreover, there was a more traditional kind of contract, the former principles of government based on the Estates-General and the *parlements*, which Louis and his advisers appeared to be ignoring, often in the attempt to make their absolutism more enlightened or to act as arbitrators in the struggle between the Estates of the realm.

The First Estate, the clergy, which used to be such a prop for divine right and for the maintenance of tradition, was now itself in turmoil. In particular, the rank and file were ranged against the upper levels of the clerical order, which struggled to maintain an exclusive hold on its property and privileges. The Second Estate, the nobility, was engaged in a similar conflict, to some extent internal but more seriously against the Third Estate. Making attack the best form of defence, the nobles attempted in their role as landed seigneurs to press their ancient feudal rights and to increase the level of their rents, while reserving to themselves as much as possible governmental posts and commissions in the armed forces. From 1781, for example, it was made more difficult for commoners to become officers in the army or navy. The inflexibility of the nobility must not be exaggerated, while its ideologues attempted to make full use of the arguments concerning the part that it should play put forward by such *philosophes* as Montesquieu. They readily accepted the argument that their Estate acted as the main prop to monarchy by assuming the functions of intermediate bodies in a polity founded on the principle of the separation of powers. Unfortunately, they took this argument so far that in such separation they would receive a preponderant share.

Some members of the nobility demonstrated their open attitude to the opportunities presented by the eighteenth century in their enthusiastic entry into activities that their fellow aristocrats could only view with disdain. That is, they attempted to make improvements in agriculture and to participate in commerce and industry. Here they would come near to sharing the views of leading members of the Third Estate, the upper bourgeoisie. Conversely, the bourgeoisie had made greater inroads into the traditional noble preserve of landholding. However, the cutting edge of the middle class, clearly discerned by Arthur Young, was in the seaports, especially by the Atlantic. Through their prosperity, they made an impact on manufacturing industry, encouraging the breakup of closed corporations that stemmed from medieval times. Ambitious craftsmen and shopkeepers, both masters and workmen alike, could join in the struggle to overthrow outdated privilege at whatever level of society. Generally speaking, a new outlook of 'free contract' was attempting to make its way through the ties and restrictions of the old regime.

However, while the old regime was not beaten, there were still many successful members of the Third Estate who were trying to join it, often experiencing frustrations in the attempt. At the lower levels of the Third Estate, formal social structure was looser, but the peasants and urban proletarians still knew their place for the most part, although there was also a collective memory of violence and revolt. As Arthur Young rightly noted, many rural areas and provincial towns did not share in the economic growth of the eighteenth century. Change in agriculture was slow and by no means, especially where increase in rents and assertion of feudal rights were concerned, always for the better. The patience of the people was traditional, but so was the possibility of their sudden fury.

Fundamentally, France in the eighteenth century was not stagnant. Great changes were occurring, including a rise in the population from the low twenties of millions at the beginning of the century to the high twenties of millions by its end. Commercial growth and at least some indications of industrial revolution were evident. As for political revolution, that was by no means definitely on the agenda. The Enlightenment had launched its attack on superstitition and abuses of the old system, rather than on its overthrow. Its ideas were used as much to defend the position of the nobility as to assert that of the bourgeoisie. From 1783, however, with the example of the American Revolution before the bourgeoisie and a growing number of financial and other problems, including the accident of poor harvests, weighing down the nobility and the monarchical establishment, the rights of man came to be a slogan that could much more easily overthrow the old order than maintain it. Fundamental questions were to emerge: who should control the state, and for what purpose? However, one final point needs to be made. Nobody could easily foretell where events would lead after the fall of the Bastille. Nobody really knew what France was letting itself in for as it embarked on its Revolution. If the pattern of the years after 1789 had been more evident, there can be little doubt that at least some of the enthusiasm at the dawn of liberty would have been more restrained.[21]

6

THE FRENCH REVOLUTION AND NAPOLEON, 1789–1815

The French Revolution and Napoleon introduced a new era not only for France but also for Europe and beyond. A considerable part of the message of 1789 and succeeding years had already been announced in the British and American Revolutions, but now it was to come over in complete form and at full blast. The rights of man were now given wider publicity than ever before, as was the vocabulary of modern politics. Admittedly, the rhetoric outweighed the implementation, and there is even a case for saying that the revolution turned full circle, for France in 1815 in many respects resembled the France of 1789. On the other hand, the weight of the past is such that high hopes for immediate and complete reversal of an old order can never be fully realised, and in the space of a few years absolute monarchy and many of its feudal trappings were swept away. Just as the sons of Charles I had found it impossible to make the Stuart restoration complete, so the brothers of Louis XVI discovered enormous obstacles in the path of restoring the inheritance of the Bourbons. While there is some truth in the argument that Napoleon developed tendencies towards centralisation and even the increase of state power that were already implicit under the old regime, they could not be maintained by absolute monarchy. If the myth of the French Revolution has been greater than the thing itself, the myth grew from the happenings of 14 July 1789 and their sequel. Before we return to an assessment of the great days, there-fore, we must attempt to describe the manner in which they unfolded. As we do this, moreover, we must not forget that they would not have taken place in the way they did had not France been affected by developments beyond its borders. Bearing this wider setting in mind, let us now consider events in France under the following head-ings: Constitutional Monarchy, 1789–92; Republic and Terror, 1792–4; Thermidor and the Directory, 1795–9. Late in 1799, the opportunity presented itself for Napoleon Bonaparte to assume power as first consul. Before briefly examining his domestic policies, we will look at the French Revolution and Napoleon's rule in the international context.

CONSTITUTIONAL MONARCHY, 1789–92

The events of 14 July 1789 were not in themselves earth-shattering, indeed rather the reverse, for the Bastille fortress was found to contain no arms and only a few prisoners. The situation was already out of hand before the famous day, however, and now as before the king could only give recognition to what had happened, while attempting to avoid a further worsening in the crisis by recalling the experienced minister Necker. Meanwhile, the electors of the Third Estate in Paris attempted to assume the leadership of the insurgents, bringing into being a protection for their assumption of power in the shape of the National Guard. Louis XVI bowed to the inevitable, and while some of his relations and supporters began the emigration of princes and nobles, the isolated monarch now found himself confronted with the National Assembly reaffirming and enlarging its aim of giving France a constitution, announcing that it had become a constituent assembly for this specific purpose.

However, for neither the first time nor the last, those who had begun a moderate revolution found themselves confronted not only by the remains of reaction but also by the beginnings of more radical revolt as unrest spread from Paris and other towns to the countryside. The desire for change aroused by the *cahiers de doléance* combined with the wor-sening economic crisis, an accelerating collapse of law and order, and growing rumours of plans for punishment by the landlords to produce in the ranks of the peasantry in many parts of France a great fear of what might happen next. Many bands of peasants therefore rose up to attack the landlords and to destroy their property, losing all sense of duty and obedience to their former masters. The fear of those who owned property, bourgeois as well as noble, now became in its own way as great as that of the lowest orders of society. What was to be done? The National Assembly's short experience was of demanding concessions, not giving them. While the representatives of the Third Estate could only worry about what might become an attack on their own position, those from the nobility obliged with a declaration of their own reduction in law which they hoped would keep their class alive and still in possession of its property. On 4 August, in a night session of great emotion and powerful oratory, all the trappings of the feudal society, all the old rights and dues of the landlords as well as Church tithes and the sale of offices, were given up. The peasants were appeased, and went about their important business of collecting the harvest, not fully realising that they would still have to pay compensation for many of the concessions that had been graciously granted to them after they themselves had rudely seized them. From a longer perspective, then, it would be apparent not only that property rights had been secured, but also that the state would now be able to tax all its citizens.

On 26 August 1789 another milestone was reached, its inscription beginning: 'The representatives of the French people, organised in the National Assembly, considering that ignorance, forgetfulness, or contempt of the rights of man are the sole causes of public misfortunes and of the corruption of governments, have resolved to set forth in a solemn declaration the natural, inalienable, and sacred rights of man.' The Declaration of the Rights of Man and the Citizen went on to say that it had been issued as 'a perpetual reminder of their rights and duties' for 'all members of the social body', as well as a regulator of the legislative and executive power and a director of the demands of the citizens, 'founded henceforth upon simple and incontestable principles ... directed towards the maintenance of the Constitution and the welfare of all'. Therefore, 'in the presence and under the auspices of the Supreme Being', the National Assembly went on to list 17 rights, all summarised in the first two:

1. Men are born and remain free and equal in rights; social distinctions may be based only upon general usefulness.

2. The aim of political association is the preservation of the natural and inalienable rights of man; these rights are liberty, property, security, and resistance to oppression.

The basic support for the authority to assert and protect these rights was not to be found in a group or an individual, since 'The source of all sovereignty resides essentially in the nation', and 'Law is the expression of the general will'. Separation of powers as well as the guarantee of rights would guarantee the basic constitution.[1] So now the French Revolution had followed in the wake of the British Revolution of 1688 and the American Revolution of 1776 as well as curing many of the ills of the French old regime. Every citizen could now speak, write, and print freely, and would pay for his protection through a common tax assessed equally on all citizens in proportion to their means.

In the new heady atmosphere, with daily political meetings in Paris and a great flood of publications in favour of the National Assembly as it set about its task of completing the constitution, Louis made one last effort to move up his troops and thus to exploit what differences could be found between the deputies opposing him and those still prepared to give him their support. A combination of this threat and an even more serious economic situation, with the all-important price of bread going up yet again, led to more of the Revolution's most famous days. On 5 October, rumours of soldiers trampling on the red, white and blue cockade that had become the most common symbol of the new order, as well as their growing concern for the welfare of their families, persuaded a crowd of Parisian women to march off to Versailles to complain to the king. Even the National Guard could not prevent the royal bodyguards being massacred, mostly by men, in the ensuing clash. On 6 October, Louis was obliged to move to Paris, where he was put under the protection of the National Assembly, whose August decrees abolishing feudalism and declaring rights he was also obliged to accept. France was now a constitutional monarchy in theory, but would their deputies in the National Assembly be able or willing to restrain the as yet unstilled disturbance of the people?

A negative answer was soon given to this question, partly because of external pressures, which we will consider below, and partly from internal developments, which we will examine now. For about a year, the constitutional monarchy struggled on, although the king and some members of the clergy and nobility wanted to put the clock back while others, mostly from the Third Estate, pushed it forward. There were further moves towards the sweeping away of the debris of feudalism. The *parlements* made their final departure from the scene, as a new judicial system and a new arrangement of provincial administration were uniformly applied throughout the length and breadth of the nation. However, there were a few discordant setbacks for liberty and equality in October 1789, the first of these mostly harmonious months: slavery was accepted as a necessity for the colonies, and restrictions on the franchise were accepted as a necessity for France. In the first case, human beings were recognised as property; in the second, human beings without property were not given full recognition. In other words, those who laboured every day for others were denied citizenship; only those citizens who paid in taxes a sum equal to the wages to be gained from three days' labour would be able to vote in future elections. To be worthy of holding offices, a citizen would need to meet a higher qualification, while those citizens who might want to protest about having no property at all were restrained by a law prescribing the introduction of martial law in the event of future popular disturbances.

The seeds of dissension were sown in the lower ranks of the Third Estate in spite of the National Assembly's attempt to stop them. Even greater immediate problems arose from the policy adopted towards the First Estate. Among the feudal dues abolished in August 1789 were the tithes that helped to pay the parish priests. The nationalisation of its lands in November 1789 removed a further source of the Church's income, while both this measure and the dissolution of monasteries and convents in February 1790 led to discussion of a more comprehensive reform of the First Estate. On the principles of reason, equality and justice, together with not a little religious devotion, a new arrangement for the Church was drawn up by the National Assembly which included such democratic principles as the abolition of redundant bishoprics and the election of the clergy. Full civic equality was granted to Protestants and Jews. Like other institutions of the old regime, however, the First Estate was not happy with the loss of its independent existence and its incorporation into the framework of the new constitution, nor could it, as a Roman Catholic body, be happy with the failure to consult its head, the Pope. In turn, the reluctance of clergymen to accept the new arrangements led by November 1790 to an impatient National Assembly imposing on them an oath of allegiance to the constitution. Barely half of the ordinary clergymen and only a handful of bishops accepted this imposition, and when the Pope broke a long silence to express his opposition to the new arrangement, these numbers decreased still further. A problem arose similar to that in seventeenth-century England, Scotland and Ireland, as those who refused to take the oath were looked on with suspicion as possible counter-revolutionaries, which is what more than a few of them actually became. This development forced the National Assembly and its supporters to ask themselves the question, on whose side was God?

The problem became more serious when doubts arose about the loyalty to the constitution of its keystone, the king, whose authority to rule by divine appointment had previously been given its essential support by the First Estate. Now that the issue of the loyalty of the clergy was becoming increasingly serious against a background of continuing, even worsening, economic depression and social discontent, Louis XVI had the opportunity to guarantee his own future by removing any doubts about his own attachment to the new order. But the weight of tradition, of the 15 previous Louis and other predecessors, as well as his own character and that of his immediate advisers, was too much for him. There ensued on 20 June 1791 another of the famous moments of the Revolution, the flight of the royal family from Paris and their capture at Varennes on their way to exile in the Austrian Netherlands.

The flight to Varennes was significant as well as colourful, for it took the Revolution further towards a radical turning. On the one hand, supporters of the old regime at home were pushed towards a firmer stand, while those abroad attempted more energetically than before to stir up a war of intervention. On the other hand, the Parisian crowd along with some politicians and many journalists agitated for the creation of a republic. Debate was almost continual in political clubs, of which the radical Jacobin was the most famous. In the middle, the majority of the National Assembly whose dissatisfaction had been settled by the creation of constitutional monarchy attempted to make excuses for the king's action. Two years and three days after the storming of the Bastille, on 17 July 1791, there occurred an event that widened the gap between conservatives and radicals even further, the killing of about 50 demonstrators in favour of a republic by the agency called into being to protect the first stage of the Revolution, the National Guard. In the next few months, the members of the National Assembly that had acted as the Constituent Assembly of the moderate new order made further attempts to preserve it. But through the idealistic gesture of forbidding their own membership of the Legislative Assembly that was to come into being after the formal declaration of the constitution on 1 October 1791, they made it even more likely that after them would come the deluge. The king himself made matters worse by his veto of two laws passed against clergymen who refused to take the oath and *émigrés* who refused to return home.

The most radical or 'Jacobin' members of the Legislative Assembly, usually called the Girondins after the region of origin of some of their leaders (the Gironde, to the south-west around Bordeaux), were therefore able to make their voices heard above the rest. Their inclination turned in the direction of the ultimate solution for disunity and disaffection, a declaration of war on 20 April 1792 against what they claimed were ever more threatening foreign enemies of the Revolution. This would make the dissidents at home either join those who had already left their native land or forget their own grievances and move over to its defence. War was also welcome to those who had gone into exile, including many noble army officers who now believed that they could bring that exile to an end by joining in the suppression of the Revolution. A smaller number of their comrades in arms who had stayed at home now believed that the moment was approaching for the introduction of martial law. Opposition to the war came from a minority of political activists, including some who believed that it would completely ruin chances of compromise with the king and others who feared that it would imperil the possibility of the Revolution's further development in a more radical direction. A leader of the latter group soon to become more prominent was Maximilien Robespierre.

REPUBLIC AND TERROR, 1792–4

Defeats following early victories in the war appeared to be making a reality of the fears of the second group, but in fact they dashed the remaining hopes of the first group. The Revolution was about to take a radical turn. Louis XVI accepted the constitutional limits on his power but also contributed to his own downfall by his use of the royal veto, while the war made its contribution by intensifying the already serious economic problems. The new demands of the crowd, in which the most vocal part was played by the *sans-culottes* (those not wearing the knee-breeches of the upper classes), were enough to frighten the breeches off those who did wear them. The *sans-culottes* were not the lowest of all in the social scale, but rather artisans and small shopkeepers who stood to gain from the fullest implementation of the Revolution's avowed aims. The crowd they led was not a seething, anarchic mob, but possessed a real enough measure of organisation and direction. It helped to give strength and purpose to the Commune of Paris, which was now to seize power from the Legislative Assembly. As the news from the front grew worse in the summer of 1792, even the Girondins could not hold the Assembly together, as it hastened its own dissolution by introducing the unpopular measure of conscription as a means of strengthening the National Guard of the capital and its provincial counterparts. On 2 June, 29 Girondins were arrested. On 10 August, an insurrection took place under the direction of the Commune in which an army of regulars and irregulars stormed the royal palace of the Tuileries. Hundreds of lives were lost in the ensuing scrap, but the Commune was victorious. It insisted that the monarchy must be overthrown and a more democratic republic brought into being through the election of a national Convention.

Before this new body could meet, the Parisian crowd decided on further action. Three years before, it had stormed the royal prison known as the Bastille to release its political inmates. Now, it attacked prisons throughout Paris to kill their political inmates, counter-revolutionary suspects who were thought to be plotting a mass, murderous break-out. A measure of the intensification of the Revolution was that while hardly any candidates for rescue could be found on 14 July 1789, well over 1000 'conspirators' were murdered on 2 September 1792. Terror had arrived by popular demand before the Republic was officially declared by the Convention on 20 September. But as better news from the front helped to restore calm behind the lines, the Convention was given a respite of several months in which to debate orderly procedures towards the furtherance of revolutionary aims. Could further terror be avoided? And, in particular, could the life of the king be saved?

The previously radical Girondins of the Legislative Assembly now found themselves playing the part of moderates in the National Convention. They sought to act as a restraint on the Commune of Paris, while another group, known as the Montagnards (men of the mountain, because of their occupancy of the high back benches in the Convention), assumed the role indicated by their position to the left of the tribune, the raised platform at the front of the meeting. They demanded that the king should be brought to justice in order to protect the new order, although everybody knew that this would mean a summary trial and execution. The Montagnards were not necessarily in favour of following every whim of the *sans-culottes*, but they quickly realised that they would have to mobilise the crowd's support in order to take the revolutionary government's policies in the direction that they wished to follow. Herein lay the reason for both their immediate success and their later downfall.

After some brief delaying actions, the Girondins and their supporters could no longer hold back the execution of the king, who went to the guillotine on 21 January 1793. While the international situation deteriorated, widespread revolt in favour of the Church and the monarchy flared up in the west, especially in the Vendée to the south of the Loire. The *sans-culottes* pressed for a more vigorous prosecution of the foreign war and an intensification of the terror at home. A Committee of Public Safety was set up and other measures for the introduction of 'revolutionary government' were taken in the early spring of 1793. In the early summer, Marie-Antoinette followed her husband to the guillotine, while over 100 Girondins were arrested by units of the National Guard, itself now under more radical leadership than at the time of its formation.

Whatever such measures may have done to raise the morale of the Montagnards and their supporters in Paris, they brought despondency and alarm to citizens of more moderate outlook in the provinces. In midsummer 1793, nearly three-quarters of the departments of France (60 out of 83) were disaffected from the central government. Accused of plotting a 'Federalism' that would destroy the Republic, the provinces were in fact far from united in their policies or actions. This circumstance left them open to suppression one by one, although it was not until the end of the year that several of the important cities of France – Bordeaux, Lyon, Marseille and Toulon (briefly occupied by the British) – had been reincorporated firmly in the Republic, a process which involved the introduction of the Terror into the provinces. In Lyon, for example, a commission set up to restore order in November issued an Instruction declaring that representatives of the people and units of the army would collaborate in order 'To punish traitors and seek out conspirators; to revive the energy of the *sans-culottes*; to assure a regular supply of food to the armies and the civil population; and, above all, to compensate the poor and suffering portion of the People for the losses caused them by the crimes of the rich counter-revolutionaries'. These aims, as well as the further fostering of national morale, would be achieved by the introduction of 'total revolution': the arrest of suspects, the revolutionary taxation of the rich and the extirpation of fanaticism. The counter-revolutionaries had relied on the rich landowners, daring to believe that 'famine would conquer France for slavery'. The edifice of this slavery had been raised up gradually over 1300 years by the priests, who were 'the sole cause of the misfortunes of France'. Therefore, the Instruction recommended the slogan on the banners of the *sans-culottes* – 'Peace with the cottages, war against châteaux', to which might almost be added, destruction to the churches.[2] Certainly there were many attacks on property in late 1793, as well as a large number of executions, over four-fifths of the death sentences during the period known as the Terror being passed in the provinces, and nearly half the executions (about 7000 out of 16,500) taking place between December 1793 and January 1794.

Meanwhile, the second half of 1793 had been eventful in Paris. The Convention hurried through a new Constitution in June, and then suspended it for the duration of the emergency. It revolutionised the national army, obliging every citizen to mobilise in its support in August. The *sans-culottes* also managed to force through their demands for more stringent controls on food prices and more energetic prosecution of suspects. In September a new calendar was introduced, with the second year of liberty proclaimed as beginning on 21 September, one year to the day from the abolition of the monarchy. There was much discussion and a considerable amount of legislation concerning 'revolutionary government', one of the more coherent views being put forward by Maximilien de Robespierre (1758–94), who emerged soon after the introduction of the new calendar as a powerful leader supported by the Committee of Public Safety. Seeing himself rather as a 'Legislator' embodying the 'General Will', Robespierre argued that a new despotism must be created to remove the remains of the old, which could not disappear immediately since it had taken many centuries to build up. Moreover, the war necessitated a suspension of the Constitution, although this did not mean the abandonment of all controls on government. Robespierre declared on 25 December 1793:

> If the revolutionary government must be forceful in its actions and freer in its movements than ordinary government, is it then any less just, less legitimate? No! It is based on the most sacred of laws, the safety of the people; on the most unchallengeable of all authorities, necessity.
>
> It too has its rules, based on justice and public order. It has nothing in common with anarchy or disorder – on the contrary, its aim is to repress them and so establish and consolidate the rule of law. It has nothing in common with arbitrary power, for it must be directed not by private passions but by public interest.[3]

Robespierre's arguments, and the man himself, have often not been taken seriously enough. The Revolution was undoubtedly in danger, and extraordinary times did indeed call for extraordinary measures. Nevertheless, in the months following his Christmas Day speech of 1793 (le 5 nivôse An II according to the new calendar), he became the victim of his own excesses. In the spring of 1794, Robespierre and the Committee of Public Safety turned the Terror into a means of consolidating their dictatorship by using it to remove the leaders of the Commune of Paris. But the strain of these policies warped the dictatorship's powers of judgement, and it did not seem to know when to stop the work of the guillotine. Doing all he could to make a virtue out of what he saw as a necessity, Robespierre organised a Cult of the Supreme Being, whom critics could not avoid identifying as the self-image of Robespierre himself. Having lost the support of the *sans-culottes*, Robespierre also withdrew from the bickering of the Committee of Public Safety. His last, long speech to the Convention on 26 July (le 8 Thermidor) made much of 'virtue' and 'purity' and the need to remove just a few more men who stood in the way of their final triumph, but it met with a deafening silence. During two days of

ensuing confusion, Robespierre was arrested along with about 20 supporters, and on 28 July he followed most of them to their last
experience, the short, sharp shock of the enlightened mode of execution invented by Dr Guillotin. About 70 councillors of the reformed
Commune also implicated in the 'Robespierrist Conspiracy' were
executed on the following day.

THERMIDOR AND THE DIRECTORY, 1795–9

The new regime has been associated with the summer month in which
it took power – Thermidor coming to signify reaction. But were the
men who overthrew Robespierre and his supporters indeed reaction-
aries, or rather sensible moderates seeking nothing more than the
restoration of peace and quiet along with the consolidation of the Revolution? They were mostly united by the desire to bring the Terror
associated with Robespierre to an end, even if this meant that they
would have to continue at least a little terror of their own. Beyond that,
whether they wanted to or not, they would certainly have to do
something, since the situation in France was still too fluid and the
international situation too dangerous for them to pursue a policy
of inaction. Therefore, after the reduction of the influence of the
Committee of Public Safety and other such bodies in the provinces,
accompanied by the liberation of thousands of 'suspects', the new
government found itself the unwitting promoter of a counter-Terror or
'White' Terror, in which those who wore knee-breeches made a return
to the streets of Paris and other towns to persecute the *sans-culottes* and
others deemed responsible for the preceding years of discomfort.
Remaining Montagnards in the Convention tried to steer a middle
course on such vexed questions as that of religion, declaring that there
was no established Church, but this did not appease the new mood
sweeping the country.

The bitter winter of early 1795 brought a renewal and intensification of economic distress, which the abandonment of price controls
did nothing to relieve. In the spring, the *sans-culottes* made a last
desperate effort to secure better supplies of food and to bring back the
Constitution of 1793 through occupation of the Convention chamber
on 1 April 1795 (le 12 Germinal An III). After some hesitation or
stalling for time, the Convention took a turn to the right by calling on

the army to suppress the *sans-culottes* and their associates. The arrest of thousands and the execution of about 20 led to the loss of confidence on the part of the rest. The Convention also accelerated its progress towards a new arrangement of government.

At the centre was the Directory, an executive body of five to be chosen by the members of a new legislature to be composed of two councils, which were to be the central features of a new Constitution of the Year III devised by the Convention. Property was to form the basis of the right to vote for the councils, and even then the elections were to be roundabout and indirect so that any last vestiges of radical sympathy might be eliminated. But the Convention was able to use the opportunity of a British-backed invasion of *émigrés* in the summer of 1795 to decree that two-thirds of the members of the new legislature would have to come from its own ranks. In such a manner, it hoped, a measure of continuity would be preserved and the road laid down, not forwards to military dictatorship, but rather backwards towards the constitutional situation of 1791 without the king. That is, the leading members of the Third Estate would resume control without their lower-class associates. But it is never more difficult to turn the historical clock back than in times of revolution, and the attempt to return to 1791 from 1795 resulted in more turmoil. Fortunately for the Directory, the opposition to it also based its aims on the irrecoverable past. Thus the royalist sympathisers, frustrated by the closure to them of the electoral route to a reconquest of power, launched a revolt in Paris in the autumn of 1795. The Directory suppressed it by releasing from prison and rearming the *sans-culottes* and other anti-royalists, and by calling in the army. On 5 October, a detachment under an ambitious young officer named Napoleon Bonaparte brought the revolt to an end. While Napoleon himself went off for more famous victories before he himself was installed in Paris, the army remained.

In the spring of 1796, as the Directory moved against the radical left, a group of conspirators composed a 'Manifesto of Equals' which declared that the French Revolution was the precursor of another, much greater and more solemn and final, in which 'the new tyrants, the new hypocrites' would be trampled like the kings and priests before them. The conspirators did not seek a division of land, but announced instead:

We demand something more sublime and more equitable, common ownership or the community of possessions. No more private property: the earth belongs to no one, its fruits belong to everyone. We can no longer suffer the majority of men working and sweating in the service and for the good pleasure of a small minority.[4]

The actual conspiracy did not get very far, and the 'Manifesto of Equals' itself was not published, although other announcements were put up around Paris. But a clumsy uprising came to nothing, the Equals were betrayed and about 30 of them went to the guillotine about a year later. Their leader, Gracchus Babeuf, made a long and spirited defence at their trial of their views which became an inspiration for others in both the shorter and the longer run.

Thereafter, the Directory attempted to preserve the gains of 1789–91 in the context of continuing counter-revolution. In elections in the spring of 1797, most of the seats went to royalists and other conservatives, and the councils proceeded to pass laws friendly to former enemies of the Revolution such as *émigrés* and priests. In September, three more moderate Directors moved to replace the other right-wing two, and to nullify some of the spring election results. In the same month, the new or second Directory took a step from which previous administrations had shrunk, the renunciation of two-thirds of its debts. In the spring of 1798, the Directors demonstrated that their inclination to the left was indeed slight by nullifying new election results in which pro-Jacobin candidates achieved good results. However, a return of war and the continuance of domestic economic and political problems, including more revolts in the provinces, made the position of the Directors difficult to maintain in the summer of 1799. To restore order, the man on the white horse who had been waiting in the political wings at the same time as occupying the centre of the military stage at last made a decisive move. On 9 November 1799 (le 18 Brumaire 1799), Bonaparte dismissed the Directors and the councils, and established himself in power.

THE FRENCH REVOLUTION IN ITS INTERNATIONAL SETTING, 1789–99

The French Revolution put at least some flesh on the ideas of the later Enlightenment. In an often confused and contradictory manner, the experience of the decade 1789–99 demonstrated that the old order represented by absolute monarchy could be overthrown. Certainly, it was replaced by an order that might not have been as new as many of those who died in the ensuing struggles might have wished. Nevertheless, it gave more influence to some members of the Third Estate and somewhat reduced the preponderance of the First and Second Estates, helping to create a more modern society. This was more than enough to cause alarm and confusion throughout Europe and beyond, even in those countries where absolute monarchy had either been overthrown or had never even existed. The fact that the Revolution had occurred in France was of prime importance, for that country had not possessed just any old absolute monarchy but what was still widely believed on the eve of its fall to be the mightiest in Europe, still the worthy continuer of the France of Louis XIV. For this reason, the shock and the anxiety that the Revolution produced were all the greater. For this reason, too, other absolute monarchies held back from early intervention, not yet believing that Louis XVI was doomed to an extent sufficient for them to sink their own differences and unite in a war against revolutionary France for his and their own protection. Meanwhile, the course taken by the French Revolution was very much influenced by the direction of international relations throughout the last decade of the eighteenth century. Therefore, to give the Revolution its full significance and to determine its essential nature, we must place it in the context of Europe, and indeed of the wider world.

Let us begin by examining the manner in which other governments were made anxious about the possible spread of the idea of revolution into their own countries, and into their empires. While the cry 'Long live Robespierre' was certainly heard in Africa,[5] most of that continent and of Asia too did not feel the shock waves that spread from Paris as much as North and South America and the rest of Europe. The United States barely avoided war with France towards the end of the eighteenth century, in spite of the advice to steer away from such difficulties contained in the farewell message of its retiring first president, George Washington. In the summer of 1798, with the support of the second president, John Adams, the US Congress passed the Alien and Sedition Acts, making the position of suspicious immigrants uncomfortable and imposing fines and even imprisonment for various kinds of opposition to the government. A crisis of Spanish rule in Mexico was to be followed by events of some importance in Latin America at the beginning of the nineteenth century.

Back across the Atlantic, in south-west Europe, the Spanish and Portuguese governments were worried about possible threats to their overseas empires, and both also exhibited considerable concern about sympathy for the French Revolution at home. There were a number of enthusiasts in Madrid and Lisbon for the new developments taking place across the Pyrenees, but the respective police forces were active in their suppression, while loyalties to 'Religion, King and Country' generally held fast, in the Spanish case especially after the French army began to invade in 1793. The various old regimes of the Italian peninsula were affected in different ways. While towns from Naples to Turin possessed their Jacobin circles of middle-class and aristocratic enthusiasts, there was little attempt at coordination between them. Moreover, the problem of establishing connections with the lower classes was difficult everywhere, and also depended on local situations that had developed over centuries. In particular, there was already a wide gap between the south, which had been under Spanish influence, and the north and centre, where the Austrians were dominant. However, at least a few stirrings of the need for Italian liberation and unification were felt.

The most immediate and greatest impact of the French Revolution was made on those countries in the immediate vicinity, France's neighbours in the north-west of Europe. The message quickly crossed the Channel, and groups of sympathisers were formed in England, Scotland and Ireland. In England, constitutional and reform societies were founded in a number of towns, while a range of older organisations adapted themselves to the new developments. In parliament, members of a Society of the Friends of the People made a response to the anti-revolutionary views being put forward by Edmund Burke and others. Outside parliament, there was evidence of the English *sans-culottes* bestirring themselves in the shape of a London Corresponding Society made up largely of tradesmen and craftsmen. The *Annual Register* for 1791 lamented that throughout Europe:

> The progress of gradual improvement stopped; manners, morals, religion on a precipice; the internal system of every country disquieted; and new factions created in all, which threaten long to agitate and

convulse this quarter of the globe, to extinguish in one extreme or the other, all love of well-regulated liberty, and to overthrow the general balance of power, so necessary to the public security.[6]

In its Preface to the 1792 volume, the *Annual Register* spoke of the period that it was discussing as 'the most critical and interesting in the present century, perhaps in the whole succession of centuries from the reign of Charlemagne'. Certainly, in that year the government under the younger Pitt decided that it was time to stop the rot, and made a number of moves against dissidents in England and Scotland. Hardest hit were a group of Scotsmen sent to exile in Botany Bay, Australia, for their part in organising a British Convention in 1793. In Ireland, there was the most widespread disaffection among urban intellectuals and peasants in the countryside, and ruthless suppression was inflicted. In the summer of 1800, in the vain hope of pacifying that troubled island, parliament passed a Bill effecting Union with it. Ireland was not the British government's only overseas problem, as we shall soon see, and its attention was often distracted from events in France by those in the empire and elsewhere in Europe.

Meanwhile across the Channel, there were stirrings in the Dutch United Provinces (Holland) and in the Austrian Netherlands (Belgium). The Dutch Patriots revived somewhat in 1789, but did not become very active until the French invasion of 1795. The Belgian revolt against Austrian domination took on new energy, but its aristocratic leadership turned against democratic rivals, and the ensuing divisions left the way open for the return of the Austrian armies at the beginning of 1790. Here also the ensuing war was to exert considerable influence. Northern Europe was not as profoundly affected as the north-west, although there were some stirrings in both Denmark and Sweden.

To the east, an earlier supporter of the Enlightenment, Catherine the Great of Russia, now turned against it, persecuting some dissident intellectuals as well as dreading a repetition of the 'Great Fear' of 1773–5, the Pugachev Revolt. Moreover, she was not alone in anxiety about Poland, where there was not only the possibility of peasant unrest but the actuality of a new constitution introduced with the support of the king. While the model was more British than French, Catherine moved to stop the rot through intervention and a second Partition with Frederick William II of Prussia early in 1793, just over

20 years after the first. From March 1794, a veteran of the American Revolution, General Tadeusz Kosciuszko, led a rising in which he encouraged the peasants to join by proclaiming the end of serfdom. But not enough support was forthcoming, either from the peasants or from the landlords, or from revolutionary France. Early in 1795, Russia, Prussia and Austria agreed a third Partition. Meanwhile, developments in France were not without their influence in the Balkans to the south-east, where the Ottoman Empire was concerned about internal stability as well as external threat.

In Austria, the death occurred early in 1790 of Joseph II. His brother and successor, Leopold II, attempted to work as a constitutional emperor through the diets and estates from Hungary to the Nether-lands. Soon conscious of the difficulties of such an approach in the face of the Jacobin sympathies to be found even in these narrowly representative bodies, Leopold became more reactionary before his death in the early spring of 1792, when he was succeeded by his eldest son. Francis II (1792–1835) was less prone to compromise. In Prussia, the successor of Frederick the Great, Frederick William II (1786–97), was not so much bothered by the support given to the Revolution by people such as Junker army officers and middle-class academics as by the opposition to his rule from peasants and others in Silesia. As far as Germany in general was concerned, French influence was strongest in the principalities of the Rhineland, where there was endemic peasant disturbance and some apprehension on the part of the authorities that middle-class activists might attempt to take advantage of the circum-stances to promote their own anti-seigneurial revolution. While we must be careful not to exaggerate the extent to which the Rhineland or any other part of Europe was likely to witness anything like a repetition of the events taking place in Paris, we must also recognise that gov-ernments throughout Europe were to a considerable degree alarmed about such possibilities and included them in their calculations of the best policies to be pursued at home and abroad.

THE FRENCH REVOLUTION AND INTERNATIONAL RELATIONS, 1789–99

The importance of international relations for the French Revolution is underlined by the bellicose words of 'La Marseillaise', which became the battle hymn of the new republic after being brought to Paris by volunteers marching from the south in the summer of 1791.

In the opening year of the French Revolution, 1789, Sweden was at war with Russia, while Russia and Austria were at war with Turkey. At the very least, these conflicts distracted the attention of the powers concerned from the events taking place in France, on which they might otherwise have tried to bring their earlier influence to bear. Equally, Britain and Prussia, to name but two, were unhappy at the extension of the influence of their rivals into the Ottoman Empire. Prussia was prepared to join in the war and mobilised its troops in Silesia on the frontier of the Austrian Empire early in 1790. If Prussia had taken its action further, much of Europe would have been involved in a great war concerned with the settlement of the Eastern Question. Intervention in France would have been altogether unlikely, and the course taken by the Revolution would therefore have been different.

Similarly, Britain was perturbed about Russian gains on the Black Sea, and early in 1791 decided to send a naval squadron there and a whole fleet to the Baltic Sea to thwart Catherine the Great's ambitions. There was a possibility of combining action with Prussian troops on the frontiers of Livonia, and an ultimatum was sent to St Petersburg. However, Dutch reluctance to collaborate, British public opposition and the younger Pitt's statesmanship averted the conflict until Russia made the Peace of Jassy with Turkey at the beginning of 1792. Pitt was also concerned about his wider imperial responsibilities, bringing to an end through the Nootka Convention of October 1790 a dispute with Spain about the share of rights of commerce, navigation and settlement on the Pacific coast north of San Francisco. As far as France in particular was concerned, Britain had made a commercial agreement with it in September 1786, according to which some tariffs between the two countries were lowered and others removed. But, as Arthur Young noted, many French merchants were not happy with the new competition. There was also alarm in Britain about the extension of French influence in the United Provinces in 1787, which was resolved by Dutch defensive treaties in April 1788 with Britain and Prussia, who also drew up a similar agreement between themselves. The attention of this combination was then drawn to developments in eastern Europe.

Just as the British Revolution of 1688 and the American Revolution of 1776 had been influenced by the international setting in which they took place, so now was the French Revolution of 1789. There were also lines of continuity going back to the Thirty Years War, to traditional French concern for the Rhineland, as well as to the location there of some of the principalities within the cumbersome framework of the Holy Roman Empire. The Emperor, Leopold II, composed the Austrian differences with Prussia in the summer of 1790. Then, after the French royal flight to Varennes about a year later, he proceeded to make a joint declaration with King Frederick William II concerning the difficult position of Louis XVI, whose wife, Marie-Antoinette, was his sister. The declaration increased the alarm in France itself about the activities of the *émigrés* in the Rhineland and elsewhere, and about their agitation for counter-revolutionary intervention in the homeland. Moreover, the dismantling of the feudal system after August 1789 had perturbed the imperial princes in Alsace by the Rhine about their position in France, and they appealed to the emperor for confirmation of their status. Leopold II delayed any decision, although he succeeded in antagonising the French revolutionaries by the manner in which he addressed them. Ambiguities about the imperial policy were removed by the death of Leopold II and the accession of Francis II early in 1792. The new emperor took a tougher line than his father, while the French government was also becoming more radical in its international outlook, and so, in April 1792, France declared war on Austria and Prussia.

Although under threat of attack from both the German and Italian sides (since Piedmont was also anxious to suppress the Revolution), France soon beat back a mostly Prussian invasion. The French stand at Valmy in September showed clearly that the new nation was capable of successful military action, and caused Goethe to declare that a new chapter in world history had begun. France now carried the fight to its enemies in the Rhineland, occupying Mainz and moving into the Austrian Netherlands. To the south, Nice and Savoy were taken over. The French government began in its own way to echo Louis XIV's expansionist view of his glory as it executed his descendant and put forward its view of the natural frontiers of the Republic. Early in 1793 it declared war on other potential enemies: Spain, Holland and Britain. The last and most powerful of these was especially alarmed at the threat posed to both the Austrian Netherlands and Holland, and attempted to force it back by instituting, in conjunction with Russia, a grain blockade on France. The French government was able to make use of this and other hostile gestures to extend the Terror in an effort to solve its domestic problems. Meanwhile, Prussia was joining with Russia in the second Partition of Poland at the beginning of 1793, while Austria watched this division with jealousy and alarm.

Impetus for carrying the war to France in a concerted fashion came from the British government, with Pitt following the traditional policy of paying subsidies to some of the lesser German states as well as to Piedmont, and attempting to revive against revolutionary France the approach that had succeeded against Louis XIV – that of alliance. The First Coalition, as it became known, was formed early in 1793, and consisted principally of Russia, Prussia, Austria, Holland, Naples, Spain and Portugal in addition to Britain. However, it was some time before the coalition moved from agreement to action, largely because of the continued preoccupation of Russia, Prussia and Austria with Poland, which they subjected to a third Partition that was finalised in the autumn of 1795. All the members of the coalition had their own special interests, even Britain, the most active of them, giving considerable attention to its overseas interests, which now included taking advantage of the French government's embarrassment at a huge slave revolt in the Caribbean island of Saint Domingue (later Haiti) in particular. Consequently the coalition was falling apart by 1795, leaving France in control of the left bank of the Rhine and of the Low Countries. In 1796, Spain switched sides to resume its previous alliance with France.

The general conscription leading to the making of the 'nation in arms' gave the French army a significant numerical as well as an ideological advantage over many of its enemies. At the cost of enormous hardships and deprivations, many victories had been won even before the appearance on the scene of the most famous victor of them all, Napoleon Bonaparte. This name began to be heard widely as France under the Directory moved against Austrian dominions in Italy, taking Piedmont out of the war on the way. The Peace of Campo Formio in October 1797 marked the Austrian recognition of its defeat in Italy and is usually taken to mark the end of the First Coalition as well. Napoleon quickly set about his first exercises in empire building, superimposing upon Italy a design which essentially made the north his own while the south retained a measure of independence. Switzerland soon became a virtual protectorate in the shape of the Helvetian Republic, and this and other developments in 1798 made France's enemies even more anxious about how far its natural frontiers would be extended.

Britain, the principal remaining enemy of France, tried to work towards the formation of a second coalition. While continuing to enjoy mastery of the seas, albeit at the expense of serious naval mutinies in the spring and summer of 1797, Pitt's government still had to overcome the problem of restraining France on land. This could only be solved through the formation of a new and more successful alliance, which Pitt and his government duly attempted to create. But the tensions in central and eastern Europe had by no means fully disappeared, and a further complication arose towards the end of 1796 with the death of the Empress Catherine of Russia. Her son Paul drew back from the commitments that his mother had appeared to be making, and aimed at keeping Russia out of war so that he could concentrate on an ambitious programme of domestic reform. However, like Catherine before him, he grew alarmed at the threat that France seemed to be posing to Russia's growing interests in the Mediterranean area through its expansion from Italy into the Ionian Islands off the west coast of Greece and into Malta. Since he had become protector of the Knights of Malta, his chivalric honour as well as the national interest obliged him to make a stand. Russia was not the only Mediterranean power alarmed at the spread of French influence. Turkey was especially apprehensive after the invasion of its dependency of Egypt on 1 July 1798. It declared war on its former ally France and made an alliance with its former enemy Russia as well as with Britain. A joint Russo-Turkish force drove the French from the Ionian Islands early in 1799. Soon, with the assistance of a British naval detachment under Nelson, Naples was to rid itself of the French invader.

Meanwhile, further to the north, another somewhat uneasy combination of the Russian and Austrian armies under the veteran commander Suvorov was driving the French out of the upper part of the Italian peninsula and moving on the Helvetian Republic in Switzerland. Still further to the north, the French were pushed back across the Rhine. The forces of what became known as the Second Coalition experienced worse fortunes in the Low Countries, however. Britain managed to land a force in Holland in the autumn of 1799, which was joined by another from Russia, but problems of supply and disease combined with disagreements among the joint leadership to turn early success into near disaster, and the invaders had to plead with the French to allow their evacuation about one month after the invasion.

There were recriminations over the Dutch campaign and over action elsewhere. Emperor Paul of Russia was hurt that the British would not allow his forces to participate in the occupation of Malta after they had retaken it in September 1798. The Austrian Emperor Francis II was suspicious of British intentions towards the former Austrian Netherlands (Belgium), while lack of confidence between his army and that of Russia made it impossible to launch a projected invasion of France from Switzerland. The British and the Russians were both unhappy about the evident Austrian intention of exploiting allied successes to reimpose a presence in Italy, as the Austrian army was sent in that direction rather than into France. The deserted Suvorov was left with his now exclusively Russian force to fight a rearguard action and then beat a spectacular retreat across the Alps into Germany. Paul left the coalition, a break with Britain soon following that with Austria. By the beginning of 1800, the Second Coalition was dead.

NAPOLEON AND INTERNATIONAL RELATIONS, 1799–1807

By this time, however, good news for the coalition's former members had come from Egypt, where another temporary answer had been given to the Eastern Question by Napoleon's return to France in August for his assumption of power in November. French forces did not finally leave until a British–Turkish force drove them out in September 1801, but even before Napoleon's departure it was apparent that victories on land could not be fully exploited while British fleets under Nelson and others succeeded from August 1798 in cutting effective French communications with Europe.

Although Napoleon could no longer emulate Alexander the Great in a march to India to strike at the British Empire, there was still ample opportunity for him in Europe to follow and even outshine Caesar. We shall now consider his spectacular progress towards such an achievement, leaving his domestic policies for later attention. Napoleon would resume his string of victories where it had begun, in Italy. In June 1800, after a somewhat untidy march across the Alps with a rapidly mustered army, he claimed a decisive victory over the Austrians at Marengo. Another French force was moving forward again in Germany and soon enjoyed victories over the Austrians there. In February 1801, with the Peace of Lunéville, France was able to recoup the gains of Campo Formio nearly three and a half years before, and to extend them, in Belgium and on the left bank of the Rhine as well as in Italy.

At the end of 1800, with French encouragement, Russia, another former member of the Second Coalition, had taken the lead in an Armed Neutrality League, in which Prussia, Denmark and Sweden also joined to counter Britain's exploitation of its mastery of the seas, which included infringement of the rights of neutral shipping. Bonaparte also hoped that the Emperor Paul might be moved by his resentment of the policies of his former British ally at sea and his former Austrian ally on land to move closer towards accommodation with him, but Paul was assassinated at the beginning of March 1801, and his successor, Alexander I, was not immediately attracted to the idea of following in his father's footsteps. A month later, Nelson's attack on the Danish fleet by Copenhagen brought the League of Armed Neutrality to an end. But Britain, so severely overextended that the dreaded income tax had to be introduced in 1799, was in no position to follow up this victory, especially since the capable younger Pitt had resigned and a determination to carry the fight to the French departed with him. Negotiations began for a peace agreement, finally signed at Amiens on 27 March 1802. Britain agreed to give up most of its recent conquests, except for Ceylon, which had been taken from Holland, and Trinidad, which had been taken from Spain. For its part, France agreed to withdraw completely from Naples to the south and also from the Papal States in the centre of Italy. Egypt would return to Turkey, and Malta to the Knights.

Napoleon could be reasonably content with the results of the first phase of his occupation of the office of first consul, which in 1802 he awarded himself for life. But he was not one for resting on his laurels, his ambition for further conquests being as certain as the smouldering resentment of his former enemies to bring about an early resumption of hostilities. Napoleon had no set plan for the conquest of Europe; he was an improviser with a keen eye for the main chance but without much thought for the future, a good short-term schemer but a rather impractical long-term dreamer. An apt illustration of his cast of mind might be found in his Proclamation to the People of Egypt of 2 July 1798: 'you will be told that I have come to destroy your religion; do not believe it! Answer that I have come to restore your rights and punish the usurpers, and that … I respect God, his Prophet and the Koran.'[7] In fact, Napoleon had gone to Egypt for a mixture of motives, among which was the extension of his challenge to the greatest empire of his own time, the British, and the pursuit of a desire to outshine the greatest empire-builders of ancient times. He himself once said to an adviser: 'My mistress is power, but it is as an artist that I love power. I love it as a musician loves his violin.'[8] But his mistress was fickle, and he was never sure of the music that he was playing. Perhaps the most harmonious suggestion was made in exile in St Helena after his great victories had been followed by great defeats. If he had won in 1812, he said, his 'constitutional reign' would have begun, since he was 'the natural mediator in the struggle of the past against the Revolution', reconciling monarchy with republicanism. He had sought peace rather than war, but his opponents had not allowed it. With more time, he would have brought more national fulfilment: 'There are in Europe more than thirty million French, fifteen million Italians and thirty million Germans. I would have wished to make each of these peoples a single united body.' He would have restored the independence of the Poles, whose division into three parts must have encouraged his inclination towards frontier rearrangement and state reconstruction. Germany presented problems in these respects, and he had therefore tried first to 'simplify their complications', while in Italy he had attempted 'to supervise, guarantee and advance the national education of the Italians'. He had misjudged the pride of the Spanish in dethroning their Bourbon dynasty as part of his programme for regenerating Spain. Generally speaking: 'Europe thus divided into nationalities freely formed and free internally, peace between states would become easier; the United States of Europe would become a possibility.'[9]

In the aftermath of the Peace of Amiens in the spring of 1802, Napoleon soon found himself in dispute about the terms of that agreement with the other partners to it, especially Britain. The British government had reduced its war expenditure and abolished income tax, but could not bring about the promised peacetime prosperity. It was not happy with the continued French dominance of the Low Countries and other parts of Europe, while French policies in the wider world were if anything even more alarming. Across the Atlantic, France had forced Spain to hand over Louisiana on the North American continent and crushed the slave revolt in Saint Domingue (Haiti). In the Mediterranean, Napoleon was reviving his expansionist plans in a menacing fashion. He was building up the French navy as a practical demonstration of his intent to transform his plans into reality. As a counter to the French menace, the British government decided to hang on to Malta, the base in the Mediterranean from which it had agreed at Amiens to withdraw, while also demanding that France should quit Holland and Switzerland.

This meant war, finally declared by Britain in the spring of 1803. As soon as hostilities began, their former pattern reasserted itself in the shape of French control of the land, British control of the sea. Napoleon tried to break this familiar deadlock by building up an 'Army of Invasion' from about the end of 1803 to near the end of 1805. In a message to one of his admirals in the spring of 1804, he declared: 'Let us be masters of the Straits for six hours and we will be masters of the world.'[10] A conclusive response was given in October 1805, when Nelson won his final victory against a combined fleet of France and its recent ally Spain near the port of Cadiz at Trafalgar. Meanwhile Pitt, who had returned to power in the spring of 1804, was trying to make progress on land by means which had been found wanting but to which there was no alternative. Working towards a third coalition, he had to resume the payment of large subsidies to potential continental allies. Even with such financial assistance, the major powers of Europe were not keen to shoulder the burden of the actual fighting against such a formidable opponent as Napoleon. Prussia, Austria and Russia all had cause to be alarmed at French expansionism, but none of them wanted to be first in the field against it, and none of them trusted the others. Russia came nearest to taking action, being especially perturbed about the French threat in the Balkans and eastern Mediterranean. Austria, newly concerned with Napoleon's assumption of the crown of Italy and his extension of its domains, also mobilised. Neither Russia nor Austria was fully prepared for war, however, and Napoleon cleverly outmanoeuvred their joint army and then defeated it at Austerlitz at the beginning of December 1805. This was almost as significant a victory on land for Napoleon as Trafalgar had been a defeat at sea a month and a half before. On hearing the news of Austerlitz, Pitt allegedly looked at a map of Europe and declared: 'Roll up that map; it will not be wanted these ten years.' He died soon afterwards, and never knew that his forecast was almost exactly accurate.

Austria left the Third Coalition, making a peace with Napoleon before the end of 1805 which removed it completely from Italy and broke its authority in Germany. Prussia was obliged by the turn of the year to give up its neutrality, but received the much coveted prize of Hanover as an inducement to promising troops for possible further action against Russia and joining the French answer to Britain's blockade of Europe – the Continental System. Humiliating treatment at the hands of Napoleon, including the possibility of a snatch back of Hanover to offer to Britain as a peace offering, however, forced Frederick William III to make a stand. In October 1806 his well-drilled army was overwhelmed in barely a week by the improvisations of its new-style French counterpart. Napoleon's manoeuvrability was just too much for generals trained to think of warfare in a much more static and deliberate manner, avoiding battle while their enemy sought it out.

However, Napoleon was to discover that easy victories led the way to overwhelming defeat. Rapid advance involving the local acquisition of supplies succeeded brilliantly while such supplies could be found. This method of approach began to founder in Spain and Poland, and was later to collapse completely in Russia. At the end of 1806, confrontation with Russia seemed an immediate possibility, since war had broken out between Russia and Turkey, which had been for some years at peace with France. Encouraged by Napoleon's military successes, Turkey moved even closer to France while taking a less conciliatory attitude towards Russia. Napoleon took his advance further into Poland at the end of 1806, but soon found the going harder there than in Austria and Prussia, while also realising that his contact with Paris was becoming less certain the further he went away from it. Meanwhile, since the death of Pitt, Britain was taking less interest in continental affairs and more in the affairs of the empire. So Russia's consciousness that it was fighting France alone was underlined by a defeat of its army at Friedland in East Prussia in the summer of 1807. It was now clear to both Napoleon and Tsar Alexander I that they needed a breathing space and consequently they made their famous accommodation at Tilsit in East Prussia on 25 June 1807. The personalities of the two emperors certainly exerted an influence on the timing of their meeting as well as lending it colour, but both had been pushed towards agreement by the weight of the developments outlined above. In a series of treaties, France and Russia made some minor rearrangement of their respective spheres of influence, and also agreed to declare war on Britain should Russian mediation fail.

NAPOLEON AND INTERNATIONAL RELATIONS, 1807–15

Napoleon gained most from Tilsit, and he was to rise still higher before taking his harder fall. Russia was pushed back from the Mediterranean, and threatened by Napoleon's creation of a satellite Grand Duchy of Warsaw, which was carved out of Prussia's share of the partitions of Poland. Prussia also lost its Rhineland possessions, which became part of a newly created Kingdom of Westphalia. Austria's losses in Italy and Germany had been marked by the formal abolition of the Holy Roman Empire in 1806. This facilitated the creation of a large Confederation of the Rhine, of which Westphalia now became a part, along with Saxony, Bavaria, Würtemburg and other former members of that empire. Russia, Prussia and Austria were obliged to declare war on Britain, which Napoleon needed to defeat in order to complete his dominance of Europe.

His principal means of achieving the submission of Britain, now that the quick blow of invasion had been ruled out, was the slower strangulation of economic exclusion. Napoleon believed that this 'nation of shopkeepers' would not haggle about the price to be paid for its livelihood if its exports to the continent were sufficiently curtailed. Unfortunately for Napoleon, even though he tried to close all ports from Lisbon to St Petersburg to British ships, the task was too vast, particularly since the Continental System embodying the boycott of British goods brought as much ruin on those countries forced to become members as on the country they were attempting to exclude. The British navy was able to maintain mastery of the seas. For example, it kept open the Baltic, from which masts and other vital naval supplies were obtained, while also helping to find alternative markets for British goods in South America and other parts of the world. One unfortunate consequence of Britain's abuse of its mastery of the seas, however, was a war against the USA from 1812 to 1814, of which more below.

Although he could not bring Britain to submission, Napoleon and his Grand Empire enjoyed their finest years following Austerlitz, at least formally, even ceremoniously, as he shared the crowns of Europe out among his relations almost as if they were counters in some great game. The emperor's sense of theatre was fully indulged, as was the more wayward side of his temperament. Napoleon had crowned himself king of Italy in 1805, as well as later detaching some parts of it to include them in the French Empire. The Kingdom of Naples was created in 1806, and ruled first by Napoleon's brother Joseph, then by his brother-in-law Murat. The Kingdom of Holland was set up in 1806 for brother Louis, who found the task too much for him, however, and so Holland was annexed to France in the summer of 1810. In 1807 the newly created Kingdom of Westphalia went to brother Jerome, to whom Napoleon wrote on 15 November of that year:

What German opinion impatiently demands is that men of no rank, but of marked ability, shall have an equal claim upon your favour and your employment, and that every trace of serfdom, or of a feudal hierarchy between the sovereign and the lowest class of his subject, shall be done away with. The benefits of the Code Napoleon, public trial, and the introduction of juries, will be the leading features of your Government. And to tell you the truth, I count more upon their effects, for the extension and consolidation of your rule, than upon the most resounding victories.[11]

Here, amid all the self-indulgent glorification of the Bonaparte family, was a description of the concepts that were to give the Grand Empire some of its strength and coherence. These achievements must not be exaggerated, however, least of all in Spain, to which Joseph was transferred as king from Naples in the late spring of 1808, by which time a revolt was already in progress making impossible the full exertion of his new royal rule.

Indeed, under their gilt exterior, all the Napoleonic kingdoms enjoyed mixed fortunes, and by 1810 their creator was considering replacing them with an imperial system embracing the whole of Europe. The greatest ulcer in his grand imperial body remained Spain, which was already wracked with guerrilla warfare by the summer of 1808, when French agonies in the Iberian peninsula were intensified by the landing in Portugal of a British expeditionary force under the future Duke of Wellington. This arrival marked a change of strategy on the part of the British government, which had previously shrunk from sending troops to the continent. At the same time, this government also expanded its former strategy of subsidy, paying more, in materials as well as money, to its European allies. The immediate focus of attention was Portugal, where Wellington established a firm footing before his second, successful, invasion of Spain in the summer of 1809. An attempt at a raid on Holland at the same time was in vain, but Wellington in Spain went from strength to strength, from stout defence to bold attack, with an army of nearly 100,000 men, during the years 1810–12.

By this time, the Peninsular War, both through the anxiety it caused Napoleon, his family and friends on the one hand and the encourage-ment that it gave to their enemies on the other hand, had made a contribution to the outbreak of even more fateful hostilities at the other end of Europe. We must switch our attention there to examine the manner in which Napoleon came to launch his fateful invasion of Russia in 1812. As noted above, the alliance between Russia and France was one of shorter-term convenience rather than longer-term sym-pathy. However, before this alliance began to fall apart, Austria rose up in a vain attempt at revenge for earlier humiliation. Declaring war in the spring of 1809, Austria was defeated before the summer was over and was then subjected to more humiliation in the shape of the Peace of Schönbrunn. This took away the Austrian share of Poland, the last remaining piece of Austrian coastline on the Adriatic Sea, and even some upper parts of Austria itself, transferring them respectively to the Grand Duchy of Warsaw, the Kingdom of Italy and the Kingdom of Bavaria. Austria's disgrace was another, if brief, concern for Napoleon, who was also disconcerted by a promise of assistance from Tsar Alexander that never materialised. The tsar in turn was not happy about the growing threat to Russia posed by the Grand Duchy of Warsaw, even though he had been able to derive some comfort from the acquisition of Finland from Sweden after a brief war in 1808–9. He was then able to derive further reassurance about his Balkan flank in October 1811 by ending the war with Ottoman Turkey that had been in progress since 1806. The formal conclusion to the war, the Peace of Bucharest of May 1812, brought Russia the Danubian province of

Bessarabia. Napoleon's earlier worries about Russia were augmented by its stranglehold on the mouth of the River Danube.

Just over a month later, without a formal declaration, Napoleon invaded Russia with an army of 600,000 men. About 100,000 of these were Poles, who mistakenly hoped that their efforts would be rewarded by the re-establishment of their homeland. Others were foreign nationals pressed into service with the Grand Army. The French – both seasoned veterans and raw recruits – amounted to less than half the total. Altogether, then, this constituted a large but somewhat unwieldy force. Moreover, Napoleon found difficulty in engaging the Russian army in battle in the vastnesses of a terrain unlike anything he had experienced before. He was hoping for a quick victory that would reinforce the crumbling Continental System, from which Russia had been a major defector. For their part, in spite of some dissension among their upper ranks, the Russians withdrew as far as they could before making a stand outside Moscow early in September at widespread demand. As the cool, strategic analysis of Clausewitz said of the general who had now assumed command: 'Kutuzov, it is certain, would not have fought at Borodino where he obviously did not expect to win. But the voice of the Court, of the Army, of all Russia, forced his hand.'[12] The spirit of national resistance clearly demonstrated itself in the numbers of those prepared to make the ultimate sacrifice: over 50,000 Russians were killed and wounded, taking out about the same number of the enemy with them. Napoleon went on to Moscow, but this glittering prize was empty and soon destroyed, partly by the barbarism of the invaders, even more by the 'scorched earth' policy of the Russians which became a 'burnt city' policy. The mild weather of autumn flattered only to deceive, and Napoleon took some time to decide that the only thing to do after marching his Grand Army to Moscow was to march it back again. The severity of the early winter and the non-stop harrying by the Russian regular and irregular forces combined to wreak a terrible havoc on the Grand Army, whose remnants on their return to Poland totalled less than a tenth of the original number.

Having discovered that nothing succeeds like success, Napoleon was now to learn the more painful lesson that nothing fails like failure. The gambler general's winning streak came to an abrupt end, as Prussia and more belatedly Austria came in on the side of Russia, whose Emperor Alexander I began to assume some of the sense of mission for the leadership of Europe that was leaving the other emperor, Napoleon I. Meanwhile Britain, the other chief member of an emerging fourth coalition, made its contribution in blood by continuing the harassment of the French in the Peninsular War, and in materials by the supply of hefty subsidies and many armaments. In October 1813, in the so-called 'Battle of the Nations' near Leipzig, Napoleon inflicted considerable losses on his enemies, but suffered a decisive defeat. The map of Europe could now be rolled out again, even though Napoleon's skill managed to keep the war going until the spring of 1814, when he abdicated on 6 April. Alexander I was a generous victor, too generous for the liking of some of his allies, who all had further cause for alarm when Napoleon returned from exile on the Mediterranean island of Elba for the famous 'hundred days'. These came to a hard-fought climax on 18 June 1815 in the Battle of Waterloo, 'the nearest run thing you ever saw in your life' in the famous verdict of one of the victorious generals, the Duke of Wellington. It was now thought too dangerous to allow Napoleon to end his life as he had begun it, on a Mediterranean island, and so the last half-dozen years or so were spent on the much more remote South Atlantic island of St Helena.

This is an appropriate point at which to put the rise and fall of Napoleon in Europe in the context of the wider world. He himself perhaps thought less of this than at least one of his main opponents: the conquest of India was a dream for him; for his British enemy the defence of India was a vital necessity. And India formed only part of worldwide British overseas concerns. The British *Annual Register* for 1811 noticed a general broadening of focus for international relations by that year, changing the title of the historical part of the volume from 'The History of Europe' to 'General History' – 'the state of the world being now such, that information would be materially defective, were it to neglect the occurrences passing in the other quarters of the globe'.[13] As we have already noted, there was a growing British commercial interest in South America, especially after 1808. Partly because of this, tension built up with the former British colonies in North America, now the United States of America, which had also become an important trading partner. Napoleon added to the size and confidence of the USA through the sale of the huge province of Louisiana in 1803, just three years after he had taken it from Spain. This marked the end of Napoleon's hopes for a great transatlantic empire.

Expansion, to the north as well as the south, was an important part of the American agenda in the early nineteenth century, and the British in Canada were thought to be inhibiting the movement of Americans westward. At least as great a cause of resentment was the interference of the Royal Navy with American and other neutral shipping, which led to the prohibition of American trade with Britain. This cut off the outlet for about a quarter of the British export of manufactures as well as the source of cotton and other important raw material imports. British economic problems at the opening of the second decade of the nineteenth century were now at their most severe level of the whole Napoleonic period, and political stability was also threatened by widespread riots in the Midlands late in 1811. Then, in June 1812, the USA declared war on Britain, which was kept busy until the end of 1815 when the Treaty of Ghent was signed, settling none of the issues that had brought the war about. This Atlantic war was not without its connections with the war also beginning in 1812 in Europe. H. W. Wilson went so far as to note in 1905:

> Napoleon was on the eve of his invasion of Russia when the United States declared war; and continental opinion anticipated his speedy success – a success the more certain if British energy were directed to a new field in America. But for the disasters of the Russian campaign, followed by the crushing defeat of Leipzig, the war of 1812 might have rung the knell of freedom in Europe for a generation.[14]

As the bells of celebration rather than mourning rang out in 1815, there were those who wished to consolidate and extend British imperial possessions, perhaps taking over the Dutch colonies in South-East Asia. Wisely, the statesman who had given the Fourth Coalition much of its vitality – Castlereagh – also saw the wisdom of not offending Britain's European allies by feeding their suspicions of its overseas greed. Out of British acquisitions retained at the end of the Napoleonic wars, only two, Guyana and Tobago across the Atlantic, were kept for reasons of commercial gain. The others – Malta, the South African Cape, the Indian Ocean island of Mauritius and the West Indian Island of St Lucia – were held for mainly strategic motives. Castlereagh's restraint was from a position of strength, for Britain's influence throughout the world was now greater than ever.

NAPOLEON AND FRANCE, 1799–1815

We cannot bid Napoleon a conclusive adieu since his influence lived on after him in the phenomenon of Bonapartism. As Michael Broers appropriately observes, 'Napoleon's genius was for seeing where power lay, and drawing it to himself', blending enlightened absolutism with terror as he did so.[15] Hence, we need to look at an important aspect of the work of Napoleon I that we have almost entirely neglected so far, his internal policy. This has often been summarised as a mixture of some features of absolute monarchy with others of revolutionary government. An equally important observation might be that this mixture changed considerably throughout the Napoleonic period and was not finally settled in 1815. In February 1800, the first use was made of an important Bonapartist device, the plebiscite, in which, by a large majority, Frenchmen approved a new constitution. This pre-scribed the indirect election of a 'national list' of delegates, from which a centrally appointed Senate would select a Tribunate to suggest laws and a Legislature to pass them. But the main legislative initiative was reserved to the first consul in consultation with a Council of State that he himself would appoint. Under him, it was this Council of State which supervised the lower ministries and departments, the most important of which was perhaps the ministry of police. The first con-sul asserted his control over the provinces by the appointment of prefects to the departments. These were officials comparable to the *intendants* of the old regime. A new financial order was set up to improve the collection of taxes and the manner in which the national income was distributed. An important feature here was the Bank of France, founded in 1800 and given the sole power to issue bank notes in 1803.

One of the more famous features of the new order was the Civil Code of 1804, renamed the Code Napoleon in 1807. This was an amalgam of the Roman law operating in the south and the customary law applied in the north. The 'Respective Rights and Duties of Husband and Wife' emphasised the power of the father and the subservience of the mother in the family, although arguably for hierarchical rather than sexist reasons. Individual property was given stronger protection, although estates were to be divided equally among all children. Napoleon was less of an egalitarian than an elitist, however: he introduced the Legion of Honour in 1802, and a more elaborate system of such rewards under the empire from 1804 onwards. His educational reforms were not so much to bring enlightenment to the broad masses as to encourage the advancement of the talented few. While primary education would be rudimentary, at the secondary level there would be a selective group of special institutions (the *lycées*) as well as more ordinary schools for the less capable students who got that far. There were to be some specialised academies for officers and technicians, and from 1808 onwards, an overseeing University of France, a kind of Ministry of Education. Napoleon hoped that this would do for secular education what the Order of Jesuits had done for its ecclesiastical counterpart. Not that he was against religion, which he believed was good for the state, observing: 'The people need a religion; this religion must be in the hands of government.' It was necessary to inculcate 'the mystery of the social order', or, to put it more simply, to teach the people to accept inequality or elitism.[16] Hence the agreement of Concordat with the papacy in 1801, according to which Roman Catholicism was recognised as the religion of the majority of Frenchmen, whose first consul would nominate bishops for the Pope's confirmation. However, this settlement did not last for long in its original form as he attempted to subject the French Church to further regulation.

Napoleon believed it necessary to take care of the bodies of the French people as well as their souls. 'I fear insurrections caused by shortage of bread', he once observed. 'I would fear them more than a battle of 200,000 men.'[17] Consequently he took particular care to ensure that food supplies were adequate and that relief would be provided in times of hardship, especially in Paris. He was also interested in the development of the French industrial economy, to some extent perhaps making a virtue out of the necessity imposed by his Continental System. But the economic hardships that struck deeply from 1810 onwards were responsible along with the military defeats for the loss of Napoleon's popularity among the middle class or bourgeoisie that had earlier brought him to the pinnacle of power.

Bonapartism as developed by the first Napoleon was primarily a device for staying in power. It derived its legitimacy from the people, a plebiscite giving overwhelming authority to the first consul in 1800 (by 3,011,007 to 1562) and another in 1802 making him consul for life with an even greater majority (3,568,000 to 8374). The legitimacy became dynastic after Napoleon made himself Emperor of the French, which was approved by a final plebiscite (3,572,000 to 2569).[18] This was a few months after the discovery of a plot to kidnap or assassinate Napoleon and also after the execution of the high-born Duc d'Enghien, who was accused of being implicated in the plot. For fear of further opposition, Napoleon now controlled the government in a more dictatorial manner, and worked more actively through censorship and police to suppress further possible sources of opposition. Frédéric Bluche comments:

> What is Bonapartism at the end of the imperial experience? This is a new formula of power, combining democracy (passive) and author-ity (active), a 'centrist' formula founded on a composite legitimacy. It is a form of authoritarian government and of centralising admin-istration. It is the rough draft of a simple doctrine, but it is no longer a powerful political current. And this is for want of a veritable army of supporters for the regime, outside of the army properly so called (officers, NCOs, sometimes soldiers). For the Empire, having not kept the promises of the Consulate, can survive only through victory. Prolonged war, in spite of the personal popularity of the emperor, contains in embryo the final defeat and collapse of the system.[19]

However, it would be wrong to finish on such a negative note confined to France at the beginning of the nineteenth century. Taking a view that is more positive, wider and longer term, Stuart Woolf writes:

> It could be argued that the model of France, perhaps even more than that of Britain, was central in this construction of the political concept of modern Europe, precisely because in the hands of the liberals national identity was combined with the leading role attributed to the state. For one of the most remarkable features of this legacy of the Napoleonic years was the growing association of liberalism

and standardizing administrative reforms as the method to forge a unified state identity. ... Thus it was not just the nation state as the modal political unit that Europe exported to the rest of the world, but its particular stated version of the Napoleonic experience.[20]

We must now move on to examine the manner in which liberalism evolved during the years after 1815.

7

FROM REACTION TOWARDS LIBERALISM, 1815–1848

THE CONGRESS OF VIENNA

In exile at St Helena, Napoleon talked of the aims for which he had worked while in power. He said that he had tried to merge the peoples of Europe into nations joined together by 'unity of codes, principles, opinions, feelings, and interest'. He had thought of setting up a central assembly on an ancient Greek or a modern American model, to take care of 'the great European family' with the guidance and protection of his empire. In spite of his defeat, he still believed that what he had worked for would ultimately be realised:

> The impulse has been given, and I do not think that, after my fall and the disappearance of my system, there will be any other great equilibrium possible in Europe than the concentration and confederation of the great peoples. The first sovereign who, in the midst of the first great struggle, shall embrace in good faith the cause of the peoples, will find himself at the head of all Europe, and will be able to accomplish whatever he wishes.[1]

Even in the long run, Napoleon's alleged dream was to fall somewhat short of realisation. More immediately, the Congress of Vienna, on which his remarks might well have been intended as a critical comment, did very little to order the affairs of the continent in anything

187

like the manner he envisaged. Then, as if realising their own shortcomings, the principal signatories of the Treaty of Vienna worked from 1815 to 1822 to build up at least the beginnings of collaboration in what became known as the Congress System.

Their emphasis remained on restoration rather than construction, however, as they made an attempt partly to go back to the Europe of the eighteenth century rather than moving fully into the nineteenth. Absolute monarchs and noble advisers attempted in such a manner to reimpose their authority over the lower orders. Unfortunately for them, the impact of the French Revolution could not be ignored, and the lower orders were not prepared to revert to the old regime. In particular, the upper middle class or *grande bourgeoisie* was able to insist on a due recognition of its right to participate in government based on a consolidation of its property and wealth. An assertion of its political power was to be found in the emerging ideology of liberalism, which was aimed basically at protecting its interests. (For a fuller discussion, see the end of this chapter.) In its turn, the upper middle class was to find that its own newly asserted predominance was under attack from the lower members of its own class, and even more from those of the proletariat, workers and landless peasants. Therefore, it was sometimes driven into alliance with the landed nobility. As for the assault on the propertied classes, while it contained traditional elements of blind fury or utopian expectation, it also moved towards a more organised and realistic outlook which was to develop later in radical directions.

As ever, the history of Europe was affected during the years from 1815 to 1848 by events unfolding in the world beyond. In this period, a special place is occupied by the Americas, where independence movements stemming from the experience of the USA and of revolutionary France were to weaken further the empires of Spain and Portugal. Back in Europe, the decline of the Ottoman Empire also made it difficult to maintain the settlement of 1815 in its original condition. The struggle for Greek independence assumed special significance. But perhaps the most compelling imperative towards political change was the continuance and spread of industrial revolution.

Before looking at the manner in which these phenomena made their presence felt in the various regions of Europe, we must return to examine the map as it was rearranged at the Congress of Vienna and its successors. The leading powers at Vienna were Austria, represented by Prince Metternich; Britain, whose delegates were Viscount Castle-reagh and the Duke of Wellington; Prussia, whose principal spokesman was the Prince von Hardenberg; and Russia, for which Tsar Alexander I acted directly, although taking advice from Counts Capodistrias and Nesselrode and Baron von Stein. By playing these powers off one against the other, Prince Talleyrand was able to secure a seat at the conference table for defeated France. The secretary-general of the Congress was the Prussian adviser to Metternich, Friedrich von Gentz, who wrote after the Final Act had been signed:

> Men had promised themselves an all-embracing reform of the political system of Europe, guarantees for peace; in one word, the return of the Golden Age. The Congress has resulted in nothing but restorations, which had already been effected by arms; agreements between the Great Powers, of little value for the future balance and preservation of the peace of Europe; quite arbitrary alterations in the possessions of the less important states; but in no act of a higher nature, no great measure for public order or for the universal good, which might compensate humanity for its long sufferings, or reassure it as to the future. ... The Protocol of the Congress bears the stamp rather of a temporary agreement than of the work destined to last for centuries. But, to be just, the Treaty, such as it is, has the undeniable merit of having prepared the world for a more complete political structure. If ever the Powers should meet again to establish a political system by which wars of conquest would be rendered impossible and the rights of all guaranteed, the Congress of Vienna, as a preparatory assembly, will not have been without use. A number of vexatious details have been settled, and the ground has been made ready for a better social structure.[2]

What were the vexatious details, and how had the ground been prepared? To look first at the provisions of the 'First Act' of 9 June 1815, former dynasties were put back on the thrones of Spain, Piedmont, Naples (the Two Sicilies) and other Italian states. Lombardy–Venetia was created as a kingdom for the Austrian emperor, and a considerable part of Poland presented in a similar manner to the tsar of Russia. At first, Russia and Prussia attempted to achieve an agreement whereby Prussia would receive compensation for losses in Poland from the absorption of Saxony and extension of its foothold on the Rhine.

In the end, Prussia retained its share of the first two partitions of Poland and received in addition the province of Posen (Poznań) and the city of Thorn (Toruń), but gave up Warsaw and its share in the third partition. Austria kept Galicia, its allotment from the first partition, but its acquisition from the third was reduced to the free city of Cracow (Kraków) and its surroundings. Prussia received much of Saxony and compensation for the rest in the northern Rhineland, Westphalia and, on the Baltic coast, former Swedish Pomerania. Austria was appeased with Salzburg as well as Lombardy–Venetia and Dalmatia on the Adriatic coast along with its hinterland. With the formal abandonment of the Holy Roman Empire, a German Confederation of some 40 states including Prussia and Austria was set up. A Diet of two chambers, similar to that of the Napoleonic Confederation, was to be presided over by Austria in a permanent location at Frankfurt.

To dominate the mouth of the Rhine, an artificial united Kingdom of the Netherlands (Belgium, Holland and Luxemburg) was created, while beyond its upper reaches, the Swiss Confederation was reborn with a guarantee of neutrality. In northern Europe, Norway was ceded by Denmark to Sweden, which not only lost its part of Pomerania to Prussia but did not regain Finland from Russia. Neither Denmark nor Sweden was henceforth as influential in the affairs of Europe as they had both been previously. As for the other great powers, France was hampered by Napoleon's return from Elba but saved by Talleyrand after Waterloo sufficiently to retain its boundaries as they had been in 1790. Britain retained Heligoland in the North Sea and Malta in the Mediterranean, the Cape of Good Hope, Ceylon and Mauritius in and near the Indian Ocean, and Tobago and Santa Lucia in the Caribbean.

The Congress of Vienna also set up procedures for the conduct of international diplomacy in general, and in particular made a number of significant decisions concerning: the free navigation of the rivers Rhine and Meuse; the extension of the rights of Jews, especially in the German Confederation; and the condemnation of the slave trade (already abolished in the British Empire in 1808).

METTERNICH AND REACTION

Having taken a broad view of the details of the Treaty of Vienna and the agreements connected with it, we can now look at the manner in which

the ground was prepared for what Gentz called a 'better social structure'. This, it must be said immediately, did not involve any wholesale
readjustments of relations between the classes, but was rather an
argument for what his master Metternich called the sole function of a
statesman, to 'prop up mouldering institutions'. Metternich made a full
'Confession of Faith' in a secret memorandum sent to the emperors
Francis I of Austria and Alexander I of Russia at the later Congress of
Troppau in 1820. Metternich declared:

> Kings have to calculate the chances of their very existence in the
> immediate future; passions are let loose, and league together to over-
> throw everything which society respects as the basis of its existence;
> religion, public morality, laws, customs, rights, and duties, all are
> attacked, confounded, overthrown, or called in question. The great
> mass of the people are tranquil spectators of these attacks and
> revolutions, and of the absolute want of all means of defence. A few
> are carried off by the torrent, but the wishes of the immense major-
> ity are to maintain a repose which exists no longer, and of which
> even the first elements seem to be lost.

What was the cause of all these evils? In Metternich's view, man's
nature was immutable, apparent differences being brought about by
influences mostly geographical. On such a basis, institutions might
come and go, but two elements were indestructible: 'the precepts of
morality, religious as well as social, and the necessities created by
locality'. Unfortunately, 'presumption' made every man substitute
individual conviction for faith and consider himself to be 'the arbiter
of laws according to which he is pleased to govern himself, or to allow
someone else to govern him and his neighbours'. It was mostly
the middle classes of society that had been affected by this 'moral
gangrene', and agitation was provoked mostly by wealthy men – 'real
cosmopolitans, securing their personal advantage at the expense of any
order of things whatever – paid officials, men of letters, lawyers, and
the individuals charged with public education'. Since 1815, their
rallying cry had been 'Constitution', which might mean different
things in different countries according to their status in that year, but
everywhere meant 'change and trouble'.

Yet in Germany and elsewhere, the great mass of the people asked
only for peace and quiet. They wanted laws protecting individuals,

families and property, and dreaded any threat to such stability. Acting according to such general wishes, governments should not be immobile, indeed they should demonstrate respect for 'the progressive development of institutions in lawful ways'. But, not giving aid or succour to 'partisans' under any disguise, they must set up a league against factions. Declared Metternich: 'Union between the monarchs is the basis of the policy which must now be followed to save society from total ruin.' Threats of destruction had always existed, but the present age 'by the single fact of the liberty of the press, possesses more than any preceding age the means of contact, seduction, and attraction whereby to act on these different classes of men'. Before the latter half of the seventeenth century, liberty of the press was unknown in the world; until the end of the eighteenth century it was restrained everywhere, one of the few exceptions being Britain – 'a part of Europe separated from the continent by the sea, as well as by her language and her peculiar manners'. Through control of the press and restriction of concessions to political parties, as well as minute attention to financial affairs and the strict maintenance of religious principles, let monarchs demonstrate that they were just, but strong; doing good, but being strict. Summing up, Metternich made the following affirmation:

> In short, let the great monarchs strengthen their union, and prove to the world that if it exists it is beneficent, and ensures the political peace of Europe: that it is powerful only for the maintenance of tranquillity at a time when so many attacks are directed against it; that the principles which they profess are paternal and protective, menacing only the disturbers of public tranquillity.[3]

Metternich's message did not fall on deaf ears, for he spoke the kind of language that both Francis I and Alexander I liked to hear. The Russian emperor had indeed put forward his own views – which went even further than those of the Austrian emperor's minister – five years or so previously, when he persuaded both Francis I and King Frederick William III of Prussia to join him in the Holy Alliance of September 1815. This somewhat mystical agreement contained the declaration that 'the precepts of Justice, Christian Charity and Peace ... must have an immediate influence on the Councils of Princes and guide all their steps'. Most other European sovereigns later signed their agreement with the principles of the Holy Alliance, although George the British prince regent (1811–20, later George IV 1820–30), concerned for the constitutional niceties of his position, would go no further than expressing his approval of its 'sacred maxims'. His foreign secretary, Castlereagh, was more dismissive, deeming the Holy Alliance 'a piece of sublime mysticism and nonsense', and even Metternich went so far as to call it 'a loud-sounding nothing'.[4] While the influence of the Holy Alliance as an agency for stability is difficult to determine, a much more positive appraisal in this respect can be given to another agreement of November 1815, the Quadruple Alliance of Austria, Russia, Prussia and Britain, which created the system of consultation that came to be known as the 'Concert of Europe'.

THE CONCERT OF EUROPE

According to the terms of the Quadruple Alliance, the four powers agreed that their representatives should meet from time to time for the purpose of consulting about their common interest and for the consideration of the measures most useful for the maintenance of the peace of Europe. Four further congresses were indeed held – at Aix-la-Chapelle in 1818, Troppau in 1820, Laibach in 1821 and Verona in 1822 – but by 1823 the powers involved had recognised that the 'Concert of Europe' had broken down. Russia, Austria and Prussia revised the Holy Alliance in the Troppau Protocol of 1820, but we have already noted what Metternich thought of the Holy Alliance, and even though he recommended the union of monarchs in his message to Francis I and Alexander I at Troppau, he was already conscious of interests that divided these two monarchs from each other as well as from Frederick William III. For example, Metternich's suspicion of Alexander I's mystical and, even worse, at least occasional liberal sentiments was overcome by about 1820, partly because of the tsar's explicit confession and renunciation of his former political deviation. However, the convert was now too enthusiastic for the preacher, as Alexander argued in favour of intervention in the affairs of other countries in order to suppress revolutions: in Spain, Portugal, Naples, Piedmont and Greece. After Alexander I's death in 1825, Nicholas I also soon showed himself to be the enemy of revolution in a manner which alarmed some of its other opponents. Meanwhile, tension of an even deeper kind increased between Russia and Austria over the Eastern Question, Austria fearing Russian expansion into the ailing Ottoman Empire. Prussia was not as apprehensive as Austria concerning Russian intentions in the Eastern Question, but was far from happy about them, nevertheless. Equally, while Frederick William generally accepted the dominance of Austria in the affairs of the German Confederation, there were already some of his subjects who believed that Prussia should assume the leadership, even if their voices were as yet largely unheard.

Tension within the Holy Alliance was never so serious as tension from without. A considerable amount of difficulty arose from the attitude of the fourth member of the Quadruple Alliance, 'a part of Europe separated from the continent by the sea, as well as by her language and her peculiar manners', to use again the phrase of Metternich. Britain was certainly not in favour of intervention against revolutions, partly because it welcomed at least some of them, partly because it wished to adhere to its traditional policy of the maximum possible degree of isolation from the problems of Europe. Castlereagh insisted that 'nothing would be more immoral or more prejudicial to the character of government generally than the idea that their force was collectively to be prostituted to the support of established power, without any consideration of the extent to which it was abused'. In the view of the British foreign secretary, the 'Concert of Europe' should devote itself to the maintenance of obligations imposed on the powers by their treaties, in particular to the preservation of the frontiers agreed by them. As the 'Concert' began to break down by the beginning of 1823, his successor, Canning, observed: 'So things are getting back to a wholesome state again. Every nation for itself, and God for us all.' In his turn, Metternich considered Canning to be 'the malevolent meteor hurled by an angry Providence upon Europe'.[5]

There was some British rapprochement with Alexander I in 1825, and with his successor Nicholas I in 1826, concerning Greece. After the Treaty of London solemnising this rapprochement in July 1827, a combined British, Russian and French fleet destroyed their Turkish counterpart in the Bay of Navarino off the Morean coast in October. Such co-operation was rare, however, and disappeared during the ensuing Russo-Turkish War of 1828–9. Even during the years 1825–7, the rapprochement had been one of convenience, Canning being anxious by means of it to exert some control over Russian expansion in south-east Europe. Meanwhile, there was even more alarm about the Russian threat growing from the Near and Middle East to central Asia. Lord Dudley Stuart spoke for many in a House of Commons debate in 1836:

> But one enthusiasm pervaded the entire population – that of advancing the pre-eminence of their country and its superior power over the rest of the world. The very climate encouraged that feeling. The population looked forward to attaining the luxuries and enjoyments denied them in their own country, but which they knew were to be procured elsewhere. The government of Russia encouraged that feeling. All their policy and arrangements were directed with that view. The moment a soldier left the country on foreign service he received four times his ordinary pay. All these circumstances united made the desire of aggression and territorial acquisition natural and necessary to the Russian empire. A reference to history would show that aggrandisement was the entire object, and had been the successful aim of a country, which, not long since, was scarcely recognised as an important Power in Europe.[6]

Britain was not the only country to view the assertion of Russia's influence in the years following 1815 with more than a little concern. Indeed, Britain's Russophobic outlook was shared to varying extents by all the other major powers of Europe for much of the nineteenth century, and beyond. In the short run, these powers included France, which gradually made its way back to its rightful place after the disgrace of 1815. With the collapse of the 'Concert of Europe' by 1823, France was again exercising its influence abroad, as it intervened against revolution in Spain, with the hope of bringing Spain back into the French or Bourbon family fold. This revived old British suspicions, which were also directed at what seemed to be a revival of French imperial pretensions in the wider world.

RUSSIA AND THE EAST

To turn back to European affairs, and to look at them in somewhat more detail region by region, we must remind ourselves that, as in other chapters, our use of the names of European states has been a shorthand device intended to convey a complex combination of governments, societies, economies and cultures. We must bear this in mind as we look at the major states in turn, beginning in the east and centre of the continent with the members of the Holy Alliance, and taking first its founder and his empire, Alexander I of Russia. There were obvious implications in the tsar's very name, which hinted at a reassertion of his country's classical inheritance and his own potential emulation of Alexander the Great. While aware of these implications, his grand-mother, Catherine the Great, had attempted to arrange his education in such a manner that he would be aware of the best ideas of the Enlightenment and capable of putting them into effect. However, the course taken by the French Revolution, even if he was initially an enthusiast, and the manner of his elevation to the throne, after the assassination of his father (even if he did not instigate it), combined to create a personality of some complexity. This helped to explain, at least in part, his attraction towards religious mysticism, overtones of which were to be found in the Holy Alliance. By the time of its proclamation in 1815, the emperor had lost most of his desire to bring about reform, which had in fact been barely implemented. The great victory over Napoleon in 1812 had encouraged him to believe that Russia was mighty enough without liberalism, indeed all the mightier for its absence. Therefore he contented himself with adjustments of the administration rather than fundamental changes: for example, the sub-stitution of ministries for the colleges from 1802 onwards and the further professionalisation of the bureaucracy among other reforms in 1810–11. However, little was done to alter the official social system, especially the institution of serfdom, except in the Baltic provinces. Elsewhere, a new kind of serfdom was introduced with the increase from 1816 in military colonies, which vainly attempted to subject cows as well as soldiers to good order and discipline.

While the peasants who made up the vast majority of the Russian Empire's population showed their discontent in riots and revolts, these were neither large nor frequent enough to cause the government much anxiety. However, at least some members of the ruling class, the nobility, were conscience-stricken enough about the plight of their fellow countrymen to discuss what should be done, and even to take action in order to put their ideas into practice. They organised them-selves secretly. Some of them, especially in the Northern Society, were liberals, anxious for the introduction of a constitutional monarchy and civil rights. Others, predominantly in the Southern Society, were more radical, republican and Jacobin. They aspired to exercise power in a manner at first dictatorial, later democratic. At the death of Alexander late in 1825 there was a hesitant and disorganised demonstration in St Petersburg which became known as the Decembrist Revolt. Five leaders were executed, and became martyrs for later revolutionaries. In the short run, there were few successors, even though the government of Nicholas I, especially his notorious private police, the Third Section of HM Chancery, looked for them everywhere. Yet numerous if small-scale peasant disturbances were enough to cause Nicholas some concern, particularly when international revolution appeared to be breaking out in 1830, even more in 1848.

For this reason, the policy of Nicholas was to shore up the old Russia rather than attempting to build anew. Not for him any vestige of liberty, equality, fraternity, but rather the slogan 'Orthodoxy, autocracy, nationality'.[7] He attempted to make the nobility into a more exclusive caste in a decree of 1845 after creating the rank of 'honorary citizen' for distinguished members of the middle class in another decree of 1832. In 1833, a *Complete Collection of the Laws of the Russian Empire* was published, while a new *Criminal Code* was issued in 1845. Nicholas also extended the Russian Code to the provinces of the southwest and west, to Ukraine, White Russia (Belarus) and Poland. In all these provinces there had been separatist agitation, especially in Poland in 1830, after which it had been made an 'indivisible part' of the empire in 1832. To the east, the government still had to worry about the pacification of the Caucasus region, while beyond the Caspian Sea insurgency was even more troublesome, and the armed forces were drawn ever further into central Asia to overcome it as well as to extend imperial ambition.

As far as foreign expansion was concerned, the Russian Empire under Alexander I had moved into Finland and the Danubian province of Bessarabia as well as across the Caucasus Mountains and the Caspian Sea. It had also consolidated its hold on Siberia, whose administration was reformed in 1822 and 1827, and spread more vigorously beyond Asia into North America. From their base in Alaska, Russian adventurers moved southwards as far as California, although a treaty drawn up with the USA in April 1824 restricted Russian territorial claims to an area somewhat to the north of Vancouver Island.

This was a few months after the announcement in December 1823 of the Monroe Doctrine, which expressed opposition to European infiltration into the Americas and also renounced the intervention of the USA in the affairs of Europe, one of the most pressing of which at the time was the fight for Greek independence. Much more than the remote USA, other European powers were concerned that this latest episode in the perennial Eastern Question should not result in further Russian expansion into the Balkans. After some co-operation with Britain and France in the expulsion of Turkey from Greece in 1827, Nicholas I alienated these temporary allies by turning from a war with Persia to another with Turkey in 1828. By the Treaty of Adrianople of 1829, Russia acquired rights of passage through the Dardanelles, ownership of the mouth of the Danube and protection over the hinterland provinces of Moldavia and Wallachia, which now were to be independent from Turkey in every way but name, as was Serbia.

What seemed to other powers to be Russian ambitions in the Balkans and the Middle East appeared to Nicholas I and his advisers to be legitimate steps towards consolidation of frontiers and of national security. Such motives were even more pressing after the Polish insurrection of 1830 and the wave of unrest that swept across Europe and beyond. Egypt now rebelled against Ottoman rule, which Nicholas moved to prop up in the Treaty of Unkiar Skelessi of 1833, sealing the friendship of Russia and Turkey. Russia joined with Prussia and Austria later that year in a formal renewal of the Holy Alliance, which led the maritime powers of Britain, France, Portugal and Spain to conclude a new Quadruple Alliance in 1834. Russophobia now grew in the outlook of Lord Dudley Stuart, Palmerston and others in Britain especially, where there were fears for the partition of Turkey as well as the penetration of India. But at least temporary rapprochement came after further insurgency in Egypt in the shape of the Treaty of London of 1840 and the Straits Convention of 1841. The treaty settled the argument between the Turkish government and Egypt with the support of Britain, Austria, Prussia and Russia. The convention brought in France to join the other major European powers in settling the vexed question of navigation through the Dardanelles. The warships of all major foreign powers were to be denied access in time of peace, an agreement which made for the maintenance of that desirable state of affairs in the short run, but which was in the not too distant future to lead to the reopening of the Eastern Question in a much more threatening manner than ever before.

AUSTRIA, PRUSSIA AND THE CENTRE

For Russia's partners in the Holy Alliance, the leading German states Austria and Prussia in the centre of Europe, there were many other problems to worry about. For Metternich, as we have seen, the principal aim was to maintain stability everywhere, at home as well as abroad. And although he claimed that for him stability did not mean immo-bility, he set his mind firmly against the kind of change that would have given Austria a better chance of successful adaptation to the pressures exerted by the nineteenth century. He had no time for civil rights and liberties, political parties or parliaments, which for him could only incite unrest, although he did allow them in the southern German states. Finding the principal location of agitation in favour of such constitutional advance in the universities, he made full use of the opportunity presented to him by the assassination of a Russian agent named Kotzebue in 1819. He obliged the German Confedera-tion to accept the so-called Carlsbad Decrees, which instituted close supervision for educational institutions, especially the universities, where idealistic student fraternities known as *Burschenschaften* were indeed concerning themselves with the question of German unifica-tion, especially according to a liberal pattern, and even some teachers were arguing for such change. Such teachers were now to be dismissed, and the *Burschenschaften* dissolved. A central investigating commission was set up to seek out revolution and quell disturbances. The decrees stressed the need for a strict censorship of the press, and for the prohibition of political meetings. In 1832, the Carlsbad Decrees were reinforced by the so-called Six Acts.

Conscious of his role as senior minister in the German Confedera-tion, Metternich was totally opposed to any federal solution for its political problems. He also believed that the empire could be kept intact only if the imperial authority was imposed on it in a uniform and unitary manner. He also attempted to maintain the previous align-ments of the Austrian Empire's social classes, refusing in particular to make any move towards the abolition of serfdom, which engulfed the vast majority of the population after reforms brought in by Joseph II during the eighteenth century had been allowed to lapse. Provincial traditions and arrangements could be maintained only if they did not threaten the basic principle of one head for one main body.

Wherever there was opposition, there would be vigorous repression, for example in Hungary in the 1820s, 1830s and 1840s. Hungary's ancient constitution included provisions that the Diet would have to pass its laws for the royal approval before it could make arrangements for the army and its upkeep. Moreover, the Diet was elected by about 10 per cent of the adult male population, a higher than average suffrage for Europe between the years 1815 and 1848, even higher than Britain before 1832. Metternich feared that Hungary might stray further from the correct path, warning that the 'subversive' opposition was trying to exploit moderate constitutionalism in order to overthrow the Hungarian polity, which was 'monarchical-aristocratic' and could not be adapted to democratic institutions.[8] He therefore attempted to take the constitution into his own hands, to control the central and local Hungarian administration through a mixture of repression and infiltration. Even terror was used in the later 1830s, with opponents accused of treason and imprisoned, but public outrage was so heated that Metternich had to moderate much police activity. The chancellor enjoyed better fortunes in the Italian provinces acquired in 1815, Lombardy–Venetia, where he was able to use his own agents to get round the formal arrangements.

Metternich's manipulation of the government in Vienna was more successful than that in Hungary, less so than that in Lombardy–Venetia. In the imperial capital, he needed to take most notice of the emperor, who was Francis I until his death in 1835 (he had been Francis II as Holy Roman Emperor from 1792 to 1806) and from then to the end of 1848 was Ferdinand. Francis agreed with Metternich on basic principles, but one of these was that he himself should have the last word, and this was often long delayed. He worked hard at reading reams of official papers, but often took years before making even trivial decisions. Ferdinand was rather the opposite, a feeble-minded embodiment of the argument against hereditary monarchy, whose reign is closely associated with the *Vormärz* or pre-March 1848 period, after which was to come a spring of discontent. Indecisive 'workaholic' or inactive imbecile, the emperor was not as helpful to Metternich in person as he was in theory. The chancellor attempted to overcome this basic problem through improvements in the efficiency of the central administration, but he encountered several difficulties and some opposition.

Metternich would have liked the emperor to be advised by a council, and then to take decisions in consultation with a ministerial conference formed by the heads of administrative departments. But the ministerial conference was never properly created, and the administrative heads were often to be found in the Council. The Council therefore tended to act more as a co-ordinator of the activities of the higher civil service than as an advisory body for the emperor. The chancellor's ambitions were also thwarted by the dominant member of the Council from about 1828 onwards, the Count Franz Anton Kolowrat-Liebstinsky, who managed to keep his hands on the imperial purse-strings and so to restrict Metternich's expenditure on the armed forces and the police. Confusion and economy in the imperial administration made it difficult for Metternich to implement his aims at home and abroad.

For him, Austria played a special part in the affairs of Europe, from the points of view of location and character. The empire was centrally placed to maintain stability on behalf of 'monarchical-aristocratic' government throughout the continent, defying all the machinations of an alleged secret committee that he suspected of fomenting revolution from St Petersburg to Lisbon. Unfortunately for his purposes, Austria was almost as much a 'geographical expression' as he claimed that Italy was, and the base for his activities was unsure. He did manage to exercise some control over Italy as a whole, intervening in Naples in 1820 and threatening intervention there and elsewhere in the peninsula on other occasions, at least until the onset of the 1848 Revolution. In the German Confederation, Metternich succeeded for the most part in giving a lead in the Carlsbad Decrees and other policies, but the seniority decreed for Austria in 1815 was already looking shaky by 1848 with the rise of Prussia. From 1833, when Tsar Nicholas I met Metternich and promised to work with him to maintain the existence of the Turkish Empire and to carry on the struggle against revolution, co-operation with Russia became closer. In the same year, the Holy Alliance of Austria, Russia and Prussia received official reassertion, with Metternich approving its secular spirit if not its mystical substance. He fully understood that Austria could not go it alone. This realisation was further forced on him by the German Confederation's relations with the rest of Europe. In 1830, 1840 and 1848, when war threatened with France, the military contribution offered by Austria was smaller than that of Prussia. The last and most serious of these crises led to Metternich's downfall, and the collapse of his policies for Austria and its role in Europe.

With the decline of Austria came the rise of Prussia, which in the reign of Frederick William III (1797–1840) was not so much political as economic and cultural. In 1815, Prussia extended its hold over the most important commercial routes by land and water. In order to make full use of this advantage and to draw its different territories from East Prussia to the Rhineland together, the Prussian government set up a customs union (*Zollverein*) from 1818 onwards. Economic growth accelerated in the 1830s and 1840s especially as transport improved with the arrival of the railroad. Prussia was still basically agricultural in its economic pursuits in 1848, but the writing was already clear enough on the factory walls for Metternich to express alarm about the influence of the *Zollverein*. This was great enough for him to fear the consequences of Austria's inclusion in it, and to attempt unsuccessfully to set up a rival customs union linking Austria and the other states of the German Confederation with northern Italy and a sea outlet on the Adriatic.

The period 1815–48 marked a chorus of the creative arts heralding the dawn of German nationalism. Already, from 1807–8 during the French occupation, the 'Father of German nationalism', Johann Gottlieb Fichte, had declared in his 'Addresses to the German Nation' that the invaders must be driven out and the natives must come together, for:

> The separation of the Germans from the other European nations is based on Nature. Through a common language and through common natural characteristics which unite the Germans, they are separate from the others. ... Those who speak the same language are joined to each other by a multitude of indivisible bonds by nature herself, long before any human art begins; they understand each other and have the power to make themselves understood more and more clearly; they belong to one another and are by nature one and inseparably whole.[9]

Before 1848, the father had many offspring, a large number of whom gave voice to their yearnings in Prussian and other accents. A powerful philosophical underpinning was given by Georg Wilhelm Friedrich Hegel, who looked upon the whole of reality as being a single process distilled in a great Spirit but embodied in peoples, especially the German.

FRANCE, BRITAIN AND THE WEST

As Prussia began its rise in the centre of Europe, France struggled in the north-west for recovery, at the start even for full restoration. It would take some time before both the French and other Europeans fully realised that France could never again be the dominant power in the continent that it had been in the reigns of Louis XIV and Napoleon I, and at some junctures between them. Under Louis XVIII (1814–24), brother to the executed Louis XVI, France regained some of its self-respect after the disasters of Waterloo and Vienna, especially through its successful intervention against a revolt in Spain in 1823. Charles X (1824–30), another brother of Louis XVI, was a more thoroughgoing reactionary, who provoked the Revolution of 1830. The July monarchy, named after the month in which it was created, was entrusted to Louis-Philippe (1830–48), a descendant of Louis XIII. The *grande bourgeoisie* or upper middle class came into its own, as even the king, with his famous umbrella, adopted its dress. Such a disguise could not save Louis-Philippe and royal government in general from overthrow in 1848. However, even though the throne was lost, this time the king kept his head.

To consider France in Europe and the world, there was a widespread and intense feeling among French people in 1815 that the national honour as well as the public purse were besmirched by the upkeep of an army of occupation and the payment of an indemnity. To paraphrase the 'Marseillaise', the impure blood of the foreigners had quitted French furrows by 1818 and the debt was cleared by 1820. But the memories of 1815 lingered on. France still wanted to break out of the containment imposed upon it, to restore its 'natural frontiers', especially on the Rhine, and to regain the full status of a first-class power with influence in Europe and beyond, in the Mediterranean especially. For such purposes, both the army and the navy would have to be rebuilt. On these basic purposes France was near to agreement, but as an accompaniment and stimulus of internal dissension there was much debate about the methods to be used for their achievement. Some royalists were for war and reaction, while most liberals were for peace and progress, but the pattern that emerged from millions of words was by no means always so clear. Even the most warmongering of patriots usually came to realise that France could not again face a coalition of enemies, while liberals usually supported rearmament for defensive purposes, which could be liberally interpreted, for expansion if not for offence.

Whatever foreign policies it was to pursue, France needed an ally or allies. Could there be a new Tilsit, an agreement like that between Napoleon and Tsar Alexander in 1807, only this time more lasting? Or a revival of the old friendship with Austria? Neither of these questions could be answered in the affirmative while the Holy Alliance continued. What about rapprochement with Britain? In the early 1830s, the prospect of the two constitutional monarchies working together was inviting. On the face of it, the new Quadruple Alliance of 1834, which brought in Spain and Portugal along with France and Britain, was a more positive response. Portugal had experienced revolution from 1820 and Spain from 1830, and there were considerable if largely unrealised hopes of liberal regimes being installed in the Iberian peninsula. However, the British government made no secret of its primary purpose of moving closer to France in order to restrain it in the Low Countries and across the Pyrenees. It was not until the Crimean War of 1854–6 that the diplomatic impasse following 1815 was broken, and France was able to emerge fully from its isolation.

Therefore, France had to move warily in order to avoid united opposition to its policies. Pursued in such a manner, the invasion of Spain in 1823 was a success. Britain alone took a stand against the ensuing restoration of King Ferdinand VII to his throne, which was welcomed by the other crowned heads of Europe. Then in 1832, after the French reoccupation of the papal port of Ancona on the western coast of the Adriatic Sea – one of the minor losses of 1815 – Austria and other European powers objected, Britain alone expressing its acceptance. Thus France was re-establishing some influence in two traditional spheres, Spain and Italy.

The Low Countries could not so easily be infiltrated. The July 1830 Revolution in Paris encouraged the French and Flemish areas of the southern Netherlands to bring to a head a movement for their independence from the Dutch, from whose domination they had become increasingly alienated ever since the compulsory union of 1815. When a revolt in Brussels in August was followed by other disturbances in provincial towns, the Dutch king, William I, sent two sons and a few thousand men in an attempt to win the Belgians back by persuasion rather than force. But independence was agreed in late October, and after elections on a limited male franchise, a new constitution was drawn up making provisions for a limited monarchy. At the beginning of 1831, an international London Conference including Britain, France, Prussia, Austria and Russia set up an independent Belgium. In the summer, Prince Leopold of Saxe-Coburg-Gotha accepted an invitation to become Leopold I of the new state. The uncle of Queen Victoria and the son-in-law of Louis-Philippe, Leopold made a mostly successful effort until his death in 1865 to guide his adopted country through a period of economic development without further major social disturbance. He put life into a constitutional monarchy with the co-operation of a liberal Catholic bourgeoisie, avoiding for the most part clashes between the French-speaking Walloons and the Dutch-speaking Flemish. Differences with Holland were not settled until 1839, when the Treaty of London guaranteed the independence of Belgium as 'a perpetually neutral state'. Both the Dutch and the French were dissuaded from over-vigorous intervention by the watchful suspicion of the other powers.

Kept out of Belgium and the Rhineland by the vigilance of its rivals, with success in Spain and Italy strictly limited, France was encouraged by many of its politicians to look outwards. If expansion could not take place by land, France must turn to the sea. Specifically, if all doors in Europe were closed, France must put its energies into its backyard – North Africa. Here, inevitably, there was a clash with Britain, the major maritime power, as well as a limited amount of co-operation: French adventurers were obliged to confine their ambition of restoring Roman Africa to Algiers, which was gradually taken over from 1830 to 1845. Further afield, or rather over the water, France accepted the Straits Convention of 1841 and did not attempt to interfere to any great extent in the Middle East, still less in places more remote. Tahiti in the south Pacific was taken in 1843, in spite of vigorous British protests, and the Ivory Coast in West Africa was adopted by the same year. But a more vigorous attempt at the revival of full imperial glory would come with Napoleon III.

Meanwhile Britain continued to rule the waves, and to contribute to the balance of power in Europe. As usual, Britain was also trying to conduct its foreign policy on the cheap – if there was any economic determinism in the nation of shopkeepers, it was to pinch pennies in the preservation of peace rather than to throw away pounds in the pursuit of war. During the period 1815–48, British fighting in Europe was on a minor scale and confined to the Iberian peninsula and Greece. On the other hand, British influence in the affairs of the continent was more marked in this period than in that which followed it, and all the other major powers were interested to know how Britain stood, or in which direction it was prepared to move.

In the years following 1815, Castlereagh worked hard to fashion the Congress System after his own image of it, seeking to use Britain's strength on behalf of balance and moderation. By 1822, however, his diplomatic disillusionment was complete, and joined with more personal problems to lead him to commit suicide. His successor as foreign secretary from 1822 to 1827, George Canning, did not like the Congress System, but did not give up all interest in the affairs of the continent. It was rather, as he said in November 1822, that 'for *Europe*, I shall be desired *now* and then to read *England'*.[10] Moreover, while taking a lively interest in developments across the Atlantic, Canning by no means completely neglected those nearer home. For example, until his death in 1827 he supported the struggle for Greek independence, attempting to reduce the influence of other powers by bringing in Britain's. His immediate successor was Wellington, who quickly showed that his talents lay more in the direction of strategy than diplomacy.

From 1830, however, the conduct of British foreign policy fell into the capable hands of Lord Palmerston, who declared that, in all eventualities of any significance, it was 'not fitting that a country occupying such a proud position as England should be a passive and mute spectator'. Palmerston spoke loudly, especially in support of liberal causes, but was restrained enough in his actions, which were basically aimed at 'the maintenance of peace and the preservation of the balance of power'.[11] For this purpose, in his view, Britain needed allies; for their part, all the major European powers at some time between 1815 and 1848 sought alliance with Britain. For Palmerston, the three former friends of 1815, Russia, Austria and Prussia, shared an outlook which was not compatible with that of Britain. Therefore, in the Quadruple Alliance of 1834, he turned to France, Spain and Portugal, although he was looking less for equal partnership than for control over France and protection of Portugal and Spain. An entente with France that seemed to be blossoming during Palmerston's absence from the Foreign Office during the years 1841 to 1846 withered on his return over the question of the Spanish marriages, an issue which seemed to be reviving the old Franco-Spanish family connection, this time through the agency of the House of Orléans rather than that of Bourbon. But it would be going too far to say that Palmerston was perturbed enough by the ambitions of the House of Orléans to engineer its downfall in 1848, or took his liberal sympathies to the extreme of fomenting the revolutions of 1848 in France or in any other country.

As before and after, British foreign policy during the years 1815–48 was directed at the wider world at least as much as at Europe. Hence the British interest in developments in the Eastern Question, although here as elsewhere the basic aim was to avoid war if possible. Peace was indeed achieved, at least for the time being, with the Treaty of London of 1840 and the Straits Convention of 1841. Similarly, successive British ministers kept a close watch on the course of events in the Americas, where there seemed to be a distinct possibility that other colonies would follow the lead of the USA in declaring their independence, even that they would use the ideology of the American and French revolutions to achieve a social overturn as well as a breakaway from the empires of Europe. The upsurge in Saint Domingue leading to the proclamation of the independent black republic of Haiti in 1804 appeared to be an ominous indication of the shape of things to come. However, the former colonies of Spain that broke away to become Mexico, Venezuela and Argentina did so in confusion rather than full revolution, while Spanish Chile and Portuguese Brazil preserved their local elites intact as they made a formal severance of the old ties. The main Spanish stronghold was Peru, which needed British support to achieve independence. In the Monroe Doctrine of 1823, the USA asserted that the powers of Europe should not take advantage of the new situation to seek new colonies for themselves in the western hemisphere, while Britain quickly extended its economic predominance with the assistance of the Royal Navy. Britain worked in unofficial alliance with the USA to preserve this advantageous state of affairs throughout most of the rest of the nineteenth century under the somewhat transparent banner of free trade.

In the shorter run, British policy in South America contributed to the breakdown of the 'Concert of Europe'. During the period 1815–48, Britain also pursued its interests elsewhere in the world. It became embroiled in the first Afghan War of 1838–42 in response to what was wrongly believed to be Russian infiltration. It countered the threat of a Burmese invasion of Bengal in a war of 1824–6 which led to the acquisition of Rangoon and part of southern Burma. Singapore and other settlements in Malaya were controlled from India after 1826 until 1867. In China, the so-called 'Opium War', 1839–42, was concluded by the Treaty of Nanking, which ceded Hong Kong to Britain for 150 years. The treaty also opened up other ports to foreign traders, especially the British with whom a commercial treaty was agreed in 1843. Much British energy and money, both governmental and private, went into the campaign against the slave trade. This helped to further British involvement in West Africa, especially the Gold Coast.

At home, the violent dispersal of a radical demonstration in Manchester in 1819, which became known as the 'Peterloo massacre', led immediately to more repression but soon to more agitation. The Great Reform Act of 1832 was a partial response, increasing the electorate by about a half, although in no way reducing the influence of urban or rural elites. The New Poor Law of 1834 demonstrated a degree of paternalist concern for the most wretched of the lower orders. William IV (1830–7) was the last monarch directly to interfere in politics, not always for the better. His famous successor, Victoria (1837–1901), learned to be more discreet.

1848: FRANCE

We move back to France, to which, especially to Paris, the eyes of would-be revolutionaries had been primarily turned ever since 1789. Although there were economic and other problems enough there at the beginning of 1848, the movement originated in February in a comparatively low-key manner. The great days of 1789 had begun with a shortage of bread, the disturbances of 1848 opened with the cancellation of a banquet. The fear that the after-dinner speeches would weaken the position of a government that had already banned political meetings persuaded it to take the provocative step. Even then, the crown of Louis-Philippe would perhaps have been safe for some time if a shot had not been fired during an ensuing demonstration. The dismissal of the unpopular minister François Guizot had already done something to reduce the anger of the crowd, which was singing happily enough as it walked up and down the boulevards on the evening of 23 February. But when a detachment of troops guarding the Ministry of Foreign Affairs made a firm stand, the good-natured crowd became an agitated crush. In the ensuing confusion, the fateful shot was fired, followed by a volley. Who fired the first shot is not known, but it is known that the volley was almost the only evidence of the army moving to the defence of the July Monarchy, which now came to an abrupt end. The 80 dead or wounded were moved back along the boulevard, and barricades were put up throughout Paris. The Parisian National Guard joined the insurgents, and was then reorganised and expanded. Louis-Philippe abdicated on the afternoon of 24 February in favour of his grandson, but the young comte de Paris was never in fact burdened with this high office.

The men who now came to the fore were for the most part not so much hard-headed realists as salon liberals dreaming of continuing or even extending the traditions of 1789 and later years. It was appropriate that one of the leading figures in a Provisional Government of ten members was the poet, historian and orator Alphonse de Lamartine. In a bold speech, he argued against the adoption of the red flag, but agreed that the tricolour should be augmented by a red rosette – an early compromise. It was also significant that under left-wing pressure three socialists and one worker were added to an original list of seven. The Provisional Government immediately proclaimed the right of universal male suffrage, and abolished slavery in all French territories for both sexes. The second move brought great hardship to the proprietors in the colonies, the first soon turned out to be far from the cure for all the ills of the metropolis.

As the Provisional Government discussed how it should allow all Frenchmen to make use of their vote, some of the unemployed in Paris began to agitate for the implementation of what they saw as another basic right, that to work. Louis Blanc, one of the socialists in the Provisional Government and the originator of the right to work formula, along with the worker member, was put in charge of a Parliament of Industry where he tried without success to advance his scheme of government-supported National Workshops. The Provisional Government was more concerned to preserve public credit, and introduced an additional tax, falling mainly on the peasantry, to bridge a gap in its budget.

Meanwhile, Alexandre Ledru-Rollin, the Minister of the Interior, was making arrangements for the election of a Constituent Assembly and doing what he could to ensure that a liberal republican majority would be secured by replacing the prefects of Louis-Philippe's administration with revolutionary commissars. The Ministry of Education strove to counter the clerical indoctrination of the parish priests through the secular indoctrination of village schoolteachers. In the election that finally took place at the end of April, the votes of the peasants, whose traditional conservatism was reinforced by the imposition of the additional tax on them, made sure that only a small minority of radical and socialist deputies was elected, the majority being either moderate royalists or moderate liberal republicans. The Provisional Government handed over its authority to the Assembly, which excluded Louis Blanc and the other left-wing ministers. It retained some of their former colleagues such as Lamartine, but he lost much of his influence by arguing for the retention of Ledru-Rollin.

Ousted from government, the left-wing politicians along with thousands of workers adopted the cause of Polish rebels recently suppressed by Prussia as the occasion for an attempt on 15 May to overthrow the Assembly so that they could tax the rich and declare war on the kings of Europe. The army and National Guard moved in to crush this movement, and the leaders soon found themselves either thrown into prison or fleeing into exile. Returning to Paris around this time, that acute analyst of the French Revolution and of American democracy, Alexis de Tocqueville, wrote: 'I saw society split in two: those who possessed nothing united in a common greed; those who possessed something in a common fear.' The gap between the two classes had produced a general awareness of 'an inevitable and approaching struggle'.[12] Frustration among the possessionless now produced a violent, disorganised protest after the closure of the National Workshops on 21 June, and the introduction of measures on the following day to enlist unmarried workers in the army, or to send them into the provinces. A bloody struggle began on 23 June, but was settled a few days later with the introduction of army detachments under the command of General Cavaignac, who was supported almost unanimously by the possessors. One of the more sensitive members of this class, the writer Victor Hugo, observed that in these June days civilisation defended itself with the methods of barbarism. Several thousand insurgents were killed, and several thousands more were summarily transported.

Now that a strong man had appeared to bring order out of chaos, the time was ripe for such a person to take over power. Cavaignac himself probably could have acquired it for the asking, but his firm constitutionalist beliefs helped to restrain him. Others feared what might now happen, when the Constitution drawn up by the Assembly included, in addition to a legislative chamber, an executive president. One of the deputies, Jules Grévy, asked:

> Are you sure that there will never be found an ambitious man, anxious to perpetuate his power, and if he is a man who had been able to make himself popular, if he is a victorious general, surrounded with the prestige of that military glory which the French cannot resist, if he is the offspring of one of the families which have reigned over France, and if he has never expressly renounced what he calls his rights, if commerce is languishing, if the people are in misery ... will you guarantee that this ambitious man will not succeed in overthrowing the republic?[13]

Lamartine and others argued that they should wait for the will of providence and the choice of the people.

Into a situation that had been tailor-made for him stepped a man identified by his clothes, as it were, and by very little else. Most observers of Napoleon I's nephew Louis Bonaparte came near to agreeing with the dismissive estimate of him made by Alexis de Tocqueville: 'an enigmatic, sombre, insignificant numbskull'.[14] But not for the first time in history, the intended dummy turned out to have a voice of his own. Up to 1848, except for a couple of abortive attempts to seize power in 1836 and 1840, Louis Bonaparte had not achieved much distinction beyond his name, although he certainly kept that going through publications such as *Napoleonic Ideas* in 1839.

Among the observations of his uncle in St Helena, let us recall, was the forecast that 'The first sovereign who, in the midst of the first great struggle, shall embrace in good faith the cause of the peoples, will find himself at the head of all Europe, and will be able to accomplish whatever he wishes'. Louis Bonaparte now believed that the moment had come for him to be such a sovereign, adapting the first Napoleon's teachings against the experience of the years from 1815 to 1848 to provide the basic ideas for himself to become Napoleon III.

1848: THE WEST

Early in 1848, there was a successful agitation for liberal constitutions in the Italian peninsula from Sicily to Piedmont. All of these were soon rescinded, however, except for a sole survivor in Piedmont, where King Charles Albert declared war on Austria in March, coming to the aid of Lombardy, where Marshal Radetsky and his forces had been driven from Milan. With little support from the other states, Lombardy and Piedmont could not hold out, and finally admitted defeat in March 1849. In 1848, after much adverse publicity, partly because of his refusal to encourage Piedmont, Pope Pius IX found it necessary to flee to Naples, leaving behind him the formation of a Roman Republic. Stoutly defended by the patriotic soldier Giuseppe Garibaldi, the republic held out against French forces until July 1849. A comparable institution in Venetia, the so-called Republic of St Mark, managed to remain in existence from March 1848 until August 1849 with fitful support from Piedmont. Although Giuseppe Mazzini, the leader of the Young Italy nationalist movement, was present in the revolt in Milan as well as becoming a member of the government of the Roman Republic, events in Italy through 1848 and 1849 were not so much a reflection of a clear desire for unification as a somewhat confusing mixture of conflicting ambitions, most of which were local or divisive. Pointing to the fact that there were more than 1000 different terms for weights and measures in the Kingdom of Naples alone as evidence for the difficulty of internal, let alone inter-state, commerce, Denis Mack Smith comments: 'Even the word "Italy" can have meant little to most southerners (or perhaps to most Italians).'[15] By the autumn of 1849, the Austrians were fully re-established in the north and centre, and the pre-war situation generally resumed elsewhere. In Italy's neighbour, Switzerland, late in 1847, liberals defeated conservatives in a brief conflict which had led by 1848 to the formulation of a new constitution, the basis for its modern confederation.

The other peninsula of south-west Europe, Iberia, was considerably affected by the great liberal cry of 1848. In Spain, there were risings in Madrid in March and May, a few leaders were executed and hundreds of followers sent into exile. Minor uprisings in other towns were more easily suppressed, and the government made a positive response to the Pope's appeal for the recapture of Rome in May 1849 just a few weeks after the French expeditionary force had landed. In Portugal, the impact of the revolutions of 1848 did not lead to action until the spring of 1851, when a new liberal ministry of 'regeneration' soon revealed itself to be moderate in a manner which reassured native and foreign businessmen.

A considerable number of the second group would be found in the British Isles, where there was mostly business as usual during 1848. The leaders of the movement for parliamentary reform known as Chartism called for a great demonstration in London in April, but the attendance was smaller than expected, and the Duke of Wellington, who had been appointed to direct the defence of the capital, experienced little call on his military talents. Such control as was necessary was left to the police augmented by special constables including Napoleon Bonaparte. Chartist demonstrations throughout Great Britain also came to very little. The 'Young Ireland' movement hoped to provoke a peasant revolt, but was a long way from immediately realising its aims, even though there had been a series of disastrous Irish potato harvests. More general excitement was probably aroused by the opening in 1851 of the Great Exhibition in the 'Crystal Palace'. Nevertheless, the degree of apprehension in 1848 must not be underestimated. It was Thomas Carlyle, after all, who en route to the London demonstration decided to catch an omnibus back home because it was raining, who wrote about the 'haggard element of fear' in the French Revolution. Alarmed by castle-burning and other events back home in Saxe-Coburg, and writing of 'Chartists every night', Prince Albert took Victoria off to

Osborne in the Isle of Wight. Even there, ramblers were mistaken for Chartists, and the royal couple soon sought more secure refuge in 'the imagined patriarchal world of the Scottish highlands' at Balmoral.[16]

In the Low Countries, nearly all was calm. A Liberal government under a constitutional monarch was already in power in Belgium, at whose frontiers a detachment of the army had no difficulty in turning back an invading band of French revolutionaries at the end of March. In Holland, the king summoned a States Commission to draw up a new Fundamental Law, which was proclaimed at the beginning of November. It made provision for representative legislative government on a limited franchise with the executive authority being retained by the hereditary monarchy of the House of Orange.

1848: THE CENTRE AND THE EAST

King Frederick William IV (1840–61), the head of the powerful absolute government in Prussia, was in no doubt about the necessity of maintaining the old order against all new threats when he addressed the United Landtag (combined meeting of the provincial governments or diets) on 11 April 1847. The king wanted to raise an international loan for the construction of a railroad, but the banks would not advance this financial aid without a guarantee from a national assembly authorising the necessary taxes. So he summoned the United Landtag, but nevertheless declared: 'Never will I allow a written document to come between God in Heaven and this land ... to take the place of ancient loyalty.'[17] However, liberals were able to use this new opportunity for spreading their views, and the unsatisfactory conclusion of the proceedings in June led to more discontent. Liberal demands in city councils for constitutional change were accompanied by demonstrations on city streets against food shortages and other financial pressures. There were serious riots in Berlin in March 1848, encouraged by the news of events in Paris and Vienna. Frederick William IV conceded the convocation of a Prussian Constituent Assembly, which from the middle of May to the beginning of December was to consider the manner in which Prussia might merge with a united Germany. The rulers of smaller German states followed Frederick William's example.

Meanwhile, at the beginning of March a group of about 50 liberals, mostly from the south-western German states, met in Heidelberg.

Although divided on the issue of the extent to which they should attempt to follow the example of France, the group was united in the decision to call for the creation of a parliament that would represent the interests of all Germany. Some believed that this move might promote revolution, others that it would avert it. The debate would continue after they agreed to call a preliminary parliament in Frankfurt, the seat of the German Confederation. This arranged for the election by male voters of nearly 600 representatives, which with a limited amount of governmental restriction, some republican opposition and a little violence was duly carried out. The National Assembly, or Frankfurt Parliament as it is more usually known, opened in mid-May. It was dominated by teachers, lawyers and civil servants, that is by middle-class professionals, who proceeded to consider the manner in which national unity might be achieved. After much argument, a Constitution was drawn up which would have realised in a federal form the ideal of national unity. Late in March 1849 the imperial crown was offered to the king of Prussia. Frederick William turned the offer down early in April, partly because of his abhorrence of the Frankfurt Parliament and everything new that it stood for, partly because of his reverence for the old traditions of the Holy Roman Empire.

Frederick William's decision soon brought about the dispersal of the Frankfurt Parliament. It also gave some comfort to the emperors of Austria and Russia at a time when they both had many other causes for anxiety. To take Austria first, riots in Vienna in March 1848 led to the resignation and departure of Metternich. The Emperor Ferdinand himself found it necessary to leave his capital in May and also to accept the convention of a Constituent Assembly, which opened its proceedings at the end of July. Like its counterparts elsewhere, it made few concrete decisions, although it did at the beginning of September pass a law completing the emancipation of peasants throughout the empire. The Constituent Assembly was dissolved early in October, and an ensuing series of political disturbances was brought to an end by force rather than by further concessions. However, early in December the Emperor Ferdinand was persuaded to abdicate in favour of his nephew Francis Joseph, who began a long reign lasting to 1916 with the completion of the restoration of the old order.

In its wider empire, the Austrian government managed to avoid disaster in central Europe in the time-honoured manner of playing off

Slav against Magyar, and recommending to the subject peoples the Austrian devil they knew as an alternative to the devils they did not know, the Russian and Prussian. Such considerations weighed heavily upon, for example, the Czech nationalist František Palacký, who in his address to the Committee of the Frankfurt Parliament in April 1848 talked of 'an empire whose preservation, integrity and consolidation is, and must be, a great and important matter not only for my own nation but also for the whole of Europe, indeed, for humanity and civilisation itself ...'. Faced on the one hand by the Russian aspiration to 'universal monarchy', which would gobble up the smaller Slav peoples, on the other hand by a unifying Germany, a Czech connection with which would be devoid of any historical or legal basis, his own people should look to Vienna. The Slavs, Wallachians and other peoples along the Danube should do the same. Palacký declared: 'Assuredly, if the Austrian state had not existed for ages, it would have been a behest for us in the interests of Europe and indeed of humanity to endeavour to create it as soon as possible.' Moreover, the peoples of the Danube must not be dominated by Hungary – 'a State which declares a man must first be a Magyar before he can be a human being'.[18] At a Slav Congress which met in Prague in June 1848, after the publication of two manifestos, one declaring loyalty to the Austrian emperor, the other making an appeal to the brotherhood of all the Slavs, Palacký composed a third which was generally accepted, calling for a general congress of nations. This was not enough for some of his fellow Czech nationalists, especially the younger elements, and a revolt broke out on 13 June. The Austrian commander Windischgrätz agreed to an armistice on 15 June even though his wife had been killed. But a resumption of the revolt on 15 June persuaded him to bomb the city into submission.

In Hungary, there was more serious trouble. On 15 March 1848, the Diet in Budapest under the leadership of the liberal nationalist Louis Kossuth adopted a programme for independent representative government which was to include union with Transylvania and the absorption of Croatia, but without recognition of their non-Hungarian peoples. The Emperor Ferdinand accepted these 'March Laws' on the last day of the month. However, unrest in Croatia grew sufficiently for a local force led by the governor and supported by the emperor to invade Hungary in mid-September. The Hungarian militia managed to withstand the invasion, even though it was joined by Windischgrätz, and on 14 April 1849, Kossuth declared that the Habsburgs were deposed from the throne of Hungary, which would now assert its independence under his governorship. However, in the summer the Hungarians found themselves opposed not only by the Austro-Croatian forces but also by a Russian army which had invaded at the invitation of the government back in Vienna. A defeat at the none too merciful hands of the Russians early in August led to the more relentless suppression of Hungarian independence under the boot of the Austrian General 'Butcher' Haynau. Kossuth went off to gain the rapturous acclaim of a wide variety of foreigners, but was never allowed home to receive the sympathy of his fellow countrymen.

Meanwhile, some of them fresh from the barricades in Paris, Romanians in the Danubian principalities of Moldavia and Wallachia, and in Transylvania, too, spoke out for radical reform and national unification. In July 1848, the Russians marched into Moldavia, in September into Wallachia. With the consent of the Turkish authorities, the occupation continued for three years. The Russians would have been fully prepared if necessary to extend their activities in Poland, but unrest was most noticeable in the Prussian and Austrian sectors.

The Emperor Nicholas I and his advisers were alert to the dangers of subversion even before the central European disturbances of 1848 began. The emperor himself composed a famous manifesto of 26 March 1848, in which he complained that rebellion and lawlessness were rampant in Prussia and Austria and menacing 'our Holy Russia'. He called on his people to rouse themselves for 'Faith, Tsar and the Motherland', expressing his confidence that God was with them.[19] An army 400,000 strong was duly deployed at the frontier, and the royal commander-in-chief was prepared to send it on a repressive mission as far as the Rhine. The alarm that such a move would have provoked even among those opposed to the revolutionary movement is difficult to imagine: even as it was, the invasion of Hungary and the Danubian principalities led to considerable unease.

With the collapse of the revolutionary movement in the rest of Europe and its failure to penetrate Russia itself to any significant level, Nicholas himself could sleep a little more easily, perhaps, but his last years were full of apprehension and foreboding. Among other measures was the prohibition of the sale of matches in quantities of less than a thousand – those who could only afford fewer were deemed most likely to set fire to mostly wooden buildings. More substantially, the emperor appealed to the nobility to remain the chief support of the autocracy, promising no alteration in serfdom or in any other aspect of the Russian system. As David Saunders forcefully argues, 'the political chasm that divided the Russian empire from the other European states was widening, not only by virtue of leftward movement in the west, but also by virtue of rightward movement in the east'.[20]

Nicholas would have liked the international situation to have reverted to the status quo of the Vienna Settlement of 1815. The Eastern Question was now becoming more complex with the steeper decline of the Ottoman Empire in south-east Europe, and the emperor deemed it all the more necessary, therefore, to keep a tight grip on Ukraine and other outlying regions. Mistakenly, he believed that his predicament was understood by Britain, which he saw as his chief hope of support against France. This misunderstanding would compound the problems leading towards the Crimean War.

To the north of Europe, the menacing spirit of the age did not appear as great in the Baltic region as elsewhere. There was certainly shouting on the streets of Stockholm and Copenhagen, and some constitutional liberalisation, but little tumult. On the other hand, war involving Denmark with the restless duchies of Schleswig and Holstein in 1848 brought in the Prussians with the support of the Frankfurt Parliament, which wanted to incorporate them in the German Confederation. Nicholas sent a Russian squadron into Danish waters, and threatened Frederick William with war unless he withdrew. The Austrian imperial government also kept a close eye on these northern developments, and exerted pressure for a Prussian withdrawal. British Baltic interests made for support of Denmark, and Britain acted as host for the drawing up of the Treaty of London of 1852, which restored the status quo.

LIBERALISM

The revolutions of 1848 seemed to have dashed the hopes of those who had believed that this was the beginning of a new era. Middle-class agitation and popular dissatisfaction had not been able to effect a successful combination. A great torrent of words had dwindled to a trickle of action in the expected direction, to some extent because few of the would-be revolutionaries wanted to repeat the pattern of events following 1789 – hardly anybody wanted the return of political execution. Nevertheless, reaction could not claim complete victory, and liberalism did not have to admit full defeat. Indeed, the future was still with those who made at least some recognition of economic and political change rather than attempting to ignore or reject them.

Liberalism was such a powerful force because it was associated with economic as well as political development, and because the ideas of Adam Smith were adapted for differing circumstances. For example, the German Friedrich List argued in *The National System of Political Economy*, first published in 1841, that Smith and his contemporaries had given insufficient attention to the necessity for nationalism. He wrote of Britain and its system of free trade: 'It is a rule of elementary prudence, when you have reached the top, to kick away the ladder you have used, in order to deprive the others of the means of climbing up after you.'[21] Other nations needed to resort to tariffs to protect their trade, until they were strong enough to open their commercial doors to outside rivals. In order to achieve the necessary progress, these nations should take legislative and administrative steps to ensure that agriculture, industry and commerce were combined in harmonious proportions. In such a manner, German and much other continental economic liberalism would differ considerably from the major British model.

Similarly, the extent to which political ideas and groups should follow the example set by the French in the years following 1789 was debated with much passion. In France itself, Benjamin Constant in his *Principles of Politics* published in 1815 attacked the power of the state, the all too clear knowledge of what Napoleon had done with it fresh in his mind. For him, man was a 'temple' possessing the divine attribute of freedom, and would therefore be happy if left completely to himself. On the other hand, Alexis de Tocqueville argued on the basis of the experiences that he distilled in his *Democracy in America* published in 1835 that equality was a stronger instinct among the masses than freedom. Therefore, the encroaching power of the state was best resisted in association, since 'it is in the commune that the strength of free peoples is lodged'.[22] In Britain, James Mill was more than anybody the founder of 'philosophic radicalism', moving from support for the rights of man towards the argument that good government could best be secured by a wide extension of the franchise. He was also a devoted disciple of Jeremy Bentham, who believed that his ideals of utilitarianism, the greatest happiness of the greatest number, were best guaranteed through emphasis on the rights of the individual and free trade. John Stuart Mill, son of James, argued in his *Principles of Political Economy* published in 1848 that state intervention was necessary to secure utilitarian ends, that the state should encourage co-operative enterprises and reduce inequality by curbing rights of inheritance. During the Irish famine of 1846–7, he went so far as to argue in favour of the creation of peasant proprietorships. More generally, he attacked the subjection of women.[23]

Restoration politics in France were on the basis of a very narrow franchise, restricted even further by 1829 in an attempt to save the Bourbon regime. Even after the 1830 Revolution, France had one elector for every 170 inhabitants while Britain after 1832 had one for every 25. The outstanding politician of the Orléanist era, Guizot, helped to extend education but was very wary about broadening the right to vote, recollecting the excesses of the sequel to the Revolution of 1789. Meanwhile, the British looked more towards 1688, as Whigs tended to become Liberals in the years following the Reform Act of 1832. This Act extended the franchise in a limited manner only, and so a People's Charter was drawn up in 1838 asking for one vote for every man, new parliaments every year and a number of other moves in the direction of equality. Chartists were killed in demonstrations in 1839, and some former Liberal supporters drew back from a movement that seemed to them to have turned too radical. An Anti-Corn Law League founded in 1839 to achieve another important Liberal aim, free trade, enjoyed more constant support and won its victory with the repeal of the protective Corn Laws in 1846. This measure split the Tory government of Sir Robert Peel, who had previously persuaded his party to accept the Reform Act of 1832 and thus to move in the direction of becoming the Conservative Party. In Germany and Italy, the liberal cause became closely involved with the struggle for national unification, while in Russia, it was identified by the government with ideas that were much more extreme.

1848 was more of a victory for reaction than for liberalism, but in the following years the struggle would be continued, as well as being made more complex by the more complete entry into the arena of nationalism, socialism and imperialism.

8

NATIONALISM, SOCIALISM, IMPERIALISM, 1848–1878

Nationalism in one form or another had been around in Europe for several centuries. Yet, during the period following the 1848 revolutions it became a powerful force in many parts of the continent – in Austria–Hungary, Germany, Italy, and in the 'sick man of Europe' – the declining Ottoman Empire. From region to region, nationalism took on different forms, and in turn these were affected by socialism and imperialism. Moreover, all three movements were influenced by the process of industrialisation that was making itself increasingly felt throughout Europe, and by the changing nature of the relationship of Europe to the rest of the world.

NAPOLEON III AND THE SECOND EMPIRE

In the fateful year of 1848, after a brief visit to Paris where he had found little or no support for his assumption of the imperial sceptre, Louis Bonaparte had returned to London to wield a baton as a special constable against the Chartists. But with the cry of 'Vive Napoléon' rising up at the beginning of the June Days, the moment had come for him to be both a man of destiny and the winner of a popular election. From June onwards, with the help of some rich patrons, Louis Bonaparte carried on a widespread publicity campaign, which led towards crushing victory in the race for president. On 10 December 1848, he secured nearly 5.5 million votes to General Cavaignac's nearly 1.5 million. Last came Lamartine, the embodiment of the spirit of 1848, with less than 18,000 votes. Next to last came the candidate of the extreme left, with just over double that number at nearly 37,000 votes. Nevertheless, it was fear of the threat posed by the poor that persuaded so many of the rich and not so rich to give their support to the authority that their candidate's name seemed to give him.

In the May 1849 elections for the Legislative Assembly, the reappointed prefects exerted considerable influence, even without which the 'party of order', as the conservatives were often called, would probably have achieved a large majority. As it was, they won about 500 out of 750 seats, although with many peasants staying away from the polls, the left managed to achieve 180 seats. There followed some more June Days, this time arising from a demonstration in favour of the Roman Republic, which French troops were about to squash. Although the demonstration was an almost complete failure, some left-wing leaders were put in jail and others went hurriedly into exile. The government moved towards entrenchment of its position through renewed support for clerical education and prefectorial control over the hiring and firing of primary school teachers. In October 1849, the supposed puppet started to pull the strings as Louis Bonaparte dismissed the ministers in the Assembly and appointed men under his own leadership from outside it. In March 1850, the left made impressive gains in some by-elections, partly as a consequence of which the government changed the electoral law in May to exclude all those deputies who had run foul of the law courts – nearly a third of the total. Louis Napoleon was still not completely sure of his maintenance of power, however, especially since he could not secure the two-thirds majority in the Assembly necessary for the constitution to be changed so that he could be re-elected president.

After much jockeying for position, Louis Bonaparte and his advisers decided to ignore the constitution and stage a coup. Army leaders without General Cavaignac's scruples were called in from Algeria, and at the beginning of December 1851 strategic points in Paris were taken over by their troops. An appeal was issued to the people accusing the Assembly of plotting to overthrow the president, the direct opposite of the truth. With remarkable ease, the Second Republic was replaced by the Second Empire. Karl Marx's explanation is persuasive:

> Just as the Bourbons were the dynasty of the great landlords, and just as the July monarchy was the dynasty of money, so the Bonapartes are the dynasty of the peasants, the smallholders who form the bulk of the French population ... For three years, the towns had been able to falsify the significance of the election of 10 December, and to cheat the peasants of their desire, the restoration of the Empire. The purpose of the election of 10 December 1848 was not achieved until the *coup d'état* of 2 December 1851.

As Marx went on to explain, the majority of the French population were peasants with their own smallholdings, each family making up an almost self-sufficient unit or atom. Then:

> A score or two of these atoms make up a village, and a few score of villages make up a department. In this way, the great mass of the French nation is formed by the simple addition of like entities, much as a sack of potatoes consists of a lot of potatoes huddled into a sack.

But the peasants could not act as an independent class, and needed the representation of a lord and master 'who will protect them against the other classes, and who will send them the rain and the sunshine from above'. Therefore they gave their support to another Napoleon.[1] In this way the peasants of the provinces were getting revenge on the town-dwellers, especially those in Paris. Because of such age-old rivalries, the great gulf between the peasants and the urban proletariat would never close in the manner predicted by Marx. Moreover, while Napoleon needed to create his own entourage and bureaucracy, the bourgeois were kept happy with tax burdens which did not seem heavy as long as there was prosperity for them.

The Second Empire was fortunate in beginning its history with an almost immediate revival from the economic difficulties that had embarrassed the July Monarchy and the Second Republic. With an amalgamation of many railway companies into as few as six, three times as much line as in 1851 was in existence by 1859. Production of coal, iron and steel all shot up, and foreign commerce almost trebled from 1855 to 1867. This expansion meant that other European nations were enjoying prosperity, too.

THE CRIMEAN WAR, 1854–6

However, industrial expansion was by no means a promoter of amicable international relations. Indeed, the reasons for the outbreak of war in the Black Sea after 40 years of nearly general peace in Europe possessed a pronounced economic aspect along with the more celebrated personal misunderstandings and arguments. In the first instance, the war appeared to arise from disputes concerning the fate of the Christian peoples and places within the fragile frontiers of the declining Muslim Ottoman Empire. The fact that the major challenge to traditional Russian rights in this sphere was issued by a descendant of Napoleon who had the audacity to call himself an emperor acted on Tsar Nicholas I like a red rag to a bull. An underlying and probably more important cause was British apprehension of Russian expansion into the Middle East and the Balkans. The Suez Canal was being actively discussed as a means of making easier what was already a vital link with India through what was already called the crossroads of half the world. The Ottoman Empire was a pliant recipient of British goods and an actual supplier of grain to some customers, a potential supplier of grain to others.Therefore, the Danube and the Straits from the Black Sea to the Mediterranean needed protection from Russia by Britain and its French ally. For Nicholas I, on the other hand, the Ottoman Empire needed protection from Western aggressors.

There were also many diplomatic acts of 'folly and blunder' before more of them followed in hostilities. As British, French and Turkish regiments entered the fray in 1854, Florence Nightingale and other nurses worked overtime at their grisly labours, which were made even more arduous by widespread disease. The fame of the incidents and personalities of the Crimean War was partly the result of the fact that this was the first international conflict widely reported in the newspapers by special correspondents, but it was also a reflection of the circumstance that this was the first such conflict since 1815. Moreover, its significance was greater than the terms of the Treaty of Paris of 30 March 1856, drawn up after an Austrian threat to join in the war against Russia at the end of 1855, might suggest. According to them, Russia was to draw back from the mouth of the Danube and Bessarabia, to give up its protectorate over Christians in the Ottoman Empire and to join with the other powers in making the Black Sea free of fortifications and warships. Napoleon III would have liked to have made a greater name for himself by promoting in the Congress of Paris as great a revision of international frontiers as in the Congress of Vienna of 1815, an answer to the questions of Europe as well as to the Eastern Question. But other powers would go no further than a secret agreement made in April 1856 with France by Britain and Austria to guarantee the Treaty of Paris, especially the integrity of the Ottoman Empire. However, in spite of the inclusion of an article obliging the sultan to bring in reforms to Turkey and its dependencies, the Ottoman Empire's health could not be restored in such a manner. Moreover, by excluding Russia and themselves from the Balkans, the signatories to the agreement had created a kind of vacuum which could only promote the rapid infiltration of nationalism. In particular, they guaranteed the Danubian principalities of Moldavia and Wallachia, which joined together in 1862 as Romania.

Nationalism in general received a considerable impetus from the Crimean War, although not in the way that Napoleon III or any of the other participants, with the possible exception of the late entrant Piedmont, could have wanted. This nationalism was promoted in an atmosphere of international tension leading to more conflict. Moreover, the struggle for nationalism and between nations was accompanied by social conflict, leading to many appearances of the spectre of communism, which in the Paris Commune of 1871 appeared to be made flesh. Yet another Congress had to meet in Berlin in 1878 in an attempt to settle the Eastern Question in a more satisfactory manner than had been achieved at the Congress of Paris in 1856.

RUSSIA

Turning to an examination of the manner in which the complex sequel to the Crimean War unfolded, let us look first at the power which, apart perhaps from the Ottoman Empire, came out of it worst. The collapse of his policies probably hastened the death of Nicholas I in 1855; certainly, the mess had to be cleared up by his eldest son, Alexander II (1855–81). Russia's social system, which had appeared to the first Alexander to have received assurance from victory over the first Napoleon in 1815, now seemed to the second Alexander to be given a negative appraisal by the virtual defeat inflicted partly by the third Napoleon 40 years on. In consequence, the new tsar and his entourage gave primary attention to domestic problems, steering away from Russia's previous attempt to act as the gendarme of Europe. They concluded that armed forces for the defence of the fatherland, and perhaps for its expansion in Asia rather than Europe, could be modernised after their poor performance in the Crimean War only if they were prepared to abolish Russia's peculiar institution of serfdom. This reform was duly implemented in 1861, although in a manner modified after much opposition from a sizeable group of the noble landlords. The peasants were to be personally free, but were still mostly tied to the commune, restricted by inadequate shares of land and overburdened by redemption payments. Therefore, there was only partial fulfilment of the intention of the emancipation edict of 1861 that the peasants 'should understand that by acquiring property and greater freedom to dispose of their possessions, they have an obligation to society and to themselves to live up to the letter of the new law by a loyal and judicious use of the rights which are now granted to them'.[2] Indeed, it was probably more through breaking the letter of the law than by living up to it that some peasants did manage to join in the movement towards industrial revolution that was taking place even in Russia, and towards some associated improvement in agricultural techniques that promoted the increase of grain surpluses. The railway began to conquer the age-old problem of vast distances, at once stimulating and benefiting from increased production of metal and coal, and helping the grain surpluses on their way to more remote markets.

Other measures in 1864 followed the emancipation of 1861: a reform of local government involving a limited amount of election and initiative for a new body called the *zemstvo*; and a reform of the judicial system, introducing the principle of equality before the law and the right to trial by jury for criminal offences. Provincial bureaucrats and lawyers everywhere benefited from the changes; their impact on the mass of the people might have been for the better but was less easily perceptible.

'The major drawback of the reforms of the 1860s', observes David Saunders, 'was not the inadequacy of particular edicts or the juxtaposition of old and new, but the tsar's refusal to establish a central representative organ in which the problems attendant upon reform might have been subject to public scrutiny.' Since the tsar alone still made the law, the reforms could have been rescinded whenever he so chose. However, Saunders suggests: 'Conceptually limited, poorly executed, incomplete, unsustained and insecure, the measures enacted by Alexander II nevertheless transformed the Russian Empire.'[3]

The death of his eldest son in 1865 probably undermined Alexander II's resolution, while any ideas of further reform were almost certainly dissipated by an attempt on his life in 1866. Nevertheless, another great change was still to come in 1874, the reorganisation of the armed forces on the basis of universal male service. Regular soldiers were better educated, and possibly helped to spread literacy after demobilisation. Certainly, they were given an early opportunity to show their professional mettle in a war against Turkey from 1877 to 1878.

Before that, they had concentrated on the maintenance of domestic order, the most flagrant breach of which was the Polish insurrection of 1863, although there was unrest in the Baltic provinces and Ukraine as well as some serious peasant and worker disturbance nearer home, too. Trouble among the non-Slavic nationalities was to be found in Asia, where Russia was pushing its frontiers outwards until it met the British or other opposition, the mountains or the sea. It withdrew from across the sea after the sale of Alaska to the USA in 1867, and the exchange with Japan of the Kurile Islands for the southern half of Sakhalin in 1875. But it took land from China with the Treaty of Aigun in 1858 and the Treaty of Peking in 1860. In 1860 it founded on the Pacific Ocean the town of Vladivostok, which means 'Lord of the East'.

Expansion to the east was partly a compensation for lack of it to the west, although it was also partly Russia's variation of a more general imperial development. Certainly, the experience of the Crimean War had indicated to Russia that it could no longer lord it over Europe after 1856 as it had done after 1815. The victory of Prussia over Austria in 1866 acted as a further deterrent, but also as a warning. In 1873, Alexander II joined in a League of the Three Emperors with William I of Germany and Francis Joseph of Austria, but, not surprisingly, this system of co-operation began to break down almost before it was set up. As we shall see as we now turn to consider the two empires of central Europe, by 1873 their interests were diverging from those of Russia while, after disagreement and even war, moving towards convergence between themselves.

AUSTRIA–HUNGARY

Of the three emperors, there can be little doubt that Francis Joseph (1848–1916) was confronted with the most serious problems after his accession. Although he liked to think of himself as the last monarch of the old school, he would never have survived as long as he did without some adaptation to the new. Having alienated Russia during the Crimean War, especially through the ultimatum of December 1855 which forced its former ally to come to terms, Austria now found itself isolated. Beset with troubles in Italy that led to war against France and Piedmont in 1859, it lost all its Italian possessions except for Venetia. At the same time, the continuing struggle with Prussia for pre-eminence in the German Confederation was taking a turn for the worse as far as Austria was concerned. We must remember that Austria was still widely looked on as the senior member of the Confederation set up in 1815, a position underlined by an agreement about it between Prussia and Austria with the encouragement of Russia in 1850. This Olmütz Pact dissolved the Erfurt Union of North German States set up by Prussia in 1849. Then early in 1861, the proclamation of a new constitution made Austria appear liberal in contrast with a reactionary Prussia, and a meeting of the princes summoned by the Austrian Emperor Francis Joseph in 1863 indicated his ascendancy over the smaller states of the Confederation. But any further strengthening of the Confederation could not be achieved without the co-operation of Prussia, which was clearly shown to be impossible after disagreements on the Schleswig–Holstein problem from 1864 to 1865 led to the Austro-Prussian Seven Weeks War of 1866.

At the Treaty of Prague which concluded this disastrous war, Francis Joseph officially gave up the seniority in Germany that his Habsburg forebears had claimed for centuries, while the upstart Prussian Hohenzollern William I extended his influence over a new North German Confederation. The last Austrian foothold in Italy, Venetia, went to Napoleon III, who handed it over to Italy at the same time as trying to ensure that neither the Prussian victory nor the Austrian defeat should be complete. Prussia would not in any case have wanted to take on the problems of administering the Austrian Empire, any infiltration into which would also have upset Russia. The southern German states were to form their own independent federation, although the process of undermining their independence was already begun by Prussia. Bohemia was excluded from Germany along with Austria, which now, in order to preserve its integrity, made concessions to Hungary.

By the end of 1867, the *Ausgleich* or Compromise had been reached, and the Dual Monarchy of Austria–Hungary was set up. Foreign affairs and the armed forces and the finance required for them were to be administered jointly. But the emperor was to go to Budapest (strictly speaking to Buda, the incorporation with Pest not taking place until 1873) to receive the old Crown of St Stephen, king and unifier of medieval Hungary from about 974 to 1038, and to take the medieval oath to the Golden Bull of 1222, the equivalent and almost exact contemporary of the English Magna Carta of 1215. Magyar, the language of the Hungarians, was given official recognition, as was their separate nationality. An Austrian in Budapest, except for King Francis Joseph, of course, would now be considered as much a foreigner as a Hungarian in Vienna.

Hungary was to include Croatia, which did not please the Croatians, even though they were given the exclusive use of their own language and a considerable degree of internal self-government in a further Compromise of 1868. Transylvania was also included in Hungary, much to the outrage of Romania, which believed it should be incorporated along with Moldavia and Wallachia. Transylvania, widely thought of in the West as the mythical home of Count Dracula, has remained a real bone of contention between Hungary and Romania down to the present day. In 1868, deprived of any compromise for themselves, the Czechs demonstrated their annoyance at the compromise with Hungary. In a Declaration of August 1868, they claimed the same traditional rights for Slavonic Bohemia as had been recognised in Magyar Hungary. The government in Vienna proclaimed a state of siege in Bohemia, whose cause was supported by the Slovaks and echoed by the Poles. In spite of all these problems, the government of Francis Joseph managed to hold on until the completion of German unification under Prussia. But the seniority of Austria in the German Confederation, which we have acknowledged by considering it first, was lost some years before 1871.

GERMANY

The achievement of German unification has traditionally been attributed to the man who became Prussia's chief minister in September

1862, Otto von Bismarck. Before then his career was not especially distinguished. Born in 1815 to a Junker father and a middle-class mother, he made no great mark at Göttingen University or afterwards as a landlord or civil servant.

As Prussian representative at the Frankfurt Parliament from 1848, Bismarck conceived a distaste for parliamentary government, and first perceived the possibility of Prussia taking the lead in German unification. Three years as ambassador to St Petersburg from 1858 convinced him that Prussia had need of Russia, and a briefer embassy to Paris in 1862 taught him that France also could help in the task of unification on which he was now set. Recalled to help Prussia out of constitutional crisis, he achieved this aim by unconstitutional action later in 1862. He was now firmly installed as chancellor.

Bismarck is well known for his many statements about how the task of German unification under Prussian leadership must be completed, the most famous being that the task would be completed through 'blood and iron'. Yet Bismarck himself was neither a military nor an industrial specialist, and achieved his reputation partly through clever diplomacy and partly through domestic political skill. To put his contribution in perspective, and even to cut it down to size, we must recall another celebrated observation, this time of the twentieth-century British economist Lord Keynes, to the effect that 'The German Empire was not founded on blood and iron, but on coal and iron'.[4] The Customs Union (*Zollverein*), which had been going from strength to strength for more than 40 years, was to prosper still further at the critical time. Moreover, the way for Bismarck was also prepared by the development of cultural nationalism: along with blood, coal and iron must be placed pen and ink, and voice. Germans did indeed write and speak the same language in reality much more than the Italians, for example, and metaphorically spoke the same language more than many other peoples.

While they agreed with Goethe and Fichte and with folk tales collected by the brothers Grimm which illustrated the unity of German culture, the German peoples were by no means agreed about the manner in which their unification would come about at the time that Bismarck came to power in 1862. Should there be a greater German (*Grossdeutsch*) or lesser German (*Kleindeutsch*) answer to the problem? The former would include Austria, although not necessarily its empire, and was generally favoured by Roman Catholics. The latter would exclude Austria and its empire and was generally favoured by Protestants. There were in addition most of the Prussian Junkers and some others who did not want unification at all. There was also a dispute among those in favour of unification about how it should be achieved. By 1862, Bismarck was decided on the lesser German solution, which he did not believe could be settled except through the aforementioned 'blood and iron'. Not that he was in favour of force while the methods of diplomacy could avert it, or until those methods had created the optimum conditions in which to resort to it.

Bismarck's diplomacy began at home. Although he often expressed his impatience with political parties and parliaments, he needed to work with them. Moreover, he also had to co-operate with the King of Prussia, William 1 (1861–88), and with his entourage composed mainly of die-hard Prussian conservatives. As he once put it: 'In order that German patriotism should be active and effective, it needs as a rule to hang on the peg of dependence on a dynasty.'[5] Although he had personal differences with the Hohenzollerns, they also helped him, not only within Germany but also outside it. For example, in 1863, the question of Schleswig–Holstein, which had been temporarily settled more than ten years previously, arose again as a new Danish king, Christian IX, announced that he was going to incorporate Schleswig and strengthen his grip on Holstein. Encouraged by the smaller German states, Prussia and Austria declared war on Denmark, and their joint armies overran the two duchies within a few weeks early in 1864. In 1848, at a time of a similar crisis, Nicholas I of Russia had sent a naval squadron to Danish waters demanding the withdrawal of Prussian troops acting on behalf of the German Confederation. Now, with some misgivings but also with gratitude for Prussian moral support at the time of the Polish insurrection in 1863, Alexander II and his entourage held back from condemning the action of King William and Emperor Francis Joseph and their administrative division of Schleswig and Holstein by the summer of 1865.

Bismarck's diplomacy made use of his experience in Paris as well as in St Petersburg, for he fully realised the necessity of gaining acceptance for his next move, against Austria, not only from Russia but also from France. He went to the French resort of Biarritz in October 1865 to conciliate Napoleon III, whom he had once described as 'a sphinx without a riddle, an unfathomed nonentity',[6] but now recognised as a mighty and ambitious emperor. We must remember here that, before the fiasco of the war against Prussia in 1870–1, France was widely looked upon as a greater power than Prussia, while Napoleon III was looked upon as more expansionist than William I. Bismarck made the appearance of agreeing with Napoleon that France's natural frontier of the Rhine could be rounded out while Germany would do the same beyond that river in central Europe. Italy agreed to engage Austria from the other flank should war break out between the two contenders for German leadership.

Bismarck attempted to extend his influence in the German Confederation by a proposal of universal male suffrage. Then, using the pretext of Austria's infringement of its agreement concerning Schleswig–Holstein, Bismarck managed to get a sufficient amount of support from the members of the Confederation to begin the war against Austria in Holstein in June 1866 and to finish it with a crushing victory over Austria and its ally Saxony at Sadowa or Königgrätz in Bohemia on 3 July 1866. Bismarck now had to restrain William I, who was anxious to march on to Vienna and complete the humiliation of Austria. Bismarck believed that such a move would alienate Russia and perhaps provoke France to the point of intervention; moreover, to dismember the Austrian Empire would bring Prussia greater responsibilities than it could handle. He also argued that 'We will one day need Austria for ourselves'.[7]

By the Treaty of Prague of August 1866 Austria was pushed out of the German Confederation, also out of Italy, and obliged to pay Prussia an indemnity. Bismarck took the opportunity of moving nearer unification by annexing small states that had opposed Prussia: Hanover and North Hesse as well as Schleswig and Holstein. He made a further step in the same direction by incorporating Saxony, which had fought on the side of Austria, into a new North German Confederation. The four southern German states, Bavaria, Würtemburg, Baden and South Hesse, were to remain independent and develop their confederation.

Even before the Treaty of Prague was signed, however, Bismarck had pushed the southern German states into making secret defence treaties with Prussia, whose army would be augmented by theirs in time of war. He also gave his approval to the formation by these states of their own customs union, suggesting that this experience would sooner or later incline them towards political integration. However, this gradual conversion was never allowed to take place, owing to the attitude of the emperor of France. Napoleon III, whose posture and rhetoric had persuaded other powers in Europe to consider him a more formidable potential adversary than he turned out to be, had himself committed an error of gross miscalculation in 1866. Fully expecting Austria to gain the upper hand in the early phases of a long war, he planned to intervene at an appropriate moment on the side of Prussia in return for the more certain fulfilment of the promise of expansion to the Rhine that Bismarck had held out before him at Biarritz. Now he and his advisers found themselves humiliated and dismayed by the suddenness of the Prussian victory. Therefore, although they were in the middle of a comprehensive military reform, they decided to press on regardless towards the promised river. As for one of the larger southern German states in the middle, a popular newspaper in Würtemburg expressed the wish: 'If only south Germany had a statesman, just a single one who had confidence in himself, confidence in the people and the confidence of the people!'[8] It also expressed apprehension about the spread of Bavarian as well as Prussian influence.

However, a greater fear was of the French dominance of the Upper Rhine. Bismarck played upon this fear while at the same time provoking the already agitated Napoleon towards desperate action. As the most accessible satisfaction of his injured reputation, the French emperor looked to the Duchy of Luxembourg, offering to buy it from Holland. Bismarck might have accepted this move, but was pushed into opposition by the patriotic declarations of the new North German Reichstag. Again, alternative French financial infiltration into Belgium was not opposed by Bismarck, indeed it was even encouraged by him to the point where he considered taking a German share in the Low Countries in the shape of Holland as an agreed counterpart to a complete French adoption of Belgium. When Britain moved to defend the continuance of Belgium as instituted in 1830, Bismarck once more backed down.

Frustrated beyond almost every limit, Napoleon attempted to create an appropriate diplomatic situation for the restraint of Prussia, even attack on it. Certainly, by this time, other powers such as Russia and Britain were becoming somewhat alarmed at the expansion being achieved by Bismarck. However, the attitudes and pronouncements of

Napoleon appeared to them to constitute if anything a graver threat. Austria was alienated by Napoleon's restraint at the time of the Austro-Prussian War of 1866, while Italy had cause to be grateful to Bismarck as well as to Napoleon, and was not happy at the continuing prospect of French troops in Rome. In any case, neither Austria nor Italy was in a position to embark on further war. The showdown between France and Prussia arose from a crisis occurring in Spain, where Queen Isabella had been pushed from her throne in 1868 by a revolution. To outflank Napoleon, Bismarck pushed the candidature of Leopold von Sigmaringen, a Roman Catholic member of the Prussian Hohenzollern family. King William I did not at first promote his distant kinsman's candidature, not wishing to antagonise Napoleon, but Leopold went ahead with Bismarck's continued support, and duly secured the position for which he had applied. However, after French protest, and the discouragement of William I, he withdrew his candidature: then, the French ambassador dared in July 1870 to approach William I in the streets of the resort of Ems, and demand that the candidature be withdrawn permanently. Such an insult was turned to his salvation by a hard-pressed Bismarck, who knew from a meeting between William I and Tsar Alexander II in Ems in June that Russia would not intervene on the side of France. Bismarck also used the wide means of publicity open to him concerning the French threat to keep Britain out as well.

Bismarck released to the press the famous Ems Telegram sent him by William I, concluding: 'His Majesty ... declined to receive the French ambassador again, and had the latter informed ... that His Majesty had nothing further to communicate to the ambassador.' There was a clear message in the midst of the diplomatic verbiage, as William I was himself to declare: 'This is war.'[9] The same message got through to Napoleon III, who ordered mobilisation to begin on Bastille Day, 14 July, and declared war on Prussia on 19 July. Bismarck immediately publicised evidence of aggressive French intentions towards Luxembourg and the Rhine, which not only kept Britain firmly out of the war but also made it sympathetic to the Prussian cause. Moreover, the southern German states were persuaded by the French threat as well as by the national sentiments expressed by liberal politicians more than conservatives to enter the conflict on the Prussian side. Localism in Bavaria took a little longer to overcome than in the smaller states of Southern Hesse, Baden and Würtemburg, but soon a united Germany was in the field against a dispirited France. After crushing defeats culminating at Sedan on 1 September, Napoleon III surrendered, and a republic was declared in Paris, against which the Prussian army instigated a siege. Alsace and Lorraine were annexed from France by royal and popular demand after the move had been initiated by Bismarck, even if he asserted later that this expansion had been forced on him. On 18 January 1871 at Versailles, the creation of the German Empire was proclaimed. Sadly for him and ominously for his future, the contribution of Bismarck was not fully recognised by William I. The king had wanted the new title 'Emperor of Germany' but was given that of 'German Emperor', which Bismarck successfully argued made more allowance for the still strong particularism of several of the German states.

As well as creating an emperor, the Franco-Prussian War deposed one, but before looking at the fall of Napoleon III and the significance of his reign, we will complete the context for it by considering the process of unification in Italy, and then other developments first in south-west, then in north-west Europe. Here, we need to begin with the observation that while Italian unification is the most important of a considerable number of other national developments that have their own distinctive interest, we will look at them all only insofar as they had an impact on Europe as a whole. In its turn, of course, Italian unification, like its German counterpart, benefited enormously from the disposition of the other European powers at critical moments.

ITALY

We have noted above how, after new hope in 1848, the Italian cause suffered disappointment in 1849. King Charles Albert of Piedmont, who has been widely quoted as coming to the conclusion that 'Italy will do it by herself', abdicated in March 1849 in favour of his son, Victor Emmanuel II, and died soon afterwards. Arguably, Charles Albert had failed because he had not acted decisively enough according to his own alleged principle. As for Victor Emmanuel II, his most abiding passions were hunting and philandering, but he was shrewd enough to work towards the still desired end along with Count Camillo Cavour, who became prime minister towards the end of 1852 and remained in office for most of the time until his death in the summer of 1861. Unlike Mazzini, the revolutionary republican, and Garibaldi, the patriotic soldier, Cavour was a realistic politician. It has well been said of this triumvirate of the *Risorgimento* or Revival that respectively they provided the soul, the heart and the brains of Italian unification. However, Cavour would not himself have agreed with this assessment. He despised Mazzini and his followers in the Young Italy movement, and found Garibaldi and his irregular Redshirts more than somewhat of an embarrassment. His methods of using both the power of the king and the authority of parliament as well as other tools at his disposal were not so different from those that would be used by Bismarck. Like the German chancellor after him, Cavour made especially good use of international opportunities as they were presented to him. He was also helped in a similar manner by a rising tide of national feeling and economic progress, although in neither case was the tide as strong as it became in Germany.

Strongly believing that Italy could not do it by herself and not even sure what he wanted Italy to do, Cavour took Piedmont into the last stages of the Crimean War. He made use of the Congress of Paris to put before the powers of Europe the evils visited upon Italy by Austria and to increase his understanding of the developing situation in Europe, 'to sniff the air' as he said. In particular, he learned that Napoleon III was prepared 'to do something for Italy' when an appropriate moment should present itself.[10] Fate seemed to have decided to remind him of his vague promise when it moved an Italian revolutionary named Orsini to make an attempt on the lives of the French emperor and empress in January 1858. In July, Napoleon invited Cavour to meet him secretly at the spa of Plombières in the Vosges Mountains, there to discuss how Austria could be provoked into a war without reviving revolution in Italy. Napoleon and Cavour also worked out the shape that Italy should assume after the war. Piedmont would take Lombardy, Venetia and part of the Papal States, another part of which would join Tuscany to form a central Italian kingdom. The Kingdom of Naples would be left untouched in the south, while the Pope would receive compensation for the reduction of his earthly inheritance to Rome and its surroundings by his appointment as president of a confederation similar to that already existing in Germany. The two conspirators also agreed that most of the fighting would have to be done by the French, in return for which they would receive the reward of Savoy and possibly of Nice, too.

A seal on the Franco-Italian accord was to be constituted by the marriage of Victor Emmanuel II's daughter to the French emperor's cousin. A secret treaty early in 1859 handed over Nice as well as Savoy and abandoned the proposal of an Italian confederation, although the Princess Clotilde was duly called upon to make her sacrifice. The guileless Garibaldi was called in to inject an appropriate degree of fervour into the impending conflict with Austria. Then, after some delay brought about by a Russian suggestion of March 1859 that Italy should be the subject of a European Congress, and some hesitation on the part of Napoleon III, the Austrian emperor sent Victor Emmanuel II an ultimatum which he rejected, leaving Austria at the end of April with no alternative to invasion. A few days after that invasion, Napoleon III declared war on Austria in defence of Victor Emmanuel II.

The combined army, although badly led by Napoleon III, performed well enough to defeat a dispirited Austrian army which was even worse led. Two bloody victories at Magenta and Solferino in June were not followed up by Napoleon III, however, since he did not want to become involved in a war of attrition and was worried about Prussia's partial mobilisation on the Rhine. Accordingly, he met Francis Joseph in July 1859 to draw up the Treaty of Villafranca. Austria retained Venetia but gave Lombardy to Piedmont via Napoleon III, who did not attempt to take Savoy and Nice at this juncture. The central duchies were left in a somewhat ambiguous position. As soon as he heard of the terms of the Peace of Villafranca of July, Cavour resigned, feeling betrayed by his king's acceptance of the terms of Villafranca on which he had not been consulted.

But Cavour returned after six months to continue and complete the next important stage in unification, which was the voluntary annexation to Piedmont of Tuscany and the other central duchies. The British government gave its support to this move, although it was far from happy that Napoleon had been won over by the previously delayed reward of Savoy and Nice. Garibaldi was also furious at this concession, and threatened a descent on Nice. Instead, he went in May 1860 to Sicily where a rising had begun against the king of Naples. Cavour was not happy with this development, but preferred to have Garibaldi in the south rather than the north or the centre, where he had stopped off en route in order to promote an attack on the Papal States. In Sicily, Garibaldi proceeded all too quickly for the liking of Cavour, who did what he could to stop the spread of the Redshirts to the mainland. In their different ways, the British and French governments were also worried about this development, each being most concerned that the other might gain an advantage. But Garibaldi was not to be stopped, duly landed on the toe of Italy in mid-August and reached Naples early in September, establishing himself as dictator in the Kingdom of Naples.

In mid-September, Cavour sent the Piedmontese army into the Papal States to forestall Garibaldi, who was being held up by troops loyal to the king of Naples. The British government supported Cavour's intervention while Napoleon desisted from intervention of his own. Late in October, Victor Emmanuel II came to the frontier of Naples, which Garibaldi soon agreed to hand over to its new king. Plebiscites gave overwhelming support to this rapid making of Italy through annexation of the other states to Piedmont. On 17 March 1861, Victor Emmanuel was officially made king of Italy by a parliament elected on a respectably narrow franchise. Cavour died in June 1861 happy with the way that Italy was being unified. (Garibaldi lived on for more than 20 years not so happy, while Mazzini returned home to die in 1872 unreconciled to the completion of unification as monarchy rather than republic.) In 1866, Venetia was taken over after the war on the side of Prussia against Austria. In 1870, Rome was assimilated when Napoleon III removed his troops to fight in the war against Prussia. Thus the process of Italian unification ended in 1870 as it began in 1848, fundamentally influenced by the course of developments elsewhere in Europe.

THE OTHER STATES AND THE REST OF THE WORLD

Elsewhere in south-west Europe, Spain and Portugal were as turbulent as Italy in the years following 1848, arguably even more so, but they impinged on the affairs of the rest of the continent even less, except perhaps when Queen Isabella of Spain was pushed from her throne in 1868. In the north-west, Britain also was aloof; because of wide if not yet always formal imperial responsibilities, the government always kept half an eye, even an eye and a half, on what was going on in the world beyond Europe. As we have seen, the single British involvement in European war between 1848 and 1878 was in the Crimea, where there were implications stretching beyond the Black Sea into the Mediterranean and beyond the Caspian. For Britain, Russia was not so much a threat in Europe as in Asia: sympathy for the Poles was not as great as concern for India.

Any immediate danger to the British island refuge was deemed to come not from Russia, but from that even older enemy, France. As early as 1845, Lord Palmerston had warned that steam had bridged the Channel, and in 1848 an anxious government looked to its defences. During the Second Empire, there were occasions when the third Napoleon was believed to be on the point of attempting to outdo the first in attacks on the British coast or even invasion. A rivermouth fort against such an eventuality was built as far north as Aberdeen in 1860, after the annexation of Savoy and Nice appeared to have whetted the French appetite for more. Britain was never at this or any other juncture as deeply involved as France in the wars for Italian unification, although its moral support had an undoubted effect on the ultimately successful outcome of that process. As for the similar process of German unification, Britain never interfered, even if Palmerston made loud but ineffectual noises on behalf of Denmark during the second Schleswig–Holstein crisis. Up to the sudden defeat and collapse of the Second Empire in its war with Prussia in 1870, most British observers of the continental scene continued to believe that the major immediate danger for their security stemmed not from Germany, but from France.

From the Crimean War onwards, such hostilities as involved British soldiers and sailors were beyond Europe, briefly and without much enthusiasm against Persia in 1856, similarly against China in 1857, when a more serious outbreak of violence occurred in the shape of the Indian Mutiny. This persuaded the British government to transfer the administration of India from the East India Company to the crown, and thus to increase enormously the size of the formal British empire. A Second Burma War had led to the annexation of the Irrawaddy Delta in 1852, while informal empire was extended through a further war with China from 1859 to 1860. This helped to widen the opportunities for British trade in Chinese markets, but also to increase the impact on industrial markets of 'cheap yellow' labour in the shape of Chinese 'coolies'. Action to discipline China was taken in collaboration with France, with which, however, there was immediate disagreement over the unification of Italy. There was then the further tension in Europe from 1863 to 1864 with Germany and Austria over Schleswig–Holstein. There was an even greater danger of involvement in the American Civil War of 1861–5. But the next actual involvement of British troops was in an expedition to Abyssinia in 1867 to secure the release of some British prisoners.

While the powerful force of nationalism exerted its strength throughout Europe, Britain also responded to the spirit of the age. While self-government was extended to New Zealand in 1852, Canada in 1867 and to individual states in Australia from 1855 to 1859, Victorian Britain was being constructed as the fount of freedom and haven of justice, even if the monarch herself was frequently a target for criticism and the full development of ceremonial did not take place until after the installation of Victoria as Empress of India in 1877. Before then, however, Lord Palmerston maintained stability at home until his death in 1865. Then, the second Reform Bill of 1867 extended the franchise to include more of the middle class in the provinces and more of the lower middle class – more prosperous artisans and workers – in the towns. There were significant reforms in the civil service, the army and the judiciary which reduced some of the old privileges, while the provision of social welfare was extended to aim at at least a minimum standard of living. The Education Act of 1870 provided for elected school boards enforcing attendance up to the age of 13. Trade unions were being formed, and radical agitation continued, but emphasis from the left was on reform, not revolution. Karl Marx was in London, but very little Marxism.

Over the Channel, in the Low Countries, there was much concern for empire, especially on the part of the Dutch concerning their holdings in South-East Asia, for which they were prepared to fight against a rising in Java in 1825–33. But Holland and Belgium also had to worry about imperial questions in a passive rather than an active sense, as they seemed to be pawns in the struggle between the great powers, of which, especially in the Belgian case, the most aggressive seemed to be France.

FRANCE: FROM THE SECOND EMPIRE TO THE COMMUNE

We have already noted much of Napoleon III's mostly unsuccessful foreign policy in Europe. His policy outside Europe, especially an expedition to Mexico in 1863, was if anything even more unsuccessful. The Suez Canal was opened in 1869, but failed to lead the way to wider influence in Asia. Nevertheless, the Second Empire was in existence for nearly 20 years, during which considerable progress was made towards continuance of the industrial revolution and social adjustment to it. After his seizure of power in December 1851 had been given overwhelming support in a plebiscite and his assumption of the imperial title had received similar approval about a year later, Napoleon III worked on the construction of a strong centralised administration supported by the Church and by a more powerful army, which almost became a new Second Estate in place of the old nobility. Using the same class alignments as had given him power in order to maintain it, he gave much emphasis to nationalism in a continued attempt to exorcise the converse spirit of socialism, which was also repressed in a more direct manner.

Towards the end of the Second Empire, Napoleon III introduced a number of liberal measures to appease his middle-class supporters. Some press restrictions were lifted in 1868, and elections held in the spring of 1869 increased the influence of opposition to the empire enough for Napoleon III to hold a plebiscite on liberal reforms in the spring of 1870. The emperor asked for an affirmative vote in order to avert the peril of revolution, establish order and liberty on a firm basis, and assure the transmission of the crown to his son. There were 7.5 million votes in favour of the emperor's request, and only 1.5 million against. But the cracks in the empire were no more than papered over. The support of the Church had diminished with the inconsistencies of Napoleon's policy in Italy, while the bourgeoisie could not hold firm in the midst of economic difficulties, which also alienated the peasants and made more resolute the disaffection of the workers. The cracks reappeared more widely under the pressure of the war against Prussia.

Therefore when Paris was subjected to a harsh siege after the defeat at Sedan and the new government formed after Napoleon's capture made a humiliating peace with the German invaders, some of the people of Paris, especially the National Guard, refused to surrender and a Commune modelled on the Jacobin-led Assembly of 1793 was set up in March. Able in previous moments of crisis to dominate the rest of France, the capital now found itself suffering from its isolation as the Commune movement did not spread quickly or completely enough elsewhere. During its brief existence of two months or so, the Commune enacted a considerable amount of legislation: if it stopped short of taking over the Bank of France, there was a strong egalitarian and co-operative element in its activity. Its membership was less working than middle class, but there was undoubtedly an heroic proletarian aspect to this 'festival of the oppressed',[11] even if it was to be romanticised as well as vilified after the ruthless suppression in May 1871 during which 100,000 were killed, imprisoned or exiled. Martyrs or devils, the Communards exercised a considerable influence over the politics of the Third Republic, from 1870 right through to 1940. In conclusion, let the Commune write its own epitaph in the shape of excerpts from its Declaration of 27 March 1871:

> The Revolution of the communes, begun by the popular initiative of 18 March, inaugurates a new era of politics – experimental, positive and scientific. ... It is the end of the old governmental and clerical world, of militarism, officialism, exploitation, speculation, monopolies, privileges, to which the proletariat owes its bondage and the country its misfortunes and disaster. ... Therefore let this dear and great country, deceived by lies and slanders, put away its fears.[12]

THE CONGRESS OF BERLIN, 1878, AND AFTER

In the mid-1870s, with the support of the Church and extreme conservatives, the Panslav movement achieved dominant influence in Russian government circles. It pressed for Russian action on behalf of those brother and sister Slavs who were still under the heel of Muslim Ottoman oppression, but developing strong desires for independence. If the object was to distract the attention of the bulk of the Russian people from their plight, it failed to arouse much popular enthusiasm. But the army had just been modernised in a sweeping reform of 1874, and at least the generals were raring to go. The none too firm agreement of Austria and the somewhat reluctant acceptance of Germany were obtained by the beginning of 1877. Advantage could be taken of the fact that several of the Ottoman provinces were already in revolt, and in apparent need of Russian assistance. An international conference in Constantinople late in 1876 had failed to solve the crisis in a peaceful manner, and the rejection of an agreement by the Ottoman government gave Russia the excuse to declare war on it in April 1877.

Hostilities ensued mainly in the Danube–Balkan region, to a lesser extent in Transcaucasia, with the badly led and not completely reformed Russian armies experiencing disasters scarcely less crippling than those inflicted on their even more incompetent enemy. At the beginning of 1878, the Ottoman government asked for peace, but it was extremely unhappy about the peace that was offered in the Treaty of San Stefano in March 1878. A virtually independent big Bulgarian principality bounded by the Black and Aegean seas and the River Danube was to be set up, as were the fully independent states of Montenegro, Serbia and Romania. Bosnia and Herzegovina and other Ottoman provinces were to receive a reformed administration while Russia was to gain control of the Danube delta and the Dobrudja region immediately to the south.

Bulgaria and Montenegro were especially pleased with the terms of the treaty, but most other powers except of course Russia were dismayed at its terms and even more at its implications. Would Russia with the help of a dependent Bulgaria now dominate the Straits and threaten Constantinople? The League of the Three Emperors set up in 1873 was not firm enough for the German and especially the Austrian rulers to refrain from expressing their displeasure at the aggrandisement of their Russian partner, while Queen Victoria and her government were also unhappy about it. Widespread denunciation of the Turkish 'Bulgarian atrocities' that had been whipped up by Gladstone in 1876 was now forgotten as the new administration under Disraeli vented equal if not more infectious alarm at the threat posed by the greedy Russian bear to the Mediterranean and the route through the Suez Canal in particular. In order to make sure that the Russians would not have Constantinople, British ships were dispatched there and troops brought up from India. Austria was also deeply disturbed, and threatened to take action, perhaps in alliance with Britain and Bulgaria's disgruntled neighbour Romania. Calls for war in London, Vienna and Bucharest were loud in March and April 1878, and received a firm response from St Petersburg.

Into the breach stepped Bismarck, who helped clear the way for the Russo-Turkish War to be brought to a more satisfactory conclusion in the same manner as it had arisen, with an international conference, this time in Berlin. Claiming to act as 'honest broker', he was also hoping to prevent rapprochement between Russia and its only possible friend at this time, France, and between Austria and Britain. The Congress of Berlin met for the first time on 13 June and for the last time on 13 July 1878. The final treaty was essentially aimed at conciliating the great powers rather than satisfying the smaller, an emphasis which stored up later trouble in the Balkans. Russia regained Bessarabia, the province to the immediate north of the Danube that had been acquired after the war of 1812 and largely lost after the Crimean War, and some other smaller areas in Asia Minor. However, Bulgaria was taken back from the Aegean Sea: it retained less than half of the territory received from the Treaty of San Stefano just a few months previously, while the other larger portion south of the Balkan range reverted to the Ottoman Empire. Bosnia and Herzegovina were taken over by Austria–Hungary. The independence of Romania, Serbia and Montenegro were confirmed, though with some reduction of the frontiers that they wanted. But Romania received the Danube delta and the Dobrudja from Russia as a compensation for the loss of Bessarabia. The vexed question of the Straits was left without clear settlement, largely owing to the ambiguous position of the British government, which, however, protected its wider imperial interests in a move without ambiguity outside the Congress of Berlin, the acquisition from the Ottoman Empire of the island of Cyprus, the 'key to western Asia'. From this base, Britain could keep a watch on the Straits and on the Suez Canal, which had become a vital lifeline for the route to India and beyond.

After the Treaty of Berlin, nationalist and imperialist feelings still ran high throughout Europe, at their most heated perhaps between Britain and Russia, whose interests clashed in Afghanistan and throughout Asia. If the Three Emperors' League experienced something of a revival in 1881 after the assassination of Alexander II, the friendship of Alexander III with Francis Joseph and William had already been undermined by Bismarck's secret treaty of 1879 for a defensive alliance of Austria–Hungary and Germany against Russia. Thus the Treaty of Berlin marked nothing more than a breathing space before the energies of the great powers of Europe were expended in rivalries throughout their home continent and away through Asia and Africa.

NATIONALISM

The question posed by the Irishman Captain Macmorris in Shakespeare's *Henry V*: 'What is my nation?' had received a variety of answers in the early modern period. At the beginning of the nineteenth century, Sir John Sinclair from the north of Scotland observed: 'National peculiarities are of great use in exciting a spirit of manly emulation. . . . It is in the interest of the United Kingdom to keep alive those national, or what, perhaps, may now more properly be called local distinctions of English, Scotch, Irish and Welsh.'[13] By this time, the French Revolution and Napoleon had both made a great impact on the nature of nationalism in the UK and throughout Europe.

The period from 1848 to 1878 is dominated by the unification of Germany. This was a triumph for a force that was growing in strength as the nineteenth century wore on, especially in areas where it had formerly been denied or repressed. As we have seen, Germany was united by nationalism of three kinds – economic, political and cultural. Often, the idea preceded the reality, as was clearly the case in Italy, where only 2.5 per cent of the people in 1860 spoke what was to become the national language. Nearly 30 years before then, Mazzini was prepared to assert broadly in his *General Instructions for the Members of Young Italy* announced in 1831 that:

> The strength of an association lies, not in the numerical cypher of the elements of which it is composed, but in the homogeneousness of those elements; in the perfect concordance of its members as to the path to be followed, and the certainty that the moment of action will find them ranged in a compact phalanx, strong in reciprocal trust, and bound together by unity of will, beneath a common banner.

Moreover, in his view Europe was already undergoing 'a progressive series of transformations which are gradually and irresistibly guiding European society to form itself into vast and united masses'.[14] Yet Mazzini's aim – a republican, unitarian Italy – and the means that he recommended to reach it – education and insurrection – were expounded in a manner that fitted the particular rather than the general case. Moreover, Mazzini asserted, if 'God has written one line of his thought on the cradle of each people', Italy was 'the land destined by God to the great mission of giving moral unity to Europe, and through Europe to Humanity'.[15] Almost by definition, other writers on nationalism would assign to their own nations a similarly superior role – hence one of the greatest difficulties in writing a history of the continent. If full allowance were made for the self-image of each and every nation, the work would never be finished!

We may make a clear distinction between those states that were already in existence at the beginning of the nineteenth century and those that were as yet nothing more than a glimmer in the eye of a few intellectuals. On the whole, with Italy a major exception, the west of the continent fits into the first category, although composed of amalgams of numbers of earlier independent units. In the centre and east of the continent there were many peoples subject to the Austro-Hungarian, Russian and Ottoman Empires. We have seen in this chapter how some of them, for example in Bulgaria and Romania, were given a new affiliation. But peasants, who predominated in these new states, were far less conscious of their nation than city dwellers. Even in the early twentieth century, according to one calculation, about 90 per cent of those living in what was to become the Ukraine had little or no awareness of it.

However, although there are artificial aspects to all nation states, we may be ill-advised to accept the notion that they are all inventions. Even if nationalism flares up and dies down in a somewhat fickle manner, such a powerful emotion cannot be dismissed. Undoubtedly, as in the case of Germany, there have been economic, political and cultural forces making for unification in both the nineteenth and the twentieth centuries. Nevertheless, from the vantage point of the early twenty-first century, at least some Europeans would want to argue that they are in process of transferring at least some of their loyalty to the continent as a whole. We shall return to this subject in our last chapter.

SOCIALISM

'When Adam delved and Eve span, who was then the gentleman?' was a rallying cry during the English Peasant Revolt of 1381. The Levellers in seventeenth-century England and the followers of Babeuf in late eighteenth-century France were among the forerunners of a movement that, like nationalism, received new definition in the nineteenth century.

Then, a comprehensive attempt to cover society, especially industrial society, as a whole was made by writers espousing the doctrines of 'socialism', a word that gained coinage in the 1830s. Its first adherents were such propagandists as Robert Owen, who attempted to set up a model community at New Lanark near Glasgow in Scotland; the comte de Saint-Simon, who argued for a 'New Christianity' led by men of science and bringing capital and labour together in harmony; and F. M. Charles Fourier, who sought a 'new industrial world' composed of communes. These two Frenchmen and their British counterpart were deemed by their more renowned successor, the German Jew Karl Marx, to be 'critical-Utopian', that is, capable of perceiving what the problems of society were, but unable to provide appropriate solutions. Together with his close associate Frederick Engels, the German manufacturer of textiles in Manchester, England, at the beginning of the Revolution of 1848 Marx set about writing the *Manifesto of the Communist Party*, the original statement of the ideology that was to become known as Marxism.

The brief introduction describes the growing power of the ideology: 'A spectre is haunting Europe – the spectre of Communism. All the powers of old Europe have entered into a holy alliance to exorcise this spectre: Pope and Tsar, Metternich and Guizot, French radicals and German police spies.' It was high time, the introduction continues, that the Communists assembling in London should set out in their various languages their views, aims and tendencies in order to meet 'this nursery tale of the Spectre of Communism with a manifesto of the party itself'.

The *Manifesto* then begins its first section, entitled 'Bourgeois and Proletarians', with a description of its basic assertion: 'The history of all hitherto existing society is the history of class struggles.' After their development through the ancient and medieval periods, those struggles were now taking on the simple shape of two great hostile camps consisting of two great classes – the bourgeoisie, or capitalist owners, and the proletariat, or wage labourers, who owned nothing but their ability to work which they sold in order to live. The discovery of America and the opening up of wider commercial possibilities in general had led, along with steam and machinery, to the establishment of modern industry and the world market, and to the intensification of the class struggle.

Historically, the bourgeoisie had played the most revolutionary part, replacing old social ties with the naked self-interest of a relationship based on cash. In other words: 'for exploitation, veiled by religious and political illusions, it has substituted naked, shameless, direct, brutal exploitation'. And yet: 'It has been the first to show what man's activity can bring about. It has accomplished wonders far surpassing Egyptian pyramids, Roman aqueducts and Gothic cathedrals; it has conducted expeditions that put in the shade all former exoduses of nations and crusades.' During the demonstration of its accomplishments:

> The bourgeoisie has subjected the country to the rule of the towns. It has created enormous cities, has greatly increased the urban populations as compared with the rural, and has thus rescued a considerable part of the population from the idiocy of rural life. Just as it has made the country dependent on the towns, so it has made barbarian and semi-barbarian countries dependent on the civilised ones, nations of peasants on nations of bourgeois, the East on the West.

Marx and Engels showed here that they shared the prejudices of their contemporaries concerning the Ancient and Middle Ages, provincial existence and the world beyond Europe. Possibly, they celebrated the achievements of the bourgeoisie in too lyrical a manner. However, they also believed that they had discerned more clearly than others the manner in which the very success of capitalism would lead to the downfall of the bourgeoisie, which was 'like the sorcerer, who is no longer able to control the powers of the nether world whom he has called up by his spells'. For 'The weapons with which the bourgeoisie felled feudalism to the ground are now turned against the bourgeoisie itself'. The necessity for ever improved methods of production in an increasingly competitive market would mean the breaking of national barriers and the daily destruction of old-established industries that would not adapt themselves to such changing demands. For a few to succeed in such a fierce struggle, many would have to fail. The large capitalists would swamp the small, and thus from all classes of the population would be recruited the mortal enemy of the bourgeoisie – the proletariat.

Workers became enmeshed in capitalism through the sale of the only cash commodity at their disposal, their ability to work. They became appendages of the machines of industry, and were crowded into factories like soldiers. Paradoxically, however, their abject humiliation led to the formation of their strength. Herded together under strict regimentation, the workers developed their class consciousness and their own organisations or unions. This process occurred more quickly and in more strained national and international circumstances than the preceding process of the emergence of the bourgeoisie. Because of the pace of change and the associated difficulties each national bourgeoisie is obliged 'to appeal to the proletariat, to ask for its help, and thus to drag it into the political arena', not only to complete the struggle against the old order but also to fight with the rival bourgeoisie of foreign countries. Willy-nilly, the bourgeoisie helps the proletariat to prepare itself for the struggle between the two classes: 'The bourgeoisie itself, therefore, supplies the proletariat with its own elements of political and general education, in other words, it furnishes the proletariat with weapons for fighting the bourgeoisie.'

The proletariat would receive further assistance from bourgeois becoming proletarians and from bourgeois ideologists able to understand in a theoretical manner the historical process as a whole. Some of these would become Communists, providing general explanations of what the workers had learned through their collective experience. Without property and without family relations based on property, the workers were stripped of every trace of national character, in Britain as in France, in the USA as in Germany. Thus, the workers had no country, while national differences and antagonisms were 'daily more and more vanishing, owing to the development of the bourgeoisie, to freedom of commerce, to the world market, to uniformity in the mode of production and in the conditions of life corresponding thereto'. When the proletariat had consolidated its position, class distinctions would disappear, too, and public power would lose its political character, since 'political power, properly so called, is merely the organised power of one class for oppressing another'. The new order would consist of 'an association, in which the free development of each is the condition for the free development of all'.

While there were utopian elements in this and other assertions of the *Communist Manifesto*, there is no doubt that Marx and Engels, while standing on the shoulders of Owen, Saint-Simon, Fourier and other predecessors, had established an interpretation of history that was much more comprehensive or, in the wider sense of the term, 'scientific'. Perhaps the biggest stumbling block to the realisation of their projections in the short run would be the persistence of that phenomenon which they saw as temporary or transient – nationalism. They believed that a forthcoming bourgeois revolution in Germany would be immediately followed by a proletarian revolution there because the conditions in which it would occur would be much more advanced than those of its predecessors in Britain and France.[16] Thirty years on, the bourgeois revolution had indeed occurred in Germany to the extent that the process of unification was complete with the creation of the German Empire in 1871. No proletarian revolution was to follow, however much it was expected and yearned for.

In 1864, following the Polish insurrection in the previous year, the International Workingmen's Association or First International was formed by British trade unionists and continental socialists. Marx and Engels dominated it for the most part, but ran into trouble after the fall of the Paris Commune of 1871. The Russian anarchist Mikhail Bakunin and his supporters were expelled in 1872 for their opposition to the seizure of state power by the workers, and the First International collapsed in 1876. Meanwhile, as well as writing a number of pamphlets, Marx continued work on what was to be his masterpiece, a 'Critique of Political Economy'. By the time of his death in 1883, however, even the first part, *Capital*, was far from finished; Marx had shown in some detail how capitalism was on the rise, but had not spelled out how it was to fall. Nevertheless, socialism, both Marxist and non-Marxist, was to gain vigour as nationalism was reinforced by imperialism.

THE NEW IMPERIALISM

Although no precise date can be given, the period from about 1878 to 1914 may be looked upon as the period of the 'New Imperialism'. To put this new variety of an age-old process in its place, let us first look at the shape it had taken in the preceding periods. Just before the beginning of the seventeenth century, the great Spanish–Portuguese era of empire gave way to the Dutch, which lasted for about three-quarters of that century, being then overtaken by the Franco-British. This was to last for about 100 years, at the end of which, after the American Revolution, there began a British–American era. Another century or so on, the European–American era, that of the 'New Imperialism', ensued down to 1914.

An accompaniment to the earlier periods of imperialism had been another age-old process, that of colonisation. The Spanish and the Portuguese had settled in the West Indies – Cuba, Hispaniola and Puerto Rico, and the North, Central and South American coastal areas, as well as in the East Indies. The Portuguese were also scattered along the African and Indian coasts. During the period of Dutch predominance, the same areas were infiltrated not only by settlers from Holland but also from France, notably in Canada, and from Britain, especially in the area that became the 13 North American colonies and in Jamaica. The French and the British then expanded their presence in North America and the West Indies, and arrived in small but significant numbers in India and to a lesser extent in Africa. During the British–American era, British immigrants joined the French in Canada and the Dutch in South Africa, while also arriving in Australia and New Zealand. After a comparatively slow beginning, the United States had expanded across the North American continent in the nineteenth century, receiving successive waves of immigrants from Europe, first British and Irish, then German. This expansion stepped up its pace even more after the Civil War of 1861–5, with Italy and eastern Europe providing most of the 'huddled masses yearning to breathe free' – to quote the inscription on the Statue of Liberty erected in New York harbour as a gift from France. Immigrants from Asia were less welcome at a time when the USA was looking increasingly outwards in that direction: at the inauguration ceremony for the statue in 1886, emphasis was given not to the grant of liberty to incomers but to the spread of liberty to other lands.

During all earlier four phases of development, we must remember, Europe was spreading overland as well as overseas. In the seventeenth century, Russia extended its penetration into Siberia and Ukraine, while Prussia acquired its name as well as an important part of its territory by expanding eastwards from Brandenburg. In the eighteenth century,

Russia acquired its substantial footholds on the Baltic and Black seas, and Prussia took Silesia, before both these powers participated with Austria in the partitions of Poland. In the first three-quarters of the nineteenth century, Russia consolidated its holdings in central Asia and the Far East while Prussia led the process of German unification at the expense of Austria, which like its Ottoman Turkish neighbour demonstrated that empires could grow smaller as well as larger.

Another phenomenon amply demonstrated in the period before 1878 was internal instability as an accompaniment to international competition. This was now to become one of the distinguishing features of the 'New Imperialism'. Lord Salisbury, one of the most enthusiastic British participants in the race for empire, observed that the general election of 1880 began 'a serious war of the classes'.[17] Joseph Chamberlain was to talk around 20 years later of his vision of an empire for the common man, of a broad patriotism that would maintain harmony between the classes. Such remarks were made elsewhere in Europe, and historians have put forward the idea of 'social imperialism', the pursuit of a vigorous foreign policy with at least the partial aim of providing a safety valve for discontent at home. We will be looking in the next chapter at possible examples of this kind of policy in Germany, Russia and France as well as in Britain.

There are a number of other features of the 'New Imperialism' that will become apparent as the chapter unfolds: economic, social, political, strategic and cultural. To put these in turn in a simple introductory fashion, a second industrial revolution of steel and chemicals and large-scale organisation pushed capitalism much more than before beyond national frontiers. Much of this investment and the accompanying search for markets and raw materials was carried out in Europe itself, but more went to Africa, Asia and the Antipodes, while the largest injection of capital was in North and South America. Emigration now became a river in flood in comparison with the former modest stream as 25 million Europeans crossed the Atlantic to the USA in the last quarter of the nineteenth century, and a considerable if much smaller number moved in other directions, including Britons to outposts of empire and Russians to Siberia. Peasants throughout the continent were flocking to the towns in an internal migration at least as significant for 'social imperialism' as external migration was for imperialism in general. Governments now attempted to make their empires formal, to a large extent in order to forestall their rivals in what was a race to extend their influence throughout the world, especially in Africa and Polynesia, the two regions yet to be fully infiltrated by Europeans. The competition as well as the arrival of steam-powered navies made it necessary to look for bases and coaling stations, and generally to consider the manner in which maritime activity could protect imperial interests. Before the end of the nineteenth century, the USA had become an important participant in the global relations of the time, across the Pacific and the Atlantic, too, as well as keeping a jealous watch on South and North America.

Americans were also bearing their share of 'the white man's burden', the illusion that Europeans and their emigrant relations shared a duty to bring their advanced culture to ignorant, backward peoples, some of whom at least were in fact the heirs of civilisations much older than the European, even if not so efficient in methods of extermination. The exterminators included at least some of the followers of the Prince of Peace, although many of the missionaries – Roman Catholic, Protestant, and to a far smaller extent, Orthodox – moving into Asia and Africa brought with them the positive as well as the negative influence of European civilisation. Evaluation in this regard must be largely a spiritual problem, but the more material point should also be made that missionaries could act as a cutting edge for empire, serving their worldly masters by creating an 'interest' which business and government could then use for their own purposes.

'Interest' of this kind had long been shown in Asia by the European powers, while in 1875 about one-tenth of the vast continent of Africa was controlled by them. Britain's authority was widespread, its presence felt in South, East, West and North Africa. Next came France, in the west and north and the offshore island of Madagascar, followed by Spain mainly to the north-west and Portugal in the east and west. The Germans and the Turks were also established in Africa, yet it was from another country that the initiative came for the first international conference on methods to be adopted for the exploration and colonisation of Africa. In 1876, Leopold II of Belgium invited to Brussels delegates from Britain, France, Germany, Austria–Hungary, Italy and Russia to join with others from the host nation in unofficial discussion of these important questions. The most concrete evidence of agreement was the foundation of the International African Association.

However, its basic idea of making the exploration and development of Africa a co-operative enterprise was never realised. The Association developed into the Congo Free State under Belgian control involving the personal sovereignty of King Leopold.

9

THE CLASH OF EMPIRES AND CLASSES, 1878–1914

In July 1879, Mr Goldie Taubman (later Sir George Goldie) formed a United African Company in order to manage the British infiltration of Nigeria. In 1880, the French explorer Count de Brazza returned to the north bank of the River Congo to make treaties with Makoko, a local chief. These treaties were ratified by the French government in the summer of 1882. The race for Africa had begun. Henry Morton Stanley, famous for his meeting with the missionary David Livingstone, was to write about the Congo of

> the novel mission of sowing along its banks civilised settlements to peacefully conquer and subdue it, to remould it in harmony with modern ideas into national states, within whose limits the European merchant shall go hand in hand with the dark African trader, and justice and law and order shall prevail, and lawlessness and the cruel barter of slaves shall be overcome.[1]

This aspiration would soon be applied to other parts of the 'dark continent'.

Although extended consideration of Africa itself is beyond the confines of a history of Europe, the point must be made, however briefly, that the colonised affected that history along with the colonisers. For example, in the late nineteenth century African producers could no

256

longer deliver goods in sufficient quantity or at low enough prices for their patrons in Europe, who for most of the last quarter of the nineteenth century were operating in conditions of intensified international competition. Hence an additional reason for taking over local societies and economies for greater efficiency within the framework of formal empire.

Within Europe itself, the working out of what contemporaries perceived as the 'Great Depression' from 1873 to 1896 assumed a shape that varied at least partly according to the relationship of any given state to the network of imperialism, which was worldwide. Generally speaking, the rural areas that were remote from it, in central and eastern Europe, suffered more than their western neighbours from the competition in agricultural produce presented by North America and Australasia. From the seventeenth century onwards, grain exports to the west of the continent had been of great importance to the predominantly farming economies of the east. Hence, the greater pressure felt from the new competitors, with ensuing implications for the intensity and nature of the social conflict in those parts of Europe comparatively remote from the most dynamic processes of imperialism.

As far as the empires were concerned, the 1880s were a decade in which governments were being driven in the direction of making those empires formal not only by economic competition but also by exploration, nationalism and militarism. In the 1890s, the emphasis was on the more deliberate extension of formal empire, which continued in the first decade or so of the twentieth century in an atmosphere of growing international competition and tension. As far as the classes were concerned, the 1880s brought a growth in the organisation of the labour movement in trade unions and political parties, along with the formation in 1889 in Paris of the Second International Workingmen's Association. The Second International concentrated at first on a debate concerning 'revisionism', the argument that the proletariat could advance its cause by changing the established order rather than overthrowing it. The debate continued through the 1890s, a decade in which strike activity grew in scale and trade unions increased their membership, and at the end of which the Second International established a formal secretariat. After 1900, the organised working class made an even more positive impact, especially in the years 1905 and 1914, on the eve of the First World War.

This important new class dimension greatly affected the evolution of political parties. Socialist parties, especially of a revisionist nature, made an appearance in the 1880s and grew apace in the 1890s and 1900s. This development caused a split in liberalism between a radical and a traditional type, while a new kind of conservatism emerged, often with a mass base. These developments all varied from region to region of Europe. For example, the persistence of a peasantry could lead to a special kind of conservatism, with religious overtones, more often Roman Catholic, but sometimes Protestant and Orthodox, too. Moreover, these developments were very much affected by economic change, by the arrival of the second industrial revolution of oil, steel and electricity before the first of coal, iron and steam had been completed in some regions, or indeed had even begun in others. The consequent migration to the towns as well as emigration from Europe, in addition to extension of transport and communication by railway and telegraph, also contained important implications for politics and society. In addition, round about the turn of the century there was an associated revolution in ideas, in the arts and the sciences (see Chapter 10).

BRITAIN

Throughout the 1870s, Britain managed to avoid involvement in the Franco-Prussian War, the Russo-Turkish War and other European conflicts, in spite of the excited publicity given to the 'Bulgarian atrocities' inflicted by the Turks in 1876 and the later Russian threat to Constantinople. All through this period, however, successive prime ministers found it necessary to wrestle with an intractable and long-running crisis that was at once domestic and colonial, in Ireland.

At the time of the Treaty of Berlin in 1878, imperial rivalry with a European power arose in the shape of a renewed squabble with Russia over Afghanistan. Benjamin Disraeli, or rather Lord Beaconsfield as he now was, attempted to impose order by sending in an expeditionary force, which could also readjust the Himalayan frontier in order to make it more 'scientific'. Unfortunately, one side's 'science' was the other's humiliation, a 'forward' policy for one army meant another's retreat. So neither the Afghans nor the Russians were reconciled to the settlement imposed by the British in 1879. Tension remained high over central Asia as the British broadly accepted arguments that strategic points in Afghanistan constituted 'the pivot to the whole eastern question' and 'the key to India', the finest jewel in the crown of Queen Victoria, Empress of India since 1877.[2] From the Russian side, there were certainly 'scientific' ideas for establishing 'forward' positions as well as at least some thinking that even a small-scale Russian military presence on the frontier of India 'would probably lead to a general uprising in India and to the ruin of the British empire', perhaps to 'a social revolution' back in the metropolis which could constitute the beginning of the fall of Britain.[3] And so the struggle for spheres of influence on the roof of the world turned full circle in its wider implications. During the late nineteenth century Britain was also consolidating its own previously established sphere in Fiji, Malaya and the Gold Coast, while Canada, Australia and New Zealand moved towards dominion status.

Another long-standing imperial interest presenting a problem at the end of Disraeli's ministry was in South Africa, where the outbreak of war with the Zulus threatened the Boer republic of Transvaal, which together with the Orange Free State had been independent since 1852 and 1854 respectively. A British proposal of 1877 for the incorporation of the Transvaal into the formal empire annoyed many Boers, while British troops in 1879 found the Zulus a much more formidable enemy than they had expected – in order to pay for their suppression, income tax had to be raised back home. A general election was impending, and the Liberal leader, Gladstone, made the most of Disraeli's imperial difficulties as well as of domestic economic and other problems. Once in power, however, Gladstone found it impossible to put into effect the policies that he had been advocating during the electoral campaign, and while he was able to come to at least a temporary agreement with the Russians concerning Afghanistan, he found himself in confrontation in South Africa with the Boers, who inflicted a number of humiliating defeats on British troops as they fought for the return to independence of the Transvaal. Gladstone finally kept the campaign promise of such independence that he had made to the Boers, but at the loss of much of his own popularity. The eternal problem of Ireland, which he had made it his mission to pacify, caused him further embarrassment, especially after the chief secretary and under-secretary for Ireland were murdered in Phoenix Park, Dublin, in May 1882. New measures of coercion were introduced rather than the relief measures that had first been contemplated.

Another headache inherited by Gladstone was Egypt, where Britain had joined with France in a Dual Control in 1876 after Disraeli's purchase in 1875 of a major interest in the Suez Canal. British influence extended into the great territory of the Sudan to the south, where Disraeli's legacy now led to Gladstone's embarrassment as a local movement arose to drive out all foreigners. The British government's response in the summer of 1882 – bombardment of Alexandria and invasion of Egypt – led to the full British takeover of administration there. Thereafter, Egypt became a pivotal area for British foreign and imperial policy, much to the annoyance of the French. Attention switched in 1883 to the Sudan, where the adherents of a Muslim revival movement led by the 'divinely guided one', or Mahdi, defeated an Egyptian army under British leadership. In order to protect its responsibilities on the Red Sea, the British government sent an army there, while early in 1884 General Gordon was recalled to the Sudan from China in order to manage a withdrawal. Gordon underestimated the size of his task and even increased it. He and a small band of devotees withstood a long siege in Khartoum, but were killed at the beginning of 1885 before a relief force could reach them. Gordon posthumously became an even greater popular hero than he had been during his lifetime, and recriminations against the government for not giving him enough support, along with a Russian victory in Afghanistan and a whole series of domestic problems, led to Gladstone's resignation.

A comprehensive Reform Act was passed with bipartisan support before a general election, in which the imperial debate was continued along with arguments about social welfare including the right of rural labourers to 'three acres and a cow' and of everybody to free education. Joseph Chamberlain more than any other politician showed that it was possible to be a Liberal radical, declaring that 'the path of legislative progress in England has been for years, and must continue to be, distinctly Socialistic' at the same time as vigorously supporting expansion overseas. Trade unionists in parliament tended to be cautious, but the left moved modestly forward from what was called in August 1884 the Social Democratic Federation (SDF). More ambitiously, one of the leaders, Henry Hyndman, fixed 1889, the centenary of the outbreak of the French Revolution, as the date for the beginning of 'the complete international Social Revolution'.[4] By that time, in fact, the influence of the SDF was falling rapidly away. Hard economic times in the mid-1880s did give it a measure of support, while less organised protest was to break out on the streets of London, but there was little support for revolution by way of the ballot box. From the general election of 1885, the Liberals emerged as the biggest single party, with the balance between them and the Conservatives held by the Irish Nationalists, a result which contributed to a necessary and immediate concentration on the problem, both imperial and internal, of home rule for Ireland. Gladstone put forward a bold measure for the creation of an Irish parliament, but without consulting his former colleagues, many of whom refused to give him their support. A further general election in 1886 meant not only defeat for Gladstone, but also the loss of Joseph Chamberlain and some other Liberal Unionists who moved over to give their allegiance to the Conservative government under Lord Salisbury.

Fully aware that, as he put it, politics were Ireland, Salisbury had to move carefully on all fronts, especially in the face of energetic Irish parliamentary agitation led by Charles Stewart Parnell until his implication in a divorce suit in 1887 broke the Irish party. In the next general election of 1892, home rule versus union was still the leading issue, with Gladstone and the Liberals securing a small majority for home rule. A modification of the Bill of 1886 went through the Commons in 1893, but was rejected by the Lords, and opposed throughout England, if not in Wales, Scotland or Ireland. Home rule was now left in mid-air, as it were, as Gladstone retired and Salisbury soon became prime minister again in 1895.

While the Irish question had been on the boil, imperial affairs were still simmering away. Even if Salisbury possessed neither Disraeli's flamboyant personality nor his room for manoeuvre, he managed first of all to make an agreement with Russia in 1885 on the brink of another war over Afghanistan during his first brief period of office before the general election in that year. From 1886 onwards, he worked to make relations smoother with the USA over the Atlantic and with France and Germany in Europe. France was not very receptive, although it agreed to a division of West Africa. Germany was too receptive, and Salisbury had to turn down Bismarck's offer of a British–German alliance in 1889. But he did conclude a British–German treaty in July 1890 with Bismarck's successor, Caprivi. In exchange for the island of Heligoland off the German coast, Britain received Zanzibar and a large part of East Africa, including the southern flank of the Nile valley leading to the Sudan and Egypt. Italy also soon agreed to stay out of that important valley, while the Portuguese were obliged to recognise a British stake in central Africa. The all-important sea routes through the Suez Canal were guaranteed against French or especially Russian encroachment by secret Mediterranean Agreements with Italy and Austria–Hungary in 1887. These preserved the status quo in the Black and Aegean seas as well as in the Mediterranean, and defended the Ottoman Empire and the Balkans against potential Russian aggression. Salisbury held back from the advice of some of his cabinet colleagues that he should seek rapprochement with Russia even to the point of giving up protection for Constantinople in exchange for guarantees concerning India. He feared that this might drive France and Germany together to Britain's disadvantage.

At home, Salisbury had to worry not only about Ireland but also about social unrest and political developments on the left. In 1889, although the SDF was in decline, a great dock strike occurred in London, which led towards the foundation of the Independent Labour Party in 1893. Also in 1889, the publication of *Fabian Essays* gave wider publicity to the ideas of the mainly middle-class intellectual Fabian Society, first founded in 1884 to propagate the message of evolutionary rather than revolutionary socialism. Until then, the trade union movement had concentrated on skilled workers, and its representatives in parliament had been very moderate in their demands. A match-girl strike led by Mrs Annie Besant in the summer of 1888 had brought new attention to the sub-human conditions in which the poor had to exist, and helped to create the strained atmosphere that brought out the dockers about a year later. Driven quickly to the point of desperation in the face of the refusal of their employers to grant demands for a minimum wage of sixpence an hour and the abolition of the harsh burden of contract work, the dockers were given fresh heart by support from as far away as Australia as well as closer at hand. Impending defeat quickly became almost complete victory, as one of their leaders, John Burns, recalled in a speech to a mass meeting on 9 September 1889 a famous moment from the Indian Mutiny, when the besieged garrison of Lucknow detected the distant glint of the bayonets of a force coming to its relief: 'This, lads, is the Lucknow of Labour, and I myself, looking to the horizon, can see a silver gleam – not of bayonets to be imbrued in a brother's blood, but the gleam of the full round orb of the dockers' tanner.'[5]

The Lucknow of Labour was soon to be followed by the establishment of its formal empire. There was a rapid growth in the membership not only of the Dockers' Union in London and other ports, but of trade unions in general, if still mainly on a craft basis. The match-girl strike was not forgotten, as at least a beginning was made towards cooperation between the trade unions and the women's movement. At the Trades Union Congress of 1890, the 'old gang' of moderate leaders were easily defeated, the Bill for eight hours a day was accepted, and a programme of state socialism to be achieved by parliamentary means was approved. The vehicle for the implementation of such a programme was created at the beginning of 1893 with the foundation of the Independent Labour Party (ILP) under Keir Hardie. The cloth cap was soon to join the top hat in the House of Commons, even though none of its candidates was successful at the general election of 1895. By then, it was already apparent that the cause of revolutionary socialism was not prospering in Britain. There was little British enthusiasm for the Second International set up in Paris in 1889, nor much revulsion against the expansion of overseas empire. Nevertheless, the ILP was to incur new unpopularity in 1899 by opposing the Boer War. A year later, with the war still raging, the ILP joined with trade union leaders and the Fabians, as well as briefly with remnants of the SDF, to form a 'Labour Representation Committee', known from the outset as the Labour Party.

The 1890s were from the beginning a decade of imperial problems which were to culminate in a number of crises, the most important of which was the Boer War. In the earlier 1890s Europe moved closer to diplomatic alignment, while Britain adhered to its traditional policy of aloofness from the continent. But the rapprochement of Britain's two main imperial rivals, France and Russia, led to fears for the Mediterranean and demands for a new build-up of the navy, the issue over which Gladstone resigned. Germany was far from happy with British policy over the disputed Samoan Islands in the Pacific, while Britain suspected the German government of stirring up the Boers in South Africa. If this were not enough to embarrass Gladstone's successors, ruthless suppression of an Armenian revolt by the Turks led to fears for the stability of the Near East, and therefore made it difficult to consolidate the understanding with the Russians reached in Afghanistan. To cap it all, France, Russia and Germany combined to influence the settlement after the war between China and Japan in 1894, cutting out Britain.

On his return to power in the summer of 1895, Salisbury was soon forced to realise that he could not give such a positive response to the Eastern Question as Disraeli had given nearly 20 years before, since the balance of European forces was now altered to Britain's disadvantage. There were also more immediate problems to be faced, concerning the boundary between British Guiana and Venezuela, which led to an acrimonious dispute with the USA from 1895 to 1896, and especially concerning the sequel to a raid on the Transvaal led by Dr Jameson, an associate of the British empire-builder Cecil Rhodes, in December 1895. The raid failed quickly and immediately. Rhodes was forced to resign as premier of Cape Colony, and the Boers were further encouraged by the telegram sent to President Kruger of the Transvaal by Kaiser William II. Disputes with the new imperial powers of the USA and Germany combined with continued suspicion of the older rivals, France and Russia, to make at least some British policy-makers wonder if they had been proud of their 'splendid isolation' with justification.

Acceleration in the imperial race from 1898 onwards was to increase such doubts. The German naval programme was launched in that year, and the crisis over Samoa intensified as the USA went to war with Spain. Germany and Russia had begun the carve-up of China in 1897, and Britain established a foothold in Wei-hai-wei in 1898 to keep an eye on this development. In Africa, Britain and France clashed after a confrontation between units of their armies at Fashoda on the Upper Nile in the Sudan. The French agreed to withdraw from the Nile by March 1899, but a worse crisis ensued in October of that year when President Kruger, annoyed at the unfriendly postures of the British colonial secretary, Joseph Chamberlain, and encouraged by words of support from Europe, sent a Boer expeditionary force against Cape Colony and Natal, the two British provinces in South Africa. Before the summer of 1900, however, the towns subject to Boer siege had been relieved, with special rejoicing over Mafeking, and the Transvaal along with its Orange Free State ally had been annexed. The Conservative government won a bitter election with an almost unchanged majority,

Salisbury promising a fight to the finish. In the autumn of 1900 the Boers reopened the war, this time adopting guerrilla tactics, and caused the government much concern and expense. Concentration camps and block houses were among the methods adopted to suppress the insurgents, but a halt had to be called to the fighting without the most satisfactory of finishes. By the Treaty of Vereeniging in May 1902, the Transvaal and Orange Free State were incorporated in the British Empire, but with the promise of self-government which was honoured in 1907, and the payment of £3 million as compensation for the widespread damage inflicted on them.

The death of Queen Victoria in 1901 and of Lord Salisbury in 1903 brought an era to an end. Edward VII (1901–10) and other statesmen would be associated with new directions. In 1904, Britain reached agreement with France on spheres of influence in North Africa, and in 1907 with Russia on spheres of influence in central Asia. The Triple Entente was now set up between Britain, France and Russia (see more on this in Chapter 10). Salisbury's foreign policy had been based not so much on splendid isolation as on prudent restraint, but now Britain was being drawn towards the kind of entangling alliance that he had sought to avoid. Similarly, his domestic outlook, that of an aristocratic patrician, could not easily accommodate the arrival of mass democracy, still less when it included the advent of the Labour Party and a widespread trade union movement, organisations about to increase their representation in parliament. The general election of 1906 brought up the issue of a pro-tariff reform, Chamberlain's Imperial Preference argument being broadened to exclude German and other foreign competitors. The Liberals argued that the continuance of free trade would produce a 'big loaf' rather than a 'little loaf', and also promised to reverse the notorious Taff Vale decision of 1901 which curtailed the right to strike. The Liberals won a vast majority, while the Labour Party, the trade unions and their sympathisers won a substantial representation of over 50 seats. The scene was set for reform and progress was soon duly made: in education, with regulation of child labour outside teaching hours, and some provision for school meals and child health; in industry, with some movement towards the eight-hour day and minimum wage, and the institution of Labour Exchanges; and in social welfare, with a new Housing and Town Planning Act, and the introduction of old-age pensions. All this and more followed in three years or so after the reversal of the Taff Vale decision in the Trade Disputes Act of 1906. But the trade unions and workers in general were not happy with prices rising faster than wages, while the Liberal majority in the House of Commons was annoyed by the restraints placed upon some of its legislation by the House of Lords.

In 1909, David Lloyd George, chancellor of the exchequer, provoked the crisis that more moderate Liberals were anxious to avoid with a budget including a land tax which would fall on many members of the House of Lords. In two general elections of 1910, the second made necessary by the reluctance of the newly acceded George V (1910–36) to put pressure on the Lords by the threat of creating more Liberal peers, the Liberals lost their majority over the Conservatives and had to depend on 84 Irish MPs and 42 Labour MPs to keep them in power. Now, it seemed, pressed additionally by industrial unrest, the government would become radical indeed. There were large-scale strikes in 1911 and 1912 and a considerable number of smaller disputes in 1913, growing in 1914 towards preparations on the very eve of war for a greater strike than ever organised by the new triple alliance of miners, railwaymen and transport workers. Even the army that had been reformed by Lord Haldane threatened rebellion, while Ireland was in uproar, and the militant movement in favour of votes for women was also making a decided impact.

Yet the government managed to hold on by keeping the Irish MPs dangling on the issue of home rule, while taming the Labour MPs as a consequence of a judicial decision even more threatening to them than Taff Vale – the Osborne Judgement of 1909, which made it unlawful for trade unions to spend money on the return of MPs or indeed on any political purpose. This was not reversed until the Trade Union (Amendment) Act of 1913, which followed the introduction of a £400 a year salary for MPs in 1911. The Labour Party, under a new leader, Ramsay MacDonald, managed to survive the difficult years before 1914. At the war's outbreak, MacDonald, who had put the blame for hostilities on both sides, was forced to resign the leadership in favour of Arthur Henderson, but once the war was under way, MacDonald and most of the Labour Party gave it their full support, going along with such sentiments as those expressed by Keir Hardie in the fateful month of August: 'A nation at war must be united ... With the boom of the enemy's guns within earshot the lads who have gone forth to fight their country's battles must not be disheartened by any discordant note at home.'[6] Hardie was soon to transfer his loyalties to the pacifists before dying of a broken heart in 1915, and MacDonald would join in the call for peace in 1916. But the majority of the Labour movement would continue to give their encouragement to the lads out in the trenches in France.

FRANCE

The progress of Britain's future ally along the path of the New Imperialism was comparable in several ways with that of Britain itself, as well as developing ideas put forward in France during the years following 1815. A passionate advocate of full French participation in the imperial race was Jules Ferry, who as premier (1880–1 and 1883–5) did much to encourage expansion in Africa and Asia. Ferry expounded his views in a concise and comprehensive manner in a speech of 28 July 1885 to the Chamber of Deputies, supporting credits for operations in Madagascar. Ferry began by agreeing that France could not be blamed for the fact that she produced fewer emigrants than any other country in Europe since 'a country which allows a large number of its citizens to emigrate is not a happy, prosperous country'. Yet capital could be sent out as well as people, and on this point, he quoted John Stuart Mill to the effect that: 'One of the best things in which an old, wealthy country can engage is colonisation.' Ferry conceded that intelligent investment would be of benefit to the capitalists, but argued that labour would benefit from the consequent accumulation, too. The French economy as a whole would also derive prosperity from the outlets for exports that were to be found through colonies. It was especially important to consider this aspect of the matter at a time of crisis such as most European industries were then enduring.

But Ferry insisted that the question was not just a material one: there was a much derided but nevertheless important humanitarian and civilising aspect to it. If the black peoples arose to attack French settlements, there would be forceful resistance and an imposition of a protectorate. 'It must be openly said that the superior races have rights over the inferior races', he declared, and these rights were justified by 'a duty to civilise the inferior races'. Those who protested that such statements should not be made in France – the country where the rights of man had been proclaimed – should stay out of Africa.

Beyond the economic and the cultural, there was the political aspect of the matter. Ferry did not care for the argument advanced in another speech that the French were 'seeking compensation in the East for the caution and self-containment which are at the moment imposed on us in Europe'. There could in his view be no compensation for the disasters suffered by the French, that is in the Franco-Prussian War. However, the containment that had been brought about by the agreements made at the Congress of Berlin should not oblige nations that had experienced great misfortunes to abdicate responsibilities and neglect opportunities. Were French governments to remain no more than spectators as other people went into Tunisia in North Africa or policed Tonkin and the mouth of the Red River in South-East Asia? Moreover, he asked: 'Are they going to leave it to others to dispute the mastery of the regions of equatorial Africa? Are they going to leave it to others to decide the affairs of Egypt which, from so many points of view, are in reality French affairs?'

The policy of colonial expansion that had taken France in all these directions as well as to Madagascar was also founded on another strategic 'truth', namely that 'our navy and merchant shipping in their business on the high seas must have safe harbours, defence positions and supply points'. Ferry declared:

> In Europe as it now exists, in this competitive continent where we can see so many rivals increasing in stature around us – some by perfecting their armed forces or navies, and others through the enormous development produced by their ever-increasing population – in a Europe, or rather in a world, which is so constructed a policy of containment or abstention is nothing other than the broad road leading to decadence! In this period in which we are now living, the greatness of nations is due exclusively to the activities they develop.

To look upon any expansion towards Africa and Asia as 'a snare and a rash adventure' would lead to the abdication of France's great power status in less time than his hearers would think. If they voted against the credits their children and grandchildren would meet the fate that had overtaken other nations 'which played a great role on the world's stage three centuries ago but which today, for all their power and greatness in the past, are now third- or fourth-rate powers'.[7]

Those who agreed with Ferry about the necessity of colonial expansion did so for different reasons. For anxious bourgeois, the alternatives were often 'Empire or socialism'. The writer Victor Hugo exclaimed: 'Go peoples! Spill out your excessive numbers into Africa and, at the same time, resolve your social questions. Change your proletarians into landowners.' Yet a liberal such as Léon Gambetta could assert that 'France must keep its role as the soldier of civilisation',[8] while soldiers themselves might be seeking nothing more than adventure and businessmen turning their attention exclusively to profits. The Church concentrated on giving its blessing.

For whatever reasons, between 1880 and 1895, the overseas possessions of France grew from 1 to 9.5 million square kilometres. Madagascar was duly annexed by the mid-1890s, while France took over much of West and Central Africa as well as extending its North African influence from Algeria formally into Tunisia and informally into Morocco. In South-East Asia, French Indo-China extended from Tonkin to Saigon. Colonial commerce increased by nearly 70 per cent in the years 1901–13, while foreign investment quadrupled between 1870 and 1914 for France to become one of the world's greatest financial powers, in Russia and Turkey as well as overseas.

Yet, except at such times as the clash with Britain over Fashoda in 1898 and with Germany over Morocco in 1905 and 1911, the French people were not generally as aroused as others by colonial and imperial questions. This was partly because far fewer of them had emigrated to add ties of blood to the patriotism of the flag, and three-quarters of the 885,000 people who had left an underpopulated France by 1914 went to Algeria. The majority of those who remained were still peasants, nationalistic enough but with horizons more limited to France itself and immediately beyond, while at least some townsmen were anti-colonial. In the aftermath of the Franco-Prussian War and the Commune, French attention was drawn largely to national political and European diplomatic issues.

Both these problems were settled in the short run by Adolphe Thiers, whose political career had first flourished during the reign of Louis-Philippe, whom he had helped persuade to accept the throne in 1830 and tried to advise to retain it in 1848. Out of favour during the Second Empire, he was chosen to be 'Head of the Executive Power' of the Third Republic in 1871, made the peace with Bismarck and regained control over Paris. Now President of the Republic until 1873, Thiers would have liked a restoration of the constitutional Orléanist dynasty, but he was opposed by Legitimists still loyal to the absolutist Bourbon line and by Bonapartists who wanted a resumption of dictatorship by plebiscite. Therefore, although monarchists together held a majority of the seats in the Assembly elected in 1871, they were unable to agree among themselves about who should wear the crown, or indeed what flag should be flown. While Orléanists and Bonapartists were in favour of the retention of the blue, white and red tricolour, the Legitimist comte de Chambord and his supporters wanted to return to the white flag of the Bourbons: what had been good enough for Joan of Arc was good enough for them There were also divisions of attitude among the monarchists concerning the Church: the Legitimists favoured a revival of the temporal authority of the Pope; the Orléanists wanted such authority to be restrained in France; and the Bonapartists sought to bypass this old controversy by the development of a strong Church that would bind society together without involving itself in matters of doctrine.

As the monarchists grew collectively weaker while divided among themselves, the republicans were making full use of a franchise widened to include nearly all males to build up their strength and solidarity in by-elections and in recruitment from the ranks of their enemies. By 1875 they were in sufficiently good heart to be able to see potential benefit accruing from constitutional changes involving the creation of a seven-year presidency and an Upper Chamber or Senate in addition to the lower Chamber of Deputies. As well as putting the ship of state on firmer course, this moderate reform also took some of the wind out of the monarchist sails. However, there remained possibilities for a 'strong man' to establish himself as president, and there was an early attempt to exploit them. Marshal Patrice Macmahon had served in the Crimea and Algeria, and in the Franco-Prussian War had been wounded and captured at Sedan in 1870 before returning to lead the troops that put down the Paris Commune in 1871. He became president in 1873, and tried to take advantage of his reinforced position after 1875 by installing the Orléanist duc de Broglie as premier in 1877. When this move failed to achieve the approval of a majority in the Chamber of Deputies, he dissolved it with the support of the Senate. His influence was not enough to secure a royalist majority in the ensuing elections, however, and he resigned at the beginning of 1879. Macmahon had failed partly because of personality weakness, and partly because of his behaviour in 1871. This helped to unite the anti-monarchists with the slogan 'No enemies on the Left' and rousing speeches from Gambetta, who had withstood at least the first part of the siege of Paris in 1870 before escaping in a balloon.

Macmahon was an ineffectual bull charging the 'red rags' of republican propaganda. His fellow general Georges Boulanger appeared at first to be made of sterner stuff. Following service in Algeria, Italy and the Franco-Prussian War, he continued a more settled military career before entering politics in 1884. As war minister from 1886, he introduced some welcome reforms as well as ordering sentry boxes to be painted in tricolour as a graphic advertisement of his patriotism. Falling from power along with the government of the day in 1887, Boulanger became involved with monarchists and other right-wing groups, who had organised themselves into a League of Patriots (not all of the blue, white and red variety) and pushed Boulanger on his black horse towards emulating the exploits of Bonaparte on his white horse. After a series of election successes, Boulanger felt strong enough to stage a coup overthrowing the constitution and making himself an all-powerful president. But his nerve failed him at the moment of truth in January 1889, and he fled into exile.

Once again, the republicans had closed ranks from centre to left, many of them joining the Society for the Rights of Man and the Citizen. Their leaders took a firm stand against Boulanger and the League of Patriots on the basis of the constitution and the law. But the troubles of the Third Republic were far from over. All the political rivalries that had fallen below fever pitch for nearly a decade broke out again in 1898 four years after the court martial for treason of a Jewish officer from the ceded province of Alsace accused of handing over secret documents from the French general staff to the Germans. With new evidence coming to light, including proof that some of the old evidence had been forged, the former Captain Alfred Dreyfus was recalled from the penal colony of Devil's Island for a retrial in September 1899. This was preceded by a vigorous campaign in his favour in which the novelist

Émile Zola accused the prosecution of rabid racialism. The ranks were drawn up with the army leaders, Church and royalists on the one hand and republicans of various kinds forgetting their differences again on the other. The verdict of the retrial was 'guilty with extenuating circumstances'. The accompanying pardon was not enough to satisfy the Dreyfusards, who pressed for acquittal and reinstatement, while the anti-Dreyfusards continued to pour out mud of the kind slung by one of their number in 1898:

> The Italian Zola, who combines Latin perfidy with Semitic rapacity, and who has for the last thirty years poured the poisoned products of his corrupt soul on everything healthy and noble which remained in our Celtic traditions, our private institutions, our habits and customary laws, comes into the category of enemies of France to be feared far more than the Bismarcks and other redoubtable warriors.[9]

In 1906 the campaign in favour of Dreyfus was finally successful, and he was taken back into the army, promoted and awarded the Legion of Honour.

By this time, a reforming government had taken steps to ensure that the army and the Church could no longer desert their primary responsibilities by turning to involvement in politics. But there was still a powerful group at work on the principle of no enemies to the right, with a new pressure group, *Action française*, taking a firm stand against Protestants and Jews as well as foreigners. On the left, the League for the Rights of Man and the Citizen continued to hold republicans of all shades together, while a Delegation of the Left was formed to keep radicals and socialists in co-operation with other republicans in the Chamber of Deputies. Outside the Chamber, the extreme left voted with trade union delegates for more direct socialist action at the Congress of the General Confederation of Labour in the fateful year of 1905. As elsewhere in Europe, there was a series of strikes in the years following, with a general strike in 1906. The Syndicalist movement started by Georges Sorel for workers' control gained a following of up to half a million, and there was considerable sympathy for its ideas among the other 10.5 million workers. But the radical Georges Clemenceau was prepared to bring in the troops against strikers in 1909, as a consequence of which both his party and other moderates received a larger vote in the general election of 1910. This was not the end of strikes and agitation from left and right, but with the arrival of war, the government was able to call with some success for a 'Sacred Union' as it urged citizens once again to take up arms and form battalions against a foreign invader.

Here was a kind of 'social imperialism', perhaps, but on the whole there was less of this phenomenon apparent in France in the years of the New Imperialism than in Britain or in Germany. France had not felt pressures towards overseas empire as strong as those in the other two major powers of Europe, partly because its economy was not developed to the same extent, partly because the realisation had sunk in after the Franco-Prussian War that times had changed in a manner that no longer allowed her as much room for manoeuvre as she had enjoyed previously. Extreme nationalism, either in monarchist or Bonapartist form, could no longer command as much support as earlier in the century, and while there were frequent changes in government and a number of crises, a continuity and coherence of administration was achieved with a solid majority for the republic. A large measure of stability was achieved by the conversion to the republican cause of a sufficient quantity of the most numerical class, the peasantry. It has been well said that 'The First Republic gave the land, the Second the vote, the Third now offered peasants schools, railways, cheaper freight rates, tariffs'.[10] However, neither the rural nor the urban picture was uniform. During the early years of the Third Republic, the previous Bonapartist majority of the Second Empire in the villages and towns was converted, according to region and temperament, to conservatism or radicalism. Provincialism, as well as clericalism, made the French situation different from that across the Channel, although not so very different from that across the Rhine.

GERMANY

From 1871, Germany was established in Alsace-Lorraine on the 'French bank' of the Rhine. This alien presence on what they considered to be their native soil persuaded many French people to harbour thoughts of revenge, but they tended to keep them quiet through realisation of the even greater tragedy that might befall France in any future war, especially if it had no powerful allies. For this reason, diplomatic understanding was arranged with Russia in 1894 and extended to Britain in 1904. In the early years following 1871, Bismarck went out of his way to be generous in victory and to do what he could to quieten French suspicions and enmity. One advantageous way of achieving this desirable end was through co-operation on colonial expansion. In 1868, Bismarck had written: 'The advantages expected from colonies for the trade and industry of the mother country rest for the most part on illusions.' In 1871, he declared: 'I do not want colonies at all', and in 1873: 'Germany's geographical position does not necessitate her development into a first-class maritime power'. The story also goes that when Bismarck was asked about German interests in Africa, he pointed to a map of Europe, especially to the position of Germany between France and Russia, and said: 'Here is my map of Africa.'[11] Undoubtedly, Bismarck's world outlook was largely centred on Europe, and his lack of interest in Africa might well have stemmed to a considerable degree from his desire to conciliate France so that Germany would not have powerful rivals on both flanks.

That is not the whole story, however, for like their counterparts elsewhere in Europe in the late nineteenth century, German commercial interests were pushing out into Africa, Asia and the Pacific, and would sooner or later bring in the government after them. Bismarck would not support German interests in the Fiji Islands in 1872, and Britain annexed them in 1874. In this year, the chancellor rejected another opportunity for pushing the interests of the German Empire, this time in Zanzibar. The resignation from the government of some of his colleagues over the introduction of tariffs in 1879 made Bismarck think again. In his typical fashion of testing the water before diving in, he floated before the Imperial Diet in 1880 the idea of coming to the financial support of a company formed for the acquisition of property in the Samoan Islands. The Diet gave a negative response, and Bismarck himself would not go in any deeper.

Various pressure groups were formed to persuade the government that it must be more positive. In 1882, a German Colonial Association published a colonial programme urging the launching of two expeditions in West Africa and the prevention of the annexation of either the Congo or the Niger rivers by any European state. Attention was drawn to British and French activity in those vast regions. Yielding to these and other such initiatives, Bismarck asked the Prussian envoy to the

Hanseatic cities to ask them for their views on what the government might do to help their activities in West Africa. The most famous of the responses came from the Hamburg Chamber of Commerce in a long memorandum of 6 July 1883. After a full description of German interests in the area as well as at least a mention of those of other countries such as Portugal, France and especially Britain, the memorandum concluded:

> German trade on the West Coast of Africa has drawn great advantage from the fact that many of these British treaties apply not only to British subjects but generally to Europeans. ... German firms acknowledge gratefully ... the willingness with which British consuls and warships have protected them recently. ... It would, however, be more in keeping with the position of the German Reich and its subjects abroad if they did not have to rely on the goodwill of foreign powers – props which might give way at any moment ...
>
> If Germany wants any practical advantage – to which it surely has the right since the Reich has supported so much scientific research and exploration in the African continent through the African Society – it must act quickly. ... It is not just a few firms who want colonies but the whole German people.[12]

One response to such arguments was Bismarck's sponsorship of a Berlin Conference from late 1884 to early 1885. This was concerned with the activities of King Leopold of Belgium's International Association in the Congo, and with the Congo and Niger basins and African coasts in general. It was attended by a large number of major and minor powers – Germany, France, Britain, Russia, Austria–Hungary, Denmark, Sweden, Norway, Belgium, Holland, Spain, Portugal, Italy, Turkey and the USA. The Conference probably did more to whet imperial appetites than to control them. It certainly allowed King Leopold to bite off as much as he could chew, and more. However, agreement was secured on the major points for discussion along the lines of a phrase used for the first time in the General Act of the Berlin Conference signed on 26 February 1885 – 'spheres of influence', an extension perhaps of the 'balance of power'.

Another phrase had been used for the first time by a Mr Parker Gillmore in an article in the London *Times* of 15 September 1884 – 'The Scramble for Africa'. A leader in the same edition contrasted the

French system of colonisation – land annexation and government control before commerce and immigration – with the British – free trade. In the view of the leader, Bismarck seemed to be holding to the British view. In a speech to the House of Commons after the Berlin Conference, a great British champion of free trade, Gladstone, declared: 'If Germany becomes a Colonising Power, all I can say is "God speed her". She becomes our ally and partner in the execution of a great purpose of Providence for the benefit of mankind.'[13] Bismarck himself had not been thinking along such lines before the Berlin Conference, which he had promoted at least partly in pursuance of conciliation of France. But now France and Britain were reaching agreement over West Africa even if France remained unhappy about the British takeover of Egypt in 1882. Bismarck began to move in the direction of Britain, and went so far as to offer an alliance against what he saw as a growing threat of agreement between the major powers on Germany's flanks – France and Russia – in spite of his secret Reinsurance Treaty with Russia of 1887. Accord between Germany and Britain was finally secured with the treaty of 1890 after the fall of Bismarck.

This important event, 'dropping the pilot' as it was called in a celebrated *Punch* cartoon, occurred in March 1890. Two courses that the pilot had tried to chart led to his departure from the ship of state, one inside Germany, the other outside. After 1871 Bismarck claimed that, as far as the Reichstag was concerned, he sought 'an understanding with the majority of the deputies that will not at the same time prejudice the future authority and governmental powers of the Crown or endanger the proficiency of the army'.[14] From 1871 to 1878 there ensued a so-called 'Liberal Era', as Bismarck brought in a number of measures that completed the process of unification: a currency reform including the creation of a national bank on the gold standard; standardisation of post, telegraph and communications in general; and the promotion of labour mobility through the reduction of guild and apprenticeship restrictions. Bismarck could have achieved these changes without the support of the Reichstag, but believed this assembly to be a useful diversion for public opinion, knowing that it could cause delay but no insuperable barrier to his policies. Throughout the 1870s, Bismarck indeed achieved the support of the large National Liberal Party, but he began to lose it as the party split in 1879 over the issue of his introduction of a tariff. He now derived his principal support from the Conservatives, the political alliance of Junker landlords with industrialists, of 'steel and rye'. But in order to continue harmonious relations with the Reichstag through the 1880s, Bismarck needed the agreement of other parties. By the election of 1885 the National Liberals were with him again as part of the race for empire. At this time, he had also managed to conciliate some of the Centre Party, which was largely Catholic and had therefore been alienated in 1873 by Bismarck's *Kulturkampf* – his 'conflict of beliefs' based on the proposition that German Catholics were insufficiently attached to Prussia, being loyal to a Rome that could promote their open opposition to him. From 1878 Bismarck established a good relationship with the new Pope, Leo XIII, and the Centre Party could now more easily vote in favour of tariffs in 1879 and work with Bismarck afterwards.

Opposition to Bismarck in the Reichstag in the 1880s came from the Progressive Party, joined by dissidents from the National Liberal Party in 1879 to form a new 'Liberal' party also known as the 'Crown prince's party' because of its association with the future Frederick III. Bismarck's espousal of the popular colonial cause helped him not only to achieve a *Kartel* or block of support in the Reichstag but also to make it impossible for Frederick III to oust him during his brief rule of little more than three months in 1888. The new emperor, William II (1888–1918), was friendly enough at the beginning, but was much more enthusiastic for further expansion than his chancellor, and believed that for this purpose it was necessary to gain widespread public support, not only from the middle class but from the working class as well. The chief proletarian political party was the socialist SPD, which Bismarck had never liked and even attempted to suppress by making it an outlaw from 1878 to 1890. He tried to reduce the influence of the SPD in 1883 through the introduction of medical care and sick pay for the workers, although they had to pay two-thirds of the costs. In 1884 he brought in accident insurance financed by the employers, and in 1889 an old-age pension scheme. But the social welfare programme did not go far enough to alleviate the great hardships following on industrialisation, partly as a consequence of which there was a vast coal miners' strike in 1889 involving some half a million workers. Kaiser William not only ordered their employers to give these workers higher wages, but also drew up a list of more extensive social reforms, including the prohibition of child and Sunday labour. Bismarck managed to delay these reforms at the beginning of 1890, and urged an approach to the SPD which was military rather than electoral. While the Kaiser disliked the socialists as much as his chancellor, he would not call out the troops against them, and they made large gains in the Reichstag elections of 1890.

The immediate reason for Bismarck's resignation in March 1890 was, however, foreign policy, specifically towards eastern Europe. German expansionists were looking to the Balkans as an area for their activities. For the chancellor, who looked on the inhabitants of the Balkans as 'fragments of peoples' and 'sheep-stealing bandits',[15] south-eastern Europe was of little concern except as an area that could be brought into calculations concerning the maintenance of the balance of power, especially as a concession to Austria–Hungary. As far as Russia was concerned, he wanted to preserve the spirit of the Reinsurance Treaty of 1887, but this was made difficult for him by widespread opposition to a Russian request for a large loan. William II's already powerful voice spoke out for moving away from Russia and closer to Austria–Hungary, which was a more important trading partner and a necessary ally in any more vigorous infiltration into the Balkans. The Kaiser made Russian troop movements in Poland in March 1890 an excuse for German mobilisation and more intimate liaison with Austria–Hungary. Bismarck managed to stop the mobilisation, and to complain that the Kaiser was conducting foreign policy without consulting the chancellor. But these were his last acts of navigation, for the opposition to him from military as well as civilian sources was now so strong that he was manoeuvred into resignation, and the pilot was duly dropped. In 1871 he had claimed that Germany had reached a good harbour, and should rest content. Twenty years later, he had been overtaken by a Kaiser and many supporters in favour of a vigorous policy of fresh departures from the harbour. For them, the empire as arranged in 1871 was not a conclusion but a beginning.

The manner of Bismarck's departure was not just a stratagem: William II really did mean to run his own show. Thus the names of later chancellors – Georg Caprivi (1890–4), Chlodwig Hohenlohe (1894–1900), Prince Bernhard von Bülow (1900–9) and Theobald von Bethmann-Hollweg (1909–17) – are not nearly as well known as that of their predecessor. Apart from the Kaiser himself, the most familiar figures from late imperial Germany are military – Count Alfred von Schlieffen – and naval – Alfred von Tirpitz: this is a clear reflection of the more aggressive stance adopted by the imperial establishment in the years following 1890. It would be wrong to go on to say that every step from then on was along the road to the First World War, a view which we will discourage here by reserving discussion of that conflict for the next chapter. Nevertheless, there is a change of gear in Germany's imperial expansion which becomes a grasp for world power.

To some extent, as in other empires, the vigour of German foreign policy appears to be prompted by pressures exerted at home. In particular, the rise of socialism that Bismarck had done so much to avert and even to suppress continued in the decade after his resignation. In its early days, the SPD did not achieve easy agreement on the manner of unification ('little German' versus 'large German') or on the manner in which socialism would be achieved (by parliamentary or revolutionary means). However, in contrast to the Gotha programme of 1875, which was in favour of the building of socialism by moderate means, the Erfurt Programme of 1891 took a much more radical stance just after the SPD had secured nearly 1.5 million votes in the Reichstag elections of 1890. The vote climbed to more than 3 million in 1903, and after a disappointing rise of about 250,000 in 1907, rose to more than 4 million in 1912. The SPD was now the single largest party in the Reichstag, although it still had less than one-third of the seats, since electoral boundaries were not revised after 1871: a seat in Berlin could have 100,000 voters, a seat in rural East Prussia only 10,000. Partly because of the SPD's failure to secure a majority in the Reichstag, partly because of the necessity for its deputies to collaborate with those of other parties if they wished to exert any influence upon the government, Edward Bernstein and others argued for the rejection of the Erfurt Programme and the adoption of a revisionist approach, the pursuit of socialism through parliamentary compromise. The gradual abandonment by the majority of the SPD of revolutionary Marxism weakened the Second International, of which it formed the largest component, and also made it easier for the government to pursue its policy of vigorous self-assertion at home and abroad. The difficulties facing William II and his entourage should not be underestimated, however. At some point in the 1890s, the population of Germany became evenly balanced, half rural and half urban, but by 1910 the population of the towns had risen to 60 per cent of the total. While the social misery involved in this mass movement was partly relieved by mass emigration, especially to the USA, there was much industrial unrest led by trade unions, which had gained a membership of about 3 million by 1914. The biggest strike was, as elsewhere, in 1905, when about 500,000 workers were involved, but then in most succeeding years up to 1914 stoppages and disorders occurred of a kind serious enough for the government and some of its opponents alike to believe that revolution was not so very far away.

From 1890 onwards, the government attempted to keep control in various ways. Karl Liebknecht, one of its most determined enemies, was no doubt guilty of some exaggeration when he dismissed the Reichstag as no more than 'a fig leaf covering the nakedness of absolutism', but many recent German historians would agree with the verdict of one of their number on William II's system – 'anachronistic semi-monarchical semi-absolutism'.[16] The Reichstag could only delay, not veto, and Bismarck's successors under the command of their imperial patron used various kinds of manipulation to exert their will. Their policy has often been described as *Sammlungspolitik*, the collection together of all groups supporting the state with the 'rye and iron' alliance of landlord Junkers and industrialists at its centre. For example, the Junkers supported the expansion of the armed forces in return for higher tariffs on grain. The old habits of command of the landlords combined with a similar outlook on the part of the 'barons' of heavy industry such as Krupp to preserve severe discipline reinforced by emphasis on duty and service. National minorities or political extremists could be used as scapegoats for the hardships visited upon the German people. The fact that the German Empire was so newly created allowed the government to play upon regional differences and to stress the need for unity.

However, the success of the government's purely internal policies should not be overestimated, and at least one reason for its energetic foreign policy was 'social imperialism', the relief of pressures within the frontiers of the empire by expansion beyond them. This is not to say that such a 'safety valve' motive was dominant, since the government in any case believed, like its major competitors elsewhere in Europe, that to stand still would be to go backwards. The grasp after world power was therefore not an option, but a necessity. A critical decision in this regard was to build up the navy to such an extent that no rival, not even the British, would want to take on the risks involved in attacking it. This decision was taken largely on the advice of Alfred von Tirpitz, who managed to become minister of marine in 1897, and made recommendations in June of that year which were duly carried out after the 'Navy Laws' of 1898 and 1900. In his Memorandum of June 1897, Tirpitz wrote: 'For Germany the most dangerous naval enemy at the present time is England. It is also the enemy against which we most urgently require a certain measure of naval force as a political factor.' Large battleships as well as smaller cruisers would soon be deployed as a counterweight against the British fleet with its Dreadnoughts and other ships: 'Our fleet must be so constructed that it can unfold its greatest military potential between Heligoland and the Thames.'[17] To counter France and Russia as well as Britain, best use would have to be made of the Kiel Canal between the Baltic and North seas, which was completed in 1895. At the same time, the Suez Canal would determine the size of the ships to be stationed in the Indian and Pacific oceans, helping to protect German imperial interests which had now become worldwide. In the early twentieth century, they took up over 2.5 million square kilometres, mainly in East and South-West Africa, the Cameroons and Togo, but also in New Guinea and other islands in the Pacific, plus Kiachow in China, which was seized in 1897. The tropical colonies provided mostly raw materials, as well as a boost for imperial pride. German imperial ambitions also included North Africa, the Middle East and the Balkans, which were gathered together in the grasp for world power in a manner well represented by the Berlin to Baghdad railway.

Germany was a most dynamic but also a rather fragile empire. It never had the opportunity to settle down after 1871, but was pushed relentlessly onwards and outwards. Internally, it suffered from a series of persistent and overlapping strains: town against country; Prussia against the other states; centre against provinces; north against south, to a lesser extent east against west; Protestants against Catholics; Prussian landed aristocrats, who feared Russian competition most, against industrial bourgeois, who saw the major threat coming from Britain; both these upper classes in the by no means harmonious alliance of 'rye and iron' against peasants and workers (who themselves rarely saw eye to eye). These strains were not only persistent and overlapping but also evolving. For example, Prussian aristocrats were losing their agricultural dominance and were looking increasingly to government military and civil service to maintain their position in society. Similarly, the old backbone of society, especially in the north, the *Mittelstand*, independent farmers and artisans, was being infiltrated by new members from the professions, teachers and lower-level officials. Hence the difficulties in keeping *Sammlungspolitik* moving, and the pressures to look outwards to relieve internal tensions as well as to pursue a vigorous rivalry with the other great empires of Europe: France and especially Britain.

RUSSIA

Russia, like Austria–Hungary, was not in the top rank of European empires in the period 1878–1914. Nevertheless, it had a significant part to play in the arrival of the First World War, which helped in turn to produce the Russian Revolution of 1917. Leaving those two subjects for later consideration, we shall attempt here to concentrate on the last years of tsarism in their own right.

After the reverses of the Treaty of Berlin, Russian nationalists, especially the Panslavists, tried to retain their interest in the Balkans, but there was the wider world to consider too. While Russia was not well placed to join in the scramble for Africa, it pursued a vigorous policy of expansion in Asia, clashing again with Britain in Afghanistan from 1878 to 1880, and with a number of European powers as well as Japan and the USA in the scramble for China at the end of the nineteenth century. When the Treaty of Shimonoseki of 1895 brought a brief war against China to an end with great gains on the mainland as well as offshore for the overwhelming victor, Japan, Russia joined with Germany and France in persuading Japan to draw back from the mainland. Russia now consolidated its sphere of influence in Manchuria, began to infiltrate Korea and took Port Arthur. After the Boxer Rebellion of 1900, Japan and Russia clashed in Korea and Manchuria, and the Russo-Japanese War of 1904–5 ensued. Russia suffered disastrous defeat, including the annihilation of the Pacific Fleet at Port Arthur and of the Baltic Fleet in the Straits of Tsushima – after sailing all the way round the world. The Treaty of Portsmouth, New Hampshire, concluded in September 1905, was less humiliating than it might have been, owing to the moderating influence of the American president, Theodore Roosevelt. But the Russians were forced to admit the supremacy of Japanese interests in Korea and to hand over to the 'yellow monkeys' Port Arthur and its peninsular hinterland, as well as the southern half of the island of Sakhalin. Later the trans-Siberian Railway was completed to take Russian colonists into Siberia (although there were more emigrants to the USA and migrants to the towns). Russia had not lost interest in the Far East, or in the Middle East, where it had made an accommodation with Britain concerning Persia in 1907, thus helping to make a Triple Entente with Britain and France in addition to the Franco-Russian agreement of 1894. But the major focus of attention was now shifted to an area that had in any case never been forgotten, the Balkans.

The Russo-Japanese War possessed a certain element of 'social imperialism', for like the other European empires, Russia at the beginning of the twentieth century was suffering considerable internal tensions that were deemed capable of relief through vigorous activity abroad. In the aftermath of the Emancipation of the Serfs of 1861 and associated reforms of the mid-1860s, Russia went through its own kind of 'liberal phase', and there was even some suggestion of the autocratic monarchy becoming constitutional. But internal problems built up again in the 1870s, leading to the emergence of a small but determined populist movement which split towards the end of that decade into terrorist and agitational wings. The terrorists managed to assassinate Alexander II in 1881, but were then driven out of existence. The agitational wing could hardly be called moderate, however, for in 1883 its members formed the Marxist Liberation of Labour organisation in Geneva. A strike in textile mills near Moscow in 1885 compelled even reactionary newspapers to admit that the 'labour question' had arrived in Russia, although Alexander III (1881–94) and his reactionary advisers did all they could to stop this question and the even more important peasant question from being openly discussed. In the latter case, in 1889 they introduced a new official, the land captain, who, in the informed judgement of Hans Rogger, 'was to check the arbitrariness of peasant over peasant by carrying the arbitrariness of St Petersburg to all'.[18] However, an irresistible momentum for change had built up even in backward Russia.

During the reign of Nicholas II (1894–1917), at least two ministers made energetic attempts to introduce policies that would enable imperial Russia to catch up with its rivals. Sergei Witte, minister of finance from 1892 to 1903, was influenced by the ideas of Frederick List, who had argued in 1846 that, during the German transition from an agrarian to an industrial economy, state controls including protection would be necessary. Witte did not seek slavishly to follow the German example, declaring: 'We must give the country such industrial perfection as has been reached by the United States of America, which firmly bases its prosperity on two pillars – agriculture and industry.'[19] However, with the aid of huge foreign loans, especially from France, he used the power of the state to follow the Prussian rather than the American path to modernity. There were significant increases in railroad construction and heavy industry.

Witte's reforms brought economic growth but also social tensions, on which the political opposition began to thrive before the humiliation of the Russo-Japanese War led to the Revolution of 1905. This signal failure of 'social imperialism' involved a huge general strike and an armed insurrection in Moscow, where workers' councils (Soviets) were set up. Moreover, there were disturbances among the peasants, the armed forces and the nationalities, especially in Poland. Witte advised Tsar Nicholas that he must either institute a military dictatorship, which the unreliability of the armed forces made extremely difficult, or concede at least the beginnings of representative democracy. The result was the Duma, even less powerful than the German Reichstag, but at least giving some airing to a large range of political views from right-wing nationalists to left-wing Social Democrats – Bolsheviks and Mensheviks. The ministerial voice now striving to make itself heard above the clamour was that of Peter Stolypin, prime minister from 1906 to 1912.

Like those of Witte before him, Stolypin's policies were influenced by the success stories of Germany and the USA, especially the former. He gave special attention to the peasant question, hoping to create a middle class of sturdy independent peasants who would provide a backbone for a new social order. At the same time, with such patriotic appeals as 'No second Tsushima', he built up the army and navy with the same kind of dual purpose in mind as had operated elsewhere. Firstly, the Russian Empire would be in a better position to defend and assert itself in an increasingly dangerous world. Secondly, opposition to the government would be stilled and support for it encouraged. Stolypin ran into all kinds of problems in the Duma as well as incurring the displeasure of the tsar and his more immediate advisers before he was assassinated in 1911. Even before the First World War made its own great contribution to the arrival of the Russian Revolution, the chances for the Russian Empire to adapt to the demands of the twentieth century while solving the old peasant and the newer proletarian problems looked slim indeed.

AUSTRIA–HUNGARY AND THE BALKANS

For at least a few years after the Treaty of Berlin in 1878, the Dual Monarchy of Austria–Hungary experienced comparative international and internal peace. The Three Emperors' League was in operation, Russia was most interested in Asia and Germany under Bismarck was not very interested in the affairs of south-eastern Europe. So Austria was now able to establish patronage over Serbia, while moving closer to Romania along with Germany, even if the other new state of Bulgaria remained in the Russian sphere of influence. Meanwhile, the constitutional arrangements set up at the same time as the Dual Monarchy in 1867 managed to hold good, with German bourgeois liberals in Austria and Magyar landlord liberals in Hungary accepting what they had been granted for fear of what they might lose.

From approximately 1890, the remains of the old Habsburg Empire came under threat from a new wave of nationalism accompanied by a new class consciousness. Agrarian society even here was in places beginning to make the transition to industrialism, while agriculture could not remain aloof from new market pressures including competition in grain production from North America. Nationalism in this region was not so much attachment to an abstract ideal or a more materialistic desire for wider markets or better jobs as 'a matter of group dynamics', replacing older ties of family, place or social position.[20] Czech nationalism in particular developed in this sense during the last years of the nineteenth century. Even in this case, however, splits soon developed in political parties, representing socialist and peasant as well as liberal interests. Thomas Masaryk attempted to provide a leadership rejecting the old idea of co-operation with the Austrian Habsburgs.

In the face of this challenge, the governments could pursue three kinds of policy: repression, reform and 'muddling through'.[21] The first, attempted in Hungary as in Russian and Prussian Poland, largely failed. Magyars were not able to keep their stranglehold on such institutions as banks and schools in addition to local and central government in the manner they had intended. Reform was attempted by the Austrian government in relation to the Czechs. For example, in 1897 their language was given equal status with German in Bohemia. But this alarmed the Germans in Bohemia while encouraging the Czechs to ask for more. Further afield, the Magyars in Hungary and Serbs along with Croats in Croatia were encouraged to seek concessions. Various kinds of federalism were suggested as the best answer to the problems of the Dual Monarchy, but the answer actually given was the 'muddling through' brand of mixed imperial–federal policies which managed to stagger on to 1914, not without their successes and humane progress or their failures and bloody reaction.

Meanwhile, although a byword for bloody reaction of an undiluted variety, the new states of the Balkans were making some efforts to adapt themselves to the demands of a new age while still in the first flush of independence. Taking the basis for its new incarnation from the old Dacian 'state' that became a Roman province, Romania under King Carol or Charles (1866–1914), a former German prince, strove to consolidate its former boundaries. Similarly Bulgaria, under two more former German princes, Alexander (1879–86) and Ferdinand (1887–1918), worked for the acquisition of as much as possible of the old 'state' that had existed in association with Byzantium from the beginning of the eighth to the end of the fourteenth centuries. Bulgaria had the more recent concern of its reduction in size at the hand of the Congress of Berlin, and managed to take a larger slice out of the Ottoman Empire in 1885. Meanwhile Serbia was the most successful of the Yugoslav or southern Slav peoples – too successful for the liking of Austria.

The Balkan states were not able to compose their many differences among themselves. Frontiers of ancient and medieval 'states' overlapped, and there were many bitter rivalries between them. The wars that were to break out in the twentieth century reflected these rivalries as well as ambitions to secure pieces of the still declining Ottoman Empire. The involvement of the great powers from outside the Balkans was to lead to the outbreak of the First World War in 1914. Before then, the largely peasant societies of the Balkans had not made many strides towards industrial development, however much major out-side powers – Germany, France and Britain as well as Russia and Austria–Hungary – had looked upon them as worthy of considerable investment.

THE REST OF EUROPE AND THE WIDER WORLD

From the 1880s onwards, the other states of Europe – Sweden, Den-mark and (from 1905) Norway to the north, Belgium and Holland to the north-west and Italy, Spain and Portugal to the south-west – proceeded in a manner which necessarily reflected the influence of the five major powers. This is not to say that they did not make their mark on the development of Europe and its relations with the world beyond. For example, the newest of them, Norway, independent from Sweden after 1905, possessed the fourth largest mercantile marine in the world after Britain, Germany and the United States. The Nether-lands made the most of the Dutch East Indies, while Belgium promoted the International African Association and infiltration of the Congo. Italy made a contribution in Africa of a more negative kind, being the only European state to suffer significant defeat there, at Adowa in 1896 at the hands of the Abyssinians. However, Italy was a force to be reckoned with in the Mediterranean and as a member from 1882 of the Triple Alliance with Germany and Austria. Portugal and Spain held on to old dreams of empire, although Spain received a rude awakening in its war with the USA in 1898.

Outside Europe, just two powers participated in the race for empire in a positive rather than a negative manner. The United States of America, from its ever stronger sphere of influence in North and South America, looked increasingly outward, especially with the war against Spain in 1898 which took it into the Philippines as well as Cuba. Commence-ment of the construction of the Panama Canal under his auspices encouraged President Theodore Roosevelt to show a combined interest in the Atlantic and the Pacific, although the canal was not actually opened until 1914. He worked to maintain the 'Open Door' for all foreign nations in China and to bring to an end the war of 1904–5 between Russia and Japan. Japan was by this time a vigorous second non-European entrant in the race for empire, and the first non-white imperialist power. This development brought some hope for their own eventual liberation to those who had become victims of European imperialism while causing alarm in Europe itself. A reassuring Japanese spokesman declared:

> there is no ground for a 'Yellow Peril'; first, because Japan is sincerely convinced of the superiority of the West; second, because we believe that a truly superior culture is the common property of all mankind; third, because European civilisation forms an invincible bulwark against any Asiatic onslaught.[22]

Strategic arguments for maintaining such a bulwark fell after 1878 into two major schools, which can be conveniently linked with two names, Mahan and Mackinder. In 1890, an American naval officer, Alfred T. Mahan, published *The Influence of Sea Power upon History, 1660–1783*, in which he took as an object lesson the manner in which Britain had arisen to great power status because of its maritime activity. The lesson was learned in the USA and in Germany especially. In 1904, Halford John Mackinder, an Oxford graduate in history whose varied career had involved travel, politics and education, gave a lecture to the Royal Geographical Society entitled 'The Geographical Pivot of History'. This gave special emphasis to the vast continent of Eurasia's 'heartland' and stressed its central importance through many centuries. The arguments of this lecture were given attention not only in Britain, but further afield.[23]

However, the Mahan and Mackinder arguments were probably more complementary than contradictory, the first originating in a land-based power that had comparatively neglected the sea and the other in a sea-based power that had comparatively neglected the land. Overseas imperial activity could not be separated from that taking place over-land. For example, the Germany attempting to build a railway and influence from Berlin to Baghdad was no different from the Germany constructing a navy and attempting to assert itself in the North Sea and other waters. Similarly, external expansion and rivalry could not be separated from the internal tensions between the classes in all of the empires of Europe. As the history of Europe and the history of the world overlapped to an extent much greater than before, the essential connections between foreign and domestic policy remained as close as ever, and even became closer.

THE RISE OF EUROPE

As early as the 1860s, an official of a telegraph company could declare: 'We hold the ball of the earth in our hand, and wind upon it a network of living and thinking wire, till the whole is held together and bound with the same wishes, projects, and interests.' He continued:

> Thus the commerce of the world will find its path ..., for the telegraph is to precede all, rapidly and cheaply we press it forward as the swift-running courier. First the adventurous merchant seeks the channel opened by this messenger; then the stately ship, soon to make way for the more rapid steamer; finally the iron way joins the circle, and girds the world with steam and electricity.[24]

The 'iron way' had added a new dimension not only to commerce but also to strategy. As Edwin A. Pratt observed in 1915 of the railways that had been constructed in Europe, North America and beyond:

> They allow of war being carried on between a number of nations at one and the same time, thus spreading the area over which the conflicts of today may extend. They encourage the cherishing of designs of world-power and dreams of universal conquest.[25]

Such designs and dreams were encouraged by other ideas being put forward in the late nineteenth century, not only concerning the rivalry between nations and conflict between the classes but also between all life forms. Charles Darwin's *On the Origin of Species*, first published in 1859, was applied several decades later to the belief that human beings banded together to ensure their own survival, and that some such groups would survive while the weaker would succumb. Thus, for example, in 1911 General F. von Bernhardi argued that the prospect for Germany was either world power or downfall.[26]

During the period of the Revolution and Napoleon, France once again provided a challenge to Europe. After 1815 the two most powerful states were Russia and Britain, which both succeeded in consolidating their empires, by land and sea respectively. Their clash was at the centre of the next major European conflict, the Crimean War in 1854–61, which resulted in a setback for Russia in Europe. This was one of the circumstances that allowed the process of German unification to be completed under Prussian leadership by 1871. By this time, Italy had also been able to make use of a favourable international situation to complete its unification. Nationalism remained a powerful force down to the end of the nineteenth century, especially in eastern Europe where new states emerged as the Austrian and Turkish empires grew weaker.

Meanwhile, the major European powers moved towards collision as they struggled for supereminence on the continent and for shares of the rest of the world. By around 1900 they had together risen to the peak of their global influence. But the rivalries between them were already leading by 1914 towards decline, a process to be accelerated by the emergence of the USA and Japan, and especially by the outbreak of the First World War.

Europe's brief moment of dominance was brought about by its development of industrial might. This process was accompanied by the formation of the ideologies of liberalism and nationalism, of socialism and imperialism. These systems of ideas and beliefs reflected the changes in social alignment, in particular the formation of the bourgeoisie and the proletariat, but also the adjustment to modern market forces of the landlords and the peasants, who still constituted the largest class. Classes new and old were to struggle with each other in a manner which threatened to bring about a revolution as far-reaching in its implications as the one that broke out in France in 1789. After many alarms at various times in other countries, the significant moment arrived in 1917 in Russia.

10

EUROPE BEFORE 1914: ORIGINS OF WORLD WAR AND THE RUSSIAN REVOLUTION

THE NEW CENTURY

Before 1914, six European great powers – Great Britain, France, Italy, Germany, Austria–Hungary and Russia – along with two others from outside the continent – the USA and Japan – 'had brought the greater part of the earth's surface, resources, and population within their respective spheres of administration, control, or influence'.[1] This in spite of the fact that the total population of the eight powers was little more than a quarter of a world population approaching 1,700 million. In five of the six European great powers, between seven and nine out of every ten persons lived on the land. Even in the exception, Great Britain, the landed interest was far from insignificant, while in the other cases it vied with the urban middle class – the bourgeoisie – in an almost exclusively male struggle for supremacy. However, nearly everywhere the bourgeoisie was on the rise, as there was a considerable movement from rural areas to the cities as peasants became proletarians. For the migrants to become competent cogs in the ever expanding industrial machine, they were obliged to change their culture, for example to work regular hours, and to master the three Rs, reading, writing and arithmetic. Male dominance was marked at all levels of European society before the First World War, one of the few positive consequences of which was to be a move towards female emancipation.

Vast crowds of people in the English-speaking world from all classes celebrated the arrival of the twentieth century at the end of 1899. They were reminded of their mistake a year later through the most common means of public communication, the daily newspapers, which also reviewed the past and looked forward to the future. The leading journal of the American establishment, the *New York Times*, warned its readers on 1 January 1901 not to be too precise: 'When men speak of the achievements of the Nineteenth Century they show disrespect for historical truth and natural law. Nature has its rhythms, and history may move in cycles, but the world's progress cannot be scanned by the artificial prosody of the calendar.'

Nevertheless men, and women too, have persisted in talking of the 'twentieth century' as an entity categorically different from those that went before, and with increasingly good reason. As for the *New York Times*, it overcame its own warning to look back at the preceding hundred years to 'call it a century of marvels, and it should be marvelous, for it is the flower of all the others'. Going even more remotely into the past, the leading editorial suggested:

> Away back in some immensely distant age there was a hairy fellow, living in a cave, who one day picked up the fallen branch of a tree and used it as a club to kill a wild goat for his dinner. If we knew him we should erect a statue to him as a father and founder of the arts that have come to such development in the Nineteenth Century, for his was one of the earliest triumphs of man over nature, a first and hopeful act that put him fairly on the way to the lordship of creation.

Here was the gospel of the survival of the fittest forming a large part of the outlook of upper-class Americans and Europeans alike at the turn of the century.

The Times of London, in similar vein, asked of the years to come: 'Will they enlarge the dominion of man over nature in the same degree or in a greater degree than the age that has gone by?' But a more pressing question for Englishmen, Scotsmen and Irishmen had to be: 'How will the new century affect the moral and material greatness of our country and of our Empire?' Australia was to become a federal commonwealth that very day, 1 January 1901, and although there continued to be difficulties in South Africa, progress was general enough throughout the empire for *The Times* to assert:

> We have a reasonable trust that England and her sons will emerge triumphant from that ordeal at the end of the Twentieth Century as at the end of the Nineteenth and that then and for ages to come they will live and prosper one united and Imperial people, to be 'a bulwark for the cause of men'.

The resolution of readers could be fortified by turning to the advertisements which reminded them that 'The Greatest Success in Dietetics in the Nineteenth Century was the Invention of Bovril' and that they should be prepared for accidents by having ready a proved remedy – Elliman's Rub. Meanwhile, solid citizens of the British Empire's most northerly large town were being urged in their daily newspaper to buy Curr's Dandelion Essence, the cure for indigestion, as well as Owbridge's Lung Tonic – 'Be sure you get it! It never fails!' In its leading editorial the *Aberdeen Journal* provided another encouraging message for those with Hogmanay hangovers:

> In the outset, it may safely be asserted that in no similar period of the world's history has there been anything approaching the progress that has characterised the period under review. ... One may even say that in some respects the past century has seen more and done more than all the previous centuries put together.

All nations and spheres of activity had been involved. There had been great political developments, with even the United States of America affected by the 'Imperial Spirit'. 'Marvellous advance' and 'amazing progress' had taken place in science and civilisation. Among the most striking features had been the introduction of steam transport by land and sea, and of electricity as a means of communication with all its wires and cables. Labour-saving machinery was to be found everywhere, while moves forward in civilisation were marked by public education, private charity and free trade. And so: 'The world today, with all its disturbing elements, is as good and as happy as it has ever been.'

For further confirmation that the new century was beginning well, the Aberdonian could turn to other pages. Law and order were being maintained, as was demonstrated by reports on proceedings in the local police court. For example, reckless driving had been curbed with the arrest of Albert Flatters, hot-potato vendor of Urquhart Road, who while the worse for liquor had taken his horse and vehicle down Union Street: he was offered the option of a 20 shilling fine or 10 days in prison. Thus reassured, the newspaper reader might decide to take his family for a New Year treat to the theatre. He would probably avoid Her Majesty's where *The Little Minister* by Mr Barrie was playing, for it had been criticised by 'Scotch and non-Scotch' alike for its caricature of 'Scotch elders', but the Palace had a good, wholesome holiday show where they could all go with better conscience. Heading the bill was the Zalva Trio, whose acrobatic feats were the talk of the patrons of the southern music halls. Colonel Gaston Bordeverry impressed with his unique shooting powers, and there was also Little Victor, the famous Italian mimic. Another favourite 'turn' was 'Gibbons' bio-tableau, an alternative name for the cinematograph. A few more hardy souls braved the boisterous elements in the weather and the crowd to watch Aberdeen Football Club, whose opponents Partick Thistle were first 'on the leather', but then overtaken by 'the holiday mood' to settle for a 1–1 draw. Among the crowd, just possibly, were one or two more prosperous and adventurous souls who had travelled to the first Olympic Games of the modern era in Athens in 1896 or the second in Paris in 1900.

TRAVEL IN EUROPE AND BEYOND

For this purpose, they might well have used the services of the tourist firm of Thomas Cook, founded in 1841, and the guidance of No. 644 of *Bradshaw's Continental Railway, Steam Transit, and General Guide, for Travellers throughout Europe*, published in 1907. In Britain, one could reach Wick and Thurso by rail if not John o'Groats, and Penzance if not Land's End. Over the Channel, one could go along the 'iron road', as it was everywhere called, from Faro in the south of Portugal with further appropriate sea crossings to Trondheim in Norway or to Noto in Sicily. To the east, routes became sparser beyond Warsaw or Vienna, but in Russia the more intrepid kind of traveller could still be on the 'iron road' out of Europe and into Asia beyond the Caucasus Mountains or the Caspian Sea or across Siberia as far as Stretensk on the further side of Lake Baikal and the town of Chita. From there, until the further laying of rails was completed, a steamboat travelled down the River Amur to Khabarovsk, head of the railway line to Vladivostok. To the southeast, trains went from Berlin to the extremity of Europe at Istanbul, but not yet to Baghdad, the line coming to an end at Konya in Anatolia in 1900 (it was still far from complete in 1914).

Tourists throughout Europe embarking on an updated version of the Grand Tour at the beginning of the twentieth century could avail themselves of that invaluable series of guidebooks published in Leipzig by the firm of Karl Baedeker, whose founder had died in 1859. In Portugal, according to Baedeker, the people were 'more humane than the Spaniard, less bigoted in religious matters, and less excitable and unruly in the political field'. However, the Portuguese language would make 'a somewhat unpleasant impression on the visitor from Spain on account of the comparative dullness of its tone and the numerous sibilant and nasal sounds'. In Spain, the stranger moving in educated circles would be impressed by the charming spontaneity of manner and the somewhat exaggerated politeness of the people. However, he should avoid all serious topics of conversation, especially religion and politics – 'The national pride of the Spaniard and his ignorance of foreign conditions render a collision in such cases almost inevitable'. The lower-class Spaniard had much more common sense than his so-called superiors, but he must be treated courteously and with patience – 'Common intercourse in Spain is marked by a degree of liberty and equality which the American will find easier to understand than the European'. The 'national pest' of Spain was begging, and its practitioners should be ignored as much as possible, especially the children among them. Other pests might be encountered at bedtime, and a supply of Persian or Keating's insect powder should be taken along. In the case of a riot or other popular disturbance, the stranger should remove himself as far and as quickly as possible, 'as the careful policemen, in order to prevent the escape of the guilty, are apt to arrest anyone they can lay their hands on'.[2] In Italy: 'As a rule the trains are very unpunctual, and booking is a provokingly slow process.' The people were easier to deal with in the north and centre than in the south, although the bark of Neapolitans was generally worse than their bite.[3]

Punctual or not, the Italian trains, like others in the south-west of Europe, enabled travellers to move considerable distances with a rapidity and degree of comfort that would have been unthinkable before their development. In this way, the whole continent may be said to have shrunk, and there was introduced into each region within reach of the railway a new ease of communication with the world beyond. This shrinkage was of great significance: local economies, cultures and societies were now open as never before to outside influences. This is not to say that a new uniformity was superimposed on Europe over- night. Even in the most advanced north-west, the inns away from the larger towns and the more fashionable watering places in northern France 'retain their primitive provincial characteristics, which might prove rather an attraction than otherwise were it not for the shameful defectiveness of the sanitary arrangements'.[4]

To the north, age-old reticence was still to the fore in Scandinavia: 'The manners of the innkeepers are quiet and reserved, but there is no lack of real politeness.' But the perils of customary modes of release from such reticence were underlined by the warning that 'Spirits are rarely obtainable at the hotels, and never in steamboat or railway restaurants'.[5] At the centre, in Germany and Austria, the railways were clean, comfortable and efficient, and all regulations were stringently enforced by the authorities. If the traveller forsook the train for the bicycle along the Rhine, he should note that: 'Some of the narrower and steeper streets in towns and villages are apt to be closed to the cyclist, and restrictions are also often made on the use of the wheel in public parks. In most cases, a numberplate has to be attached to the bicycle, and the police have the right to demand the exhibition of the cyclist's club-ticket or passport.'[6] Cycling in Austria was not recom- mended, 'for the steam-roller is unknown in that country', while 'The further east one goes the worse the roads become'.[7]

Moreover, in the same direction, the police, although less efficient, became more obtrusive. In the east, in Russia, a passport was 'indis- pensable' and if it was not in order, 'its unhappy owner has to re-cross the frontier, the train by which he came waiting for the purpose'. Other kinds of care needed to be taken: for example, 'unprinted paper only should be used for packing, to avoid any cause of suspicion'. And: 'The taking of photographs near fortresses is naturally forbidden; and even in less important places the guardians of the law are apt to be over-vigilant.' As far as travel within Russia was concerned, the roads were bad, and to move along them in the available carriages and carts ('resembling a rude edition of the American buckboard') was 'very rough and often painful'. The trains, of four inches wider gauge than was standard in Europe, were frequently late and often overcrowded, but comfortable enough first class. The *provodnik* (attendant), who gave out bedding and made himself useful in many kinds of ways, 'like the negro porter in Pullman cars, expects a fee for his services'.[8]

By the beginning of the twentieth century, Baedeker was offering advice to those European travellers intrepid enough to cross the Atlantic and experience American buckboards and Pullman cars for themselves. The advantages and disadvantages of the American open-carriage trains were fully set out: peace and quiet were difficult to obtain, but much amusement could be derived from watching one's fellow passengers. In general, travelling in the USA was now as safe 'as in the most civilized parts of Europe', and the carrying of arms was as unnecessary here as there, although in many western towns 'it is advisable to avoid the less reputable quarters and to refrain from entering any shops, barber's rooms, or the like except those undeniably of the best class'. The 'average Englishman' would probably find greatest discomfort in the dirt of city streets, the roughness of country roads, the winter overheating of hotels and railway-cars, the dust, flies and mosquitoes of summer and, in many places, the habit of spitting on the floor – 'but the Americans themselves are now alive to these weak points and are doing their best to remove them'.

The Baedeker of 1904 found it necessary to include a glossary of American words and usages, for although 'the cultivated American' would differ little in speech from 'the cultivated Englishman', such people as railway officials, cabmen and waiters would not understand some British expressions, although there would be considerable regional variation. Among the items deemed necessary for inclusion in the glossary were:

bed-spread, coverlet, counterpane.
boss, master, head, person in authority.
chore, odd job about a house done by a man.
dumb, (often) stupid (Germ. *dumm*).
fix, to arrange, make, put in order, settle, see to, etc.

> *mad*, vexed, cross.
> *parlor*, drawing-room.
> *right away*, directly.
> *shortage*, deficiency.
> *take out*, An American takes a lady 'out' to dinner, while an English-
> man takes her in.

Just a few years on, even a dumb Englishman would be mad right away at any suggestion that he suffered from any shortage of understanding of these items from the glossary. Having emerged from the bed-spread and fixed the chores assigned to him in the parlor and elsewhere by his boss, he might take her out to dinner, not in, so far had the Americanisation of English progressed in so brief a time. Of course, at least some of this 'Americanisation' could have been re-Anglicisation, for the debate was already in progress about who spoke the oldest version of the language, and Baedeker in at least one of the items of its glossary, '*deck*, pack of cards', was anxious to point out that the word had been used in this sense by Shakespeare.[9]

No such ambiguities would worry those travellers bold enough to go by steamer beyond Europe and the English-speaking world. Africa was the 'dark continent' and the Orient was 'inscrutable': it was rare at the beginning of the twentieth century for regions outside the familiar North Atlantic to be considered on their own terms rather than according to the degree to which they had accepted 'civilisation', by which was meant essentially 'Europeanisation'. Japan, therefore, was recognised in this regard to some extent, even if in a somewhat grudging manner. Nevertheless, most of the globe had been 'discovered' before the First World War, and more than a little of it penetrated not only by explorers but even by tourists. Only the most intrepid had reached the Arctic and Antarctic, however.

SIR DONALD MACKENZIE WALLACE'S *RUSSIA*, 1905

The first edition of Sir Donald Mackenzie Wallace's *Russia* published in 1877 soon gained for its author the reputation of being one of the most perceptive of foreign authors on this difficult subject. In his Preface to a new and enlarged edition in 1905, Sir Donald wrote that changes in the previous quarter of a century had been neither so numerous nor so important as he had supposed: certainly, there had been much progress, but nearly all along old lines. Therefore, while revising his old chapters, Mackenzie Wallace decided to add just five entirely new ones: three on the revolutionary movement that had arisen since 1877; one on the industrial progress with which the latest phase of the revolutionary movement was closely connected; and one on the main lines of the situation as it appeared at the time of going to press – for better or worse, in the middle of Russia's first major revolution.

Travel had been made easier by the development of railways to St Petersburg and Moscow, and thence to Odessa, Sevastopol, the lower Volga, the Caucasus, central Asia and Siberia. The trains never attained a high rate of speed, partly explained by the fact that 'In Russia time is *not* money; if it were, nearly all the subjects of the Tsar would always have a large stock of ready money on hand, and would often have great difficulty in spending it'. However, the railways had been built by the state primarily for a purpose that could become urgent – 'the railway map of Russia presents to the eye of the strategist much that is quite unintelligible to the ordinary observer'. Communication by river and canal had also greatly improved, although the climate often impeded navigation because of ice in the winter and lack of water in the summer. Roads were nearly all of 'the unmade, natural kind', although winter use could be more pleasant than summer since 'snow and frost are great macadamisers'.

The vast, monotonous spaces of European Russia were divided into two principal zones by a line stretching eastwards from St Petersburg, with forest and morass to the north, and arable land broken by occasional patches of sand or forest to the south. Apart from St Petersburg, Moscow and other towns, population was most dense in a band broadening from Moscow to Kiev and Kharkov in Ukraine and then narrowing down to Odessa on the Black Sea. Between 85 and 90 per cent of the people were peasants, setting great importance on the Orthodox sacraments and observing rigorously the lengthy fasts, but showing little respect for the priests, who were almost as poor as themselves. Their medicine was a mixture of the magical and the scientific. Bound together by extensive household links, and in many areas by the commune, too, the peasants could also be involved in an *artel* (co-operative association) for the pursuit of small-scale or even larger-scale manufactures – 'Though the peasants may continue for a time to work at home for the wholesale dealers, they cannot in the long run compete with the big factories and workshops, organised on the European model with steam-power and complicated machinery, which already exist in many provinces'. The bulk of the peasants scorned those who prospered as exploiting *kulaki* (fists) – 'Russians of all classes have, in fact, a leaning towards socialistic notions, and very little sympathy with our belief in individual initiative and unrestricted competition'. Nevertheless, entrepeneurs of a new type vied with merchants of a more traditional kind. Similarly, the nobility could be divided into modernisers and traditionalists.

According to the census of 1897, there were 104 towns with more than 25,000 inhabitants and only 19 with more than 100,000. The official town population at this time, not allowing for an incalculable number of seasonal workers and other unofficial inhabitants, was about 14 per cent of a total of just over 125 million. (In Britain at that time, 72 per cent of the population lived in towns.) As far as native language was concerned, the census showed the following approximate percentages: Russian – 45; Ukrainian – 18; Turkic – 11; Polish – 6; Belarussian – 5; and Jewish – 4, followed by many others.

Mackenzie Wallace found it necessary to utter a word of warning about some of these statistics, in particular about classes. On the one hand, Russians might well deny that there were classes in their country, and declare that legal categories were 'mere administrative fictions'. For visitors, on the other hand, class distinctions formed 'one of the most prominent characteristics of Russian society': there was no mistaking nobles, clergy, burghers and peasants. The problem centred round the term *soslovie* – usually translated now as 'estate'. If *soslovie* were taken to mean 'an organised political unit with an *esprit de corps* and a clearly conceived political aim', none could be found, because there were 'no distinctions of race and no impassable barriers'. However, to claim that social classes had never existed was 'a piece of gross exaggeration'. Because of Russia's peculiar development of 'an almost exclusively agricultural Empire with abundance of unoccupied land' controlled by an 'irresistible autocratic power' keeping all social groups in check, there was 'almost no trace of those class hatreds' that were appearing so conspicuously elsewhere in Europe. (No doubt Mackenzie Wallace would have changed his mind on this particular point after 1917!) Moreover, the tsar was not only the secular autocrat but also, to quote the law, 'the supreme defender and preserver of the dogmas of the dominant faith' whose 'autocratic power acts in the ecclesiastical administration by means of the most Holy Governing Synod created by it'. Mackenzie Wallace commented that the tsar 'is merely the defender of the dogmas, and cannot in the least modify them; but he is at the same time the chief administrator, and uses the Synod as an instrument'.[10]

The immobility of the central administration could be illustrated by the nature of the papers produced by the commissions invariably appointed whenever there was talk of reform. One of them, on the subject of benevolent institutions, began with a philosophical discussion before proceeding with some remarks on the Talmud and the Koran, then on the treatment of paupers in ancient Rome and Athens, before proceeding to 'the Anglo-Saxon domination' of King Egbert and King Ethelred and 'a remarkable book of Icelandic laws, called Hragas'. Conclusions were drawn from the so-called 'latest results of science' – in fact a mass of raw, undigested materials drawn from the work of respected names in Germany, France and Britain. Such papers were of no help to those considering the reform nor to those trying to gain information on the actual state of the country.

Mackenzie Wallace found it equally difficult to weigh up the long-term consequences of the Emancipation of the Serfs of 1861. The educated classes were 'unduly disposed to represent to themselves and to others the actual condition of the peasantry in a very unfavourable light' while 'very few peasants ever put to themselves the question: Am I better off now than I was in the time of serfage?' Nevertheless, it could be said with confidence that some had prospered while others had become impoverished as the old way of life began to yield to the pressures of industrialisation – 'This change in rural life is so often referred to that, in order to express it, a new, barbarous word, *differentsiatsia* (differentiation), has been invented'. While the peasantry was becoming impoverished and 'therefore more likely to listen to the insidious suggestions of Socialist agitators', in the towns, for any future revolutionary movement, 'the Proletariat would naturally supply recruits'.

Following 1861, other reforms undoubtedly made an impact. The *zemstvo* attempted to look after the material and moral well-being of the provincial population, while the law courts struggled to resist encroachments from the central bureaucracy while overcoming age-old prejudices on the part of the peasants and other classes alike. While liberals tried to improve the system, others sought to overthrow it. Mackenzie Wallace suggested that the revolutionary movement had passed through four stages – the academic, the propagandist, the insurrectionary and the terrorist. By the early twentieth century, two parties predominated: the Social Democrats, essentially doctrinaires, thoroughgoing disciples of Karl Marx, concentrating on agitation especially in the towns; and the Socialist-Revolutionaries, more empirical, but extending their activity to the countryside in the belief that the peasantry would play an important part in the revolution while continuing to believe that the use of terrorism could accelerate the arrival of political liberty.

Of course, the Revolution of 1905 and its sequel would change the nature of political parties in Russia. In the appraisal he made at the beginning of that momentous year, Mackenzie Wallace remarked on Russia's 'irrepressible tendency to expand', on which 'we should keep a watchful eye'. Vigilance was particularly necessary because a further motive – 'to acquire new markets for her manufactured goods' – had been added to those already in existence – 'spontaneous colonisation, self-defence against nomadic tribes, and high political aims, such as the desire to reach the sea-coast'. In conclusion, Mackenzie Wallace expressed the hope that the emperor would adopt the liberal programme and that 'a strong man will be found to take the direction of affairs'. Close as he was to events, he does not seem to have appreciated fully the part played by the disastrous war of 1904–5 against Japan in bringing the Revolution about, nor the seriousness of the situation that was emerging in 1905.[11]

In a further revised edition of *Russia* in 1912, Mackenzie Wallace paid special attention to the period since 1905, in particular 'to the rise and development of parliamentary institutions which must exercise a great influence on the future destinies of the country'.[12] However, he criticised the impatience of the liberal members of the Duma – the Kadets (from the Russian letters 'ka' and 'de' – Constitutional Democrats). He suggested that they should have given support to Stolypin's reform efforts, for example. Soon after the outbreak of the First World War in 1914, Mackenzie Wallace produced a pamphlet entitled *Our Russian Ally*. He conceded that 'in the general march of civilisation Russia long remained far behind her West-European sisters' and had 'not yet quite overtaken them'. While again criticising moderate members of the Duma for not giving the government more support, he praised Nicholas II for his 'keen, sympathetic interest in the material and moral progress of his country', and his readiness 'to listen attentively and patiently to those who are presumably competent to offer sound advice on the subject'. During 'the revolutionary agitation' of 1905, he had steered a middle course. As far as the expansionist tendencies of his empire were concerned, the tsar had shown moderation, and in particular turned a deaf ear to suggestions for provocative action against Great Britain on the frontier of Afghanistan.[13]

By 1917, the First World War had hastened the end of tsarism, as we shall see in the next chapter. In this manner, Mackenzie's hopes for the continued pursuit of 'a middle course' were dashed. Nevertheless, he had discerned with acute insight the significant cultural and economic developments that were taking place not only in Russia but throughout Europe as a whole.

FROM ROMANTICISM, 1815–71

The high culture of medieval Europe was shared by Christians who knew Latin, although the Greek Orthodox constituted an important exception. The Age of Reason and the Enlightenment were more secular, and more widespread. The nineteenth century was to produce a broader culture with greater quantities of both print and readers.

The nineteenth century also introduced produced many -isms in the wake of the French Revolution and Napoleon. These included feudalism and absolutism, which were devised to describe earlier developments. On the period since 1789 itself, as T. C. W. Blanning has observed:

> With amazing speed the revolutionaries created a whole new political culture, quite different in theory and practice from even the most liberal polities of Europe. Underpinned by the principle of national sovereignty, it was an ideology with a short past but a great future, for it wrapped into one explosive package the three great abstractions of modern politics – the state, the nation and the people.[14]

Since the present was messier than the past, the -isms adopted to describe aspects of what was going on in the nineteenth century itself were often inexact. We cannot do without these terms, but equally we cannot be as precise as we would like in our use of them, as we have seen in earlier discussion of liberalism, nationalism and socialism.

However, there might be wide agreement not only that Romanticism was promoted by the French Revolution and Napoleon, but also that it was a reaction to neoclassicism. According to one of many definitions within 'a chaos of rival and competing Romanticisms', it emerged in 'a Europe recovering from a French domination which could pretend to *universal* progress and rationality'. In contrast, 'Romantics aimed to uncover a national character and even "racial" continuities through which the past, embodied in living memory, could speak to, guide, and nurture the present'. Moreover, Romantics 'conjured up myths of the glories of the past, the drama of the inner self as hero, spiritual voyages into the religious and the transcendental, and a communion with the mountains'. Living writers became 'a new priesthood' exerting 'a cultural influence hitherto unthinkable'. Among their contributions was an encouragement of patriotism and nationalism.[15]

Romanticism is most closely associated with artists, poets, novelists and musicians: for example, the Frenchman Eugène Delacroix, the Englishman William Wordsworth, the Scotsman Walter Scott and the German Ludwig van Beethoven respectively. Delacroix painted subjects natural, mythical and historical, catching the swirl and impetus of revolution in *Liberty Guiding the People* soon after the events of 1830 in Paris. Wordsworth declaimed that to be young at the time of the French Revolution was very heaven and that earth had nothing to show more fair than the view from Westminster Bridge in London. But he devoted much more of his attention to catching the beauty and spirit of the Lake District to the north. Even further north, 'Scotland, through its images, played as important a part in the whole romantic movement as it did through its ideas in the eighteenth-century Enlightenment'.[16] Following the great vogue for the Highland bard Ossian at the turn of the century, Walter Scott set out great chronicles of Highland and Lowland history in his Waverley novels. In music, Beethoven set the tone by withdrawing the dedication to Napoleon of his Third Symphony after disillusionment with his former hero. To take another example, the music of Fryderyk (Frédéric) Chopin 'remains the purest and the most universally accessible expression of Polish Romantic feeling',[17] all the more poignant for being composed in exile.

Just as we must avoid too many -isms, we must not allow ourselves to lapse into a mere list of names. However, to take just one more individual, the English artist Joseph Turner's atmospheric rendering of light and colour pointed the way towards later, non-figurative painting, while his *Rain, Steam and Speed* could be viewed as a precursor not only of Impressionism but also of Futurism.

The English words 'scientist' and 'physicist' were coined in 1840 by the English philosopher William Whewell, who also observed the tendency of the sciences towards separate specialisation, from amateur towards professional research. However, in his *Cours de philosophie positive*, completed in six volumes by 1842, Auguste Comte suggested that six sciences – mathematics, astronomy, physics, chemistry, biology and sociology – had reached their third and final, positive stage (after fictional and abstract stages). In 1843, Commissioner Henry L. Ellsworth of the United States Patent Office concluded a report to Congress with the observation that 'The advancement of the [mechanical] arts, from year to year, taxes our credulity and seems to presage the arrival of that period when human improvement must end'.[18]

The Great Exhibition of 1851 in London was more a celebration of achievement than a visionary pointer to progress. However, by the time of the Universal Exhibition in Paris in 1867, a change of tone can be detected in a 'Paris Guide' of that year writing of 'the opening of a new era':

> World exhibitions are a part of that vast economic progress which includes railways, the electric telegraph, steam navigation, the piercing of isthmuses and all those great public works, all the discoveries of science, and which will bring an increase in moral welfare, that is, more freedom, as well as an increase in material welfare, that is, more affluence, to the benefit of the majority.[19]

In general, then, the period from about 1850 to 1870 was one of transition, including a quest for synthesis. No less a figure than the patron of the Great Exhibition of 1851, Prince Albert, observed in 1850: 'Nobody, who has paid any attention to the particular features of our present era, will doubt for a moment that we are living at a period of the most wonderful transition, which tends to the accomplishment of that great end to which, indeed, all history points – the realization of the unity of mankind.'[20] Seeking synthesis through a combination of sound, poetry and gesture, Richard Wagner sought to evoke the German national spirit by means of a quartet of operas devoted to the Nordic myth of *The Ring*. In science, one very important date was 1859, the year of the publication of *The Origin of Species*. Building on his own researches and making use of the research of others, on a wide range of subjects from the study of fossils and micro-organisms (especially by Louis Pasteur and Joseph Lister) to economics and sociology, Charles Darwin put forward the argument that all living species had evolved through adapting themselves to their environment: the struggle for survival had led to natural selection, some species adapting successfully, others failing. Darwin's bold propositions came at a time of great confidence in science, but also helped to undermine that confidence. By the time of the publication of his *The Descent of Man* in 1871, Church leaders and others were putting forward passionate objections. To collect fossils and make suggestions about their history was one thing; to assert that human beings themselves were part of a vast process involving all life forms was another.

Influenced by scientific discovery and technical change in general, and by the development of photography in particular, some artists joined in a movement away from Romanticism, caught by the Frenchman Gustave Courbet setting out his stall in the open air at the time of the Paris Exhibition of 1855 under the sign 'Realism'. Courbet was also taken by socialist ideas, arguing that 'one must give art a popular content'.[21]

TO FUTURISM, 1871–1914

Just as Romanticism was promoted by the French Revolution and Napoleon, so another major phase in the development of European culture was probably influenced by the completion of the process of Italian and German unification. Certainly, science in a united German Empire was to play a bigger role than it did in the states that constituted it. Possibly, it was more than coincidence that in 1871, the year of the final formation of that empire, the physicist James Clerk Maxwell noted the widely held opinion that the only occupation left to scientists would be to carry on current measurements already in progress to a further place of decimals. But he went on to argue that this was a pessimistic view in the face of the 'unsearchable riches of creation' and the 'untried fertility of ... fresh minds'.[22]

Of course, both quantification and classification remained central to science, but fresh, fertile minds could perform wonders with them. Under such a heading could be placed the arrangement of the elements in order of atomic numbers in the Periodic Table completed by the Russian chemist Dmitrii Mendeleev in 1871. However, Clerk Maxwell's own electromagnetic theory of light put forward before his death in 1879 led on to the measurement of the velocity of electromagnetic waves by the German Heinrich Hertz by 1886 and the discovery of X-rays in the associated area of radioactivity by another German, Wilhelm Röntgen, in 1895. In 1896, the Frenchman Antoine Becquerel demonstrated that uranium produced a similar sort of ray. In 1898, another Frenchman, Pierre Curie, and his Polish wife, Marie, isolated radium. (The individual contributions of Clerk Maxwell and the others were all recognised in the naming of units of measurement after them.) The relationship between matter and energy was being revealed, with awesome – if still to be perceived – implications for the future of warfare as well as more peaceful pursuits such as radio, telecommunications and radiotherapy.

Generally speaking, the turn of the century marked great scientific progress, with physics remaining at the forefront. Two successors to Clerk Maxwell at Cambridge made great contributions to a revolutionary theory of the structure of the atom. Building on the contributions of German physicists, J. J. Thomson discovered what he called 'corpuscles' but have since become known as electrons. Ernest Rutherford suggested that electrons revolved around the nucleus of the atom like planets round the sun. At the turn of the century, too, the German Max Planck put forward the theory that the energy of radiation consists of 'quanta' depending on the frequency of oscillation of the electrons. In 1905, a patent office clerk in Bern, Switzerland, Albert Einstein, began to put forward his astounding theory of relativity, mathematics joining physics in revealing the secrets not only of the structure of the atom but of space–time. Newton's mechanical view of the atom and of the universe was radically revised.

A significant development in chemistry was the emergence of biochemistry. In 1897, for example, the German Eduard Buchner discovered that sugar could ferment even though the accompanying crushed yeast contained no living cells. This led to the realisation not only that a dead chemical substance – the enzyme (meaning 'in yeast') – caused fermentation but that similar substances brought about most other chemical reactions taking place in living matter. As a by-product of the work on dyestuffs in German industrial laboratories, chemical pharmacology began to provide remedies for such ailments as syphilis and sleeping sickness. Another offshoot of the dyestuffs industry was the explosive trinitrotoluene (TNT), which meant termination for all the ills of those in the vicinity of its detonation, and was often harmful to the health of those engaged in its manufacture. In biology, the Moravian Abbé Gregor Mendel had explored the processes of heredity through crossing various kinds of peas as long ago as the 1860s. However, his contribution was not fully appreciated until further contributions on heredity from the German August Weismann and others towards the end of the nineteenth century.

No less than science, 'eternal art' was also culture-bound. That is not to say that either is confined within national frontiers. For example, as we have just seen, work carried out on synthetic dyestuffs in German industrial laboratories could aid science in other countries. Impressionism may have begun with an exhibition in Paris in 1874 devoted to the work of Claude Monet, attempting to catch the play of light on water, but it was soon reflected elsewhere. Art would never be quite the same, either in France or throughout Europe and across the Atlantic. Neo-Impressionism and Post-Impressionism followed, with a French accent, even more explicit in the *fin-de-siècle*, *art nouveau* and the *avant-garde* of the turn of the century. However, Cubism is most closely associated with the Spaniard Pablo Picasso. Expressionism, anticipated by the Dutchman Vincent van Gogh and the Norwegian Edvard Munch, found homes for itself in two German cities, Dresden and Munich. And Futurism, calling for an art that would do away with the past and create a new dynamism that would capture the beauty of speed, energy and the machine, originated in Italy and made a great impact in Russia. Although its ambition was far greater than its achievement, Futurism also provided a telling contrast with Romanticism, which was comparatively static and even backward-looking. Of course, there were new aspects to early twentieth-century art: for example, greater receptivity to the work of other continents, in particular Africa. Nevertheless, a clear line of development could be traced from Turner's treatment of a train in *Rain, Steam and Speed* to Marinetti's attempt to capture the movement of an automobile.

Similarly in music, there is a clear progression from Beethoven through Wagner to the late Romantic Gustav Mahler. Even more than art, nineteenth-century music reflects the spirit of nationalism, even though its 'language' is international. For example, Peter Tchaikovsky called Mikhail Glinka's *Kamarinskaia* the acorn from which the oak of Russian music grew. In Czech Bohemia, Antonin Dvořák and Bedřich Smetana were among those to tap another source of Slavonic melody and rhythm. Italy was distinguished by the operas of Giuseppe Verdi and Giacomo Puccini, while Claude Debussy and Maurice Ravel provided echoes of French Impressionism; virtually every European country produced its distinctive school before the nineteenth century was over. Some of the music sounded rather strange to foreign ears, for example the works of the Hungarians Béla Bartók and Zoltán Kodály. In the early twentieth century, however, those whose knowledge of the subject went no further than 'doh' to 'doh' in the tonic sol-fa were taken further aback by the arrival of the twelve-tone scale and even atonal music. The Austrians Arnold Schönberg and Alban Berg were leading protagonists, but the new music was too abstract to have an easily identifiable home.

To take the novel as our major example of literary activity, this certainly has a specific location conditioned by language as well as history. Following Sir Walter Scott and other models, virtually every European country produced before 1914 writers not only telling great stories from the national past but also depicting more recent developments in society. We must avoid a long list, and thus can only give a few examples. In England, Charles Dickens depicted life in London in *Oliver Twist*, while Mary Ann Evans, writing as George Eliot, explored the social boundaries between a provincial town and its rural hinterland as well as between the classes and the sexes in the aptly entitled *Middlemarch*. In Germany, Theodore Fontane approached Berlin and Brandenburg in a comparable manner in *Effie Brest* and Thomas Mann anatomised a prosperous Lübeck family in *Buddenbrooks*. A French line could be traced from Gustave Flaubert's *Madame Bovary* to Émile Zola's *Germinal*, a Russian from Lev Tolstoy's *Voina i mir* (*War and Peace*) to Fedor Dostoevsky's *Prestuplenie i nakazanie* (*Crime and Punishment*). Henryk Sienkiewicz produced an epic trilogy on Poland's turbulent seventeenth-century history, while Bolesław Prus anatomised tensions between Polish and German peasants in *Placówka* (*The Outpost*). Many more tales could be unfolded from Portugal to Romania, from Italy to Sweden.

HISTORY AND CULTURE

Accurate mirrors of society before 1914 were provided by novelists depicting life in the encroaching city; composers catching the music of disappearing rural society; painters inspired by the industrial revolution or apprehensive of its implications; and so on. Moreover, there was enough in common and interaction between the various national cultures for contemporaries to talk of a distinctively European culture, even of a Western culture combining European with American. However, the First World War and the Russian Revolution led to the lasting disruption of European culture and the ultimate ascendancy of American.

What about those whose professional concern was to note such developments? At the beginning of the twentieth century, historians were not only continuing to amass vast collections of data, they were also attempting to analyse and synthesise them in grand collective works. The Germans and the French were first in the field, but the British did not lag far behind. *The Cambridge Modern History*, whose first volume was published in 1902, was arranged according to the plan of the late Lord Acton so that 'the history of each people should be taken up at that point at which it was drawn into the main stream of human progress, as represented by the European nations'. Therefore, Russia did not make its entrance until volume V, entitled 'The Age of Louis XIV', where the conclusion to a chapter on its history from 1462 to 1682 included the observation that during the seventeenth century, 'access to Western ideas was within the reach of the Russians, and this explains the fact that a Peter the Great could arise'. The next chapter was devoted to 'Peter the Great and his Pupils'. For the United States, entrance into the mainstream was said to have taken place in the latter half of the eighteenth century, although it was only more recently that 'its people have definitely, because inevitably, taken their place among the Great Powers of the world'. Therefore, the whole of volume VII was devoted to the USA. Volume XII, entitled 'The Latest

Age' and coming out in 1910, brought in Asia and Latin America to a much greater extent than hitherto, largely no doubt because, as the first sentence of its first chapter put it, 'In this period the History of Europe becomes in a sense the History of the world'. Later chapters demonstrated a new breadth not only in geographical coverage but also in thematic approach: the modern law of nations and the prevention of war, social movements, the scientific age, and the growth of historical science.[23]

Similarly, the eleventh edition of the *Encyclopaedia Britannica* declared that it was 'dominated throughout by the historical point of view': that is, it attempted to consider a whole range of subjects 'in continual evolution ... so that the salient facts up to the autumn of the year 1910 might be included throughout, not merely as isolated events, but as part of a consistent whole, conceived in the spirit of the historian'. Statistics were used, and comparisons were made in the same spirit, while it was considered 'no less essential that the spirit of science should move over the construction of the work as a whole'. In order to achieve objectivity, contributors of all shades of opinion and of several different nationalities had co-operated, especially on controversial questions, and while individual judgements as to their relative claims might naturally vary, 'The general estimates which prevail among the countries which represent Western civilization are, however, in practical agreement on this point, and this consensus is the only ultimate criterion'.

Historical-scientific consensus was thus confidently asserted, and those thinkers who had already challenged such an approach made little or no appearance in the eleventh edition's 28 volumes. There was one column on Nietzsche, whose free-thinking atheism led him to preach proudly a new 'master' morality and to incite the 'over-man' (superman) to trample the great herd of lesser beings. But there was no entry in the eleventh edition on either Einstein or Freud, who had already published some of their important findings, nor on relativity or psychoanalysis. Also unlisted were Benedetto Croce, whose anti-scientific views of history had already been clearly expressed, and Max Weber, the father of modern sociology, whose subject was presented as progressing through 'English utilitarianism ..., as influenced by the English theory of the rights of the individual on the one hand', and 'Marxian Socialism as influenced by the Latin conception of the omnipotence of the State on the other'. Marx himself was given four pages of exposition and analysis, while the major revisionist Edouard Bernstein, who argued for the possibility of an evolutionary rather than a revolutionary road to socialism, went unmentioned.

This neglect of important continental thinkers could be attributed partly to the circumstance that, although there were at least some continental contributors to the *Encyclopaedia Britannica*, its primary focus, like the majority of the contributors, was British–American. However, the neglect could also result from the sheer impossibility of assimilating all the features of a rapidly changing world. Could the encyclopaedia aiming at comprehensive coverage have passed its peak even before the onset of the First World War? In other languages, too, the heyday of the encyclopaedia was before 1914, for example the *Grand Dictionnaire Universel* edited in Paris by Larousse and the *Conversations-Lexikon* produced in Leipzig by Brockhaus, which led in collaboration with Efron to the production of the Russian *Entsiklopedicheskii Slovar* in St Petersburg. By the outbreak of the First World War, there were comparable publications in Spanish and Italian, Danish and Swedish, Polish and Czech, Hungarian and Romanian.

Throughout our discussion of culture, the emphasis has been on the high rather than the low. That is to say, we have neglected popular culture, whose more traditional aspects were under threat towards the end of the nineteenth century. Even before 1870, France and Prussia were well on their way to constructing a system of modern education; by 1914, virtually every European state had made arrangements for compulsory primary schooling. This remarkable spread of modern enlightenment did not take place without a struggle, not only against the dark forces opposed to mass education of any kind but also between Church and state, throughout continental Europe and even in Great Britain. This does not mean that Churches always refused to move with the times: Pope Leo XIII, for example, made a spirited attempt to come to terms not only with the idea of popular education but also with socialism in such encyclicals as *Rerum novarum* (*Of New Matters*) in 1891.

One important consequence of the spread of literacy was the rise of the popular newspaper, with the Parisian *Le Petit Journal* reaching a circulation of 1 million by 1890. In 1898, the historian Gabriel Monod lamented that the French press was now 'little more than an agent of moral disintegration, a fomenter of hatred and of future civil wars'. The London *Daily Mail* sold a million copies during the Boer War. The economist J. A. Hobson was moved to publish *The Psychology of Jingoism* in 1901, finding the 'chief engine' of the phenomenon in 'a biased, enslaved, and poisoned press'. In 1900, with the Boxer Rebellion in China in mind, the historian G. M. Trevelyan considered that the 'yellow peril' was less a threat to European civilisation than the 'white peril' consisting of 'the uniform modern man ... creature of the great cities' moulded by 'the uprooting of taste and reason by the printing press'. At the end of the First World War, the philosopher Bertrand Russell considered that the press encouraging racism and nationalism had been one of its causes.[24] In all these comments, there is an element of 'not in front of the servants', that is to say, certain subjects should be considered by the *Times*-reading educated elite exclusively.

THE SECOND INDUSTRIAL REVOLUTION AND ITS CONSEQUENCES

We must not exaggerate the extent of the changes achieved by human beings soon after 1900. The eleventh edition of the *Encyclopaedia Britannica* (published in 1910–11) spoke somewhat tentatively of the aeroplane as creating widespread interest 'both as a matter of sport and also as indicating a new departure in the possibilities of machines of war'. This was a few years after the Wright brothers had flown their motor-driven aircraft for nearly a minute in 1903 and just after Wilbur Wright had flown about 55 miles at approximately 37 miles per hour in 1908 and the Frenchman Louis Blériot had flown the Channel from Calais to Dover in a little over half an hour in 1909. Even the landbound motor vehicle still had some way to go before its presence in Europe ceased to be a rarity, although total British registrations including motor-cycles and motor-cars showed an increase deemed remarkable from 1905 – just under 75,000 – through 1908 – something over 150,000 – to 1909 – more than 180,000. Increasing familiarity with such vehicles meant that the Red Flag Act (restricting their speed in towns to 2 miles per hour and only then if accompanied by warning flags) had already become an object of ridicule since its repeal in 1896. But traffic accidents were also now common, an early fatality in Paris being Pierre Curie, the French scientist. France was at first the centre of the motor-car industry in Europe, but from 1906 the world leader was the USA, which produced nearly 115,000 cars in 1909 as opposed to France's tally of just over 45,000. As far as public transport was concerned, most cities in Europe possessed tramways, to an ever increasing extent electrified, to supplement the longer distance railways, but for the most part they were confined to the major thoroughfares, beyond which horse-drawn transport was still the norm.

Developments in travel had been remarkable enough, but there had been considerable progress in other forms of communication, too: for example, 'of electricity', as the *Aberdeen Journal* had put it, 'with all its wires and cables'. Telegraphy had first been used as an accompaniment to the railway from about 1840, but with the laying of the Atlantic cable from 1865 and of the Pacific cable from 1901 the whole world was encompassed, with many overland lines as well, while Marconi began transatlantic wireless telegraphy in 1902. Meanwhile, the telephone developed in the 1870s by the Americans Bell and Edison was being used mostly in the United States, followed by Germany, Britain, France and Switzerland. According to the American Baedeker in 1904, there were 3000 million telephone messages in the USA, 725 million in the British Isles and 766 million in Germany. While there was as yet no public broadcasting by wireless or radio, home entertainment of the traditional kind was being supplemented by the phonograph with its cylinders and the gramophone with its discs, while the cinematograph was entering the world of public entertainment, first as a music-hall turn, then in its own right. Soon, the 'movies' or the 'flicks' would be offering a considerable challenge to 'live' theatre, just as the still photograph had already made enough appearances in the family album to supplement and even replace the painted portrait.

While it is important to observe what Europeans did with their leisure hours at the beginning of the twentieth century, it is even more necessary to note what they did at work. For towards the end of the nineteenth century, there occurred the second industrial or scientific revolution, with the age of coal and iron giving way to that of steel and electricity, of oil and chemicals. New materials and methods increased the pace of development of the factory and the city, especially in combination with the ever-expanding railways and allied means of transport and communication. The mass market was born.

Now that the Great Depression of 1873–96 was at last over, price rises from 1896 to 1914 in both agricultural and industrial products encouraged the growth of credit and investment to supply it. New technologies demanded vast amounts of capital as well as large-scale organisation – hence the formation of joint-stock corporations often forming national and international cartels and trusts and using their strength to direct government policies on tariffs and trade unions, even on foreign and colonial policy. Hence, too, a 'managerial revolution' involving educated 'white-collar workers' to organise and plan the activities of skilled and unskilled 'blue-collar workers'.

All these changes made a considerable social impact, although it varied from one part of the continent to the other. To take Europe as a whole at the turn of the century, the largest class was still the peasantry, and the agrarian way of life was the most common. And although it was by now the smallest class, the landed aristocracy retained much of its influence not only in the provinces but also at the centre. The relationship of lord to peasant continued to hold a high degree of significance for the nature of the completion of the process of modernisation in any given state: when it broke down before a new basis of stability could be built up, there ensued the danger of social dislocation of an extreme kind.

This would become an even greater likelihood if accompanied by disturbances in the cities, which also varied greatly in nature. London already had a population of over 2 million by 1850, and by mid-century, 28 towns each with more than 50,000 inhabitants contained between them approximately one-fifth of the total population of Britain. By about this time, agriculture ceased to be the major occupation of the British people. Much of the north and north-west of the continent soon reached the same point, but in parts of eastern, south-eastern and south-western Europe, such a changeover did not occur until well into the twentieth century. Just as the relationship between lord and peasant was of central importance in most rural areas of Europe, so the relationship between the bourgeoisie and the proletariat was dominant in the towns. Again, the rate at which these two classes grew and the manner in which they managed to establish some kind of equilibrium between them, however temporary, was of key significance in the maintenance of urban stability.

Some factory workers were recent immigrants from the countryside, some were following the footsteps of their parents and grandparents. Equally, the bourgeoisie contained some families established in the class for several, even many, generations, and others whose wealth was only recently acquired. Experience and attitudes could vary enormously within the wide frameworks of the class that owned property and the class that owned none. It was not difficult to discern the wide gap between the two in all European cities, not easy to appreciate all the gradations within each of them depending on variations of race, language and religion. For a full understanding, documents have to be supplemented by recollection, by oral history.[25]

Women, especially from the upper and middle classes, often remained at home, supervising the activities of their domestic servants whose drudgery was as yet little relieved by the advent of labour-saving devices such as the vacuum cleaner, washing and sewing machines. But many working-class women were employed for as many hours as their menfolk in the textile and other industries.

DIPLOMATIC COUNTDOWN

In 1914, a distinguished professor of history at Aberdeen University wrote a short pamphlet explaining the origins and significance of the war that had broken out early in August of that year. In *Germany and Her Neighbours, 1871–1914*, Charles Sanford Terry wrote: 'The governing fact in the life of Europe for the past half-century is the emergence of a unified mid-Continental State with an exterior policy of its own and the material power to enforce it.' He went on to assert that: 'The characteristic note of Imperial Germany has been consistent and blatant assertiveness. It is founded, in the main, upon an unblushing inventory of German virtues, a complacent appraising of German *Kultur*, and a humourless conviction of moral and mental superiority.' Even in 1870, at the time of the outbreak of the war with France, the historian Treitschke had insisted that Germany was fighting a holy war for the liberation of the world. After that conflict had been brought to an end and the German Empire created, 'Treitschke's chauvinistic exposition of German destiny was inspiring University common-rooms and class-rooms with the conviction that Germany is predestined by an appreciative Providence to *Weltreich* at other nations' expense'. What Treitschke had taught about *Weltreich*, or world empire, to a generation of students was now in 1914 the creed of all Germans. In 1911, General Bernhardi had declared that there were only two alternatives for Germany, the attainment of that world power or decline, and now the Germans had launched an aggressive war on that supposition. Professor Terry concluded:

> Not less for Germany than for her neighbours it is essential to exorcise the new spirit in her by a round drubbing – the only form of discipline her perverted character can appreciate. Looking out on the situation to-day we can say confidently that the discipline has begun.

Professor Terry's views would have met with wide acceptance among the British people and their allies in 1914. If, however, they had known what it would cost for the discipline to be completed, they might have paused to consider whether or not allowances and adjustments for Germany's imperial ambitions should have been made in the years preceding 1914. For the realisation soon began to dawn that not only Germany was suffering grievous losses as a result of the war, so were all of the other powers involved in it. At least one of them, tsarist Russia, was to experience a profound revolution, and the others were to undergo much social and political dislocation.

Such international stability as there had ever been had centred on the elusive and flexible concepts of the 'concert of Europe' and the 'balance of power', which had been restored to real enough existence in the years following 1815 after the disturbances of the years of the French Revolution and Napoleon. But then the equilibrium was upset by the rise of Prussia, which in 1866 with surprising rapidity defeated its rival for central European domination, the Austrian Empire. The response to defeat in Vienna was to share power with Budapest: in other words, the Dual Monarchy of Austria and Hungary was created. While this distribution of power and responsibility certainly made for a greater measure of efficiency, it also aroused in the other nationalities of the empire, especially the Czechs and other Slavs, a resentment and a growing ambition for their own participation in government. As the

Ottoman Empire grew weaker, the Dual Monarchy's interest in developing its influence there could not be realised without making its own internal problems more serious. For the Balkans were largely populated by yet more restless Slavs, while the antagonism was aroused of the government of the mightiest Slav people of them all, the Russians.

Meanwhile, the crowning in 1871 after the defeat of France of the German emperor William I at Versailles was another, even clearer pointer towards conflict. And so, with echoes of the Holy Alliance of crowned heads in 1815, some of their successors spoke up for further maintenance of the fraternal monarchical ideal in the Three Emperors' League of Germany, Austria and Russia in 1873. But the other two emperors were soon alarmed that the third of them might top the league, for in 1877 Alexander II of Russia took advantage of revolts within the Ottoman Empire to go to the relief of his little brother Slavs by carrying war to Turkey. The Treaty of San Stefano which brought the war to an end early in 1878 appeared to be making Russia, the Slav big brother, more powerful than ever, especially with regard to the protectorate that it exercised over Bulgaria. Austria was especially alarmed by a threat building up near its very frontiers, while, among the other nations of Europe, Britain showed especial concern at the possibility of Russia establishing itself as a major force on the Mediterranean at a time when it was already making alarming progress in central Asia towards India. So Bismarck took upon himself the role of honest broker at the Berlin Conference held later in the year 1878, and it was agreed that Russian influence would be diminished in the Balkans while Austrian influence increased there. Britain was enabled to keep a watch on the eastern Mediterranean and routes to Asia by occupying Cyprus.

Since the honest broker was obliged to keep a watch not only on the Rhine but also on the Vistula, to look in both directions from the German Empire, he stood to gain a considerable percentage of any benefits gained from the Treaty of Berlin. To insure himself against further difficulties, he took the special relationship that he was developing with Austria–Hungary to the point of a Treaty of Alliance in October 1879. The two high contracting parties solemnly promised mutual defence against Russia, which had threatened war, according to Bismarck in an explanatory conversation with the French ambassador to Berlin. Moreover, Bismarck claimed, the Dual Alliance was necessary to protect Austria–Hungary both for its own sake and for that of what was left of the balance of power. Then in 1882 a Triple Alliance, adding to the Dual Alliance rather than replacing it, was agreed with Italy, which was concerned about French involvement in Tunisia. This new agreement protected the southern flank of the German and Austro-Hungarian empires, but could possibly increase the suspicion of France and drive it towards some accommodation with Russia. Fearful of such an eventuality, Bismarck continued to try to breathe new life into the Three Emperors' League, but further clashes over Bulgaria in the mid-1880s made such artificial respiration extremely difficult. Therefore in 1887 he resorted to another approach, a Reinsurance Treaty with Russia, promising support if Austria–Hungary should attack in return for a guarantee in case of a French attack on Germany. Technically, this did not infringe the Dual Alliance, which was also defensive, but Austria–Hungary was pleased in 1887 to receive some additional promises of support in the Mediterranean, from which it agreed with Britain and Italy to exclude Russia.

Having charted such a complicated course for Germany, the pilot was dropped in 1890. To Bismarck's further disappointment, the eventuality that he had worked so hard to avoid, the coming together of the great powers on both flanks, soon ensued in the shape of the Franco-Russian Alliance of 1894. Again, this was an ostensibly defensive agreement, although there was a secret military convention added to it. Moreover, Russia sought French assistance not only in case of war but also in her drive towards modernisation, and negotiated a large loan for this second purpose. Ten years later, the diplomatic approach to the First World War took a further step forwards as France reached agreement with Britain in the Entente Cordiale of 1904. This particular passage was by no means as smooth as its bare announcement might suggest. Indeed, the old imperial rivals had been arguing over their respective rights in the wider world with an intensity increased by their awareness of the problems developing in Europe. In 1898 they had nearly come to blows when their spheres of influence clashed at Fashoda on the Upper Nile in the Sudan. However, that crisis had blown over, and the Anglo-French Entente of 1904 settled some other outstanding disputes as well as agreeing to assign Egypt to the British sphere and Morocco to the French. In 1907, an understanding was reached between Britain and Russia defining spheres of influence in Persia and relative interests in Afghanistan and Tibet. The Dual Entente became the Triple Entente, and Britain followed France in the extension of loans to its new partner. The pound sterling now followed the franc down the drain of tsarist modernisation, as the Russian side of the triangular relationship of the Triple Entente in the wake of the Revolution of 1905 showed itself to be far less than the equal of either the French or the British sides.

The diplomatic geometrical arrangement of the major powers was complete, and the proof of an appalling theorem was growing closer. Talk of 'spheres of influence' could do little to extend the European balance, itself fragile enough, to the outside world. Already in 1905 there had been not only abortive revolution in Russia but also the first Moroccan crisis, when Germany looked for a place in the North African sun already reserved by agreement with Britain for France. In 1908–9, trouble that had never really gone away made itself all too apparent again in the Balkans. Then in 1911 there was another Moroccan crisis, as the German government attempted gunboat diplomacy to make its influence felt in the small port of Agadir. In October 1912, Bulgaria, Serbia, Montenegro and Greece attacked Turkey, and enjoyed rapid success. But the victors fought among themselves in 1913, Bulgaria making war on Serbia and Greece, which it suspected of plans to divide Macedonia among themselves. Romania and Turkey joined in to make certain the defeat of Bulgaria. Consequently the Treaty of Bucharest of 1913 duly divided most of Macedonia between Serbia and Greece, and compelled Bulgaria to give the southern Dobrudja to Romania. Montenegro increased in size, as did Serbia and Greece, while Bulgaria and Turkey were left reduced in size but swollen in anger. With Russia and Austria–Hungary at each other's throats as they took opposite views on the solution of the Balkan crisis, the warning bell for combat was sounded by the assassination of the heir to the Austrian and Hungarian thrones on 28 June 1914.

The Archduke Francis Ferdinand was shot by a fervent Serbian nationalist. On 5 July, the Emperor William II of Germany had an audience with the Austrian ambassador to Berlin, urging the adoption of a strong line towards the small Balkan state of Serbia, and promising firm support should Russia go to the aid of its Slav brother. From 20 to 23 July, the French President Poincaré paid a visit to St Petersburg, assuring the Russian government that he would maintain his obligations to them. On 23 July, the Austro-Hungarian authorities sent a humiliating ultimatum to Serbia, which could not fully accept it, and therefore on 28 July Austria declared war on Serbia. On 31 July, Russia began full mobilisation after Nicholas II's advisers convinced him that his own preference for partial mobilisation could not be realised. Austria–Hungary also now began general mobilisation, and France and Germany followed suit on 1 August. Ultimata to Russia and France having been rejected, Germany declared war on Russia on 1 August and on France on 3 August. Meanwhile Italy declared that there was no case yet for abandoning neutrality, and Britain was hoping to remain aloof also. But German rejection of a British ultimatum concerning Belgian neutrality was rejected, and Britain declared war on Germany on 4 August. The delayed Austro-Hungarian declaration of war on Russia came on 6 August; Britain and France declared war on Austria–Hungary on 10 August. The First World War had begun.[26]

THE GREAT POWERS

Arguably, it was not a world war from the beginning, although the European empires stretching around the globe were involved from almost the very start. True, Japan came in on the Allied side almost immediately, but perhaps it was not until the later American entry in 1917 that the conflict took on its full significance. (The entry of Italy and other smaller European powers made less of an impact.) Certainly, before it was over, the Great War, as many called it, fully deserved the label of world war. Moreover, the first such conflict led to the second. Therefore, in examining its origins we must bear its ultimate nature and its sequel in mind. And so, having looked at the diplomatic count-down, we will now turn to consider the wider interests of the major belligerents and the manner in which they came to be deeply involved in the international crisis that led to the arrival of large-scale hostilities.

We begin with the non-European states, Japan and the USA, both of which helped to bring about the final catastrophe by acts of omission as well as commission. In 1894, Japan took a major step towards its emergence as a great power in war against China. In 1902, it made a significant alliance with Britain that was to last until 1921. In 1904–5, it confirmed its status as a great power in war with Russia. Indeed, the unexpectedly easy Japanese victory was of truly global significance, producing hope among the colonised peoples of Asia, concern on the part of the American and European governments and agony for the defeated tsarist regime in Russia. Having infiltrated and then annexed Korea in the aftermath of the 1904–5 war, Japan took advantage of the European preoccupations of her imperial rivals a decade onwards in the First World War to strengthen her interests on the Asiatic mainland at the expense of Germany and even more of China. Japan's former enemy Russia moved towards further accommodation, sharing railway concessions in Manchuria, for example, while her current ally Britain was more than a little alarmed. Meanwhile, the USA under President Woodrow Wilson did what it could to maintain its Chinese policy of the 'Open Door' – equal access for all interested parties. However, in 1914 Wilson was most interested in keeping the door closed on the major American sphere of influence, Latin America, and was especially concerned with Mexico, where there was the threat of revolution.

As the world's leading industrial power, the USA might have brought more influence to bear over the Atlantic. But reluctance to become involved in European squabbles, a line of policy indicated by Washington's Farewell Message and the Monroe Doctrine, was too powerful a national sentiment for easy adaptation. As for Japan, its interest in the West from its vantage point of the Rising Sun was not yet to any significant degree direct. However, its indirect influence on the outbreak of the war was considerable, since after the humiliation of its war with Japan, Russia was no longer in a position to follow the advice of the German Kaiser and to carry the white man's burden in Asia. Having burned his fingers there, the Russian bear returned to his more traditional honeypot in Europe. Meanwhile in the Balkans, as we have seen, Austria–Hungary, which had nowhere else to look now that it had lost its major holdings in Italy, was obliged to make its last stand even irrespective of the promptings of Germany.

In the last resort, the responsibility for the outbreak of the war must be shared among its major European participants, Britain, France and Germany: the most serious decisions were taken in London, Paris and Berlin rather than in St Petersburg, Vienna or Rome. The problem with Britain was that it was by no means certain even at this late stage that the affairs of Europe were as important as those of the British Empire, on which the sun would never set even if the continental lights were going out. Top priority was the maintenance of British imperial pre-eminence, as was indicated in the speeches of the foreign secretary, Sir Edward Grey, and also in a *Memorandum on the Present State of British Relations with France and Germany* produced at the beginning of 1907 by a Foreign Office official, Eyre Crowe. Regarding the foreign policy of Britain's chief rival for mastery of the seas and apparent leader in the struggle for control of Europe, Crowe wrote:

> Either Germany is definitely aiming at a general political hegemony and maritime ascendancy, threatening the independence of her neighbours and ultimately the existence of England; Or Germany, free from any such clear-cut ambition, and thinking for the present merely of using her legitimate position and influence as one of the leading Powers in the council of nations, is seeking to promote her foreign commerce, spread the benefits of German culture, extend the scope of her national energies, and create fresh German Interests all over the world wherever and whenever a peaceful opportunity offers, leaving it to an uncertain future to decide whether the occurrence of great changes in the world may not some day assign to Germany a larger share of direct political action over regions not now a part of her dominions, without that violation of the established rights of other countries which would be involved in any such action under existing political conditions.[27]

With a German mother and a German wife, Eyre Crowe almost certainly had a deeper understanding of the German problem than most of his colleagues. Yet even he did not understand that the hypothetical and delayed nature of the concessions that he was prepared to allow Germany would have been far too little to satisfy that expanding empire's aspirations. Germany was not prepared to wait for 'an uncertain future' for the growth of its dominions, especially since the world had already been carved up among the imperial powers to such an extent that there was no room for further growth without violation of somebody's right of prior occupation.

While Britain was determined to remain number one in the wider world, France had no desire forever to yield the primacy of place on the continent of Europe which she had lost in the Franco-Prussian War of 1870–1. However, by 1914 the memory of past humiliation was fading, and the nationalistic urge for revenge was supported by a minority of voters in the spring when legislative elections gave a majority to peace-loving radicals and socialists. The outstanding leader Jean Jaurès had put his position clearly in a speech in Berlin in 1905:

> Let nobody mistake what we are saying. We socialists are not afraid of war. If it breaks out, we shall be able to face events, and do our best to make them serve the cause of the independence of nations, the liberty of peoples, the liberation of the workers. ... Now, in peace, the growth of democracy and socialism is assured. Out of a European war, revolution may spring, and the ruling classes will do well to keep this in mind; but there may also come a long period of counter-revolutionary crises, wild reaction, exasperated nationalism, stifling dictatorships, monstrous militarism – a long chain of reactionary violence, base hatreds, reprisals, enslavements. For our part, we do not want to engage in such a monstrous game of chance.[28]

Nevertheless, as war fever spread in the summer of 1914, Jaurès was finding it difficult to keep the contagion away from his supporters when he was assassinated by a fanatical nationalist on 31 July. At that time, President Poincaré was on his way back from an official visit to St Petersburg, where he had learned of widespread social unrest and given the Russian government reassurances of French support, to such an extent indeed that some analysts at the time and others since have attributed to him a major share of responsibility for the outbreak of the war. Certainly, Poincaré was determined that if France was to be involved in another conflict with Germany, Russia would have to join in so that pressure on the French front could be relieved. Whether or not he can be blamed for provoking the Russian government into full mobilisation is a different and difficult question.

It is of course yet another question whether or not the Russian mobilisation was the crucial milestone on the road to war. Is it not rather the case, as has been argued in recent years along the same lines as Professor Terry's pamphlet of 1914, albeit in more moderate language, that the formation of the German Empire in 1871 upset the European equilibrium and that the successors of Bismarck, far from trying to right it, asserted their desire for predominance in an even more aggressive manner? The voices of scholars like Treitschke and generals such as Bernhardi were certainly accompanied by those of businessmen and politicians all demanding for Germany a greater measure of influence in the affairs of Europe than rival powers would be prepared to accept. Moreover, the build-up of the navy from the end of the nineteenth century onwards had been a clear indication that German ambitions went beyond the continent and aimed at not only catching up rivals in the race for empire but also overtaking them. At sea, the chief rival was Britain, on land Russia, and when, much to Germany's surprise, the whale and the bear managed to accommodate their differences from 1907 onwards, the feeling grew among members of the government that Germany would have to strike first before the strength of its rivals became overwhelming. The bear's rearmament programme gave Chancellor Bethmann-Hollweg a particular fear of Russia: 'It grows and grows and hangs over us ever more heavily like a nightmare', he declared in the year that the war broke out.[29]

Still in 1914, but in September after hostilities had begun, Bethmann-Hollweg sketched out the shape of Europe as it would be reformed after the expected German victory. A central European economic association would be created, incorporating its neighbours, some of whom would also lose pieces of their territory to their conqueror. Although the appetite of the other belligerents grew as the war stretched on, none of them was quite as ambitious as Germany at the war's commencement. Here too, then, is evidence of Germany's expansionist ambition, which must certainly be given heavy weighting in any distribution of responsibility for the outbreak of the catastrophe. However, more fundamental still is the mutual lack of understanding of what full-scale conflict among fully industrialised states would entail. Moreover, even before the war had started, by no means every German was always confident of the final outcome, the Kaiser himself expressing doubts in a minute of 28 July 1914:

My function is at an end. Wantonness and weakness are to engulf the world in the most terrible of wars, the ultimate aim of which is the ruin of Germany. For now I can no longer doubt that England, France, and Russia have conspired to fight together for our annihilation ... and so the notorious encirclement of Germany is at last an accomplished fact ... England stands derisive, brilliantly successful in her long-meditated, purely anti-German policy – a superb achievement, stirring to admiration even him whom it will utterly destroy. The dead Edward is stronger than the living I.[30]

The living Francis Joseph of Austria and Nicholas of Russia were certainly weaker than Wilhelm of Germany, and no crowned or even uncrowned head of state could be completely confident of his position on the eve of war. From one end of Europe to the other, there were pockets of unrest in town and country alike, partly caused perhaps by the preoccupation of governments with the international crisis but partly also the result of the process of modernisation. Leaving the dead Edward aside, we could argue that his successor, George, was in a stronger position than most because that process was nearest to completion in Britain, although even there 1914 brought strikes of formidable proportions. In Russia, there was a widespread sense of living 'on a volcano' early in 1914, but historians are divided about the likelihood of revolution without war.[31]

At the outset of hostilities, however, social stability returned: there were great demonstrations in London and other capitals but these were not in favour of international brotherhood and the advancement of the cause of the working class. On the contrary, nearly everybody was swept up in a huge wave of patriotism and backwash of xenophobia (a word for hatred of foreigners appropriately coined at about this time). The Almighty was called upon to intercede on behalf of the just cause by the clergy of all the warring nations, and believing that God as well as their own united people were on their side, millions of young men went off to do their bit, never to return. Thus society at all levels was deprived of the longer-term services of many of the most vigorous male members of a whole generation. Meanwhile, women did much more than weep and keep home fires burning, putting their shoulders to the wheels of industry as a practical example of the need for their emancipation.

Far from solving the problems of Europe, the First World War made them greater. The principal loser, Germany, was pushed into deep resentment, the chief European victors, Britain and France, were considerably weakened. The great power that gained by far the most was outside Europe – the USA. Moreover, as Dick Geary has observed, 'What happened during and after the First World War was that many of the previous impediments to protest disintegrated; and the European working class attempted to seize this chance to improve its lot.' Before 1914, the vast majority of European workers belonged to no economic or political organisation. Nevertheless, the 'wave of pre-war militancy and radicalism seems to have been generated by some of the same phenomena that have been held responsible for the even greater upheavals at the end of the First World War'.[32] The threat to skilled workers from the influx of new, at best semi-skilled, workers necessitated by the onset of the second industrial revolution grew with the need to produce the materials of war. Nowhere was this more so than in Russia, where it combined with other difficulties to provoke a political revolution that was to confront Europe and the world with an additional problem for most of the twentieth century.

11

THE FIRST WORLD WAR AND THE RUSSIAN REVOLUTION, 1914–1921

THE WESTERN FRONT

The plans for action of both sides depended on attack. The most famous of them, the German Schlieffen Plan, called for a quick strike at Paris after outflanking the French defences through Belgium and Luxembourg, while on the Eastern Front the army would mark time until reinforcements could be brought over from the West. However, as Hew Strachan makes clear, Schlieffen had retired in 1905, and by 1914 'There was no single solution, no one plan', and more concern for French intentions.[1] The French Plan 17, which replaced others responding more directly to German intentions, concentrated on mobilising much more efficiently than in 1870, stopping the German attack from Lorraine or through Belgium and demonstrating flexibility in both defence and counter-attack. Meanwhile, the Russians hoped to move rapidly to secure their flanks in East Prussia and Galicia before advancing from their Polish salient towards Berlin. For their part, the Austro-Hungarians were intent on advance from Galicia against the Russians as well as on completion of the punishment of insubordinate Serbia. Britain was in a somewhat exceptional position, preoccupied by imperial concerns and by no means as committed to the continent as its allies. The small professional army was to cross the Channel to assist the French while the navy was to concentrate on keeping the high seas free of the enemy. In such a manner, the British government hoped that the enemy would be denied participation in international trade and thus be starved into submission.

Now that the military and naval deterrents had proved ineffective, the plans of action that had looked so convincing on paper could not be realised in battle. Although French losses were considerable as their plan was adapted to meet the German invasion, enough men were moved to the defence of Paris to save the capital from a repeat of the humiliation of 1870. Moreover, the concentration of the invaders on Paris had led to their neglect of the Channel ports, which the French were able to retain as a means of communication with Britain, from which more recruits were sent over for the British Expeditionary Force. But the Germans had been able to seize the most important industrial region of north-east France, whose iron and steel were vital in the years of attrition that followed in place of the expected quick victory. Along the Western Front, which moved by no more than a few miles in either direction from the end of 1914 to the beginning of 1918, from Ypres to Verdun there stretched the undulating territory that was to become drenched with the blood of millions of soldiers as their com-manders – Haig, Foch and the others – called for effort after effort to break the stalemate. No words can describe the carnage with any adequacy, although the poet Wilfred Owen perhaps came closest, and the prose writer C. E. Montague also succeeded in conveying some of the desolation:

> The winter after the battle of Loos a sentry on guard at one part of our line could always see the prostrate skeletons of many English dead. They lay outside our wire, picked clean by the rats, so that the khaki fell in on them loosely – little heaps of bone and cloth half-hidden now by nettles and grass. If the sentry had been a year in the army he knew well enough that they had gone foredoomed into a battle lost before a shot was fired.[2]

Many of the fatal shots were fired by machine guns, which from defensive emplacements often well protected against heavy artillery barrage could easily mow down advancing infantrymen as they attemp-ted to cut their way through thickets of barbed wire. Behind the lines railways usually gave the advantage to the defending side, since they could move troops to any sector under pressure before breakthrough could be achieved. The aeroplane was of importance here too as an observer of attacks in preparation (rather than as a dropper of bombs on the enemy, a subordinate role). On occasion, fleets of trucks could be used to bring up large numbers of men with surprising rapidity, to stem the German advance at Verdun early in 1916 for example, but the wheels that did most in the end to break the deadlock were those that moved the caterpillar tracks of those new war machines first built for the navy as 'land ships' and then ordered for the army under the code-name 'tank'. Tanks made their first big impact on the war in November 1917 at Cambrai, and helped to bring the great conflict on the Western Front to its conclusion a year later. Another important new element in the last months of the struggle was the arrival of reinforcements from the USA. Among a large range of methods used in earlier years to achieve victory, the employment of gas was initially perhaps the most terrifying, but not in the end the most effective, owing to the absence of favourable winds and the general use of efficient gas masks. A means of fighting the war at sea at first considered to be equally barbaric was the submarine, which came near to winning the war for Germany, but then contributed directly to its defeat.

THE EASTERN AND OTHER LAND FRONTS

While the Western Front is most familiar to us, we must not neglect the Eastern, where there was certainly more movement and possibly more significance for Europe as a whole. In the beginning, the Russian 'steamroller' did indeed bear down on Germany, where there was alarm of sufficient proportions for some troops to be transferred to the Eastern Front from the Western. So some of the pressure on Paris was relieved at the critical moment. But then one Russian army was destroyed at Tannenburg in late August and another routed at the Masurian Lakes by mid-September. One of the Russian generals shot himself, while the German commanders Hindenburg and Ludendorff acquired wide fame. Two months later, Turkey was persuaded to join the war against Russia, which now felt itself beleaguered in the Black Sea and the Caucasus as well as in Poland. In March 1915, in answer to an earlier Russian appeal, British and Anzac (Australian and New Zealand Army Corps) forces launched an expedition to Gallipoli, the

rocky peninsula adjacent to the Dardanelles, the narrow passage leading from the Mediterranean to the Black Sea. Istanbul and European
Turkey were to be cut off, thus leaving the way open to the Balkans and
relief of the Russians. In spite of a considerable amount of heroism,
a series of errors and misfortunes led to disaster before withdrawal at
the beginning of 1916. The Russian steamroller was now moving most
of the time in reverse against German attacks through Poland and the
Baltic provinces. However, to the south General Brusilov pushed back
the Austro-Hungarian forces from June to September, encouraging
Romania to join in the war on the Allied side. Once again German
forces had to be brought over from the Western Front during important
battles around Verdun and on the Somme. But now the Russian army
could no longer renew its efforts, because of the onset in March 1917 of
the Revolution, which we will consider below.

There were other land fronts besides the Western and Eastern in
the First World War. After much hesitation, Italy entered the conflict
in the spring of 1915, not on the side of its German and Austro-
Hungarian fellow members of the Triple Alliance, but against them.
Italy was promised by the Western Allies extensions of its frontiers to
include the Tyrol in the Alps and most of Dalmatia round the Adriatic
Sea. Thus, it made a contribution to the Allied victory in its engagement
of the historic enemy, Austria–Hungary, as it sought to cash in on those
promises. Serbia at first managed to resist punitive attacks by Austria–
Hungary, but was finally late in 1915 overwhelmed by a joint force of
Austria–Hungary, Germany and a new combatant Bulgaria – lured into
fighting by the promise of revenge expansion in Macedonia. However,
near the very end of the war in September 1918, an Allied force
including troops from Greece, which had been obliged by an Allied
invasion and coup to enter the war in September 1916, pushed the
Bulgarian army out of Macedonia.

In the Middle East, mainly British troops kept the Turks busy in
Mesopotamia (the region between the rivers Tigris and Euphrates with
Baghdad at the centre, soon to become Iraq), in Syria and in Palestine.
Already in May 1916, the Sykes–Picot agreement arranged for a division
of spheres of influence, with France dominant in Syria and Britain
dominant in Iraq. On 2 November 1917 the British foreign secretary,
A. J. Balfour, declared to Lord Rothschild and his fellow Zionists that
'His Majesty's Government view with favour the establishment in

Palestine of a national home for the Jewish people'.[3] Further south, in South-West and especially in East Africa, campaigns were mounted against the German colonies, not so much for strategic reasons as for those of negotiation, to give the Allies 'a card to play in any peace discussions against claims for European territory by the Central Powers'.[4]

In the even more remote Pacific Ocean, Australia and New Zealand launched expeditions against Samoa and other German islands, while, more significantly, Japan moved early on in the war to take the German base in China, Kiaochow (Tsintau), and other German possessions and interests in the adjacent Shantung Peninsula. From this basis, Japan moved in 1915 to impose 'Twenty-One Demands' on China, involving parts of South Manchuria and Inner Mongolia as well as Shantung. Japan's friends, especially the USA, were now almost as alarmed as some of its enemies.

THE WAR AT SEA

Having moved around the world, we are now prepared to leave the land for another important aspect of the war, what occurred and threatened to occur at sea. At the outbreak of hostilities, as we have seen, it was fundamental to British strategy to use the mastery of the Royal Navy to impose a blockade upon Germany and thus to starve her into submission. Since there were 20 British Dreadnoughts to 13 German big battleships of this type, there was no immediate major challenge to the strategy. The blockade was intensified as the war progressed to the maximum level possible without causing a rupture in relations with the USA, ever sensitive about British interference with neutral shipping. It did not become complete until the entry into the war in April 1917 of the USA, which was brought about largely by the efforts of German submarines to counter the naval barrier.

Britain was in a more vulnerable maritime position than its principal enemy, since at the outbreak of war it needed to import almost two-thirds of its foodstuffs by sea, while Germany had to import less than a quarter of its foodstuffs, much of which could come in by land. The use of the submarine (*Unterseeboot*) was widely considered to be illegal and immoral, especially when civilians were involved, but the German government came round to the view that it was the best way of achieving victory. In May 1915, the British liner *Lusitania* was sunk off the west coast of Ireland, with the loss of over 1000 lives, including about 100 Americans. President Wilson declared that 'There is such a thing as a nation being too proud to fight'. However, on this and on other minor occasions in the summer of 1915 and the spring of 1916, he sent the German government curt notes culminating in the ultimatum that if submarine warfare against ships carrying passengers and freight were not abandoned, he would have no choice but to sever diplomatic relations with the German Empire altogether. This brought an accommodating response in May, and Wilson went on to gain a narrow victory in the presidential election late in 1916 with such slogans as 'He kept us out of war' and 'Wilson and Peace with Honor'.[5]

The only major surface naval battle of the First World War occurred at the end of May 1916, off Jutland, Denmark. Both sides claimed victory: it did little or nothing to reduce British supremacy in the North Sea, but on the other hand it ended all hope of opening up the Baltic Sea to the Royal Navy. While the German fleet was by no means as cowed as British propaganda suggested, its chief of staff came to the conclusion that: 'A victorious end to the war at not too distant a date can only be looked for by the crushing of English economic life through U-boat action against English commerce.'[6] Some of the best German officers and men were transferred to the U-boats, and the morale of the High Seas Fleet degenerated through inaction towards eventual mutiny. Then, on 1 February 1917, after widespread arguments in its favour had reached an almost irresistible level of intensity, unrestricted war on seaborne commerce was declared by the German government. The government was taking a calculated risk, even gambling its last card. 'If it is not trumps', said one of its officials, 'Germany is lost for centuries.' The basic aim, shown to be a mathematical certainty in a lengthy memorandum from the German Admiralty, was to starve Britain into submission within six months. With at least five times as many submarines at its disposal as in 1915, the German Admiralty did indeed have good reason to believe that it had got its sums right.[7]

THE ENTRY OF THE USA AND THE WAR'S END

Some unforeseen factors multiplied with others that had been foreseen to render the German equation sufficiently inaccurate for British starvation to be avoided and the ultimate victory to go to the Western Allies rather than the Central Powers. It was realised that unrestricted use of U-boats would bring the USA into the war, but the speed with which that entry could be made effective was underestimated. Right from the beginning of the war, most American sympathies had been with Britain and France, and now that tsarism had been overthrown in the Russian Revolution at the beginning of 1917, Russia could be brought more fully into an alliance fighting to make the world safe for democracy. Hostility towards the Central Powers had been whipped up by an efficient British propaganda machine, which had given all possible emphasis to the infringement of Belgian neutrality and exaggerated the all-round beastliness of the Hun. The direct threat posed by such a monster to the security of the USA was underlined by the publication on 1 March 1917 of the Zimmermann Telegram – a message from the German foreign secretary, Arthur Zimmermann, to the German minister in Mexico urging the invasion of the USA for the recapture of territories lost in earlier wars and indicating that Japan might be persuaded to change sides and attack American interests in the Pacific. Sensitive as always about these interests and all too conscious of recent problems involving Mexico and necessitating American military action there, Congress and the public were caught up in a strong wave of emotions culminating in the declaration of war on Germany on 6 April 1917. Amid the outrage and the fever there was also cold rationality: the almighty dollar demanded protection, since the financial neutrality proclaimed at the beginning of the war had not been maintained. A. J. P. Taylor suggested that:

> Soon businessmen complained that the chance of great profits was being lost. Large funds were extended to the Allies. Copper, cotton, wheat poured across the Atlantic. Factories worked overtime on British and French orders. The economy boomed. If the German submarines stopped this trade, there would be depression, crisis. If the Allies lost the war, the American loans would be lost also. In the last resort, the United States went to war so that America could remain prosperous and rich Americans could grow richer.[8]

But the involvement of the USA in the First World War was not exclusively a matter of financial gain. There were other kinds of contribution, and sacrifices, too. During the summer of 1917, the introduction of the convoy system led to a steep decline in the losses inflicted on Allied shipping by the dreaded U-boats. Whether or not the original idea was American or British remains a matter of controversy: certainly, American ships played a full part along with those of the Royal Navy. Now, food and other necessary supplies got through to Britain in a less interrupted manner. Moreover, after some delays in mobilisation, tens of thousands of American troops were brought over the Atlantic without one single loss at sea to make a considerable impact on the final outcome of the war on the Western Front. There, mutiny or perhaps rather a 'professional strike', occurred during the early summer in the French army. The new French commander-in-chief, Pétain, said: 'We must wait for the Americans and the tanks.'[9] The new machines enjoyed their first full success in November, the new men in the spring of 1918, when the Germans launched a last desperate offensive towards the Maine River, only 50 miles from Paris. Here and elsewhere, the Yanks did their bit in helping to turn the German advance into a retreat leading by 11 November to the Armistice.

At home, like most Europeans, Americans also lost a considerable number of their much-treasured civil liberties, as legislation concerning sedition and sabotage was given a wide interpretation. But if the reckoning is to be made in terms of the numbers who made the final sacrifice, the sufferings of the USA must be accounted much smaller than those of the other major belligerents. American war dead reached a total of about 100,000, while the British approached 1 million, the French and Austro-Hungarian exceeded it and the Russian and German numbers were both nearer to 2 million. Still connected with the deprivation and dislocation of war as well as with continued hostilities were the deaths of well over 20 million civilians in the years of the war and those immediately following. Most of these perished in a vast epidemic of influenza; many others were Armenians massacred by the Turks; yet more were Russians and members of the former tsarist empire who succumbed during the Russian Revolution and its aftermath.

THE LAST YEARS OF TSARISM

In a famous passage at the beginning of his work on the assumption of power by Louis Napoleon in 1851, Karl Marx wrote:

Men make their own history, but not just as they please. They do not choose the circumstances for themselves, but have to work upon circumstances as they find them, have to fashion the material handed down by the past. The legacy of the dead generations weighs like an alp upon the brains of the living.[10]

In 1917, the alp of the Russian past became a volcano, as was pointed out later by one of the major performers in the first act of the great drama, Paul Miliukov:

just as a powerful geological cataclysm playfully casts down the crust of the latest cultural strata and brings to the surface long-hidden strata recalling the dim past – the ancient epochs of the earth's history – so the Russian Revolution laid bare for us all our historical structure, only thinly hidden by the superficial layers of recent cultural acquisitions.[11]

Miliukov went on to suggest that the movements led by Lenin and Trotsky after the fall of tsarism had more in common with the 'peasant wars' of the seventeenth and eighteenth centuries than with the most recent developments in European socialist ideology. This put it too strongly, Miliukov's far-sighted view being jaundiced by the circumstance that he personally was swept aside by the momentum of the events of spring 1917. On the other hand, it is equally true that analysis of the Russian Revolution on the basis of simple Marxist terminology alone cannot provide a full understanding of those events that followed the abdication of the tsar or that led to the assumption of power by Lenin, Trotsky and their associates.

The outbreak of the First World War gave the old regime in Russia some relief as a wave of unrest was washed over by another wave of patriotism. However, the Russian army 'steamroller' failed to function in the expected manner after some early success. Paris was saved by pressure on the Eastern Front in the autumn of 1914, but before long a greater threat was being posed to Petrograd – the empire's capital having been renamed in a more Slavonic manner in order to avoid the Germanic associations of St Petersburg. Fear and suspicion that the influence of the Huns had penetrated as far as the royal family were unfounded, but there can be little doubt that the tsar contributed to

his own downfall by pursuing some policies which were if anything overpatriotic. His insistence at the commencement of the war
that prohibition must be introduced made it more difficult not only
for millions of Russians to acquire their favourite beverage, but also for
treasury officials, deprived of substantial excise taxes, to manage the
budget, already thrown off balance by departure from the gold standard. The economy in general was hampered by problems not so much
of production as of distribution: if, as has been suggested, the First
World War had a close connection with railway timetables, Russia was
increasingly unable to keep up with the schedule.

A vehicle of a different kind was suggested by a contemporary politician as a striking analogy for the tsarist government, which he likened
to a car being driven down a precipitous road at breakneck speed by a
mad driver: should the passengers try to take the wheel, or would this
move only make disaster more certain? During the war, various kinds
of semi-official groups loosely connected to the Duma and to industry
did their best to keep the car on the road, but the driver took an even
firmer grip on the wheel by deciding in the summer of 1915 to assume
personal command of the army. A large part of the weight of the past
bearing down on Nicholas II was his consciousness of his responsibility
for keeping intact the inheritance not just of his father but also of other
ancestors stretching back to 1613, the date of the foundation of the
Romanov dynasty. The empress greeted her husband's decision as
the beginning of a 'glorious page' in tsarist history:[12] in fact, far from
turning a new leaf, the decision was to help bring the old story to an
abrupt end.

Nicholas himself might not have been quite so incapable as he has
often been described, although his attitude to both strikers and Jews, to
name but two of the groups that he despised, made him far less lovable
than has been suggested in some of the more romantic biographies.
Moreover, the tsar and his advisers must bear their share of the
responsibility for the unseemly 'ministerial leapfrog' of the war years,
as minister after minister, none of them as astute as Witte and Stolypin,
was given the task of keeping the state on its right course. Members
of the Duma, which was not given the confidence of the government,
lost whatever confidence they had in return. At the same time as
Nicholas went off to the front, a so-called Progressive Bloc of politicians
attempted to arrange again a parliamentary government responsible

to the Duma and enjoying the confidence of the nation. But the Empress Alexandra, who had taken over from her absent husband, paid more attention to an embodiment of Russian traditions older than the Romanov dynasty itself. This was Rasputin, often called the 'mad monk', although he was in fact neither. As aware of Rasputin's influence as any of his colleagues and sharing their suspicion of pro-German elements at the court, the historian and liberal politician Paul Miliukov made a bold and bitter speech before the Duma in November 1916, attacking the 'dark forces' behind the throne and ending each in a series of accusations with the question: 'Is this stupidity or is this treason?'[13] Rasputin was assassinated in December, but the year 1916 ended without any satisfactory response by the government to the questions raised against it by Miliukov and others.

RUSSIA IN 1916 AND THE ORIGINS OF THE RUSSIAN REVOLUTION

By now, too, it was not just the politicians who were putting tsarism to the test. Even among the peasants, who were remote from the latest news and rumours, suspicion was growing of the 'little father', and a simple belief as ancient as the folk wisdom dispensed by Rasputin was again coming to the surface: the land was theirs. And while the vast majority of the Russian people in the provinces were beginning to agitate for their rights, that small but significant minority in Petrograd and other cities were already more active in pursuit of justice for the workers. Economic dislocation including a high level of inflation and a low level of supplies was widespread by 1916. The response took the form of strikes, involving over a million workers, and often of a dis-organised, 'wildcat' nature, sometimes revealing tensions between the skilled and the unskilled. The rootless, restless nature of urban disturbances was coloured by the circumstance that they involved many recent immigrants from the countryside. But there were many towns-people of longer standing, too, and a few of them at least would have been descended from participants in the revolts in St Petersburg and Moscow of 1905 and earlier years. Bolsheviks, Mensheviks, Socialist Revolutionaries and other left-wing radicals, although not well orga-nised in their respective parties, did succeed in helping to give some shape to the labour movement. A third category of opposition to tsarism was arising among the non-Russian nationalities: individuals and groups among them were showing their dissatisfaction with their incorporation into the empire, even though this had sometimes occurred centuries before. For example, some feelings of separatism were apparent in the Ukraine, much of which had been joined with Russia as far back as 1654, as well as in the Baltic provinces incorporated by 1721. But the most violent opposition to the central government arose in 1916 in the more recently taken over central Asia, where the local inhabitants rose up in protest at their mobilisation. Generally speaking, of course, conscription into the armed forces aroused despair, for the Russian peasant and worker families as well as for those of other nationalities. However, the success of the Brusilov offensive in the summer of 1916 not only brought relief for the Allies on the Western Front but did something to restore morale on the Eastern Front; Russian military spirits were probably at their lowest ebb behind the lines.

Stephen Graham, a sympathetic British visitor to Russia in 1916, found it 'remarkably cheerful'. He gained the impression that the Russians had become accustomed to the thought of a long war, and were 'brightly optimistic' after a period of depression. However, there was 'a strange silence': there was 'as yet no promise of the future anywhere'. Graham was not happy with the changes taking place under the influence of the war:

> I believe in Holy Russia, and as far as Russia is concerned do not care for anything else. I hate to see her being commercialised and exploited, and to see her vulgar rich increasing at the expense of the life-blood of the nation. Without any question the new class of middle-rich coming into being through Russia's industrial prosperity is the worst of its kind in Europe. They are worse than anything in Germany, and it is they who are beginning to have the power in Russia. It is the green and inexperienced who think that the power wrested from the Tsar and his Court is grasped by the idealists of Russia. It is grasped by the capitalists, often by foreign capitalists, by business interest in any case.

While the rich got richer, the poor got poorer. There was a severe shortage of necessities, including wood, boots and all kinds of foodstuffs. What could be bought in Moscow had risen steeply in price during the war: mutton by 281 per cent; pork by 142 per cent; bread by 45 per cent; and sugar by 57 per cent. The introduction of ration cards had not been an unqualified success, especially in the countryside: 'in one village a rumour spread that the Anti-Christ had arrived in Russia and was giving these out. It is said that one inhabitant of foreign origin bought up all the cards from the peasants at a low price, and they now contentedly buy their provisions from him when he has them.'[14]

The picture built up by the British visitor was confirmed and supplemented by that drawn in October 1916 in Petrograd by the Ministry of the Interior. The populations of the capital and large cities were already suffering from hunger. Various committees concerned with such problems as the care of refugees, supply of food and relief of the poor had without exception expressed their belief that Russia was on the eve of important events 'compared to which those of 1905 are a mere trifle'. At the front, tsarist Russia was holding together:

> The brilliant success of the offensive of General Brusilov in the spring of the present year and the current solution of the problem of supplying the army proved convincingly that the task undertaken by the Government and the community has been fulfilled more than successfully. The question of the organisation of the army supply may be held to have been satisfactorily settled.

It was 'the disintegration of the rear, that is of the whole country' that had reached such monstrous and extreme proportions that it had begun to undermine the success achieved at the front.[15]

Meanwhile, in exile in Switzerland, Lenin was completing one of his longer works, *Imperialism: The Highest Stage of Capitalism*. In this, he presented a composite picture of the international relationships of the world's major powers on the eve of the First World War. He described a struggle for the division of the world, for the acquisition of colonies and the creation of spheres of influence for finance capital. Against such a background, the showdown of 1914 appeared inevitable. By 1916, although Lenin in Zurich could not clearly discern developments at home, Russian society was breaking up under the strain of the great conflict and heading towards revolution. Perhaps the greatest difference between events in Russia in 1917 and those in France in 1789 lay here: the French Revolution occurred at a time of comparative peace, the Russian in the middle of the greatest war in history up to that time.

THE FEBRUARY REVOLUTION

On International Women's Day, Thursday 8 March 1917 (23 February Old Style – there were 13 days between the Old Style and New Style calendars), mostly female members of queues for bread lost patience and began demonstrations that linked up with a mostly male industrial strike movement already in progress. During the next day, the size of the crowds out on the Nevsky Prospect and other streets of Petrograd grew and demands for bread mingled with outcries against the government. By Saturday 10 March, the strike movement had become general, and socialists played an increasingly vigorous part in its direction. The Revolution may not have been centrally planned, but neither was it spontaneous, and momentum was building up for the formation of a soviet or council after the pattern of the Revolution of 1905. On the government side, some beleaguered policemen fired on the demonstrators, who killed two of their chiefs. General Khabalov, the commander of the Petrograd Military District, acted on orders sent from headquarters by his commander-in-chief, Tsar Nicholas II, to suppress the uprising, more than 100 alleged leaders of which were arrested. The tsar's representatives also began to discuss the crisis with representatives of the Duma.

A few soldiers had already defected before 11 March, which became known as Bloody Sunday after still loyal troops had accounted for more than 50 of the demonstrators. A reprieve for tsarism appeared to be granted by the following lull, but Nicholas did not help his own cause by proroguing the Duma against the advice of its president, M. V. Rodzianko, who had been hoping for the creation of a 'ministry of trust'. Before nightfall, one whole company of soldiers had broken its oath of loyalty and joined the cause of revolutionary treason. On Monday 12 March the deserters were joined by many of their comrades, and some army weapons fell into the hands of the civilian strikers. These insurgents contributed further to the breakdown of law and order by storming the prisons of Petrograd and freeing thousands of the inmates, as well as arresting some government ministers. The Soviet of Workers' Deputies held its first meeting, the Duma formed a Provisional Executive Committee. Urgent if contradictory messages were sent to his headquarters by remaining supporters of the tsar such as Khabalov, whom Nicholas promptly dismissed just before setting off home to the palace of Tsarskoe Selo. On Tuesday 13 March, Khabalov joined the number of those arrested as virtually all those previously under his command went over to the opposition. This was now beginning to form its own militia and to elect deputies to the Soviet, which opposed the Duma's continuing efforts to create a ministry of trust. On Wednesday 14 March, the soldiers began to attend the Soviet and to demand their rights. The leaders of the Soviet and Duma continued to jockey for position as the Revolution spread to Moscow and to the Baltic fleet. On Thursday 15 March, the historian P. N. Miliukov, who had taken over from Rodzianko as the leading influence in the Duma, attempted to persuade the grand duke Michael to succeed his brother Nicholas, who had abdicated for himself and his son. The grand duke refused Miliukov's offer and so the Romanov dynasty came to an end in 1917 as it had begun in 1613, with the cry 'Long live Michael'.

On Friday 16 March a proclamation was issued, beginning:

> Citizens, the Provisional Executive Committee of the members of the Duma, with the aid and support of the garrison of the capital and its inhabitants, has triumphed over the dark forces of the Old Regime to such an extent as to enable it to organize a more stable executive power.[16]

Here, a would-be official stamp was given to a version of events distorting what actually had happened to an almost ludicrous degree. The 'dark forces' consisting of the Romanovs and their adherents had indeed been overthrown, but those citizens who constituted the garrison of Petrograd and its inhabitants could claim this achievement for themselves rather than in 'aid and support' of the Provisional Executive Committee of the Duma. For these members of the Duma had been worried spectators of the street demonstrations rather than leaders of them, concerned lest the volcano get completely out of control and bring about the overthrow of society along with the government. To declare themselves constituted to bring about a new stability was an expression of hope rather than confidence, especially since the Provisional Government was obliged from the first to coexist with another candidate for the same position, the Soviet of Workers' Deputies.

Those who had actually brought about the Revolution were not included in the Soviet Executive Committee, and when sailors and peasants as well as workers and soldiers became involved in Soviets, not only in Petrograd but also in Moscow and elsewhere, they began to wonder if they were not exchanging one master for another. They were especially suspicious of the Provisional Government and Miliukov's attempts to preserve tsarism, and only partly mollified by the Soviet Executive Committee's guarded support of the Provisional Government and the inclusion in it of one of its members. This was A. F. Kerensky, who was given an appointment aiming at the creation of a new law and order to replace the old, the Ministry of Justice. And so, along with the emergence of an uneasy 'dual power' of Soviet and Provisional Government, there persisted an anarchic 'third force' of popular impatience. Even a Socialist intellectual in Petrograd, S. D. Mstislavsky, could write that it had been easy for his colleagues to make speeches 'in the name of the proletariat' but 'when ... this theoretical proletariat stood here, side by side, in full height, in full power of its emaciated flesh and of revolting blood ... unintentionally the words of inquietude, instead of militant slogans, began to be mumbled from the pale mouths of the "leaders"'.[17] In Mstislavsky's view, the leaders of both the Soviet Executive Committee and the Duma Executive Committee shared a fear of the masses, and collaborated through fear of continued revolution from below as well as of counter-revolution from outside. By presenting a united front, they could encourage a national solidarity.

Indeed, the volcano was capped, but for all too many reasons it soon burst forth again with if anything greater intensity than before. In the first place, the context of the February or March Revolution must be emphasised – that is, its relationship to the other great issues of early 1917, war and peace. While all was fairly quiet on the Eastern Front, and there was even less action in the Baltic states after the German forces had established themselves there, enforced idleness itself was a breeder of discontent. We have already seen that the soldiers of the Petrograd garrison cracked before those facing the enemy. We must now note in addition that the naval bases of Kronstadt, Helsingfors and Reval experienced early discontent because, partly as a consequence of Russian strategy, Russian ships had been kept in port during the summer months as well as being frozen into harbour throughout the winter. The German blockade was important, too. 'While the comparative failure at Jutland did nothing to impair British supremacy in the North Sea', wrote C. R. M. F. Cruttwell of the abortive naval battle at the end of May 1916, 'it ruined all hope of opening the Baltic to Russia. ... Thus Jutland may be reckoned among the many converging causes which brought the March Revolution of 1917.'[18] Support for Nicholas and his adherents was already on the wane among naval men and their officers, one of whom, present at Jutland, wrote later: 'I had never been an admirer of Tsardom, with its leaning towards political suppression and national chauvinism. ... and the favour enjoyed by ambitious men ... had always been abhorrent to me.'[19]

For similar or for other reasons, quite a few of the officers of both navy and army were prepared to follow their men in coming to terms with the Provisional Government. If they had not been so prepared, there would have been a rapid deterioration towards more violent upheaval led by the armed forces. As it was, good order and discipline declined with some speed in any case, the rot starting to set in on 15 March with the publication of Order No. 1, which Trotsky called 'the single worthy document of the February Revolution' and which, General Denikin claimed, 'gave the first and chief blow to the disintegration of the old army'.[20] Introducing the ideas of election of committees and, by implication, of officers as well as of representatives to the Soviet, and abolishing many of the traditional formalities, Order No. 1 spread quickly from Petrograd to the front and to the Baltic.

The minister of war, A. I. Guchkov, along with the Provisional Government's most forceful personality, the minister of foreign affairs, P. N. Miliukov, believed that social cohesion as well as political advantage could best be achieved by keeping faith with the Allies and pushing on towards victory. Thus, the new regime could gain wider frontiers for Russia and even realise the age-old aim of the acquisition of Constantinople. Now, a split developed in the 'dual power', for in contrast to the Provisional Government the Soviet was calling for a defensive war without annexations or indemnities. The split was reinforced in mid-April by the return to Petrograd of Lenin, by no means the dictatorial leader of a tightly disciplined Bolshevik party, but already able to put forward a powerful argument: fraternisation with the enemy meantime and prosecution of the war only if it turned against imperialism as the Revolution intensified and spread. In his *April Theses* and at greater length in *The State and Revolution*, both produced in 1917, Lenin drew a clear picture of the old bourgeois order being overthrown completely by a new society in which the proletarian workers and peasants would establish not a parliamentary republic but a more complete democracy based on the Soviets.

Demonstrations against the policies of Miliukov and Guchkov led to their resignations in mid-May. A new coalition including moderate socialists was set up a few days later, appearing at first to give the 'dual power' a united strength with such appointments as Kerenskv as minister of war. But soon, although they retained some of the style and language introduced by the Soviet, his policies were to reveal more affinity with those of Miliukov and Guchkov than with those of Lenin and other radicals. For example, he published on 24 May a Declaration of Soldiers' Rights which had some faint echoes of Order No. 1 but then in its final point stated without reservation that the appointment and dismissal of commanders at all levels was the exclusive right of the High Command. A few weeks later, after some attempts at clarification and compromise, there was a widespread demonstration on 1 July with such slogans as 'Down with appointments from above, long live the elective principle' and 'All power to the Soviets', as well as 'End of the war' and 'Down with the capitalist ministers'.[21]

THE OCTOBER REVOLUTION

On that same day, 1 July, an offensive began in Galicia as a further Russian contribution to the Allied cause in the war. It had been well prepared by the generals and enthusiastically supported by Kerensky, who hoped that the morale of the army and the situation on both Eastern and Western fronts would be improved by successful action. However, less than two weeks later, the offensive ground to a halt. General L. G. Kornilov was made commander of the southern front including Galicia, and successfully demanded stern measures against the reluctant troops, including the reduction in the influence of the committees and the restoration of the death penalty. On 31 July, General Kornilov was made commander-in-chief. Meanwhile, back in Petrograd, from 16 to 19 July there had been an armed revolt in favour of the Soviet. It had been inaugurated by military members of the 'third force', the rank and file, demanding that the Soviet Central Executive Committee take over from the Provisional Government. The demand met with refusal along with condemnation of the revolt as a stab in the back for the gallant army. Even Lenin and the Bolsheviks, who believed the action premature, were reluctant to assume its leadership, and did what they could to bring it to an end. Nevertheless, the Bolsheviks were now branded as German spies stirring up trouble on behalf of the enemy: Lenin had to go into hiding; another returned exile, Trotsky, was among those arrested.

Ironically, some members of the Provisional Government soon resigned because they considered some of its policies too left-wing. But a new coalition set up on 6 August tried to keep to the middle of the road, even veering to the right in the attempt. Kerensky himself was appointed prime minister as well as remaining minister of war, and at his new residence in the Winter Palace he planned various kinds of councils and conferences, while promising iron rule. However, Kerensky could not play the part of Napoleon, which seemed more appropriate for General Kornilov. During discussions and speeches throughout August and early September, there appeared every possibility that the eloquence of Kerensky and the discipline of Kornilov could combine in a new, personal 'dual power', but mutual suspicion and clashing ambition made continued co-operation impossible when the crunch came in mid-September. It was brought on by the German occupation of Riga on 3 September and the subsequent threat to Petrograd itself. Kornilov believed that the time had come for order to be restored behind the lines, especially since there were rumours of further Bolshevik insurgency. Kerensky rightly or wrongly became convinced that the general was trying to oust him as prime minister, and therefore dismissed Kornilov on 8 September. The next day the air became thick with recriminations and denunciations, and Kornilov instigated a mutiny. Kerensky had appealed for the support of the Bolsheviks and the workers' militia, or Red Guard, as well as that of the Soviets, and when Kornilov attempted to lead his troops on the capital, they showed no readiness to follow, while the railwaymen refused to transport them. Thus the counter-revolutionary mutiny came to an abrupt end before it had really started.

'And now the Provisional Government found that it had been mortally wounded through its own victory', Cruttwell observed, with the explanation:

> The extremists believed that it had acted in collusion with the
> leaders of the insurrection, the exceedingly lenient treatment of

whom confirmed that view. The danger to Petrograd spread visibly like a thundercloud. The Germans, anxious to restore the spirit of their navy, lately cankered by mutiny, equipped an amphibious expedition, which seized the islands at the mouth of the Gulf of Riga. Thus the enemy stood over against the arsenals of Kronstadt and Helsingfors, whose sailors were the most ardent and ruthless instruments in Bolshevik hands.[22]

The left was made stronger by the reluctance of the Red Guard to disband as well as by the release on bail of Trotsky and other Bolshevik leaders. On 13 September, the Bolsheviks became the majority party in the Petrograd Soviet, achieving the same dominance in the Moscow Soviet on 19 September.

Meanwhile, Kerensky was attempting to keep himself in power through a number of increasingly desperate measures. Soon after the dismissal of Kornilov, the prime minister appointed himself commander-in-chief. On 14 September, he took Russia out of its constitutional limbo by declaring a republic, a measure anticipating the decision of a Constituent Assembly, whose election was now hurried through after having been previously delayed. On the same day, he appointed a Directory of five close advisers. Kerensky's apologists, who included himself on many occasions, have argued that his basic aim was to ensure the progress of revolutionary Russia to its new order with all the due process of legality and democratic decision. His own policies in the last month of his tenure of office, including the formation of another unstable coalition on 8 October, did much to undermine such a case.

Fundamentally, Kerensky and his successive attempts at government failed because he refused to recognise that the Revolution was social as well as political. The peasants believed that the land was theirs, and were seizing it before land committees could make allocations. Urban workers wanted a measure of control in the factories as well as a decent standard of living. Nationalist yearnings in Ukraine, the Baltic provinces and elsewhere were frustrated by policies that often appeared as Great Russian in emphasis as those of the tsar. In addition, the desertion of millions from the armed forces underlined a widespread preference for peace over a war described as for defence, for democracy or whatever.

The predicament of the navy was perhaps not quite so serious as that of the army, although at the beginning of November the British Admiralty was asked for support by the Russian fleet, whose commanding officers were reported as stating that 'the whole German Fleet was operating in the Baltic, and that the lack of support of any kind from the Allies was having a depressing effect both upon the morale of the Fleet and upon public opinion'.[23] There was a response in the shape of the penetration of the Kattegat outer entrance to the Baltic by a British flotilla, but this was too little too late. Already Lenin was gaining a ready response to his claim that Kerensky and the Russian bourgeoisie were determined to surrender Petrograd to the Germans and that the capital was also under threat from the preparation of a second Kornilov revolt. Such arguments attracted to the Bolsheviks any residual will to fight on the part of soldiers and sailors.

Lenin had returned from exile in Switzerland to argue that the Russian Revolution had only just begun; he now emerged from hiding in Finland to argue that it should be brought to completion. Because of the external and internal dangers confronting the Bolsheviks, their allies and supporters, the move must be made at once, or history would never forgive them. The Bolshevik Party was still by no means as tightly disciplined as has often been suggested, and even its central committee was by no means unanimously enthusiastic about Lenin's resolutions. Some members wanted to wait for the second all-Russian congress of the Soviets which was to meet on 8 November, and at least a few were against armed insurrection in any circumstances. Nevertheless, under Trotsky, who was already the chairman of the Petrograd Soviet, a military revolutionary committee was set up by the end of October for the declared purpose of safeguarding the revolutionary defence of Petrograd against the openly prepared attack by the military and civilian supporters of Kornilov. Lenin appeared at Smolny, formerly an exclusive girls' school and now headquarters of the Petrograd Soviet and Bolshevik Central Committee, on the evening of 7 November.

Preparations for the insurrection were at best an open secret, and far from being the clandestine conspiracy of some accounts. Kerensky certainly knew about it, and on the morning of 7 November he attempted to rearrest Trotsky and other Bolshevik leaders for breaking the conditions of their bail, among a number of other steps to forestall his overthrow. But the Bolshevik sailors of the cruiser *Aurora* refused to accept the order to put to sea, while Bolshevik soldiers defended the offices of their party's newspapers. The prime minister worked himself up into a final oratorical flurry, while immediately after his return, Lenin worked with Trotsky and others to give what direction they could to the actions of the Red Guard, the sailors and soldiers. There was no 'blueprint' for the insurrection, and by no means completely co-ordinated action. The success of the nocturnal operations of 7–8 November was largely due to the circumstance that there was virtually no opposition to them. By the morning of 8 November, such strategic objectives as the state bank, telephone exchange and post office had been seized along with railway stations and bridges. In the middle of the morning, having talked in vain for support throughout the night, Kerensky left the Winter Palace ostensibly to secure military reinforcements, in fact never to return. There followed the historic storming of the Winter Palace, which was not completed before the early morning of 9 November and was in reality much more undirected and confused than in epic reconstructions.[24]

Nevertheless, the October Revolution, as it is known (Old Style was not replaced by New Style in the Soviet calendar until March 1918), has at least as much right as February to be considered a signal moment in European and world history. The second all-Russian congress of Soviets gave it the stamp of approval, just as it had made a reality of the much heard slogan 'All power to the Soviets'. Similarly, before dispersing after just two sessions on 8 and 9 November, the congress ratified a series of decrees aimed at making a reality of the other popular slogans. The decree on peace called for an immediate armistice of three months, and invited all peoples and governments at war to begin immediate negotiations for a just and democratic peace. In such a spirit, the new Russian government would support its renunciation of annexations and indemnities with the publication of all the secret agreements of its predecessors made between March and November 1917. It also appealed for the support of the workers of Britain, France and Germany. The decree on land abolished without compensation the private ownership of large estates. All alienated land was to go into one national fund that would be distributed among the toilers by local democratic bodies. Hired labour would be prohibited, but individual citizens and their families would be entitled to use the land as long as they could cultivate it. A third decree confirmed the Council of People's Commissars as the new supreme executive authority in Russia.

In the short run, there was no great opposition to the new regime. Dissident socialists left the congress quietly, and Kerensky had no great success in gathering support for his now generally discredited cause. Lenin and his associates had succeeded in bringing the volcano of social revolution under control by directing the main lava flow rather than by attempting to stem it, not by parliamentary methods but by those of the more direct Soviet method:

> The Bolsheviks came to power not because they were superior manipulators or cynical opportunists but because their policies as formulated by Lenin in April and shaped by the events of the following months placed them at the head of a genuinely popular movement.[25]

Now that they had established themselves in power, Lenin and his associates attempted to implement their first decrees and generally to carry out their promise of establishing a new order. The Constituent Assembly duly convened early in 1918 according to the programme drawn up by Kerensky, but was quickly dismissed, Lenin arguing that the establishment of the republic of Soviets signified the implementation of a higher democratic principle. Much has been made of the fact that the Bolsheviks did not secure victory in the elections to the Constituent Assembly, especially among the peasantry. But the Socialist Revolutionary Party, which received most votes, was in no state to assume power, even if the Bolsheviks gaining the majority in Moscow and Petrograd had been prepared to relinquish it. Moreover, the dissolution of the Constituent Assembly was nothing more or less than the last kick at what had been something of a political football for all parties throughout 1917. Now, in the spring of 1918, the government moved the capital back from beleaguered Petrograd to a more secure Moscow. The party changed its official title from Social Democrats to Communists (to escape the opprobrium heaped on those Social Democrats who had betrayed the cause of the international workers' movement at the beginning of the First World War). In the summer, the former empire was given the title of Russian Soviet Federated Socialist Republic.

THE CIRCUMSTANCES OF PEACE

The English-speaking world's basic strategic concept at the beginning of the twentieth century was maritime: top priority was control of the seas, as was indicated in theory by the writings of Admiral Mahan and in practice by the American navy's circumnavigation of the world in 1907 as well as by the widespread voyages of the British navy at all times. However, the Anglo-Russian struggle in and around Afghanistan was at least one good reason for not forgetting completely the significance of the land, whose importance was underlined by Halford John Mackinder. Mackinder returned to his theme in a book written just after the First World War, *Democratic Ideals and Reality: A Study in the Politics of Reconstruction*, and first published in 1919. Essentially, Mackinder argued, the continents of Europe, Asia and Africa formed a 'World Island', to which the other continents were peripheral satellites. The 'World Island' possessed a central 'Heartland' which stretched from the Volga to the eastern Siberian and Manchurian highlands and from the Arctic Ocean to the Himalayan Mountains. And the key to the 'Heartland' was eastern Europe.

Although paying full tribute to the manner in which the war had been won, Mackinder argued that it had very little to do with the manner in which the peace would have to be established. The conflict had not been between eastern and western Europe so much as between German and Slav. Moreover:

> Had Germany elected to stand on the defensive on her short frontier towards France, and had she thrown her main strength against Russia, it is not improbable that the world would be nominally at peace today, but overshadowed by a German East Europe in command of all the Heartland. The British and American insular peoples would not have realised the strategical danger until too late.

Now it was essential that their statesmen worked for a peace including 'a balance as between German and Slav, and true independence of each', for:

> Who rules East Europe commands the Heartland:
> Who rules the Heartland commands the World-Island:
> Who rules the World-Island commands the World.[26]

Mackinder's book brought him to the attention of at least some of these statesmen, and the British foreign secretary, Lord Curzon, invited him in October 1919 to become British high commissioner in South Russia, where he could give advice and support to the White Russian General Denikin in the fight against the Reds. The British government soon announced that military assistance to Denikin would be brought to an end by 31 March 1920, but Mackinder nevertheless set out on a fact-finding mission in eastern Europe. He came back in January 1921 to advise the cabinet to 'range up all the anti-Bolshevist forces from Finland to the Caucasus, giving them a certain amount of support', partly because there was a danger of Bolshevism if unchecked 'sweeping forward like a prairie fire' towards India and beyond.[27] The cabinet did not accept Mackinder's suggestion of further intervention, but certainly remained alive to the dangers of expanding Bolshevism, fear of which had been one of the dominant motives in the drawing up of the Treaty of Versailles which was signed on 28 June 1919.

In order to put that treaty as well as the balance between German and Slav in their context, we must go back to the beginning of 1918, if not even further, for the American president had already made some peace initiatives in 1916 and 1917. On 8 January 1918, Woodrow Wilson's Address to Congress noted that the 'sincere and earnest' Russian representatives had broken off negotiations with those of the Central Powers because they could not entertain the proposals that had been handed out to them 'of conquest and domination'. The Western Powers would remain steadfast of purpose in the face of such provocation for there was among them 'no uncertainty of principle, no vagueness of detail'. But there was 'a voice calling for these definitions of principle and purpose which is, it seems to me, more thrilling and compelling than any of the moving voices with which the troubled air of the world is filled'. This was the voice of the Russian people, to which the people of the United States would want their president to respond 'with utter simplicity and frankness'.

Woodrow Wilson went on to give the precise detail of his 'program of the world's peace' in the famous Fourteen Points, six of which were of general application, three concerned western Europe and five eastern Europe. Diplomacy was henceforth to be open, while navigation of the seas and international trade were to be as free as possible. Armaments were to be kept at the lowest possible level, while all colonial claims would be impartially adjusted with equal weighting for the interests of the populations concerned. In the final point, the president declared that 'a general association of nations must be formed under specific covenants for the purpose of affording mutual guarantees of political independence and territorial integrity to great and small states alike'. With regard to western Europe, France should be given back the 'invaded portions' of Alsace–Lorraine, Belgium should be 'evacuated and restored' and the frontiers of Italy should be readjusted along clear lines of nationality. As far as eastern Europe was concerned, the peoples of Austria–Hungary were to receive the best possible opportunity for autonomous development and those of the Balkan states were to be guaranteed their political and economic independence. The Turkish portions of the Ottoman Empire would be assured 'a secure sovereignty', and an independent Polish state should be set up with access to the sea. In the longest of the Fourteen Points, Wilson gave his response to the voice of the Russian people: all their territory should be evacuated so that they could determine their own political development. Russia would be given 'a sincere welcome into the society of free nations under institutions of her own choosing' as well as every kind of assistance. The American president observed:

> The treatment accorded Russia by her sister nations in the months to come will be the acid test of their good will, of their comprehension of her needs as distinguished from their own interests, and of their intelligent and unselfish sympathy.[28]

PEACE AND WAR IN THE EAST

Before proceeding to see how this 'acid test' proceeded during the decision of peace in the West, let us look at how it was settled in the East. The Russian civil war and the allied intervention, like the October Revolution before them, were closely connected with the questions of war and peace. The White forces dedicated to the overthrow of the Reds formed themselves into a Volunteer Army on the Don in loose alliance with local dissident Cossacks. The new Red Army managed to push the Whites back towards the Caucasus early in 1918, but were then obliged to leave Ukraine in March as a consequence of the treaty reluctantly and hesitatingly arranged by the government with the advancing Germans.

Negotiations between the Soviet Russian Republic and the Central Powers had begun at Brest-Litovsk in December 1917. The first people's commissar for foreign affairs, L. D. Trotsky, was hoping to abandon diplomacy of a traditional kind, and put forward to his comrades a formula of 'neither war nor peace'. Another leading Bolshevik, N. I. Bukharin, was in favour of 'revolutionary war', while Lenin, at first in a minority in the government, held out for what he saw as an appalling necessity, the acceptance of the harsh terms imposed by the Central Powers. After Trotsky and his fellow Soviet delegates delayed acceptance for two months and more, the terms grew even harsher, as the enemy armies resumed their advance and the response from sympathisers in Austria–Hungary and Germany was not forthcoming. Therefore on 3 March 1918 the Russian government contracted in the Treaty of Brest-Litovsk to pull its frontiers back from the Baltic states and Finland as well as from Poland, the Caucasus and Ukraine. At about the same time, Romania pushed the south-eastern frontier back by taking Bessarabia.

The Germans could now give their fuller energies to the spring offensive on the Western Front, while Allied interventionists, who had first come into Russia in the summer officially to help keep the Eastern Front going, now more explicitly gave their support to the White cause. The Reds were additionally weakened by the loss of some left Socialist Revolutionary (SR) collaborators, who believed that Brest-Litovsk revealed the Bolsheviks to be soft on capitalism. To the north and along the Volga, Left and Right SRs attempted to collaborate without lasting success against the Reds, who were opposed also by some thousands of Czecho-Slovak prisoners of war who revolted while being transported along the Trans-Siberian Railway. In the summer of 1918, the first British forces landed in the north, soon seizing the port of Archangel, which became their headquarters. In the Far East, Japanese and British forces were followed by American. In Siberia, where the situation was complicated by the presence of rebellious Czecho-Slovak prisoners of war, the interventionists and the SRs agreed on Admiral Kolchak as supreme commander. To the south, in Ukraine, there was an intervention by France, in Transcaucasia by Britain. There were also a number of Allied secret service operations throughout Russia fortified by considerable amounts of money. Against the intervention forces open and clandestine were ranged the troops of the Red Army and agents of the Cheka (the acronym of the All-Russian Extraordinary Commission for the Suppression of Counter-Revolution, Sabotage and Profiteering, the secret police). Already there were a Red Terror and a White Terror in operation, mass as well as individual murders on both sides, in addition to bitter if sporadic fighting.

Bolshevik fortunes revived late in 1918. The Germans left the Ukraine and the Caucasus at the end of the war in the west in November, and the puppet regime that they had installed there collapsed almost immediately. In the same month, the international proletarian movement appeared to be spreading with the outbreak of revolution in Germany. Beginning with a mutiny in the navy in late October, the revolution soon included workers in northern ports and then in inland cities as well, especially Berlin. At first the republican government that had taken over from the Kaiser found it difficult to resist the opposition, especially from the left-wing radical group known as the Spartakists led by Rosa Luxembourg and Karl Liebknecht. However, Friedrich Ebert, the leader of the principal socialist party, the SPD, gave his support to army regular and irregular units in order to restore stability, and this aim was achieved in January 1919 with the murder of Luxembourg and Liebknecht and the killing of thousands of their supporters.

Back in Soviet Russia, the execution of the promised sweeping reforms was hampered by the Russian civil war and allied intervention. In their place was a hand-to-mouth emergency programme given a title to make a virtue out of necessity – War Communism. In spring 1919, the Whites under Denikin broke into Soviet territory from their base on the River Don, but were pushed back by a more numerous Red Army by the autumn. Kolchak in Siberia was defeated and executed by February 1920. Most of the interventionists had left by the spring. Meanwhile, however, German irregulars were helping the Baltic states to remain independent, and in the spring of 1920 the Poles invaded Ukraine, hoping to widen the boundaries of their newly recreated republic. The Reds counter-attacked and reached Warsaw, yet again reviving hopes for the extension of the Revolution, but then they fell back again. The Treaty of Riga of March 1921 fixed the Russo-Polish frontier considerably to the east of the line suggested by Lord Curzon in an attempt to stem the Red tide in the summer of 1920. By the spring of 1921, the Soviet government had also accepted the independence of Finland, Lithuania, Latvia and Estonia around the Baltic Sea, while still complaining about the incorporation of Bessarabia into Romania down by the Black Sea. Thus the Soviet Republic constituted a much smaller presence in Europe than its tsarist predecessor, although after some further years of fighting in Siberia and elsewhere it was able to restore the previous dimensions of the empire in Asia in time for the creation of the Union of Soviet Socialist Republics (USSR) at the end of 1922. Through superior numbers, better strategy based on its central position and full use of available railways, and a more coherent ideology, the Reds had achieved victory over the Whites and other internal opponents, and foreign interventionists. But the agonies of the years 1917–21 would leave a bitter legacy.

In the West, there would have been widespread and lasting agreement with the conclusion of a British commission of investigation in 1919 that 'Bolshevism in Russia offers to our civilisation no less a menace than did Prussianism, and until it is as ruthlessly destroyed we may expect trouble, strikes, revolutions everywhere'. The situation would grow worse where Bolshevism and Prussianism were in collaboration, assisted by propaganda and secret service activity.[29] Such fears concerning Bolshevism were never fully realised, but they never completely disappeared. On the other hand, at least a little remained of the high hopes held out for the world revolution by many people in Europe and other continents. As for the historians, even those unsympathetic to the October Revolution recognise its outstanding significance: G. H. N. Seton-Watson observed that 'The Bolshevik Revolution was unquestionably one of the greatest events in all human history'; and Richard Pipes suggested that 'a convincing case can be made that the Russian Revolution was the single most consequential event of the twentieth century, whose repercussions have been felt in every corner of the world'.[30]

Indeed, we must not forget the wider setting of the great changes that occurred in Russia in 1917 and the years immediately following. The major European imperial powers had become exhausted in the struggle among themselves, bringing the period of European world dominance closer to its end. The greatest world power from 1918 onwards was the USA, which had moved during the second industrial revolution to first position in economic strength, a position confirmed at the end of the First World War by its assumption of leadership in financial affairs. These basic facts were real enough, although disguised in the short run by the more dramatic nature of the Russian Revolution and by the USA's retreat towards isolation. The USA's full emergence as a superpower would not take place until after the Second World War. Meanwhile, by external force and by internal inclination, the Soviet Union had been cut off from Europe. Some years later than the USA, it too emerged after the Second World War as a superpower, sharing control over Europe with its American rival.

Back in 1918 this rivalry was predicted by, among others, the German-born Swiss essayist and playwright Hermann Kesser, who wrote in October of that year:

> in one deed, the only truly great statesman-like deed, the first signal of world improvement rang out: Wilson announced the League of Nations; he foresaw that without it the peoples could no longer carry on their existence. The second attempt at world improvement ... has been undertaken in Russia, and it is yet too soon to pronounce upon it. ... There can be no question that ... Wilson and Lenin will appear merely as men with different methods. It is certain that mankind must make up its mind either for Wilson or for Lenin.[31]

THE PEACE CONFERENCE

The German revolution had virtually failed by the beginning of 1919, but in March the Third Communist International (the Comintern) held its first congress in Moscow. In an atmosphere of great excitement, it vowed to avoid any repetition of the acceptance of nationalism by members of the Second International in 1914. It condemned the treachery of the SPD and other social democrats in 1918–19, declaring a determination to continue the struggle for the seizure of power by the proletariat. Hopes rose again with the creation of a Soviet republic under Béla Kun in Hungary which managed to continue in existence from the spring to the summer. There were disturbances and threats of disturbances throughout Europe and the wider world in 1919, by the end of which, after several reverses, the Red cause was emerging victorious in Russia itself.

The Allied response was to attempt to keep the Bolshevik regime in quarantine, and then to create a safety zone or *cordon sanitaire* along the still retracted Russian frontiers. Policy towards Soviet Russia in general remained an important background theme to the major task of dealing with Germany at the peace conference, which met from January 1919 to January 1920 in Paris. The location was doubly appropriate because of the proximity of much of the war and the presence of the Allied Command. It also made easier the choice of Premier Clemenceau as chair of the conference rather than Woodrow Wilson, whose idealistic approach and high moral tone aroused the suspicion of his European allies. Clemenceau himself observed that when God Almighty had only Ten Commandments, Wilson's Fourteen Points were too many, and even before the conference convened at least two of these points had needed revision. Germany was informed that the freedom of the seas was a concept open to various interpretations, some of which the Allies could not generally accept. Also, the Allies agreed that no doubt should be allowed to exist about the proposal that invaded territories must be restored as well as evacuated and freed, making it clear that Germany must pay compensation for all damage done to the civilian populations of the Allies and to their property by its aggression on land and sea and from the air.

Therefore, excluded from the Paris conference, the German government had little expectation of being offered a just peace, and its apprehensions were strengthened by the decision of the Allies to maintain their blockade until the peace was concluded. Of course, there was always the threat that the German High Command might resume hostilities to secure more favourable terms, and it was less than co-operative in schemes to relieve the ever wider distress in the confusion that followed the Armistice. So by no means all the blame for the hunger and discomfort could be laid at the door of the Allies. On the other hand, the chances of realisation for Wilson's Fourteen Points, even in their amended form, were slight in the absence not only of Germany but also of the other ex-enemies as well as of the former ally, Russia. Moreover, the American president's express hope that justice would be secured by great and small states alike was also reduced by the dominance over the conference proceedings established almost immediately by a council representing five great powers, the USA, Britain, France, Italy and Japan. Even among the five, the first three were much more influential than the other two in the council.

The Big Three were all subject to domestic pressures. In the USA, the opposition Republicans had gained control of both houses of Congress after the Democratic President Woodrow Wilson had made the mid-term elections of 1918 a vote of confidence for his domestic and foreign policies. He came to Paris against most advice and all precedent – it was the first time that a serving president had left the USA on a journey to Europe – and he had to return home for a month in the middle of the conference to perform necessary executive duties. In Britain, Lloyd George had won a resounding victory in the so-called 'Khaki Election' of December 1918, but amid a storm of such slogans as 'Hang the Kaiser!' and 'Make Germany Pay!' The British prime minister also had to return home on several occasions, and even though London was nowhere near as far from Paris as Washington was, these journeys took toll of his time and concentration. In France, Clemenceau had been given a huge vote of confidence by the Chamber of Deputies, but again to the accompaniment of xenophobic attacks on the Germans. He was also the subject of an assassination attempt that incapacitated him temporarily. In addition to the different backgrounds to their attitudes at Paris, the Big Three faced the difficulty of mutual incomprehension of a linguistic kind. This was smoothed over to some extent by the fact that Clemenceau spoke English as well as French, but nuances of meaning would be lost on him as well as between Woodrow Wilson and Lloyd George, who themselves did not speak quite the same language. Also, to put it bluntly, the Big Three probably did not like each other very much.

Although the principal actors in the drama were accompanied by large retinues of advisers and experts, the range and complexity of the questions demanding a solution were just too much for them. In a speech that he gave at about this time, Lloyd George referred to the town of Kharkov as one of the leaders of the Bolsheviks: none of the statesmen making the great decisions appeared always to be clear about exactly what it was they were deciding. Moreover, while it would have been difficult enough for the conference to conclude the peace if hostilities had completely ceased, war of varying kinds continued to rage not only in Russia, Poland and the Baltic States, but also in many other parts of eastern Europe. While Béla Kun's Red government in Hungary was in combat against both Czechs and Romanians, there were also heated border controversies between the Czechs and the Poles and the Austrians and the Yugoslavs, all of these peoples arguing about the manner in which the old empire of Austria–Hungary should be dismantled against the background of the possible spread of Red revolution or right-wing counter-revolution. A loud accompaniment to these struggles was created by starvation and disease.

Largely for these reasons, the peace conference took upon itself the tasks of relief and reconstruction as well as of peace. Woodrow Wilson's close adviser, Colonel House, observed that the Supreme Economic Council set up at the American president's suggestion 'was especially concerned with the problem of relieving the famine-stricken areas of Eastern Europe – a situation recognised as dangerous to political stability and likely to encourage the spread of Bolshevism'.[32] Special Commissions created by the peace conference dealt with a vast range of subjects including labour legislation and territorial questions. But the most important was that on the League of Nations, whose Covenant was seen by Woodrow Wilson as the solemn embodiment of his Fourteenth Point. A general proposal from Japan for 'the equality of nations' (by implication without regard for race or colour) was turned down. The small powers did not receive equality with the large powers; special allowance was made for the USA's Monroe Doctrine protecting the Americas and for Britain's maritime interests, to give two examples. However, an essential guarantee of lasting peace for all was given in Article X of the Covenant, whereby the contracting parties undertook 'to respect and preserve as against external aggression the territorial integrity and existing political independence of all Members of the League'.[33]

Colonel House observed in 1926 that 'It is only in retrospect that historic events are seen at their just value. Those who are making history sometimes exaggerate the importance of some things and underestimate the importance of others.' At the time, he believed, undue stress had been laid on enemy disarmament and reparations: from the vantage point of 1926 it seemed to him that 'questions like the League of Nations and the security of France reach to the heart of peace and war, and are vital if Western civilisation is to live'.[34] A half-century and more later, after a Second World War and under the shadow of a third, the perspective would change again.

THE TREATIES

Having established the League of Nations, the Treaty of Versailles (or German Treaty) went on to make changes in the frontiers of Germany.

On the western side, Alsace and Lorraine were returned to France, and the Saar river valley was placed under an international commission with its coal mines ceded to France for 15 years, at the end of which there was to be a plebiscite on its future. Belgium and Luxembourg were restored and strengthened, while the Rhineland was demilitarised. To the north, the frontier with Denmark was amended in conformity with a local plebiscite, such as Bismarck had promised in 1866 but never in fact given. Further plebiscites to the east divided Silesia between Germany and Poland, and gave certain districts to East Prussia, but no local agreement was sought for the transfer of other territory to Poland. This included the corridor between East Prussia and Brandenburg giving Poland access to the sea at Danzig or Gdańsk, which was made a free city administered by the League except for its foreign relations, which would be controlled by Poland. The city of Memel or Klaipeda and its hinterland were ceded to the Allies but were to be handed over in 1924 to Lithuania, which actually seized them in 1923. Altogether, the German Republic lost about 6 million of the population of the former empire, although less than half of these were actually German. At least as serious was the loss of iron and other mineral deposits. Germany was also deprived of all its overseas colonies, which were divided among the Allies as mandates of the League of Nations: those in tropical Africa went to France, Belgium, Britain and the Union of South Africa, those in the Pacific went mostly to Japan, Australia and New Zealand. In addition, Germany lost all its overseas property and concessions, even German missionaries coming under the complete earthly control of the mandatories. (The territories of the former Turkish Empire were placed in a different category of mandate, Britain being made responsible for seeing Iraq, Transjordania and Palestine through to eventual independence while France was to do the same for Syria and Lebanon.) The German army was reduced to 100,000 men with appropriate equipment, the navy to half a dozen battleships and an assortment of other craft, enough for coastal defence and no more, with submarines strictly forbidden.

Moreover, there were severe moral and financial penalties. Provision was made for the trial of William II, the former German emperor, for a supreme offence against international morality and the sanctity of treaties. In fact, 'Kaiser Bill' sought refuge in the neutral Netherlands, which refused to hand him over and allowed him to live on there until he was 'liberated' by the invading German army at the beginning of the Second World War shortly before his death. More widely, arrangements were drawn up for the trial of Germans 'accused of having committed acts in violation of the laws and customs of war', and a list was compiled of about 100 such criminals. In fact, only a few of them were brought to trial and even fewer were convicted by the Germans themselves, who refused the claims of the Allies for extradition. When Field-Marshal von Hindenburg, one of the 'war criminals' on the original list, was elected president of the Republic in 1925, there was no formal protest from the Allies. If the Germans saved their necks, their pride and their pockets were certainly hurt by the famous or infamous Article 231, which stated:

> The Allied and Associated Governments affirm and Germany accepts the responsibility of Germany and her allies for causing all the loss and damage to which the Allied and Associated Governments and their nationals have been subjected as a consequence of the War imposed upon them by the aggression of Germany and her allies.[35]

Payments in cash and in kind were to rub salt into the deep wound of national humiliation.

The payment of reparations was in fact not fixed until 1921. The total was to be £66,000 million plus interest, but it was modified later in the 1920s and abandoned completely in the early 1930s. Similarly, war guilt was to be reduced during the same period to such an extent that most of it was transferred to the consciences of the Allies, who were to lean over backwards to appease Germany in the middle and later 1930s. With the longer perspective at their disposal, at least some historians were arguing a further 40 years on that the Treaty of Versailles was nowhere near as harsh as the German Republic's representatives coldly argued at the time and Hitler would claim with great heat soon afterwards. The territorial losses inflicted on Germany in defeat were far smaller than those that it would have imposed on its neighbours in the event of victory. Moreover, since most of the fighting had not been on German soil and the material damage had been inflicted mostly on the Allies, especially France, it was only right that Germany should pay compensation. And it was not the burden of reparations that later caused the Weimar Republic its financial problems so much as its own financial policies. As for the moral opprobrium heaped on the Germans, this was not so much at the insistence of the Allied statesmen as at that of their respective public opinions, formed not only by war propaganda but also by decades of aggressive pre-war German nationalism. Perhaps, then, for greater effect, the Treaty of Versailles should either have been more lenient or much more disciplinary, reducing Germany permanently to its pre-imperial fragmentation and pre-industrial agrarianism.[36]

Regarding the second of these alternatives, the South African leader General Smuts spoke for many when he put what seemed to him a couple of 'quite clear and elementary' points to Lloyd George in March 1919:

1.   We cannot destroy Germany without destroying Europe;
2.   We cannot save Europe without the co-operation of Germany.

But the destruction of Germany was nevertheless being prepared in Paris, and Smuts feared 'that the Paris Conference may prove one of the historic failures of the world; that the statesmen connected with it will return to their countries broken, discredited men, and that the Bolshevists will reap where they have sown'. What had become of Wilson's Fourteen Points as Germany was about to be dismembered? And had not the Spartakist Revolt demonstrated that a weakened Germany would be a prey to anarchy? Who could protect Poland, Bohemia and Romania against the Hungarian and Russian Reds? In the view of Smuts, Germany should be neither impoverished nor disarmed: he believed that it should be made to join the League of Nations from the beginning, and that 'her appeasement now may have the effect of turning her into a bulwark against the oncoming Bolshevism of Eastern Europe'.[37]

In March 1919, Lloyd George himself was thinking of leniency towards Germany, until a 'round-robin' telegram of 8 April sent by 370 MPs caused him to stiffen his attitude. But Smuts, Lloyd George and other like-minded statesmen were to have their views at least indirectly vindicated in the series of treaties that dealt largely with eastern Europe. We take these in turn as they followed the Treaty of Versailles, which was reluctantly signed by German representatives on 28 June 1919. The Treaty of Saint-Germain was concluded with the heart of the old Habsburg Empire – Austria – on 10 September 1919. Austria lost Bohemia and other provinces to the newly created Czechoslovakia; Bosnia and other provinces to the enlarged Serbia that became Yugoslavia; and further areas to Italy and Romania. The new Austria possessed only a quarter of the territory and a fifth of the population of its predecessor, and was expressly forbidden union with Germany. On 27 November 1919 the Treaty of Neuilly was agreed with Bulgaria, which approximately resumed its immediately pre-war shape. On 4 June 1920 the Treaty of Trianon was arranged some months after the fall of Béla Kun's Red Republic with a more respectable Hungary, which nevertheless lost a vast amount of land and people to Romania. Romania also benefited from the determination of the Allies not to allow the blue Danube to become Red.

These treaties together with those between the Baltic states and Poland on the one hand and Soviet Russia on the other created a safety zone (*cordon sanitaire*) against Bolshevism in the years immediately following the conclusion of the First World War in eastern Europe. A more difficult problem in the immediate vicinity, however, was that of the stability of the south-east, where the collapse of the Ottoman Empire was bringing to a head a whole range of difficulties: how to accommodate a resurgent Greece and other movements in the Balkans as well as Arab nationalism and Jewish Zionism around the corner of the Mediterranean? It was not until Greek and Turkish conflict had come to an end and several frontier and other questions had been at least temporarily settled with the new nationalist Turkish government of Kemal Ataturk that the Treaty of Lausanne was signed on 24 July 1923. Turkey was now firmly settled in Anatolia in Asia and in Constantinople on the other side of the Bosporus with a considerable European hinterland. Meanwhile, the extensive kingdom of Saudi Arabia had taken shape. There was agitation for the independence of other Arab states, while Zionists exerted pressure for 'the establishment in Palestine of a national home for the Jewish people' as promised in the Balfour Declaration of 1917. Thus, in the Middle East as in Europe, the peace arranged in the years following the First World War was to lead to later conflict.

12

THROUGH DEPRESSION AND ISOLATION TOWARDS ANOTHER WORLD WAR, 1921–1939

THE ARRIVAL OF 'NORMALCY'

In the decade or so that followed Versailles and the immediately accompanying treaties, relations between European states and with other powers beyond Europe were essentially shaped by the agreements made in the years 1919–21. Even though the greatest world power, the USA, did not sign the treaties or enter the League of Nations, in spite of all Woodrow Wilson's valiant efforts, American interest in maintaining post-war stability remained constant. In July 1921, President Harding signalled his desire to support what he called 'normalcy' by inviting Japan, China, Britain, France, Italy, Belgium, the Netherlands and Portugal to a conference in Washington on the limitation of naval armaments with special reference to the Pacific and the Far East. After a series of negotiations from November 1921 to February 1922, some significant treaties were signed. A ratio was instituted of $5:5:3$ for the capital or larger warship tonnage of the principal naval powers, the USA, Britain and Japan respectively. The 'Open Door' in China was reasserted through a collective guarantee of its independence and the withdrawal of Japan from its foothold in Shantung. However, the Soviet government protested vigorously at its exclusion from the discussions in Washington, as well as at the continued presence of

Japanese troops in Vladivostok, which they did not leave until October 1922. From the strategic point of view, the Washington conference did for the seaborne concept of Mahan what Versailles and other treaties did for the land-based idea of Mackinder.

Beyond the other extremity of the Heartland in Europe, a conference assembled in Genoa in the spring of 1922 to discuss the renewal of relations between Soviet Russia and the other European states along with some non-European (although the United States declined an invitation). The principal outcome was indirect and unwelcome to the former Allies: the signing on 6 April at nearby Rapallo of a separate treaty by the two major powers kept out of the League, Soviet Russia and Weimar Germany. These two pariah states had already moved some distance towards reconciliation with a provisional agreement in the spring of 1921. Now, dealing mainly with diplomatic recognition and economic readjustment, they laid the foundations for mutually advantageous recovery.

However, in 1922 Germany was unable to do anything to resist pressure resulting from default on payment of reparations. Then, at the beginning of 1923, when French troops occupied the industrial region of the Ruhr, there could be no active resistance except through sabotage. More than 100 Germans were killed, several thousands were imprisoned and about 140,000 deported, while reparations to the value of millions of gold marks were extracted. To ease this difficult problem, another conference was held in London to approve and put into effect a plan worked out by an international committee under the chairmanship of the American General Charles G. Dawes. The basis of the Dawes Plan of April 1924 was the extension to Germany of a loan of 800 million gold marks to assure currency stability and to finance essential deliveries in kind. As soon as the plan was adopted, the French began to make arrangements for the evacuation of the Ruhr, and this was completed about a year later.

By now more negotiations were in progress concerning European security, this time culminating in a meeting at Locarno, a resort town on the shores of Lake Maggiore in Switzerland. A final Protocol signed in October 1925 comprised what was called the Locarno Pact and consisted of four main parts. The first was the Rhine Guarantee Pact assuring the inviolability of the German–Franco-Belgian frontiers and reaffirming the demilitarisation of the Rhineland. Secondly, there were

Conventions between Germany on the one hand and France, Belgium, Poland and Czechoslovakia on the other regarding the maintenance of general peace. Thirdly, there were Treaties of Guarantee between Czechoslovakia and Poland and France concerning mutual security. Fourthly, there was a collective note regarding adjustments of the Covenant of the League of Nations with a view to the admission of Germany into the League. Britain and Italy were to act as guarantors of the commitments undertaken by the other European states regarding Germany's western frontier, but France was left by herself as guarantor of Germany's eastern frontier. On the whole, the success of Locarno was an illusion: the question of Germany's western and eastern frontiers had by no means been fully solved.

As for the League of Nations, although Germany became a member in 1926 and joined Britain, France, Italy and Japan as a permanent member of the Council, the USA continued to remain aloof and the USSR was still excluded. However, the USSR and Germany reaffirmed the Treaty of Rapallo in 1926. In 1927, the USA responded positively to an overture from the French foreign minister, Aristide Briand, suggesting their mutual renunciation of war; indeed, Secretary of State Frank B. Kellogg proposed that all nations be invited to join in. Several of them accepted the invitation in August 1928 when the Kellogg–Briand Pact or Pact of Paris was drawn up, condemning and renouncing recourse to war as an instrument of national policy or a solution of international dispute. Quite soon, no fewer than 65 states including the USSR had agreed to outlaw war. As in earlier agreements, the USA insisted that the Monroe Doctrine concerning the Americas would have to be observed and Britain made a similar reservation concerning the security of the British Empire.

Generally speaking, the 1920s were coming to an end with widespread high hopes for the preservation of peace. Another meeting concerning reparations presided over by the American banker Owen D. Young in Paris in the summer of 1929 reduced the scale of payments to about a quarter of the total first demanded, while the British government argued for the end of the Allied occupation of the Rhineland. The French minister for war, André Maginot, received initial approval for the construction of the defensive line that was to bear his name. And in central Europe, the so-called 'Little Entente' of Czechoslovakia, Romania and Yugoslavia consolidated itself in an alliance of May 1929 to maintain stability after a series of earlier agreements stretching back to 1920. At first, they had been concerned principally with possible threats from Austria and Hungary, now they were more concerned with Germany and the Soviet Union. But there was no cause for immediate alarm, either in Europe or in the wider world. However, the deepening of the global economic crisis in 1929 was to make a disturbing impact on international relations all too soon.

This is not to say that European ships of state sailed smoothly through the 1920s, their passengers celebrating the return of peace in a non-stop Charleston. Certainly there was dancing in the streets when the good news came in 1918. And while homes fit for heroes were not built in the quantities that the returning soldiers would have liked, there were some positive steps forward such as the extension of the right to vote, especially to women, in the United Kingdom and elsewhere. Some long-standing problems were given a solution that may not have been permanent but was certainly less temporary than what had been achieved previously: for example, the partition of Ireland in 1921 between the Free State and Ulster. The newest of the major European democracies, the German Weimar Republic, managed to survive a series of crises, as did the Republic of France, even though there was little if anything left of the social harmony of the early war years. No country escaped grave problems, even Britain, which possessed the oldest and probably the most stable of parliamentary regimes, encountering a major problem in the General Strike of 1926. More generally, it experienced considerable difficulties in adapting to the decline of the Liberal Party and the rise of the Labour Party.

Meanwhile, elsewhere in Europe the general tendency was away from democracy. Taking advantage of some of the errors made in the war and insults supposedly handed out in the immediate peace, Mussolini rose to power in Italy after a march on Rome in 1922. His Fascist government soon eliminated vestiges of political opposition. According to the new leader, 'The Doctrine of Fascism'

> is opposed to classical Liberalism, which arose from the necessity of reacting against absolutism, and which brought its historical purpose to an end when the State was transformed into the conscience and will of the people ... Outside the State there can be neither individuals nor groups ... Therefore Fascism is opposed to Socialism,

which confines the movement of history within the class struggle and ignores the unity of classes established in one economic and moral reality in the State ... Fascism desires the State to be strong, organic and at the same time founded on a wide popular basis. The Fascist State has also claimed for itself the field of economics and, through the corporative, social and educational institutions which it has created, the meaning of the State reaches out to and includes the farthest off-shoots; and within the State framed in their respective organizations, there revolve all the political, economic and spiritual forces of the nation.[1]

Agreement with Mussolini's strong-arm methods if not necessarily with all his ideas spread throughout many sections of Europe, especially the south-west, the centre and the east. In Spain there was General Primo de Rivera, proclaiming himself dictator in 1923 with the support of the king, the army and a substantial section of big business. In Portugal, with similar backing, General Carmona carried out a coup in 1926. In Poland, Marshal Pilsudski assumed supreme power in 1926 and developed 'a secular authoritarian system of government of a non-fascist type',[2] while in Hungary, Admiral Horthy continued his land-locked dominance. The tendency towards authoritarianism under various guises was also noticeable in Austria and Yugoslavia, the Baltic and the Balkan states.

Most threatening of all developments for many observers were those to be seen not on the right but on the left, in the Union of Soviet Socialist Republics, which was set up officially in December 1922. By that time, some kind of 'normalcy' had arrived in Soviet Russia with the introduction in the spring of 1921 of the New Economic Policy (NEP). Before then, the title War Communism had more than flattered the series of improvisations and requisitions making up the government's policies during the years of the Russian civil war and Allied intervention. At least a few enthusiasts had argued that virtue could be made out of necessity: for example, if there was no money around, the transition could immediately be made to the exchange of goods in a co-operative manner without the use of cash. As it turned out, however, War Communism consisted of little more than forcing peasants to give up their grain and other produce to feed the army and the towns. Lenin argued that by the spring of 1921, with peace returning and considerable evidence of popular discontent, the neces-sity had arisen for a peasant Brest-Litovsk. One step backwards must be taken for two forwards. Under NEP, farmers would now be allowed to sell surpluses on the open market once they had paid a tax in kind, that is, made a delivery to the state of a proportion of their foodstuffs. Trade and manufacture would be freed from most restrictions, although the government would retain control of the 'commanding heights' of international commerce and heavy industry.

Worn down by wounds and illness, Lenin was out of action for some time before his death at the beginning of 1924, and his place was increasingly taken by the general secretary of the Communist Party, Joseph Stalin. Diplomatic relations were restored between the USSR and Britain in 1924, about three years after a trade agreement between the two powers. But relations soon deteriorated, official contacts being broken off in 1927 amid some talk even of war. The scare was real enough in Moscow and London too. By this time, the Soviet Union had been recognised by a number of other European states, and had signed non-aggression and neutrality treaties with most of its neigh-bours. Nevertheless, as Stalin's hold over the party became stronger, apprehension about the nature of the Soviet Union became keener. The 'normalcy' of which President Harding had spoken was turning out to be a strange phenomenon indeed.

THE DEPRESSION AND THE USA

Discussion of the Depression of 1929 and succeeding years is some-times set against a background assumption that the norm for most people in the industrialising world had always been prosperity. In fact, the reverse was nearer the case, even in those periods when the panics, crashes and slumps of earlier years had been overcome. Still the basic problem remained the same, the maldistribution of wealth, too few rich and too many poor. As ever, if the whole world were included in the discussion, the gap would appear even wider, the imbalance even greater. There were some special features to the situation in 1929, nevertheless, most of which arose from the First World War and its immediate aftermath. The great conflict had accelerated the emer-gence of the USA as the world's leading financial power while the major states of Europe spent their treasure in attempting to blow each other to bits. American loans went to all the major belligerents, and more were extended after the Armistice of 1918. The problem then became compounded as the passionate desire to make Germany pay led to the imposition of reparations which Germany soon found it impossible to keep up with, and so once again the dollar had to step in. A vicious financial triangle arose, as the USA lent money to Germany to make its reparations to Britain and France so that they in turn could send at least some of the money they owed back to the USA.

Therefore, when frenzied speculation on the American stock market came to an abrupt end on Black Friday, 23 October 1929, the echoes of the Wall Street Crash were heard over both the Atlantic and the Pacific. Instead of attempting to solve through international co-operation what was undoubtedly an international problem, the major powers turned in upon themselves. President Herbert C. Hoover welcomed the increase of the American protective tariff to a record level in 1930, and blamed the Depression on the lax monetary standards of Europe. He became all the more convinced that the root of the trouble lay beyond him and outside the USA as the financial problems of Europe intensified. In the summer of 1930, he proposed a postponement for one year on all payments of reparations and all repayments of inter-governmental loans. While Britain and Germany were quick to agree, France, which had not been consulted and was suspicious of the proposal, delayed acceptance, and the general predicament, especially of Germany, grew worse. Now the medicine was not strong enough to cure the ill, and standstill agreements meant retreat. By the end of 1931 every major power except the USA, France and Italy had followed Britain's abandonment of the gold standard. International trade, like international finance, was grinding to a halt.

There ensued in 1932 an attempt at a solution of the kind that had sometimes worked in the 1920s, an international conference, this time at Lausanne in Switzerland. Britain and France were in the end persuaded that Germany could no longer be made to pay, and that reparations should be more drastically reduced than before. However, they made the proviso that their own war debts must be scaled down accordingly, which was too much for the American Congress and president to accept in the climate of the times. Consequently, delay led to default, distrust to bitterness and recrimination. Hoover now agreed to yet another international meeting, the London Economic

Conference that convened in the summer of 1933. But by this time he had been replaced as president by Franklin D. Roosevelt. Hoover had been hoping for restoration of the gold standard, but Roosevelt would not accept such a proposal or an alternative proposal for the stabilisation of international currency through the replacement of gold by the dollar. The new president denounced the 'old fetishes of the so-called international bankers' and withdrew American representatives from the conference. International financial co-operation of a regular kind now came to an end.

The USA under Roosevelt did not give up the rest of the world completely. By the summer of 1934, after much presidential arm-twisting, the Congress passed a law providing that reciprocal trade agreements could be drawn up with other nations in such a manner that tariff barriers could be lowered by as much as a half. Considerable use was made throughout the 1930s of the new law, in Latin America and elsewhere. However, for the most part, Roosevelt's famous New Deal was in favour of internal consumption only, neither for exports, nor especially for imports. This trading reduction not only damaged economies in Europe but also in other parts of the world, not least in Asia. Japan especially had depended heavily on the American market, in which, for example, most of its exported silk was sold. The northern part of Honshu, the main island, was hit especially hard, and its distress was made worse by a crop failure in 1931. With restricted opportunities for emigration and other peaceful means of relief, the Japanese looked to a more aggressive solution for their problems, beginning with their conquest of Manchuria in September 1931. They saw no reason to change their policies as the decade wore on.

GERMANY AND THE RISE OF HITLER

In Europe also, the Depression brought harsh remedies for severe problems, especially in Germany, and even more, if less directly, in the Soviet Union. In Germany, the middle and later 1920s had not been the most settled of periods before the Depression, but compared with the turbulent years immediately following the Armistice of 1918, they had been peaceful enough. Attempts from both the Left and the Right to seize power did not get very far. While the Communist Party (KPD) enjoyed solid if minority support, the Nazi Party (National Socialist

German Workers' Party or NSDAP) enjoyed no more than a minimum of success. Although, like the Fascists under Mussolini in Italy, the Nazis under Hitler had borrowed some of the Left's ideas to gain followers among the lower orders of society on behalf of the Right, their message at first made little headway. However, the economic difficulties that arose at the end of the 1920s changed the political situation both considerably and quickly, with the NSDAP acquiring support from two unexpected directions. First, some of those who followed the plough began to adopt the Nazi emblem of the swastika and warmed to the Nazi idealisation of rural life as decline in agricultural prices brought impoverishment to many peasant farmers. Secondly, mutual discontent as far as the Young Plan for payment of reparations was concerned brought about an alliance of opposition to it between the Nazis and the conservative Nationalists, whose leader Hugenburg also owned a large newspaper chain which gave extremist views wide publicity. Now civil servants, teachers and tradesmen joined with the middle class in the alliance, particularly in the Protestant north and east. They tended to share the view of the peasant farmers that they were becoming superfluous; therefore they also possessed a keen sense of grievance. Meanwhile, the cutting edge of the Nazi movement, the SA (*Sturmabteilung*) stormtroopers, was mostly made up from the vast ranks of the unemployed, bully boys not just working class but also petty bourgeois in origin. A further source of the Nazi Party's energy was its youth: 70 per cent of those joining it between 1930 and 1933 were under 40, more than 40 per cent were under 30. The Hitler Youth movement founded in 1926 was also of increasing importance, although its most rapid growth in membership came in the year after the seizure of power, from just over 100,000 to more than 3.5 million from 1933 to 1934. The leader (*Führer*) himself was comparatively young for a politician – he was not yet 45 years old when he became chancellor – and the average age of his party's elite was lower.

Although the NSDAP's support came mostly from outsiders, there were nevertheless some important elements in its appeal and its success that came from inside German traditions. These included vague and even artificial memories of a Golden Age, whether in the nineteenth century at the time of the Second Reich or back as far as the ninth century and the First Reich of Charlemagne, even stretching back to a prehistoric folk past. Then, there was the love of ceremonial – flags, uniforms and parades – involving above all the heroic leader who embodied nationalist aspirations and the purity of the race. Moreover, the rapid pace of Germany's modernisation process in the 50 years or so before 1914, as well as the joys and agonies of the war period, 1914–18, gave the emotions of its superficially stolid people both intensity and instability. None of this, however, it must be repeated and emphasised, would have become as explicit and dominant without the economic crisis. This brought Hitler's movement the support of many great land-owners and of some big businessmen, especially from the coal and iron industries: such groups would not otherwise have been able to sink their suspicions of some of the Nazi ideas and some of the SA actions. Much the same might be said of the army, except that at least some of its officers had seen positive advantages accruing from association with the SA: certainly, the army helped to prepare the way for the Nazi takeover in June 1932 when it suppressed the civilian government in the province of Prussia, where Socialists, Communists and others were holding out for the preservation of the Weimar system.

Even at this stage, power was by no means there just for the asking: a gamble still had to be taken. In the presidential election of the spring of 1932, ex-corporal Hitler gave Marshal von Hindenburg an insubordinately close contest. The ensuing parliamentary elections in the summer gave the Nazi Party more than a third of the total vote. The Communists also made gains and the Socialists held firm, but most of the other parties were in disarray. Strikes and violence in Berlin led to more parliamentary elections in which the Communist Party continued its rise but the Nazis fell back to just under a third of the total vote. Hitler realised that the moment was approaching when a bold move would have to be made to save Germany from Bolshevism by ruling it through Nazism. At first, he demonstrated his political skill, or possibly just his fanatical determination, in his refusal to compromise. Conservative groups in agriculture, industry and politics came round to agreeing that Hitler could be controlled, that restrained right-wing revolution was infinitely preferable to a cataclysm giving control to the Communists. Thus at the beginning of 1933, the Nazi leader was made chancellor in close association with Hugenburg and the Nationalists.

Again, Hitler did not play for safety, but staked everything on a concerted move to overthrow the Weimar Republic and to establish his own dictatorship. He first killed the old regime with its own weapons, applying its emergency regulations for the preservation of order in general to avert an alleged Communist 'plot' in particular. This was discovered in what was actually the deranged action of one individual, the burning down of the Reichstag building. Communists were now ejected from the parliament and Hitler manipulated the other deputies to get for himself four years of supreme power in which he could issue laws without their consent. In this way all the opposition parties soon found themselves prohibited. Now, the Führer took another bold step, this time against his own most vigorous supporters, the SA brownshirts. In the 'Night of the Long Knives' at the end of June 1934, he stabbed these Nazi zealots in the back and made himself the close associate of the more respectable regular army. Irregular duties of suppressing opposition passed to the SS (*Schutzstaffel*) protection squads and the Gestapo (*Geheime Staatspolizeiamt*) secret police, who were virtually united in their sinister activities under a cloak of legality. With power assured, Hitler and the Nazis gave full voice on radio and film as well as in the press to their assertions of Aryan superiority and the subhuman inferiority of Jews, Slavs and Bolsheviks. They denounced this vile trinity as deserving despite and destruction, so that the master race might live in the space and comfort it deserved.

Before the drive for such *Lebensraum*, however, there had to be economic recovery in the cramped conditions of Germany within the frontiers imposed by the much hated Treaty of Versailles. Fortunately for the Nazis, the industrial base established before the First World War had not been totally destroyed. They were helped further by the fact that an upturn had begun and schemes for accelerating it had been composed during the last years of the much despised Weimar period. This led to a degree of comparative prosperity although there was no 'economic miracle' during the years following 1933. How much of this recovery can be directly attributed to Nazi policies is difficult to assess. Hitler declared in 1936 that 'German business will understand the new economic tasks, or it will prove incapable in this modern age, in which a Soviet government erects a gigantic plan, of existing any further'.[3] But the Nazi Four Year plans never in fact approached the all-embracing scope of their Soviet Five Year counterparts, since they represented essentially a development of state control of the economy as practised in Weimar and imperial Germany. German banking and business were not the tools of Hitler and his associates any more than, as has some-times been alleged, the reverse was the case. Finance and industry could profit on terms that were partly their own and partly the government's, with priorities overlapping. The search for autarky (self-sufficiency), which could be achieved only by expanding the Reich's frontiers, was not unwelcome to at least some economic interests, which were often prepared to accept forced labour and other compulsory means of achieving the desired end. As for the farmers, they were to find that the glorification of their way of life in Nazi ideology was no guarantee of prosperity, while the workers remained widely discontented. But for the time being, even after 1936 when recovery was sufficiently attained for a concerted drive on rearmament to begin, there was at least some butter along with the guns, for skilled labour in particular.

THE SOVIET UNION AND THE STALIN REVOLUTION

Meanwhile, as what Hitler called the 'fight against Jewish world Bolshevisation' was being prepared, there was no lack of awareness of the approaching attack in the principal target for his denunciations and diatribes, the Soviet Union. In a famous speech at the beginning of 1931, Stalin talked of the need for the Soviet regime to overcome Russia's historic backwardness, declaring that: 'To slacken the tempo would mean falling behind. And those who fall behind get beaten. But we do not want to get beaten. No, we refuse to be beaten. ... We are fifty or a hundred years behind the advanced countries. We must make good this distance in ten years. Either we do it, or they crush us.'[4] Just over ten years later, Hitler launched 'Barbarossa', the codename for the invasion of the Soviet Union by the Third Reich taken from one of the rulers of the First Reich. Certainly, there was a long historical dimension to the struggle between Slav and Teuton, as both Stalin and Hitler each in his own way understood, just as they both knew it had taken on a new and more dangerous dimension with the First World War and the Russian Revolution that could not be overridden by their temporary alliance of convenience at Rapallo in 1922.

An even more recent event of significance for the Soviet Union as well as Germany was the Depression. True, Stalin with his policy of 'socialism in one country' was attempting to achieve autarky within the Soviet Union's frontiers while Hitler's similar attempt could not be successful on such terms – there was never a 'Nazism within one country', since Germany was more closely integrated with the global capitalist economy than was the Soviet Union. Nevertheless, the level of transformation indicated in the First Five Year Plan begun in 1928 could not be reached without active participation in international trade. Therefore the collapse of that trade in the years following 1929 struck Soviet hopes a severe blow, especially since prices for grain, their chief export, declined sharply in comparison with those for the most important import, machines: by 1930 twice as much grain as in 1928 had to be exported per unit of machinery imported. Worse was to come, for although the agricultural year of 1930–1 brought nearly 6 million tons of grain exports, the highest total for one year since the Revolution, the price that could be obtained for wheat in the world market at the beginning of 1931 was little more than a third of that obtainable at the beginning of 1930, while the prices of machines and other imports fell much less steeply.[5] If German autarky was a deliberate policy, Soviet autarky was largely an enforced necessity.

Throughout the 1920s, foreign trade had not produced as much capital as Stalin and his associates would have liked, and the debate about whether or not to continue the NEP had been conducted around the central question of how to extract the maximum profit from the peasants: should the individual farm be tolerated, encouraged or discouraged, even eliminated? The question was brought to a head when NEP was abandoned and the First Five Year Plan was launched in 1928, when the delivery of grain fell somewhat short of what was expected. The decision was soon taken to force the pace of the collectivisation of agriculture along with the elimination of the kulaks, those who employed their fellow peasants or were deemed to exploit them in some other way. And so, at the same time as the workers of the industrialised societies were losing their jobs in the Depression, the rank-and-file inhabitants of the Soviet Union were being subjected to an even worse fate. During the years of the First and Second Five Year Plans, 1928–37, a large number of Soviet citizens lost their lives and an even larger number lost their homes, many of the surviving peasants moving to the towns, whose population more than doubled as that of the rural areas declined. The hunger, misery and suffering involved in this vast social change defy description, but there was voluntary as well as compulsory sacrifice, some real 'labour heroism' as well as some invented. Towns like Magnitogorsk in the Urals and Komsomolsk on the Amur River in the Far East were built virtually from scratch, and many factories were constructed to produce tractors and trucks, and increasingly tanks and planes as well. By around 1937 the basis of an industrialised economy had been created, even if the problems of agriculture remained less than completely solved: it was even more difficult than training a peasant to work at a lathe to persuade him to exchange the individual family farm for a share in a collective *kolkhoz*.

The scale and pace of the Soviet achievement were remarkable enough; even more significant perhaps was its nature. The state bank (*Gosbank*) closely supervised all financial operations and the responsibility for the control of the economy as a whole was taken by *Gosplan*, the state planning commission, which co-ordinated the activities of a number of commissariats. This is not to say that the First and Second Five Year Plans were an unmitigated success. Bribery and corruption, much waste and inefficiency, a considerable amount of incompetence and even some deliberate sabotage (if not as much as the government asserted) were the companions of harsh methods in the achievement of ever-increasing production figures. And the growth could be made to appear all the more remarkable because it was from a very low level: the more mature capitalist industrial economies were experiencing their difficulties at a considerably higher level.

THE REST OF EUROPE

Like the Soviet Union, perhaps even more so, most of the states of eastern Europe depended on the export of agricultural produce for their livelihood, and rapidly falling prices brought huge problems in their wake. There was a large amount of industrial and even more agricultural distress and unrest, a persistent and often bloody struggle. The response of governments could be as harsh as that of Stalin and Hitler, with much repression and no little persecution. As for the excuses given for such inhumanity, the ideological basis was generally more akin to Nazism than Communism, with denunciations of impure and alien elements in society. These were quite often Jewish, although by no means invariably so since all the states of eastern Europe had substantial minorities living within the frontiers often artificially created at the Paris peace conference or soon afterwards – yet another cause of inflamed passions. Along with the diatribes against the Jews and other 'outsiders' went celebrations of the dominant nationality, including appeals to some kind of romantic past: heroes from the classical period or even before were given biographies embellished or even invented in order to make these peoples love themselves and hate their neighbours more.

In Poland, Marshal Piłsudski was laid to rest at the side of the kings of Poland in 1935, and his adherents argued among themselves about the succession and the meaning of his ideas. They could at least agree that worker and peasant unrest should be suppressed as well as German, Belorussian and Ukrainian nationalism. The Hungarian leader from the end of the Red Republic in 1919 to nearly the end of the Second World War in 1944, Admiral Horthy, dispensed a view of the superiority of his people in the Danube valley and persecuted left-wing and alien elements. Considerable sympathy for Nazi Germany developed while antipathy towards Czechoslovakia and Romania continued. As the Arrow-Cross movement grew up in Hungary, the equally pro-Nazi Iron Guard legion built up its strength in Romania. There, King Carol had destroyed the political parties, at the same time silencing dissident national minorities: Russians in Bessarabia and Hungarians in Transylvania, for example. And the Romanians liked to think that the Danube was theirs rather than belonging to the Hungarians or other neighbours. Other royal dictatorships with Nazi sympathies were established in Bulgaria by King Boris and in Yugoslavia by King Alexander, although they argued about frontiers with each other as well as with Greece. Alexander had the additional problem of opposition to his pro-Serb policies: he was assassinated by an extreme Croatian nationalist in 1934, and his cousin Paul became chief regent. An exception to what was almost an invariably authoritarian eastern European rule was comparatively democratic Czechoslovakia, from 1919 until the end of 1935 under the firm but not harsh guidance of President Thomas Masaryk. Czechoslovakia was the only state of eastern Europe to have an agrarian minority rather than majority, although this did not help it to avoid the impact of the Depression, which hit as hard as anywhere in the Sudetenland, where many of the 3.5 million strong German national minority were ready to listen to pro-Nazi propaganda. The less developed Slovaks were also especially discontented with their lot at the other end of the country, which was dominated from the centre by the Czechs. Meanwhile, Austria in central Europe was reeling under the impact of the Depression and becoming ripe for Nazi takeover.

To the north, authoritarian governments were to be found in the Baltic states, but the Scandinavian countries gained something of a reputation for having devised a middle socialist way between Communist and Nazi extremes. This is not to say that Norway, Denmark and Sweden, as well as Finland, did not have problems in the 1930s with their economies, or on occasion with their social stability. Much the same might be said of Britain and France, Belgium and the Netherlands in the north-west of Europe. Again, it must be emphasised, this is to speak comparatively. Those on the spot would have found it difficult to remain confident that difficulties arising from the Depression in the north-west of Europe were less serious than in many other parts of the continent. But a glance over the Rhine could have been reassuring, equally across the Alps and the Pyrenees. For while Hitler was consolidating the Nazi hold on power, Mussolini was using the excuse of economic problems to entrench his Fascist state. Spaniards who shared his beliefs were submitting the republic newly created in 1931 to persistent assaults and Dr Salazar was moving from economic reform to the establishment of dictatorship in Portugal after taking over from General Carmona in 1929.

Generally speaking, the Depression had made a deep impression on Europe and the wider world. True, many difficulties were already apparent before 1929, but there can be no doubt that the Wall Street Crash and all the other ramifications of financial and commercial collapse made them more onerous and the appropriate solutions appear more extreme. A further consequence was a move away from the international approach to serious ills towards attempts at curing them within the national framework. Depression had led to isolation: the next stage of Europe's agony through the 1930s would be breakdown.

THE 1930s: THE USA AND THE USSR

In the 1930s, Europe's place in the world was indeed less prominent than it had been a half-century or so previously, partly because of the rise to world power of the USA and to a lesser extent of Japan, partly because of the exclusion of the Soviet Union. But even thinking

Europeans, among whom must be numbered at least some statesmen, still tended to look inwards. According to a later analysis, the British historian R. H. Tawney 'found the Russian Revolution interesting; toward America he was . . . vaguely curious, open-minded and a shade condescending. But neither country impinged upon Tawney's Britain, which he saw as a fixed "middle kingdom".' And Pertinax, a reputable French journalist of the period, has been quoted to the effect that: 'I knew well and understood the international politics of Europe, but going beyond Germany one arrived at the Soviet Union, and it was indefinite, while towards the west there were the United States, and they were another world.'[6] Generally speaking, the outlook of European statesmen had not adapted to changing times. They did not see sufficiently clearly that the 1930s were not pre-1914, and they contributed to the arrival of the Second World War by attempting to avoid the mistakes that had led to the First.

That is far from the whole story, for the two great figures on the horizon imperfectly understood by Tawney, Pertinax and their contemporaries 100 years later were not yet in a position to play their major part in the world's affairs. They too were looking inwards, concentrating on the Five Year Plans in the construction of 'socialism in one country' and on the New Deal in the restoration of what we might call 'capitalism in one country'. While isolationism has been most explicitly attributed as a policy to the USA, in reality if not so much in theory it was also the policy of the USSR. As a former official at the German Embassy in Moscow said of the local policy at the beginning of the 1930s, the Soviet Union 'concealed an ironclad isolationism behind a facade of intensified Comintern activity which was designed in part to detract attention from her internal troubles'.[7]

Appropriately enough, one of the first moves by President Roosevelt after his inauguration early in 1933 was towards recognition of the USSR. Brushing aside the negative advice of some State Department officials, and dismissively suggesting at one point that they were more worried about the spelling of the word 'commissar' than the real issue confronting them, FDR argued that it was an unnecessary inconvenience to have no direct official contact between the United States and the Soviet Union. Secretary of State Cordell Hull declared: 'The world is moving into a dangerous period both in Europe and in Asia. Russia could be a great help in stabilising this situation.'[8]

As diplomatic relations were established between the United States and the Soviet Union in November 1933, it could indeed be hoped that some new global balance of power could be achieved. In fact, the expectations, economic as well as political, were soon dashed by American fears of Soviet Communist infiltration in Latin America and even in the USA, while British alarm at the prospect of Soviet–American rapprochement grew to such an extent that the counterweight of a British–Japanese accommodation was seriously considered, until Japanese demands were taken to be exorbitant. Contacts between the USA and the USSR were to remain minor until Joseph E. Davies cleared the way for wartime co-operation in an embassy lasting from 1937 to 1938.

Isolationism may be the best single-word definition of American foreign policy in the 1930s, but it needs to be qualified in several ways in order to be adequately appreciated. In one of the few references to non-domestic matters in his inaugural address of March 1933, Roosevelt asserted: 'In the field of world policy, I would dedicate this Nation to the policy of the good neighbor – the neighbor who resolutely respects himself and, because he does so, respects the rights of others – the neighbor who respects his obligations and respects the sanctity of his agreements in and with a world of neighbors.'[9] This general remark was quickly associated with the USA's most important sphere of traditional interest, Latin America. The exclusive Monroe Doctrine itself was still very much alive, and there was widespread determination to deter infiltration not only from the Soviet Union but also from Germany, Japan and wherever. In the Far East, FDR pursued his predecessor Woodrow Wilson's policy of the Open Door, which, about six years after the conquest of Manchuria, Japan appeared to be attempting again to slam in the USA's face with renewed invasion of China in July 1937. By this time, dangerous developments in Europe as well as in Asia called for a change in direction. The terms of a Neutrality Act of 1935 were relaxed somewhat in May 1937, and the president made an appropriate speech in October in isolationist Chicago, in effect sorting out good neighbours from bad. With a new metaphor, Roosevelt declared that there was an 'epidemic of world lawlessness' from which, if it continued, 'let no one imagine America will escape'. To avert disaster, the USA would introduce 'quarantine', isolation not so much of the USA as of potential enemies.[10] Offering more moral than physical support to attempts made by Britain and other friends to deal with the epidemic, the president was also making certain that the USA would be in a position to fight when necessary. At the very beginning of his administration in 1933 he had launched a large-scale programme of naval construction, and he later expanded both navy and army, especially from 1938 onwards. According to some estimates, rearmament helped the USA to emerge from the Depression more than the New Deal.

While the USA's road to involvement in the Second World War was similar to the one that led it into the First, there was less continuity apparent in the approach of Europe's other peripheral giant, where the foreign policy of Joseph Stalin in the 1930s was not closely comparable to that of Nicholas II before 1914. This was certainly a consequence of the difference in internal regime, but it also stemmed from the contraction of the western frontier. Before 1914, even from the reign of Peter the Great and before, tsarist Russia had formed an integral part of the European state system. The Russian Revolution meant exclusion from the councils of Europe to a point unknown for 200 years or more. The consequences of this reversion to isolation were seen in the Rapallo Treaty and its aftermath, bringing Russia together with Germany, the other major outcast from the Paris peace conference. But we must also remember, as well as Versailles, the 'forgotten peace' of Brest-Litovsk and later treaties, which resulted in the subtraction from revolutionary Russia of vast areas of the pre-war empire. Finland, the Baltic Provinces, Poland and Bessarabia were all lost, and the siege mentality of the years of the Russian civil war and Allied intervention from 1917 to 1921 therefore remained in existence, in spite of a growing number of diplomatic contacts and treaties of non-aggression and neutrality.

Nazi Germany's agreement of a Non-Aggression Pact with Poland at the beginning of 1934 appeared to signal an end to the Rapallo agreement between Germany and Russia. Although economic relations between Germany and Soviet Russia continued, the USSR's concerns for its safety intensified. The extent of these concerns may be measured by the switch in policy towards the outside world which was now made by the Soviet Union and the Comintern. Recognised by the USA at the end of 1933 and entering the League of Nations with French aid in September 1934, the Soviet Union proceeded to make pacts with both France and Czechoslovakia in May 1935. And in the summer of

1935, the Seventh and last Congress of the Comintern gave its seal of approval to the policy of 'collective security' that the Soviet government had been working towards in the preceding agreements. Stalin did his best to reassure visitors such as the American newspaper owner Roy Howard that international revolution was no longer on the Soviet agenda, and that the top Soviet priority was a European version of the 'good neighbor' policy.

Stalin's anxiety about the deterioration in international stability combined with his struggle for the retention of power to produce the trials and purges of the 1930s. These, in their turn, reinforced the outside view that the Soviet Union could not be taken completely seriously as a military power, especially after the execution of Marshal Tukhachevsky and other senior officers in the summer of 1937 seriously weakened its high command. This low estimation, combined with the fundamental antipathy throughout the capitalist world to what was still seen as the headquarters of world communism, put the Soviet Union at a considerable disadvantage in its dealings with the other states of Europe and elsewhere. For although our attention is on Europe, we must not forget that the extension of the USSR through Asia over to the Pacific coast brought it into conflict with Japan, which had subjected its tsarist predecessor to a humiliating defeat in 1905 and had been the last of the interventionist powers to withdraw after 1917. The Japanese invasion of Manchuria in 1931 again raised the spectre of simultaneous involvement in war on two fronts, which good relations with Mongolia and China did little to dispel.

Such anxieties were compounded by the limited extent of Stalin's 'totalitarianism', and by the forced pace of the fulfilment of the Five Year Plans. A standard image is of Stalin as a devilish master puppeteer holding the lives of all Soviet citizens by tiny threads, aided and abetted by a series of sinister henchmen: Yagoda, Ezhov and Beria. These police chiefs were undoubtedly as villainous as the titles of their organisations looked innocent (the United State Political Administration, OGPU, was introduced in 1922 and absorbed in 1934 by the People's Commissariat of Internal Affairs, NKVD). Stalin himself remains a repulsive figure to most Western eyes, while even his undoubted continuing popularity for some citizens of the former Soviet Union no longer rises to such heights of adulation as those achieved by a speech at the Seventh Congress of the Soviets in 1935:

Centuries will pass, and the generations still to come will regard us as the happiest of mortals, as the most fortunate of men, because we lived in the century of centuries, because we were privileged to see Stalin, our inspired leader ... because we are the contemporaries of a man who never had an equal in world history. ... I shall be eternally happy and joyous, all thanks to thee, great educator, Stalin. Everything belongs to thee, chief of our great country. And when the woman I love presents me with a child the first word it shall utter will be: Stalin.[11]

A devil deified or whatever he was, Stalin could not control Soviet society as much as he would have liked. The techniques of surveillance at the disposal of his secret policemen were not sufficiently well developed for them to know for certain what was going on in Moscow, let alone the surrounding expanses. This, after all, was still the age of the informer and the double agent with all their human failings: the electronic equipment that makes a more complete totalitarianism possible was not developed until well after the Second World War. The solemn formality of the show trials of 1936–8 could not disguise the flimsiness of hard evidence concerning the crimes of the accused. Links between political functionaries and the exiled Trotsky or foreign powers were never proved, and the confessions for the most part rang untrue. The random nature of the purges at lower levels has been well described in the works of Evgenia Ginzburg and Nadezhda Mandelstam, among others. Nobody, however innocent and devoted, could be certain of avoiding arrest and accusation.

For this reason, even the mundane business of provincial government was conducted in a far from rational and calm manner. The records for the Smolensk province show that both the *obkom* (regional Party committee) and the *raikom* (district Party committee) worked in confusion and haste, knowing that 'success or failure, even life or death may depend on their ability to satisfy the expectation of their chiefs'.[12] At these lower levels there were the lesser members of the new elite, the little Stalins, protecting their patronage networks at the same time as bullying those who comprised them. They in their turn were at once protected and bullied from above by higher officials, and so on, up to the very top. Equally, the insecurity in the Central Committee as indicated by the show trials and the fate of respective police chiefs was repeated in the *obkom* and *raikom*. As for Stalin himself, apparently serene above all the protection rackets and party in-fighting, it is by no means certain that even he slept peacefully at night.

All this turmoil, we must remember, involved the Soviet Union from Smolensk in the west through Siberia to Vladivostok in the east, a vast country with long frontiers and all kinds of geographical and historical variations within them, attempting to reach the optimistic targets of the Five Year Plans. The Soviet Union must catch up with the advanced countries in ten years, Stalin had said in 1931, or go under. In spite of the purges and the forced labour camps there was also widespread agreement with him. As well as several million inmates of the notorious GULAG, there were others who voluntarily gave their energies to what they saw as a great cause. Probably a majority of the population was struggling on as best it could in the traditional patient manner, although non-Russian nationalities from the Baltic to the Pacific almost certainly felt the strain more than the Russians. For everybody, conditions of day-to-day existence might have eased somewhat in the middle 1930s. However, by the end of the decade they were as hard as ever. Now no worker could change jobs without permission, and even lateness of arrival was deemed to be absenteeism, while the welfare system, already rudimentary, became almost primitive. Within such restrictive conditions, heavy industry was in process of construction, with the percentage devoted to defence increasing from 3.4 in 1933 through 16.5 in 1937 to 32.6 in 1940.[13] Was rearmament as much of a boost to the economy in the USSR as it was in the USA?

THE 1930s: JAPAN, GERMANY AND ITALY

Responsibility for the increasingly grave international situation in the 1930s is usually attributed to the three most explicit enemies of the Soviet Union, the signatories of the Anti-Comintern Pact in 1936 and 1937, Japan, Germany and Italy. To take the non-European power first, Japan began to emerge from its Depression at the beginning of the decade with its invasion of Manchuria in 1931. Condemnation by the League of Nations of the Japanese creation of the puppet state of Manchukuo led to Japan's withdrawal from the League in 1933. Then in 1934 Japan made a none too indirect threat against any state attempting to counter its growing influence in China. Since it was natural that the responsibility for keeping the peace in eastern Asia should fall to Japan, its Foreign Office announced:

> We oppose, therefore, any attempt on the part of China to avail herself of the influence of any other country in order to resist Japan; we also oppose any action taken by China calculated to play one Power against another. Any joint operations undertaken by foreign Powers even in the name of technical or financial assistance at this particular moment ... are bound to acquire political significance ... supplying China with war aeroplanes, building aerodromes in China, and detailing military instructors or military advisers to China or contracting a loan to provide funds for political uses would obviously tend to alienate friendly relations between Japan, China, and other countries and to disturb peace and order in Eastern Asia. Japan will oppose such projects.[14]

Alarm grew in Europe and in the USA as news filtered through from Japan of further projects for expansion in China and also in South-East Asia, a valuable source of oil, tin and rubber. European states were concerned for the security of their empires, while the USA could see formidable obstacles to the continuance of the traditional 'Open Door' policy. Japan's 'isolationist expansionism' had few supporters in the wider world, except for the two European states that found themselves faced with a similar predicament, Nazi Germany and Fascist Italy.

What about their policies? In retrospect, more method has often been put into Hitler's madness than was probably there at the time. He was as much an improvising showman as a cool calculator, and it was only an astonishing early run of success that made his foreign policy appear astute and discerning. Nevertheless, there were some persistent themes in the thinking of the Führer and his collaborators. An important question here is, how important was the element of continuity with previous German governments? Hitler's own heroes, as well as the gods and demigods of mythical antiquity, included Frederick the Great of eighteenth-century Prussia. His Third Reich contained some distant echoes of the First, notably, as we have already seen, in his adoption of the twelfth-century Emperor Frederick I's nickname as codename for the invasion of the Soviet Union, Operation Barbarossa. However, the most meaningful discussion of continuity does not go further back than the Second Reich, the German Empire formally created in 1871, which having established itself as a unified, mid-continental state developed the ambition for world power that helped bring about the First World War. Just before the disastrous conclusion to that conflict on the Western Front, an indication of a further road forward had been given to Hitler and others by successes on the Eastern Front. A revived Germany could push again to the east in order to find its *Lebensraum* and in this manner grasp a second time at world power. There were those in the Weimar government who thought along such lines without contemplating Nazi methods, even before the Nazi government began to move to put the idea into action. Hitler believed that this expansion would have to take place in collaboration with Italy, the heir to Rome, the greatest even if now dead empire of classical antiquity, and especially with Britain, the actual if declining greatest empire of modern times. D. C. Watt has written: 'There are only two elements common to his words in *Mein Kampf* and his deeds in the period 1933–1941, the drive for living-space and the attempt to reach an understanding with Britain and Italy.'[15] In a sense, perhaps, the Führer was attempting to show old Europe how it could co-operate under his direction in order to reassert its world power both ancient and modern against those peripheral upstarts, the USSR and the USA. Both of these had been corrupted by an admixture of Jewish blood, he alleged, and as long as they could restore and maintain their own racial purity, the German people would retain their pre-eminence, especially as they achieved their full reunification. In fact, as far as world power was concerned, Hitler's foreign policy aims were mostly confused by the impossibility of their realisation. Germany had arrived on the scene too late to be the leading empire of Europe, and could not now by itself constitute a superpower.

Hence the need for *Lebensraum*, which would help provide autarky. Hence, too, the need for direction and control, and for a forcing of the pace before it was too late. Not that the Nazi government was anywhere near as efficient and unified as is sometimes alleged. As K. D. Bracher has written of its structure:

> The *Führer* constituted the only definite link between and above the jurisdictional thicket of party agencies and state machinery. The omnipotence of his position rested not least on the ill-defined

relationship of party and state; he alone was able to solve the costly jurisdictional conflicts which were part of the system. Regardless of whether this was an unavoidable dilemma of totalitarian dictatorship, the widespread idea about the better organized and more effective 'order' of totalitarian one-man rule is a myth all too easily believed in crisis-ridden democracies.[16]

Moreover, red tape and delay were everywhere. The Nazi government was founded on paper. 'There is an elaborate system', wrote Stephen Roberts, 'of chits and counter-chits – of forms to be filled in duplicate and of halves that must be minuted and returned and filed.'[17] If information, and especially misinformation, flew thick, fast and in multiple copy, the truth became even more elusive than usual. However, both later analysis and contemporary observation are agreed on the limits of totalitarianism and the inefficiencies of the Nazi government.

Similarly: 'The economy of Nazi Germany was neither a war nor a peace economy, but both at the same time. The resources were not sufficient to maintain this dualism indefinitely.' From 1936 onwards, rearmament had been given greater emphasis than before: responsible for less than 25 per cent of public expenditure in 1935, it accounted for more in 1936 and 1937, and in 1938 amounted to 17.2 out of 37.1 billion marks, nearly 50 per cent. Even then, however, the emphasis was on *Blitzkrieg* (lightning war) rather than on sustained war, and the warning went out in 1939 after such a war had begun that 'we shall never defeat England with radio sets, vacuum cleaners and cooking utensils'.[18] The inadequacies of the German economy, even after its expansion by early conquests, became all the more apparent after the invasion of the Soviet Union in 1941. Hitler's appetite for world power had quickly grown in the eating, and now he had bitten off more than he could chew.

While Germany's isolation had been forced upon it in the aftermath of the First World War, Italy drew away from its wartime allies through its own choice, or rather at the order of its leader, Mussolini. Italy had not enjoyed the best of wars, and of all the victors it emerged least happy from the peace. The treaties allowed a certain amount of frontier readjustment in the Alps, but too little down the Adriatic coast, which hurt the national pride, and none at all in Africa, which insulted it. Consequently, in his foreign policy Mussolini aimed at avenging these alleged wrongs in Europe and beyond, giving increasing emphasis to the Mediterranean and the continent on the other side. This concentration of focus was at least partly the result of the circumstance that, having begun as the senior partner in the Fascist attack on the Versailles settlement, Mussolini was beginning to sense that Hitler was overtaking him, that the revival of the German Reich was a more dynamic force than that of the Roman imperium. He was especially worried about a Nazi takeover in Austria, and then in the Balkans.

THE 1930s: THE REST OF EUROPE

While the USA and the USSR were doing their best to preserve their isolation, and Japan, Germany and Italy were beginning to break out from theirs, Britain was caught in a middle position. That is, it would have liked to be left to attend to its own domestic and imperial concerns, but it was being pushed towards more involvement in European questions, especially under pressure from France. Recovering from the Depression, British society was still convalescent, the working class still worried about prospects of employment and reduction of social services, the middle class insecure in the superficially calm suburbs. Anxiety was reflected in the abdication of Edward VIII and the succession of George VI (1936–52). The National Government, first under the Labour renegade Ramsay MacDonald, then under the Conservative Stanley Baldwin, managed to retain a large measure of popular support, and won a clear victory in a general election of November 1935 with such slogans as: 'A million new houses built, a million more employed'. At least some of the new jobs were connected with rearmament, which, as elsewhere, was given more emphasis from the mid-1930s onwards. In the face of the Italian invasion of Ethiopia (Abyssinia), which took place a month or so before the general election, Baldwin and his supporters professed their support for the principle of collective security and the policies of the League of Nations. However, at least some of their opponents were sceptical about the government putting its muscle where its mouth was.

Equally, across the Channel there was considerable French doubt about the lengths that the British would be prepared to go to in co-operation for the preservation of peace. While Baldwin had declared in 1934 that the British frontier was on the Rhine, the French continued to derive more reassurance from the concrete of the Maginot Line than from what they often understood to be the hot air of the spokesmen of the offshore islands. After the crisis of the Stavisky scandal and ensuing riots in February 1934, a succession of right-wing governments tried to combine financial stability with continued rearmament, while challenged by strikes from the Left and Fascist agitation on the extreme Right. These threats subsided somewhat after an election in May 1936 and the formation of a Popular Front administration under France's first Socialist prime minister, Léon Blum.

Whether they wanted to or not, neither Britain nor France could avoid playing central roles in the countdown to another world war. No other state to east or west could resist German and Italian expansion by itself, while Spain and Portugal welcomed it.

FROM MANCHURIA TO SPAIN, 1931–8

Europe was now firmly on the road to the Second World War. It had set off soon after the First World War but took a turn towards deeper crisis in the 1930s. There were difficulties enough for the maintenance of peace in the earlier part of the decade following the Japanese occupation of Manchuria in 1931. There were already those in the West who believed in a policy that was to become notorious, that of appeasement, for example L. S. Amery speaking in the House of Commons in February 1933:

> When you look at the fact that Japan needs markets and that it is imperative for her, in the world in which she lives, that there should be some sort of peace and order, then who is there among us to cast the first stone and to say that Japan ought not to have acted with the object of creating peace and order in Manchuria and defending herself against the continual aggression of vigorous Chinese nationalism? Our whole policy in India, our whole policy in Egypt, stand condemned if we condemn Japan.[19]

In that same month, however, the Assembly of the League of Nations took a more disapproving stance with its adoption of the Lytton Report condemning the aggressor for its armed seizure of Chinese territory and recommending that its forces should withdraw from it. Japan would not accept the report's findings and gave notice of intent to quit the League, at the same time extending its influence up to the Great Wall of China and beyond.

Such developments in the Far East did little to help the work of a Disarmament Conference, which was aimed at the reduction of armaments in accordance with the Covenant of the League of Nations. Over 60 nations, including non-members of the League such as the USA and the USSR, were represented at the conference, which opened in February 1932 in Geneva and reopened there a year later with renewed hopes of progress. Perhaps the biggest stumbling block in the first year of the conference's existence was Germany's desire for equality, which was recognised in a Draft Convention submitted by the British prime minister Ramsay MacDonald in March 1933. The Draft Convention, which also went so far as to propose the total abolition of naval and military aircraft, managed to secure provisional acceptance by June 1933. During the subsequent recess, there were considerable attempts to overcome further objections, which originated particularly from the new German chancellor, Herr Hitler, and from the French government. Hitler refused to accept the maintenance of armaments at their existing level, and took Germany out of the conference, then from the League of Nations in October. The French became even more concerned about guarantees for their security, and refused to accept German terms for return to the conference, which included a German conscript army of 300,000 men and the restoration of the Saar region. Early in 1934, the British government made some last vain attempts to reconcile the differences between Germany and France, and the Disarmament Conference met for a final inconclusive session, adjourning indefinitely on 11 June. Before the year was over, all the leading European nations were committed to a policy of army and air force expansion.

At the beginning of the month during which the Disarmament Conference came to an end, on 1 June 1934, Mussolini declared: 'I absolutely disbelieve in perpetual peace. It is detrimental and negative to the fundamental virtues of man, which only by means of a struggle reveal themselves in the light of the sun.' The Italian leader was probably concerned to take the mind of his people off continued economic and social problems at home by pursuing a more vigorous policy abroad, wherever it might lead: 'better one day as a lion than a hundred years as a sheep' ran a slogan of the time.[20] The moment was approaching for him to fulfil his promise of reviving the Roman Empire, while the way forward as far as defiance of the League of Nations was concerned had been prepared by Japan and Germany. Ever since the late nineteenth century, Italy had possessed colonial interests in north-east Africa, especially in the coastal regions of Eritrea and Somaliland. If they could be joined through the conquest of the Abyssinian hinterland, Italy would acquire a large unified possession strategically useful as a counterweight to British influence from the eastern Mediterranean through the Suez Canal and Red Sea on to India and the Far East. In December 1934, the first serious clash occurred between a unit of the Italian army, comparatively well prepared and largely mechanised, and another of the Abyssinian army, poorly armed and inadequately trained. In January 1935, Emperor Haile Selassie made an appeal on behalf of Abyssinia to its fellow members of the League of Nations for support in the struggle against Italian aggression. There was no positive response. Indeed, at a meeting in Stresa on the banks of Lake Maggiore in April, Italy, the host nation, agreed to work with France and Britain in a 'Stresa Front' for the maintenance of stability in Europe, and was not warned about any consequences of taking its Abyssinian expedition further. Mussolini gained additional encouragement as Britain was alarmed at the signing of the Franco-Soviet Pact in Moscow in May, while France was dismayed at the British acceptance of the Nazi violation of Versailles in the British–German Naval Agreement in June.

The full Italian invasion of Abyssinia took place early in October 1935. It received the condemnation of the League of Nations, which attempted to institute economic sanctions against Italy in November. However, discussion of an oil embargo which would have stopped the Italian mechanised advance in its tracks came to nothing, largely because France was against it and the necessary co-operation of the USA was not forthcoming. Early in May 1936, Haile Selassie was obliged to go into exile and King Victor Emmanuel III of Italy was proclaimed emperor of Abyssinia in his place.

Together, France and Britain could have halted the aggression. Their lack of appropriate joint action was a consequence partly of mutual suspicion and partly of domestic pressures. Moreover, from 7 March 1936 they had an additional problem of aggression to worry about far nearer home than the wilds of Abyssinia, for it was on that fateful day that Hitler sent his troops into the demilitarised zone of the Rhine-land. His action violated both the Versailles and Locarno treaties, but was explained by him on the basis that the Franco-Soviet Pact of May 1935 was itself in breach of Locarno. The Führer had also cleared the way for his action by seeking rapprochement with Mussolini, who was weaned away from the 'Stresa Front'. Again, Franco-British mobilisation would probably have pushed the German troops back from the Rhineland just as the joint imposition of an oil embargo would have halted the Italians in Abyssinia. Certainly, Hitler's advisers had believed that France would make a counter-move into the Rhineland. Why was no such action forthcoming? Fundamentally, the general mood was not favourable either in France or in Britain: in both countries there were influential groups arguing that Germany's grievances were justified; the counter-argument that a stand had to be made before it was too late received very little support, especially in view of the expense involved at a time of continuing economic hardship. The French, including the military leaders, had already adopted the defensive posture associated with the Maginot Line. The British were even less enthusiastic about risking war for the Rhineland, which they did not really think of as their own frontier and looked on more as Hitler's backyard than as France's front entrance. In retro-spect, it might seem clear that this was the moment to contain Nazi expansion before it gathered momentum; at the time, such a con-sideration was far from obvious, indeed barely visible.

France now moved closer to Britain, but France's potential allies in the east, especially Czechoslovakia, Poland and the Soviet Union, could not rely any longer on a French offensive in the event of further Nazi aggression. Meanwhile, after the establishment of the Berlin–Rome Axis in October 1936, Germany signed an anti-Comintern Pact with Japan in November, thus increasing the threat to the Soviet Union from both sides and intensifying its isolation. Such an alignment of forces was to be encouraged by the Spanish Civil War, which had begun in July 1936 with the revolt of the army in Morocco under the command of General Francisco Franco. In August the prime minister made the following declaration:

The present situation in Spain has been provoked by the military, the clergy and the Fascists in an open rebellion against the Republic and the legitimate Government elected by the people. The existing Madrid government is republican, without one Socialist or Communist minister, but with the support of these parties.

And a counter-declaration soon followed from the 'National Government' at Burgos, the insurgent capital in Old Castile:

On 18 July General Franco and the other leaders declared the National revolt to free Spain from the Communist domination. Secret orders issued by Communist headquarters for the formation of a National Soviet have been discovered ...[21]

Such 'secret orders' almost certainly never existed, but there is no doubt that Franco and his associates managed to colour the republican administration with the Red brush. Consequently, the German Nazis and the Italian Fascists were encouraged to follow what was their natural inclination and to give the Spanish opposition their firm support. The French and British administrations held back from giving aid to the government. The Soviet Union got just enough response from the government and gave just enough aid to it to make the allegations about its subversive aims appear credible, but not nearly enough to counterbalance the men and materials coming from Germany and Italy.

Transported from Morocco by the German air force, Franco's army managed to gain control of over half of Spain, including the south and west, by the end of 1936. Madrid managed to hold out during the next year, but the opposition encroached along the north sufficiently to take Bilbao, the capital of the separatist Basques. Throughout 1938 Madrid still managed to withstand a persistent siege, but at the very end of the year another separatist region to the east, Catalonia, began to give way. At the beginning of 1939 the cessation of Soviet aid to the government combined with the continuance of German and Italian help to the opposition to bring about a rapid conclusion to the Civil War. In January, Barcelona, the capital of Catalonia, fell, and the surrender of Madrid followed towards the end of March. Already, on 27 February 1939, France and Britain had given official and unconditional recognition to General Franco. Such was the logical consequence of their policy of non-intervention, which they had resolutely followed while other European powers flagrantly infringed it.

French and British policy towards the Spanish Civil War was not so much an indication of dispassionate neutrality as of reasons of state. Although Léon Blum, the Socialist prime minister at the head of a 'Popular Front' government in France since the summer of 1936, might have been expected to give more positive support to the Spanish republican government, he was concerned lest such an action would endanger domestic stability as well as expose France to the danger of war on three fronts, the Mediterranean and the Pyrenees as well as the Rhine. To the west of the Rhine, the Maginot Line was more exposed since the German remilitarisation of March 1936 to the east and the Belgian reassertion of neutrality in the autumn of the same year to the north. As for Britain, Stanley Baldwin had given way as Conservative prime minister to Neville Chamberlain in 1937, but there was no break in policy, owing to the persistence of the traditional British reluctance to become involved in European squabbles because of prior imperial responsibilities and the newer apprehension of the Communist menace. There was also the fear of attack, especially from the air, as well as the desire to win the next general election. Meanwhile, both Mussolini and Hitler were emboldened to take their aims for expansion further, especially since their aggression in Spain had been answered by appeasement. For the so-called 'Gentlemen's Agreement' of January 1937 included British recognition of Italy's equal rights in the Mediterranean.

'With dictators nothing succeeds like success', Hitler had observed in May 1936,[22] and the unfolding of the Spanish Civil War had appeared to support his assertion not only for Hitler himself but also for Mussolini and for Franco. Moreover, in the Far East the Japanese military dictators unleashed war on China in the summer of 1937, while their submarines were venturing far enough away from home base to attack French and British ships trading with the Spanish Republic. In November 1937 Italy joined the anti-Comintern Pact concluded between Germany and Japan a year previously, and the threat to international stability was becoming global.

FROM MUNICH TO POLAND, 1938-9

France and Britain were increasingly aware of the dangers of isolation, but neither was ready to move closer to the Soviet Union and neither was capable of fully arousing the United States. Negotiations between France and the Soviet Union for a military convention were carried on in secret from 1936 to 1937, but the French general staff itself argued against it. The outlook of the British government was clearly expressed by the prime minister on 20 March 1938:

> with Franco winning in Spain by the aid of German guns and Italian planes, with a French government in which one cannot have the slightest confidence, and which I suspect to be in closish touch with our Opposition, with the Russians stealthily and cunningly pulling all the strings behind the scenes to get us involved in war with Germany (our Secret Service doesn't spend all its time looking out of the window), and finally with a Germany flushed with triumph, and all too conscious of her power, the prospect looked black indeed.[23]

This was a week after the German army had marched into Austria to cement the union (*Anschluss*) that had been expressly forbidden in the peace settlement following the First World War but was soon passively accepted as part of the policy of appeasement, the alarm of the Little Entente powers of eastern Europe notwithstanding. And so the Red menace still took precedence over the black prospect. As for the United States, its officials showed little confidence in France, whose continued financial crises persuaded the secretary to the Treasury, Henry Morgenthau, to compare lending money to France with pouring money into the Atlantic, adding the assertion that 'someone has to tell the French that they are a bankrupt, fourth class power'.[24] In any event, the Neutrality Act of 1935 helped to inhibit the USA from collaborating with the British Empire to restrain Japan in the Far East, or from supporting Britain in its European embarrassments. An important further consideration here was the suspicion on the part of the British government of the encroachment of American power into its own spheres of influence both in the wider world and nearer home.

With rearmament already under way, Hitler and his advisers agreed on a more aggressive foreign policy during the course of the winter preceding the *Anschluss* with Austria on 12 March 1938. However, there was no definite plan or timetable, rather the determination to take fuller advantage of opportunities that came along. For the observation that for dictators nothing succeeds like success concealed the difficulty that success had to be repeated or continuous for dictators not to appear before their peoples as failures. Once begun, the Nazi drive for living space could not pause for breath. Therefore, as soon as Austria was taken, preparations began for the seizure of Czechoslovakia, the most formidable obstacle in the way of further expansion to the east. Already, the French government now under Edouard Daladier and the British government under Chamberlain were determined to continue appeasement to any lengths short of what they perceived as their own dishonour. Chamberlain took the lead in wanting to accommodate Hitler, perhaps, but Daladier was by no means reluctant to abandon the commitments that France had made to Czechoslovakia. Therefore all was virtually over before the signing of the Munich agreement on 30 September 1938. According to the agreement made by Chamberlain and Daladier with Hitler and Mussolini, the Germans were to occupy the area dominated by their co-nationals, the Sudetenland, and allowance was to be made for other claims on Czechoslovak territory by the Poles and Hungarians stemming from the post-First World War settlement. An international commission was to supervise the takeover of the Sudetenland, with the Czechs being held responsible for any damage to their own defences. The Four Powers were then to guarantee the new reduced state of Czechoslovakia.

At a heavy price including the greater likelihood of future war, present war had been averted. The Germans had mobilised, and so had the Czechs, while the French had partially mobilised. The British fleet was alerted, while Roosevelt had sent a cable to Chamberlain encouraging him to stand firm and had kept some American cruisers in British waters as a show of force to Hitler. Roosevelt also encouraged the Führer to come to the conference table, although he did not send any American representative to it. As for the other peripheral great power, the Soviet Union, its basic attitude at the time of Munich has been well caught by Keith Robbins:

> In fact, Soviet policy most closely resembles British. Just as Chamberlain felt that there was little to choose between Germany and the Soviet Union, the Soviet Union at least advertised that there was little to choose between Britain and Germany ... Both the Soviet Union and the British Empire adopted fundamentally defensive positions towards Europe. They both oscillated between trying to reach

agreement with Nazi Germany, trying to forget its existence and trying to arrange an alliance against Hitler. If the Russians suspected Britain of trying to involve them in a war with Hitler, this suspicion was fully shared on the other side. ... Each side found the other's policy peculiarly wicked.[25]

However, the additional point must be made that the Soviet Union also mobilised, put out appeals to the Western powers for consultation on collective security and declared its readiness to adhere to the terms of the Soviet–Czechoslovak Treaty of Mutual Assistance of 16 May 1935, which obliged the USSR to assist Czechoslovakia in the event of a German attack provided that France also gave its help. France not only withheld its aid from Czechoslovakia but also collaborated in the exclusion of both Czechoslovakia and the Soviet Union from the conference that met to decide the fate of the Sudetenland. Moreover, in December 1938 France followed the example of Britain in drawing up what amounted to a non-aggression pact with Germany. The British–German Declaration of 30 September 1938, which Chamberlain discussed and signed with Hitler without informing Daladier, had declared that their mutual relations were of prime importance for 'the two countries and for Europe' and that the two countries would never go to war with one another again, solving any disputes by a mutually arranged method of consultation. This was the piece of paper that the British prime minister waved on his return from Germany, promising 'peace in our time'. At this point, the British oscillation was very firmly in the direction of agreement with Germany, and away from accommodation with the Soviet Union beyond the strengthened barbed wire on the other side of a rearranged *cordon sanitaire*. However, in 1939 the pendulum began to swing in the other direction, even if late and slowly.

13

THE SECOND WORLD WAR AND THE DIVISION OF EUROPE, 1939–1945

EUROPE IN 1939

During the period leading up to the Second World War, nearly every-body in Britain and France was hoping that it would not come, or at least would take place elsewhere. Encouragement for such hopes was provided by the mass media, old and new. Until towards the end of the 1930s, many of the newspapers asserted that peace was secure. Similarly, radio broadcasts and cinema newsreels did not sound many notes of alarm before the final fateful years; nor did television, which was still in its infancy and reaching no more than a small number of viewers.

As far as travel was concerned, rail and sea were still much more common than air, even if the road was increasing in importance – in 1938, there were nearly 30 million motor vehicles in the USA, nearly 2.5 million in Britain and nearly 2.25 million in France. For Germany, the figure was just over 1.5 million,[1] and the importance of movement by road was recognised there in the construction by the end of 1938 of 3000 kilometres of *Autobahn*, with 14,000 more kilometres planned. The *Autobahn* system, the Baedeker Official Guide or *Führer* of the German Automobile Club for 1939 tells us, was the most modern network on earth and the brainchild of another guide or leader, the Führer himself, Adolf Hitler.

Hitler's name was frequently to be found in the pages of this work, entitled *Deutsches Reich* (*Grossdeutschland*). The foreword tells us that in a short span of time the Führer had performed 'colossal, world historical deeds'. He had changed the map of *Mitteleuropa* (central Europe) in a spirit of 'justice, reason and love of peace'. In such a manner, the *Lebensraum* of Germany had become greater with the 'incorporation' of Austria following the 'homecoming' of the Sudeten-land, the establishment of a 'protectorate' over Bohemia and Moravia and the 'reintegration' of Memelland. Now German tourists could the more easily become acquainted with the greater 'homeland' while foreign tourists could get to know and understand, love and marvel at the largest and most populated state of Europe.[2] Any foreign tourists attempting to accept the Baedeker invitation in the summer of 1939 might well have found themselves on the *Autobahn* in company with German armoured divisions making their way to launch an attack on Poland. For Germany under Hitler was extending its gamble for dominance in Europe; in such a manner, it would accelerate the continent's downfall.

About six months later, the historian L. B. Namier remarked that Hitler was able to make the progress he did in the late 1930s because 'Mankind was intellectually and emotionally unprepared to re-enter a major conflict', while the Western democracies were also technically unprepared. Hitler alone could ignore 'the war-weariness and fears of his own people'. He was 'an a-moral paranoiac' in control of 'a mechanised nation', exerting a 'hypnotic paralysis' upon the German people through his exploitation of the 'stab in the back' of the Versailles treaty.

Hitler and his associates must have known that as their demands grew, so did the likelihood of war. Probably they hoped to avoid war as long as possible, to 1942 or even later, but such was the global nature of their ambitions, extending far beyond Europe, that a showdown first with the Soviet Union, then with the United States, was virtually inevitable. L. B. Namier posed the question: 'Is the present war a World War? Will it last, will it grow?' He provided his own answer: 'a war in which the issue is world hegemony *versus* a European balance of power has to be fought to the bitter end'.[3] But even Namier could not foresee that the post-war European balance of power would be exercised not by the former great powers but by the Soviet Union and the United States, and as part of a new struggle for world hegemony.

Back in the winter of 1938–9, Britain had drawn still closer to France amid rumours of further aggressive action by Germany and Italy now that the Spanish Civil War had come to an end. Moreover, criticism of the policy of appeasement grew even if hampered by censorship and direction of the news media. Hitler's occupation of Prague on 15 March and the immediately subsequent dismemberment of what was left of Czechoslovakia by Germany, Poland and Hungary prompted speedy joint reaction by Britain and France in the shape of guarantees to Poland, then to Greece and Romania, and later to Turkey. In the middle of April discussions were begun with the Soviet Union in an atmosphere of growing international crisis. By this time Hitler had seized Memel (Klaipeda) in Lithuania and was putting forward claims to Danzig and threatening Romania, while Mussolini had invaded Albania. The Japanese counterparts were on the move again, too, on land and by sea: after a skirmish with the Red Army at the Soviet border in the summer of 1938 there was another clash in the spring of 1939, just after Roosevelt had given orders for the American fleet to move from the Atlantic to the Pacific to counter the Japanese maritime challenge.

British–French–Soviet military staff talks in Moscow broke down on 14 August after just two days, the chief stumbling block being Soviet right of access to Poland and Romania to counter further Nazi aggression. In reply to persistent questioning from Marshal Voroshilov, the commissar for defence, the British representative, Admiral Drax, could only reply:

> If Poland and Romania do not ask for Soviet help they will soon become German provinces, and then the USSR will decide how to act. If, on the other hand, the USSR, France and Britain are in alliance, then the question of whether or not Romania and Poland ask for help becomes quite clear.[4]

'Are we to be obliged to beg for the right to fight the common enemy?' Voroshilov asked.[5] The evasiveness of the replies given by the British and French representatives as well as the fact that they were not the Chiefs of Staff persuaded Voroshilov and Stalin that the Western Allies were playing for time rather than preparing to commit themselves to alliance. As Jonathan Haslam observes, 'Clearly the British and French had themselves to blame for missing an opportunity which, judging by their reaction, they would not have let slip had they been more aware that Berlin intended an agreement with Moscow.'[6]

For, from the Soviet point of view, the next logical step was the conclusion of an agreement with the Nazi government, which did seem prepared for commitment, culminating in the Nazi–Soviet non-aggression pact of 23 August 1939. Widely advertised in the West as a shocking act of treachery and wickedness, for Stalin and his advisers the pact constituted a certain means of recovering territory lost after 1917 and an apparent quietus of the fear of a German invasion through the Baltic. There is little or no evidence to support the view that Stalin had always intended to do a deal with Hitler, rather more to suggest that the failure of the British–French–Soviet military negotiations left him with no alternative.

Both Stalin and Hitler probably meant what they said in denunciation of each other and their respective ideologies. However, in his speech to the Eighteenth Party Congress on 10 March 1939, Stalin was drawing on Russian experience before 1917 as well as since the Revolution. For example, in expressing determination 'not to permit our country to be drawn into conflicts by warmongers who are accustomed to having others pull the chestnuts out of the fire for them',[7] he was probably thinking of his own apprehension concerning the involvement of the Soviet Union in Asia and of the action taken by the tsarist army in 1914 and 1916 to relieve pressure on the Western Front. Going back in history even further, he would probably have agreed with those of his colleagues who believed that the Munich agreement and the subsequent British and French non-aggression pacts with Nazi Germany had pointed the way not only to a Soviet counterpart but also to a new partition of Poland, this time between Hitler and himself.

For Hitler, the Nazi–Soviet pact certainly presented an opportunity for applying greater pressure on Poland, where another sizeable German minority was to be found. He was also coming round to believe that having cried wolf in response to his earlier acts of aggression, the British and French governments would not now attempt to keep him out of the Polish corridor, especially if he continued to dress in sheep's clothing. Thus, up to the very end, there were protestations of wanting to settle claims peacefully at the same time as build-up for war. The

British and French governments did indeed still want to avoid war, and seriously considered last-minute proposals to this end from both Hitler and Mussolini, whose Pact of Steel concluded in May was still not as hard and fast as it may have appeared.

Appearances in general were deceptive, and when British and French ultimata were delivered to Germany after its invasion of Poland on 1 September 1939, nobody seems to have been certain whether after their expiry on 3 September Europe would again be fighting, almost exactly 25 years after the previous great conflict had begun. Isolation had led through misunderstanding and deception to a breakdown of communication and war. However, as the German forces overran Poland, the British and French were powerless to make any move to help as the Soviet army moved in from the east to make a reality of the forecast of a new partition.

PHONEY WAR: FROM POLAND TO FRANCE, 1939–40

In the beginning, the war was more than European but not yet world-wide. While the action was taking place in Poland, even some of the short-term strategic considerations centred elsewhere. For example, the British government continued to give top priority to the security of its empire, and the Soviet Union was still concerned about the possibility of further attacks by Japan in the Far East, hence the apparently absent-minded fluctuations in British policy towards the crisis on the continent, and the Soviet determination to avoid fighting on two fronts for as long as possible. The clash with Japan on the frontier of Outer Mongolia was not brought to an end until September, although reversals there as well as the rapprochement between the Soviet Union and Nazi Germany persuaded the Japanese government to adopt a new policy. This consisted of non-involvement in the European war and a more serious consideration of the southern strategy as far as its own plans for expansion were concerned. Here, opposition would be met not only from the European empires but also from the United States of America, as anxious as ever to maintain the Open Door in the Far East. To look back from the USA at Europe, nearly two-thirds of the American people were in favour of the maximum amount of aid short of war to Britain and France, but less than a third of them were in favour of the USA joining in the war even if Britain and France were near to surrender. Sensitive as ever to public opinion, President Roosevelt early in November accepted a revision of the Neutrality Act so that the arms trade was now placed on a strict cash-and-carry basis. This was to the advantage of the British and French governments, although there was as yet no American desire completely to alienate Nazi Germany, in which American investment had been heavy.

After the Nazi invasion on 1 September 1939, Poland managed to hold out for a period much shorter than it anticipated but at least a little longer than is sometimes recollected. A large-scale battle began on 8 September and lasted for nearly a week; in an ensuing siege, Warsaw managed to hold out for two weeks. Ironically, the courage of the Poles gave just about enough time for the Red Army to effect its hurried invasion from the east, taking as much of Poland in this one partition as Catherine the Great had taken in three. The Red Army met the German army at Brest-Litovsk, a reminder of the more recent carve-up of 1918. Before the final Polish surrender, the victors met to redistribute their spoils, so that Nazi Germany would acquire central Poland and Soviet Russia would retain Lithuania. Thus the revival of old fears that Russia would penetrate deep into central Europe was stemmed and the traditional Russian concern for the security of its frontiers was accommodated. This concern was reflected further in treaties of 'mutual assistance' imposed by the beginning of October not only on Lithuania but also on the other Baltic republics of Estonia and Latvia. Finland, encouraged by the Western powers as well as by Germany, held out against Soviet demands that its border with the USSR be moved back another 30 kilometres from the 30 kilometres or so that already separated it from Leningrad. Deadlock led to the Winter War which broke out at the end of November 1939 and lasted to mid-March 1940.

This was the only significant land action immediately after the defeat of Poland: except for some isolated episodes, there was little more at sea or in the air. Attention was then drawn to gallant little Finland, doubly popular in the USA as the only European country to have repaid its debts in full, and attractive to some in the West as an eleventh-hour possibility for launching a pan-European anti-Soviet crusade. Hitler in particular was encouraged by Finland's doughty performance to think more boldly about an invasion of the Soviet Union. Meanwhile, however, he was making more peace overtures towards Britain and France, partly at least for home consumption since the war was by no means universally popular within Germany itself during these early days. Generally speaking, the mood of the German people was more volatile than that of their enemies, as Howard K. Smith, an American reporter, pointed out:

> The graph of German morale is not a graceful, snaky thing which slithers upwards in long rises and downwards in slow, calm declines like the graph of almost any people living in peace. It is a low, jagged line which leaps spasmodically upwards in one instant and collapses into sharp depressions in the next. The reason for its abrupt contours is the unmitigated fear of this war which afflicts the German people, and their gullible readiness to believe anything, however fantastic, which indicates an early end to it.[8]

In contrast, there was an underlying confidence and calmness in Britain, even though the Nazi propaganda machine was much more efficient than its British counterpart. In London, the Ministry of Information conducted an unnecessarily harsh policy of censorship, attempting to fire the patriotism of the people with photographs of Bond Street mannequins in steel helmets or of Mr Chamberlain walking in St James's Park with his famous umbrella and being saluted by a couple of soldiers. At the very beginning of the war there was no enthusiasm of the August 1914 variety and concern was great enough for many children to be evacuated from London and other likely targets to more remote areas. But there was no widespread alarm, and citizens proceeded in orderly fashion to shelters with their gas masks and iron rations as the air-raid sirens rehearsed their wailing warning. In France, an atmosphere of relaxation and complacency grew behind the false security of the Maginot Line; the preface to a competent book describing the war's origins could suggest in December 1939 that:

> Looking back over the years since Versailles, the historian may feel that one name stands out in the struggle to protect the west from attack, that of the ex-serviceman and Minister of War who built a wall of steel and concrete to save France and the civilization of Europe from the aggressor – André Maginot.[9]

American journalists, who provided some of the most vivid description of the period, called it the 'phoney war', while the Germans named it the *Sitzkrieg* or 'sit tight war' and Chamberlain talked of the 'twilight war'. It was certainly twilight for him and his French counterpart, as they continued to talk, but not fight. In December 1939, the League of Nations broke precedent and expelled a state condemned as an aggressor, doing to the Soviet Union what it had previously failed to do to Japan, Italy and Germany. In the same month, the British–French Supreme War Council decided to render aid to embattled Finland. Such help would have to be given by way of Scandinavia, where Norway and Sweden were attempting to assert their neutrality. Somewhat ironically, the Western Allies were preparing to defend the rights of one small country by infringing those of two others when Finland relieved them of their embarrassment by making peace with Soviet Russia on 12 March 1940. Edouard Daladier, the French prime minister, fell first, his successor Paul Reynaud promising more dynamic leadership and coming to London to make some reality of his promise. The British agreed to break Norwegian neutrality in order to cut the winter supply route of iron ore from Sweden to Germany and were beginning to lay mines for this purpose when the Germans moved swiftly to take both Norway and Denmark on 9 April. The British retaliated and inflicted considerable damage on the German navy but could not retain their footholds in Norway. After a dramatic debate on the Norwegian situation in the House of Commons, Chamberlain was forced to resign. His policy of appeasement could no longer command a sufficient measure of support, even if it was by no means as weak and stupid as it has sometimes been made to appear since. L. S. Amery, who was among the fiercest opponents of Chamberlain, was not himself without the sin of inconsistency, since his empire loyalism combined resistance to Germany with accommodation of Japan.

BLITZKRIEG: THE FALL OF FRANCE AND AFTER, 1940–1

The new prime minister was no less enthusiastic about the British Empire than the old, but believed in resisting aggression wherever it was encountered. While the greatness of Winston Churchill was as yet by no means universally recognised, and it required the support of the

Labour Opposition for him to overcome the reservations of his own Conservative colleagues in the House of Commons, the opportunity for decisive action was immediately presented to him. On the morning of 10 May 1940, the very day that he took up his new appointment, Nazi Germany invaded Belgium and Holland. Three days later, *Blitzkrieg* flashed over the frontier into France, and in hardly any time at all, forked around the Maginot Line. The fundamental strategy of the British–French forces was broken before it could be fully adapted to the surprise attack through the undulating wooded plateau of the Ardennes. In spite of the fact that Belgium had been neutral since 1936 and had therefore made impossible the kind of co-operation on which that strategy depended, a defensive, immobile attitude persisted through the months of the phoney war. Almost before they knew what was hitting them, the ten divisions of the British Expeditionary Force and considerable detachments of their French comrades were driven back to the port of Dunkirk, from which little boats joined with larger ships to effect an epic evacuation from 27 May to 4 June 1940. Having offered his fellow countrymen nothing but 'blood, toil, tears and sweat' on the day that France was invaded, Churchill now promised that they would fight on the beaches and beyond but never surrender.

Churchill's powerful rhetoric was supported by the telling circumstance that *Blitzkrieg* could not easily be carried across the Channel. Moreover, not only the weakness of Hitler's navy but also a lack of resolve appears to have dissuaded him from attempting an immediate invasion of Britain. As on several previous occasions, indeed, he might well have been prepared at this point to make some kind of accommodating peace with the British government, if Churchill and his coalition had not been made of sterner stuff than the Chamberlain administration. Certainly, the olive branch was soon extended in the direction of France, and after several other changes in the command structure, Premier Reynaud resigned in favour of Marshal Pétain, who was prepared to accept it. Now that all attempts to repeat the stand of 1914 on the Western Front and elsewhere had failed, the highest responsibility was given to the First World War hero for bringing the Second World War to as satisfactory a conclusion for France as possible. Out-of-date strategy and lack of will to fight on the part of France had combined to bring Germany into a dominant position where it could have demanded unconditional surrender, but the terms offered were in fact lenient. Germany would occupy northern France and the Atlantic coast, but the area to the south of the River Loire was to be under the civil authority of a French government established in the town of Vichy. Italy, which had joined in the war on 10 June to get its hands on the spoils, in fact received no more than a token amount. A token of incalculable proportions was the location of the signature of the armistice of 22 June 1940, the same railway coach in which the First World War Armistice had been agreed on 11 November 1918. A British injury was now added to the German insult, when after a series of misunderstandings in which the old entente had become less and less cordial, the Royal Navy destroyed the French fleet in its North African harbour. About 1300 sailors were killed because their admiral had refused to sail for a British or American port. Before this unhappy event, a hitherto obscure army colonel named Charles de Gaulle crossed to London to head the Free French in exile, while brave souls carried the resistance to the invaders on home territory.

The defeat of France was Nazi Germany's finest moment. War had not been especially popular in Germany at the beginning, even after *Blitzkrieg* had triumphed for the first time in Poland. Anxiety and pessimism could be detected during the ensuing lull, and the most positive excitement was roused by rumours of peace at the time of Chamberlain's resignation. There was a certain lifting of some spirits at the news of the invasion of Denmark and Norway, but much indifference. By the beginning of the campaign against France, there had been a severe decline in the general mood. Even after Dunkirk, the crippling stalemate of 1914 was recalled as the German armies halted for just one day to get their breath back for the final blow. Then, after the new armistice reversing the humiliation of the old, there was no immediate elation; some time elapsed before the message got through that the war was apparently over, that what had previously taken four years and ended in defeat had now lasted about six weeks and culminated in victory. According to Howard K. Smith:

> About a month later, an extraordinary thing happened. The graph reached its all-time high. It was the only occasion in the better part of six years I have spent in Germany that I saw real, uninhibited enthusiasm, with Germans weeping and laughing from pure, spontaneous joy. It had never happened before and it has never

happened since. A division of Berlin infantry had returned from France. ... Children broke through the police cordon and carried little bouquets of flowers to the marching soldiers, while a dozen military bands, punctuating the ranks of the marchers, played martial music. It was truly a glorious day. And in every happy heart lived the belief that this was the end of it all.[10]

Even the great German historian Meinecke, brought to despair by the Nazi regime and stripped of his academic honours, could not forbear from expressing to a former pupil his deep satisfaction at the return to Germany of Strasbourg, a revival of an emotion stretching back beyond 1914.[11]

Blitzkrieg's greatest triumph was followed first by celebration, then by a return of apprehension as Operation Sea-Lion, the invasion of Britain, met with delays. Hitler did not give it his highest priority, already turning his mind towards the next great land battle with the Soviet Union while his army, navy and airforce commanders squabbled among themselves about how best to bring the defiant offshore islands to submission. Hopes of defeating Britain came to rest in the short run largely with the Luftwaffe, whose aircraft would soon be so thick over London, according to Marshal Goering, that the famous English sparrows would have to go on foot. In his view, Eagle, the *Blitzkrieg* from the air, would render Sea-Lion unnecessary. The admirals and generals continued to think that there was a role for them to play in the conquest of Britain, while the attention of the Führer continued to be mainly elsewhere.

Fear of attack by the Luftwaffe had contributed to the persistence with the policy of appeasement in the 1930s. The Joint Planning Committee of the Chiefs of Staff had reported in 1936: 'We are convinced that Germany would plan to gain her victory rapidly. Her first attacks would be designed as knock-out blows.' Unofficially but seriously, the distinguished military analyst Major-General J. F. C. Fuller emulated the imaginative forecast of H. G. Wells in his *The Shape of Things to Come*. With just one air raid, in Fuller's view:

London for several days will be one vast raving Bedlam, the hospitals will be stormed, traffic will cease, the homeless will shriek for help, the city will be a pandemonium. What of the Government at Westminster? It will be swept away by an avalanche of terror.[12]

Reality appeared to be making such forecasts all too accurate with air raids such as that on Shanghai in 1932 and Guernica in 1937. Consequently, when Eagle began on 15 August, there was a widespread feeling that a moment of important decision had indeed been reached. The next month showed that Britain could take it, and also that the RAF could give better than it got. Nevertheless, the Luftwaffe came near to achieving the aim set for it when it concentrated on attacks on airfields. When, after an RAF sortie against Berlin, the Luftwaffe switched its attention to London, the chance of quick victory was lost, and the limitations of *Blitzkrieg* were revealed. The Battle of Britain had been won by the famous few, and the anonymous many had shown that air attack was not as destructive of the civilian population as had been feared. This lesson was underlined in the following winter during a further series of air attacks on London and other targets, mainly on London and at night – the Blitz as it became generally if somewhat inaccurately known. Hundreds of thousands of houses were destroyed, but no more than 30,000 lives were lost, far fewer than in pre-war calculations, and a new spirit of national unity was gained.

Although there were some false alarms, there was in the end no need to activate 'Cromwell', the codename for Britain's response to an invasion, nor Churchill's suggestion for a slogan, 'Take one with you!' But the war was far from over, indeed it had hardly begun, and there were other developments from September 1940 onwards influencing its nature and outcome, beyond the domestic and imperial security of Britain, the only power remaining in the fight against Germany and Italy. On 27 September these two members of the Anti-Comintern Pact joined with the third, Japan, in a Tripartite Pact whereby each promised to join the war if another was attacked by a new enemy. Here was another indicator, if such were still needed, that the conflict would become global. Meanwhile, the action was centred around the Mediterranean and in the Atlantic. As ever, Britain was concerned for Suez, and conscious of the need to protect European responsibilities in the Middle East that it had previously shared with France. In September, an Italian army invaded Egypt from Libya, but a Commonwealth army under Wavell pushed it back by the end of the year. In October, another Italian force invaded Greece from Albania, only again to be repelled. Hitler had to intervene to help Mussolini out. In the spring of 1941, bringing a none-too-reluctant, would-be expansionist Bulgaria into the struggle for the Balkans, the German forces quickly took most of Yugoslavia. They then began to push the British forces and their local allies down through Greece, driving them from their last foothold in the island of Crete by the end of May. By this time, there was more failure for Italy in North Africa, where the British Commonwealth army liberated Abyssinia, making Hitler think of extended intervention as a counter.

While managing to keep the Mediterranean sea routes open in the face of heavy air attacks on Malta and Gibraltar, Suez and Alexandria, the Royal Navy also worked hard in the Atlantic to maintain the convoy system against the threats of German submarines and mines. These threats were all the greater because of German access to bases on the Atlantic coast of France, which along with Nazi domination of most of the continent made impossible any repetition of the First World War blockade. Britain was helped by a 'destroyer for bases' agreement with the USA in September 1940, even if, in the manner it was carried out, many of the American ships proved unusable while American infiltration into the Caribbean and western Atlantic alarmed those jealous of encroachments into British spheres of influence. Such anxiety persisted and became even greater early in 1941 when President Roosevelt, re-elected for a third term, was authorised by the Lend-Lease Act of March 1941 to give aid to any state whose security was considered vital for that of the USA. Britain was the main beneficiary, but its dependence on the USA meant that it was no longer a world power, however persistent the illusion.

FROM *BLITZKRIEG* TO ATTRITION: BARBAROSSA, PEARL HARBOR AND AFTER, 1941–3

At the cost of near financial ruin, Britain had bought and borrowed enough supplies to keep going, and therefore won some of that most valuable commodity – time. In this way, it made its most significant contribution to the outcome of the war, engaging the enemy until its allies joined in. Air attacks on Berlin and other strategic targets probably resulted in more losses to the RAF than damage to German industry and morale, and the mind of the Führer was given only fitfully to the British problem. Nevertheless, at least some attention was diverted in the year that followed the fall of France from what was increasingly seen as the main German task, the invasion of the Soviet Union. By June 1940, or soon afterwards, Nazi Germany had established control over all Europe west of the expanded Soviet frontier. Some of its allies – Bulgaria, Romania, Hungary and especially Italy – still retained a measure of independence, and, albeit temporarily, so did some of the countries that it had invaded, Holland, Norway, Denmark and especially Vichy France. Of the neutrals, Spain and Portugal tended to favour Nazi Germany, while Sweden, Switzerland and Turkey found it advisable to do so, too, during the years of Nazi ascendancy. (Ireland was the exception to prove the rule, so to speak, maintaining a stricter neutrality while secretly favouring the Western cause, especially after the entry into the war of the USA. And many Irishmen volunteered for service in the British armed forces.)

Many of the aims of imperial Germany as set out in 1914 had already been realised. Now, apart from the nagging persistence of Britain, however, there remained another problem that had brought to an end an earlier attempt at European domination, that of Napoleon. For Hitler to outdo this predecessor, as well as to guarantee the prosperity of his New Order in Europe and fulfil his aims as set out in *Mein Kampf*, he had to march on Moscow.

The invasion of the Soviet Union, Operation Barbarossa, was launched on 22 June 1941. This was over a month later than first planned, partly because of the diversion arising from Italian weakness in the Balkans and North Africa, largely because of the difficulty of preparing the supplies for a huge force of more than 150 divisions. Even if this was to be another *Blitzkrieg*, it would be on a scale greater than during the two previous years, and with more uncompromising aims, as Hitler decreed a 'War of Race Annihilation'. As it turned out, the *Blitzkrieg* failed, and the war became one of attrition. Hitler was to find out, like Napoleon before him, that to invade Russia was easy, to defeat it much more difficult. Blame for the failure has been attached to the delay in the launch of the attack, and to the early onset of winter. Moreover, the immediate directions of the invasion have been criticised: Hitler and his generals should perhaps have made their major drive towards the oil-rich Caucasus rather than ordering a three-prong attack against the major Soviet cities of Moscow, Leningrad and Kiev. However, the overall superiority of the Soviet Union was more clearly revealed the longer the war went on, even though the Soviet leadership allowed Hitler to add to the list of his successes in the war's first few months. Stalin had blown hot and cold during the months of the Nazi–Soviet pact, making concessions to Hitler and demands on him. Through such inconsistency, he himself probably made a contribution to the decision on Barbarossa. However, there is no concrete evidence that he himself was preparing a war of aggression, much more that he dismissed intelligence reports from many sources that Hitler's attack was imminent. Just days before the launching of Barbarossa, he shouted at his generals: 'If you're going to provoke the Germans on the frontier by moving troops there without our permission, then heads will roll, mark my words.'[13]

The German people were far from exultant about the early progress made by their invading army. Indeed, that careful observer Howard K. Smith noted: 'The graph of German morale struck, in the last days of September, the lowest point it had reached in almost nine years of Nazi domination.' Military triumph was not enough, the people wanted decisive victory bringing the war to an end, and could not accept the exaggerated claims of the propaganda machine, especially as the hardships of war were inflicted on them with unprecedented severity. From the beginning, there had been rationing, but no great shortages. Now, after what Smith called 'The Great Watershed' of the Russian invasion, first the quality of supplies declined, and then the quantity. Food and other necessities had to be sent eastwards to supply the huge army advancing into scorched earth, as the Red Army destroyed everything within reach. The graph sank even lower, and to alleviate the sufferings of the people, the government began to look for a scapegoat. It turned to the Jews, who although already underprivileged and disqualified had not been physically persecuted since the great pogrom of 1938, when their shops all over Germany had been smashed. An ominous note was struck on 19 September, when it was decreed that every Jew in Germany and Bohemia would be compelled to wear a yellow six-pointed Star of David inscribed in black hebraic script: *Jew*. The Nazi newspaper, the *National Observer*, explained the necessity for the decree in the following manner: 'The German soldier has met in the Eastern Campaign the Jew in his most disgusting, most gruesome form. This experience forces the German soldier and the German people to deprive the Jews of every means of camouflage at home.' As things got worse, the Führer himself made a blanket threat that could cover Jews and other supposed sources of evil or opposition:

> Should anyone among us seriously hope to disturb our front – it makes no difference where he comes from or what camp he belongs to – I will keep an eye on him for a certain period. You know my methods. That is always the period of probation. But then there comes a moment when I strike like lightning and eliminate that sort of thing.[14]

Now that *Blitzkrieg* was failing on the steppes of Russia, it would be brought home to the Jews and domestic 'traitors'.

German apprehension became still greater in December, when there were reverses for the army not only in the Soviet Union but also in Africa. Hitler himself privately confessed that victory could no longer be won, but made defeat even more certain on 11 December by joining Italy in declaring war on the USA five days after the Japanese attack on Pearl Harbor. The war was becoming truly global, as we shall now see. Stalin was not among those statesmen who had neglected the Far East, since, whatever his errors and misjudgements in the west, especially with regard to the Nazi invasion, his wartime policies in Asia from a Soviet standpoint were correct and well considered, turning Japan away from attacks on the Soviet Union. In April 1941, he had signed a neutrality pact with the Japanese foreign minister who was on his way back to Tokyo after conversations in Berlin with Hitler. The Führer was in favour of such an agreement, since it would keep Japan out of the Soviet Union which he believed was about to become his own greatest prize. By this time, the inclination of the Japanese government was in any case towards South-East Asia, the area where it hoped to develop its own New Order. Further encouragement for expansion in this direction came from the collapse of two European countries with extensive empires in the area, Holland and France, and from the straitened circumstances of a third such imperial power, Britain. The American government decided that the time had come for firmness by July 1941, taking a lead in reducing Japan's trade and cutting off its oil supplies.

The Japanese Imperial Conference resolved that it could not give way in the face of American restrictions. Even though the option of further expansion to the north at the expense of the Soviet Union had been rejected, the surprise manner of Japan's great success against tsarist Russia in 1904–5 was still well remembered. And considerations were put before the Conference reminiscent of the dictum of Clausewitz that:

> A small state which is involved in a contest with a very superior Power, and foresees that each year its position will become worse should make use of the time when the situation is farthest from the worst if it considers war to be inevitable. The small state in this position is advised to attack.[15]

Thoughts such as those of the Prussian general blended with the Japanese concepts of honour and self-sacrifice in a just cause to produce strong military demands for action, and war minister Tojo became prime minister. So the decision was taken for pre-emptive strike, for Japan's own version of *Blitzkrieg* in the shape of an air attack on the USA's principal Pacific naval base at Pearl Harbor on 7 December 1941, soon followed by other raids in the Pacific and South-East Asian regions. The Imperial Conference believed that the move was taken to protect the integrity of Japan. As so often in the past, self-defence was given as a reason for aggression. Certainly, the way was now open for the development of the Greater Asia Co-Prosperity Sphere, the updated version of Japan's New Order.

The United States and Britain, along with China, the British Dominions and other Western allies, immediately declared war on Japan, the Soviet Union holding aloof in adherence to the neutrality pact drawn up in April 1941. Arguably, on this occasion, Roosevelt and Churchill were at fault in not being sufficiently alert to the likelihood of a Japanese attack. In August 1941, when the American president and the British prime minister had their first meeting, Roosevelt was most interested in the drawing up of a statement embodying the political ideals of the English-speaking peoples, the Atlantic Charter, which he hoped would encourage more American citizens to favour war with Germany. He did not want to discuss the Far East, where he believed that American firmness, with no more appeasement, would be enough to keep the peace. Churchill was no more alert to the threat from Japan, possibly in a British tradition well established in the 1930s. Just a few days before Pearl Harbor, he expressed the belief that war with Japan was no more than a remote possibility. Since many members of the American administration shared such an outlook, neither Roosevelt nor anybody else can be singled out for special blame for the surprise nature of the Japanese air strike. Roosevelt received intelligence warnings but appears less culpable in the case of Pearl Harbor than was Stalin in that of Barbarossa; both leaders can to some extent be exonerated because of the large element of surprise possessed by the two types of *Blitzkrieg*.

Whatever errors had been made by the Allied leaders in 1941, already by the end of that year discerning observers including Hitler and Churchill could note that *Blitzkrieg* was no longer enough. Held up before Moscow, Hitler confessed: 'Victory can no longer be achieved'. Soon after Pearl Harbor, Churchill declared: 'So we had won after all',[16] believing that the Grand Alliance of the Soviet Union, the United States and Britain would comprise too much power for the enemy opposition, as long as the technical expertise and political judgement of the two sides was roughly at the same level. If the Axis had developed the atomic bomb or manufactured a larger supply of V-2 rockets, there might have been a different outcome. Strategic decisions, the level of morale and other variables could still play their part, too. It was generally agreed, if not without dissension, that victory would be pursued first in Europe and the Atlantic, then in Asia and the Pacific. But it was by no means clear in the year 1942 that the thoughts of Hitler, Churchill and others at the end of 1941 were to be justified.

On the eastern European front, the German and associated forces were able to recover from the reverses before Moscow and elsewhere to press their advance further. Leningrad was subjected to a determined siege: 'in the winter of 1941–2, more Leningraders starved to death every month than the total of British civilians killed by German bombs in the entire war; the 1 million premature deaths in this one city greatly exceeded the combined military and civilian casualties of the British Empire and dominions and of the United States'.[17] But Leningrad held out; and so the principal successes of the invaders were to the south, where they moved forward about 150 miles in two weeks of the late spring of 1942. Beyond the River Don, they approached the city of Stalingrad on the Volga and the Caucasus Mountains, and their force grew to more than 150 divisions. There was no front in western Europe, but there was peripheral action in North Africa involving four divisions of the German army under Rommel, in collaboration with 11 Italian divisions. Rommel pushed on to El Alamein in Egypt by June, threatening Alexandria, Cairo and the Suez Canal. By this time, after lengthy talks, the British and Americans had agreed to make their first joint major effort in North Africa, and Churchill went to Moscow to tell Stalin that there could be no opening of a second front in western Europe before 1943. Meanwhile, in the Far East the Japanese were pushing all before them on the mainland, with Singapore falling in February and most of Burma following by May. They had no difficulty in crossing seas to take the islands constituting the Dutch East Indies and the Philippines during the same months. India and Australia seemed to be under threat, and the Pacific Ocean wide open.

By now, however, the superior might of the USA began to show itself in two naval victories, in the Coral Sea to the east of Australia early in May and off Midway Island to the west of Hawaii early in June. The limits of Japanese expansion were set. Later in the year in North Africa, after a powerful army had been assembled under Montgomery, Rommel was pushed back from El Alamein by the beginning of November – the first significant victory on land. A few days later, a British–American force landed in French North Africa, not without confusion and delay but nevertheless obliging the Vichy government to throw in its lot more completely with the German–Italian Axis.

The climax to the war of attrition was reached on the east European front, where during the same month of November the Red Army managed to effect a pincer movement around the enemy before Stalingrad and cut it off from its lines of supply. Hitler insisted on the continuance of the attack rather than withdrawal, for reasons of prestige and of strategy – withdrawal would mean disaster on other Soviet fronts as well. The epic battle of Stalingrad continued throughout the winter until the surrender of Field-Marshal Paulus on 31 January 1943. In the authoritative view of John Erickson, 'Stalingrad set the Soviet Union on the road to being a world power'. Erickson also catches the desperate nature of the battle: 'horrifyingly savage battles were fought for cellars, rooms, staircases and corners of walls. Lacking food and sleep, small units, the "garrisons" of Stalingrad, went out to seek water and battled to death over drainpipes.'[18]

UNCONDITIONAL SURRENDER: FROM STALINGRAD TO HIROSHIMA, 1943-5

There were three days of mourning in Germany, while the Allies had more occasion to rejoice. The war was still far from over, but there could now be at least preliminary thoughts about how it was to be brought to an end. Progress was sufficient in North Africa for Churchill and Roosevelt to meet in Casablanca in mid-January 1943. After a week and a half of difficult discussion, they agreed to give full recognition to de Gaulle as leader of the Free French, to postpone again the opening of the second front in Europe but to subject Germany meantime to heavy bombing, and to insist on 'unconditional surrender'. This announcement came as no great surprise, since after rumours of negotiation in the first year or so of the war, the Allies made it clear that they would fight on to the end. And it was impossible to be more specific at this juncture, owing to the fact that Stalin was preoccupied with Stalingrad and in no position to join in bargaining about the post-war settlement. Even if he had been at Casablanca, there could hardly have been any agreement among the Big Three on long-term aims. And so, for the time being, the Western Allies would continue to send aid to the Soviet Union via the arduous North Sea route and the less dangerous overland road across Persia, and to hope that this would compensate for the failure to open up a second front.

For their part, the enemy powers had never adopted the policy of 'unconditional surrender', although it might have come to that before the New Orders in Europe and Asia were completely constructed. For while many of the early victories were concluded with moderate peace treaties, especially with Vichy France, Nazi Germany treated its Western conquests with greater harshness as the war dragged on. It treated the Soviet Union in a bestial manner from the beginning, as indicated by Hitler's declaration of a 'War of Race Annihilation' at the time of the launching of Barbarossa. When the army showed no opposition, even some attraction, to such a policy, it developed without further prompting from the Führer. As Christian Streit, a thorough German scholar, has pointed out, the army was not only concerned to maintain its own authority within the political system:

> Rather the active acceptance of the extermination policy as an un-
> avoidable 'stretch of dirt', was based on a thoroughgoing ideological

agreement between the Generals and the National Socialist leadership, in which it was precisely the relative vagueness of the objective
in conquering the East that specifically enabled it to be integrated.
The traditional component of Eastern-imperialistic National Conservative thinking, the 'traumatic fear of Bolshevism', the internalised
equating of Jews with Socialists, and the consequent uncontrolled
Anti-semitism, had already been the determining factors for the
German Generals before the Russian campaign. This explains why,
after the Spring of 1941, the annihilation policy in which the Army
participated became increasingly more radical. This was reflected in
an extension of categories of the victims, in almost geometrical
progression from the 'Bolshevist leaders' down to the mass of all Jews
and Soviet intelligentsia, not only among the prisoners of war but
amongst the civilian populace too.[19]

Before the end of the war, millions of ordinary Soviet citizens were
deliberately exterminated.

Some of the notorious gas chambers of the Final Solution were first
tried out on the Soviet prisoners of war, over 3 million of whom
perished in captivity. Those who survived were treated severely for
suspected cowardice or treason by Stalin's government on their return
to their motherland, while over a million German prisoners of war
died in Soviet camps. If neither as systematic nor as thorough as their
Nazi counterparts, the Soviet authorities demonstrated their inhumanity as clearly during the war as they had during the preceding purges.

The Western Allies, too, were far from innocent with their indiscriminate 'saturation' bombing of German civilians culminating in the
virtual destruction of Hamburg, Dresden and other cities. The police
president of Hamburg made the following report on 1 December 1943
about the raids of the preceding July and August:

> The streets were covered with hundreds of corpses. Mothers with
> their children, youths, old men, burnt, charred, untouched and
> clothed, naked with a waxen pallor like dummies in a shop window,
> they lay in every posture, quiet and peaceful or cramped, the death-
> struggle shown in the expression on their faces. The shelters showed
> the same picture, even more horrible in its effect, as it showed in
> many cases the final distracted struggle against a merciless fate.

Although in some places shelterers sat quietly, peacefully and untouched as if sleeping in their chairs, killed without realization or pain by carbon monoxide poisoning, in other shelters the position of remains of bones and skulls showed how the occupants had fought to escape from their buried prison. No flight of imagination will ever succeed in measuring and describing the gruesome scenes of horror in the many buried air raid shelters. Posterity can only bow its head in honour of the fate of these innocents, sacrificed by the murderous lust of a sadistic enemy.[20]

At the time, many British and American people believed that the Germans were getting nothing more than a taste of their own medicine, but the worthlessness of 'saturation bombing' as well as its inhumanity have been indicated in later analysis. This kind of attack was for the most part counter-productive, since it was conducted at enormous cost in men, machines and money while not achieving success in its aims of destroying German industry or morale. And then there was the dropping of the atomic bomb on Hiroshima and Nagasaki, an awesome technical device for advancing the war against Japan. By this time, the Japanese had given more than adequate proof that barbarity was not the exclusive attribute of European and American civilisation. So degraded had the general standards of decency and honour become that indiscriminate submarine warfare, looked upon with horror at the beginning of the First World War, was now carried on without much qualm or question.

Whether or not a negotiated peace as sought by Japan and Germany before 1945 would have reduced the suffering is difficult to say. Certainly, it was never seriously contemplated by the Allies from the beginning of 1943 onwards as they continued the task of what was now generally agreed to be 'total war'. During the rest of 1943, the Allied forces continued by such means to take several steps forward, although not without at least a few back. On the eastern European front, the persistence of the attack on Stalingrad had allowed the German army on other fronts to prepare itself for the inevitable counter-attack, while weapons manufactured behind the Urals could now be put to full use by the Red forces along with the materiel sent in by the Allies. So there were several large-scale battles, notably near the town of Kursk in July, with about 1500 tanks on each side as the

Germans attempted another offensive. Although the Germans were pushed back again, they were still far from broken, and resisted the Soviet advance all the way through Ukraine and from Moscow and Leningrad. There was significant action in western Europe, too, although not yet the opening of the second front. After the German and Italian forces had finally been defeated in North Africa in April, the Allies decided to work their way into the Nazi 'Fortress Europe' through Sicily and Italy, beginning in July. As before, German units put up much heavier resistance than Italian ones, which had never cared much for fighting and were now completely giving up. Spirits sank low enough for Mussolini to be ousted before the end of July, and the successor government accepted unconditional surrender early in September. Although their former friends now turned on them, and there was a considerable amount of guerrilla action by a powerful Italian partisan movement behind the lines, the Germans fought on. In the Far East, the mainly American amphibious forces hopped from island to island over vast distances in the Pacific, while a motley army hacked its way through the jungles of Burma on the Asiatic mainland.

At the other end of the continent, the Big Three met for the first time at Tehran, Persia, in November. Much attention was given to the question of the strategy to be adopted to bring the war to an early end. Should pressure be applied to Turkey to join the Allies so that Germany could be attacked through the Balkans? Churchill, remembering his Dardanelles strategy from the First World War and wanting to forestall the Russians, argued for an attack on what he called the 'soft underbelly' of Europe. In fact Turkey did not declare war on Germany until March 1945, and there were problems of access to the Balkans, therefore. Stalin argued that in general the Mediterranean was not as promising or as important a springboard for attack on Germany as France, and Roosevelt agreed with some enthusiasm, Churchill with a certain reluctance. Finally, the Western Allies promised to open up the second front in France no later than May 1944. Stalin was to co-ordinate with them an advance from the east. There was preliminary discussion about the shape of post-war Europe, especially Poland, which was to be reconstituted on a less muddled ethnic basis, losing some territory to the Soviet Union but receiving compensation from Germany, which would be partitioned. Firmly agreed on unconditional surrender, the

Big Three went back to their respective headquarters to make their various contributions to its attainment.

1944 was the year when the New Orders in Europe and Asia began to crumble. In the spring, hard-won progress continued on the east European front, where the Red forces removed the enemy from the Crimea and thus regained control of the Black Sea, gaining access to the Balkans. In the summer, the Balkans were taken over without much resistance from the Axis satellites, which had never fought with as much tenacity as their German patrons, who withdrew to nearer their own homeland. Romania quickly switched sides; Bulgaria, which had never fought against the Soviet Union, collapsed in a few days, and Hungary followed, albeit not without a fight, by February 1945. The Red forces passed through Yugoslavia, where their ally Tito was attempting to establish his authority. But they kept out of Greece, where civil war broke out late in 1944, and Albania, where another Communist, Enver Hoxha, was gaining power. By this time, further north, the Soviet advance had moved along the Baltic Sea as far as the frontier of Prussia. Finland kept its independence in an armistice made in September, but Estonia, Latvia and Lithuania were reincorporated in the Soviet Union. In Poland, the Soviet forces reached as far as the banks of the River Vistula facing Warsaw, and then paused, allegedly because the troops needed a rest, probably because the Soviet authorities did not want to assist the mainly anti-Communist uprising in the Polish capital. Certainly, a Soviet-backed provisional government was set up in the city of Lublin.

Pressure on the east European front was relieved by the much delayed opening of the Second Front in the West with the launching of Operation Overlord on D-Day, 6 June 1944, under the unified command of an American, General Eisenhower. Preparations had been thorough, involving many men and much technology, and the Germans were caught somewhat by surprise. Nevertheless, some of the cross-Channel landings were made with difficulty, and progress through the summer and autumn was by no means smooth, even after another invasion of France from the south in August. Part of the blame must be attributed to wranglings between the British and American generals, some must be placed on the Allied suspicion of the French partisans, especially the Communists among them. Although they had no great love for de Gaulle, the Allied leaders were relieved when he rather than the Communists was able to assume the leadership of liberated France. Similarly, the final stages of the war in Italy were drawn out partly through Allied distrust of the Italian partisans right up to the spring of 1945, when they captured and shot Mussolini. At the same time, as ever, the German armies on both sides of the Alps were still fighting stoutly, and were indeed still in good enough heart to launch a counter-offensive in the Ardennes near the French frontier in December.

Before that, from the summer onwards, the Germans were making a final attempt at a technical knock-out of Britain through their pilotless aircraft or V-ls and their even more formidable rockets or V-2s. The V-2s in particular created widespread alarm in London in particular, and revived thoughts of its evacuation. Concerned about another threat, the spread of Communism in eastern Europe, Churchill went to Moscow in October, and made an unofficial deal with Stalin and Molotov on spheres of influence. Some figures were agreed: Romania 90 per cent Soviet; Greece 90 per cent British; Bulgaria and Hungary 80 per cent Soviet; Yugoslavia 50–50.

The Red menace was seen to be raising its ugly head in the other principal theatre of war, where the Americans discovered as they established a presence in China that Chiang Kai-shek was more concerned with suppressing Mao Zedong than defeating Japan. Nevertheless, from the summer of 1944 onwards the American Air Force was able to use bases in China for attacks on Japanese cities. Meanwhile, from the direction of the Pacific, enough islands had been hopped for air attacks to be made there, too. In October, General MacArthur and his army returned to the Philippines in a huge amphibious operation accompanied by a victory at sea in what has been called 'history's last great surface contest'[21] in and around Leyte Gulf. Back on the mainland there was further Allied success in Burma, and Singapore was now in reach of British aircraft.

The year 1945 brought great Allied celebrations with the final surrender of Germany and Japan. But its unconditional nature brought problems for the victors, who extended their disagreements about the post-war settlement. In Europe, the year began in a most amicable manner, as the Red forces complied with a Western request to relieve the pressure caused by the Ardennes counter-attack, and hastily launched a large-scale winter offensive. But cracks in the Grand Alliance were visible at the Yalta Conference in February, of which more below. The Red offensive enjoyed hard-won success on all fronts early in 1945. By March, most of East Prussia and Poland had been cleared of the enemy, as well as the eastern part of Austria including Vienna. There remained the formidable task of breaking the deep defensive line along the Oder and Neisse rivers, where the majority of the remaining German forces gathered for a last stand. After some final bitter fighting the Soviet victory banner was raised on the Reichstag on 1 May, the day after Hitler's suicide.There were still a few pockets of resistance in Prague and southern Czechoslovakia, but they were quickly crushed.

From the west, after the collapse of the Ardennes counter-attack, the British and American forces moved towards a meeting with their Soviet allies. Heavy bombing was still preparing the way for them, and was extended in order to ease the path of the Soviet forces. Dresden was virtually destroyed, and other towns such as Halle and Dessau very badly damaged. Bickering continued between Montgomery and the American generals, with Eisenhower insistent on an orderly advance rather than a quick strike to arrive in Berlin before the Russians. When the victorious armies did meet, there were warm embraces, but also an early realisation that the Allies did not speak the same language in more ways than one after the Nazi capitulation on 8 May.

In the Far East, the Soviet Union entered the war against Japan on 8 August three months after the conclusion of the war in Europe. Welcomed as a promise earlier in the year, the Soviet advance was not so agreeable a fact. The losses of the tsarist war against Japan of 1904–5 were recouped at little cost, and the occupation of southern Sakhalin and the Kuril Islands in particular was to lead to later disagreements. The use of the atomic bomb on 6 and 9 August over Hiroshima and Nagasaki respectively obliged the emperor to force the Japanese war cabinet to accept unconditional surrender by 14 August, and probably prevented further Soviet gains. Certainly, there was immediate Allied resentment that the Soviet Union had gained so much at so little cost. For their part, Stalin and his associates believed that they had already made much more than their fair contribution to the winning of the war in Europe, but the existence of the atomic bomb helped to soften their protests about their exclusion from peace discussions with Japan. As the Second World War came to an end, then, there was an ominous indication of what might be involved in a Third, as well as of some of its potential origins.

On 2 April 1945, Hitler gave his own farewell view of the future, now that the New Order would not be set up either in Europe or Asia:

> With the defeat of the Reich and pending the emergence of the Asiatic, the African and perhaps the South American nationalisms, there will remain in the world only two Great Powers capable of confronting each other – the United States and Soviet Russia. The laws of both history and geography will compel these two powers to a trial of strength either militarily or in the fields of economics and ideology. These same laws make it inevitable that both powers should become enemies of Europe.[22]

During the last few months of the war, Hitler and his associates did all they could to foment dissension between the Allies, posing as guardians of the European civilisation which they had in fact done all too much to destroy. Nevertheless, after the death of the Führer and his 12-year Reich, even without his help at least some of his forecast turned out to be accurate, as Europe became divided as never before between the USA and the USSR.

THE END OF THE GRAND ALLIANCE: YALTA AND POTSDAM, 1945

In February 1945, at Yalta in the Crimea, President Franklin D. Roosevelt, Marshal Joseph V. Stalin and Prime Minister Winston S. Churchill talked together for a week or so to decide impartially the fate of the world – or so they and many others appear to have believed. In fact, as well as giving an individual flavour to the proceedings of the conference, each of the Big Three was expressing a national viewpoint developed from many years of experience.

To take them in order of the power at their disposal, Franklin D. Roosevelt argued that with regard to the principal problem, that of Germany, it would be utopian to talk of decentralisation, even though the administration had been decentralised during his visit to the country some 40 years previously. Now that the administration was concentrated on Berlin, he could see no other solution to the problem but dismemberment, into half a dozen or so separate parts. The German people should not be forced to starve, but the USA did not want German living standards to be higher than those in the USSR. Regarding the question of Poland, which was somewhat more immediate than that of Germany, the American president pointed out the necessity of maintaining the support of his people, especially the 6 million Poles among them, particularly since elections were imminent. While favouring the Curzon Line drawn up after the First World War as the boundary between Poland and the Soviet Union, therefore, he hoped there might be some consideration of concessions to the Poles in its southern sector. In general, he hoped that a government of Polish national unity could be formed, with representatives of all Polish parties. As far as the wider world was concerned, FDR probably aimed at some kind of New Deal on a global scale. Although he made no specific recommendation for such a policy at Yalta, he seems to have wanted the old world of empires to pass away. He certainly believed that a new world based on the freedoms enunciated in the Atlantic Charter would be guaranteed through the creation of the United Nations Organisation. Moreover, he was fully aware that the economic power of the USA was much greater than that of all its allies and rivals. He understood therefore that the USA would have the largest influence in the councils of the great powers in the years following 1945, especially if the Open Door of international economic opportunity could be maintained.

Who came next to Roosevelt in the sheer physical might at his disposal, Stalin or Churchill? This is not the easiest of questions to answer. Stalin was all too conscious of a level of destruction in the Soviet Union far higher than his allies could understand. He probably did not realise that in little more than ten years the Soviet Union would emerge as the world's second superpower, in at least some respects rivalling the United States. As for Churchill, he seems to have overestimated the strength of the British Empire and to have possessed little inkling of its imminent dissolution. Problems of precedence arose at Yalta itself, even when alphabetical, for in Russian Stalin comes before Churchill. Here, putting future potential before past performance, let us also take Stalin first.

Somewhat surprisingly for an adherent of Marxism–Leninism, not so surprisingly considering his record, the Soviet leader put heavy emphasis on the role of the individual in history, declaring to his two colleagues: 'as long as the three of them lived, none of them would involve their countries in aggressive actions'. But in ten years, they might all be gone, and 'A new generation would come into being not knowing the horrors of the present war'.[23] In fact, as we know, two of the Big Three were to go within a year, Roosevelt through death and Churchill via the ballot box. Both these events shook Stalin considerably: he had not realised that Roosevelt was so ill, and had expressed his belief that the British Labour Party would never come to power. But he was not sustained by confidence in his colleagues alone: he also expressed belief in historical forces apart from the individual or beyond. For example, he argued that Russia had been attacked twice in 30 years and that the frontiers needed to be constructed in such a manner that future attacks might be discouraged. If their leaders were to accept proposals for concessions to the Poles in the south, the Soviet peoples might say that Stalin and Molotov had turned out to be less reliable defenders of the Russians and the Ukrainians than Curzon and Clemenceau at the end of the First World War. Regarding the United Nations, Stalin expressed a certain amount of apprehension based on the Soviet experience of the League of Nations, but he found some consolation in the new organisation's award of three votes to the Soviet Union (Ukraine and Belarus as well as Russia). With reference to the Far East, Stalin went back even further than the First World War to the Russo-Japanese War of 1904–5 for justification of his present policy. As far as the other areas were concerned, Stalin expressed some interest in Fascist Italy, but was much more anxious that Nazi Germany should be made to pay in full for the damage that it had inflicted on the Soviet Union.

Agreeing with this last point, Churchill also referred to the difficulties that the Allies had experienced in collecting reparations from Germany at the end of the First World War. He may have harboured thoughts about the Soviet Union more akin to those following the Russian Revolution of 1917 when he had been militantly anti-Communist than to those during the Second World War when he had been a loyal ally of the USSR. The idea of the 'iron curtain' was already in his correspondence even if he was not to proclaim it to the wider public before his famous speech in Fulton, Missouri, in March 1946. More at the front of his mind at Yalta, however, was the determined attitude to matters nearer home expressed at an earlier speech in the

Mansion House, London, in November 1942: 'I have not become the King's First Minister in order to preside over the liquidation of the British Empire.' And at Yalta the British prime minister's suspicions were directed not only at the Soviet Union but also towards the United States, whose independence after all had been the first milestone on the road to that imperial decline that Churchill feared most. An American proposal concerning United Nations trusteeship over colonial and dependent peoples disturbed him greatly, although he was somewhat reassured by the American declaration that the proposal concerned enemy colonies only. Nevertheless, Churchill's vision of an English-Speaking Union incorporating the USA as well as the British Empire remained partially clouded over by the apprehension that the USA and the USSR were in at least tacit alliance to dismember every empire but their own. On European questions, the British prime minister also had strong views. Regarding the division of Germany, he feared in particular the strength of Prussia – the arch evil – and believed that if Prussia were separated from Germany, the chances of future European war would be much reduced. Such a rearrangement of frontiers could be to the advantage of the Poles, in the view of Churchill, who also showed some support for Roosevelt's hopes that there could be a readjustment of the south-eastern sector in Poland's favour. Here, he might well have been thinking of another of his concerns going back to 1917 and after, that the Balkans should be protected as much as possible from Soviet infiltration.

The Protocol, or official statement of agreement, of the Yalta Conference announced the convocation of another, wider conference of the United Nations in the USA in April 1945. The Big Three would become the Big Five with the addition of France and China, and they would have permanent seats in a Security Council, other lesser powers being represented in a General Assembly. France would be given a zone of occupation in Germany. The Big Three agreed that Germany must pay reparations in kind, half of which would go to the Soviet Union. The question of war criminals would be discussed by the three foreign secretaries. Problems of territorial trusteeship would be looked at by the Big Five. Civilians and prisoners of war would be returned home. Among the other points of the Yalta Protocol was a Declaration on Liberated Europe asserting that: 'The establishment of order in Europe and the rebuilding of national economic life must be achieved by processes which will enable the liberated peoples to destroy the last vestiges of Nazism and Fascism and to create democratic institutions of their own choice.' There were more specific provisions summarising the positions of the Big Three on Germany and Poland as well as on the United Nations and Yugoslavia. There was also a secret agreement regarding the entry of the Soviet Union into the war against Japan, which was to take place two or three months after the surrender of Germany. The Kuril Islands should be handed over to the Soviet Union, while 'the former rights violated by the treacherous attack of Japan in 1904' would be restored.[24]

In April 1945, the first full meeting of the United Nations in San Francisco brought together delegates of 50 nations to adopt unanimously by June 1945 a Charter adapted from the Atlantic Charter and to resolve to collaborate in the maintenance of peace. All members would participate in the General Assembly. The Security Council was to consist permanently of the USA, USSR, UK, France and China, along with temporarily elected members.

When the next conference of the Big Three was held in Potsdam in mid-July 1945, Roosevelt was already dead and Churchill was about to be defeated in a general election. The new American president, Harry S. Truman, wrote home to his wife the day after the conference opened that he had already taken a liking to Stalin and was glad that the Soviet Union was entering the war: it would be shorter and the boys home all the sooner.[25] The new British prime minister, Clement R. Attlee, also got on well with Stalin and Truman. Byrnes, Molotov and Bevin worked happily enough together in the beginning of a now formally constituted Council of Foreign Ministers, in which they were to be joined by the representatives of France and China, the other two of the Big Five. There were certainly items on the agenda that divided the Big Three: for example, Poland and other eastern European states; Germany, Italy and Spain; and the Middle East. But the new Polish frontiers were accepted for the fact that they had become, as was the division of Germany and of reparations. Stalin maintained a poker-face when Truman told him of the A-bomb, probably because he knew about it already.

The eventuality that goodwill was not maintained on all sides was not so much to do with the individual failure of statesmen as with the irreconcilability of the interests of their respective states in the task of reconstruction out of the ruins left by the war. In a sense, too, Hitler was correct in his assertion that the laws of both history and geography compelled the United States and the Soviet Union to a trial of strength.

THE LOSSES

Before we look at the beginnings of this contest in the context of reconstruction, we must carry out the sad exercise of estimating the extent of the ruins. To take the human losses first, the approximate European totals were as follows: the Soviet Union, at least 20 million (6 million killed in battle, 14 million murdered by the Germans and their allies); Poland, more than 6 million (0.3 million killed in battle, 5.8 million murdered by the Germans and their allies); Germany, 5 million (3.5 million killed in battle, 1 million dying in Soviet captivity and 0.5 million in air raids); Yugoslavia, 1.5 million (0.5 million killed in battle, 1 million murdered by the Germans and their allies). Up to 6 million Jews were systematically exterminated in the Holocaust, most of them from eastern Europe (3 million from Poland, 1.25 million from the Soviet Union). Along with the Jews, a large number of gypsies, Communists and other anti-Nazis, and 'deviants' – homosexuals, for example – also perished. Losses in western Europe, no less grievous for those concerned, were considerably smaller than in the First World War: about 0.6 million French people, mostly civilians; about 0.4 million British, mostly combatants; and about 0.3 million Italian, again mostly combatants. Outside Europe, the greatest human losses were sustained in China, although even a rough figure is hard to come by, and estimates vary between 3 and 13 millions, mostly civilians. Japan suffered more than 1 million battle deaths and more than 0.5 million from air raids, about 1.6 million altogether. Least affected was the USA, with about 0.3 million battle deaths, virtually none of which were civilian (but still by no means a negligible amount, and many Americans were involved in the war in some way, 16 million of them serving in the armed forces).[26]

To these grisly figures of mortality must be added millions more of the wounded and maimed. Moreover, because of the great destruction and dislocation, vast numbers in Europe were obliged at the war's end to undergo a miserable existence to which at times death must have seemed almost preferable. Firstly, there were prisoners of war and other exiles sent home often against their will, including not only hundreds of thousands of Red Army soldiers who had fought alongside the Soviet Union's enemies under General Vlasov and other traitor commanders but also millions of prisoners of war and civilians drafted into forced labour. Many of these were kept in forced labour on their return to the Soviet Union, and more than a few executed. Thirdly, there were about 25 million displaced persons (DPs), with about 10 million Germans being moved on from reconstituted Poland, Czechoslovakia, Hungary and Romania as well as the Baltic states. There were also somewhat smaller quantities of other nationalities expelled from their place of residence: Poles moved westward with the frontier of their country, Greeks from Bulgarian Macedonia, Hungarians from Czechoslovakia, Romania and Yugoslavia, Slovaks from Hungary into Czechoslovakia, and so on. The Crimean Tatars and Volga Germans who had been uprooted in the Soviet Union during the war were still under suspicion and not allowed to return home. Retribution was exercised in the shape of the death sentence for 12 Nazi leaders and seven Japanese leaders after trial, sometimes without trial for many others less well known and for collaborators at other places. A few were spared because of the valuable intelligence information or technical expertise at their disposal, and some of those guilty of war crimes escaped unpunished.

To the human death and discomfort must be added the material damage, the virtual destruction of some cities, the extreme dislocation of transport, and shortages of food and even of drinkable water. The suffering would have been far worse from 1943 to 1948 had it not been for the operations of the United Nations Relief and Rehabilitation Administration (UNRRA). Tons of supplies were distributed throughout west and east Europe alike, if not so much in the Soviet Union, by UNRRA and by other UN agencies. Unfortunately, however, almost from the beginning, the carrying out of even-handed policies was made difficult by the approaching shadow of what was to become known as the Cold War.

14

THE COLD WAR AND DECOLONISATION, 1945–1968

THE FALL OF EUROPE

As well as the vast losses, there were the huge costs. For example, the British foreign debt was six times as great as before – the largest in the world, while trade had shrunk to a third of its former level. France was faced with the formidable problem of how to regain its stature after the years of occupation. Germany and Italy had to begin again from scratch after their comprehensive defeat. Indeed, Europe as a whole had completely lost the dominance that it had enjoyed before the First World War. There could be no more talk of a balance of power arranged exclusively by European diplomats. For now, by a wide margin, the USA was *the* global power, with the Soviet Union in second place largely because of its occupation of a vast amount of strategically situated land.

Two interconnected processes, the Cold War and decolonisation, were to give new emphasis to the downfall of Europe. However, in 1945 and immediately afterwards, hopes were held out for revival of the situation that had existed before the Second World War, with even some echoes of the situation before the First. Although there was widespread recognition that the UK would depend on loans from the USA, there was still the hope in the Foreign Office that the British lion was not yet in his dotage. Indeed, his strength should be increased in

433

two ways: 'cooperation between the three World Powers' (USA, USSR and UK); leadership of the Dominions, France and the smaller European powers.[1] Needless to say, General de Gaulle would not be happy with such an approach, although he soon realised that France would have to come to terms with the USA if it wished to regain anything like its former stature.[2] The Italian foreign minster, Carlo Sforza, confessed that Italy's days as a great power were over, observing: 'I am not at all sure that England is an iron vessel, still less so that France is, but I am certain of the fact that we are only a poor earthernware vessel.'[3] The German liberal democrat Theodor Heuss held out some hopes that his country could act as a bridge between East and West.[4] But the two defeated Axis powers also appealed quite soon for support from across the Atlantic.

While Europe welcomed dollars, it attempted to resist US cultural influence: 'It's true *they* have the money bags, But *we* have all the brains' said a note circulating within the British delegation to the post-war loan talks,[5] anticipating the more dignified but no less arrogant observation of Harold Macmillan that the UK constituted Greece to the USA's Rome. High culture held out more successfully: Paris in particular made a strong comeback with the development of the philosophy of existentialism by Jean-Paul Sartre and others. But the vigour and persistence of transatlantic cinema and popular song could not be resisted, as, for example, a series of American entertainers packed out the London Palladium. In ironic riposte, Jacques Tati's film *Jour de Fête* (*Holiday*) depicted a rural postman attempting to adopt American efficiency, while Vittorio de Sica's *Ladri di Biciclette* (*Bicycle Thieves*) showed its hero vainly attempting to erect a poster of a film star.

ORIGINS AND IMPACT OF THE COLD WAR, 1945–9

At the end of the Second World War, Winston Churchill asserted that we would not make the same mistakes again: we would make different ones. This prediction turned out to be all too true. Furthermore, we did make the same mistakes again, in the sense that the lesson that we tried to learn from the past was how not to repeat it. In other words, since the root cause of the Second World War was seen in appeasement, we would avoid the repetition of that policy at all costs. The principal costs turned out to be the Cold War and the increasing risk of a third world war. Thus, history did repeat itself not for the first time as statesmen ran the risk of another conflict through a policy of attempting to avert a conflict that had already been brought to an end.

However, that was not the whole story, for the Cold War had been on the way for some time, arguably for about a century and a half, especially to the extent that it involved a confrontation between America and Russia. At the beginning of Europe's rise from the late eighteenth century, even before, astute observers could discern that these two future superpowers on Europe's flanks were heading towards a shared dominance of the world amid probable conflict. Such an observation is reinforced in the context of the realisation that these two new empires were rising up on the shoulders of the old. Britain, France and other European states were losing not only their continental but also their overseas influence to these rivals, who struggled with each other to fill as much as possible of the resulting power vacuum. To put it simply, the Cold War was intimately linked with decolonisation, the other principal characteristic of the years following 1945.

The Cold War was not a completely new type of conflict. Indeed, the term had been used by a Spanish writer describing the struggle between Christians and Muslims as far back as the fourteenth century: 'War that is very strong and very hot ends either with death or peace, whereas cold war neither brings peace nor gives honour to the one who makes it.'[6] Almost certainly the Greeks and Romans had a word for it, too. What was new about the Cold War that arose after 1945 was its global scale and the very extensive nature of the death that would follow should it ever become hot. Similar to the fourteenth-century mutual hatred of Christian and Muslim was that of capitalist and Communist, which did much to bring about the disruption of the Grand Alliance, made a mockery of the United Nations, and impeded balanced historical assessment. Certainly, neither extreme of interpretation is correct. Whatever the enormity of his crimes and the depths of his depravity, Stalin did not have a master plan to take over eastern Europe, then western Europe, later the world. On the other hand, while the businessmen of the USA were hoping for greater profits in the post-war period, they were not conspiring for an 'Open Door' of free enterprise so wide that it would immediately take over the economy of the Soviet Union and of all other European states for their own purposes.

However powerful the Soviet Union might have appeared to some observers at the end of the Second World War, its armed forces were in no position to carry the fight to its former allies. Early in 1946, a US navy memorandum pointed out that:

> The Red Fleet is incapable of any important offensive or amphibious operations ... a strategic air force is practically non-existent either in material or concept ... economically, the Soviet Union is exhausted. The people are undernourished, industry and transport are in an advanced state of deterioration, enormous areas have been disloca-ted ... Maintenance of large occupation forces in Europe is dictated to a certain extent by the necessity of 'farming out' millions of men for whom living accommodations and food cannot be spared in the USSR during the current winter.[7]

At the very most, Soviet aggressive postures were confined to eastern Europe and other lands contiguous to the USSR, while President Truman had at his disposal not only the atomic bomb but also the express desire 'to enforce the peace of the world'. Undoubtedly, too, the USA was in a dominant financial position, as its former allies had discovered at a conference at Bretton Woods, New Hampshire, in July 1944. An International Monetary Fund (IMF) and an International Bank for Reconstruction and Development (IBRD, World Bank) were set up in such a manner that the other trading currencies were effec-tively tied to the dollar. Lord Keynes complained after attending a further conference of the two new agencies at Savannah, Georgia, in March 1946: 'I went expecting to meet the world and all I met was a tyrant.'[8] Similarly, the United Nations Relief and Recovery Adminis-tration (UNRRA) and other such agencies were dependent on largely American finance, and so the American influence in their administra-tion was greatest. For example, in 1945 the Soviet Union made a request to UNRRA for funds to relieve the much stricken republics of the Ukraine and Belarus as Lend-Lease was coming to an end and negotiations for more credit appeared to have failed. The sum asked for was drastically reduced and grudgingly given. In April 1945, even before going to Potsdam, Truman had shocked Molotov by telling the Soviet foreign minister that no aid would be given to the Soviet Union unless it accepted the American version of the Yalta agreements.

In spite of these and other problems, in spite of references to the 'iron curtain' by Churchill and others even before his famous speech of March 1946, the Cold War did not break out fully before 1947, at the beginning of which an appropriately harsh winter was raging. The effect of the weather on the economy of the UK, which had been carrying out its traditional imperial role of policing the Mediterranean since the end of the war, was disastrous. Into the breach thus caused stepped the USA, as on 12 March 1947 President Truman asked Congress for $400 million worth of aid for Greece and Turkey, both of which were experiencing severe internal difficulties. Elevating his request into what became known as the Truman Doctrine, the president declared that thenceforth it must be American policy 'to support free peoples who are resisting attempted subjugation by armed minorities or outside pressure. If we falter, we may endanger the peace of the world and we shall surely endanger the welfare of our own nation.' Howard K. Smith, as acute an observer of the post-war scene as he had been of that pre-war, argued that, although Truman's appeal had been necessary, it was also bad foreign policy, since it stirred up suspicions and animosities in the minds of the Russians that could not easily be stilled:

> I was in Moscow at the Foreign Ministers' Conference on Germany at the time, and the change in our Soviet hosts' attitude from one of some amicability to a stubborn resistance on every detailed point of discussion was perceptible. In Russian eyes, the meaning of the new doctrine was clear. America – which President Truman himself had said was heading for depression – was going to avoid a crisis by stirring up warlike anti-Communist emotions in the West European vacuum: a rearmament programme, they concluded, would follow.[9]

On the other hand, needless to say, Soviet policies since 1945 and before had already stirred up many suspicions and animosities in the West, as we shall see further below. Less than three months after the enunciation of the Truman Doctrine, however, came another, conciliatory, American speech, this time from the new secretary of state. On 5 June 1947, George C. Marshall outlined a scheme of long-term recovery for European civilisation through integration and planning backed by American aid. The Marshall Plan (European Recovery

Programme) was discussed in Paris by the British, French and Soviet foreign ministers. However, albeit after some serious consideration by Stalin and his advisers back in Moscow, the Soviet Union decided to reject the plan for itself, and, after some hesitation, for the east European states within its sphere of influence, too.

Not all the initiatives came from Moscow. While there were those in Poland, Hungary and Czechoslovakia who were inclined to enter Marshall's Programme, the Yugoslav and Romanian governments rejected it from the first. A more general, enforced unanimity came with the foundation in September 1947 of the Cominform (Communist Information Bureau). Stalin and his advisers, especially Andrei Zhdanov, played a predictably important part in this replacement for the Comintern that had been dissolved in 1943. In addition, however, strong opposition to the popular front policies of some European Communist parties was led by Tito and the Yugoslavs. (Ironically, Yugoslavia would soon be the first state to be ejected from the Cominform.) Zhdanov's keynote speech contained the exposition of the two-camp thesis, the rejection of the argument that there could be any reconciliation of capitalism and Communism, and assertion of their fundamental enmity. The launch of the Cominform was preceded in June 1947 by the announcement of the Molotov Plan, a series of bilateral trade treaties between the Soviet Union and the other states of eastern Europe.

In April 1948, the Organisation for European Economic Cooperation (OEEC) was set up in western Europe as the US Congress approved the implementation of the Marshall Plan. Would it have done so had the Soviet Union decided to participate? However, we cannot linger on alternative possibilities. Instead, we must look at the manner in which the various areas of Europe became involved in the Cold War during the years 1945 to 1949.

The south-west

Let us begin our survey of Europe as before in the south-west, where the Iberian peninsula was entirely a Fascist region during the Second World War but managed for the most part to stay out of it. Portugal was still under the dictatorship of the former professor of economics Dr Oliveira Salazar, who announced in 1945 that 'the flag of victory is blowing in a democratic breeze', but then sailed as close as he possibly could to the wind. That is, he conceded the appearance of liberalism rather than the reality. Although some prosperity had been derived from the provision of a safe place of refuge and from the sale of wolfram, a mineral used in the making of tungsten steel, little of the wealth had trickled through to the mass of the people, most of whom scratched out a bare living from the soil or snatched it from the sea. The vast empire in Africa was retained less as a source of wealth than as an outlet for emigrants and a proud reminder of the great imperial past, an image protected by the status of 'Britain's oldest ally', and by the acceptance of the wider western community at the onset of the Cold War.[10]

Like its Iberian neighbour, Spain under General Francisco Franco had quite a good war. For the most part, it was not involved in the conflict, although a Blue Legion fought alongside the German army in the Soviet Union and there were plans interrupted by the invasion of the Soviet Union for a German–Spanish seizure of Gibraltar. Spain managed to exploit its 'neutrality' in a manner economically and diplomatically useful for the Axis, and facilitated the escape of many suspected war criminals. The Big Three agreed at Potsdam in August 1945 to keep Franco's Spain out of the United Nations, citing 'its origins, its nature, its record and its close association with the aggressor states', and there was some talk of bringing the government down by economic sanctions and diplomatic isolation, then forcing it to become more democratic. Franco was possibly somewhat anxious, but unmoved by the pressure. When a visiting American representative suggested to the dictator that Spain should have a Christian Democratic party along the lines of the Roman Catholic parties in Italy and France, Franco allegedly replied: 'But we are all one party in Spain; and it *is* Christian!' He managed to hold out until the opening of the Cold War, which brought Spain into the strategic thinking of the American National Security Council. Soon landing rights were negotiated on Spanish airfields, and there was some consideration of the establishment of American bases in Spain. But American prosperity was not brought in for most of the Spanish people. Meanwhile, except for Morocco and lesser holdings in Africa, the empire had now shrunk to nothing. And if some Latin American states worked in the late 1940s for the entry of Spain into the United Nations, this was probably less the result of filial piety towards the mother country than a response to pressure from the neighbouring USA, which wanted Spain to be firmly in the Western camp.[11]

Such rehabilitation of Franco's Spain was something of an embarrassment to moderate politicians in Italy, especially in the spring of 1948, when the Italian Communist Party looked set for some success, even for outright victory, in the impending general election. However, Italy's neo-Fascists were not yet a large enough party for old fears to be revived, while the loss of empire was not widely lamented. Therefore, a combination of the internal support of the Vatican and the upper class and that of the USA from outside was enough to return a coalition dominated by the Christian Democrats. However, such economic problems as rural overpopulation, backward agriculture and ailing industry persisted after the war. Meanwhile, the traditional north–south split had perhaps even been widened by the manner in which the south had been liberated and a conservative caretaker government been set up while predominantly left-wing partisans were still fighting the Germans to the north. The size of the division had been revealed in a referendum on the monarchy in the summer of 1946, most of the south supporting the institution, the large majority of the north rejecting it. Had it not been for Marshall Aid and the broad support given by the USA to the government under the leadership of Alcide de Gasperi, former librarian of the Vatican, Italy might have succumbed at the beginning of the Cold War. Instead, the former coalition colleagues of the Christian Democrats and of their moderate allies, the Communists, were now obliged to concentrate on trade union activity.

The north-west

A similar danger to the reviving old order was perceived in the largest state of north-west Europe, France, where the Red menace seemed poised to take power by the ballot box. After de Gaulle had restored order out of chaos at the end of the war, the first elections in October 1945 for seats in a Constituent Assembly put the Communists just ahead of the Catholics and Socialists. Then, when a complex series of arguments about the form to be taken by the Fourth Republic was over, the Socialists fell away in the elections for a new government, while the Communist and Catholic parties were more or less equally balanced.

The political instability of the Fourth Republic was intensified in 1947 as the Catholic voters turned towards de Gaulle's conservative Rally of the French People (RPF) and the prime minister, Paul Ramadier, expelled the Communist members from his cabinet. As the French Communists, like their Italian counterparts, put their major energies into the trade union movement, de Gaulle's influence increased. The threat from the Right appeared as great as that from the Left. Through the first difficult years of the Fourth Republic, however, an element of continuity was supplied by the extension of public ownership to key industries and the introduction of the Monnet Plan involving in particular major commodities such as coal, electricity, steel and cement. This interference in the economy, as much in the tradition of Louis XIV and Napoleon as a response to left-wing pressure, combined with the impact of the Marshall Plan to allow a mostly Catholic–Socialist 'Third Force' government to survive. Its internal problems were compounded by those of Europe, even more by those of the empire. France struggled to maintain a presence in Indo-China, where war broke out in 1946. In Africa, however, there were less violent manifestations of the desire for independence. This was partly because recommendations for a return to a united empire, albeit with some reforms appearing to give a greater measure of equality to its members, had been adopted at a conference at Brazzaville in the French Congo in February 1944.[12]

Like most French people, their neighbours in north-west Europe believed that restored empires were an important foundation of post-war recovery, especially in the Belgian Congo and Dutch Indonesia, and they were prepared to use police repression and even armed struggle to keep them. Internally, too, the problems of its neighbours were comparable to those of France, although Belgium was much more prosperous than the Netherlands, having done well out of the last years of the war through the port of Antwerp and comparatively undamaged industry, especially steel. The large Catholic party was somewhat embarrassed by the support that it gave to the return of the exiled King Leopold III, who was suspected of Nazi sympathies. But after the Communists left the government at about the same time as their Italian and French counterparts, the Catholic party formed an important part of the support for the moderate Socialist prime minister, Henri Spaak. Now the principal source of internal conflict became again what it had been earlier, the split between the French-speaking Walloons and the Flemish-speaking Flemings. In the Netherlands, Rotterdam and Amsterdam were not as immediately prosperous as Antwerp and destruction of industry had been greater than in Belgium. Communist, sectarian and linguistic problems were smaller than across the border, but the colonial question was more starkly posed in Indonesia than in the Congo, partly because the Japanese had set up an independent regime there, with at least some autonomy. Along with Luxembourg, the Netherlands and Belgium moved towards the much-discussed formation of Benelux. However, the first tangible step was modest, the establishment of a common tariff policy at the beginning of 1948.

Like many states on the other side of the Channel, Britain was a recipient of Marshall Aid and of other loans previously. It differed from them in having no Catholic party and only a very small Communist party, and also in its assumption of wide international responsibilities at the end of the war, not just throughout the British Empire but also in Europe, especially in the Mediterranean. This world role was not unwelcome to at least some members of the Labour government, and the former union leader who was now foreign secretary, Ernest Bevin, gave every indication of thriving on it. But just as his health was being undermined by overwork, so the superficially convincing might of the Royal Navy was not supported by a prosperous economy. Britannia could no longer afford to rule the waves, and her weakness became clear early in 1947:

> If ever a nation was paralysed it was Britain in her winter crisis. Millions were unemployed. War-time blackout was reintroduced over 80% of the country. Domestic use of electricity for heating was restricted on pain of heavy fines. A newspaper stated the alarming truth that at that moment a country so small and weak as Portugal could have invaded and conquered England, prostrated by cold.[13]

Britain had been transformed from a lender to a borrower nation, with overseas investments, merchant marine and industry all in disarray. But its Labour government was introducing the welfare state and carrying out a programme of nationalisation at the same time as attempting to discharge what it saw as its international duties. The burden was too much to bear, and the British people were so weighed down by the hardships imposed on them (far lighter than those inflicted throughout most of the rest of Europe though they may have been) that they almost failed to notice the empire beginning to slip away in August 1947 with the loss of India, the finest jewel in the crown.

The north

To the north of Europe, in Scandinavia, Sweden had benefited from its neutrality during the war, for example by selling iron and other essential supplies to Germany, while Denmark and Norway had suffered from much of the unpleasantness of occupation. All three countries shared in the economic problems of the immediately post-war period, and found it advisable to join in the Marshall Plan, but all three shrank from closer union with the rest of Europe. In their efforts to preserve neutrality, they sometimes appeared to be leaning over backwards to appease the Soviet Union, by making trade agreements with it and by including Communists in their governments. However, after the Communist takeover in Czechoslovakia in February 1948, Communists were ejected from governments, trading agreements with the Soviet Union were not renewed, and all three Scandinavian governments increased their military expenditure. None of them was worried about wider imperial concerns, Denmark alone possessing them in Greenland and the Faroe Islands after allowing Iceland and the Virgin Islands their independence. Therefore the perceived threat was exclusively from the far left, Sweden's Socialist prime minister, Tage Erlander, observing on May Day 1948 that 'The *coup* in Czechoslovakia was a testing time not only for Prague, but also for Stockholm'. There was now more urgency to discussions concerning the possibility of the three Scandinavian socialist constitutional monarchies following the lead of the Benelux countries and moving towards more thorough association.[14]

On the other side of the Baltic, the former tsarist provinces of Estonia, Latvia and Lithuania were now incorporated into the Soviet Union as republics. A slice of Prussia centred on Königsberg, renamed Kaliningrad, became a detached section of the Russian Republic. It was partly because the eastern Baltic had been made safe from the Soviet point of view that the treatment meted out to Finland was less severe than elsewhere. The Finns were obliged to pay reparations and to adopt a neutral foreign policy, but there was no interference in their internal government or any attempt to engineer an increase in the falling support for the Communist Party.

The centre

To turn to the centre of the continent, a word first on Switzerland, which had benefited from neutrality during the war even more than Sweden, and suffered less from post-war problems. For this reason, it guarded its neutrality jealously, keeping its ministers away from many conferences. However, in 1948 it did become a founder member of the OEEC for the administration of Marshall Aid.

Meanwhile, Germany was attempting to recover from unconditional surrender, the move of its eastern frontier to the Oder–Neisse line and its division into four zones of occupation. The Morgenthau Plan for permanent partition and de-industrialisation was not implemented, however, and social revolution for the most part was avoided, to the extent that many former Nazis retained their positions. The most complete change was in the Russian sector, where there was a sweeping land reform and insistence on full reparations. But programmes for democratisation and re-education were vigorously pursued in the other zones.

From the beginning, there were disagreements and readjustments among the occupying powers, and the most stubborn of them was not always the Soviet Union. Smarting from its exclusion from the Potsdam Conference and still very sensitive about the national humiliation of 1940, France insisted on the full implementation of its rights of occupation, including reparations, and went beyond them to virtually annex the Saar. But Britain had taken on more than it could manage in the most populous northern zone including the Ruhr, and found it necessary to agree to a merger with the American zone to the south on 1 January 1947.

After the failure of the meeting of the Council of Foreign Ministers in Moscow in May 1947, the Western zones as a whole were merged and soon brought into the Marshall Plan. The Soviet Union suspected that West Germany was being transformed into an arsenal for an imperialist assault. The focus of contention became Berlin, divided like the rest of Germany into four sectors but located deep inside the Soviet zone and tenuously linked with the zones of the Western powers.

On 30 March 1948, the Soviet authorities issued new 'traffic regulations' which made communications even more difficult. Western reform of the currency coupled with an improvement in living conditions and talk of 'Western union' led to the further reduction of communications to two narrow corridors on 24 June. The way was being prepared for the first major Berlin crisis.

Austria, now detached from Germany, benefited more than most other states from the arrival of the Cold War, even though the country and its capital, Vienna, were divided among the four powers, or rather perhaps because of this division, which acted as a damper on class, regional and religious conflicts. Hungary, the other part of the former Habsburg Dual Monarchy, was not so fortunate behind the Iron Curtain, although arguably it too derived at least some benefit from its own frontier situation. At least it was treated fairly leniently immediately after the war, even though it had fought on the Nazi side. However, the Smallholders Party, which had won nearly three-fifths of the post-war vote in elections after the redistribution of great landed estates, was pushed aside in favour of the Communist Party after the failure of the Moscow Conference of Foreign Ministers in May 1947. Opposition to this move centred around the Roman Catholic Church, especially Cardinal József Mindszenty, but for the time being at least it did not lead to any widespread manifestations of unrest.

About nine months after the Communist takeover in Hungary, another took place in March 1948 in Czechoslovakia. Since 1945, with a mixture of Roman Catholic and Marxist allegiance, Czechoslovakia had appeared to be charting a middle course between East and West, but as early as 1946, Sheila Grant Duff wrote: 'For Russia, as for Germany, Bismarck's old saying is correct, "The master of Bohemia is the master of Europe." Russia will allow the Czechs to be masters in their own home only so long as this does not constitute a danger to her safety.'[15] Such a danger was perceived from March 1947 with the announcement of the Truman Doctrine followed by that of the Marshall Plan, along with the ejection of Communists from the governments of France, Italy and elsewhere. Taking advantage of a poor harvest and other economic problems towards the end of 1947, and exploiting the age-old suspicions between the Czechs and the Slovaks as well as the newer distrust of the West since the desertion of Czechoslovakia in the Munich agreement of 1938, the Communist Party was able to arrange a mostly bloodless coup by March 1948, followed by elections arranged to accept its assumption of government in May.

Stalin's thorniest external problem, and also probably the original unwitting prompter of the Cold War, was Poland. After nearly 200 years of increasing involvement in the Russian orbit, Poland appeared to be escaping from it between the two world wars. But the end of the Second World War brought an even more complete connection to the Russian, now Soviet, neighbour, and the proud Poles did not feel compensated for the loss of their eastern provinces by the acquisition of a large slice of Germany. We have already seen how unhappy the Western Allies were at Yalta and Potsdam about the manner in which the affairs of Poland were being arranged in 1945 by the Soviet 'liberator'. However, the course of events had been conditioned by recent and not so recent history, as was pointed out by Stalin to Roosevelt and Churchill and conceded in a very different manner by Stalin's bitter opponent, the prime minister of the Polish government in exile, Stanisław Mikołajczyk, who wrote: 'In the morbid suspicions of the Kremlin, the plains of Poland had become a smooth highway over which the armour of the West might some day roll. Thus much of our nation must be incorporated into the USSR, and the rest made into cannon fodder to resist such an advance.'[16] Mikołajczyk was allowed to return to his country and to join in coalition government with the Lublin Communists that had been installed already, but he and his Peasant Party were pushed and shoved by uncompromising means into a tight corner from which the only escape was renewed exile. Poland after the war was not as badly treated as during it. Soviet repression did not begin to equal that of the Nazis, but many Poles could not but feel that they had escaped the fire only to be landed in the frying pan. On the other hand, the minority who believed that there was no realistic alternative in the Polish predicament to at least a measure of co-operation with the Soviet Union managed to arrange for themselves, and to a lesser extent for their fellow Poles, a degree of recovery under the leadership of Władysław Gomułka.

The south-east

While much of central Europe had been pushed into the Communist camp by the summer of 1948, the Soviet Union was already confident of its control over the two Balkan states closest to it. Although Bulgaria had refused to fight against the Soviet Union, it was quickly and ruthlessly cleared of opposition to Communist government at the end of the war. Romania, the home of the Fascist Iron Guard and Nazi Germany's most fervent ally, was also summarily dealt with, perhaps with more justification. But while it lost some of Bessarabia to the USSR, it gained Transylvania from Hungary. While thoughts of independence from Soviet rule were harboured, especially in Romania which was non-Slav with none of the fellow-feeling exhibited by Bulgaria, no possibility existed of any action in that direction as the Cold War was beginning.

The rigidity of the Iron Curtain became even greater after Marshal Tito asserted that it should not be drawn around Yugoslavia. During the war, he and his fellow partisans had been fighting not only against the invaders and their collaborators but also against other domestic rivals. Although the final victory was assisted by the Red Army, Tito and his followers had not fought for independence and revolution only to become the unquestioning subordinate of Moscow. And so they clashed with the Soviet Union as well as with the West over such questions as the exclusion from their country of the city of Trieste. Pursuing its obstinate middle way, Yugoslavia was expelled from the Soviet bloc in June 1948, and all evidence of freethinking 'Titoism' was ruthlessly suppressed in the remaining satellites. In the summer of 1948, these included Albania, one of Yugoslavia's southern neighbours, but certainly not Greece, the other neighbour, which after years of civil war was firmly in the Western camp, if far from being a democracy. For that form of government, which was said to have been born in the Greek city states, was not revived after 1945 owing to the overriding fear of Communism on the part of the liberating British, who had given their support to right-wing elements, several of them Nazi, in order to avert the perceived greater evil from the Left. This heritage was passed on to Truman in March 1947, announcing his Doctrine on behalf of Greece and its neighbour and enemy to the east, the even less democratic Turkey. The inclusion in the Western camp of Turkey, with its dominance of the route from the Mediterranean to the Black Sea and many other strategic and historical associations, was of great significance as the battle lines of the Cold War were drawn, however embarrassing to the West's ideals the nature of its internal regime might be. Like the defection of Tito, the alienation of Turkey encouraged Stalin and his entourage to think even more single-mindedly about keeping the walls of the eastern European fortress strong and rooting out potential traitors within them.

The Soviet Union

Meanwhile, Big Brother himself was going from strength to strength, if the following appraisal published in 1947 is anything to go by:

> Stalin is the brilliant leader and teacher of the Party, the great strategist of the Socialist Revolution, military commander, and guide of the Soviet state. An implacable attitude towards the enemies of Socialism, profound fidelity to principle, a combination of clear revolutionary perspective and clarity of purpose with extraordinary firmness and persistence in the pursuit of aims, wise and practical leadership, and intimate contact with the masses – such are the characteristics of Stalin's style. After Lenin, no other leader in the world has been called upon to direct such vast masses of workers and peasants.[17]

In fact, the post-war Stalin was not the man he had been before the war or during it, according to observers such as Milovan Djilas, the Yugoslav politician and intellectual, who noticed a steep decline in the 'brilliant leader' between 1945 and 1948. A more recent historian writes: 'By most accounts Stalin was a lonely man who craved company. Much of his time with Politburo colleagues was spent sitting through Westerns or endless dinners marked by a conspicuous lack of policy-oriented discussions.' Yet, although he insisted on collective responsibility, the old man still had the last word when policy was discussed.[18] The spirit of the post-war years was more clearly distilled perhaps in the policies of the minister of culture, A. A. Zhdanov, who kept a close eye for deviations in the writing of history, economics, philosophy and imaginative literature. During the war a certain amount of latitude had been allowed in these fields and extended in particular to the Orthodox Church. Now extreme care had to be taken by intellectuals and believers alike in order to avoid persecution from the censors and the police. These were also the years in which returning prisoners of war and citizens who had been taken away into forced labour were given the harsh treatment of the GULAG or even execution.

The economic problems of recovery were enormous, while the amount of aid received from the West was nowhere near proportionate to the relative scale of such problems. Here the Soviet government itself shared much of the responsibility, for its representatives invariably displayed an inflexible self-righteousness and profound suspicion that could do nothing to win friends and influence people abroad. Such poor public relations decisions as the refusal to send a unit of the Red Army to take part in the Victory Parade in London in 1946 or to allow the Soviet brides of British soldiers to join their husbands in Britain tarnished the Soviet image, which had been bright during the war. All too conscious of its weakness before the West, concerned with its internal problems of staggering severity, the Soviet government had more to worry about than the attitude of its former allies, which in any case was assumed to be hostile. Stalin and his henchmen looked outside the Soviet Union with apprehension and even alarm. Far from plotting the overthrow of the rest of the outside world, as was often alleged in the West, they gave the highest priority to protecting themselves from it, and the truculence of their language disguised the mania for security that governed their domestic and foreign policy. Similarly, Marxism–Leninism–Stalinism was adapted as an ideology for the primary purpose of achieving cohesion in the Soviet camp. The Cominform was set up in 1947 for this purpose.

The USA

As Howard K. Smith observed in 1949:

> The nation that has expanded most since the outbreak of World War II has not been Russia, but America. The most distant of Russia's new areas of dominance are 600 miles from her borders. The farthest of America's are 7,000 miles. Since 1942, America has displaced Britain as ruler of the seas, including even that most British of all waters, the eastern Mediterranean. America is said to have a lien on some 400 world-wide naval and air bases. This means that any empire linked to its motherland by water exists on American sufferance, as it did in the past on British sufferance. Russian influence over other governments

is blatantly visible. American influence is like an iceberg: only the smaller part can readily be seen by the naked eye.[19]

The economic penetration of the world had been tremendous. Three-quarters of the capital invested throughout the world was American, a reflection of the circumstance that two-thirds of the world's industry was to be found within the USA. American grants and loans had tied not only the factories but also the farms of many other countries to the economic policies of the USA, while political agreements leading towards treaties had done the same for their foreign relations and made the USA the final arbiter of world politics. The rapidity of the USA's emergence as a superpower was disconcerting to its potential enemies, especially the Soviet Union, which would not fully assume the same status for another ten years or more, if ever. At the same time, it bewildered and confused its European friends, whose previous predominance it appeared to be supplanting, while even the USA itself was not immediately comfortable with its new might and responsibility. However, by the end of 1947 President Truman was certain of the road that he wanted to travel, with the advice and support of such new bodies as the National Security Council, in which the armed services had a powerful voice. The majority of the American people seemed persuaded that their own well-being could be protected only through militant anti-Communism and a somewhat narrow conception of what constituted pro-American and unAmerican activities. For its own protection and prosperity, the USA was seeking to create a world after its own image.

DECOLONISATION, 1945–9

If the presence of Soviet power was the major factor determining the post-war development of eastern Europe, the presence of American power was no less important in determining that of the western half of the continent. But how about the world outside Europe, which had largely been divided up among European empires? What was happening there in the years immediately following the Second World War? What were the origins of decolonisation and how were they influenced by the arrival of the Cold War? It is only through an answer to such questions that we will be able to arrive at a full picture of the position of

Europe in the post-war world. We will approach the wider world as we considered Europe, via its regions.

The Middle East

Let us begin with the Middle East, the region closest to Europe, and also one in which the European empires, especially the French and the British, had been dominant since the collapse of their German and Ottoman rivals at the end of the First World War. Roosevelt served notice at the Yalta Conference that he did not expect the former situation to be recreated at the end of the Second World War, and underlined his point by flying home from the Crimea via the Middle East and conferring there with King Farouk of Egypt, King Ibn Saud of Saudi Arabia and Emperor Haile Selassie of Ethiopia. Churchill was disturbed by such meddling in what he considered still to be a Franco-British sphere of influence and attempted to maintain as such both at Yalta and at Potsdam. But American oil interests quickly developed in the region, and the American navy was sailing the Mediterranean to protect them some time before the announcement of the Truman Doctrine on Greece and Turkey in March 1947. A crisis in Iran (as Persia was now generally called) immediately after the war was also connected with oil, agreement on which had been made with the Soviet Union, still maintaining a military presence there after Britain and the United States had moved their troops out. When, under great pressure, the Soviet Union withdrew, the Iranian government renounced its former commitment and made a new oil agreement with the USA, which sent over both financial aid and military advisers, and ultimately transformed Iran, like neighbouring Turkey, into an American satellite. There was tension over this development with the USA's European allies, especially with Britain, which had a longer-lasting interest in Iran and became apprehensive about its possible exclusion.

Britain retained a dominant interest in Egypt for the time being, but a further source of disagreement with the USA was neighbouring Palestine. The British government sought to discharge what it saw as its duty concerning its mandate, and the American government pushed towards the creation of the state of Israel, which was finally achieved in May 1948. The Soviet Union recognised Israel, but was most unhappy about other Middle Eastern developments. From the Soviet point of view, American infiltration into both Turkey and Iran as well as into Greece constituted a threat from an interloper, while Russian interests in the Mediterranean and its hinterland went back to the Revolution of 1917 and centuries before.

Africa

At the first meeting of the Council of Foreign Ministers in London in September 1945, soon after the end of the Potsdam Conference, Molotov put forward a claim for Soviet trusteeship of at least part of the former Italian colony of Libya. Facetiously perhaps, Molotov suggested that if that trusteeship should not be forthcoming, the Soviet Union would be satisfied with the Belgian Congo. This remark appears to have persuaded the British and the Americans that the Russians were seeking mineral deposits, especially uranium, as well as the 'eventual destruction of the British Empire'.[20] Possibly, as in the case of the interest in Italy that he and Stalin had expressed at Yalta and Potsdam, Molotov was in an indirect manner supporting the argument for spheres of influence, indicating that if the Soviet Union were to stay out of Africa, western European states as well as the USA should not interfere in eastern Europe. Probably, he would also have been aware that the USA was beginning to show an interest in Africa. Certainly, the Soviet proposal alarmed the South African prime minister, Jan Smuts, who had spoken of the danger of the spread of Bolshevism soon after the Russian Revolution of 1917 and who was now reported to have warned the British government that the Soviet Union should not be given any trusteeship in Africa in case Stalin and his associates used it to 'stir up the tribes'.[21] In fact, for the moment at least, although there was some social disturbance, Soviet influence did not spread into the continent.

India

Rather more surprisingly, Soviet influence did not reach beyond its own frontiers into the neighbouring regions of Asia. We have seen already how it was pushed out of Turkey and Iran. In the first few years after the war, there was little or no active Soviet interest in the Indian subcontinent, where independence was negotiated for Pakistan and India with the Muslim League and the Indian National Congress. In the communal violence that accompanied the partition of the subcontinent and the formal transfer of power on 15 August 1947, neither the local Communist parties nor their Soviet patron played any significant part. As for the USA, it gave a welcome to the creation of Pakistan and India, and moved quickly into economic contacts with them, showing special interest in Indian deposits of manganese, a vital mineral that it had previously imported largely from the USSR.

In *The Discovery of India*, the book that he wrote while interned by the British in 1944, the future prime minister Jawaharlal Nehru gave a fairly even-handed treatment to the USSR and the USA, which both seemed to him destined to play a vital part in the future: 'They differ from each other almost as much as any two advanced countries can differ, and even their faults lie in opposite directions. All the evils of a purely political democracy are evident in the USA; the evils of the lack of political democracy are present in the USSR.'[22]

While feeling little if any sympathy for the Japanese during the Second World War, Nehru and most of his colleagues were nevertheless impressed by their successes, and a group led by Subhas Chandra Bose went as far as military collaboration with the Japanese. Before the advancing armies, the British colonial empire had indeed cracked up with amazing rapidity. Was this proud structure, then, just a house of cards with no foundations or inner strength? Disappointed by the restricted and conditional offers made to them by the British government during the war, Mahatma Gandhi and the Indian leaders were emboldened by the British difficulties to ask for more.

South-east Asia

Similarly, those parts of South-East Asia that had been occupied by the Japanese during the war, French and Dutch colonies as well as British, were also encouraged to press for independence at the war's termination, holding before them the models of the former democratic and proletarian revolutions. One of the earliest and most persistent struggles was in French Indo-China, where Ho Chi Minh made a declaration of independence on 2 September 1945, basing his remarks on the American Declaration of Independence and the French Declaration of the Rights of Man and the Citizen, and expressing the conviction that 'the Allied nations which have acknowledged at Tehran and

San Francisco the principles of self-determination and equality of status will not refuse to acknowledge the independence of Vietnam'.[23]However, French troops reoccupied Saigon on 23–24 September 1945 after the departure of the Japanese, and the long Vietnamese War began, with Ho Chi Minh and his followers moving politically to the left. In Indonesia the Dutch, assisted at first by the British, attempted to regain control at the end of the war of a republic declared on 17 August 1945 by President Sukarno after the departure of the Japanese, who had given encouragement to the independence movement for their own purposes. Years of fighting were necessary before independence was finally achieved in 1950. As far as the countries under British control were concerned, Burma struggled towards independence by the beginning of 1948 without much resistance from the imperial power, while Malaya was overtaken in the summer of that year by a guerilla war under local Chinese leadership which the imperial power strongly resisted. A settlement satisfying both Chinese and Malays was not reached before 1957. Generally speaking, in South-East Asia as a whole the tendency was for the Soviet Union to support the nationalist movements, often labelled Communist by themselves, their friends or their enemies, and for the United States to push the imperial power towards the grant of independence to as moderate a government as possible. Vietnam constituted the most unfortunate exception.

Japan and China

To turn to the two great powers of east Asia, both had considerable influence on the early nature of the Cold War and of decolonisation. We have already seen how the occupation of South-East Asia by the Japanese during the war accelerated the process of decolonisation. At the war's end, the United States was in control of Japan and excluded the Soviet Union. But swift advance from 8 August 1945 onwards brought the Soviet forces into south Sakhalin and the Kuril Islands, more temporarily into Manchuria and North Korea. There was no agreement between the USA and the USSR about a peace treaty with Japan any more than with Germany, and the seeds of war in Korea and dissension elsewhere were firmly sown.

In China, liberation from Japan brought chaos with the attempt at the restoration of its power by the Kuomintang government under

Chiang Kai-shek. American aid was given reluctantly to the Kuomintang, while Soviet support was given only grudgingly to the principal opposition, the Chinese Communist Party under Mao Zedong. On 1 October 1949, after four more years of widespread fighting, Mao proclaimed the foundation of the Chinese People's Republic. The United States was appalled and began to develop a fear of a Moscow–Peking agreement to take over the whole world. In fact, Stalin and his advisers remained suspicious of Mao, who in turn was not very pleased about the treatment meted out to him and his followers by the Soviet Union. Mao was also unhappy about the division of Korea into a North dominated by the USSR and a South included in the sphere of influence of the USA.

The Pacific, the Atlantic and Latin America

To complete our rapid world tour, we may pass by Australia and New Zealand, firmly in the Western camp, and the Philippines, not so firmly there as a guerrilla movement developed after the grant of independence by the USA in 1946. Little need be said in the present context about Latin America on the other side of the Pacific Ocean. Although there was some general fear of the Red menace spreading to the western hemisphere via the Pacific or the Atlantic Ocean, there was no specific focus of alarm in the years immediately following 1945, and a confident enough belief that the states of Latin America would be loyal to the USA in the United Nations and more local organisations. Similarly, in the same period, there was no concern on the part of the USA and its Western allies that any serious threat was posed by the Soviet Union in the major seas and oceans of the world, with the possible exception of the Mediterranean. But no chances were taken, American fleets taking over much of the policing role previously exercised by the British Royal Navy and American bases being maintained from the North Atlantic in Greenland to the South Pacific in Polynesia.

In such a manner, the USA came to be the first political unit in world history to deserve fully the designation of 'superpower' at a time when the power of the Soviet Union beyond its borders was confined to the east of Europe and the Far Eastern regions taken from the Japanese.

FROM BERLIN AND CHINA TO HUNGARY AND SUEZ, 1949–56

In 1949, the Berlin crisis made the greatest impact in Europe. The Berlin air-lift, with supply-laden planes taking off at frequent intervals, undoubtedly remained one of the Cold War's epics until Stalin agreed to end the blockade in May. Less dramatically, in January, the USSR established Comecon along with Albania, Bulgaria, Czechoslovakia, Hungary, Poland and Romania to coordinate trade and development in eastern Europe. In April, NATO (the North Atlantic Treaty Organisation) was formally set up in Washington: the USA joined with Canada in North America and the Benelux states, Britain, France, Denmark, Norway, Iceland, Italy and Portugal in Europe as a 'shield' for the principles of the UNO Charter. A vast programme of US military aid to Europe was introduced just in time to greet the USSR's first explosion of an atomic bomb. The division of Germany was completed by the creation of the Federal Republic (FRG) in the West in May followed by the creation of the Democratic Republic (GDR) in the East in October.

The arrival of American nuclear bombers in the UK in 1950 was just the beginning of a new stage in the updated armament of Western Europe as a whole. By no means every Briton was flattered by the comment that their country was an 'unsinkable aircraft carrier'. In April, the US National Security Council approved Report NSC 68 describing the USSR as a 'totalitarian dictatorship' with 'a new fanatic faith', 'inescapably militant' with a 'fundamental design' to destroy the USA and to dominate the Eurasian land mass. Armaments, thermonuclear, conventional and moral, must be built up to defend the USA and achieve victory over the USSR.[24]

In the world as a whole, the most important event of the year 1949 was the completion of the Chinese Revolution with the institution of the People's Republic of China (PRC) under Mao Zedung. The PRC would go on to play a most significant part in the Cold War and in decolonisation, immediate appearances to the contrary. At the end of 1949, the US National Security Council extended the Truman Doctrine as it reported that the USSR threatened to dominate Asia for the foreseeable future 'through the complementary instruments of communist conspiracy and diplomatic pressure supported by military strength'. Soviet influence and power in Asia must be contained and even reduced 'to such a degree that the Soviet Union is not capable of threatening the security of the United States from that area'. [25] There was anxiety, too, as we have seen, about a Moscow–Beijing conspiracy for world revolution, which appeared to be indicated by the almost simultaneous recognition by the USSR and the PRC of Ho Chi Minh's government in North Vietnam in January 1950.

Confirmation seemed to come with the North Korean invasion of the South in June 1950. In fact, although Stalin supported the invasion and then the Chinese intervention in October, he was anxious to avoid direct confrontation with the US and other UN forces, and held back from full commitment. At the time, fears of the conflict widening were real enough, while the bloody conflict led to between 3.5 and 4 million deaths, more civilians than combatants, before an armistice line was agreed near to where the conflict had started in July 1953. In September 1954, Secretary of State John Foster Dulles announced that the 'hands off' policies of the Monroe Doctrine were being extended to Asia as the USA joined with the UK, France, Australia, New Zealand, Thailand, Pakistan and the Philippines in the formation of the Southeast Asia Treaty Organization (SEATO).

Back in Europe, during the Korean War, NATO was joined by Greece and Turkey in 1952. To the east, the death of Stalin in March 1953 encouraged hope for better days. A general strike against demands for higher productivity in Berlin and other GDR cities brought out the Soviet tanks. In 1955, in a gesture of solidarity, the USSR, Bulgaria, Romania, Hungary, Poland and Albania signed the Warsaw Treaty of Friendship, Co-operation and Mutual Assistance (the Warsaw Pact), having all just signed similar treaties with the GDR. However, a new furore broke out in 1956 following the denunciation of Stalin in the 'secret speech' of his successor, Nikita Khrushchev, in February and the abolition of Cominform in April. Unrest in Poland, especially in Poznań, led to a compromise solution in which a new leader, Władysław Gomułka, managed to revive workers' councils and regain some control over the armed forces. But, alarmed by the lack of an invitation to attend a meeting of the Polish Communist Party Central Committee in Warsaw, Khrushchev and his colleagues sent out a warning against any repetition of Yugoslavia's defection in 1948. The crunch came in Hungary, where a nationalist movement developed in October under the leadership of Imre Nagy, who announced his country's defection from the Warsaw Pact on 1 November, and called for international protection. There were large-scale demonstrations and some police officials were lynched before the Soviet tanks rolled in 'to restore order' on 4 November. Nagy was executed, and a more loyal regime installed under János Kádár.

Supportive words but no action came from the West, partly because of reluctance to risk a third world war, partly because of another crisis in the Middle East. In July 1956 the Egyptian leader Gamal Abdel Nasser, who had seized power in 1954 two years after the overthrow of King Farouk, nationalised the Suez Canal, arguing that the West had failed to deliver previously promised aid. In October, in close co-operation, Israel, France and the UK launched attacks at the very time that the Hungarian uprising was being crushed. Concerned with his campaign for re-election as well as wider issues, President Eisenhower trod warily. Vice-President Richard M. Nixon spoke for the adminis-tration in a speech of 2 November:

> In the past the nations of Asia and Africa have always felt we would, when the pressure was on, side with the policies of the British and French Governments in relation to the once colonial areas. For the first time in history we have shown independence of Anglo-French policies towards Asia and Africa which seemed to us to reflect the colonial tradition. That declaration of independence has had an electrifying effect throughout the world.[26]

Khrushchev went so far as to suggest a joint Soviet–US settlement of the crisis, which prompted the USA to push for a UN solution, which was agreed by December 1956.

Nasser had discussed with Tito and Nehru the possibility of a third world force consisting of Yugoslavia, India and Egypt. Further afield, Mao Zedong had supported the Polish reform, opposed the Hungarian uprising and encouraged Nasser's policies. This was in the wake of the PRC's assertion of 'peaceful coexistence' along with India at the conference of non-aligned states in Bandung, Indonesia, in April 1955. As the process of decolonisation contributed to the formation of what became known as the Third World, however, the PRC was to differ with India as well as with the USSR.

While the Cold War raged and the process of decolonisation intensified, western Europe was taking its first important steps towards integration with the encouragement of the USA. Would it take the 'unionist' road of a consultative assembly or the 'federalist' path consisting of a supra-national body? In fact, in the short run, a third, more gradual 'functionalist' approach was adopted, following the ideas of Jean Monnet, who had first set out a plan for a mixed French economy in 1946. The first Council of Europe had been created in 1949, and the formation of the European Payments Union and creation of the Benelux Economic Union in 1950 pointed the way towards further action. But it was a declaration made by the French statesman Robert Schuman with the advice of Jean Monnet on 9 May in Paris that made the most significant step forward. Europe would not be made all at once, nor according to a single plan, Schuman argued, proposing that the first aim should be the elimination of the age-old opposition of France and Germany through the creation of a 'High Authority' to coordinate coal and steel production. The European Coal and Steel Community (ECSC) was formally created in 1951 by France, Germany, Italy and the Benelux countries. The United Kingdom became an associate member in 1954.

From 1945 to 1956, the countries of Europe to east and west effected a recovery from the devastation inflicted by the Second World War. There was further to go in the east, not only because the ruin of war had been much greater there, but also because the economies of the region were comparatively backward before the war, too. Taking a tour from Romania to Germany late in 1945, the Soviet writer Ilya Erenburg found not only destruction but also the desire for reform as well as recuperation, noting the huge gap between life in such cities as Bucharest, Sofia, Prague and Belgrade on the one hand and much of the surrounding countryside. However, Fascism had bequeathed 'not only the taste for blood but also the taste for easy profit', and so reform would not be achieved without opposition – hence some of the excuse, and even some of the reason, for later turmoil.[27]

In agriculture, there was opposition from the peasants themselves to collectivisation. By the early 1950s, only Bulgaria had subjected more than half of its farming land to this process, the figure for Hungary and Yugoslavia being nearer to a quarter, and for Romania, Poland and Czechoslovakia even lower. Nationalisation of industry was more complete, and there were many grandiose plans for heavy and light industry, as demonstrated by Soviet-style Five-Year Plans.

In western Europe, nationalisation was also widespread. In Britain, the state takeover of major fuel industries and public transport, to give some major examples, was introduced by a Labour government but not rejected by its Conservative successor, while there was general acceptance of the welfare state, with the National Health Service and free education at its centre. France took as its point of departure Jean Monnet's Plan for the Modernisation and Equipment of France in 1946, with emphasis on key industries but no major reform of agriculture. The Benelux countries exercised firm state controls, too, while Italy gave its major emphasis to law and order. The Scandinavian countries were closely watched for their pursuit of a middle way between socialism and free enterprise. For the time being, Spain and Portugal held themselves apart.

Under the firm control of Christian Democrat chancellor Konrad Adenauer and economics minister Ludwig Erhard, the German Federal Republic achieved an 'Economic Miracle' (*Wirtschaftswunder*) through their policy of a 'social market' with emphasis on a stable currency, low taxation and liberal trade, especially exports. A member of NATO since 1955, the FRG soon had to address the question of rearmament.

A decade or so after the end of the Second World War, then, Europe as a whole could be said to be on the road to economic recovery, but with many questions hanging over its future.

TO BERLIN AND CUBA, 1956–62

After the troubles of 1956, eastern Europe went relatively quiet for some years. In Hungary, for example, having suppressed the rebellion, János Kádár went on to lead his country towards reform and himself towards at least some popularity. On the other hand, Władysław Gomułka, who had come in on a wave of public support in Poland in 1956, became less popular as he failed to introduce enough reform. Under Nicolae Ceauşescu, Romania engineered a degree of independence from the Soviet bloc, while Albania broke from it in 1961.

In 1957, the Polish foreign minister submitted to the UN General Assembly a plan for central Europe including the whole of Germany to become a zone free of nuclear armaments. In 1958, Czechoslovakia and the GDR joined Poland in reiterating their support for the Rapacki Plan after the FRG's parliament asked for the most modern weapons, including nuclear. There was considerable alarm in Western Europe: 'whose finger on the trigger?' was a popular slogan of the time. Khrushchev, who had consolidated his power in the Soviet Union, put pressure on the Western powers to evacuate Berlin and make it a 'free city'. But the USA under the second-term leadership of Eisenhower rejected both the Khrushchev proposal and variants of the Rapacki Plan.

After Suez, governments in western Europe were prepared to accept their reduced role in the world. An exception was General de Gaulle in France, who took a firm stand after returning to power in 1958 to solve a crisis provoked by severe colonial problems in Algeria. He created the Fifth Republic and devised a new constitution for it giving the president preponderant power over parliament. He sought to make French foreign policy more independent, supported by a nuclear deterrent – *force de frappe*. British Prime Minister Harold Macmillan told the British people in the election of 1959 that they had 'never had it so good' and a majority agreed with him, content to go along with the myth of an 'independent nuclear deterrent' bought from the USA.

Meanwhile, the two superpowers were racing each other up the escalator of Mutually Assured Destruction (MAD). In 1957, the contest took on a new dimension with the launching of the first space satellite – the Soviet *sputnik* – and of the first Inter-Continental Ballistic Missile (ICBM) – again Soviet. In 1959, a Soviet rocket hit the moon (*lunik* – from *luna*, the Russian word for moon). In 1961, Iurii Gagarin became the first person to orbit the earth. In fact, the Russian lead over the USA in the space race was not as great as first appeared. Moreover, the 'missile gap' complained of by politicians, service chiefs and businessmen was something of an illusion after the nuclear stockpile tripled from 6000 to 18,000 between 1958 and 1960, when the first of 14 commissioned nuclear submarines, named *Polaris*, went into service. In his farewell address soon afterwards, Eisenhower was to warn against 'the acquisition of unwarranted influence, whether sought or unsought, by the military–industrial complex' in a context where 'The potential for the disastrous rise of misplaced power exists and will persist'.[28] His words went largely unheeded, both in the USA and in the USSR, where a comparable situation existed.

In 1960, a summit meeting between Eisenhower and Khrushchev scheduled for May in Paris collapsed after an American U2 spy plane had been shot down over the Soviet Union. In 1961, a new crisis arose in Berlin after the USSR announced its intention of signing a separate peace treaty with the GDR. In June, Khrushchev met the new US president, Kennedy, in Vienna. There was heated disagreement about policy towards Germany and Europe and about 'wars of liberation' in the wider world. In August, the Berlin Wall was hastily erected to stop emigration from the GDR.

A new Berlin crisis was nothing compared to what was soon to happen in Cuba. Ever since Fidel Castro had come to power in 1959, he had sought to escape decades, even more than a century, of US control indicated by dominance of the economy as well as the possession of a base at Guantanamo. When the American government put the squeeze on, Castro moved closer to the Soviet Union. In April 1961, the recently inaugurated President Kennedy agreed to a previously prepared invasion of Cuba by an army of exiles with US air cover. The landing at the Bay of Pigs was a disaster, but enough to provoke Khrushchev into sending medium-range missiles to protect Cuba against further threats. Not just the superpowers, but Europe and the rest of the world, too, came closer to disaster than at any time since the Second World War.

Together, the Berlin and Cuban crises demonstrated that the Cold War and decolonisation were becoming part of the same global problem. There was already a considerable amount of evidence pointing in the same direction. Most notably, as the French withdrew from attempting to maintain control of their former colony in Vietnam, the Americans became more involved. Of course, successive administrations were not worried about this problem in isolation. But Eisenhower warned against all of the states in Indo-China and elsewhere in the Far East falling in turn like a stack of dominoes to the Communist threat posed by the USSR and the PRC together. In fact, if not without difficulties, Burma, Indonesia and Thailand managed to consolidate independence and Malaysia to gain it in 1957. Khrushchev and Mao were drawing apart in the late 1950s before their open split in 1961.

In Africa, the greatest problems were to the north and south. The long struggle to retain Algeria came near to causing civil war before General de Gaulle took over in 1958 and negotiated its formal breakaway by 1962, although Tunisia and Morocco had achieved the transition to independence relatively easily by 1955. Arab nationalism continued to smoulder as Israel became more assertive. South Africa became a republic in 1960 and was forced to leave the British Commonwealth in

May 1961, its policy of racial segregation (*apartheid*) keeping it some-what apart in international relations, too. In equatorial West Africa, the former British colonies Ghana and Nigeria became independent in 1957 and 1960 respectively, while French possessions were integrated in the French Community. In East Africa, the Mau Mau movement fought the British in Kenya, while White governments hung on in the Rhodesias. But the greatest conflict broke out in the Belgian Congo, at the centre, where there was serious conflict with international ramifications from independence in 1960 onwards.

As empire went, the movement for European integration gathered momentum. A climax was reached by 1958 with the Treaty of Rome signed by the Six – West Germany, France, Italy, Belgium, the Nether-lands and Luxembourg. Although the treaty created the European Economic Community (EEC) with the main objective of creating a customs union, to some sceptical observers the EEC was primarily a device to protect German industry and French agriculture. In 1960, the UK joined Norway, Denmark, Sweden, Switzerland, Austria and Portugal (and later Finland and Iceland) in a somewhat looser organisa-tion known as the European Free Trade Association (EFTA). In 1960, too, the OEEC set up in 1948 was replaced by the Organisation for Economic Cooperation and Development (OECD) including the USA and Canada.

While the formal structure of Comecon remained the same in eastern Europe, there was significant economic development. Plans continued, notably in the Soviet Union, but there was some loosening of controls as more emphasis was given to the consumer industry. Some members of the bloc, notably Romania and Hungary, attempted to establish trade links outside Comecon, while there were attempts to introduce profit motive and incentives throughout.

Back in the West, the German economic miracle continued to astonish, with high rates of growth and low rates of unemployment. Less spectacularly, France also prospered, but peasants and shopkeepers were among those concerned with the encroachments of large-scale operations. Benelux joined in the prosperity, as did northern Italy, but not the southern regions. Spain and Portugal had yet to join the main economic stream. The UK was affected by 'stop–go' economics of suc-cessive Labour and Conservative governments, and still weighed down by the costs of victory, which included retaining faith in the old ways.

While other parts of Europe had been forced to accept radical changes, many of the subjects of Queen Elizabeth II (1952–) did not want to reform the monarchy or any other venerable institution.

TO CZECHOSLOVAKIA AND VIETNAM, 1962–8

From 1962 to the summer of 1968, eastern Europe avoided major political upsets, except in the USSR itself, where Nikita Khrushchev was removed from power in 1964 for 'adventurism', both at home and abroad. His policies on domestic reform, which included dangerous tinkering with the structure of the party, and on international relations, notably the Cuba episode, were both considered too risky. His replacement , Leonid I. Brezhnev, restored stability, even to the point of stagnation.

Unease in the Soviet bloc at first registered most clearly in Romania. An official name change in 1965 from Romanian People's Republic to the Socialist State of Romania, with a new constitution giving emphasis to the role of the Communist Party, was harmless enough. But in 1966 Ceauşescu appeared to be going the way of Tito when he declared that Romania was an independent state within the bloc. In 1967, Romania established diplomatic relations with the FRG in West Germany, arousing the anger of the GDR in East Germany in particular, which responded by signing a number of treaties with other members of the Soviet bloc. Superficially stable, the bloc was to be rocked in 1968 by events in Czechoslovakia.

All was comparatively quiet before 1968 in western Europe, too. In the United Kingdom, a number of scandals involving cloak and dagger culminated in the bed when the secretary of state for war, John Profumo, was forced to admit having an affair with a young woman who had also been friendly with an attaché from the Soviet Embassy. The Conservative government under Harold Macmillan fell to a Labour government under Harold Wilson in 1964. The new prime minister promised an energetic response to 'the white heat of technological revolution', but the economy was too sluggish to allow radical change. Should trade unions be restrained, and/or management be made more professional? Or should the UK even take the fateful step of continuing to apply for entry into the European 'common market'? Meanwhile, to look at the brighter side, these were the 'swinging sixties' when the

Beatles, at first neatly dressed in collars and ties, led a pop export drive, and the Union Jack became a fashion accessory in Carnaby Street and far wider afield. New heights were reached for some with England's football victory in the 1966 World Cup.

Italy had already shown the way to the 'sweet life' (*la dolce vita*) accompanied by remarkable economic growth involving Fiat cars and Olivetti typewriters as well as a tourist boom (enjoyed also by other Mediterranean countries such as Spain, Greece and Yugoslavia). The state played its part through ownership of nearly a third of industry, but, as ever, the south lagged behind, with some of its unemployed taking advantage of labour mobility in the EEC to seek a living elsewhere.

The smaller European countries in both the EEC and EFTA joined in the general prosperity, most of them with a mixed economy combining state and private enterprise. France seemed to be heading in the same direction under the leadership of de Gaulle, who recognised the progress made by Germany in a treaty of friendship signed by himself and Adenauer in 1963. In 1966, de Gaulle announced his country's departure from NATO, as he argued in favour of not only the *force de frappe* but also of a *Europe des patries* stretching from the Atlantic to the Urals (but not across the Channel – he feared that Britain's entry into the EEC would turn it into an Atlantic community.) NATO headquarters moved to Brussels, but France remained a signatory of the Atlantic Pact and maintained relations with the USA, too close for some. Soon, foreign as well as domestic policy was to produce a flare-up, as Paris joined Prague in 1968 as a centre of revolution.

Relations between the superpowers, and further steps along the road of decolonisation, also contributed to 1968. In the short run after the Cuba crisis, the hotline of the red telephone connected the White House directly with the Kremlin. Now that the USA had more than 1000 ICBMs and the USSR nearly 900, both sides agreed to slow down the arms race if not quite to halt it. In 1963, the nuclear powers agreed a Test Ban Treaty; in 1967, the superpowers signed a non-proliferation treaty, to which nearly 60 other powers subscribed in 1968. But a formidable obstacle to more complete peace was Vietnam, where the superpower rivalry continued, complicated by apprehensions on both sides about the intentions of Mao and the PRC. The necessity to restrain China appeared clearly late in 1962, when there was a brief war with India over a border dispute. Before Kennedy's assassination in November 1963, the USA was already strengthening its position in Indo-China, not only in Vietnam but also in Laos whose neutrality had been agreed at Geneva in 1962 as part of a settlement for the whole region. As the Vietnam War intensified under Lyndon B. Johnson, Soviet 'advisers' aided the forces of Ho Chi Minh while keeping a watch on the activities of the PRC.

During the 1960s, there were problems for the USA in its own special area of interest, Latin America. In spite of the introduction of the Alliance for Progress, to which Kennedy pledged $20 million, and the creation of the Peace Corps consisting of young volunteers, both in 1961, not to mention the ongoing training of anti-guerrilla forces, unrest continued, notably in the Dominican Republic from 1965 to 1966. But it was anxiety about and opposition to the Vietnam War that combined with ghetto riots back in the USA to produce widespread disturbances at home from April 1968, soon to be echoed abroad.

In Europe, unrest was also promoted by developments in Czechoslovakia. There, in January, the Slovak Alexander Dubček became first secretary of the Communist Party, which proceeded to announce in April a progamme of economic and political liberalisation. 'The Group of Five' consisting of the Soviet Union, Bulgaria, Hungary, Poland and East Germany soon registered their opposition to the Prague Spring, and, concerned as before about a possible 'domino' effect, presented a number of severe warnings before invading Czechoslovakia in August. However much the vast majority of the people wanted to retain 'socialism with a human face', there was far less bloodshed in Prague in 1968 than in Budapest in 1956.

To the west, in May 1968, nearly all France downed tools and pens as workers and students joined in the most widespread general strike in European history against the authoritarian methods of the bosses and the professors. There was unrest in Germany, and to a lesser extent throughout western Europe. The resignation of de Gaulle helped to restore order in France, but urban terrorism by the Red Army Faction and other groups in Germany helped to pose the question: was there a future for capitalism even with a human face?

In retrospect, that question might seem facetious, but it did not seem so in 1968. Although the movements of that year remain the subject of considerable controversy, the argument is still put forward that the year marked a significant watershed in European and world history. According to Immanuel Wallerstein, who had already written a series of books about the development of the world system since medieval times, the primary protest of 1968 was against US hegemony, with a more passionate, but secondary, protest about Stalinism. The debate on the fundamental strategy of social transformation, in which new minorities based on gender or race or 'green' priorities would play an important part, would be central to human concerns for the next 20 years, Wallerstein predicted.[29] In 1989, with the collapse of the Soviet bloc, that prediction would be at least partly fulfilled.

15

GLOBALISATION: COLLAPSE IN THE EAST, READJUSTMENT IN THE WEST, 1968–1991 AND AFTER

GLOBALISATION

Before the arrival of early civilisations, so-called primitive peoples were great travellers, and moved freely around and between Eurasia, Africa and Europe. In a sense, therefore, the process of globalisation began early. The classical and medieval periods saw significant connections, too. The Greeks and the Romans penetrated central Asia, for example, while the Vikings crossed the Atlantic Ocean. From the point of view of European discovery and colonisation in particular, however, the sixteenth century marked an acceleration in awareness of the world as one, and this realisation developed along with the expansion of empire in later years. In turn, the two world wars of the twentieth century both began in Europe but then exerted a powerful globalising influence, as did the Cold War and the decolonisation that followed. As we have just argued, the events of 1968 and the ensuing debate promoted the idea that 'local happenings are shaped by events occurring many miles away and vice versa'.[1] An extremely important feature of this new stage in the process was the spread of news by television. For example, the fact that the Vietnam War was the first to be widely shown as well as reported had much to do with its growing unpopularity throughout the USA, Europe and the rest of the world.

Peace came to Vietnam in 1973, a year which also saw an oil crisis brought about by another conflict, this time in the Middle East. Generally, the 1970s and 1980s were decades without major political disturbance in Europe itself, although it continued elsewhere. To take again the Middle East, the Shah of Iran was driven from power in 1979 by the Muslim fundamentalist Ayatollah Khomeini, while the Soviet Union sought to protect what it saw as its interests by invading nearby Afghanistan, and staying there for a decade. The spirit of the 1980s was exuded by such individuals as Ronald Reagan, Margaret Thatcher and Mikhail Gorbachev, and the policies of various kinds of 'freedom' associated with them. Freedom appeared to triumph throughout eastern Europe in 1989 and in the Soviet Union in 1991, although the question would soon be posed: liberation for whom, and for what? And, back in the Middle East, what was the significance of the Gulf War against Saddam Hussein's Iraq in 1991?

We will return to the questions after taking note of the varied experiences of the years following 1968 in the major sections of the world. And, as a reminder of Europe's loss of dominance, we will take it last, proceeding in the following series: the superpowers – the USA and the USSR; the Far East – Korea, Japan and China; from South-East Asia to the Middle East; Africa; Latin America and the Pacific; Europe – south-west, north-west, north, central, south-east and east.

THE USA

In his Farewell Address of 1961, Republican President Dwight D. Eisenhower had warned of the danger of unwarranted influence being acquired by 'the military–industrial complex'. John F. Kennedy came to power in the same year with a stirring inaugural address calling for New Frontiers on earth and in the heavens. Then, almost as soon as he became president in 1963, Lyndon Baines Johnson attempted to stamp his initials everywhere, from a domestic Great Society to assertive international policies. With the escalation of the war in Vietnam, and the race for the moon (won by 1969), the power of 'the military–industrial complex' grew throughout two Democratic administrations.

The successful Republican candidate in the election of 1968 promised pacification from the jungles of Vietnam to the cities of the USA, while maintaining the strength of the 'free', that is, non-Communist, world. As president, Richard M. Nixon soon caused more bombs to be dropped on Vietnam and neighbouring South-East Asia than ever before (a ton a minute from 1969 to 1973 according to one calculation), while organising withdrawal from Vietnam and some reduction of the presence of US forces elsewhere along with the abolition of the draft. However, overt and covert operations continued throughout the Third World, while Nixon talked in 1972 to the Communist leaders of the PRC and then the USSR about the necessity for détente. Here, he was guided not only by a taste for high-level diplomacy but also by the realisation that the once all-powerful dollar was being undermined by the overextension of American commitments. Although the USA was not to recognise the PRC officially until 1979, Nixon and Mao put out a joint declaration that no power should be allowed to establish hegemony in Asia and the Pacific. The implied target for the declaration, the Soviet Union, was less capable of such dominance than either of its rivals. Interestingly enough, when Nixon went to Moscow later in 1972, Brezhnev allegedly tried to convince him that 'we the whites' and 'we Europeans' should collaborate in the restraint of their common rival before it became 'a superpower'.[2] Although there was no such collusion, the summit meeting led to no fewer than four significant agreements, two on armaments and two on other aspects of the relationship. The most significant of these, probably, followed strategic arms limitation talks (SALT I) aimed at restricting the number of ICBMs and the range of anti-ballistic missile systems (ABMs).

In 1974, 'Tricky Dicky' fell victim to his own penchant for surveillance as the 'Watergate tapes' put on record his involvement in attempts to undermine the Democratic campaign in the election of 1972. His successor, Gerald Ford, inherited financial and other problems at home, difficulties in relations with allies and even potential enemies abroad. Not surprisingly, he was defeated in 1976 by the Democratic candidate Jimmy Carter, who spent four years doggedly trying to unravel all the complex details of the Federal Government's activities. He finished with spectacular failure, increasing the military budget after trying to cut it, and unable to make a convincing response to the Soviet invasion of Afghanistan and the takeover of Iran by the Ayatollah Khomeini. Carter was succeeded by the Governor of California and former actor Ronald Reagan, who gave a polished performance in the election campaign and achieved an impressive Republican victory.

From 1981 to 1989, President Reagan played his role with consummate showmanship as TV appeared to replace reality: again and again, a few widely screened words accompanied by the appropriate expression kept the USA happy, as if there was nothing to worry about but worry itself. It is still difficult to make an objective appraisal of Reagan and his years in power. Some observers have seen him as a statesman of vision and them as the centrepiece of a great world movement towards freedom, allowing American business to prosper and peoples throughout the rest of the world to begin to share the benefits of the market economy. Others have emphasised the increases in US government expenditure and the Federal debt, the decline of the part played by central government in social policies. An early dream was nothing less than to make the cosmos safe for democracy with the grandiose 'Star Wars' (SDI – Strategic Defense Initiative) project, while the main down-to-earth aim was to roll back the 'evil empire' controlled by the Soviet Union. In other parts of the world, the USA would lend its support to 'freedom fighters' (any forces opposed to Communism). Then, in a reversal of direction from 1985 onwards, through a series of summit meetings with the Soviet leader Mikhail Gorbachev, President Reagan brought about many proposals for arms reduction and all-round détente.

Coming into the White House in 1989 on the coat-tails of Ronald Reagan, George Bush found the preceding act difficult to follow. This was partly because of the widespread realisation that the USA was threatened by 'imperial overstretch', as a consequence of which 'decision-makers in Washington must face the awkward and enduring fact that the sum total of the United States' global interests and obligations is nowadays far larger than the country's power to defend them all simultaneously'.[3] Nevertheless, the new president moved on from apparent early bewilderment to a series of attempts to stamp his own personality on an overstretched USA in a rapidly changing situation, especially over in Europe, but also in other parts of the globe. Most dramatically, and most bloodily, the unleashing of Operation Desert Storm against Iraq in retribution for its invasion of Kuwait in February 1991 allowed President Bush to speak of 'a new world order' of 'peace and security, freedom and the rule of law'.[4]

THE USSR

A decade or so of adventurous, even reckless, action under Khrushchev was to be followed by nearly two decades from 1964 of careful, barely perceptible movement forward under Leonid Ilich Brezhnev. Indeed, these years were to become known as those of 'stagnation'. Such a label was not fully deserved, and derived too much from the contrasting personalities of the two leaders, perhaps. On the other hand, global circumstances were changing at a rate too fast for the Soviet system to accommodate – this much became increasingly apparent. The USA caught up and overtook the USSR in the space race, most notably with Armstrong's first steps on the moon in 1969, while maintaining a huge lead in nearly every other direction. Insubordination continued in the 'socialist camp', most notably in the 'Prague Spring' of 1968, which led to the announcement of the Brezhnev Doctrine – that members of the Warsaw Pact could intervene if any of them appeared to be threatening their general integrity. This Doctrine cast a shadow over the Helsinki Conference on European Security held in 1975, making it very difficult for the East and the West to agree either then or subsequently on what was meant by human rights. Included in the 'Final Act' along with methods of preventing accidental collisions of the two power blocs and proposals for economic and technological collaboration, respect for human rights provoked profound disagreement at the first sequel to the Helsinki Conference in Belgrade, 1977–8. Understanding and collaboration proved elusive in a continent still basically divided.

Within the frontiers of the USSR, Brezhnev cracked down on dissidents as any signs of 'thaw' disappeared. The basic idea seemed to be that the Soviet system was firmly in place, and that there should be no challenge to it. The influence of the Party should be maintained and strengthened, along with the accompanying *nomenklatura*, the system of appointment to a whole range of positions throughout all 15 republics. An assertion of the advances made from 1917 in general and from 1964 in particular came with a new Constitution in 1977. This announced that the October Revolution of 1917 had created a new kind of state, which had launched humanity on 'the epoch-making turn from capitalism to socialism'. Sixty years on, allegedly, it was possible to talk of a society of mature socialist social relations, in which, on the basis of the drawing together of all classes and social strata and of the juridical and factual equality of all its nations and nationalities and their fraternal co-operation, a new historical community of people has been formed – the Soviet people.

This people was guaranteed a wide range of rights and freedoms, although their enjoyment 'must not be to the detriment of the interests of society or the state, or infringe the rights of other citizens'. Moreover, every able-bodied citizen had to work conscientiously and with strict observance of labour discipline – 'Evasion of socially useful work is incompatible with the principles of socialist society'. In preparation for citizenship, there was a single, universal organisation serving 'Communist education'.

In the 'Brezhnev Constitution', the USSR was defined as 'an integral, federal, multinational state' of 15 republics, each of which had the right of free secession, although there was no expectation that this would ever be used. At the same time, 'the leading and guiding force of Soviet society and the nucleus of its political system' remained the Communist Party of the Soviet Union, which 'exists for the people and serves the people'.[5] In 1977, there was little apprehension that government for the people would not long endure if it was not also of the people and by the people. Brezhnev went to his grave in 1982 probably oblivious that the Soviet system was about to collapse, and neither of the two old invalids who followed him, Iurii V. Andropov and Konstantin U. Chernenko, could have had much inkling of the way events would unfold from 1985 onwards.

Even Mikhail Sergeevich Gorbachev, their comparatively youthful and much more dynamic successor, did not suspect that, less than 15 years after the Constitution of 1977 had been drawn up, and little more than five years after his much publicised announcement of *glasnost* and *perestroika* (openness and reconstruction), the Soviet Union and its Communist Party would collapse. In retrospect, it appears that he might have saved the first if he had been prepared to sacrifice the second. But there would have been no certainty of success for such a high-risk strategy, and the system might have been on the point of collapse in any case. The disastrous meltdown at Chernobyl nuclear power station north of Kiev in April 1986 was a tragic example of the parlous state of the Soviet economy, which continued in steep decline.

In short, unequal competition with the other, more advanced super-power in a globalised context had fatally weakened its less advanced rival. The Soviet gross national product, which had appeared to be catching up in the 1960s, had now shrunk to a third of the US equivalent, or even lower. Moreover, the decline was qualitative as well as quantitative. That is to say, the Soviet Union was falling behind most quickly in the race to adapt to the third industrial revolution, symbolised by the computer. Even with regard to an older form of communication, according to one calculation, if the installation of telephones had continued at the rate achieved in the last 20 years of the USSR's existence, to reach the same level as the USA in 1989 would have taken 160 years.[6] Even though Gorbachev sought to reverse the USSR's 'imperial overstretch' by withdrawing from external commitments, especially from Afghanistan, and pursuing all-round détente with the USA, collapse was imminent. Gorbachev's limited support for the Gulf War in 1991 probably hastened his own downfall.

KOREA, JAPAN AND CHINA

The Korean War (1950–3) had reinforced the dictatorship of Kim Il Sung in the North and encouraged an attempt to establish a dictatorship in the South by Syngman Rhee. Successful for some years, Rhee was overthrown in the April Revolution of 1960. However, big business quickly adapted itself to the new domestic circumstances and to expanding foreign opportunities. Europe was soon to feel the impact of the Korean and other Asian 'tiger economies'.

The greatest of these was the Japanese. Again, the Korean War had played a major part. In 1951, a bilateral Security Pact solidified ties with the USA. The conflict also accelerated the Japanese economic recovery: from 1953 to 1965, the gross national product grew by an astonishing 10 per cent each year. There were anti-American protests from time to time, in 1968 and 1969, for example. There was also a considerable amount of soul-searching about the part to be played in Asia and beyond. To take the most important question: should there be rearmament, and to what extent? By the early 1970s, Japan's rise to a kind of economic superpower was causing concern in the USA, which felt it was being treated like an underdeveloped region. With the end of the Vietnam War in 1973, and US rapprochement with China, Japan was, to a degree unprecedented since 1945, on its own.

The development of a Chinese atom bomb by 1964 and hydrogen bomb by 1969 underlined the potential of the PRC to exercise global influence independently, and the 'cultural revolution' from 1966 to 1969 carried the thoughts of Chairman Mao as contained in his Red Book throughout the People's Republic and much further afield. Intervention in the Vietnam War seemed a distinct possibility. A member of the United Nations from 1971, the PRC began to look more like a conventional great power, especially after the Nixon–Mao meeting of 1972 and the end of the Vietnam War in 1973. After the death of Mao in 1976, his successors opened up China's doors to capitalist investors, and there was soon reason to believe that at last the sleeping giant would fully awake. However, economic liberalisation was not accompanied by comparable relaxation in the political sphere. Opponents of the regime were ruthlessly crushed, most publicly in the bloody suppression of the pro-democracy movement in Tiananmen Square in Peking in June 1989. As the 1990s opened, the road forward for nearly one-quarter of the world's population looked better economically if not politically. Meanwhile, Taiwan, a home for Chinese exiles after the Revolution of 1949, was also able to develop business interests, regarded with some jealousy by the PRC, which regarded Taiwan as an integral part of China.

FROM SOUTH-EAST ASIA TO THE MIDDLE EAST

South-East Asia, for the most part, faced a more difficult future after a worse past. Here, more than in any other part of the world, the process of decolonisation had brought agony for the peoples involved, mostly in Indo-China but also elsewhere. Some of the wounds were self-inflicted, but others were the result of the American 'crusade' against Communism. Singapore, like Hong Kong to the east, became an important centre of international commerce, drawing on the Malaysian hinterland as well as the rest of the region for its activities, and encouraging the emergence of more 'tiger economies'. This upsurge was now overtaking any lingering sense of imperial interest as far as Europe was concerned.

Meanwhile, the many different languages and customs of the Indian subcontinent were striving to coexist, not without much communal violence and frontier disputes, especially over Kashmir. Somehow or other, although at times it was touch and go, all-out conflict was avoided between the two major states, India and Pakistan. East Pakistan became the independent Bangladesh in 1971. Until his death in 1964, Nehru continued to press for a 'third way', which remained the aim of his successors, even though India at times seemed to be entering the Soviet orbit. Pakistan, not far short of military dictatorship although avoiding the excesses of Muslim fundamentalism, managed to attract the support of both China and the USA, not least during the years of the Afghan War from 1979 to 1989.

Afghanistan was among those states that assumed a wider importance than they might have possessed at times other than those of Cold War, decolonisation and globalisation. The Western suspicion grew that the Soviet Union aimed to use it as a means of acquiring access to the Indian Ocean and the oil-rich Middle East. The year 1979 was of special significance, not only for the Soviet intervention in Afghanistan but also for the coming to power of Saddam Hussein and the Ayatollah Khomeini in Iraq and Iran respectively, soon followed by long years of war between them, 1980–8. Already, there had been a great shock in the world oil market in 1973. In October of that year, Egypt and Syria launched an attack with the aim of regaining what they had lost in the Six-Day War of 1967. Israel fought back to take more territory than before in what it was to call the Yom Kippur War. In 1979, after the fall of the Shah of Iran and the arrival of the Ayatollah Khomeini, another oil crisis ensued. Although the USA was now the major Western player in the region and their own years of predominance there were long past, the United Kingdom, France and other European powers could not escape intimate involvement.

AFRICA

Decolonisation in tropical Africa failed nearly all expectations in the context of previous history as well as of the more recent Cold War. Civil conflicts were frequent in states formed on the basis of imperial partition rather than African tradition, and the participants often sought support from the USA and former colonial powers on the one hand and the Soviet Union, the PRC and Cuba on the other. Violent in the extreme, these conflicts were accompanied by famine and disease. AIDS (Acquired Immune Deficiency Syndrome) in particular became widespread by the early 1990s. However, hopes were high for South Africa from 1990, when Nelson Mandela was freed after having spent more than 25 years in prison and worked for the institution of a democratic republic.

LATIN AMERICA AND THE PACIFIC

Castro remained in power in Cuba, while elsewhere, the USA made certain that Communism did not penetrate the Latin American mainland. The overthrow of President Allende in Chile in 1973 was one of the more dramatic pieces of supporting evidence for this observation. Equally, the most appalling testimony that the 'wretched of the earth' were not confined to Asia and Africa was probably to be found in the Amazon basin, where the insatiable maw of 'progress' not only ripped up tropical rainforest but rubbed out indigenous peoples, undisturbed since pre-history.

Generally speaking, the Third World was to be found in the south, whose global division from the north appeared to be overtaking that between West and East as the dual process of the Cold War and decolonisation came to an end. On the other hand, arguably, apart from outposts in Australia, New Zealand and South Africa, Europe was most involved in the north, even during the high tide of imperialism and the following decline towards decolonisation. This is not to deny shifts in emphasis, most significantly perhaps from the Atlantic as a centre of prosperity over to the Pacific. There was much talk of the tiger economies of Asia playing an important part in a vast economic zone on the Pacific Rim.

The end of the Cold War, if it really was the end, opened up new possibilities for Europe and the rest of the world during the 1990s. For example, would Russia turn out to be an important link for the north between the Atlantic and the Pacific? Or would the collapse of the Soviet Union lead to dislocation and instability throughout northern Asia?

EUROPE

As already indicated, from the end of the 1960s till towards the end of the 1980s, there was no major political turmoil in Europe. Major regime changes occurred, however, especially to the south-west.

The south-west

The story goes that when General Franco was dying, and some close associates came to bid him farewell, he asked them where they were going. The Spanish Caudillo or head of state did indeed die in 1975, but those succeeding him did indeed have to think about their sense of direction. Some years before, in 1969, Franco had already made provision for the succession by nominating as his heir the grandson of the king who had gone into exile in 1931. The Caudillo was no doubt soon turning over in his grave as King Juan Carlos allowed the legal return of political parties, including the Communist, but he might have rested a little more securely when the first general election to be held since 1936 gave a majority to the moderate Democratic Centre Party in 1977. The army made certain that the new government did not go off the rails, although in 1978 and 1981 disaffected officers led abortive coups. A greater and more constitutional threat to the status quo came from the moderate left, and the Socialist Party duly achieved power by general election in 1982, the year in which Spain joined NATO. The transition from Fascism to democracy appeared complete, and Spain continued with relative peace and prosperity to rejoin Europe, entering the EEC formally early in 1986 along with Portugal.

Meanwhile, Franco's boast of the unity of the peoples and lands of a Spain that was one, great and free was being revealed as a sham. At least, as the apparatus of the Fascist state was dismantled, a considerable measure of genuine freedom was restored, the desire of many of its peoples and lands having been shown to be for more autonomy, even in some cases for complete independence. The most extreme passions were raised among the Basques, some of whom resorted to terrorism in pursuit of their aims, but feelings also ran high among the Catalans. After much debate, the appropriate Article 2 of the Constitution of 1978 asserted that it was 'based upon the indissoluble unity of the Spanish Nation, common and indivisible fatherland of all Spaniards'. However, this Article also said that the Constitution recognised and guaranteed 'the right to autonomy of all the nationalities and regions within it and the need for solidarity between them'. In the continuing argument about where to place the emphasis, the separatist Left asserted that they would say 'unity for the state and autonomy for the nations', where the centralist Right would talk of 'unity for the nation and autonomy for the regions'. Some believed that Spain should follow the German concept of cultural community leading to statehood, others were for the French idea of the nation as a consequence of state power.[7]

While Spain continued to occupy itself with the problem of the right balance between unity and autonomy, the other states of Europe, old and new, considered the same sort of problem with varying degrees of intensity from the Atlantic to the Urals. In Portugal, feelings on this question ran less high, although there was no shortage of strong feelings on others. In 1974, with discontent at home and vexing conflict with the colonies of Angola and Mozambique abroad, a 'Revolution of Flowers' led by a left-wing 'Armed Forces Movement' paved the way for the reintroduction of democracy about six years after Dr Salazar had given up power after a stroke. The first general election in 1976 produced no clear majority, and a minority Socialist government could not hold out for much more than two years. The resulting period of considerable confusion was followed by another of relative stability. To be sure, the hopes for sweeping reforms that had accompanied the 'Revolution of Flowers' by no means came to complete fruition, but, while regional tensions certainly existed, they were not felt in as acute a form as in Spain or Italy. Already a member of NATO and EFTA, Portugal joined the EEC in January 1986.

If the Italian peninsula be likened to a leg, there is no doubt that the thigh was not happy with the situation at the knee and below, while Sicily became something of a political football. After some initial relative prosperity in the years leading up to and following the creation of the Common Market, recession and unemployment were more of a problem from the late 1960s onwards. While the Christian Democrats continued to constitute the largest party, the Communists began to catch up through a series of municipal elections before giving their opponents a real run for their money in a general election in 1976. In the late 1970s, there appeared to be a real possibility of the breakdown of constitutional order, with the Mafia continuing its traditional covert activity from the south while the 'Red Brigade' conducted terrorist activities mostly in Rome and cities to the north. However, political parties continued to share out the spoils, both following the rules for the allotment of jobs and evading them, while the public appetite for politics in general waned sharply. As the Cold War seemed to be coming to an end, the confrontation grew less sharp between Christian Democrats on the one hand, suffering from a decline in Roman Catholicism in general, and less radical socialists and Euro-communists breaking away from Soviet direction and revolutionary traditions on the other. A measure of consumer luxury for many was a further diluter of earlier political enthusiasm. However, amid further scandals and crises, a Northern League (Lega Nord) was formed in 1991 to protect the interests of the regions above Rome.

The north-west

The spirit of post-war France was to be found in General Charles de Gaulle; or so he liked to think, and from time to time a consider-able number of his fellow citizens agreed with him. To be sure, the Fourth Republic managed to last from 1946 to 1958 without too much interference from the strong presidential authority that de Gaulle advo-cated, but the threat of civil war over the Algerian question brought him back to power in 1958 with massive support from a referendum. A new Fifth Republic was formed, giving great power to the president. However, ten years later, another referendum removed de Gaulle from power, as the disturbances of 1968 showed him to be as much out of touch with the situation as he had been in touch with it in 1958. He died two years later, but something of his spirit lived on with the Fifth Republic.

Under de Gaulle's successors, French agriculture remained a problem in spite of the supports given it, while trade and industry went through the ups and downs of the business cycle. Under the supervision of a series of presidents from Pompidou to Mitterand, something like normal political activity continued, without any centrifugal pull as strong as in Spain and Italy, and without full realisation of a series of challenges from the extreme Right. France went into the 1990s with its spirit still strong, but with some intimation that the *Europe des Patries* favoured by de Gaulle might not last forever.

Certainly, in some frontier regions such as the Saar–Lor(raine)–Lux(embourg) at the crossroads of France, Germany and the Benelux countries, there was a clear indication of the road that a new Europe might follow. Of course, while on the one hand the Benelux might by itself constitute something of the shape of things to come, it could also show age-old sources of tension in the Belgian split between the Walloons and the Flemish, for example, which sometimes cast a shadow over activities in the European capital, Brussels. The Netherlands was as concerned as ever with threats from the sea as well as with newer problems arising towards the end of the twentieth century, ranging from anarchy to right-wing nationalism.

Over the sea, the United Kingdom of Great Britain and Northern Ireland (although on occasion in apparent danger of losing that last constituent part) continued to wrestle with the vexed question of its degree of commitment to Europe. Although the British Commonwealth was coming to mean less, and the 'special relationship' with the USA was shown to be weaker, there were still many who wanted the UK to go it alone, or at least without suffering the slightest loss of sovereignty. After many internal misgivings and some external vetoes, the UK joined the EEC in 1972. After a series of Labour and Conservative governments (mainly the latter) through the 1950s, 1960s and 1970s, a most radical departure in British politics was marked by the arrival as prime minister in 1979 of Mrs Margaret Thatcher. Asserting her own strong will in the name of her party and country, she achieved the full realisation of her influence after the Falklands conflict with Argentina in 1982. Her great admiration for market forces allowed a considerable part of manufacturing to collapse while financial activities flourished. There was an occasional surge of nationalism in Scotland, where some politicians argued that the relationship with Europe could be direct, and some analysts made comparisons with regions in Italy, Germany and elsewhere. With more reluctance than enthusiasm, after the ejection by her own party from power in 1990 of Mrs Thatcher, the UK edged closer to the Europe from which it had throughout much of its history held itself aloof.

The north

The three Scandinavian countries, Sweden, Norway and Denmark, were managing to achieve an exceptional degree of internal integration and to sink old enmities and rivalries between themselves to a considerable extent before they joined other non-EEC states in EFTA, which came into existence from 1959 to 1960. Also from the north, Finland became an associate member in 1961, while Iceland came in as a full member in 1970. Along with the UK, Denmark left EFTA at the end of 1972 to join the EEC, while EFTA as a whole entered into closer relations with the EEC.

The above movements caught some of the essence of north European relationships among themselves and more widely. Finland and Iceland were peripheral to the Scandinavian core, while Denmark was of the three core countries the most closely linked to the European mainland. However, as world alignments changed by the beginning of the 1990s, so did ideas of what constituted the European north. A vision opened up for some of the links between the Baltic and North seas with the White and Barents seas.

Looking to the post-Second World War past, we can see how the Scandinavian countries became a byword for 'pink' democratic socialism, combining welfare programmes with free parliamentary elections. Unfortunately for such an image, those very elections brought to an end many decades of left-wing government throughout Scandinavia in the 1980s. By that time, too, another generally accepted idea, that of 'Finlandisation', had also fallen into disuse. There would be little fear of the Soviet Union restricting the policies of its neighbours in central, south-eastern and eastern Europe; indeed, the former apparent cohesion was quickly dissolving by the late 1980s, and the centrifugal forces were becoming far stronger than any of those to be found in the north-west or south-west. In other words, a deep-set pattern of European history was reasserting itself.

The centre

Christian Democratic central control continued in the Federal Republic of Germany until 1969, when the Social Democrats led by Willy Brandt took over after a period of 'grand coalition'. Almost immediately, he inaugurated his *Ostpolitik*, reiterating the assertion of his predecessors that Germans had the same right to self-determination as any other people, but adding that the FRG and the GDR were not foreign countries and must therefore have a special relationship. In 1970, Brandt signed the Treaty of Moscow with the USSR and the Treaty of Warsaw with Poland, both recognising the Oder–Neisse line as the frontier between the GDR and Poland. On the latter occasion, he fell on his knees at the Warsaw ghetto memorial in a widely publicised penitential gesture. At the end of 1972, the FRG and GDR signed a 'Basic Treaty' of practical if not yet legal recognition, and more agreements were soon made by Brandt and his successor, Helmut Schmidt, with other countries in the East. At home, there was a fair measure of continuity and little fear of constitutional crisis in Bonn through the 1970s and 1980s, although the Christian Democrats were to return to power in 1982. Differences in the Federal parliament were of degree rather than of fundamental principle, although the heat of some exchanges in the Bundestag belied that fact. Away from Bonn in the ten *Länder* or constituent states of the FRG, however, the picture could be different. In Bavaria, for example, there was something that looked to some anxious eyes more like the rebirth of Nazism than the desire for autonomy. From the turbulent year of 1968 for about four years a 'Red Army Faction' was the best-known of several left-wing urban guerrilla groups opposed to the excesses of capitalism and the continued presence of US forces. Later, before they were elected to the Bundestag, even after, the Greens, concentrating on ecological issues, were of concern to those in the somewhat self-satisfied mainstream of Federal politics in the 1980s.

Meanwhile, the much smaller German Democratic Republic had much larger problems. Its 'socialist construction' enjoyed some patches of success, but could not begin to compare with the 'economic miracle' of its Federal counterpart. From the Berlin blockade of 1948–9 up to the erection of the Berlin Wall in 1961 and beyond, there were many signs of discontent at the imbalance in standards of living between the two Germanies, accompanied by growing government apprehension about developments elsewhere in the Soviet bloc from the 'Prague Spring' of 1968 onwards. Having been a determined proponent of intervention in Czechoslovakia in 1968, the GDR leader, Erich Honecker, asserted that the focus of fresh unrest, Poland, belonged inseparably to the socialist camp whose other members would ensure that there was no defection from it. He also exploited apprehension about German rearmament and reunification among those who had suffered most at the hands of Nazi Germany.

When Czechoslovakia began to show 'socialism with a human face' in 1968, a veil was quickly drawn over it by a Warsaw Pact invasion.

Alexander Dubček, the leader of the would-be reform movement, was sent home to a minor post in his native Slovakia. In 1969, Slovakia and the Czech Republic were declared equal and sovereign members of a federal socialist republic, a reassertion of an unhappy state of convenience born of the First World War and the Russian Revolution. In 1969, too, a student named Jan Palach set himself alight in Wenceslas Square in protest at the return of what might be called a 'Prague Winter'. Palach soon died, but his name lived on as a stifling orthodoxy continued. A Charter '77 Group to protest against violations of the Helsinki act on human rights was formed by the playwright Vaclav Havel and other dissidents at the beginning of 1977. Havel and five others were given prison sentences in October.

In Poland, a new regime under the former dissident Władysław Gomułka more or less kept the peace until the end of 1970 attempting to steer a middle course between the Soviet government's determination not to allow any repetition of the events of 1956 in Poland, Hungary or anywhere else and the Polish government's assertion of a certain measure of nationalistic policy in order to achieve that desirable end. Then, in December, a series of riots sparked off by increases in the price of food and taking place mainly in the Baltic cities of Gdańsk, Gdynia and Szczecin led to the ejection of Gomułka and his replacement as head of the party and government by Edward Gierek. The new regime managed to stay in power for a further decade, albeit with further food price riots in 1976 and a rising tide of dissidence largely although not entirely centred around the Roman Catholic Church and encouraged by the election of Cardinal Karol Wojtyła as Pope John Paul II in 1978.

And then in 1980, after a wave of strikes throughout Poland, a new movement, Solidarity (*Solidarność*), sprang up with the Gdańsk shipyard electrician Lech Wałęsa elected leader. Gierek made concessions on free trade unions and other demands but was soon forced into retirement, to be followed by early 1981 as prime minister by General Wojciech Jaruzelski. Under the leadership of the general, attempts at suppression of Solidarity and other opposition movements alternated with attempts at conciliation. From shipyard to peasant farm, many of the old national traits could still be discerned, all symbolised by adherence to the Roman Catholic faith. Towards the end of the 1980s, old traits and new features were both to assume fresh force in Poland and elsewhere.

In Hungary, clampdown followed the Rising of 1956, but János Kádár managed in the following years to combine loyalty in international relations to the Soviet Union with measures for reconciliation and comparative liberalisation at home. There was a measure of private enterpise within the state economy according to what became known as the 'Hungarian model'. In the 1970s and early 1980s, there was even talk of a 'cola-communism' combining some of the features of the capitalist West into the command system. It was considered almost as dangerous for Soviet citizens to visit Budapest as Paris. However, like other members of the Soviet bloc, Hungary ran into severe economic problems, including mountains of debt and troughs of inefficiency. Like other leaders in the people's democracies, Kádár was swept away by the democratic popular movement of the late 1980s after making some attempt to swim with the tide. For example, multi-candidate elections were launched in 1985.

To some extent, Hungary was able to make use of its historical relationship with Austria. Not without some echoes of its Nazi as well as its imperial past, Austria became a good European, joining EFTA at its inception in 1959 and then applying for membership of the EEC in 1989. Its neutrality enabled Austria to play the role of honest broker between East and West, and Vienna was the location for several important meetings, as well as the first destination for many refugees.

Towards the end of the 1980s, the trickle of those seeking what they believed would be a better life in the West became a flood. The cracks were showing not only in Communism but also in the divisions of the European continent. Age-old questions were re-opened: what constituted the centre, the south-east and the east? Could the somewhat arbitrary arrangement still be employed with any confidence?

The south-east

Certainly, the cracks would appear deepest in the south-east, the pre-First World War tinderbox where the situation threatened to become inflammatory again. By the early 1990s, old ghosts had returned from the beginning of the twentieth century and earlier, recalling not just the struggle between the Habsburg and Ottoman empires but also that between Christian and Muslim at the time of the crusades, involving even ancient history.

After Stalin's death, the Albanian leader Enver Hoxha began to transfer his allegiance to China, and became closely associated with the Red Far East until the late 1970s. By 1978, however, he had fallen out with the PRC as he had with the USSR previously. Insomniacs could now be bored to sleep by recitations of what were proclaimed to be the only true Marxist doctrines broadcast loud and clear every night by Radio Tiranë. Not long after Hoxha's death in 1985, his system began to fall apart in the midst of attempts to reform itself. By this time, the Albanian minority in Yugoslavia was only one of many groups to show their restlessness at the maintenance of the state cobbled together to unite southern Slavs with others as part of the peace settlement following the First World War.

For more than 30 years after his break with Stalin in 1948, Tito had managed to remain at the helm of the multinational Yugoslav ship of state. Not without many difficulties, he even managed to convey to the outside world an image of a successful middle way between Soviet socialism and Western capitalism. However, at his death in 1980, Serbian and other kinds of nationalism began to reassert themselves. In 1987, for example, President Slobodan Milošević gained popularity for his defence of fellow Serbs against alleged persecution by the Albanian Kosovo police.

Yugoslavia's neighbours grew agitated, notably Greece, where there were many nationalists anxious to claim the whole of Macedonia, the native land of Alexander the Great. The birthplace of democracy continued to experience difficulties in remaining true to its ancient inheritance. In 1973, the 'Colonels' then in power formally declared a republic not long before they themselves fell in 1974 against a background of popular dissatisfaction with their handling of the dispute with Turkey over Cyprus. There was some fear that Greece might become too socialist and/or too nationalist, and eject the NATO navy from its bases. However, following its first application to join the EEC in 1975, Greece finally managed to join the community in January 1981.

Greece was in dispute not only with Turkey and Yugoslavia but also with Bulgaria, which in turn asserted its rights against Turkey, Yugoslavia and Greece, to name but three. Preaching a mixture of hard-line Soviet communism and Slav nationalism, Todor Zhivkov managed to remain in power and achieve a measure of economic growth from the mid-1950s until the late 1980s. Although Gorbachev dubbed Zhivkov the 'Chinese Emperor of Bulgaria', the cult of his personality was not taken to the level of that surrounding Nicolae Ceauşescu in neighbouring Romania. Here also, a classical heritage was asserted in order to bolster up a dictatorship both internally and internationally. Ceauşescu built a huge palace for himself and his wife in Bucharest, while forcing thousands of peasants to leave their homes in a grandiose attempt to combine old villages in new towns. In a vain attempt to pay for such ill-judged schemes for industrialisation by means of exports, Ceauşescu brought his people to the verge of starvation and ruin. Protests against deprivation erupted towards the end of 1987 in Brasov and other Romanian cities.

Romania strongly resisted Hungarian claims to Transylvania, reinforced in 1988 by demonstrations in Budapest against the destruction of villages containing large elements of the Hungarian minority. Meanwhile, the Danube remained a bone of contention for Romania, Bulgaria and other states upstream.

The east

Frontiers fluctuated in the east of Europe much more than in the centre or even the south-east. Much of Poland including Warsaw was incorporated in the Russian Empire for well over a century and the prime strategic significance of the various shapes assumed by Poland since the First World War were among the reasons for making a decision about the east that would be unacceptable to Poles, and others. 'Others' would include the inhabitants of the three Soviet Baltic republics, Latvia, Estonia and Lithuania, who looked back not so much to their involvement in the Russian Empire for as much as 200 years as to the independence which, along with Poland, they had enjoyed between the two world wars. Certainly, at the end of the 1980s and beginning of the 1990s, thoughts about what constituted the east would have to be drastically revised as not only the states just mentioned but also other former Soviet republics asserted their independence as Belarus, Ukraine and Moldova.

COLLAPSE IN THE EAST, 1989–91

While it would be wrong to attribute responsibility for these events to one man or one movement, there can be little doubt that at least some of their origins must be found in the *perestroika* and *glasnost* made famous by the last Soviet leader, President Mikhail Gorbachev. A 'Moscow Spring' helped to bring a thaw to what at times had looked like frozen immobility throughout the whole Soviet bloc.

There were already rumblings in 1988. In August, after strikes broke out again in Poland, Lech Wałęsa and Solidarity began to negotiate with the government. In Hungary, alternative political parties were allowed from November onwards. Then, with astonishing rapidity, one surprise followed another from the spring of 1989 onwards. Poland and Hungary led the way. In April, Solidarity and the government agreed that there should be independent trade unions and new elections. In June, Solidarity won most of the seats open to it and then went on to dominate the government set up in August. In April, the Soviet Army started to leave Hungary, where the frontier with Austria was opened from May onwards. This measure prompted thousands of East Germans to emigrate to the West via Hungary in September, followed by thousands more leaving via Poland and Czechoslovakia in October. The focus now switched to the GDR itself, where early in October Gorbachev criticised the government for its failure to reform while insisting that decisions about its future must be taken in Berlin. Massive demonstrations in favour of free elections and the removal of the Wall followed in Berlin itself and in other cities, especially Leipzig. On 9 November, the GDR government was resigning as the Wall tumbled down and the path opened up towards German reunification. There was now no stopping popular movements throughout the crumbling Soviet bloc. By the end of November, it was all over bar the shouting in Czechoslovakia, while Zhivkov had resigned in Bulgaria. On Christmas Day, the Ceauşescus were executed in Romania after trying to put up a final fight. This was the end of one of the most remarkable years in European history.

In 1990, there were elections throughout the former Soviet satellites as the Soviet army continued its withdrawal, and the reunification of Germany as a federal state was completed on 3 October. By the summer of 1991, the process of change was completed nearly everywhere in the socialist camp, with the formal dissolution of Comecon and of the Warsaw Pact. Those who had previously broken with the camp did not escape, a Communist-led government falling in Albania, and the collapse of Yugoslavia issuing in civil war.

The summer of 1991 also brought the beginning of the end for the former Soviet Union, as the president of the Russian Federation, Boris Yeltsin, emerged the victor over a 'Gang of Eight' attempting an 'old guard' coup while the Soviet President Mikhail Gorbachev was held captive in his Black Sea retreat. On his return to Moscow, Gorbachev presided over little more than the disintegration of the USSR, while Yeltsin and others were far from fully successful in their attempt to set up a Commonwealth of Independent States (CIS). Lithuania, Latvia and Estonia, having already in 1990 severed their official connections with their former sister Soviet republics, did not join the CIS; nor did Georgia, which had followed them into separation earlier in 1991. Even the founder members of the CIS found it difficult to see eye to eye, while problems of Russian and other minorities created unease in all the 'European' ex-Soviet republics from Moldova in the south-east through Ukraine and Belarus up to the three republics by the Baltic.

Where should Lithuania, Latvia and Estonia now be placed? However difficult it proved to achieve complete separation from the East, they would much prefer to be seen as part of the north, or even as an outpost of the West. Without a doubt, our previous demarcation of the continent falls under yet more suspicion. As Timothy Garton Ash wrote in 1989 under the first impact of the great changes: 'Like Europe itself, no one can quite agree where Central Europe begins or ends ... As with the whole of Europe, the most difficult frontier to locate is the Eastern one.'[8] In the early 1990s, two further points could certainly be made. The first is that, after the flag-waving and cheers at the discovery of freedom, the peoples of the former Soviet Union, and of its former satellites and neighbours, were to realise the limitations placed on that freedom by shortages and inflation, even to the point that some of them would talk of the 'good old days' before 1989. The second point to be made with confidence is that, wherever its divisions were made, the whole continent of Europe was more interdependent than ever before, and more closely associated with the rest of the world.

READJUSTMENT IN THE WEST, 1968–91

If the east of Europe collapsed suddenly under the strains of globalisation, the West was subject to severe strain over a longer period before achieving consolidation. Indeed, for much of the 1970s and 1980s,

'Eurosclerosis' set in. In August 1971, President Nixon brought to an end the financial system based on the convertibility of the dollar first set up at Bretton Woods in 1944. Some Europeans dubbed this measure the Marshall Plan in reverse. After a considerable amount of debate, EEC finance ministers agreed in April 1972 to set up what became known as 'the snake in the tunnel', that is, to allow national currencies strictly limited fluctuation against the dollar.

By no means all of the original six members of the EEC welcomed the increase of their number to nine in 1972 as they were joined by the UK, Ireland and Denmark. Would the offshore islands in particular be prepared to join in the move towards closer integration? However, such longer-term considerations receded into the background in the face of further immediate crisis.

The dollar and all other currencies were severely hit in the aftermath of the Yom Kippur War of October 1973 as the Organisation of Petroleum Exporting Countries (OPEC) announced a ban on the export of oil to all those countries deemed to be supporting Israel. This embargo, accompanied by a steep rise in oil prices, was at least as much of a blow to western Europe as the end of Bretton Woods. Further pressures were exerted by global competition in other commodities, including cheaper coal, iron and steel. The Common Agricultural Policy (CAP) was also under strain with cheaper foodstuffs flowing in from outside the EEC. Widespread recession was followed by a slower rate of growth, industrial decline, rural dislocation and a rise in unemployment. Such stagnation was accompanied by inflation, leading to 'stagflation'.

While the EEC now contained over 300 million consumers and accounted for more than a fifth of the world's commerce, its economic problems impeded the consolidation of the market. There were arguments over such important questions as the CAP, distribution of regional development funds and fishing quotas. While there was collaboration on some scientific and environmental questions, introducing elections for the European Parliament from 1974 did not immediately make for harmony on political objectives.

In 1978, the EEC decided to create its own monetary system, which was to consist of Economic and Monetary Union (EMU) and the European Currency Unit (ECU). The decision would be taken in 1995 to call the single currency the Euro, and the launch of the Euro followed on 1 January 2002.

Greece joined the EEC in 1981, Spain and Portugal in 1986: the nine were now twelve. However, the linchpin of the community remained its first members, especially France and Germany. In 1986, they were among a majority in favour of the Single European Act, which moved on from the Treaty of Rome to closer collaboration not only on the market but also on technology, the environment and social issues. The UK under Margaret Thatcher joined Denmark in expressing some reservations, especially concerning the extension of the decision-making powers of the European Parliament.

The famous advocates of the 'free market', Ronald Reagan and Margaret Thatcher, left office early in 1989 and late in 1990 respectively, soon followed by economic deluge. A confrontation with Iraq over its invasion of Kuwait led in 1991 to the Gulf War. Meanwhile, the European Community would find it very difficult to move to the closer union agreed at Maastricht in 1991. The treaty of 7 February 1992 resolved to mark a new stage in the process of European integration. Recalling earlier divisions in the continent and the need for new construction, the signatories confirmed their attachment to the principles of liberty and democracy, respect for human rights, fundamental freedoms and the rule of law. They also expressed their desire to deepen the solidarity between their peoples to the point of establishing a common citizenship while respecting their history, their culture and their traditions. People should be free to move around the EC as long as general safety and security remained intact. While stating their determination to achieve the strengthening and convergence of their economies, in addition to the establishment of an economic and monetary union including a single currency, the signatories also sought to promote social as well as economic progress along with environmental protection. Most ambitiously, the Maastricht Treaty 'resolved to implement a common foreign and security policy including the eventual framing of a common defence policy, thereby reinforcing the European identity and its independence in order to promote peace, security and progress in Europe and in the world'.[9]

Whatever the material reality of a smaller world, the spirits of nationalism and regionalism were far from dead in the west, even if they were not as assertive as to the east. In other words, whatever was new about Europe and the world as they approached the new millenium, there could be no neglect of previous centuries of history in any attempt at full comprehension.

HISTORIES REAL AND IMAGINED, 1991–

In his State of the Union address at the end of January 1991, President George Bush spoke of 'a new world order – where diverse nations are drawn together in common cause, to achieve the universal aspirations of mankind: peace and security, freedom and the rule of law'. To repel lawless aggression threatening this new world order, an international coalition against Saddam Hussein had been formed consisting of the forces of 28 nations from 6 continents bound together by 12 Resolutions of the United Nations. The end of the Cold War had been a victory for all humanity, and Europe had become whole and free. Democratic ideas had triumphed in Latin America, too. But most Americans knew instinctively that 'we had to stop Saddam now, not later. They know that this brutal dictator will do anything, will use any weapon, will commit any outrage, no matter how many innocents suffer. They know we must make sure that control of the world's oil resources does not fall into his hands, only to finance further aggression.' George Bush predicted: 'We will succeed in the Gulf. And when we do, the world community will have sent an enduring warning to any dictator or despot, present or future, who contemplates outlaw aggression.'[10] Operation Desert Storm was launched on 27 February, and was deemed to have been completed satisfactorily soon afterwards.

By the end of the year, however, Bush's vision of 'a new world order' did not appear to be clear. Saddam Hussein was still in power in Iraq, while in Europe, some of the excitement and hope aroused by the fall of the Berlin Wall was dying down. Nevertheless, the collapse of the Soviet Union at the end of the year brought about a calmer but still strong belief that a new era was dawning. If this book had been written then, rather than ten years or so later, the conclusion would have been more optimistic than it can be now.

To record the events of the period from 1991 onwards is certainly part of the historian's task. However, to separate what may appear significant in the long run from what will seem unimportant in later years is virtually impossible. Without the perspective given by the passage of time, historians can find no certain sense of direction for their narrative. This certainly does not mean that there is no basic story or master narrative, as is asserted by many postmodernist theorists.

Moreover, we can be fairly certain that '9/11', the terrorist attacks on New York and Washington, DC, in September 2001, will continue to influence the course of world events well into the new millennium. Consequently, distinctive emphasis is given to the process of globalisation, and new impetus to the study of geopolitics. Nevertheless, Europe retains identity and significance within such a framework, however much it has fallen from the zenith reached early in the twentieth century.

At the beginning of the 1990s, 'Europe' was an economic association within a cultural tradition accompanied by a debate on how far its constitution should approach political union. In 1992, the European Community redesigned itself, becoming the European Union in 1993. In the same year, the European Council set up the Copenhagen criteria, which all countries wishing to join the EU would have to fulfil before their applications could be successful. They would have to possess a functioning market economy and to transpose all EU laws into their national legislation. But that was not enough. They would require also stable political institutions guaranteeing democracy, the rule of law, human rights and the protection of minorities. This was an assertion of distinctive elements within the cultural tradition as well as of possible implications for a political union.

A number of programmes were launched to help candidates meet the criteria. Cyprus and Malta had already submitted their applications in 1990. They were followed in 1994 by Hungary and Poland, in 1995 by Bulgaria, Estonia, Latvia, Lithuania, Romania and Slovakia, in 1996 by the Czech Republic and Slovenia, and in 1999 by Turkey. In 2000, the Nice Treaty charted the course for accession negotiations by determining the number of votes in the European Council, the number of seats in the European Parliament and the number of commissioners in the European Commission. At the end of 2002, the Copenhagen Council confirmed the successful conclusion of negotiations with all those listed above, with the exception of Bulgaria and Romania, which were set a target date of 2007, and of Turkey, which was urged to fulfil more completely the political criteria for membership. The ten new members joined the EU on 1 May 2004.

Three of them had not existed in 1989. The Czech Republic and Slovakia became separate states at the end of December 1992. Slovenia declared its independence from Yugoslavia, as did Croatia, in the summer of 1991, and these two states were recognised by the EU at the insistence of Germany at the beginning of 1992. The process of the dismemberment of Yugoslavia continued through the 1990s accompanied by bloody conflict, as a lot of old wounds inflicted during the Second World War and long before opened up. Internecine warfare brought in the United Nations as a peacekeeper and NATO as an enforcer. Passions continue to run so high that objective historical evaluation remains elusive for all those involved. Certainly, the post-First World War settlement aimed at the pacification of the Balkans had fallen apart.

To the east, with the collapse of another post-First World War creation, the Union of Socialist Soviet Republics had broken into its 15 constituent parts. In Europe, these included, from north to south, Estonia, Latvia, Lithuania, Belarus, Ukraine and Moldova. Beyond them, in the Caucasus region, were Georgia and Armenia, worthy of inclusion, too, from some historical points of view. And of course, we must not forget Russia, freed from imperial responsibilities and therefore in a position to realise its true self, according to some well-wishers.

However, we must restrain our benevolence as well as other kinds of partiality as we seek an objective perspective on the recent past. Here, we must recall the fact that there are imagined elements in the histories of all countries. While the emergence of nation states since the beginning of the twentieth century must be seen 'as a consequence of a very long formative process', at the end of a decisive stage from the eve of the French Revolution to that of the unification of Germany and Italy, 1780–1870, 'there existed in Europe only eight established state-nations, all of them having their "own" state, ruled by ethnically homogeneous elites (including an aristocracy and an emerging industrial bourgeoisie) and having a highly developed national culture and literary language: English, French, Dutch, Portuguese, Spanish, Danish, Swedish'.[11] Even in these cases, it must be said, there was a large amount of invention of tradition, for example concerning the Gothic origins of Denmark and Sweden.

In the latest stage of the emergence of nation states, since 1989, the imaginative element has played an even greater role. During the Soviet period, especially from 1945 to 1989, there was considerable economic and cultural progress, but much political frustration. The release of pent-up energy from 1989 onwards produced not only great celebration but also an idealisation of the pre-Soviet past adding to the subsequent hangover. For example, Attila Ágh wrote in 1995 of the 'infantile disorder' of the transitional period, of the exorbitant price paid for 'this five years' excursion in the Glorious Past That Never Was'.[12]

Nevertheless, the past that did exist, glorious or inglorious, would remain an important influence on later developments. Of the ten countries due to join the European Union in May 2004, eight could rightly claim to be rejoining Europe. The three 'Baltics', Estonia, Latvia and Lithuania, had all enjoyed an independent existence in Europe between the two world wars. Before 1914, since the time of Peter the Great in the early eighteenth century, Estonia and Latvia had been significant provinces in the Russian Empire. They were joined during the reign of Catherine the Great in the later eighteenth century by Lithuania. The Baltics were important to the Russian Empire not only for their strategic situation but also for their economic and cultural contributions. Before their incorporation, Lithuania had been part of a joint commonwealth with Poland since 1569, while Estonia and Latvia had been under the influence of Prussia and Sweden.

In various ways, five more of the successful candidates for EU membership – Poland, the Czech Republic, Slovakia, Hungary and Slovenia – had been part of what some historians have called 'east-central Europe',[13] an area forming a halfway house between Germany and Russia. The label has been applied not just because they were parts of the German, Russian or Austrian empires, but also because they possessed distinctive socio-economic characteristics midway between the urbanised West and rural East. The Mediterranean islands of Malta and Cyprus have many ties with the continent to the north.

To the south-east of Europe are Romania and Bulgaria, aiming at their own accession in 2007. These two states could rightfully claim historical membership of Europe, even if sometimes inventing their own pasts to an extent greater than many of their fellows, at least partly as a reaction to their inclusion in a distinctive category of Balkan powers. Beyond them, Turkey awaits initiation of accession negotiations subject to the fulfilment of the political Copenhagen criteria. Already, opponents of this candidacy are arguing that it would be entertained largely for strategic reasons, and that Turkey can in no way claim to be part of the European cultural tradition.

We need to recall that the EU does not equal Europe, however. To the north, Iceland, Norway and Finland remain apart. To the east, there are Belarus, Ukraine and Moldova, arguably Georgia and Armenia too, as well as Russia, all fragments of the former Soviet Union. The history of the first three is somewhat problematic, since none of them enjoyed an independent existence during the modern period. Nevertheless, they all claim deep historical roots: Belarus as a more or less autonomous part of the Grand Duchy of Lithuania with its own language; Ukraine as the home of ancient Rus centred on Kiev, again with its own language. Moldova presents more difficulty, since it has been part of Romania and contains assertive ethnic minorities. Georgia and Armenia both have interrupted pasts but also strong traditions reaching back to the early reception of Christianity.

The most problematic former Soviet republic from the point of view of Europe as a whole is Russia. Still stretching from the frontier of Norway to that of North Korea, it remains the largest country in the world. As before, its occupation of North Asia raises the question about how completely it should be considered part of Europe. For some analysts, it constitutes a distinct 'Eurasia' apart from other continents. The majority, however, see its future in Europe, possibly in association with the EU or with a Nordic–Baltic group of states.

PATHS TO A NEW EUROPE

Another way of illustrating the nature of historical perspective central to our understanding of the recent past is to take the viewpoint of a distinguished commentator as it was set out a decade after the end of the Second World War. Arnold Toynbee was perhaps best known for *A Study of History*, a multi-volume exposition of a cyclical view of history, describing the manner in which civilisations have risen and fallen in accordance with challenge and response. Yet he also helped point the way towards a more balanced view of *The Realignment of Europe*, a work published in 1955 as a volume in the Survey of International Affairs series, with which he had been associated for more than 30 years. Arguably, Toynbee's classical learning and broad historical sweep were put to better use in *The Realignment* than in

A Study. Of the partition of Europe that occurred at the conclusion of the Second World War, Toynbee wrote that the line dividing the two spheres 'corresponded rather closely, though not exactly, to an older line that was not military or political, but cultural and social'. He continued:

> The Anglo-American sphere embraced most of those European countries in which the middle class was numerous, competent, and powerful and in which the institution of parliamentary government was well established and effective, whereas the Russian sphere embraced most of those European countries in which the middle class was small, inexperienced, and weak, in which parliamentary government had been exotic and perfunctory.

The principal exceptions were two countries of the 'Western' type, Finland and Czechoslovakia, in the Russian sphere, and two of the 'Eastern' type, Greece and Italy (the southern part), in the Anglo-American sphere. (Presumably, Toynbee would have added Spain and Portugal here if he had included them in his discussion.)

The realignment of Europe reflected the contemporary realities of military power, Toynbee suggested, since 'the agreed line of demarcation approximately coincided with the line along which the Russian power was in equilibrium with North American power transmitted to the Continent through a pumping station in the British Isles'. Moreover, at least some of the frontiers of Europe were now more rational. The new western frontier of Poland was 'the shortest line that could be drawn across the great North European plain anywhere to the east of the Ardennes', and the eastern frontier meant a neater distribution of the Slavonic peoples. But this rearrangement was not achieved without 'an appalling price in terms of human misery' for about 10 million Germans and numerous Slavs and others, constituting the largest displacement of eastern European population since the great migrations from the fourth to the seventh centuries AD. Consequently: 'The total effect of these sweeping and devastating transfers of population in Eastern Europe was to cancel the ethnic effects of a thousand years of German, Polish and Lithuanian conquest and colonisation, and to restore the ethnic map to something like the status quo ante AD 1200.' Here again there was an exception, in the shape of Austria.

There was ample precedent for the reduction of Germany in particular. The victory of Napoleon over the Prussians at Jena in 1806 and the Armistice of 1918 were 'two strident warnings to the victors of 1945 that the most apparently crushing victories over Germany were apt to be wasting assets'. Toynbee asked: 'Why was it that, after V-E Day 1945, a knowledge of historical facts that were known to every schoolboy did not hold the latest anti-German alliance together?' He quoted a British government paper of 1919 to the effect that the successor states set up at that time following the collapse of the Austro-Hungarian Empire between a mutilated Germany and a mutilated Russia were unable 'to stand by themselves under the strenuous conditions of the Modern World'. The collapse of Hitler's empire meant an even greater vacuum.

Now, unfortunately, 'the new dispensation, under which Europe found herself partitioned between two camps, each under the command of a non-European Super-Power, brought with it, for Europe, a further bout of political rivalry and tension that threatened to discharge itself in a third world war with Europe as its arena'.[14] Full of insight though Toynbee's remarks were, like everybody else who has written about history, the passage of time, he himself was time-bound. Considering the situation after the Second World War, he could hardly forget his observations on the First, concerning the impact of the German war on 'the lives and property of the civil population' in Belgium and the 'terrible outrages upon the civil population' in France. Equally, Toynbee's assumption of 'a knowledge of historical facts that were known to every schoolboy' after 1945 must have been based to some extent on his own recollections of what he had written about the world after the peace conference of 1919, 'that the task of holding down a country which had been the strongest member of their class had left the victors a slender margin of energy for other commitments'.[15] Undoubtedly, too, what every schoolboy allegedly knew after 1945 was very different to what every young person might have been aware of after a number of later dates: 1962, 1968, 1991, 2001.

For nearly 45 years, although it revived considerably from its nadir of 1945, Europe remained under this new dispensation, in the line of fire between two forces so unprecedented in their organisation and in their armaments that their arrival on the scene constituted a fresh departure in history. There was now something new under the sun, and a term describing it had to be minted. 'Superpower' succeeded in conveying at least some of the manner in which the USA and the USSR transcended frontiers more than the states and empires that had exerted power in the world before them, not only economically, but politically and culturally too, and most of all strategically. Einstein warned in 1945 that we must change our modes of thinking. The use of the term 'superpower'[16] is just one small way of continually reminding ourselves that what happened between 1945 and 1991 was categorically different from all preceding history.

For if the years leading up to and including the First World War constituted one of the more important changes in the history of Europe, what must be said about those including and following the Second World War? Looking back at 1945, do we not see in the A-bomb a device that appears almost primitive in comparison with the weapons of destruction at the command of the USA and the USSR in the 1980s? With concepts of strategy reaching out into space, the ideas of Mackinder and Mahan on land and sea, still appropriate up to 1945, lost much of their relevance. This did not mean, however, that the study of geopolitics was abandoned after the end of the Cold War; on the contrary, as we shall see below, it was to become more important.

While the totally unprecedented mortal threat of any third world war involving the superpowers remained the greatest reason for considering the history of Europe after 1945 categorically different from what had gone before, there were other supporting considerations which must be at least briefly noted. These included a third industrial revolution involving computers of more compact size but much greater intricacy than those developed during the Second World War, as well as biological engineering beyond the wildest dreams of 1939–45. In global terms, the first and second industrial revolutions were outstripped in quantity as well as in nature by the third such transformation accompanied by a steep rise in the world's population. The unprecedented demand for raw materials meant that some of the world's supplies no longer seemed inexhaustible, while intensive processing led to widespread pollution of the atmosphere. The extension of television and other electronic communications led to the creation of what came to be called the global village. This development also brought problems of heavy bias in the distribution of information and the spread of cultural patterns, with implications of brainwashing.

So many and complex have been the problems arising from the sweeping changes that have taken place since 1945 that at least one American historian suggested in 1978 that the citizens of the USA and the USSR 'may well find themselves looking back with a certain amount of nostalgia, some years hence, to the "good old days" of the Cold War, when all the world had to worry about was the prospect of mutual, instantaneous annihilation'.[17]

The manner in which the states of Europe had made their partial recovery since the low point of their fall in the immediate post-war years at the same time as attempting to make an accommodation with their Soviet and American patrons was also to be explained by an understanding of their past histories. Arnold Toynbee declared:

> A synoptic view of the diverse experiences of the realigned countries in the early post-war years made it evident that the character of a country's native cultural and political heritage counted for more, in the determination of its political fate, than the character of the foreign power within whose sphere it now happened to find itself included.[18]

Even after the harrowing experiences of the period 1945–89 in Europe, especially in the east of the continent, whose history had generally been more uncomfortable than that of the west, there remained an important element of truth in that observation, as the events of 1989–91 and their sequel were to reveal.

Both in its buildings and in other aspects of its culture, Europe remains a complex patchwork. The great French historian Fernand Braudel rightly spoke of a diverse France within a diverse Europe. For example, the Haute-Savoie where he wrote much of his work has been a thoroughfare and a crossroads for French, Italian and German cultures, with some enclaves such as Samoëns retaining a distinctive local language well into the twentieth century. However, along with other peasant ways of life from the Atlantic to the Urals, that of Alpine villages is on its way out.[19] There may well be a rapidly ongoing process of convergence that will erase regional and national variations to produce a continent replacing diversity with uniformity, or at least with a postmodern, post-statist network. Certainly, the division into sections, south-west, north-west, north, centre, south-east and east, becomes less useful at the end than it was at the beginning of this book.

Whatever future lies in store for all continents will have to be considered within the context of globalisation. And great configurations of power, wherever and however to be found, will always tend to dominate.

What such configurations will be in the 2090s, even in the 2010s, is impossible to predict. While the basic story of most of the twentieth century is now clear, the sequel of the twenty-first century is yet to emerge. In the early 2000s, there is considerable debate about the nature of the world situation now that the Cold War between the two superpowers appears to be over. On the one hand, many would say that the position is clear: while the collapse of the Soviet Union has reduced Russia to lower rank, the power of the USA has grown to such an extent that another new description could be applied – hyperpower. This means that the concepts of geopolitics need rethinking. For Zbigniew Brzezinski in 1997, 'with the Europe of Yalta gone, it is essential that there be no reversion to the Europe of Versailles'. There should be no return 'to a Europe of quarrelsome nation-states' but instead 'a larger and increasingly integrated Europe, reinforced by a widened NATO and rendered even more secure by a constructive security relationship with Russia'. The USA's 'central geostrategic goal' could be simply summarised: 'to consolidate through a more genuine transatlantic partnership the U.S. bridgehead on the Eurasian continent so that an enlarging Europe can become a more viable springboard for projecting into Eurasia the democratic and cooperative order'.[20]

On the other hand, at least a few analysts would want to argue that while the USSR collapsed because of relative backwardness, the USA has been confronting problems of considerable magnitude at a higher level of development. In other words: in society – how to reconcile the rights of the individual with the attempt to guarantee 'homeland security' from outside threats and to maintain stability in the face of internal pressures; in the economy – how to preserve the dynamic of the market in the context of the struggle of the previously almighty dollar to maintain international financial stability along with other currencies; in culture – how to make certain that electronic information and images do not numb the human brain at a time of great intellectual challenge.

11 September 2001 dealt a great blow to the 'new world order' equilibrium, which later events did little to restore. Moreover, concerns

for the elimination of terrorism have led to the comparative neglect of other pressing issues: for example, the reduction of starvation and disease and the supply of clean water. In a worst-case scenario for the future, the planet could go up in smoke, either of industrial pollution or nuclear war, or humankind perish from ineradicable plague. Trying to look on the brighter side, we may hope for a twenty-first century and even a third millennium of human improvement. Certainly, in the near future, Europe will remain a cultural tradition, an economic association and, at least for some, a political aspiration. There are those who would like to see Europe as a full federation, who would like to develop a European defence force. Others favour an association of independent nation states, and believe that NATO is sufficient for defence purposes, even if conceding that the inclusion of the Czech Republic, Hungary and Poland from 1999 was viewed with alarm in Russia.

However, in a harmonious future, Europe including Russia could spread to incorporate all the territory from the Atlantic to the Urals, even to the Pacific. But to stretch the boundaries so far is perhaps to destroy the idea, or to merge it with others, of an Atlantic and a Pacific community, even a truly global association. For the moment, combining an assertion with a question, let us agree with what Paul Kennedy wrote a decade ago: 'Even in the early 1990s, it is clear that Europe cannot stand apart from the rest of the world's problems. How much clearer will that be in 2010 or 2030?'[21] Meanwhile, many of us, like David Hume in the eighteenth century, will want to strive to be citizens of Europe with regard to Britain (or whichever state), but with regard to Europe, to become citizens of the world.

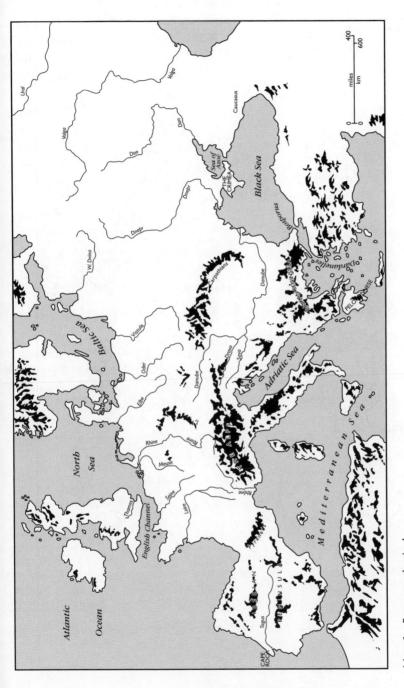

Map 1 Europe: physical

503

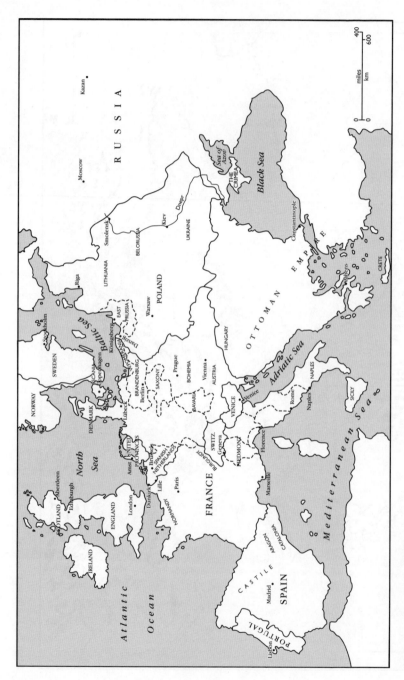

Map 2 Europe in 1648

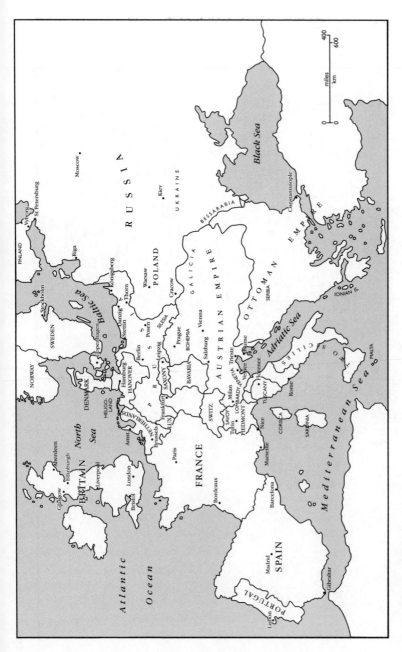

Map 3 Europe in 1815

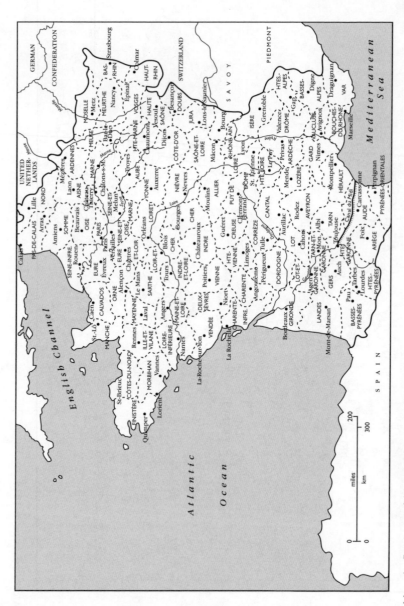

Map 4 France and its neighbours from 1815

Map 5 Europe and the Atlantic world by 1830

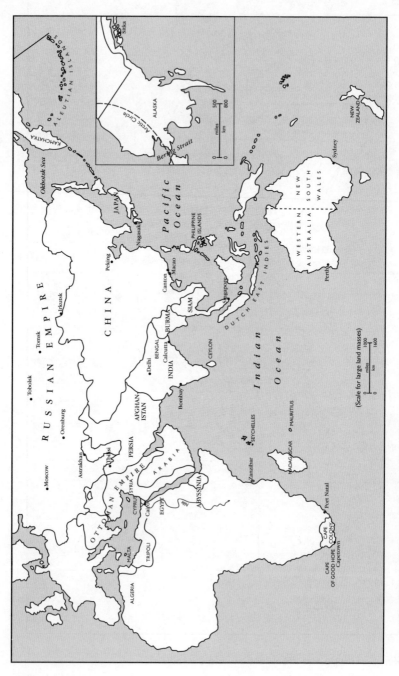

Map 6 Europe and the eastern world by 1830

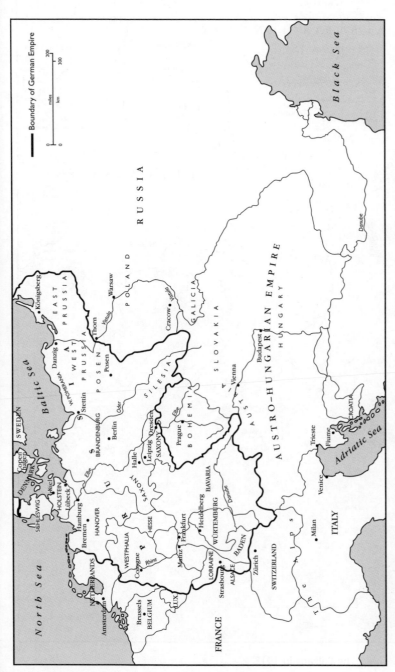

Map 7 The German Empire and its neighbours, 1871

Map 8 The Balkans in 1913

Map 9 Europe and the Atlantic world by 1914

512

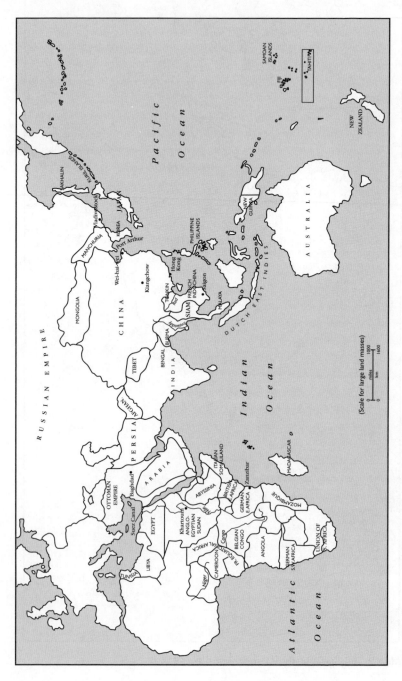

Map 10 Europe and the eastern world by 1914

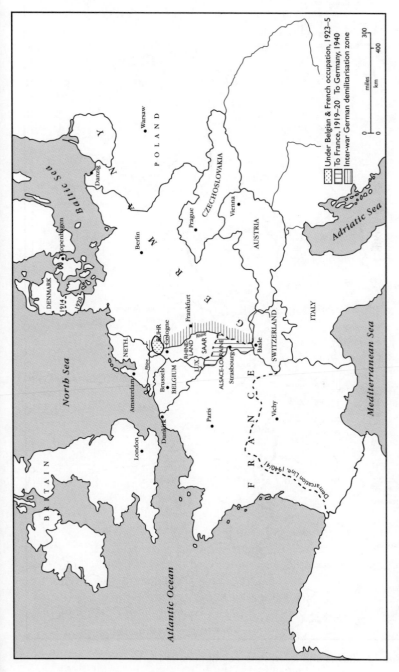

Map 11 France and Germany, 1914–40

Map 12   Russia and its western neighbours, 1914–40

Map 13   Europe and the Atlantic world after 1945

516

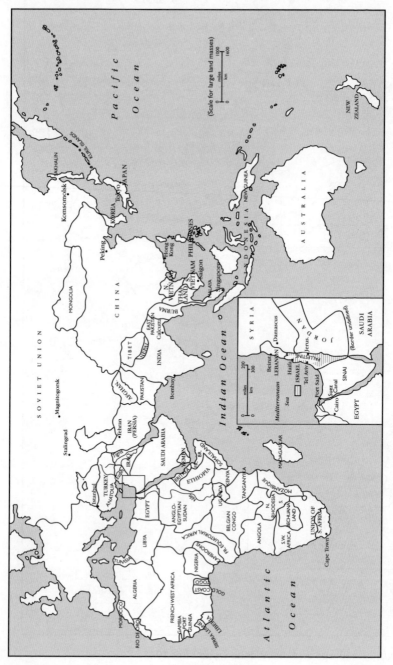

Map 14 Europe and the eastern world after 1945

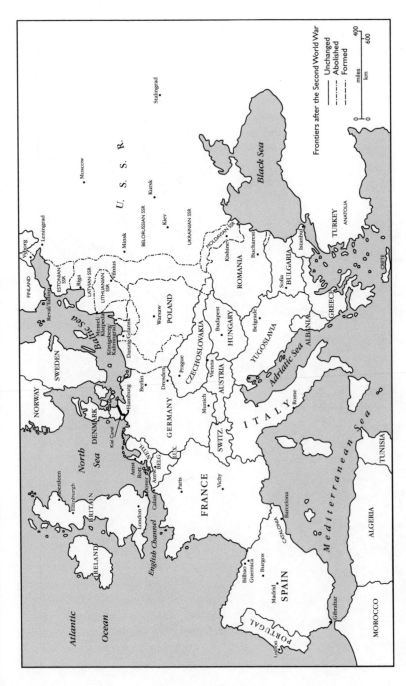

Map 15 Europe in 1945

518

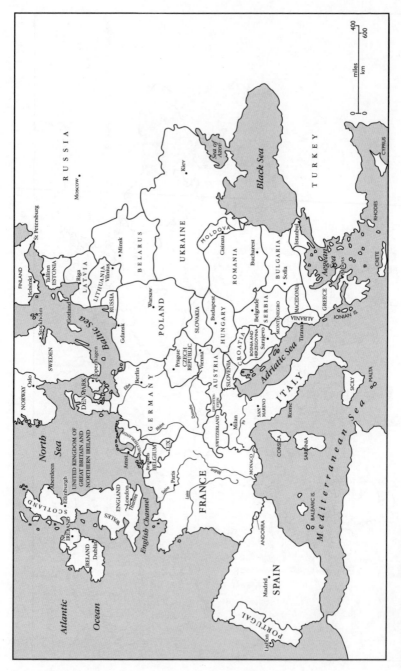

Map 16   Europe in 1995

NOTES

1 ORIGINS: EUROPE BEFORE 1648: MID-CENTURY CRISIS

1   Peter Rietbergen, *Europe: A Cultural History* (London, 1998) 246–7, 255–6.

2   B. F. Porshnev, *Tridtsatiletniaia voina i vstuplenie v nee Shvetsii i moskovskogo gosudarstva* (Moscow, 1976) 110. For a translation of pages 168–404 of this work see B. F. Porshnev, *The Thirty Years' War and the Entry of Sweden and Muscovy*, trans. Brian Pearce, ed. Paul Dukes (Cambridge, 1995).

3   Quoted by Geoffrey Parker, *Europe in Crisis, 1598–1648* (London, 1979) 219.

4   John Elliott, 'War and Peace in Europe, 1618–1648', in Klaus Bussmann and Heinz Schilling (eds.), *1648: War and Peace in Europe*, I, *Politics, Religion, Law and Society* (Münster-Osnabrück, 1999) 39. The preceding quotations from Heinhard Steiger, 'Concrete Peace and General Order: The legal meaning of the treaties of 24 October 1648', are to be found in ibid., 443. According to Margaret Aston, *The Fifteenth Century: The Prospect of Europe* (London, 1968) 87, Pope Pius II (1458–64) coined the adjective 'European'.

5   J. J. C. von Grimmelshausen, *Simplicius Simplicissimus* (Indianapolis, 1965) 41.

6   G. Perjes, 'Army Provisioning, Logistics and Strategy in the Second Half of the Seventeenth Century', *Acta Historica Academiae Scientarium Hungaricae*, 16 (Budapest, 1970) 1–14.

7   Pierre Chaunu, 'Réflexions sur le tournant des années 1630–1650', *Cahiers d'histoire moderne et contemporaine*, 12 (1967).

8   C. S. Terry, *The Life and Campaigns of Alexander Leslie, First Earl of Leven* (London, 1899) Chapters 3–8; John Morrill, 'Introduction', in John Kenyon and Jane Ohlmeyer (eds.), *The Civil Wars: A Military History of England, Scotland and Ireland, 1638–1660* (Oxford, 1998) xx. And see the database by Steve Murdoch and Alexia Grosjean, Scotland, Scandinavia and northern Europe, 1580–1707, http://www.abdn.ac.uk/ssne.

9   S. R. Gardiner (ed.), *Letters Relating to the Mission of Sir Thomas Roe to Gustavus Adolphus, 1629–1630* (London, 1875) 2.

10 P. Cluver, *Introductionis in universam geographiam* ... (Lugduni Batavorum, 1629) 47. Steven Gunn, 'War, Religion, and the State', in Euan Cameron (ed.), *Early Modern Europe: An Oxford History* (Oxford, 1999) 102–3, observes that 'The first map of Europe to attempt to show state borders was not printed until 1602'.
11 Rietbergen, *Europe*, 205.
12 Quoted by Moritz Brosch, 'Papal Policy, 1590–1648', in A. W. Ward and others (eds.), *The Cambridge Modern History*, 12 vols. (Cambridge, 1902–10) (hereafter *CMH*), vol. 4 (1907) 688.
13 Edward Hyde, Earl of Clarendon, *The History of the Rebellion and the Civil Wars in England*, ed. W. D. Macray (Oxford, 1888), vol. 6, 2–3.

2 THE FRENCH CHALLENGE: RESPONSES EAST AND WEST, 1648–1721

1 G. Zeller, 'French Diplomacy and Foreign Policy in their European Setting', *New Cambridge Modern History* (hereafter *NCMH*), 5 (1964) 214.
2 *NE*, 27.
3 John Stoye, *Europe Unfolding, 1648–1688* (London, 1969) 295.
4 Ibid.; 'Bossuet', *EB*, 4.288.
5 Giorgio Spini, 'Italy after the Thirty Years War', *NCMH*, 5 (1964) 461.
6 *NE*, 31–2.
7 Charles Wilson, quoted by E. N. Williams, *The Ancien Regime in Europe* (London, 1973) 53.
8 A. N. Kurat, 'The Ottoman Empire under Mehmed IV', *NCMH*, 5 (1964) 513–14.
9 R. R. Betts, 'The Habsburg Lands', *NCMH*, 5 (1964) 497–8.
10 John Carswell, *The Descent on England: A Study of the English Revolution of 1688 and Its European Background* (London, 1969) 100. See also Paul Dukes, 'How the Eighteenth Century began for Russia and the West', in A. G. Cross (ed.), *Russia and the West* (Newtonville, MA, 1983); Andrew Lossky, 'The General European Crisis of the 1680s', *European Studies Review*, 10 (1980).
11 Quoted by Carswell, *The Descent*, 81.
12 *NE*, 21–4.
13 Lindsey Hughes, *Russia in the Age of Peter the Great* (London, 1998) 248. There are excellent biographies with the title *Peter the Great* by Lindsey Hughes (London, 2002) and Paul Bushkovitch (New York, 2003).
14 Gilbert Burnet to Revd Dr Fall, Bodleian Library, Oxford MSS, Eng. th. c. 23.
15 *NE*, 32–3.
16 Antony Lentin, *Peter the Great: The Law on the Imperial Succession in Russia, 1722* (Oxford, 1996) 33.
17 Perry Anderson, *Lineages of the Absolutist State* (London, 1974) 226–7; Hajo Holborn, *A History of Modern Germany, 1648–1840* (London, 1965) 196–7; E. J. Feuchtwanger, *Prussia: Myth and Reality* (London, 1970) 49.

18 Jonathan J. Israel, 'The Emerging Empire: The Continental Perspective, 1650–1713', in Nicholas Canny (ed.), *The Origins of Empire: British Overseas Enterprise to the Close of the Seventeenth Century*, vol. 1 of *The Oxford History of the British Empire* (Oxford, 1998) 444.

3 THE GROWTH OF EMPIRE, 1721–1763

1 Bruce Lenman, *An Economic History of Modern Scotland* (London, 1977) 51.
2 On this point and much else, see Linda Colley, *Britons: Forging the Nation, 1707–1837* (London, 1992) 130 and throughout.
3 E. N. Williams, *The Eighteenth Century Constitution* (Cambridge, 1960) 189.
4 E. P. Thompson, *Whigs and Hunters: The Origin of the Black Act* (London, 1975) 260.
5 *NE*, 101–2.
6 F. L. Carsten, *Princes and Parliaments in Germany*, quoted in Anderson, *Lineages of the Absolutist State*, 255. This section draws generally on Anderson's work.
7 H. M. Scott, 'Europe Turns East: Political Developments', in Cameron (ed.), *Early Modern Europe*, 342.
8 Colley, *Britons*, 101.
9 W. L. Dorn, *Competition for Empire, 1740–1763* (New York, 1940) 2–3.
10 Michael Sheehan, *The Balance of Power: History and Theory* (London, 1996) 16.

4 ENLIGHTENED GOVERNMENTS, THEIR CONFLICTS AND THEIR CRITICS, 1763–1789

1 Alexander Gieysztor and others, *History of Poland* (Warsaw, 1979) 267.
2 O. A. Omelchenko, 'The System of State and Law in Eighteenth-Century Russia and the Political Culture of Europe: Some Historical Interactions', *Slavonic and East European Review*, 80/2 (2002) 222. See also O. A. Omelchenko, 'Enlightened Absolutism in Russia', in Paul Dukes (ed.), 'Eastern Approaches to European Culture', *Coexistence*, 30/1 (1995) 35–6 for a summary of the reforms of enlightened absolutism in policies social or estate, legal and state-administrative, and the assertion that its ideology 'had little in common with the ideology of the Enlightenment'.
3 Quotations in the preceding three paragraphs from T. C. W. Blanning, 'Frederick the Great and Enlightened Absolutism', in H. M. Scott (ed.), *Enlightened Absolutism: Reform and Reformers in Later Eighteenth Century Europe* (London, 1990) 268, 271, 277–8.
4 Holborn, *A History of Modern Germany*, 273.
5 Edmund S. Morgan, in John Blum and others, *The National Experience: A History of the United States* (New York, 1973) 83.
6 J. P. Kenyon, in a talk to the Aberdeen University History Society, 1983.

7   G. D. H. Cole and Raymond Postgate, *The Common People, 1746–1946* (London, 1949) 98–108; Williams, *The Ancien Regime in Europe*, 497.

8   Edmund Burke, 'Thoughts on French Affairs, 1791', *Works*, 4 (London, 1907) 346–7.

9   *NE*, 52–4.

10 Alexis de Tocqueville, *The Ancien Regime and the French Revolution* (Glasgow, 1966) 194.

11 William Doyle, *The Old European Order, 1660–1800* (Oxford, 1992) 322.

12 Edmund Burke, 'Letters on the Proposals for Peace with the Regicide Directory of France', *Works*, 6 (London, 1907) 156–7.

13 T. C. W. Blanning, *The Culture of Power and the Power of Culture: Old Regime Europe, 1660–1789* (Oxford, 2002) 52.

14 Quoted in Benjamin F. Wright (intro. and ed.), *The Federalist* (Cambridge, MA, 1966) 141–2.

15 Paul Dukes, *World Order in History: Russia and the West* (London, 1996) 32.

5   EUROPE BEFORE 1789, AND THE ORIGINS OF THE FRENCH REVOLUTION

1   W. E. Mead, *The Grand Tour in the Eighteenth Century* (Boston, MA, 1914) 398–9.

2   Jeremy Black, *The British and the Grand Tour* (London, 1985) 22–3 points out that the number of British tourists going to Spain, Portugal, Italy south of Naples, eastern Europe, the Balkans and the Baltic increased during the century but remained small, nevertheless.

3   R. S. Lambert (ed.), *Grand Tour: A Journey in the Tracks of the Age of Aristocracy* (London, 1935) 60.

4   Quotations in the two previous paragraphs are from Mead, *The Grand Tour*, 252, 271, 345, 356–7.

5   Lambert, *Grand Tour*, 143.

6   N. M. Karamzin, *Letters of a Russian Traveler, 1789–1790*, ed. and trans. Florence Jonas (London, 1957) 218–21.

7   Lord Macartney, *An Account of Russia, 1767* (London, 1768) 49–51.

8   Bernard Lewis, *The Muslim Discovery of Europe* (London, 1982) 168. Daniel Goffman, *The Ottoman Empire and Early Modern Europe* (Cambridge, 2002) 224, writes that nearly all eighteenth-century European travellers in the Ottoman Empire 'shared with many of today's tourists an absolute disinterest in contemporary indigenous peoples and societies'. He adds: 'By the end of the seventeenth century, the Ottoman Empire was as integrated into Europe as it would ever be.'

9   M. Betham-Edwards (ed.), *Travels in France by Arthur Young during the Years 1787, 1788, 1789* (London, 1890) xxv–xxvii, lv–lvi, 18, 22, 27, 28, 33, 41–2, 45–7, 55, 56, 57–8, 60, 66, 67, 69, 71, 77, 82–5, 90, 92, 97–8, 103–5, 107–8, 112, 113, 123, 125, 129, 131–2, 134, 137, 139–40, 142–3, 146.

10 René Descartes, *Discourse on Method and the Meditations*, ed. and trans. F. E. Sutcliffe (Harmondsworth, 1985) 30–1. I owe this reference to the late George Molland.

11 Thomas Hobbes, *Leviathan*, ed. Richard Tuck (Cambridge, 2002) 51, 67–8, 89, 90, 91–2, 120–1, 129, 145, 159, 175–6, 414, 459, 482.

12 John Locke, *Two Treatises of Government*, ed. Peter Laslett (Cambridge, 1970) 261.

13 Norman Hampson, *The Enlightenment* (Harmondsworth, 1968) 109.

14 Prospectus, *NE*, 48–52; other material on encyclopaedias, *EB*, 9.377.

15 Dorinda Outram, *The Enlightenment* (Cambridge, 1995) 85–6, 95.

16 Williams, *The Ancien Regime in Europe*, 204–5.

17 *Travels in France by Arthur Young*, 153.

18 Ibid., 113.

19 *NE*, 56–64.

20 *Travels in France by Arthur Young*, 193, 201, 214–15, 229, 234, 241–3. Quotation from 201.

21 The preceding summary closely follows the first part of Michel Vovelle, *The Fall of the French Monarchy, 1787–1792* (Cambridge, 1984).

6 THE FRENCH REVOLUTION AND NAPOLEON, 1789–1815

1 *NE*, 65–7.

2 *NE*, 67–77.

3 *NE*, 78–9.

4 *NE*, 80.

5 John D. Hargreaves, 'Assimilation in Eighteenth-Century Senegal', *Journal of African History*, 6 (1965) 183.

6 *Annual Register*, 33 (1791) 102.

7 *NE*, 105.

8 F. M. H. Markham, *Napoleon and the Awakening of Europe* (London, 1954) 92. Harold T. Parker identifies six elements mixing in Napoleon's consciousness: 'his desire to be first and master of all situations; the noble officer ethic of glory ("a dazzling fame") and honour; his youthful enthusiasm for historical characters who (for him) personified masterly qualities; his own brilliant victories and civil achievements which could be related to such characters; the opportunity to match such examples of past renown in the eyes of his own and of future audiences; and his inner, compelling feeling of being a man of destiny and of good fortune'. Parker's assessment as summarised by Geoffrey Ellis, *The Napoleonic Empire* (London, 1991) 112.

9 Markham, *Napoleon*, 171.

10 Ibid., 77.

11 *NE*, 88.

12 C. von Clausewitz, *The Campaign of 1812 in Russia* (London, 1843) 142.

13 *Annual Register*, 53 (1811) vii.

14 H. W. Wilson, 'The War of 1812–1815', *CMH*, 7 (1905) 336.

15 Michael Broers, *Europe under Napoleon, 1799–1815* (London, 1996) 5–6, 273.

16 Markham, *Napoleon*, 60.

17 Ibid., 114.

18 These figures from Ellis, *The Napoleonic Empire*, 22. Ellis observes that these huge majorities 'disguised a widespread apathy among the 5 million eligible electors'.

19 Frédéric Bluche, *Le Bonapartisme* (Paris, 1981) 29.

20 Stuart Woolf, 'The Construction of a European World-View in the Revolutionary–Napoleonic Years', *Past & Present*, 137 (1992) 100–1.

7 FROM REACTION TOWARDS LIBERALISM, 1815–1848

1 W. Alison Phillips, 'The Congresses, 1815–22', *CMH*, 10 (1907) 1.

2 Ibid., 2.

3 *NE*, 122–6.

4 Alan Palmer, *The Penguin Dictionary of Modern History, 1789–1945* (Harmondsworth, 1964) 155.

5 Phillips, 'The Congresses', 37.

6 *Hansard*, 3rd series, vol. 31, 615–16.

7 The slogan was coined by Count S. S. Uvarov, minister of education from 1833 to 1849.

8 Alan Sked, 'The Metternich System, 1815–48', in Alan Sked (ed.), *Europe's Balance of Power, 1815–1848* (London, 1979) 112.

9 Ian R. Mitchell, *Bismarck and the Development of Germany* (Edinburgh, 1980) 7.

10 Christopher Bartlett, 'Britain and the European Balance, 1815–48', in Sked (ed.), *Europe's Balance*, 150.

11 Ibid., 152.

12 Alfred Cobban, *A History of Modern France*, vol. 2 (Harmondsworth, 1961) 141.

13 Ibid., 145–6.

14 Ibid., 149.

15 Denis Mack Smith, 'The Revolutions of 1848–1849 in Italy', in R. J. W. Evans and Hartmut Pogge von Strandmann (eds.), *The Revolutions in Europe, 1848–1849: From Reform to Reaction* (Oxford, 2000) 56.

16 Ian R. Mitchell, *On the Trail of Queen Victoria in the Highlands* (Edinburgh, 2000) 25–6.

17 F. Meinecke, 'Liberalism and Nationality in Germany and Austria', *CMH*, 11 (1909) 57.

18 *NE*, 136–40.

19 W. Bruce Lincoln, *Nicholas I: Emperor and Autocrat of All the Russias* (London, 1978) 287.
20 David Saunders, 'A Pyrrhic Victory: The Russian Empire in 1848', in Evans and Strandmann (eds.), *The Revolutions*, 141, 153.
21 Quoted in Jacques Droz, *Europe between Revolutions, 1815–1848* (Glasgow, 1967) 55.
22 Ibid., 48–53.
23 *EB*, vol. 18, 453–9.

8 NATIONALISM, SOCIALISM, IMPERIALISM, 1848–1878

1 Karl Marx, *The Eighteenth Brumaire of Louis Bonaparte* (London, 1926) 132–3.
2 Basil Dmytryshyn, *Imperial Russia: A Source Book* (New York, 1967) 225.
3 David Saunders, *Russia in the Age of Reaction and Reform, 1801–1881* (London, 1992) 263–9.
4 Mitchell, *Bismarck*, 52.
5 Stephen J. Lee, *Aspects of European History, 1789–1980* (London, 1982) 89.
6 Mitchell, *Bismarck*, 16.
7 Ibid., 29.
8 Helmut Böhme, *The Foundation of the German Empire: Select Documents* (Oxford, 1971) 198–9.
9 Mitchell, *Bismarck*, 39.
10 J. A. S. Grenville, *Europe Reshaped, 1848–1878* (London, 1976) 229, 243–5.
11 H. Lefebvre, quoted by Roger Magraw, *France 1815–1914: The Bourgeois Century* (London, 1983) 202.
12 *NE*, 142.
13 Sir John Sinclair, *An Account of the Highland Society of London* (1813), quoted by Colley, *Britons*, 374.
14 *NE*, 128–9.
15 Bolton King, *The Life of Mazzini* (London, 1929) 306, 310.
16 Karl Marx and Friedrich Engels, *Manifesto of the Communist Party* (Moscow, 1969) 39–40, 45, 47–8, 49–50, 56, 71, 72, 75, 89–96.
17 Norman Stone, *Europe Transformed, 1878–1919* (London, 1999) 25.

9 THE CLASH OF EMPIRES AND CLASSES, 1878–1914

1 *EB*, vol. 1, 336.
2 See, for example, Paul Kennedy, *The Realities behind Diplomacy: Background Influences on British External Policy, 1865–1980* (London, 1981) 82–101.
3 Michael T. Florinsky, *Russia: A History and An Interpretation*, vol. 2 (New York, 1955) 985–6.
4 Chamberlain and Hyndman quoted in Cole and Postgate, *The Common People*, 411, 416.

5   Ibid., 430.
6   Ibid., 506–7.
7   *NE*, 174–9.
8   Hugo and Gambetta, quoted by Magraw, *France*, 234–45.
9   *NE*, 149.
10 Magraw, *France*, 351.
11 Mitchell, *Bismarck*, 111–12, and in a lecture to the Aberdeen University History Department, 1983.
12 *NE*, 171–4.
13 John D. Hargreaves, *The Partition of West Africa*, vol. 1, *The Loaded Pause* (London, 1974) 44.
14 Mitchell, *Bismarck*, 111.
15 Mitchell, in his lecture of 1983.
16 Bruce Waller, 'Hans-Ulrich Wehler on Imperial Germany', *British Journal of International Studies*, 1 (1975) 65. More generally, see David Blackbourn and Geoff Eley, *The Peculiarities of German History* (Oxford, 1984).
17 Jonathan Steinberg, *Yesterday's Deterrent: Tirpitz and the Birth of the German Battle Fleet* (London, 1965) 209.
18 Hans Rogger, *Russia in the Age of Modernisation and Revolution, 1881–1917* (London, 1990) 72.
19 T. H. Von Laue, 'A Secret Memorandum of Sergei Witte on the Industrialization of Imperial Russia', *Journal of Modern History*, 26 (1954).
20 Robin Okey, *Eastern Europe, 1740–1980: Feudalism to Communism* (London, 1982) 142.
21 Ibid., 147.
22 Alfred Stead, *Great Japan: A Study of National Efficiency* (London, 1906) 469.
23 See, for example, Paul Kennedy, 'Mahan versus Mackinder: Two Interpretations of British Sea Power', in *idem, Strategy and Diplomacy, 1870–1945* (London, 1983). On the spread of geopolitical ideas, see Holger H. Herwig, *'Geopolitik:* Haushofer, Hitler and Lebensraum', in Colin S. Gray and Geoffrey Sloan (eds.), *Geopolitics, Geography and Strategy* (London, 1999).
24 O. H. Palmer, *Statement of the Origin, Organization and Progress of the Russian–American Telegraph Western Union Extension* ... (Rochester, NY, 1866) 33, 165.
25 Edwin A. Pratt, *The Rise of Rail-Power in War and Conquest* (London, 1915) 356.
26 General F. von Berhardi, *Germany and the Next War* (London, 1914) Chapter V.

10   EUROPE BEFORE 1914: ORIGINS OF WORLD WAR AND THE RUSSIAN REVOLUTION

1   Arnold J. Toynbee, *The World after the Peace Conference* (London, 1926) 12.
2   *Spain and Portugal* (Leipzig, 1898) xxi, xxiv–xv, 502, 508.
3   *Italy: From the Alps to Naples* (Leipzig, 1909) xii, xxii.

4 *Northern France* (Leipzig, 1899) xx.
5 *Norway, Sweden and Denmark* (Leipzig, 1912) xxiv–xxvi.
6 *The Rhine: From Rotterdam to Constance* (Leipzig, 1906) xiv, xviii–xix.
7 *Austria, including Hungary, Transylvania, Dalmatia and Bosnia* (Leipzig, 1900) xiii.
8 *Russia, with Teheran, Port Arthur and Peking* (Leipzig, 1914) xvii–xix, xxi, xxiv, xxviii.
9 *The United States* (Leipzig, 1904) xx–xxi, xxx–xxxiii.
10 Sir Donald Mackenzie Wallace, *Russia*, vol. 1 (London, 1905) vii–viii, 1–4, 17, 26, 35, 73–5, 80, 102, 109, 115, 118–19, 121, 125, 135, 137, 144–5, 148, 160–1, 169, 178–9, 185, 226–8, 243, 368, 451–6.
11 Ibid., vol. 2, 26–7, 197–201, 235–6, 289–90, 353–4, 374–6, 391–6, 420, 439, 473–4.
12 Sir Donald Mackenzie Wallace, *Russia* (London, 1912) vii.
13 Sir Donald Mackenzie Wallace, *Our Russian Ally* (London, 1914) 2, 11, 17–18, 22–3.
14 T. C. W. Blanning, 'Epilogue: The Old Order Transformed, 1789–1815', in Euan Cameron (ed.), *Early Modern Europe: An Oxford History* (Oxford, 1999) 372.
15 Roy Porter and Mikuláš Teich (eds.) in their Introduction, *Romanticism in National Context* (Cambridge, 1988) 1–7.
16 Asa Briggs and Patricia Clavin, *Modern Europe, 1789–1989* (London, 1997) 186.
17 Jerzy Lukowski and Hubert Zawadski, *A Concise History of Poland* (Cambridge, 2002) 137.
18 Eber Jeffery, ' "Nothing Left to Invent" ', *Journal of the Patent Office Society*, vol. 22, no. 7 (July 1940) 479–81, quotation from 480.
19 *NE*, 146.
20 Prince Albert, speech given at a dinner given by the Lord Mayor of London for all the mayors of the United Kingdom, Mansion House, 21 March 1850, quoted in 'Introduction', *Official Descriptive and Illustrated Catalogue of the Great Exhibition of the Works of Industry of All Nations*, vol. 1 (London, 1851) 3. I owe this reference and much else in this chapter to Nicholas Fisher, cultural historian at the University of Aberdeen.
21 Gina Pischel, *A World History of Art* (Oxford, 1976) 600.
22 Lawrence Badash 'The Completeness of Nineteenth-Century Science', *Isis*, 63 (1972) 50. Badash asks: 'can we establish any connections between completeness and influences beyond science, such as cultural, intellectual, philosophical, literary, historical, or artistic trends?'(58).
23 *CMH*, vol. 1, v–viii; vol. 5, 517; vol. 7, v–vii; vol. 12, 1.
24 This paragraph from Patrick Brantlinger, 'Mass Media in *fin-de-siècle* Europe', in Mikuláš Teich and Roy Porter (eds.), *Fin de siècle and its Legacy* (Cambridge,1990) 105.
25 Information in this section from *EB*. See also Geoffrey Barraclough, *An Introduction to Contemporary History* (Harmondsworth, 1967), esp. Chapter 2,

'The Impact of Technical and Scientific Advance'. On oral history, see Paul Thompson (ed.), *Our Common History: The Transformation of Europe* (London, 1982).

26 For a more complete exposition, see for example Richard Langhorne, *The Collapse of the Concert of Europe: International Politics, 1890–1914* (London, 1981).

27 *NE*, 202–8.

28 *NE*, 200–1.

29 Gordon A. Craig, *Germany, 1860–1945* (Oxford, 1978) 334. See also Fritz Fischer, *World Power or Decline: The Controversy over Germany's Aims in the First World War* (London, 1974).

30 C. R. M. F. Cruttwell, *A History of the Great War, 1914–1918* (Oxford, 1934) 66n. For the wider Russian context, see D. C. B. Lieven, *Russia and the Origins of the First World War* (London, 1983).

31 Hans Rogger, 'Russia in 1914', *Journal of Contemporary History*, 1/4 (1966) 95–6.

32 Dick Geary, *European Labour Protest, 1848–1939* (London, 1981) 125–6.

11   THE FIRST WORLD WAR AND THE RUSSIAN REVOLUTION, 1914–1921

1 Hew Strachan, *The First World War*, vol. 1, *To Arms* (Oxford, 2001) 164, 180.

2 C. E. Montague, *Disenchantment* (London, 1922), as in *NE*, 212. On the Western Front, see more generally Paul Fussell, *The Great War and Modern Memory* (Oxford, 1975). Fussell makes little or no reference to the Eastern Front or to the Russian Revolution.

3 Balfour Declaration as in *NE*, 298.

4 Cruttwell, *A History*, 73n.

5 Ibid., 200–3; John M. Blum and others, *The National Experience: A History of the United States* (New York, 1973) 549–54.

6 Cruttwell, *A History*, 336.

7 Ibid., 376, 382.

8 A. J. P. Taylor, *The First World War: An Illustrated History* (Harmondsworth, 1966) 171.

9 Cruttwell, *A History*, 415–16.

10 Marx, *The Eighteenth Brumaire of Louis Bonaparte*, 23.

11 P. N. Miliukov, *Istoriia vtoroi russkoi revoliutsii*, quoted by Arthur E. Adams, *The Russian Revolution and Bolshevik Victory: Why and How?* (Boston, 1960) 1.

12 M. T. Florinsky, *Russia: A History and an Interpretation*, vol. 2 (New York, 1953) 1362.

13 Ibid., 1365, 1373.

14 Stephen Graham, *Russia in 1916* (London, 1917) 35, 37, 73–4, 90–1, 146–7.

15 Michael T. Florinsky, *The End of the Russian Empire* (New York, 1961) 133–5.
16 *NE*, 224–5; Tsuyoshi Hasegawa, *The February Revolution: 1917* (Seattle, 1981) 554–67.
17 Ibid., 425.
18 Cruttwell, *A History*, 337.
19 Commodore G. von Schoultz, *With the British Fleet: War Recollections of a Russian Naval Officer* (London, 1925) 274.
20 Hasegawa, *The February Revolution*, 402; L. D. Trotsky, *The History of the Russian Revolution* (London, 1934) 291.
21 The preceding account from Hasegawa, Trotsky and Arthur Ransome in *EB 13*, vol. 3, 412–15.
22 Crutwell, *A History*, 433.
23 Schoultz, *With the British Fleet*, 306–7.
24 Ransome, *EB 13*, vol. 3, 412–15; A. Rabinowich, *The Bolsheviks come to Power* (London, 1976).
25 Ronald G. Suny, 'Towards a Social History of the October Revolution', *American Historical Review*, 88 (1983) 58. Suny goes on to suggest that the fury of the civil war led to authoritarianism.
26 Halford J. Mackinder, *Democratic Ideals and Reality: A Study in the Politics of Reconstruction* (Harmondsworth, 1944) 112–13.
27 Brian W. Blouet, *Sir Halford Mackinder* (Oxford, 1975) 38–40.
28 *NE*, 216–19.
29 *NE*, 239.
30 G. H. N. Seton-Watson, *The Russian Empire, 1801–1917* (Oxford, 1967) x; Richard Pipes in *Times Literary Supplement*, 20 July 1984.
31 Arno J. Mayer, *Political Origins of the New Diplomacy, 1917–1918* (New York, 1970) 393.
32 'Paris, Conference of' by Colonel Edward M. House, *EB 13*, vol. 3, 55–6.
33 'Covenant', *EB 13*, vol. 1, 754; *NE*, 257.
34 'Paris', *EB 13*, vol. 3, 61.
35 'Versailles, Treaty of' by H. W. V. Temperley, *EB 13*, vol. 3, 948.
36 John Maynard Keynes, *The Economic Consequences of the Peace* (London, 1920) argued for reduction of reparations. Etienne Mantoux, *The Carthaginian Peace, or, The Economic Consequences of Mr. Keynes* (London, 1946; repr. North Stratford, NH, 2000) argued 25 years later, towards the end of the Second World War, that the terms of Versailles had been too lenient.
37 *NE*, 221–3.

12 THROUGH DEPRESSION AND ISOLATION TOWARDS ANOTHER WORLD WAR, 1921–1939

1 *NE*, 261–4.
2 Jerzy Lukowski and Hubert Zawadski, *A Concise History of Poland* (Cambridge, 2002) 216.

3 S. Pollard and C. Holmes (eds.), *Documents of European Economic History*, vol. 3 (London, 1973) 482.

4 J. V. Stalin, 'The Tasks of Business Executives', *Works*, vol. 13 (Moscow, 1955) 33–44.

5 R. W. Davies, *The Industrialization of Soviet Russia*, vol. 1 (London, 1980) 107, 360.

6 Ross Terrill, *R. H. Tawney and His Times*, quoted by Anthony P. Adamthwaite, *The Making of the Second World War* (London, 1977) 23; Pertinax quoted by Raymond Aron, *Le spectateur engagé* (Paris, 1981) 39–40.

7 Quoted by George F. Kennan, *Soviet Foreign Policy, 1917–1941* (New York, 1960) 80.

8 John Richman, *The United States and the Soviet Union: The Decision to Recognize* (Raleigh, NC, 1980) 246; John M. Blum and others, *The National Experience: A History of the United States* (New York, 1973) 659.

9 Blum, *The National Experience*, 655.

10 Ibid., 664.

11 Martin McCauley, *Stalin and Stalinism* (London, 1983) 97.

12 M. Fainsod, *Smolensk under Soviet Rule* (Cambridge, MA, 1958) 92.

13 A. Nove, *An Economic History of the USSR* (Harmondsworth, 1972) 227–8.

14 John P. Mackintosh, *The Paths that Led to War: Europe, 1919–1939* (London, 1940) 204.

15 Adolf Hitler, *Mein Kampf*, intro. D. C. Watt (London, 1974) xxxiv.

16 K. D. Bracher, *The German Dictatorship: The Origins, Structure and Consequences of National Socialism* (Harmondsworth, 1973) 297.

17 Roberts, *The House*, 101.

18 T. W. Mason, 'The Legacy of 1918 for National Socialism', in A. J. Nicholls and E. Matthias (eds.), *German Democracy and the Triumph of Hitler* (London, 1971) 225, 231; R. J. Overy, *The Nazi Economic Recovery, 1932–1938* (London, 1982) 50.

19 Mackintosh, *The Paths*, 206.

20 Ibid., 277; Denis Mack Smith, *Mussolini's Roman Empire* (London, 1976) 47.

21 Both quotations from Mackintosh, *The Paths*, 307–8.

22 Adamthwaite, *The Making*, 72.

23 Ibid., 183.

24 Ibid., 65.

25 K. G. Robbins, *Munich, 1938* (London, 1968) 336.

13 THE SECOND WORLD WAR AND THE DIVISION OF EUROPE, 1939–1945

1 *Encyclopaedia Britannica Book of the Year, 1939: Being a Survey of the Principal Persons, Events, and Developments in Various Spheres of Knowledge and Affairs during the Year 1938* (London, 1939) 437.

2 *Baedekers Autoführer, Deutsches Reich (Grossdeutschland)* (Leipzig, 1939) iv, xxi.

3   L. B. Namier, *Conflicts: Studies in Contemporary History* (London, 1942) 54, 56–8.

4   *NE*, 279.

5   Quoted by Donald Cameron Watt, *How War Came: The Immediate Origins of the Second World War, 1938–1939* (London, 1989) 457.

6   Jonathan Haslam, *The Soviet Union and the Struggle for Collective Security, 1933–39* (London, 1984) 226.

7   Kennan, *Soviet Foreign Policy*, 176.

8   Howard K. Smith, *Last Train from Berlin* (London, 1942) 66.

9   John Mackintosh, *The Paths that Led to War: Europe, 1919–1939* (London, 1940) vi.

10   Smith, *Last Train*, 67–9.

11   Gerhard Hirschfeld, in a lecture to Aberdeen University History Department, 1983.

12   Quoted by John Terraine, 'The Spectre of the Bomber', *History Today* (April 1982) 5, 8.

13   Gabriel Gorodetsky, *Grand Delusion: Stalin and the German Invasion of Russia* (London, 1999) 299.

14   *National Observer* and Hitler quoted in Smith, *Last Train*, 85, 133, 196.

15   Chihiro Hosoya, 'Japan's Decision for War in 1941', *Hitosubashi Journal of Law and Politics*, 5 (1967) 15.

16   A. J. P. Taylor, *The Second World War: An Illustrated History* (London, 1975) 125.

17   John Barber and Mark Harrison, *The Soviet Home Front, 1941–1945: A Social and Economic History of the USSR in World War II* (London, 1991) 40.

18   John Erickson, *The Road to Stalingrad* (London, 1985) 537; *The Road to Berlin* (London, 1985) 57.

19   Christian Streit, *Keine Kameraden: Die Wehrmacht und die sowjetischen Kriegsgefangen, 1941–1945*, as reviewed by Hans Mommsen, *Bulletin of the German Historical Institute, London*, 1 (1979) 18–19.

20   *NE*, 285. And see the discussion of works by Jörg Friedrich, Klaus Rainer Röhl and W. G. Sebald in the *Times Literary Supplement*, 25 April 2003.

21   Gerhard L. Weinberg, *A World at Arms: A Global History of World War II* (Cambridge, 1994) 852.

22   John Lukacs, *1945: The Year Zero* (New York, 1978) 36.

23   *Foreign Relations of the United States: Diplomatic Papers: The Conferences at Malta and Yalta, 1945* (Washington, 1955) 665–6. Other information from 571, 612–13, 614, 617, 620–1, 622, 664–5, 667, 668, 669, 712, 766, 788, 844, 846, 849, 896, 901–2, 903–4, 905, 921–3.

24   Ibid., 975–84.

25   Daniel Yergin, *The Shattered Peace: The Origins of the Cold War and the National Security State* (Boston, 1978) 119.

26   Taylor, *The Second World War*, 229–30. John Erickson, 'Soviet War Losses', in John Erickson and David Dilks (eds.), *Barbarossa: The Axis and the Allies* (Edinburgh, 1994) 256–8 notes that 'direct loss' estimates have reached

26–27 million, while 'global loss' including 'birth deficit' has been accepted at about 48 million. Figures on the Holocaust from Lucy S. Dawidowicz, *The War against the Jews, 1933–1945* (New York, 1976) 544. See also Michael R. Marrus, *The Holocaust in History* (London, 1987).

14 THE COLD WAR AND DECOLONISATION, 1945–1968

1 Anthony Adamthwaite, 'Britain and the World, 1945–1949: The View from the Foreign Office', in Josef Becker and Franz Knipping (eds.), *Power in Europe? Great Britain, France, Italy and Germany in a Postwar World, 1945–1950* (Berlin, 1986) 12–13.

2 René Girault, 'The French Decision-Makers and their Perception of French Power in 1948', in ibid., 47–51. A British–French treaty of 1947 led nowhere.

3 Brunello Vigezzi, 'Italy: The End of a "Great Power" and the Birth of a "Democratic Power"', in ibid., 67–8.

4 Manfred Overesch, 'Senior West German Politicians and their Perception of the German Situation in Europe, 1945–1949', in ibid., 118–21.

5 R. A. C. Parker, 'British Perceptions of Power: Europe between the Superpowers', in ibid., 449.

6 Fred Halliday, *The Making of the Second Cold War* (London, 1983) 5. After the Second World War, the first uses of the term were in 1947, by the American financier Bernard Baruch and journalist Walter Lippmann.

7 Thomas G. Paterson, *Soviet–American Confrontation: Postwar Reconstruction and the Origins of the Cold War* (London, 1973) 8–9.

8 Ibid., 153.

9 Howard K. Smith, *The State of Europe* (London, 1950) 86. For a historian's corroboration, see Daniel Yergin, *Shattered Peace: The Origins of the Cold War and the National Security State* (Boston, MA, 1978) 301: 'The Moscow Council marked for the Americans the final rejection of Franklin Roosevelt's tentatively optimistic approach to postwar Soviet–American relations.'

10 Smith, *The State*, 196–7.

11 Ibid., 251–6.

12 On France since 1945, see for example John Ardagh, *The New France, 1945–1977* (Harmondsworth, 1977).

13 Smith, *The State*, 21.

14 Ibid., 179–83.

15 Sheila Grant Duff, 'Czechoslovakia in World Affairs', in James Callaghan and others, *Czechoslovakia: Six Studies in Reconstruction* (London, [1946]) 14.

16 Stanisław Mikołajczyk, *The Pattern of Soviet Domination* (London, 1948) 23.

17 Martin McCauley, *Stalin and Stalinism* (London, 1983) 100.

18 Ibid., 102; Yoram Gorlizki, 'Stalin's Cabinet: The Politburo and Decision Making in the Postwar Years', in Christopher Read (ed.), *The Stalin Years* (Basingstoke, 2003) 200.

19 Smith, *The State*, 66–7.

20 J. D. Hargreaves, *Decolonization in Africa* (London, 1988) 88–9.

21 Yergin, *Shattered Peace*, 123–4, 435 n. 34.

22 Jawaharlal Nehru, *The Discovery of India* (New York, 1960) 360.

23 *NE*, 310–12.

24 Ibid., 401–3; Walter LaFeber, *America, Russia, and the Cold War, 1945–1996* (New York, 1997) 96–7.

25 Yergin, *Shattered Peace*, 404–5.

26 *NE*, 323.

27 Ilya Erenburg, *Dorogi Evropy* (Moscow, 1946) 142.

28 LaFeber, *America, Russia*, 210.

29 Immanuel Wallerstein, *Geopolitics and Geoculture: Essays on the Changing World-System* (Cambridge, 1991) 13–14, 65–83.

15 GLOBALISATION: COLLAPSE IN THE EAST, READJUSTMENT IN THE WEST, 1968–1991 AND AFTER

1 Anthony Giddens, quoted by Roland Axtmann in his editorial introduction to *Globalization and Europe: Theoretical and Empirical Investigations* (London, 1998) 2.

2 Walter LaFeber, *The American Age: United States Foreign Policy at Home and Abroad since 1750* (New York, 1989) 616.

3 Paul Kennedy, *The Rise and Fall of the Great Powers: Economic Change and Military Conflict from 1500 to 2000* (New York, 1988) 515, 521, 525–6.

4 Bush quoted by Walter LaFeber, *America, Russia and the Cold War, 1945–1990*, 6th edn (New York, 1991) 340.

5 Paul Dukes, *A History of Russia, c.882–1996* (London, 1998) 315–16.

6 Valentin Kudrov, *Soviet Economic Performance in Retrospect: A Critical Reexamination* (Moscow, 1998) 52, 71–2, 92, 123–4. On telephones, see V. S. Smirnov, 'Ekonomicheskaia predrevoliutsionnoi Rossii v tsifrakh i faktakh', *Otechestvennaia istoriia*, 2 (1999) 10.

7 José Amodia, 'Democracy, Nationalism and Autonomy in Spain: An Overall View', in José Amodia (ed.), *The Resurgence of Nationalist Movements in Europe* (Bradford, 1991) 137–50.

8 Timothy Garton Ash, *The Uses of Adversity: Essays on the Fate of Central Europe* (Harmondsworth, 1989) 167–8.

9 http://europa.eu.int/abc/obj/treaties/en/entoc.htm

10 *Congressional Record*, S1216–S1219, 29 January 1991.

11 Miroslav Hroch and Blanka Ríchová, 'How much does state formation depend on nationalism?', in André Gerrits and Nanci Adler (eds.), *Vampires Unstaked: National Images, Stereotypes and Myths in East Central Europe* (Amsterdam, 1995) 119.

12 Attila Ágh, 'Hungary: After the Five Years' Excursion to the "Glorious Past"', in Bogdan Góralczyk, Wojciech Kostecki and Katarzyna Żukrowska (eds.), *In Pursuit of Europe: Transformations of Post-Communist States, 1989–1994* (Warsaw, 1995) 66.

13 See, for example, Jenö Szücs, 'The Three Historical Regions of Europe', *Acta Historica Academiae Hungaricae*, 29 (2–4) (1983). Hans-Heinrich Nolte, 'The Alleged Influence of Cultural Boundaries on Political Thinking: Images of Central Europe', in Gerrits and Adler, *Vampires Unstaked*, pp. 41–2, is sceptical about the arguments put forward by Milan Kundera concerning east-central Europe as 'part of the West kidnapped by the East'.

14 Arnold and Veronica Toynbee (eds.), *The Realignment of Europe: Survey of International Affairs, 1939–1946* (London, 1955) 2–3, 7, 12–13, 15, 20.

15 Arnold J. Toynbee, *The German Terror in Belgium* (London, 1917) 1; *The German Terror in France* (London, 1917) 1; *The World after the Peace Conference* (London, 1926) 45.

16 The first use of the word in a political sense was by W. T. R. Fox, *The Super-Powers* (New York, 1944). And see Paul Dukes, *The Superpowers: A Short History* (London, 2000).

17 John Lewis Gaddis, *Russia, the Soviet Union and the United States: An Interpretative History* (New York, 1978) 279.

18 Toynbee, *Realignment*, 32–3.

19 Fernand Braudel, *L'identité de la France: Espace et Histoire* (Paris, 1986) 48; John Berger, 'Historical Afterword', *Pig Earth* (London, 1979), 195–7.

20 Zbigniew Brzezinski, *The Grand Chessboard: American Primacy and Its Geostrategic Imperatives* (New York, 1997) 43, 61, 86.

21 Paul Kennedy, *Preparing for the Twenty-First Century* (London, 1993) 288.

Suggestions for Further Reading

WEBSITES

http://europa.eu.int/futurum/forum The repository for all contributions from European and national organisations to the work of the Convention.

http://european-convention.eu.int The website of the Convention, with all the official Convention documents.

http://www.europarl.euint/europe2004/ The Parliament's dedicated site on the future of the EU.

REFERENCE

Belchem, John and Price, Richard, *A Dictionary of Nineteenth-Century History* (London, 1996).

Black, Jeremy and Porter, Roy (eds.), *A Dictionary of Eighteenth-Century History* (London, 2001).

Cook, Chris and Bewes, Dickon, *What Happened Where? A Guide to Places and Events in Twentieth-Century History* (London, 1997).

Palmer, Alan, *The Penguin Dictionary of Twentieth-Century History* (London, 2002).

Townley, Edward, *A Dictionary of Twentieth-Century History* (London, 1999).

Townson, Duncan, *The New Penguin Dictionary of Modern History, 1789–1945* (London, 2001).

Townson, Duncan, *A Dictionary of Contemporary History* (Oxford, 1999).

Webb, Adrian, *Central and Eastern Europe since 1919* (London, 2002).

Williams, E. N., *The Penguin Dictionary of English and European History, 1485–1789* (London, 1980).

MAPS

Barnes, Ian, *The History Atlas of Europe* (New York, 1998).

Black, Jeremy, *Maps and History: Constructing Images of the Past* (London, 2000).

Hupchik, Dennis P. and Cox, Harold E., *The Palgrave Concise Atlas of Eastern Europe* (London, 2001).
Magocsi, Paul R., *Historical Atlas of Central Europe* (Seattle, Wash., 2002).
The Economist Atlas of the New Europe (New York, 1992).
The Hamlyn Historical Atlas, ed. Moore, R. I. (London, 1981).
The Penguin Atlas of World History, ed. Kinder, Herman (London, 1995).
The Times Atlas of World History, ed. Barraclough, G. (London, 1993).

GENERAL

Alcock, Antony, *A Short History of Europe* (London, 2002).
Barraclough, Geoffrey, *An Introduction to Contemporary History* (Harmondsworth, 1967).
Blanning, T. C. W. (ed.), *The Oxford History of Modern Europe* (Oxford, 2000).
Bridge, F. R. and Bullen, Roger, *The Great Powers and the European States System, 1815–1914* (London, 1980).
Briggs, Asa and Clavin, Patricia, *Modern Europe, 1789–1989* (London, 1997).
Cameron, Euan (ed.), *Early Modern Europe: An Oxford History* (Oxford, 1999).
Davies, Norman, *Europe: A History* (London, 1997).
Doyle, William, *The Old European Order, 1660–1800* (Oxford, 1978).
Ferguson, Niall, *The Cash Nexus: Money and Power in the Modern World, 1700–2000* (London, 2002).
Hobsbawm, E. J., *The Age of Revolution, 1789–1848* (London, 1962).
Hobsbawm, E. J., *The Age of Capital, 1848–1875* (London, 1975).
Hobsbawm, E. J., *The Age of Empire, 1870–1914* (London, 1987).
Hobsbawm, E. J., *The Age of Extremes: The Short Twentieth Century* (London, 2000).
Joll, James, *Europe since 1870: An International History* (London, 1990).
McKay, Derek and Scott, H. M., *The Rise of the Great Powers, 1648–1815* (London, 1983).
Marks, Sally, *The Ebbing of European Ascendancy: An International History of the World, 1914–1945* (London, 2002).
Merriman, John, *A History of Modern Europe*, 2 vols. (New York, 1998).
Roberts, J. M., *The Penguin History of Europe* (London, 1997).
Thomson, David, *Europe since Napoleon* (London, 1990).

REGIONAL

Anderson, M. S., *The Eastern Question, 1774–1923* (London, 1966).
Bideleux, Robert and Jeffries, Ian, *A History of Eastern Europe* (London, 1998).
Jelavich, Barbara, *History of the Balkans*, 2 vols. (Cambridge, 1983).
Longworth, Philip, *The Making of Eastern Europe* (London, 1997).
Mazower, Mark, *The Balkans* (London, 2001).
Okey, Robin, *Eastern Europe: Feudalism to Communism, 1740–1980* (London, 1982).

Pearson, Raymond, *National Minorities in Eastern Europe, 1848–1945* (London, 1983).

Silberschmidt, Max, *The United States and Europe: Rivals and Partners* (London, 1972).

Stone, Daniel, *A History of East Central Europe* (Seattle, Wash., 2001).

Todorova, Miranda, *Imagining the Balkans* (Oxford, 1997).

Urwin, Derek, *A Political History of Western Europe since 1945* (London, 1997).

ECONOMIC

Aldcroft, Derek, *Europe in the International Economy, 1500 to 2000* (London, 1999).

The Cambridge Economic History of Europe, 7 vols. (Cambridge, 1963–7).

Henderson, W. O., *The Industrialization of Europe, 1780–1914* (London, 1969).

Kemp, T., *Historical Patterns of Industrialisation* (London, 1978).

Kenwood, A. G. and Lougheed, A. L., *The Growth of the International Economy, 1820–2000: An Introductory Text* (London, 1999).

Tipton, Frank B. and Aldrich, Robert, *An Economic and Social History of Europe*, 2 vols., 1890–1939, 1939– (London, 1987).

Wallerstein, Immanuel, *The Modern World-System* (London, 1974–).

Woodruff, William, *Impact of Western Man: A Study of Europe's Role in the World Economy, 1750–1960* (London, 1966).

SOCIAL

Ariès, Philippe, *Centuries of Childhood* (London, 1979).

Ariès, Philippe, *Western Attitudes towards Death from the Middle Ages to the Present* (Baltimore, MD, 1974).

Branca, Patricia, *Women in Europe since 1750* (London, 1978).

Briggs, Asa and Burke, Peter, *A Social History of the Media* (Oxford, 2001).

Foucault, Michel, *The History of Sexuality* (London, 1981).

Geary, Dick, *European Labour Protest, 1848–1939* (London, 1981).

Gillis, John R., *Youth and History: Tradition and Change in European Age Relations, 1770 to the Present* (London, 1974).

Kamen, Henry, *European Society, 1500–1700* (London, 1984).

Stearns, Peter N., *European Society in Upheaval: Social History since 1750* (London, 1975).

Weber, Eugen, *A Modern History of Europe: Men, Cultures and Societies from the Renaissance to the Present* (London, 1973).

Wolf, Eric R., *Europe and the People without History* (London, 1982).

CULTURAL

Blanning, T. C. W., *The Culture of Power and the Power of Culture: Old Regime Europe, 1660–1789* (Oxford, 2002).

Cipolla, Carlo, *Literacy and Development in the West* (London, 1969).
Dukes, Paul and Dunkley, John (eds.), *Culture and Revolution* (London, 1990).
Lowenthal, David, *The Past is a Foreign Country* (Cambridge, 1985).
Mosse, G. L., *The Culture of Western Europe: The Nineteenth and Twentieth Centuries* (Chicago, 1974).
Rietbergen, Peter, *Europe: A Cultural History* (London, 1998).
What is Europe?, 4 vols. (London, 1993): Boer, Pinden and others, *The History of the Idea of Europe* (London, 1993); Schröder, Konrad and others, *Aspects of European Cultural Diversity* (London, 1993); Rieu, Alain-Marc and others, *European Democratic Culture* (London, 1993); Waites, Bernard and others, *Europe and the Wider World* (London, 1993).

MILITARY AND STRATEGIC

Best, Geoffrey, *War and Society in Revolutionary Europe, 1770–1870* (London, 1982).
Black, Jeremy, *European Warfare, 1660–1815* (London, 1994).
Bond, Brian, *War and Society in Europe, 1870–1970* (London, 1984).
Childs, John, *Armies and Warfare in Europe, 1648–1789* (Manchester, 1982).
Corvisier, André, *Armies and Societies in Europe, 1494–1789* (London, 1979).
Dehio, Ludwig, *The Precarious Balance: The Politics of Power in Europe, 1494–1945* (London, 1963).
Gooch, John, *Armies in Europe* (London, 1980).
Howard, Michael, *War in Modern European History* (Oxford, 1976).
Kennedy, Paul, *Grand Strategies in War and Peace* (London, 1991).
Kennedy, Paul, *The Rise and Fall of the Great Powers: Economic Change and Military Conflict from 1500 to 2000* (London, 1989).
Kiernan, V. G., *European Armies: From Conquest to Collapse, 1815–1960* (London, 1982).
McNeill, W. H., *The Pursuit of Power: Technology, Armed Forces and Society since AD 1000* (Oxford, 1982).
Strachan, Hew, *European Armies and the Conduct of War* (London, 1983).

DISCUSSIONS OF HISTORY

Bloch, Marc, *The Historian's Craft* (Manchester, 1954).
Carr, E. H., *What is History?* (London, 1990).
Elton, G. R., *The Practice of History* (London, 1969).
Gardiner, Juliet (ed.), *What is History Today?* (London, 1988).
Ferro, Marc, *The Use and Abuse of History* (London, 1984).
Marwick, Arthur, *The New Nature of History* (London, 2001).
Plumb, J. H., *The Death of the Past* (London, 1969).

NATIONAL

Albania

Pollo, Stefanaq, *The History of Albania* (London, 1981).
Sully, Melanie A., *A Contemporary History of Albania* (London, 1990).
Vickers, Miranda, *The Albanians: A Modern History* (London, 1999).

Austria

Evans, R. J. W., *The Making of the Habsburg Monarchy, 1550–1700* (Oxford, 1979).
Jelavich, B., *Modern Austria: Empire and Republic* (Cambridge, 1987).
Macartney, C. A., *The House of Austria: The Later Phase, 1790–1918* (Edinburgh, 1978).
Taylor, A. J. P., *The Habsburg Monarchy, 1815–1918* (London, 1948).
Wangermann, Ernst, *The Austrian Achievement, 1700–1800* (London, 1973).

Baltic states (see also Russia)

Allworth, Edward (ed.), *Nationality Group Survival in Multi-Ethnic States: Shifting Support Patterns in the Soviet Baltic Region* (New York, 1977).
Misiunas, Romuald and Taagepera, Rein, *The Baltic States: The Years of Dependence, 1940–1990* (London, 1993).
Rauch, Georg von, *The Baltic States: Years of Independence, 1917–1940* (Berkeley, CA, 1974).
Vardys, V. Stanley and Misiunas, Romuald, *The Baltic States in Peace and War* (University Park, PA, 1978).

Belarus (see also Russia)

Zaprudnik, A., *Belarus: At a Crossroads in History* (London, 1993).

Belgium (see also Netherlands)

Cook, Bernard A., *Belgium: A History* (New York, 2002).

Bosnia-Hercegovina (see also Yugoslavia)

Malcolm, N., *Bosnia: A Short History* (London, 1996).
Lovrenovic, Ivan, *Bosnia: A Cultural History* (New York, 2001).

Britain

Black, Jeremy, *Convergence or Divergence? Britain and the Continent* (London, 1994).
Hill, Christopher, *Reformation to Industrial Revolution* (London, 1969).
Jones, Harriet and Butler, Larry, *Britain in the Twentieth Century* (London, 1994).
Kishlansky, Mark, Cannadine, David and Clarke, Peter, *Penguin History of Britain* (London, 1997).
Marwick, Arthur, *British Society since 1945* (London, 2003).
Morgan, Kenneth O., *The Oxford History of Britain* (Oxford, 2001).
Schama, Simon, *A History of Britain* (London, 2002).
Speck, W. A., *A Concise History of Britain* (Cambridge, 1993).

Bulgaria

Crampton, R. J., *A Concise History of Bulgaria* (Cambridge, 1997).
Evans, Stanley G., *A Short History of Bulgaria* (London, 1960).
McIntyre, Robert J., *Bulgaria: Politics, Economics and Society* (London, 1988).

Croatia (see also Yugoslavia)

Goldstein, Ivo, *Croatia: A History* (Montreal, 1999).
Tanner, M. C., *A Nation Forged in War* (London, 1997).

Czechoslovakia (including Czech Republic and Slovakia)

Henderson, Karen, *Slovakia* (London, 2002).
Kirschbaum, Stanislav J., *A History of Slovakia* (London, 1996).
Krejčí, Jaroslav and Machonin, Pavel, *Czechoslovakia, 1918–92: A Laboratory for Social Change* (London, 1996).
Skilling, H. Gordon, *Czechoslovakia, 1918–1988* (London, 1991).
Stone, Norman and Strouhal, Eduard (eds.), *Czechoslovakia: Crossroads and Crises* (London, 1989).

Denmark (see also Scandinavia)

Jones, W. Glyn, *Denmark: A Modern History* (London, 1986).
Lauring, Palle, *A History of the Kingdom of Denmark* (Copenhagen, 1960).

Estonia (see also Baltic states)

Parming, Tonu and Elmar, Jarvesoo, *A Case Study of a Soviet Republic: The Estonian SSR* (Boulder, CO, 1978).
Raun, Toivo, *Estonia and the Estonians* (Stanford, CA, 1987).
Uustalu, Evald, *The History of the Estonian People* (London, 1952).

Finland (see also Scandinavia)

Jussila, Osmo, *From Grand Duchy to Nation State: A Political History of Finland since 1909* (London, 1999).
Jutikkala, A. H., *History of Finland* (London, 1962).
Singleton, Fred, *A Short History of Finland* (Cambridge, 1998).
Wuorinen, John H., *A History of Finland* (New York, 1965).

France

Cobban, Alfred, *A History of Modern France*, 3 vols. (London, 1965).
Doyle, William, *Old Regime France, 1648–1788* (Oxford, 2001).
Goubert, Pierre, *The Course of French History* (London, 1991).
Johnson, Douglas, *A Concise History of France* (London, 1971).
Magraw, Roger, *France 1815–1914: The Bourgeois Century* (London, 1983).
Price, Roger, *A Concise History of France* (Cambridge, 1993).

Germany (including Prussia and the Federal and Democratic Republics)

Berghahn, V., *Modern Germany* (Cambridge, 1987).
Carr, W., *A History of Germany, 1815–1985* (London, 1987).
Childs, David, *The GDR, Moscow's German Ally* (London, 1983).
Craig, Gordon, *German History, 1866–1945* (Oxford, 1981).
Fulbrook, Mary, *A Concise History of Germany* (Cambridge, 1990).
Holborn, Hajo, *A History of Modern Germany* (London, 1992).
McCauley, Martin, *The German Democratic Republic since 1945* (Basingstoke, 1983).
Sheehan, James J., *German History, 1770–1866* (Oxford, 1990).

Greece

Bury, J. B. and Meiggs, Russell, *A History of Greece* (London, 1977).
Clogg, Richard, *A Concise History of Greece* (Cambridge, 1992).
Dakin, Douglas, *The Unification of Greece* (London, 1972).
Kourvetaris, Yorgos A. and Dobratz, Betty A., *A Profile of Modern Greece in Search of Identity* (Oxford, 1987).
Woodhouse, C. M., *Modern Greece: A Short History* (London, 1999).

Hungary

Bartá, István and others, *A History of Hungary* (London, 1976).
Hönsch, Jorg K., *A History of Modern Hungary, 1867–1994* (London, 1996).

Kantler, Laszlo, *A History of Hungary* (London, 2002).
Molnár, Miklós, *A Concise History of Hungary* (Cambridge, 2001).
Sugar, P. F. and Hanak, Peter, *A History of Hungary* (London, 1990).

Iceland

Karlsson, Gunnar, *The History of Iceland* (Minneapolis, MN, 2000).
Lacy, Terry G., *Ring of Seasons: Iceland – Its Culture and History* (Ann Arbor, MI, 2000).

Ireland

Cronin, Mike, *A History of Ireland* (London, 2001).
Curtis, Edmund, *A History of Ireland* (London, 2002).
Foster, R. F., *The Oxford History of Ireland* (Oxford, 2001).
Killeen, Richard, *A Short History of Ireland* (Dublin, 1994).
Moody, T. W., Martin, F. X. and Byrne, F. J., *A New History of Ireland* (Oxford, 1991).
Ranelagh, John O'Beirne, *A Short History of Ireland* (Cambridge, 1995).

Italy

Clark, M., *Modern Italy, 1871–1982* (London, 1984).
Duggan, Christopher, *A Concise History of Italy* (Cambridge, 2002).
Hearder, H., *A Short History of Italy* (Cambridge, 1963).
Mack Smith, Denis, *Italy: A Modern History* (London, 1969).
Seton-Watson, C., *Italy from Liberalism to Fascism* (London, 1972).
Woolf, S. J., *A History of Italy, 1700–1860: The Social Constraints of Political Change* (London, 1979).

Latvia (see also Baltic states)

Bilmanis, Alfred, *A History of Latvia* (Princeton, NJ, 1951).
Spekke, Arnolds, *A History of Latvia: An Outline* (Stockholm, 1951).
Watson, H. A. G., *The Latvian Republic* (London, 1965).

Lithuania (see also Baltic states)

Chase, Thomas G., *The Story of Lithuania* (New York, 1946).
Jurgela, Constantine R., *History of the Lithuanian Nation* (New York, 1948).
Senn, Alfred E., *The Emergence of Modern Lithuania* (New York, 1959).

Macedonia (see also Yugoslavia)

Danforth, L. M., *The Macedonian Conflict: Ethnic Nationalism in a Transnational World* (Princeton, NJ, 1996).
Errington, R. Malcolm, *The History of Macedonia* (New York, 1994).
Hammond, N. G. L., *A History of Macedonia* (Oxford, 1988).
Pettifer, James (ed.), *The New Macedonian Question* (Basingstoke, 1999).

Moldova (see also Russia)

Hegarty, Thomas, *Moldova* (London, 2003).

Montenegro (see also Yugoslavia)

Stevenson, F. S., *A History of Montenegro* (New York, 1970).

The Netherlands

Boxer, C. R., *The Dutch Seaborne Empire, 1600–1800* (London, 1965).
Geyl, Pieter, *A History of the Dutch-Speaking Peoples* (London, 2001).
Israel, Jonathan I., *The Dutch Republic: Its Rise, Greatness and Fall, 1477–1806* (London, 1995).
Kossmann, E. H., *The Low Countries, 1780–1940* (Oxford, 1978).
Schoffer, Ivo, *A Short History of the Netherlands* (Amsterdam, 1973).
Wintle, Michael, *An Economic and Social History of the Netherlands, 1800–1920* (Cambridge, 2000).

Norway (see also Scandinavia)

Danielson, Rolf, *Norway: A History from the Vikings to Our Own Times* (Oslo, 1995).
Derry, T. K., *A History of Modern Norway* (Oxford, 1973).
Midgaard, John, *A Brief History of Norway* (Oslo, 1963).

Poland

Davies, Norman, *God's Playground: A History of Poland,* 2 vols.: –1795, –1980 (Oxford, 1981).
Halecki, O., *A History of Poland* (New York, 1988).
Leslie, R. F. (ed.), *History of Poland since 1863* (London, 1980).
Lukowski, Jerzy and Zawadski, Hubert, *A Concise History of Poland* (Cambridge, 2001).
Reddaway, W. F. (ed.), *The Cambridge History of Poland,* 2 vols.: –1696, –1935 (Cambridge, 1971).

Portugal

Birmingham, David, *A Concise History of Portugal* (Cambridge, 1999).
Boxer, C. R., *The Portuguese Seaborne Empire* (London, 1969).
Livermore, H., *A New History of Portugal* (Cambridge, 1976).
Paine, Stanley, *A History of Spain and Portugal*, 2 vols. (Madison, WI, 1973).

Romania

Deletant, Dennis, *Romania under Communist Rule* (Oxford, 1999).
Otetea, Andrei (ed.), *A Concise History of Romania* (London, 1985).

Russia

Dawisha, Karen and Parrott, Bruce, *Russia and the New States of Eurasia: The Politics of Upheaval* (Cambridge, 1994).
Dukes, Paul, *A History of Russia, c.882–1996* (London, 1998).
Hosking, Geoffrey, *Russia and the Russians: A History* (London, 2001).
Keep, John, *A History of the Soviet Union, 1945–1991* (Oxford, 2002).
Riasanovsky, N. V., *A History of Russia* (Oxford, 1999).
Service, Robert, *The History of Twentieth-Century Russia* (London, 1998).
Seton-Watson, G. H. N., *The Russian Empire, 1801–1917* (Oxford, 1967).
Westwood, J. N., *Endurance and Endeavour: Russian History, 1812–1992* (Oxford, 1993).

Scandinavia

Derry, T. K., *A History of Scandinavia* (Cambridge, 1995).
Donner, Joakim, *The Quaternary History of Scandinavia* (Cambridge, 1995).
Griffiths, Tony, *Scandinavia: A Modern History* (London, 2000).
Hovde, B. J., *The Scandinavian Countries, 1720–1865*, 2 vols. (Boston, MA, 1943).

Serbia (see also Yugoslavia)

Cox, John K., *The History of Serbia* (London, 2002).
Judah, Tim, *The Serbs* (London, 2000).
Pavlowich, Stevan K., *Serbia: The History behind the Name* (London, 2002).

Slovenia (see also Yugoslavia)

Benderly, J. and Kraft, E. (eds.), *Independent Slovenia: Origins, Movements, Prospects* (London, 1995).
Gow, James and Carmichael, Cathie, *Slovenia and the Slovenes* (London, 2000).

Spain

Carr, R., *Spain, 1808–1939* (Oxford, 1966).
Kamen, H., *A Concise History of Spain* (London, 1973).
Paine, Stanley, *see* Portugal.
Parry, J. H., *The Spanish Seaborne Empire* (London, 1966).
Romero Salvadó, Francisco J., *Twentieth-Century Spain: Politics and Society in Spain, 1898–1998* (Basingstoke, 1999).
Shubert, Adrian, *A Social History of Modern Spain* (London, 1990).

Sweden (see also Scandinavia)

Andersson, Ingvar, *A History of Sweden* (London, 1956).
Scott, Franklin, *Sweden, The Nation's History* (Minneapolis, MN, 1977).

Switzerland

Bonjour, Edgar and others, *A Short History of Switzerland* (Oxford, 1952).
Dame, Frederick W., *History of Switzerland* (Lampeter, 2001).

Ukraine (see also Russia)

Hrushevsky, Michael, *A History of Ukraine* (Hamden, CN, 1970).
Magocsi, Paul R., *A History of Ukraine* (Seattle, Wash., 1996).
Subtelny, Orest, *Ukraine: A History* (Toronto, 2000).
Wilson, Andrew, *The Ukrainians: Unexpected Nation* (London, 2002).

Yugoslavia

Benson, Leslie, *Yugoslavia: A Concise History* (London, 2001).
Clissold, Stephen, *A Short History of Yugoslavia* (Cambridge, 1966).
Dedijer, V., *History of Yugoslavia* (New York, 1974).
Lampe, John R., *Yugoslavia as History* (Cambridge, 1996).
Singleton, F., *Twentieth Century Yugoslavia* (London, 1976).

CHAPTER 1   INTRODUCTION: EUROPE BEFORE 1648

Bartlett, Robert, *The Making of Europe: Conquest, Colonization and Cultural Change, 950–1350* (London, 1994).
Cameron, Euan (ed.), *Early Modern Europe: An Oxford History* (Oxford, 1999).
Frost, Robert, *The Northern Wars, 1558–1721: War, State and Society in Northeastern Europe, 1558–1721* (London, 2000).

Parker, Geoffrey, *Europe in Crisis, 1598–1648* (London, 1979).
Parker, Geoffrey (ed.), *The Thirty Years War* (London, 1984).

CHAPTER 2 THE FRENCH CHALLENGE: RESPONSES EAST AND WEST, 1648–1721

Cameron, Euan, as in Chapter 1.
Doyle, William, *The Old European Order, 1660–1800* (Oxford, 1992).
Dukes, Paul, *The Making of Russian Absolutism, 1613–1801* (London, 1982).
Frost, Robert, as in Chapter 1.
McKay, Derek and Scott, H. M., *The Rise of the Great Powers, 1648–1815* (Harlow, 1983).
Mettam, Roger, *Government and Society in Louis XIV's France* (London, 1977).
Parker, David, *The Making of French Absolutism* (London, 1983).
Rabb, T. K., *The Struggle for Stability in Early Modern Europe* (Oxford, 1975).
Stoye, John, *Europe Unfolding, 1648–1688* (London, 1969).

CHAPTER 3 THE GROWTH OF EMPIRE, 1721–1756

Behrens, C. B. A., *The Ancien Regime* (London, 1967).
Black, Jeremy, *Eighteenth-Century Europe* (London, 1999).
Cameron, Euan (ed.), as in Chapter 1.
Canny, Nicholas (ed.), *The Oxford History of the British Empire,* vol. 1, *The Origins of Empire* (Oxford, 1998).
McKay, Derek and Scott, H. M., as in Chapter 2.
Marshall, P. J. (ed.), *The Oxford History of the British Empire,* vol. 2, *The Eighteenth Century* (Oxford, 2001).
Rudé, George, *Europe in the Eighteenth Century* (London, 1964).
Williams, Glyndwr, *The Expansion of Europe in the Eighteenth Century* (London, 1966).

CHAPTER 4 ENLIGHTENED GOVERNMENTS, THEIR CONFLICTS AND THEIR CRITICS, 1763–1789

Amann, Peter (ed.), *The Eighteenth-Century Revolution: French or Western?* (Boston, MA, 1963).
Black, Jeremy, as in Chapter 3.
Cameron, Euan (ed.), as in Chapter 1.
Hufton, Olwen, *Europe: Privilege and Protest, 1730–1789* (London, 1980).
McKay, Derek and Scott, H. M., as in Chapter 2.
Rudé, George, *Revolutionary Europe, 1783–1815* (London, 1964).

Scott, H. M. (ed.), *Enlightened Absolutism: Reform and Reformers in Later Eighteenth-Century Europe* (London, 1980).

CHAPTER 5 EUROPE BEFORE 1789, AND THE ORIGINS OF THE FRENCH REVOLUTION

Black, Jeremy, as in Chapter 3.
Cameron, Euan (ed.), as in Chapter 1.
Doyle, W., *Origins of the French Revolution* (Oxford, 1999).
Hampson, Norman, *The Enlightenment* (Harmondsworth, 1968).
Outram, Dorinda, *The Enlightenment* (Cambridge, 1995).
Porter, Roy and Teich, Mikuláš (eds.), *The Enlightenment in National Context* (Cambridge, 1981).

CHAPTER 6 THE FRENCH REVOLUTION AND NAPOLEON, 1789–1815

Broers, Michael, *Europe under Napoleon, 1799–1815* (Oxford, 2002).
Doyle, William, *The Oxford History of the French Revolution* (London, 2002).
Ellis, Geoffrey, *The Napoleonic Empire* (London, 1991).
Hampson, Norman, *A Social History of the French Revolution* (London, 1963).
Hampson, Norman, *The Life and Opinions of Maximilien Robespierre* (London, 1974).
Markham, F. M. H., *Napoleon and the Awakening of Europe* (London, 1954).
Roberts, J. M., *The French Revolution* (Oxford, 1978).
Rudé, George, as in Chapter 4.
Rudé, George, *The Crowd in the French Revolution* (London, 1959).
Simms, Brendan, *The Impact of Napoleon* (Cambridge, 2002).
Woolf, Stuart, *Napoleon's Integration of Europe* (London, 1991).

CHAPTER 7 FROM REACTION TOWARDS LIBERALISM, 1815–1848

Anderson, Benedict, *Imagined Communities: Reflections on the Origin and Spread of Nationalism* (London, 1983).
Bridge, F. R. and Bullen, Roger, *The Great Powers and the European States System, 1815–1914* (London, 1980).
Broers, Michael, *Europe after Napoleon: Revolution, Reaction and Romanticism, 1814–1851* (Manchester, 1996).
Jacques Droz, *Europe between Revolutions, 1815–1848* (London, 1967).
Evans, R. J. W. and Strandmann, Hartmut Pogge von, *The Revolutions in Europe, 1848–1849: From Reform to Reaction* (Oxford, 2000).

Laven, David and Riall, Lucy (eds.), *Napoleon's Legacy* (London, 2001).
Sked, Alan (ed.), *Europe's Balance of Power* (London, 1979).
Sperber, Jonathan, *The European Revolutions, 1848–1851* (Cambridge, 1994).
Stearns, Peter N., *1848: The Revolutionary Tide in Europe* (New York, 1974).
Walker, Mack (ed.), *Metternich's Europe, 1813–1848* (New York, 1968).

CHAPTER 8 NATIONALISM, SOCIALISM, IMPERIALISM, 1848–1882

Bridge, F. R. and Bullen, Roger, as in Chapter 7.
Cole, G. D. H., *A History of Socialist Thought*, 4 vols. (London, 1953–60).
Grenville, J. A. S., *Europe Reshaped, 1848–1878* (London, 1976).
Hearder, H., *Europe in the Nineteenth Century, 1830–1880* (London, 1966).
McClelland, David, *Karl Marx: His Life and Thought* (New York, 1973).
Smith, Anthony D., *Nationalism: Theory, Ideology, History* (Oxford, 2001).
Taylor, A. J. P., *The Struggle for Mastery in Europe, 1848–1918* (Oxford, 1971).
Woolf, Stuart, *Nationalism in Europe* (London, 1995).

CHAPTER 9 THE CLASH OF EMPIRES AND CLASSES, 1882–1914

Bridge, F. R. and Bullen, Roger, as in Chapter 7.
Gollwitzer, Heinz, *Europe in the Age of Imperialism, 1880–1914* (London, 1969).
Langhorne, Richard, *The Collapse of the Concert of Europe: International Politics, 1890–1914* (London, 1981).
Porter, Andrew, *The Oxford History of the British Empire*, vol. 3, *The Nineteenth Century* (Oxford, 2001).
Smith, Woodruff D., *European Imperialism in the Nineteenth and Twentieth Centuries* (Chicago, IL, 1982).
Stone, Norman, *Europe Transformed, 1878–1919* (London, 1999).
Taylor, A. J. P., as in Chapter 8.

CHAPTER 10 EUROPE BEFORE 1914: ORIGINS OF WORLD WAR AND REVOLUTION

Barraclough, Geoffrey, *An Introduction to Contemporary History* (Harmondsworth, 1967).
Bridge, F. R. and Bullen, Roger, as in Chapter 7.
Geiss, I. (ed.), *July 1914: Selected Documents* (London, 1967).
Hughes, H. S., *Consciousness and Society* (Brighton, 1979).
Joll, James, *The Origins of the First World War* (London, 1990).
Koch, H. W. (ed.), *The Origins of the First World War: Great Power Rivalry and German War Aims* (London, 1972).

Kochan, Lionel, *Russia in Revolution, 1890–1918* (London, 1970).
Strachan, Hew, *The First World War*, vol. 1, *To Arms* (Oxford, 2001).

CHAPTER 11 THE FIRST WORLD WAR AND THE RUSSIAN REVOLUTION, 1914–1921

Carr, E. H., *The Russian Revolution from Lenin to Stalin* (London, 1980).
Figes, Orlando, *A People's Tragedy: A History of the Russian Revolution* (London, 1998).
Fitzpatrick, Sheila, *The Russian Revolution, 1917–1932* (Oxford, 1984).
Joll, James, as in Chapter 10.
Kochan, Lionel, as in Chapter 10.
Read, Christopher, *From Tsar to Soviets: The Russian People and their Revolution* (London, 1996).
Robbins, Keith, *The First World War* (Oxford, 1984).
Strachan, Hew, as in Chapter 10.
Taylor, A. J. P., *The First World War: An Illustrated History* (London, 1966).
White, James D., *The Russian Revolution, 1917–1921: A Short History* (London, 2002).

CHAPTER 12 THROUGH DEPRESSION AND ISOLATION TOWARDS ANOTHER WORLD WAR, 1921–1939

Adamthwaite, Anthony P. (ed.), *The Making of the Second World War* (London, 1977).
Hiden, John W., *Republican and Fascist Germany* (London, 1996).
Kershaw, Ian, *Hitler* (London, 2001).
Mack Smith, Denis, *Mussolini* (London, 1983).
Mawdsley, Evan, *The Stalin Years* (Manchester, 2003).
Preston, Paul, *Franco: A Biography* (London, 1990).
Robertson, Esmond M. (ed.), *The Origins of the Second World War* (London, 1971).
Taylor, A. J. P., *The Origins of the Second World War* (London, 1963).
Ward, Chris, *Stalin's Russia* (London, 1993).
Watt, D. C., *How War Came* (London, 2001).

CHAPTER 13 THE SECOND WORLD WAR AND THE DIVISION OF EUROPE, 1939–1945

Calvocoressi, Peter, Wint, Guy and Pritchard, John, *The Penguin History of the Second World War* (London, 1999).
Erickson, John, *The Road to Stalingrad* (London, 1975).
Erickson, John, *The Road to Berlin* (London, 1984).

Gilbert, Martin, *The Second World War* (London, 2000).

Taylor, A. J. P., *The Second World War: An Illustrated History* (Harmondsworth, 1976).

Weinberg, Gerhard L., *A World at Arms: A Global History of World War II* (Cambridge, 1994).

CHAPTER 14   THE FALL OF EUROPE: ORIGINS OF THE COLD WAR AND DECOLONISATION, 1945–1968

Calvocoressi, Peter, *World Politics, 1945–2000* (London, 2000).

Crouzet, Maurice, *The European Renaissance since 1945* (London, 1970).

Grimal, Henri, *Decolonization: The British, French, Dutch and Belgian Empires, 1919–1963* (London, 1978).

Hargreaves, J. D., *Decolonization in Africa* (London, 1988).

Holland, R. F., *European Decolonization, 1918–1981* (London, 1985).

LaFeber, Walter, *America, Russia and the Cold War, 1945–1996* (New York, 1997).

Swain, Geoffrey and Nigel, *Eastern Europe since 1945* (London, 1993).

Vaughan, Richard, *Post-War Integration in Europe* (London, 1976).

CHAPTER 15   GLOBALISATION: COLLAPSE IN THE EAST, READJUSTMENT IN THE WEST, 1968–1991 AND AFTER

Ash, Timothy Garton, *History of the Present: Dispatches from Europe* (London, 2000).

Axtmann, Roland (ed.), *Globalization and Europe: Theoretical and Empirical Investigations* (London, 1998).

Bremmer, Ian and Taras, Ray, *Nations and Politics in the Soviet Successor States* (Cambridge, 1993).

Calvocoressi, Peter, as in Chapter 14.

Fawn, Rick and White, Stephen, *Russia after Communism* (London, 2002).

Glenny, Misha, *The Rebirth of History: Eastern Europe in the Age of Democracy* (Harmondsworth, 1990).

LaFeber, Walter, as in Chapter 14.

Swain, Geoffrey and Nigel, as in Chapter 14.

INDEX

Page numbers in *italics* refer to maps

551